GERMAN
A Structural Approach
FOURTH EDITION

GERMAN
A Structural Approach
FOURTH EDITION

Walter F. W. Lohnes
STANFORD UNIVERSITY

F. W. Strothmann

William E. Petig
STANFORD UNIVERSITY

W·W·NORTON & COMPANY
NEW YORK   LONDON

The text of this book is composed in Trump, with display type set in Gill Sans. Composition by JGH Composition. Manufacturing by Halliday. Book design by Margaret Wagner.

Layout by Ben Gamit.

"Wenn die Haifische Menschen wären" and "Freundschaftsdienste," from *Prosa I* by Bertolt Brecht. Copyright © 1965 by Stefan S. Brecht. All rights reserved by Suhrkamp Verlag, Frankfurt am Main.

"If Sharks Were People" and "Good Turns," translated by Yvonne Kapp. Reprinted from the copyrighted works of Bertolt Brecht by permission of Methuen & Company, Ltd. Copyright © 1962 by Methuen & Company Ltd. Translation copyright © 1962 by Stefan S. Brecht.

"Sachliche Romanze" and "Das Eisenbahngleichnis" by Erich Kästner, from *Gesammelte Schriften für Erwachsene*. Copyright © by Erich Kästner Erben, München.

"Heimkehr," "Gibs Auf!," and "Die Prüfung" by Franz Kafka, from *Beschreibung eines Kampfes*. Copyright © 1946 by Schocken Books, Inc. Copyright renewed © 1974 by Schocken Books, Inc. Reprinted by permission of Pantheon Books, a division of Random House, Inc.

"Netter Nachmittag" by Angelika Mechtel, from *Das Mädchen und der Pinguin*. Copyright © 1986 by Paul List Verlag.

"Das Gleichnis vom verlornen Sohn," reprinted from *Die Heilige Schrift (Zurcher Bibel)*, Verlag der Zurcher Bibel, 1954.

"Demokratie" by Mathias Schreiber. Reprinted by permission of the author.

"Ostkontakte," from *Neues (&) altes) vom Rechtsstaat & von mir. Alle Epigramme.* Copyright © 1978 by Arnfrid Astel, Vertrieb Zweitausendeins, Frankfurt am Main.

"Das Märchen vom Spiegel" by Kurt Held, from *Die schönsten Gute Nacht Geschichten*. Copyright © 1983 by Verlag Ullstein.

"Der Mauerspringer" by Peter Schneider, from *Der Mauerspringer*. Copyright © 1984 by Hermann Luchterhand Verlag, Darmstadt und Neuwied.

"Zugauskunft" by Peter Handke, from *Die Innenwelt der Außenwelt der Innenwelt*. Copyright © 1969 by Suhrkamp Verlag, Frankfurt am Main.

"Luzern" by E. Y. Meyer, from *Die Rückfahrt*. Copyright © 1980 by Suhrkamp Verlag, Frankfurt am Main.

"Wie wäre es wenn . . ." by Barbara Bayerschmidt. Reprinted by courtesy of the author.

Cover art: Lyonel Feininger, Teltow II (1918). Courtesy of Staatliche Museen zu Berlin Nationalgalerie, DDR.

ISBN 0-393-95464-1

W.W. Norton & Company, Inc., 500 Fifth Avenue, New York, N. Y. 10110
W.W. Norton & Company Ltd., 37 Great Russell Street, London WC1B 3NU

2 3 4 5 6 7 8 9 0

TABLE OF CONTENTS

UNIT 3 The Structure of German Sentences—Verbal Complements—Negation with *nicht* and *kein*   68

UNIT 4 Modal Auxiliaries—Contrast Intonation—Prepositions with Accusative   102

Preface

This Fourth Edition of *German: A Structural Approach* is the most thorough-going revision to date. Our basic approach, however, still rests on the belief that an adult learner is best served by combining active use of the language with an intellectual understanding of grammatical structure. Our method has always been eclectic: in the Fourth Edition, we have worked to integrate new developments in strategy with an approach that has proved successful in our teaching and influential in the teaching of German in this country.

Teachers familiar with previous editions will immediately notice the changes in content. Each of the eighteen units has been reorganized into more manageable subdivisions. Pattern sections have been shortened and, where possible, contextualized. Many grammatical analyses have been completely reformulated and rewritten; many have been streamlined. Some perennial problems, such as time phrases and subjective modals, are now presented in what we hope is a simpler and clearer fashion. Conversation sections in each unit now have more exercises that encourage personal response and role-playing; in addition, a list of conversational gambits has been added in every fourth unit to encourage a more authentic use of the language. A number of new readings have replaced old selections; several other readings have been shortened. We have glossed all but five of the 26 readings; those five are fully translated to help students at an early stage in their learning of German. Unit vocabularies have been thoroughly reworked; each unit now contains approximately 100 high-frequency words for active use. Throughout the text we have made an effort to do away with sexual stereotypes and to achieve a balance of gender-specific language.

Teachers will also note an increased emphasis on culture in the German-speaking countries. New to the Fourth Edition are culture notes—two or three brief discussions per unit accompanied by ample illustrations—that introduce students to popular culture, geography, arts, politics, among other topics, in Central Europe. New photographs, line art, and print messages emphasize language in action and provide additional sources for classroom discussion.

These changes, we think, make the Fourth Edition a better balanced and more inviting introduction to spoken and written German. Successful completion of this course will lead to intermediate proficiency in all skills.

The book continues to allow for a great deal of flexibility in teaching. We recognize that teaching situations and the number of contact hours per week vary widely from course to course and that teachers need to tailor a text to meet their needs. To help with this task, we have included alternative syllabi in the *Teacher's Manual* that accompanies the Fourth Edition.

We wish to express our gratitude to all those who helped us prepare the Fourth Edition. Special thanks go to Marian Sperberg-McQueen (University of Illinois at Chicago) and Robert D. Hummel (University of Chicago) for their many contributions during the development of the manuscript. Gertrude B. Mahrholz (Stanford University) graciously permitted us to "run things past her" and offered invaluable advice. We are grateful to Uta Hoffmann (German Information Center, New York) for her assistance in preparing the new illustration program. Karen Kramer (Stanford-in-Berlin) provided us with a number of illustrations. Many new photographs were generously furnished by the German Information Center, the Austrian National Tourist Center, and the Swiss National Tourist Office. Some of the GDR illustrations were supplied through the Liga für Völkerfreundschaft in Berlin.

We also wish to thank these additional reviewers for their comments and suggestions on the final manuscript: D. L. Ashliman (University of Pittsburgh), Frank L. Borchardt (Duke University), Bruce Duncan (Dartmouth College), Marion Lois Huffines (Bucknell University), Michael W. Jennings (Princeton University), Sigrun D. Leonhard (Carleton College), Deborah McGraw (Cornell University), Gail Newman (Williams College), Anthony J. Niesz (Yale University), Thomas J. O'Hare (University of Texas at Austin).

F. W. Strothmann died in June 1982, a few weeks before his seventy-eighth birthday. He was still actively involved in the production of the Third Edition, and as we wrote this edition we often wondered how he would have reacted to some of the changes. We are confident that he would have agreed.

We dedicate this edition to his memory.

W.F.W.L.
W.E.P.

Stanford, California
September 1988

Introduction

German: A Structural Approach, Fourth Edition, shares the basic aims of earlier editions: developing speaking, reading, and writing, while at the same time giving students a clear understanding of the structures of the language. Our experience has shown that the combination of the "how" and the "why" of language acquisition produces good results. An introductory course that makes adult students aware of how language is structured can be far more stimulating than one that is limited to language practice alone.

No matter by what method adults are taught a language, they will search for the underlying structure. For this reason, we systematically present German syntax and frequently contrast it with the structure of English. This way students acquire a thorough foundation in the language, which will allow them, upon completion of the course, to achieve an advanced level of proficiency quite rapidly.

Each *UNIT* consists of several parts. Pattern sentences, grammatical analysis, and practice exercises are subdivided into two or three sections. These are followed by conversations and conversational exercises (including many that prompt personal response and open-ended discussion), reading selections, review exercises, and lists of basic vocabulary. Interspersed in each unit are two or three culture notes. Throughout each unit there are ample illustrations of both cultural and linguistic value.

PATTERN SENTENCES systematically introduce elements of German grammar that are described in corresponding analysis sections. Each pattern group contains a sufficient number of examples to illustrate a grammatical point, and there are marginal cross-references to the related analysis section. Many of the pattern sections are contextualized and have a kind of narrative flow in order to present language in a more natural setting. The German used is always authentic contemporary German. It reflects not only the written language, but also idiomatic spoken German used by educated people in everyday speech. Colloquial and literary German are recognized as equally acceptable.

ANALYSIS sections are detailed discussions of grammatical points. We have avoided short, terse explanations that require further elaboration in the classroom. The analysis sections should be assigned as outside reading as the new patterns are introduced in class, so that students, while they work on the patterns, will know what they are doing and why they are doing it.

In the analysis, our first and foremost concern is syntax. Adult students will acquire the language more rapidly and efficiently if they deal with entire sentences and their underlying structure from the very beginning. German structures are frequently contrasted with corresponding English structures throughout the book in order to call attention to those features of English that differ from German and are therefore a significant cause of error.

EXERCISES are provided for each unit. Analysis sections are followed by practice exercises that reinforce students' control of each structural element. Their sequence is the same as that of the patterns and the analysis sections. In addition, review exercises appear at the end of each unit. A separate set of laboratory exercises keyed to each unit is contained in the *Study Guide*. Students are given full instructions for these exercises, but their texts appear only on the tapes.

CONVERSATIONS are an integral part of each unit; they demonstrate patterns of the spoken language in context. On the assumption that the only time students are *forced* to speak German is when they encounter a German speaker who knows no English, we have provided a number of situations in which the teacher is asked to play the role of a native German. Units 4, 8, 12, 16, and 17 review conversational gambits introduced in the preceding units; these high-frequency phrases should be used in student-generated conversations as much as possible. In order to build students' confidence and willingness to go beyond the confines of the text in their speaking, each unit also contains **Fragen an Sie persönlich** (*Questions to you personally*). As the book progresses, we have added an increasing number of skeletal conversational outlines for students to flesh out; and finally, in the last few units, topics are suggested for discussions of a more substantive nature.

READING selections are included in every unit except Unit 1. Some introduce topics of contemporary Central European culture; others offer a sample of twentieth-century literature. Many of the readings reinforce major grammatical topics; all are carefully graded in length and difficulty. In some cases, readings will exceed the students' active control, but they should read them for overall comprehension. Our experience has been that students will surprise themselves with how much they actually do understand. Some early readings have been translated; but later on, they are glossed in the margins.

WRITING should be practiced from the very beginning. At first students should be encouraged simply to copy from the text. Dictations should be given regularly. A number of laboratory exercises are dictations as well. In the second half of the book, we have provided a number of structured compositions, based on the material of the conversations and the reading.

VOCABULARY study is essential to the successful completion of a German course. In the pattern sections the vocabulary has purposely been restricted so that students can concentrate on learning the sentences introduced. All vocabulary is presented in the context of whole sentences and should be *practiced* in context only. We do, however, strongly recommend that students memorize the approximately 100 new words at the end of each unit. Less frequently used words and phrases appear in the end vocabulary or are glossed where they occur in the text.

CULTURE NOTES are interspersed in all units. Together with the cultural reading selections, they provide glimpses of contemporary Central Europe and frequently draw connections with American culture, sharpening students' awareness of common ground and differences.

ILLUSTRATIONS, three-fourths of which are new to this edition, are closely tied to text discussions. Many demonstrate language in action.

The *APPENDIX* contains a complete list of principal parts of strong and irregular weak verbs; a German-English vocabulary, which is complete except for some words that are glossed only in the margins; an English-German vocabulary that contains all English words in the Express-in-German exercises; and an index to the topics treated in the analysis sections.

SUPPLEMENTARY MATERIALS

To help serve the needs of students, instructors, and teaching assistants, several supplementary materials are available with the text.

For the Student

The *Study Guide* contains a summary of important grammatical points under the heading "Grammar in a Nutshell," each followed by a series of programmed exercises that should be used in conjunction with the study of the analysis. Through these exercises, students can check their own mastery of the material in the text. All answers to the programmed exercises are contained in the *Study Guide*. In addition, there are a number of tear-out exercises that can be assigned as homework and handed in if the instructor so chooses.

The *Study Guide* also contains instructions for lab exercises and, new to this edition, a selection of additional cultural and literary readings as well as nine poems. Instructors can assign these as supplemental or substitute readings for selections in the text.

The *Audio Program* consists of ten cassettes of pronunciation drills, some listen-and-repeat exercises from early units, selected conversations and readings, and dictations for each unit. Many of the exercises are structural transformation drills, the texts of which do not appear in the book. The exercises are recorded by native speakers from various parts of Central Europe.

Computerized Datasets, developed specifically for use with *German: A Structural Approach*, Fourth Edition, are available to each department adopting the text. The datasets are designed to reduce time spent in class on drill and practice; they provide, for each unit, ten sets of exercises covering essential areas of grammar. Students receive immediate feedback in the form of hints for error correction, tutorial windows for rapid review, and cross-references to the analysis in the text for more detailed study. Written using the CALIS authoring system and class-tested at Duke University, the datasets are available for IBM PC and compatible microcomputers.

For the Instructor

The *Teacher's Manual* has been thoroughly revised in its new edition. It offers sample lesson plans and teaching suggestions for every unit in the text and alternative syllabi for courses with varying numbers of contact hours as well as complete instructions for lab exercises. To help with test preparation, the *Manual* also includes cumulative vocabulary lists for each unit and sample examinations.

THE SOUNDS OF GERMAN

This book emphasizes throughout the intonation of complete German sentences. This section addresses the pronunciation of the individual sounds that make up those complete sentences. In order to master the sounds it is essential that you practice them by listening to the tapes that accompany the text. You will want to review this section frequently as you work through the book. After a few weeks or perhaps a few months you will find this section on pronunciation even more useful than at the outset.

We have provided a large number of contrastive drills to show the distinction between two or more different German sounds which, to the ear of American students, may sound alike at first hearing. Many German sounds are sufficiently similar to English sounds so as not to cause the beginner great trouble. Our main concern will be those German sounds which either have no equivalent at all in English or tend to cause an American accent if pronounced like their English spelling equivalents. In many cases, an American accent will not make the German sound unintelligible (though you shouldn't take this as an excuse to retain an American accent); in some cases, however, the wrong pronunciation of certain sounds will produce unintended results. If you mispronounce the **ch**-sound in **Nacht**, as many Americans tend to do, you will not produce the German word for *night*, but the word **nackt**, which means *naked*.

Good pronunciation is essential if you want to speak German correctly and naturally. With patience and lots of practice, you should easily be able to overcome your initial difficulties. Don't worry about making mistakes at the beginning; you'll learn more from them than from not speaking at all.

German Vowels

German has long and short vowels, as well as diphthongs. The distinction between long and short vowels is very important, but unfortunately it is not always indicated by spelling. As a rule of thumb, however, you can assume that a vowel is short if it is followed by a double consonant (for example, **bitte**) or by two or more consonants (**binde**). German vowels are either quite long or very short.

Drill 1 contains all German vowel sounds.

DRILL 1

	LONG	SHORT	UNSTRESSED ONLY
a	**Saat**	satt	
e	**Beet**	**Bett**	
/ə/[1]			-be (gebe)
/ʌ/[1]			-ber (Geber)
i	**ihn**	**in**	
o	**Ofen**	**offen**	
u	**Buhle**	**Bulle**	
ä	**bäte**		
ö	**Höhle**	**Hölle**	
ü	**fühle**	**fülle**	

	DIPHTHONGS
au	**Baum**
ei (ai)	**kein (Kain)**
eu (äu)	**Heu (Häuser)**

NOTE: The two dots over **ä**, **ö**, and **ü** are called umlaut. Occasionally, especially in names, these sounds are spelled **ae**, **oe**, **ue**.

As the table shows, there are twenty different vowel sounds, of which two occur only in unstressed positions. These two are here represented by the symbols /ə/ and /ʌ/, which are not letters in the German alphabet, but are written as **-e** and **-er**.

All German vowels are "pure"; that is, they are monophthongs and do not have any diphthongal glide at the end as do the English letters *a* and *o*. As you hear the following examples, the difference will become clear.

DRILL 2

ENGLISH *a*	GERMAN LONG **e**	ENGLISH *o*	GERMAN LONG **o**
gay	**geh**	moan	**Mohn**
ray	**Reh**	tone	**Ton**
stay	**steh**	tote	**tot**
baited	**betet**	boat	**Boot**

LONG **a** VS. SHORT **a**

Many American students have real difficulty in hearing the difference between these two sounds and consequently have trouble pronouncing them. Yet very often the difference between long **a** and short **a** is the difference between two totally unrelated words, as the following examples show.

[1]We are using phonemic symbols here; in the alphabet /e/ is **-e** and /ʌ/ is **-er**.

LONG **a**	VS.	SHORT **a**
Saat (planting)		**satt** (satisfied)
rate (guess)		**Ratte** (rat)
Rabe (raven)		**Rappe** (black horse)
Wahn (insanity)		**wann** (when)
fahl (pale)		**Fall** (fall)
kam (came)		**Kamm** (comb)
Maße (measures)		**Masse** (mass)
Bahn (track)		**Bann** (ban)

Say these words again, but stretch the long **a** sound. Instead of **Saat**, say **Saaaat**, etc. You cannot do this with the short **a**: if you stretch the words in the second column, you have to stretch the consonant; for example, **Kamm** will become **Kammmm**.

LONG **e**, LONG **ä**, SHORT **e** AND **ä**, UNSTRESSED **e** /ə/ AND **er** /ʌ/

This group of vowel sounds will need your special attention.

Remember that the long **e**, like all other vowels, does not end in a glide: **geh**, not *gay*.

Some Germans do not really distinguish long **ä** from long **e**, except where there is a difference in meaning, for example, in **Gräte** (fishbone) vs. **Grete** (the girl's name Greta).

Short **e** and short **ä** represent the same sound: the **e** in **Kette** is indistinguishable from the **ä** in **hätte**.

The unstressed /ə/ occurs most frequently in endings and in prefixes; it is quite similar to the unstressed English *a* in *the sofa*. If /ə/ appears in front of final **-n**, it often all but disappears; thus **nennen** sounds like **nenn'n** and **kommen** like **komm'n**. These forms are hard to hear and hard to distinguish from forms without the **-en** ending. Yet very often it is essential to realize the distinction, as in **ihn** vs. **ihn(e)n**, **den** vs. **den(e)n**.

The unstressed /ʌ/, which is written as **er**, is one of the most difficult sounds for most Americans to produce. At first, you will have difficulty hearing the difference between /ə/ and /ʌ/, but the distinction is there and may be crucial, as in **bitte** (*please*) vs. **bitter** (*bitter*).

The following drills are designed to show you the differences between the various sounds of this group.

LONG **e**	VS.	SHORT **e**		LONG **e**	VS.	SHORT **e**
Beet		**Bett**		**wen**		**wenn**
Wesen		**wessen**		**den**		**denn**
reden		**retten**		**stehen**		**stellen**

Note again that short **e** and **ä** represent the same sound:

DRILL 5

SHORT **e**	VS.	SHORT **ä**
Wetter		Blätter
kenne		sänne
hemme		Kämme
Schwemme		Schwämme

DRILL 6

LONG **ä**	VS.	LONG **e**	VS.	SHORT **e** OR **ä**
Gräte		Grete		rette
Ähren		ehren		Herren
bäte		bete		bette
wähne		Vene		Wände

DRILL 7

/ə/	VS.	/ʌ/		/ə/	VS.	/ʌ/
bete		Beter		gute		guter
Rede		Reeder		Güte		Güter
nehme		Nehmer		Liebe		Lieber
gebe		Geber		Spitze		Spitzer
Esse		Esser		Pfarre		Pfarrer
Messe		Messer				
Summe		Summer		gehören		erhören
Hüte		Hüter		gearbeitet		erarbeitet
führe		Führer		gegessen		vergessen
Kutte		Kutter		gestört		zerstört

LONG **i** AND **ü**, LONG AND SHORT **u**

The two **i**-sounds are not very difficult to produce. They resemble the English vowel sounds in *bean* and *bin*.

The **ü**-sound, on the other hand, does not exist in English. To produce it, say **i** (as in English *key*); then freeze your tongue in that position and round your lips; or, to put it another way, say English *ee* with your lips in the English *oo* position. If you are musical and can get B above C above middle C on a piano, whistle it, and your tongue and lips will be in perfect **ü**-position. The letter **y**, which occurs mostly in foreign words, is usually pronounced like **ü**.

The long **u**-sound is similar to English *oo* in *noon*; the short **u**-sound is—to oversimplify matters a bit—just a very short version of the same English *oo*-sound, but again both sounds are much more clearly articulated in German.

LONG **i**	VS.	SHORT **i**				DRILL 8
Miete		Mitte				
biete		Bitte				
riete		ritte				
ihnen		innen				

LONG **i**	VS.	LONG **ü (y)**				DRILL 9
Miete		mühte				
Miete		Mythe				
Kiel		kühl				
schiebe		Schübe				
Stiele		Stühle				

SHORT **i**	VS.	SHORT **ü**	SHORT **i**	VS.	SHORT **ü**	DRILL 10
Kissen		küssen	Liste		Lüste	
missen		müssen	Gericht		Gerücht	
sticken		Stücken	springe		Sprünge	
Bitte		Bütte	Kiste		Küste	

LONG **ü**	VS.	SHORT **ü**	LONG **ü**	VS.	SHORT **ü**	DRILL 11
Hüte		Hütte	Wüste		wüßte	
rügen		rücken	Düne		dünne	
pflügen		pflücken	Füßen		Füssen	
kühnste		Künste	fühle		Fülle	

LONG **u**	VS.	SHORT **u**	LONG **u**	VS.	SHORT **u**	DRILL 12
Mus		muß	schuf		Schuft	
Ruhm		Rum	spuken		spucken	
sucht		Sucht	Buhle		Bulle	
Fuder		Futter	Buße		Busse	

LONG **u**	VS.	LONG **ü**	LONG **u**	VS.	LONG **ü**	DRILL 13
Mut		Mythe	Schub		Schübe	
Hut		Hüte	tuten		Tüten	
gut		Güte	Huhn		Hühner	
Schwur		Schwüre	Kuhle		Kühle	

SHORT **u**	VS.	SHORT **ü**	SHORT **u**	VS.	SHORT **ü**	DRILL 14
Mutter		Mütter	mußte		müßte	
Kunst		Künste	wußte		wüßte	
durfte		dürfte	Bund		Bünde	
kurze		Kürze	Luft		Lüfte	

LONG AND SHORT **o**, LONG AND SHORT **ö**

Remember that the German **o**-sound does not end in a glide toward **u**: **Mohn**, not *moan*. To produce an **ö**, say a long German **e**, then freeze your tongue and round your lips. Note also the clear distinction between German **a** and German **o**. An American would be likely not to distinguish between **Bann**, **Bahn**, and **Bonn**, but the three sounds are clearly different.

LONG **o**	VS.	SHORT **o**
wohne		Wonne
Schote		Schotter
Ton		Tonne
Lote		Lotte

DRILL 15

SHORT **o**	VS.	LONG **a**	VS.	SHORT **a**
Bonn		Bahn		Bann
komm		kam		Kamm
Sonne		Sahne		Susanne
hoffen		Hafen		haften
Schollen		Schalen		schallen
locken		Laken		Schlacken
ob		gab		ab

DRILL 16

LONG **e**	VS.	LONG **ö**
redlich		rötlich
heben		höben
bete		böte
lege		löge

DRILL 17

LONG **o**	VS.	LONG **ö**
Ton		Töne
Lohn		Löhne
Hof		Höfe
Not		Nöte
Bogen		Bögen

DRILL 18

SHORT **e**	VS.	SHORT **ö**
stecken		Stöcken
Recke		Röcke
westlich		östlich
helle		Hölle

DRILL 19

LONG **ö**	VS.	SHORT **ö**			DRILL 20
Goethe		**Götter**			
Schöße		**schösse**			
Öfen		**öffnen**			
Höhle		**Hölle**			

LONG **ö**	VS.	LONG **ü**	VS.	LONG **i**	DRILL 21
Söhne		**Sühne**		**Kusine**	
löge		**Lüge**		**liege**	
Öl		**kühl**		**Kiel**	
schöbe		**Schübe**		**schiebe**	

SHORT **ö**	VS.	SHORT **ü**			DRILL 22
Stöcke		**Stücke**			
schösse		**Schüsse**			
Röcken		**Rücken**			
Hölle		**Hülle**			

SHORT **u**	VS.	SHORT **ü**	VS.	SHORT **i**	DRILL 23
mußte		**müßte**		**mißte**	
Stuck		**Stück**		**Stickstoff**	
Kummer		**Kümmel**		**Kimme**	
Kunde		**künde**		**Kinder**	

DIPHTHONGS

There are three German diphthongs, two of which can be spelled in two different ways: **ei (ai)**, **eu (äu)**, and **au**. They will not present much of a problem. They are similar to *i* in English *light*, *oi* in English *foible*, and *ou* in English *mouse*, but, like all German vowels, they are more precise, more clearly defined, and not as drawn-out as their English counterparts.

ei (ai)	eu (äu)	au	DRILL 24
leiten	läuten	lauten	
freien	freuen	Frauen	
zeigen	zeugen	saugen	
leise	Läuse	Laus	
Meise	Mäuse	Maus	

You will be bothered by the fact that the combination **ei** represents a diphthong, but the combination **ie** is simply a long **i**. The following drill should help you overcome this difficulty. To keep the two sounds straight, think of the English phrase *The height of my niece* or of the German phrase **Wein und Bier**.

ei	VS.	**ie**		**ei**	VS.	**ie**
meine		Miene		Zeit		zieht
deine		diene		bereiten		berieten
leider		Lieder		keimen		Kiemen
reimen		Riemen		verzeihen		verziehen

Read the following words, distinguishing carefully between **ei** and **ie**:

viel, Kleid, sieben, Liebe, Leib, leider, Lieder, Seife, siegen, zeigen, liegen, schieben, scheiden, Tier, einheitlich, einseifen, einfrieren, vierseitig, Bierseidel, Zeitspiegel, Spieglein, Meineid, Kleinigkeit

eier
Vielerlei aus einem Ei

German Consonants

In presenting the German vowel system, we have, of necessity, had to use almost all German consonant sounds. As you worked through the preceding section, you doubtless noticed that some German consonants, such as **m** and **n**, differ hardly at all from their English equivalents. Others, such as **z**, have probably surprised you because they are not pronounced the way you expected them to sound. The combination of sounds represented by German **z**, however, does exist in English: if you can say *cats* in English, you should be able to say **"Tsoh"** in German, even though it is spelled **Zoo**.

There are only two consonant sounds in German which have no equivalent in English; they are both graphically represented by **ch**.

The following notes and drills will introduce the German consonants and show you where you will encounter difficulties. We shall start with the two **ch**-sounds.

ch AFTER **a, o, u, au**

This sound is relatively easy for Americans to produce; it corresponds to the **ch** in the Scottish word *loch*. To produce it, start with the sound **h**, let the air flow freely, and then, without diminishing the air flow, reduce the space between the back of your tongue and the roof of your mouth.

Most Americans tend to substitute a *k* for this **ch**-sound. The following drill will show you the difference. Note that the vowels preceding the **ch** are sometimes long and sometimes short.

LONG VOWEL	SHORT VOWEL	DIPHTHONG	
nach	**Bach**	**auch**	DRILL 26
hoch	**noch**	**Lauch**	
Buch	**Bruch**	**Bauch**	

<u>k</u>	vs.	<u>ch</u>	<u>k</u>	vs.	<u>ch</u>	
nackt		**Nacht**	**Kokken**		**kochen**	DRILL 27
Akt		**acht**	**Pocken**		**pochen**	
Laken		**lachen**	**zuckt**		**Zucht**	
lockt		**locht**	**pauken**		**brauchen**	
dockt		**Docht**				

ch IN COMBINATION WITH OTHER LETTERS; **chs**

For most Americans, this is the most difficult German consonant to produce. There are several ways of learning how to produce it. Say the English word *you* with an extended *y*: *y-y-y-you*. This *y* is a voiced sound; if you take the voice out of it, you'll produce something very close to this second **ch**-sound. (You can figure out the difference between a voiced and an unvoiced consonant by comparing the *s*-sounds in English *see* and *zee* (the letter *z*) or *Sioux* and *Zoo*.) Another way of getting at this second German **ch** is by starting with a word like *Hubert* or *huge*. Strongly aspirate the *h* and stretch it out: *h-h-huge*; the result will be quite similar to the **ch**-sound. Try the following combinations:

a human   DRILL 28
say Hugh
the hue
see Hubert

Again, you must be careful not to substitute *k* for **ch**:

DRILL 29

<u>k</u> vs.	<u>ch</u>	<u>k</u> vs.	<u>ch</u>
Bäcker	**Becher**	**siegt**	**Sicht**
Leck	**Lech**	**nickt**	**nicht**
schleckt	**schlecht**	**Brücke**	**Brüche**
häkeln	**hecheln**		

The following drill contrasts the two **ch**-sounds. The words in the second column are the plurals of the words in the first column.

DRILL 30

Dach	**Dächer**	**Buch**	**Bücher**
Bach	**Bäche**	**Bruch**	**Brüche**
Loch	**Löcher**	**Brauch**	**Bräuche**

In the following drill, the **ch**-sound occurs after consonants.

DRILL 31

München	**solcher**
mancher	**Milch**
welcher	**Furcht**

Another difficulty arises when the **ch**-sound appears initially, as in the suffix **-chen**. Note that if the preceding consonant is an **s** or **sch**-sound, the **ch** in **-chen** is pronounced almost like an English *y*.

DRILL 32

Männchen	**bißchen**
Frauchen	**Häuschen**
Säckchen	**Tischchen**

Finally, the combination **chs** is pronounced like English *x*.

DRILL 33

sechs	**Sachsen**
Luchs	**wachsen**
Lachs	**Büchse**

<u>b, d, g AND p, t, k; pf, ps, ng, kn</u>

You will have no trouble pronouncing these sounds, but there is one area where you must watch out: if **b**, **d**, **g** appear at the end of a syllable or in front of **t**, they are pronounced like **p**, **t**, **k**. In the following drill, the German words are not translations of the English words.

DRILL 34

ENGLISH	vs.	GERMAN
b, d, g		**b, d, g**
glib		**gib**
glide		**Kleid**
lied		**Leid**
lead		**Lied**
bug		**Bug**

Compare the pronunciation of **b**, **d**, **g** in the following two columns:

DRILL 35

b, d, g	vs.	**p, t, k**		**b, d, g**	vs.	**p, t, k**
lieben		**lieb, liebt**		**kriegen**		**Krieg, kriegt**
heben		**hob, hebt**		**fliegen**		**flog, fliegt**
sieben		**Sieb, siebt**		**lügen**		**log, lügt**

b, d, g	vs.	**p, t, k**		**b, d, g**	vs.	**p, t, k**
Abend		**ab**		**beobachten**		**Obdach**
loben		**Lob, lobt**		**aber**		**abfahren**
leiden		**Leid**		**radeln**		**Radfahrer**
Lieder		**Lied**		**Tage**		**täglich**
baden		**Bad**		**sagen**		**unsagbar**
Süden		**Süd**				

Now read the following words:

Bad Soden, Abendland, wegheben, abheben, Aberglaube, Staub-wedel, Abwege, Feldweg, Feldwege, Waldwege, Laubwald, Laub-wälder.

The **p** in the combination **pf** and initial **ps** is always pronounced; the latter occurs only in foreign words:

DRILL 36

Pfeife	**Psychologie**
Pfarrer	**Psychiater**
hüpfen	**Psalm**
Köpfe	**Pseudonym**
Topf	
Napf	

The combination **ng** is pronounced as in English *singer*, not as in *finger*.

DRILL 37

Finger	**lange**
Sänger	**England**
Ringe	

The **k** in **kn** must be pronounced.

DRILL 38

ENGLISH	GERMAN	ENGLISH	GERMAN
knave	**Knabe**	knee	**Knie**
knack	**knacken**	knight	**Knecht**
knead	**kneten**	knob	**Knopf**

z

The German letter **z** represents the combination **ts**, which, in English, does not occur at the beginning of words. To learn to produce it in initial position start with the English word *cats*; say it again, but make a break between *ca-* and *-ts*. Then do the same with *Betsy*: *Be/tsy*. If you only say *tsy*, you almost have the first syllable of the German word **Ziege**.

DRILL 39

INITIAL	MEDIAL	FINAL
ziehen	**heizen**	**Kranz**
zog	**duzen**	**Pfalz**
gezogen	**geizig**	**Salz**
zu	**Lanze**	**Kreuz**
Zug	**Kanzel**	**Malz**
Züge	**Kerze**	**Pelz**
Zahn	**Kreuzung**	**stolz**

However, if it occurs in the middle or at the end of a word, the **ts**-sound is usually represented by **tz**.

DRILL 40

Katze	**Platz**
putzen	**Fritz**
sitzen	

s, ß, sp, st, sch

German **s** does not present much of a problem. It is neither as strongly voiceless as the English *s*-sound in *see* nor as strongly voiced as the *s*-sound in *zoo*.

DRILL 41

INITIAL	MEDIAL	FINAL
so	**lesen**	**das**
sie	**blasen**	**los**
sagen	**gewesen**	**Glas**
sicher	**Käse**	**Mus**

The *s*-sound may be represented by the symbol **ß** (instead of **ss**). It is called an **s-z** (**ess-zet**) and is used:

(a) between two vowels of which the first is long:

LONG VOWEL + **ß**	SHORT VOWEL + **ss**
Maße	**Masse**
Buße	**Busse**
Straße	**Rasse**
große	**Rosse**

(b) after a vowel or a diphthong before a consonant (mostly in verbs whose stem ends in **-ss**):

weißt	**paßt**
mußt	**heißt**

(c) in final position:

Fuß	**weiß**
Roß	**daß**

Many Germans no longer use the **ß** symbol, but write **ss** instead.

The **s** in German **sp** and **st** at the beginning is pronounced like English *sh*.

Spaß	**Start**	**Strand**
Sport	**stehen**	**Strom**
spät	**still**	**streng**
Spinne	**Stock**	**streichen**
Spule	**Stück**	**streuen**

German **sch** is pronounced like English *sh*.

schön
waschen
Busch

sch	VS.	ch
Tisch		**dich**
mischen		**mich**
Esche		**Echo**
Büsche		**Bücher**

w, v, f

There is no German equivalent of the English *w*-sound as in *water*.
German **w** is pronounced like English *v*.

wann	**wie**
wer	**warum**
wo	

German **v** is usually pronounced like English *f*.

Vater	**voll**
verliebt	**von**
viel	

In some foreign words, German **v** corresponds to English *v*.

Vase
Villa

German **f** always corresponds to English *f*, as does the *ph*-sound in foreign words.

fallen	**fünf**
Fell	**Philosophie**
fliegen	**Physik**

w	vs.	**f**		**w**	vs.	**f**
Wein		**fein**		**Wort**		**fort**
Wand		**fand**		**Wunde**		**Funde**
winden		**finden**				

l AND r

These two consonants are mispronounced by most Americans. Such mispronunciations will normally not lead to a misunderstanding, but they do in large measure contribute to a "typical American accent." Constant practice with these two consonants is therefore essential.

The English *l* is a "dark," back *l*, and the German **l** is a "clear," front **l**. Listen to the difference:

DRILL 46

ENGLISH *l*	vs.	GERMAN **l**		ENGLISH *l*	vs.	GERMAN **l**
feel		**viel**		hell		**hell**
stool		**Stuhl**		lewd		**lud**
mall		**Mal**		light		**Leid**
fall		**Fall**		long		**lang**
toll		**toll**		bald		**bald**
still		**still**		built		**Bild**

In some parts of Germany, the **r** is trilled, but the preferred sound is a uvular **r**. To produce it, say **Buchen**, with the **ch**-sound as far back as possible. Then add voice to it and you should be saying **Buren**.

ENGLISH *r* VS.	GERMAN **r**		ENGLISH *r* VS.	GERMAN **r**	DRILL 47
run	**ran**		fry	**frei**	
rudder	**Ruder**		fresh	**frisch**	
reef	**rief**		creek	**Krieg**	
rest	**Rest**		warn	**warnen**	
ray	**Reh**		start	**Start**	
row	**roh**		stork	**Storch**	
brown	**braun**		worst	**Wurst**	
dry	**drei**				

We introduced the **er**-sound (ʌ) under the vowels. Many Germans use this same sound for **r** before **t**.

er fährt	**er bohrt**	**er knurrt**	DRILL 48
er lehrt	**er irrt**		

INITIAL **r**	**r** AFTER CONSONANT	MEDIAL **r**	**r** BEFORE **t**	FINAL **r** (ʌ)	DRILL 49
raffen	**graben**	**fahren**	**fahrt**	**fahr'**	
Rebe	**Bregenz**	**Beeren**	**fährt**	**Bär**	
riefen	**Friesen**	**vieren**	**viert**	**vier**	
rot	**Thron**[2]	**Toren**	**bohrt**	**Tor**	
Ruhe	**Bruder**	**Uhren**	**fuhrt**	**Uhr**	

ch VS.	**r**		**ch** VS.	**r**	DRILL 50
Buchen	**Buren**		**Sucht**	**surrt**	
suchen	**Suren**		**Dach**	**dar**	
fachen	**fahren**		**Loch**	**Lohr**	
Acht	**Art**		**Tuch**	**Tour**	
Docht	**dort**				

l VS.	**r**		**l** VS.	**r**	DRILL 51
wild	**wird**		**Spalt**	**spart**	
Geld	**Gert**		**spülen**	**spüren**	
halt	**hart**		**fühlen**	**führen**	
hold	**Hort**		**fallen**	**fahren**	
bald	**Bart**		**tollen**	**Toren**	

<u>h</u>

At the beginning of a word or syllable, **h** is pronounced as in English *house*. It is never silent as in English *honor*. The symbol **h**, however, is also used to indicate that the preceding vowel is long.

---

[2]The combination **th**, which occurs in a few German words, is always pronounced as **t**: English *throne*, German **Thron**.

sehen	**seht**	**steh'**	DRILL 52
fehlen	**fehlt**	**geh'**	
Lehrer	**lehrt**	**Reh**	

q

As in English, **q** appears only with a following **u**, but it is pronounced like English *kv*, not *kw*.

ENGLISH	GERMAN	
		DRILL 53
quicksilver	**Quecksilber**	
quadrant	**Quadrant**	
Quaker	**Quäker**	
qualify	**qualifizieren**	
quality	**Qualität**	
quarter	**Quartier**	

j

This letter is pronounced like English *y*.

ENGLISH	GERMAN	
		DRILL 54
yes	**ja**	
year	**Jahr**	
young	**jung**	
youth	**Jugend**	
yacht	**Jacht**	
yoke	**Joch**	

The Glottal Stop

The glottal stop is a phenomenon much more common in German than in English. In certain parts of the eastern United States, the word *bottle* is pronounced *bo-'l* with a very short open *o*, after which the glottis is closed and then suddenly reopened. This sudden release of air occurs in German in front of all initial vowels: **ein alter Affe**. Most Americans tend to run these words together: [**einalteraffe**]; this is another element of the "typical American accent." If you neglect to use the glottal stop, you may get yourself into embarrassing situations. For instance, if you don't use the stop in front of -'**au**, you will interpret the name of the village of **Himmelsau** as *Celestial Pig* instead of *Heavenly Meadow*.

ein alter Affe	**alle anderen Uhren**	DRILL 55
Himmelsau	**es erübrigt sich**	
der erste Akt	**es ist aber veraltet**	
ein alter Omnibus	**eine alte Eule sitzt unter einer alten Ulme**	
er aber aß Austern		

Note the difference in

vereisen (*to get covered with ice*)   and   **verreisen** (*to go on a trip*)
verengen (*to narrow*)   **verrenken** (*to sprain*)

Syllabication

German syllabication is considerably simpler than English syllabication. A few basic rules will suffice to see you through this book.

German words are divided before single consonants and between double consonants.

Va · ter	**kom · men**
Da · me	**reg · nen**
Te · le · fon	**Mün · chen**

The only exception to this rule is **st**, which is never separated.

fe · ster
mei · stens
Fen · ster

Unlike English, German does not consider suffixes independent units; thus it is **Woh · nung**, not [**Wohn · ung**].

Compound words are divided according to their individual parts.

Brief · trä · ger
Glas · au · ge
Sams · tag

Punctuation

Generally speaking, most German punctuation marks are used as in English. Only the use of the comma is different. The comma may be used to separate main clauses if the second clause contains a new subject, especially in front of coordinating conjunctions. The comma *must* be used to separate dependent clauses from main clauses. Relative clauses are dependent clauses, and German does not distinguish between restrictive and nonrestrictive relative clauses. In contrast to English, the comma is not used in front of **und** in series: **Männer, Frauen und Kinder.**

The first of a pair of quotation marks in German appears below the base line in writing or printing, the second appears at the top: "Be quiet!" **„Sei ruhig!"**

GERMAN

A Structural Approach

FOURTH EDITION

Unit 1

Personal Pronouns—The Present Tense of Verbs—Basic Structure—Sentence Intonation—Plural of Nouns

Where is German spoken?

The German language area is not identified with, nor identical to, a single nation state. German is spoken in five different countries: Austria, parts of Switzerland, the tiny principality of Liechtenstein (which is located between Switzerland and Austria), and the two states into which Germany was divided after the Second World War: the Federal Republic of Germany (West Germany, **Bundesrepublik Deutschland** or **BRD**, for short) and the German Democratic Republic (East Germany, **Deutsche Demokratische Republik** or **DDR**).

While there are many differences between these countries in their political and economic systems, in regional customs and local dialects, they still share a common element, the German language. Some people are unaware that German is spoken beyond the borders of Germany. The fact that one tends to think only of the Federal Republic when the word German is mentioned, reflects a lack of awareness of the German Democratic Republic and its social and political realities. Study the end maps to acquaint yourself with the German-speaking parts of Europe.

Köln am Rhein

Heidelberg am Neckar

PATTERNS ONE

1/Personal Pronouns and the Present Tense of Verbs

KARIN: Ich komme aus Bonn.[1] Und du? Kommst du auch aus Bonn?

I'm from Bonn. And you? Are you from Bonn too?

INGRID: Ja, ich komme auch aus Bonn. Aber Erika kommt aus Köln.

Yes, I'm from Bonn too. But Erika is from Cologne.

KARIN: Nein, sie kommt aus Düsseldorf. Hans kommt aus Köln.

No, she is from Düsseldorf. Hans is from Cologne.

KARIN: Ingrid und ich, wir kommen beide aus Bonn.

Ingrid and I, we are both from Bonn.

Und ihr? Kommt ihr auch aus Bonn?

And you? Are you from Bonn too?

HELGA: Ja, wir kommen auch aus Bonn. Aber Petra und Doris kommen aus Köln.

Yes, we're from Bonn too. But Petra and Doris are from Cologne.

KARIN: Nein, sie kommen aus Düsseldorf.

No, they are from Düsseldorf.

Andrea und Gisela kommen aus Köln.

Andrea and Gisela are from Cologne.

Straßencafé in Eisenach (DDR)

[1]The verb **kommen** means *to come*; **kommen aus**, *to come from*, is also used to express the idea *to be from*.

SCHMIDT:	Ich wohne in Hamburg. Und Sie?	I live in Hamburg. And you?
	Wohnen Sie auch in Hamburg?	Do you live in Hamburg too?
MÜLLER:	Nein, ich wohne in Bremen.	No, I live in Bremen.
	Und wo wohnen Sie, Herr Meyer?	And where do you live, Mr. Meyer?
MEYER:	Ich wohne in Lübeck.	I live in Lübeck.

2/Variations in Personal Endings

RICHARD:	Ich heiße Richard. Wie heißt du?	My name is Richard. What's your name?
INGRID:	Ingrid. Und sie heißt Erika.	Ingrid. And her name is Erika.
RICHARD:	Und wie heißt er?	And what's his name?
INGRID:	Er heißt Hans.	His name is Hans.
PROFESSOR:	Wie heißen Sie, bitte?	What's your name?
STUDENT:	Ich heiße Schmidt, Kurt Schmidt.	My name is Schmidt, Kurt Schmidt.
SCHMIDT:	Ich arbeite jetzt in München. Und du? Wo arbeitest du jetzt?	I'm working in Munich now. And you? Where do you work now?
MÜLLER:	Ich arbeite in Frankfurt. Meyer arbeitet auch in Frankfurt.	I'm working in Frankfurt. Meyer works in Frankfurt too.

3/The Present Tense of *sein*

Wo bist du heute abend, Inge?
Heute abend bin ich zu Hause.
Doris ist heute abend auch zu Hause.
Fritz und Dieter, wo seid ihr morgen?

Wir sind morgen in Köln.
Doris und Hans sind morgen auch in Köln.

Und wo sind Sie morgen, Herr Meyer?

Wie ist das Wetter?
—Es ist kalt und es regnet.
—Es ist warm.

Where are you (going to be) tonight, Inge?
Tonight I'll be home.
Doris will be at home tonight too.
Fritz and Dieter, where are you (going to be) tomorrow?

We will be in Cologne tomorrow.
Doris and Hans will be in Cologne tomorrow too.

And where are you (going to be) tomorrow, Mr. Meyer?

How's the weather?
—It's cold and it's raining.
—It's warm.

ANALYSIS ONE

1/Personal Pronouns

	SINGULAR		PLURAL	
FIRST PERSON	**ich**	I	**wir**	we
SECOND PERSON	**du, Sie**	you	**ihr, Sie**	you
THIRD PERSON	**er** **sie** **es**	he she it	**sie**	they

Note that the pronoun **ich** is never capitalized, except at the beginning of a sentence.

ENGLISH *you*: GERMAN **du, ihr, Sie**

Modern English has just one form (*you*) for the second person. English *you* is both singular and plural, formal and informal. In German, there are three mutually exclusive forms:

1. **du** is singular. It is used to address family members, close friends, and all children up to the age of about fourteen or fifteen. It is also used among members of certain social groups, such as students, blue collar workers, and soldiers.

2. **ihr** is the plural of **du**, that is, it is used when speaking to two or more people whom one addresses individually by **du**.

3. **Sie** is used in speaking to all those one does not address by **du**, that is, the majority of people one comes in contact with. It *must* be used with anybody addressed as **Herr, Frau, Fräulein,** or with other titles.[2]

The pronoun **Sie** is used whether addressing a single person or more than one; it is always capitalized and takes the same verb form as the plural **sie** (*they*).

Trinkst du Kaffee, Karl?	Du you drink coffee, Karl?
Trinkt ihr Milch, Kinder?	Do you drink milk, children?
Trinken Sie Bier, Frau Meyer?	Do you drink beer, Mrs. Meyer?

[2]Germans, and especially Austrians, are fond of titles. If **Herr Meyer** and **Frau Meyer** have earned any kind of doctorate, they are addressed as **Herr (Frau) Doktor** and are referred to as **Herr (Frau) Dr. Meyer** or as **Dr. Meyer.** It is not unusual for a letter to be addressed to **Frau Prof. Dr. Katharina Meyer** or **Herrn Prof. Dr. Gustav Meyer.**

NOTE: The word **Herr** means *Mr.* or *gentleman*; **Mann** means either *husband* or *man*. The word **Frau** means either *Mrs.* or *Ms.* or *wife* or *woman*, and **Fräulein** means *Miss.* The choice of **Frau** vs. **Fräulein** used to be clear-cut: a **Frau** was married, a **Fräulein** was not, except that older unmarried women could elect to call themselves **Frau**. In recent years, that age limit has been lowered considerably so that today a single woman in her late teens may legitimately and properly be called **Frau**, the closest German has come to the American *Ms.* While **Herr** and **Frau** are never abbreviated, **Fräulein** can be abbreviated as **Frl.** The term **Fräulein** is being used less and less.

2/The Infinitive and Inflected Verb Forms

The *infinitive* is that form of the verb which is used as a dictionary entry.[3] Most German infinitives end in **-en: kommen, lernen, wohnen**. The part of the verb that precedes this infinitive ending is called the *stem*. The verb **sein** and a few others have the infinitive ending **-n** instead of **-en**.

In German, as in English, a verb must "agree" with its subject. Just as one says *I learn*, but *she learns*, so in German one must select a verb form to agree with the subject. These forms are called inflected or finite verb forms.

The present tense of regular verbs is formed as follows:

		PRONOUN	STEM +	PERSONAL = ENDING	INFLECTED FORM
SINGULAR	1.	**ich**	**lern-**	e	**ich lerne**
	2.	**du**	**lern-**	st	**du lernst**
		Sie	**lern-**	en	**Sie lernen**
	3.	**er**			**er**
		sie }	**lern-**	t	**sie } lernt**
		es			**es**
PLURAL	1.	**wir**	**lern-**	en	**wir lernen**
	2.	**ihr**	**lern-**	t	**ihr lernt**
		Sie	**lern-**	en	**Sie lernen**
	3.	**sie**	**lern-**	en	**sie lernen**

The German present tense serves a number of functions:

Ich gehe ins Kino.	I go to the movies.	SIMPLE PRESENT
	I'm going to the movies.	PROGRESSIVE
	I'll go to the movies.	FUTURE
	I do go to the movies.	EMPHATIC

[3]In English the infinitive forms are frequently preceded by the marker *to*; thus *go* or *to go*, *be* or *to be*.

Geht ihr heute abend ins Kino?

The simple present is timeless: *I go to the movies often.* The progressive denotes an activity currently going on: *Where are you going? I'm going to the movies.* By adding a time phrase, the present tense can refer to the future: *I'm going (I'll go) to the movies tomorrow.* The emphatic is a strong affirmation of the verb: *Yes, I really do go to the movies.*

3/Variations in Personal Endings

In the case of **er lernt** or **er kommt**, the ending **-t** is easily pronounced and heard. However, in the case of such verbs as **arbeiten** and of all other verbs whose stems end in **-d** or **-t**, the vowel **-e** is inserted between the stem and the endings **-st** and **-t** to make these endings clearly audible. For similar reasons (so that the second syllable of all forms of **regnen** starts with an **n-**), it is **es regnet**. Verbs with stems ending in an *s*-sound have the same form in the **du**-form and **er**-form.

NORMAL VERBS	VERBS WITH STEMS IN -d OR -t	VERBS WITH STEMS IN S-SOUNDS
du lernst	du arbeitest	du heißt
er ⎫ sie ⎬ lernt es ⎭	er ⎫ sie ⎬ arbeitet es ⎭	er ⎫ sie ⎬ heißt es ⎭
ihr lernt	ihr arbeitet	ihr heißt

Note that English has no exact equivalent of the verb **heißen** which expresses the notion *to be called* or *to have the name of.*

4/The Present Tense of **sein**, *to be*

Sein and *to be* are among the most frequently used verbs in German and English; they are also the most irregular. It is very important, therefore, that you learn the present tense forms thoroughly.

ich bin	**wir sind**
du bist	**ihr seid**
er	
sie } **ist**	**sie sind**
es	

PRACTICE ONE

A. Conjugate in the present tense in all persons, singular and plural. For the third person, use pronouns or names, but not **es**, *it*.

1. Ich heiße Meyer.
2. Ich komme aus Berlin.
3. Ich wohne in Köln.
4. Ich bin heute zu Hause.
5. Ich lerne Deutsch.
6. Ich arbeite in Hamburg.
7. Ich trinke Milch.
8. Ich arbeite heute.

B. Form statements from the following elements. Note that not all combinations make logical sense.

Fritz arbeitet in Berlin.

Fritz		heute abend
sie		jetzt
Sie		morgen
wir	arbeiten	hier
Frl. Müller	wohnen	in Berlin
ihr	sein	Stuttgart
du		München
er		Zürich
Frau Dr. Müller		zu Hause

C. Give the German equivalent. Remember that German does not have emphatic and progressive forms.

1. She's coming today.
2. We're living in Cologne.
3. You live in Hamburg. (3 forms)
4. He works here.

5. We do work.
6. I'll be at home.
7. You're coming today. (3 forms)

8. My name is Doris.
9. They drink coffee.
10. You are in Munich. (3 forms)

What does *studieren* mean?

The German verb **studieren** has a more limited meaning than the English verb *to study*; **studieren** means *to be enrolled at a university*; **lernen** means *to acquire a skill:* **Sie lernt Deutsch,** *She is learning German,* but **Sie studiert Deutsch,** *She is a German major,* and **Sie studiert in Frankfurt,** *She goes to the University of Frankfurt.*

There is no German equivalent of the American college and of the American distinction between undergraduate and graduate work. After completing the university preparatory track in secondary school, German students go directly to a university to begin their chosen field of study.

The German university system dates back to the late Middle Ages. Some of the most famous universities are also the oldest: Vienna (1365), Heidelberg (1386), Cologne (1388), Erfurt (1392), Leipzig (1409), Freiburg (1457), Basel (1460), Tübingen (1477).

Since World War II, the number of universities and the number of students attending have risen dramatically.

Heidelberg University 1502

PATTERNS TWO

4/Structure of Assertions

Fritz ist leider in *Mün*chen.[4]
    Leider ist Fritz in *Mün*chen.

Doris kommt heute nach *Hau*se.[5]
    Heute kommt *Do*ris nach Hause.

Doris wohnt jetzt *auch* in München.
    Jetzt wohnt Doris *auch* in München.

Sie arbeiten jetzt in *Mün*chen.
    Jetzt arbeiten sie in *Mün*chen.

Sie bleiben übrigens heute abend zu *Hau*se.[5]
    Heute *a*bend bleiben sie übrigens zu *Hau*se.
    Übrigens bleiben sie heute abend zu *Hau*se.

Fritz geht natürlich morgen abend ins *Ki*no.
    Morgen *a*bend geht Fritz natürlich ins *Ki*no.
    Na*tür*lich geht Fritz morgen abend ins *Ki*no.

Unfortunately, Fritz is in Munich.

Doris is coming home today.

Doris lives in Munich too now.

They're working in Munich now.

By the way, they're staying home tonight.

Fritz, of course, is going to the movies tomorrow night.

[4]Throughout the book, italics are used occasionally to indicate stress.

[5]Both **nach Hause** and **zu Hause** mean *home*. If you can place *at* before *home*, you must use **zu Hause**: *I'll stay (at) home tonight.* If *at* cannot be added, you must use **nach Hause**: *I'm going home tonight.* With **nach Hause** there is always motion or direction involved.

5/Structure of Questions

Ist Herr Keller in Berlin?	Is Mr. Keller in Berlin?
Ja, er ist in Berlin.	Yes, he's in Berlin.
Nein, er ist in Köln.	No, he's in Cologne.
Heißt sie Müller?	Is her name Müller?
Ja, Ingrid Müller.	Yes, Ingrid Müller.
Ja, sie heißt Ingrid Müller.	Yes, her name is Ingrid Müller.
Heißen Sie auch Müller?	Is your name Müller too?
Nein, ich heiße Schmidt.	No, my name is Schmidt.
Arbeitet Werner Keller in Köln?	Does Werner Keller work in Cologne?
Ja, er arbeitet in Köln.	Yes, he works in Cologne.
Wer ist das?	Who is that?
Das ist Thomas.	That's Thomas.
Wann kommt Thomas nach Köln?	When is Thomas coming to Cologne?
Morgen.	Tomorrow.
Er kommt morgen.	He's coming tomorrow.
Thomas kommt morgen.	Thomas is coming tomorrow.
Thomas kommt morgen nach Köln.	Thomas is coming to Cologne tomorrow.
Wo ist er jetzt?	Where is he now?
In München.	In Munich.
Er ist in München.	He's in Munich.
Jetzt ist er in München.	Now he's in Munich.
Warum ist er in München?	Why is he in Munich?
Er studiert da.	He is studying there.
Was studiert Thomas?	What is Thomas studying?
Medizin.	Medicine.
Er studiert Medizin.	He is studying medicine.
Wie ist das Wetter in München?	How is the weather in Munich?
Schlecht.	Bad.
Das Wetter ist schlecht.	The weather is bad.

6/Structure of Imperatives

Kommen Sie bitte.	Please come.
Gehen Sie nach Hause.	Go home.
Bleiben Sie heute abend zu Hause.	Stay home tonight.
Studieren Sie Psychologie.	Study psychology.
Trinken Sie Milch.	Drink milk.
Seien Sie glücklich.	Be happy.

ANALYSIS TWO

5/The Structure of Assertions

In English assertions, the subject is usually position-fixed; it precedes the inflected verb. Some other syntactical units may also precede the inflected verb, so that the verb may be the second, third, or even the fourth element in the sentence.

	She		*lives*	in Munich.
	She	now	*lives*	in Munich.
Now	she		*lives*	in Munich.
Fortunately	she	now	*lives*	in Munich.

> In German assertions, *the inflected verb is always the second syntactical unit.*

There are no exceptions to this rule. This means that German cannot imitate the word order of the last three English sentences above. The verb **wohnt** can be preceded by either the subject *or* the time phrase, but not by both the subject *and* the time phrase. The sentence

Jetzt wohnt sie in München.

where the subject *follows* the verb is just as correct as

Sie wohnt jetzt in München.

where the subject *precedes* the verb. If pronoun subjects like **ich, er, wir** do not precede the inflected verb, they *must* follow it immediately. Noun subjects usually also follow directly after the inflected verb.

THE FRONT FIELD

The area preceding the inflected verb is called the front field. A number of elements other than the subject can occupy the front field of German sentences, but some elements cannot. In order to determine which elements *can* appear in the front field, follow this rule of thumb:

Only those elements that can precede an *English* verb can normally also precede a *German* verb:

Tonight we are going to be at home.

can result in two German sentences:

Heute abend sind wir zu Hause.
Wir sind heute abend zu Hause.

Conversely, any syntactical element that cannot normally precede an English verb cannot normally precede a German verb either:

[At home we are going to be tonight.][6]

NOTE: Adverbial phrases like **heute abend** are *never* set off by a comma.

6/The Structure of Questions

In English, questions are formed in one of two ways:

1. most verbs require a form of *to do*:

He speaks German.   Does he speak German?

2. the verb *to be* and modal verbs (*can, shall*) do not require *to do*:

Is he working?   *Can* you help me?   When *shall* I call you?

German never uses a special auxiliary or helping verb (like *to do*) to form a question. Instead of *Do you live here?* a German says [*Live you here?*] **Wohnen Sie hier?** Similarly, a German says [*Where works she?*] **Wo arbeitet sie?** instead of *Where does she work?*

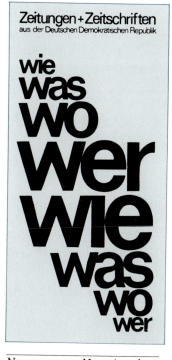

Newspapers + Magazines from the German Democratic Republic

YES-OR-NO QUESTIONS

Questions which can be answered by **ja** (*yes*) or **nein** (*no*) start with an inflected verb in both English and German:

Arbeitet sie in Berlin?   Does she work in Berlin?
Trinkst du Kaffee?   Do you drink coffee?

WORD QUESTIONS

In English and German, word questions (questions that require more than a yes or no answer) are introduced by interrogatives (question words). Among the most common are:

wann	when	**wer**	who
warum	why	**wie**	how
was	what	**wo**	where

---

[6]Brackets are used to indicate unacceptable constructions.

In word questions, the inflected verb immediately follows the interrogative.

Wann kommt ihr?	When are you coming?
Warum lernst du Deutsch?	Why are you learning German?
Was trinkst du?	What are you drinking?
Wer ist das?	Who is that?
Wie ist das Wetter?	How is the weather?
Wo wohnt sie?	Where does she live?

NOTE: Do not confuse **wer** (*who*) with **wo** (*where*).

QUESTIONS STRUCTURED LIKE ASSERTIONS

In both English and German, any assertion can be changed into a yes-or-no question simply by changing its intonation (see Sounds of German, p. xxi).

Er wohnt in München.	He lives in Munich.
Er wohnt in München?	He lives in Munich?

Questions structured like assertions, however, are not interchangeable with verb-first yes-or-no questions. They usually imply something like *Is it (not) true that . . .?* In fact, many such questions end with the phrase **nicht wahr?** (*not true?*); they presuppose a positive answer.

Er wohnt in München, nicht wahr?	He lives in Munich, doesn't he?

7/Questions and Answers

The answer to word questions, especially in spoken German, is usually just a word or phrase; thus, the answer to **Wo ist Fritz heute?** could be **hier** or **in München**. If the answer is a whole sentence, this word or phrase cannot be in the front field. In contrast to English, this word or phrase usually appears at the end of the sentence.

Wo ist *Fritz* heute? —*Hier.*
                   In *München.*
                   Fritz ist heute *hier.*
                   Heute ist Fritz in *München.*

This rule does not apply to questions with **Wer** (*who*). Such questions ask for the subject of a sentence and can be answered in two ways:

Wer kommt morgen?
***Fritz* kommt morgen. — Morgen kommt *Fritz*. — or simply: *Fritz*.**

In both cases, the subject has the main syntactical stress.

Questions with **warum** are usually answered with a complete sentence:

Warum bleibt ihr heute abend zu Hause? — Das Wetter ist schlecht.

For the time being, do not try to answer a **warum**-question with **weil** (*because*).

NOTE: From now on we will occasionally indicate syntactical stress by printing the stressed syllables in italics. For a discussion of syntactical stress, see Anal. 10, p. 19, and Sounds of German, p. xxi.

8/The Structure of Imperatives

The English imperative is identical with the infinitive. One can say *Be my guest* no matter whether one calls the person addressed *Julia* or *Dr. Able*. German distinguishes between the **du**-form, the **ihr**-form, and the **Sie**-form of the imperative. At this point, we introduce only the **Sie**-form, which looks like the infinitive plus **Sie**, for example, **Kommen Sie! Gehen Sie!** The only exception is the imperative of **sein**: **Seien Sie!**

Imperatives, like yes-or-no questions, have verb-first position; the remainder of the sentence is structured like an assertion and may be followed by an exclamation point.

You may hear your teacher use imperatives like these:

Schreiben Sie.	Write.
Lesen Sie.	Read.
Machen Sie Ihr Buch auf.	Open your book.
Machen Sie Ihr Buch zu.	Close your book.
Gehen Sie an die Tafel.	Go to the blackboard.

Summary of Types of Sentence Structure

VERB SECOND POSITION

Assertions	**Sie gehen ins Kino.**
Word questions	**Wann gehen Sie ins Kino?**
Assertion questions	**Sie gehen ins Kino, (nicht wahr)?**

VERB FIRST POSITION

Yes-or-no questions	**Gehen Sie ins Kino?**
Imperatives	**Gehen Sie ins Kino!**

PRACTICE TWO

D. Repeat each sentence, starting as indicated.

1. Petra kommt heute. Heute _kommt Petra_ .
2. Morgen geht sie nach Hamburg. Sie _geht morgen nach Hamburg._
3. Sie heißt übrigens Müller. Übrigens _heißt sie Müller_
4. Sie studiert jetzt Medizin. Jetzt _studiert sie Medizin._
5. Petra arbeitet leider heute abend. Leider _arbeitet Petra heute abend._
   Heute abend _arbeitet Petra leider._
6. Morgen abend ist sie natürlich zu Hause. Sie _ist natürlich morgen abend zu Hause._
   Natürlich _ist sie morgen abend zu Hause_

E. Change the following assertions into yes-or-no questions.

Sie gehen nach Hamburg.	Gehen Sie nach Hamburg?

1. Silvia kommt heute abend.
2. Dieter ist morgen abend zu Hause.
3. Sie arbeitet in Köln.
4. Er heißt Keller.
5. Thomas studiert Medizin.
6. Ruth geht heute abend ins Kino.
7. Frau Dr. Rücker wohnt in Bielefeld.
8. Ihr bleibt heute abend zu Hause.
9. Monika lernt Deutsch.
10. Du trinkst Bier.

F. Write down word questions which could be answered by the statements.

Wo ist Erika?	Sie ist in Bonn.

1. Wo _____ ?   Sie wohnt in Köln.
2. Wer _____ ?   Petra kommt aus Düsseldorf.
3. Wie _____ ?   Erika Schmidt.
4. Wann _____ ?   Morgen abend.
5. Was _____ ?   Medizin.
6. Warum _____ ?   Er arbeitet hier.
7. Wie _____ ?   Es ist kalt.

G. Provide several answers to the following questions.

Wann kommt Fritz nach Köln?	**Morgen.**
	Er kommt morgen.
	Fritz kommt morgen nach Köln.

1. Wer ist das?
2. Was studiert Claudia?
3. Wie heißen Sie?
4. Wo arbeitest du jetzt?

5. Wie ist das Wetter?
6. Wo wohnt ihr?
7. Wann gehst du ins Kino?
8. Warum sind Sie in Zürich?

H. Using imperatives, ask Frau Braun to do the following:

1. To come tomorrow morning.
2. To go to the movies.
3. To stay home tonight.

4. To learn English.
5. To drink milk.
6. To be happy.

PATTERNS THREE

7/Sentence Intonation: Assertions

Practice reading the following sentences aloud to get used to the intonation patterns. Stress points are printed in italics.

Das ist *Milch/Wein/Bier/Tee.*
Das Wetter ist *gut/schlecht.*
Es ist *warm/heiß/kalt.*

This is milk/wine/beer/tea.
The weather is good/bad.
It is warm/hot/cold.

Hans kommt morgen.
*Do*ris ist hier.

Hans is coming tomorrow.
Doris is here.

Fritz und Erika *Mül*ler wohnen in Deutschland.
Fritz studiert *Deutsch* und Psycholo*gie.*[7]
*E*rika studiert Medi*zin.*
Nächsten *Som*mer gehen sie nach A*mer*ika.

Fritz and Erika Müller live in Germany.

Fritz is studying German and psychology.
Erika is studying medicine.
Next summer they are going to America.

8/Sentence Intonation: Questions

Was *ist* das?
  Das ist *Kaf*fee.
Wer ist *das*?
  Das ist Fritz *Mül*ler.
Wo *wohnt* er?
  Er wohnt in *Köln.*
Was machen Sie nächsten *Som*mer?
  Nächsten *Som*mer bleibe ich zu *Hau*se.

What is that?
  That's coffee.
Who is that?
  That's Fritz Müller.
Where does he live?
  He lives in Cologne.
What are you doing next summer?
  Next summer I'm staying home.

---

[7]Some English words are spelled with an initial *ps-*, but drop the *p* when pronounced; in German, however, both the **p** and the **s** are sounded. Try to say *harpsichord* without the initial *har-*, and you get the **ps-** of **Psychologie.**

Geht Hans heute ins *Ki*no?

Ja, er geht heute ins *Ki*no.
Nein, er geht *mor*gen ins Kino.

Wohnt Peter in *Ham*burg?

Ja, er wohnt in *Ham*burg.
Nein, er wohnt in Ber*lin*.

Ist Kurt *Arzt*?[8]

Ja, er ist *Arzt*.
Nein, er ist *Leh*rer.

Ist Inge *Ärztin*?

Ja, sie ist *Ärztin*.
Nein, sie ist *Lehr*erin.

Lernt Claudia jetzt *Deutsch*?

Ja, sie lernt jetzt *Deutsch*.
Nein, sie lernt jetzt *Eng*lisch.

Erika ist heute in *Stutt*gart?

Ja, sie ist heute in *Stutt*gart.
Nein, sie ist heute in *Köln*.

Erika ist *heute* in Stuttgart?

Ja, sie ist *heute* in Stuttgart.
Nein, sie ist *mor*gen in Stuttgart.

*E*rika ist heute in Stuttgart?

Ja, *sie* ist heute in Stuttgart.
Nein, *Gi*sela ist heute in Stuttgart.

9/The Particle *denn*

Wer *sind* Sie?
  Wer *sind* Sie denn?

Ich bin Jane *Ray*.

Wie *hei*ßen Sie?
  Wie *hei*ßen Sie denn?

Ich heiße *Ray*, John Ray.

Wann gehen Sie nach *Hau*se?
  Wann gehen Sie denn nach *Hau*se?

Um *eins*. (Um *ein* Uhr.)
  Um *zwei*. (Um *zwei* Uhr.)

Was machen Sie heute *a*bend?
  Was machen Sie denn heute *a*bend?

Ich gehe heute abend ins *Ki*no.
  Heute abend gehe ich ins *Ki*no.

Wo sind Sie *mor*gen abend?
  Wo sind Sie denn *mor*gen abend?

Zu *Hau*se.
  In *Köln*.

Studieren Sie Psycholo*gie*?
  Studieren Sie denn Psycholo*gie*?

Ja, natürlich.
  Nein, Medi*zin*.

10/Plurals of Nouns

This section introduces singular and plural forms of objects found in your classroom. To practice these forms, point out such objects with your book closed.

Was ist das? —Das ist der Tisch.
Hier ist ein Tisch. Da sind zwei Tische.

What is that? —That is the table.
Here is a table. There are two tables.

[8]Note that German does not use the indefinite article when identifying professional status, see Anal. 25, p. 55.

Das ist die Tafel. (*blackboard*)
    eine Tafel.
    zwei Tafeln.

    das Fenster. (*window*)
    ein Fenster.
    zwei Fenster.

    der Stuhl. (*chair*)
    ein Stuhl.
    zwei Stühle.

    die Tür. (*door*)
    eine Tür.
    zwei Türen.

    das Buch. (*book*)
    ein Buch.
    zwei Bücher.

ANALYSIS THREE

9/Word Stress

Most German words stress the first syllable: **A'bend, ar'beiten, heu'te**. Words composed of two parts (compound nouns) stress the first part much more strongly than the second: **Haus'hund** (house dog), **Hun'dehaus** (doghouse). Words of non-German origin frequently do not stress the first syllable: **natür'lich, studie'ren, Psychologie'**. The vocabulary lists indicate which syllable is stressed in these cases.

10/Syntactical Stress

Looking at the sentence as a whole—that is, as one single unit of thought—we find that, although each word retains its word stress, there is also syntactical stress. In each sentence, the speaker singles out at least one word that carries the major *news value* and which therefore receives such a strong emphasis that all other syllables can be regarded as unstressed. This syntactical stress, by which the speaker distinguishes between important and unimportant words, overshadows word stress; and whereas word stress is fixed, syntactical stress can shift from one word to another, depending on which word the speaker wants to emphasize most strongly. The stressed syllable of this important word is called the *stress point* of the sentence.

If you look at a written sentence, especially if you do not know the context, you will often not be able to determine its stress point. The sentence

Doris ist heute in Bonn

turns out to be at least three spoken sentences which are not interchangeable. Each of them is used in a situation where the others cannot be used:

Doris ist heute in *Bonn.*	Doris is in *Bonn* today.
Doris ist *heute* in Bonn.	Doris is in Bonn *today.*
Doris ist heute in Bonn.	*Doris* is in Bonn today.

Some sentences may have more than one stress point:

Sie fährt *morgen* nach *München.*   She's going to *Munich tomorrow.*

11/Syntactical Stress and Sentence Intonation

Sentence intonation and syntactical stress are closely connected. Both English and German are intonated on three levels of pitch with the syntactical stress point having either the highest or the lowest pitch.

Assertions usually start on level 2, move up to level 3 for the stress point, and fall to level 1.

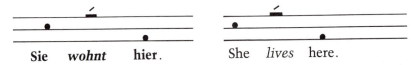

Sie *wohnt* hier.   She *lives* here.

This basic intonation pattern remains unchanged even in longer sentences. As demonstrated in Analysis 10, p. 19, the stress point can be shifted; it can be the first or the last syllable of a sentence, and frequently there can even be more than one stress point.

Questions can be intonated like assertions or they can have "upside-down" intonation, that is, the stress point receives the lowest, rather than the highest, pitch. Assertions intonated as questions *must* have upside-down intonation.

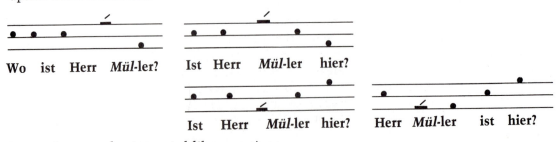

Imperatives are also intonated like assertions.

12/The Particle *denn*

Idiomatic German is characterized by the very frequent use of "flavoring particles" which, in addition to their definable dictionary meaning, have a psychological meaning sometimes hard to define. One of these is **denn**.

Consider the simple question **Wie heißen Sie?** with and without **denn**. Without **denn**, it takes on the character of interrogation; with **denn**, it expresses interest and concern on the part of the speaker.

The use of **denn** is so frequent in spoken German that most word questions contain it. It follows the inflected verb and the personal pronouns, and it may even follow unstressed nouns. However, it precedes the first stressed element of importance unless the inflected verb is stressed.

> **Wo *ist* das Büro denn?**
> **Wo ist denn das Bü*ro*?**

In yes-or-no questions, **denn** is rarely used; if it is used, it usually implies a feeling of surprise or incredulity.

Arbeitet Fritz denn *heu*te?	(I thought he was working tomorrow.)
Arbeitet *Fritz* denn heute?	(How odd! I thought Kurt was working today.)
***Arbeitet* Fritz denn heute?**	(I can't believe it. On a Sunday?)

NOTE: The particle **denn** occurs only in questions and never in assertions, not even in assertions intonated as questions. Do not repeat **denn** when responding to a question that uses it.

Most German particles do not have literal English equivalents. However, without them, a very characteristic element in the language is missing, especially in conversational German. As you go through the book, pay special attention to how and when they are used; listen to how your teacher uses them, and you will gradually develop the ability to incorporate them into "real" German.

13/Gender

Both English and German have three genders: masculine, feminine, and neuter. But English and German differ greatly in the way they treat gender.

When speakers of English refer to persons, they use *he* and *she*, but when they refer to things, they usually use *it*; we can say that English has "natural gender."

German, like many other languages, has "grammatical gender"; human males and human females are masculine and feminine, but animals and things can be either masculine, feminine, or neuter.[9]

In German, both the definite and indefinite articles have separate forms for the three genders.

MASCULINE		FEMININE		NEUTER	
der **Mann**	*the* man	*die* **Frau**	*the* woman	*das* **Kind**	*the* child
ein **Mann**	*a* man	*eine* **Frau**	*a* woman	*ein* **Kind**	*a* child

While it is obvious that **Mann** should be masculine and **Frau** feminine, it seems absurd from an English point of view to think of a *spoon* as masculine, a *fork* as feminine, and a *knife* as neuter, but that is exactly what happens in German.

> *der* **Löffel**   *the* spoon   *die* **Gabel**   *the* fork   *das* **Messer**   *the* knife

All German nouns are either masculine, feminine, or neuter and must be referred to with the personal pronouns **er** (*he, it*), **sie** (*she, it*), and **es** (*it*). Note that all German nouns are capitalized.

Wo ist *der* Käse? *Er* ist hier.	Where is the cheese? *It* is here.
Wo ist *die* Butter? *Sie* ist hier.	Where is the butter? *It* is here.
Wo ist *das* Brot? *Es* ist hier.	Where is the bread? *It* is here.

14/Plural of Nouns

Most English nouns form the plural by adding -*s* or -*es* to the singular. In German, unfortunately, the situation is complicated, since there are several ways of forming plurals.

Because there are no simple rules, it is important that, as you memorize the singular with its article, you also learn the plural form.

The plural forms are indicated in the vocabulary as follows:

der Lehrer,·	means that the plural of **der Lehrer** is **die Lehrer**		
der Mann,⸚er		**der Mann**	**die Männer**
die Frau,-en		**die Frau**	**die Frauen**
das Kind,-er		**das Kind**	**die Kinder**

[9]The seemingly inconsistent neuter nouns **das Fräulein** and **das Mädchen** (*girl*) are neuter because all German nouns with the diminutive suffixes **-lein** and **-chen** are neuter.

The article for plural nouns is the same for all three genders: **die**.

Some, but not all, nouns referring to females have a separate feminine form ending in **-in**, plural **-nen**.[10] They usually add an umlaut.

die Ärztin,-nen	from	**der Arzt,̈e**
die Lehrerin,-nen		**der Lehrer,-**
die Studentin,-nen		**der Student,-en**
die Amerikanerin,-nen		**der Amerikaner,-**

Nouns of non-German origin may have a plural ending in **-s**:

das Auto,-s　　　　**das Büro,-s**　　　　**das Kino,-s**

PRACTICE THREE

I. Read the following sentences aloud, using the correct intonation patterns. Do not be afraid to overemphasize stress in this exercise.

1. Wer bist du? —Doris.
2. Doris Müller? —Nein, Doris Schmidt.
3. Und wo ist Hans Schmidt?
4. Ist Hans auch hier? —Nein.
5. Nein? —Er ist in Köln.
6. Er wohnt jetzt in Köln.
7. Und wo arbeitet er? —Auch in Köln.
8. Wir arbeiten jetzt beide in Köln.
9. Aber morgen sind wir beide hier in Bonn.
10. Inge und Peter kommen auch.

J. Read the sentence on the right three times with sentence intonation appropriate to the three questions on the left.

Wo?	
Wann?	Hans ist heute in Bonn.
Wer?	

K. Read each of the following sentences aloud and shift the stress point as often as possible. Then explain how these shifts in stress change the meaning of the sentence.

1. Er heißt Helmut Schmidt.
2. Nächsten Sommer gehen wir nach Deutschland.
3. Herr Meyer arbeitet auch in Frankfurt.

[10]These nouns double the **-n** in the plural in order to keep the **-i-** short.

L. Supply the correct plural form.

1. Herr Meyer kommt aus Lübeck. Herr Zöllner kommt auch aus Lübeck.
   Die _Herren_ kommen beide aus Lübeck.
2. Und Frau Meyer und Frau Zöllner? Kommen sie auch aus Lübeck?
   —Nein, die zwei _Frauen_ kommen aus Bremen.
3. Fritz ist Student. Kurt und Erich sind auch _Studenten_
4. Petra ist Studentin. Andrea und Gisela sind auch _Studentinnen_
5. John Ray ist Amerikaner. Jane Ray und Nancy Davis sind
   Amerikanerinnen
6. *Der* Mann arbeitet in *München,* und *der* Mann arbeitet *auch* in München. Die _Männer_ arbeiten beide in München.

Hello and good-bye

Like every language, German has its own stereotyped phrases for basic social interaction. You may know the German phrase **Wie geht's** and think that it is the exact equivalent of English *How are you?* Usually, however, *How are you?* or *Hi!* are simply social noises, whereas German **Wie geht's** is a more or less honest inquiry of someone you know fairly well and comes closer to English *How are you doing?* The English *How do you do?* has nothing to do with the real meaning of the phrase; it is simply the polite thing to say when first meeting someone. It has no German equivalent, and you cannot use **Wie geht's** in its place. When Germans meet for the first time, they say **Guten Morgen, Frau Schmidt** (*Good morning, Mrs. Schmidt*), **Guten Tag, Herr Meyer** (*Good day, Mr. Meyer,* even though you never hear this in America), or **Guten Abend** (*Good evening*).

Guten Tag, Hedi. Wie geht's?

Most English *How do you do's?* are accompanied by a handshake; thereafter Americans rarely shake hands. Germans, however, shake hands every time they meet, but usually without saying **Wie geht's?** They shake hands again when saying good-bye (**Auf Wiedersehen** or **Tschüß**), even if the meeting has lasted only a minute or two.

CONVERSATIONS

In German, as in English, conversations do not always consist of strings of questions followed by answers in "complete sentences," but of series of utterances that can be either assertions or questions. Frequently, the verb is assumed, not spoken. Thus, if someone says **Ich bleibe heute abend zu Hause**, do not hesitate to reply **Ich auch** (*Me too*), rather than **Ich bleibe heute abend zu Hause**. Also, as in English, German uses many stereotypical phrases that are integral parts of almost any conversation, for example, *by the way, as far as I'm concerned*, or even *for example*. With such conversational gambits you can connect exchanges or buy time while sorting out your thoughts. Whenever such phrases are introduced in this book, memorize them without worrying about their grammatical form. You will be able to reuse these gambits in all sorts of other situations.

Memorize the following brief exchanges; then recombine their elements
into new exchanges.

HEIDI:	Guten Morgen, Gabi.	Good morning, Gabi.
GABI:	Morgen Heidi. Wie geht's dir denn?[11]	Morning, Heidi. How are you doing?
HEIDI:	Danke, gut. Und dir?	OK, thanks. And you?
GABI:	Auch gut, danke.	Fine, too, thanks.
FRAU BRAUN:	Tag, Frau Schulz.	Hello, Mrs. Schulz.
FRAU SCHULZ:	Guten Tag, Frau Braun. Wie geht's Ihnen denn?	Hello, Mrs. Braun. How are you?
FRAU BRAUN:	Danke, gut. Und Ihnen?	OK, thanks. And you?
FRAU SCHULZ:	Danke, auch gut.	Fine, too, thanks.
FRITZ:	Auf Wiedersehen, Peter. Bis morgen.	Good-bye, Peter. See you tomorrow.
PETER:	Wiedersehen, Fritz. Mach's gut.	Bye, Fritz. Take care.
INGE:	Also, mach's gut, Doris. Bis Montag.	Well, take care, Doris. See you Monday.
DORIS:	Du auch, Inge. Tschüß.	You, too, Inge. Bye.
FRAU DR. KLEIN:	Wie heißen Sie denn, bitte?	Excuse me, what is your name?
ERIKA MÜLLER:	Ich heiße Müller, Erika Müller.	My name is Müller, Erika Müller.
FRAU DR. KLEIN:	Sie wohnen hier in Frankfurt, nicht wahr?	You live in Frankfurt, don't you?
ERIKA MÜLLER:	Ja, ich wohne hier. Fichardstraße 23.	Yes, I live here. 23 Fichardstraße.
FRITZ MÜLLER:	Entschuldigung! Sind Sie Frau Dr. Klein?	Excuse me, are you Dr. Klein?
FRAU DR. KLEIN:	Ja, —und Sie sind Fritz Müller, nicht wahr?	Yes—and you are Fritz Müller, aren't you?
HANNELORE:	Übrigens, ich bin Hannelore Schulz. Und wie heißt du?	By the way, I'm Hannelore Schulz. And what is your name?
JOHN:	John Ray. Ich bin Amerikaner.	John Ray. I'm an American.
HANNELORE:	Oh, wirklich?	Oh, really?
LUTZ:	Wie ist denn das Wetter in Hamburg heute?	How is the weather today in Hamburg?

[11]Note the following distinctions:

Wie geht es dir (**du**-form)?	**Es geht mir gut.**	How are you? I'm fine.
Wie geht es euch (**ihr**-form)?	**Es geht uns gut.**	We are fine.
Wie geht es Ihnen (**Sie**-form)?	**Es geht mir/uns gut.**	I'm/We are fine.

| JÜRGEN: | Schlecht, natürlich. Es regnet schon wieder. | Bad, of course. It's raining again. |
| LUTZ: | Hier in Frankfurt ist das Wetter gut. Es ist warm, und die Sonne scheint. | Here in Frankfurt the weather is good. It's warm and the sun is shining. |

Fragen an Sie persönlich

Each unit contains a set of questions addressed "**an Sie persönlich**"—to you personally. These questions are designed to elicit your own responses and thus to contribute to the beginning of real conversations. If at times you are hard put to answer these questions, feel free to invent and let your imagination run, as long as it runs in German.

1. Wie heißen Sie?
2. Wohnen Sie hier auf dem Campus?
   In einer Wohnung (*apartment*)? Im Studentenheim (*dorm*)? Zu Hause?
3. Wo kommen Sie her? (*Where are you from?*)
   Aus Kalifornien? Aus Kanada? Aus Kalamazoo?
4. Wo sind Sie denn zu Hause?
   In Los Angeles? In Wichita? In New Jersey?
5. Was studieren Sie?
   Mathe*matik*? Phy*sik*? Bio*logie*? Che*mie*? Philoso*phie*? Psycho*logie*?
   Sozio*logie*? *Eng*lisch? Ge*schich*te (*history*)?
   Poli*tik*wissenschaft (*political science*)?
6. Was machen Sie heute abend?
                    morgen abend?
7. Was machen Sie nächsten Sommer?
   Gehen Sie nach Deutschland?
                    nach Europa?

Now ask the same questions of other members of your class. Don't forget that you have to shift from **Sie** to **du**.

REVIEW EXERCISES

M. Repeat each sentence, starting as indicated.

1. Ich bleibe zu Hause. Heute _bleibe ich zu Hause_
2. Er bleibt morgen zu Hause. Morgen _bleibt er zu Hause._
3. Es regnet. Hier _regnet es_ .
4. Wir arbeiten. Heute _arbeiten wir._
5. Herr Meyer trinkt Milch. Natürlich _trinkt er Milch,_
6. Frau Meyer trinkt Bier. Übrigens _trinkt er Bier._
7. Doris studiert jetzt Psychologie. Jetzt _studiert Doris Psych._
8. Nächsten Sommer gehen wir nach Deutschland. Wir _gehen nächsten Sommer nach Deutschland._

N. Write down answers to the following questions:

1. Wohnen Sie in Berlin? Ja, _ich wohne_ *Berlin*. Nein, _ich wohne_ in München.
2. Ist Fritz zu Hause? Ja, _er ist zu Hause_. Nein, _er ist_ im Büro.
3. Wer ist das? Das _ist Graff_.
4. Wo arbeiten Sie? Ich _arbeite hier_.
5. Bleibst du heute abend zu Hause? Ja, _ich bleibe_. Nein, _ich gehe_ ins Kino.
6. Studiert sie in Heidelberg? Ja, ~~sie studiert~~. Nein, _sie studiert_ in München.
7. Wann kommt ihr denn? Wir _kommen morgen_.
8. Arbeiten Sie in Köln? Ja, _ich arbeite_. Nein, _ich arbeite_ in Bonn.
9. Wohnen Schmidts *auch* in Köln? Ja, _sie auch_ Nein, ~~sie wohnen~~ in München.
10. Wo ist Fritz? _Er ist in Köln_

O. Write down yes-or-no questions which could be answered by the assertions.

Gehst du nach Stuttgart?	**Nein, ich bleibe zu Hause.**

1. _Wohnt ihr in Köln?_   Nein, wir wohnen in Berlin.
2. _Arbeiten sie heute?_   Ja, sie arbeiten heute.
3. _Ist das Frau Schmidt?_   Nein, das ist Frau Meyer.
4. _Wie ist das Wetter?_   Natürlich ist das Wetter schlecht.
5. _____   Ja, sie (Erika) ist schon hier.
6. _____   Ja, sie (Erika) wohnt *auch* in München.
7. _____   Nein!
8. _____   Ja!

P. Write down one or more word questions which could be answered by
the following statements.

Wo arbeitet Frau Schmidt?	**Sie arbeitet in Berlin.**

1. _Wo wohnt ihr_ ?   Wir wohnen in Berlin.
2. _Wo_ ?   Zu Hause!
3. _Wo bist du_ ?   Ich bin in Köln.
4. _Wer ist das_ ?   Herr Meyer.
5. _Wann kommst du_ ?   Ich komme morgen.
6. _Was studiert er_ ?   Er studiert Psychologie.
7. _Wer kommt heute_ ?   Herr Meyer kommt heute.
8. _Wer bist du_ ?   Ich bin Anna Meyer.

Q. Form statements from the following elements. Note that not all combinations make logical sense.

| **Erika wohnt in Berlin.** | | |

Erika	wohnen	in Berlin
du	studieren	hier
Herr Dr. Schmidt	lernen	zu Hause
wir	bleiben	Psychologie
er	arbeiten	nach Hause
Frau Koch	sein	Deutsch
ihr	gehen	nach Köln

R. The following exercise consists of "dehydrated sentences." They are arranged in logical order, except for the verb which appears in infinitive form at the end. Form sentences from the elements given: begin with the first element, insert the correct form of the verb, and supply the article where necessary.

| **Inge / jetzt / in Wien / studieren.** | **Inge studiert jetzt in Wien.** |

1. Hans / heute / nach Berlin / gehen. *geht*
2. Natürlich / ich / Milch / trinken. *trinke*
3. Heute / das Wetter / schlecht / sein. *ist*
4. Erika / in Stuttgart / wohnen. *wohnt*
5. Ihr / in Köln / arbeiten? *arbeitet*
6. Sabine / aus Köln / kommen. *kommt*
7. Fritz / morgen abend / hier / sein? *ist*
8. Wie / Sie / denn / heißen?
9. Um zwei Uhr / er / nach Hause / kommen. *kommt*
10. Morgen / ich / zu Hause / bleiben. *bleibe*
11. Hans und Erika / jetzt / Deutsch / lernen.
12. Du / auch / Deutsch / lernen? *lernst*

S. Express in German.

1. I'm at home.
2. I'm going home.
3. The sun is shining.
4. The weather is bad.
5. It is cold.
6. Hans will come tomorrow.
7. We are studying psychology.
8. What are you doing tomorrow, Fritz?
9. Tomorrow night we're staying home.
10. Fritz and Hans are working tonight.
11. They are both drinking tea.
12. We are also going to Munich.
13. Is it raining in Hamburg?
14. When are you coming to Bonn, Mr. Koch?
15. Do you live in Bonn? (Use **du, ihr,** and **Sie**)
16. What is your name? (Use **du, ihr,** and **Sie**)
17. Claudia is a doctor; she's from Bonn.
18. Excuse me, are you Mr. Meyer?

T. Interview one or more members of your class: find out their name, where they come from, what they'll be doing this evening, etc. Remember to use **denn** whenever possible. Use **du/ihr** with your fellow students, but **Sie** if you interview your teacher.

NOTE: Additional exercises can be found in the *Study Guide.*

VOCABULARY

Verbs

arbeiten	to work
bleiben	to stay, remain
gehen	to go; to walk
Wie geht's?	How are you?
Wie geht es dir / euch / Ihnen?	How are things going?
heißen	to be called
Wie heißen Sie?	What's your name?
Ich heiße Meyer	My name is Meyer; I am Mr. Meyer
kommen	to come
kommen aus	to be from
lernen	to learn
machen	to do; to make
mach's gut	so long; take care; see you
Machen Sie Ihr Buch auf/zu.	Open/close your book.
regnen	to rain
scheinen	to seem; to shine
die Sonne scheint	the sun is shining
sein	to be
sein aus	to be from
studie'ren	to study, to attend a university, to be a student (at a university)
trinken	to drink
wohnen	to live, to reside

Nouns

MASCULINE

der Abend, -e	evening
(guten) Abend	good evening
der Arzt, ̈e	physician, doctor (*m.*)
die Ärztin, -nen	physician (*f.*)
der Dok'tor, die Dokto'ren	doctor, physician
der Herr, -en	man; gentleman; Mr.
Herr Meyer	Mr. Meyer
der Kaffee (*no pl.*)	coffee
der Löffel, -	spoon
der Mann, ̈er	man; husband
der Morgen, -	morning
(guten) Morgen	good morning
der Sommer, -	the summer
nächsten Sommer	next summer
der Student, -en	student (*m.*)
die Studentin, -nen	student (*f.*)
der Stuhl, ̈e	chair
der Tag, -e	day
(guten) Tag	hello
der Tee (*no pl.*)	tea
der Tisch, -e	table
der Wein, -e	wine

FEMININE

die Entschuldigung, -en	excuse
Entschuldigung	excuse me
die Frage, -n	question
die Frau, -en	woman; wife; Mrs., Ms.
Frau Meyer	Mrs. Meyer, Ms. Meyer
die Gabel, -n	fork
die Medizin'	medicine; science of medicine; study of medicine
die Milch (*no pl.*)	milk
die Psychologie'	psychology
die Sonne, -n	sun
die Tafel, -n	blackboard
die Tür, -en	door
die Uhr, -en	clock, watch
um ein Uhr	at one o'clock
um eins	

NEUTER

(das) Amerika	America	Fräulein Meyer	Miss Meyer
der Amerikaner, -	the American (*m.*)	(*abbreviated:* **Frl.**)	
die Amerikanerin, -nen	the American (*f.*)	das Haus, ⸚er	house
das Auto, -s	car, automobile	Ich gehe nach Hause.	I am going home.
das Bier, -e	beer	Ich bin zu Hause.	I am at home.
das Buch, ⸚er	book	das Kind, -er	child
das Büro', -s	office	das Kino, -s	movie theater
(das) Deutsch	German (language)	Wir gehen ins Kino.	We are going to the movies.
(das) Deutschland	Germany		
(das) Englisch	English (language)	das Land, ⸚er	land; state; country
(das) Euro'pa	Europe	das Messer, -	knife
das Fenster, -	window	das Wetter (*no pl.*)	weather
das Fräulein, -	young (unmarried) woman		

Days of the week

der Montag	Monday	der Samstag	Saturday
der Dienstag	Tuesday	(der Sonnabend)	(Saturday; *used in Northern Germany*)
der Mittwoch	Wednesday		
der Donnerstag	Thursday	der Sonntag	Sunday
der Freitag	Friday		

Months

der Januar	der April	der Juli	der Oktober
der Februar	der Mai	der August	der November
der März	der Juni	der September	der Dezember

Adjectives

beide	both	nicht wahr?	isn't that so? aren't you? don't you? right? etc.
glücklich	happy		
gut	good; OK		
heiß	hot	warm	warm
kalt	cold	wirklich	real; really
schlecht	bad		
wahr	true		

Articles and Pronouns

der	the (*masc.*)	**du**	you (*sing.*)
die	the (*fem.*)	**er**	he; it
das	the (*neuter*)	**sie**	she; they; it
ein, eine, ein	a; one (*indef. article*)	**Sie**	you
eins	one (*number*)	**es**	it
		wir	we
das	that (*demonstrative*)	**ihr**	you (*pl.*)
ich	I		

Interrogatives

wann	when, at what time	**wie**	how
warum	why	**wo**	where
was	what	**woher (wo . . . her)**	from where, where . . . from
wer	who		

Prepositions

aus	out of, from	**nach Deutschland**	to Germany
bis	until; up to; as far as	**nach zwei Uhr**	after two o'clock
in	in	**um**	at; around
nach	to, toward; after		

Adverbs

		morgen abend	tomorrow night
da	there	**bis morgen**	until tomorrow, see you tomorrow
heute	today		
heute abend	this evening, tonight	**schon**	already, earlier than expected; yet
hier	here	**wieder**	again
jetzt	now	**auf Wiedersehen**	see you again; good-bye
morgen	tomorrow		

Numbers

eins	one
zwei	two

Other Words

aber	but, however	**natürlich**	natural, naturally; of course
also	well; therefore; in other words	**nein**	no
auch	also, too	**so**	so
bitte	please	**tschüß**	bye
danke	thank you	**übrigens**	by the way, incidentally
denn	(see p. 21)	**und**	and
ja	yes		
leider	unfortunately		

Unit 2

Irregularities in the Present Tense of Verbs— The Nominative and Accusative Cases

The Federal Republic of Germany

The FRG was established in 1949; its territory consists of what had been the British, French, and American zones of occupation after World War II, plus West Berlin. The FRG is firmly tied to the West; it is a leading member of the 12-nation European Community (EC) and has been a member of NATO since 1955 and of the UN since 1972. It ranks with the U.S. and Japan as one of the top three economic powers in the Western world.

Federal Republic
of Germany

The Federal Republic, including West Berlin, has a population of about 61.5 million, of whom over 4 million are foreigners. West Germany has the lowest birthrate in the world.

The federal capital is Bonn. There are ten federal states (**Bundesländer**) plus West Berlin, the special status of which derives from the Four-Power-Agreement of 1971. The **Länder** range from the tiny city-state of Bremen (pop. 680,000) to North Rhine-Westphalia with a population of 17 million. Some **Länder** have centuries-old histories and traditions, such as the **Freistaat Bayern** and the **Freie und Hansestädte** Hamburg and Bremen; others, especially the hyphenated **Länder**, were created after WW II.

BUNDESLAND (*state*)	HAUPTSTADT (*capital*)	THE LARGEST CITIES IN THE FRG	POPULATION (1983)
Baden-Württemberg	Stuttgart		
Bayern	München	Berlin (West)	1,870,000
Berlin (West)		Hamburg	1,623,000
Bremen		München	1,285,000
Hamburg		Köln	1,010,000
Hessen	Wiesbaden	Essen	642,000
Niedersachsen	Hannover	Frankfurt	618,000
Nordrhein-Westfalen	Düsseldorf	Dortmund	600,000
Rheinland-Pfalz	Mainz	Düsseldorf	583,000
Saarland	Saarbrücken	Stuttgart	568,000
Schleswig-Holstein	Kiel	Duisburg	561,000

Schleswig Holstein	Hamburg	Lower-Saxony	Bremen	North Rhine-Westphalia	Hesse	Rhineland-Palatinate	Baden-Württemberg	Bavaria	Saarland	Berlin (West)

PATTERNS ONE

1/The Present Tense of *haben*

Ich habe Hunger.	I'm hungry. (*lit*. I have hunger.)
Hast du auch Hunger?	Are you hungry, too?
Nein, aber ich habe Durst.	No, but I'm thirsty.
Herr Meyer hat immer Durst.	Mr. Meyer is always thirsty.
Es ist ein Uhr, und wir haben Hunger.	It is one o'clock, and we're hungry.
Und natürlich habt ihr auch Durst, nicht wahr?	And of course you're also thirsty, aren't you?
Sie haben immer Durst.	They're always thirsty.

2/Verbs with Vowel Change

Wohin[1] fahren die Leute?	Where are the people going?
Wohin fährt der Zug?	Where is the train going?
Ich gehe heute morgen in die Stadt.[2]	I'm going downtown this morning.
Fährst du oder läufst du?	Are you driving or are you walking?

Fahren die Leute nach Stuttgart? — Nein, sie fahren nach München. Er fährt nach München. Sie fährt auch nach München.

---

[1] German must use **wohin** rather than **wo** if it corresponds to English *where* = *whereto, whither*.

Wohin?	in die Schweiz	Wo?	in der Schweiz
	nach Berlin		in Berlin
	nach Deutschland		in Deutschland
	nach Hause		zu Hause

[2] Both **in die Stadt** and **in der Stadt** can correspond to English *downtown*; **in die Stadt** must be used if it is the equivalent of (in)to the city (**wohin?**); **in *der* Stadt** is the equivalent of *(with)in the city* (**wo?**). For now, learn these two phrases as idioms.

Ich glaube,[3] ich laufe. Das Wetter ist
heute so gut.

I think I'll walk. The weather is so nice
today.

Aber Hans fährt heute nachmittag in die
Stadt.

But Hans is going to drive downtown
this afternoon.

Ich bin heute nachmittag *auch* in der
Stadt.

I'll be downtown this afternoon, too.

Heute abend fahren Hans und ich zusammen nach Hause.

Tonight Hans and I will drive home together.

Was essen sie? —Sie essen Brot und
Wurst.

What are they eating? —They are eating
bread and sausage.

Er ißt Brot und Wurst und trinkt Bier.

He's eating bread and sausage and is
drinking beer.

Sie ißt *auch* Brot und Wurst, aber sie
trinkt Wein.

She's eating bread and sausage, too, but
she's drinking wine.

Was ißt du? —Ich esse Käse, und ich esse
auch Wurst.

What are you eating? —I'm eating cheese,
and I'm also eating sausage.

Wann eßt ihr heute? —Wir essen um
zwölf.

When are you eating today? —We'll be
eating at noon.

Herr und Frau Anders sind zu Hause und
lesen.

Mr. and Mrs. Anders are at home reading.

Herr Anders liest ein Buch, und Frau
Anders liest die Zeitung.

Mr. Anders is reading a book, and Mrs.
Anders is reading the newspaper.

Frau Anders fragt: „Was liest du denn?"

Mrs. Anders asks, "What are you reading?"

Herr Anders antwortet: „Ich lese ein Buch
von Heinrich Böll."

Mr. Anders answers: "I'm reading a book
by Heinrich Böll."

Heinrich Böll (1917–85)
Nobelpreis für Literatur
1972

Wie wird das Wetter morgen?

How is the weather going to be tomorrow?

Heute ist das Wetter schlecht; es ist kalt
und es regnet.

Today the weather is bad; it is cold, and
it is raining.

Morgen wird es aber bestimmt gut; morgen scheint sicher die Sonne.

But tomorrow it'll certainly be good; I'm
sure tomorrow the sun will be shining.

[3]The basic meaning of **glauben** is *to believe*, but it is often used with the meaning
to think as in this sentence.

*Ist das Herr Meyer?—
Das weiß ich nicht; ich
kenne ihn nicht.*

Wie alt bist du denn, Rudi?—Ich bin fünf, aber morgen werde ich sechs.	How old are you, Rudi?—I'm five, but tomorrow I'll be six.
So, du wirst morgen sechs Jahre alt.	So, you'll be six years old tomorrow.
Und Fritzchen wird nächsten Samstag drei.	And Fritzchen will be three on Saturday.

3/**wissen** and **kennen,** *to know*

Wer ist das?	Who is that?
Wissen Sie, wer das ist?	Do you know who that is?
Nein, das weiß ich nicht.[4]	No, I don't know (that).
Das ist Erika Müller. Kennen Sie Erika?	That's Erika Müller. Do you know Erika?
Nein, ich kenne Erika nicht; ich weiß nicht, wer sie ist.	No, I don't know Erika; I don't know who she is.
Weißt du, wer sie ist?	Do you know who she is?

ANALYSIS ONE

15/**Irregularities in the Present Tense of Verbs**

THE PRESENT TENSE OF **haben,** *to have*

ich habe	**wir haben**
du hast	**ihr habt**
er	
sie } **hat**	**sie haben**
es	

---

[4]For the time being, do not use **nicht** in your own sentences.

VERBS WITH VOWEL CHANGE

The English verb *do* changes the sound of its stem vowel in the third person singular: *I do, you do,* but *he does.* In German, a number of very common verbs change their stem vowel not only in the third person singular (the **er**-form) but also in the second person (the **du**-form). These verbs and their changes will be listed in the vocabulary as follows: **fahren (du fährst, er fährt).** There are two major types of changes: from **e** to **ie** (or **i**) and from **a** to **ä** (or **au** to **äu**).

sehen to see	nehmen to take	essen to eat	fahren to drive	laufen to run
ich sehe	ich nehme	ich esse	ich fahre	ich laufe
du siehst er sieht	du nimmst er nimmt	du ißt er ißt	du fährst er fährt	du läufst er läuft
wir sehen ihr seht sie sehen	wir nehmen ihr nehmt sie nehmen	wir essen ihr eßt sie essen	wir fahren ihr fahrt sie fahren	wir laufen ihr lauft sie laufen

NOTE: **fahren** always implies that a vehicle is used: *to drive, to go* (*by car,* etc.); **laufen**, *to run*, is also used with the meaning *to walk, to go*, especially in Southern Germany; **gehen** has the basic meaning of *to walk, to go* (*on foot*), (**zu Fuß**) **gehen**, but it also means *to go* without specifying the mode of movement.

Ich fahre in die Stadt.	I'm driving downtown. or: I'm going downtown (by streetcar, bus, etc.).
Ich gehe in die Stadt.	I'm going downtown. (means undetermined)
Ich laufe in die Stadt.	I'm walking downtown.

STEMS ENDING IN AN **s**-SOUND

Remember that after a stem ending in an *s*-sound (**-s, -ss, -ß, -z,** or **-tz**), the **du**-form adds **-t** rather than **-st**. Thus, **du**-form and **er**-form are identical.

lesen to read	essen to eat	heißen to be called	sitzen to sit
ich lese	ich esse	ich heiße	ich sitze
du liest er liest	du ißt er ißt	du heißt er heißt	du sitzt er sitzt

werden AND **wissen**

The verbs **werden**, *to become*, and **wissen**, *to know*, have peculiarities of their own. Note that the **er**-form **er wird** is the only third-person singular form in German that ends in **-d** and that the **er**-form of **wissen** does not end in **-t**.

ich	werde	ich	weiß
du	wirst	du	weißt
er	wird	er	weiß
wir	werden	wir	wissen
ihr	werdet	ihr	wißt
sie	werden	sie	wissen

16/**wissen** and **kennen,** *to know*

Both these verbs correspond to English *to know*, but German makes a clear distinction between *to know facts* (**wissen**) and *to be acquainted with persons or things* (**kennen**). The use of **wissen** in main clauses is largely restricted to such sentences as

Das weiß ich.
Ich weiß es.

Frequently, the object of **wissen** is a short clause, such as

Ich weiß, Meyer wohnt in München.
Ich weiß, er kommt morgen.

If **Ich weiß** is followed by a question word like **wer, wo, wann**, as in

Ich weiß, wer er ist.
Er weiß, wo wir sind.
Weißt du, wann er kommt?

← ———— verb
not subj!

then the inflected verb *must* stand at the end. For the time being, use only the few examples introduced here.

The verb **kennen** expresses personal acquaintance with people, places, or objects.

Kennen Sie Herrn Meyer?
Kennen Sie Innsbruck?
Kennen Sie das Buch?

Note the difference:

Ich weiß, wer er ist, aber ich kenne ihn nicht.
I know who he is, but I don't know him (haven't made his acquaintance).

17/**auch**, *also*, *too*

German **auch** is either unstressed or stressed. When unstressed, it refers to a following *stressed* element and immediately *precedes* that element.

Erika fährt nächsten Sommer auch nach Österreich.	Erika is also going to *Austria* next summer.
Erika fährt auch *näch*sten Sommer nach Österreich.	Erika is going to Austria *next* summer, *too*.

However, if the stressed element is an inflected verb, the unstressed **auch** must follow it because only one element can precede the inflected verb.

Er *wohnt* in Wien und er *arbeitet* auch in Wien.	He *lives* in Vienna, and he also *works* in Vienna.

When stressed, **auch** refers to a preceding element, usually the subject.

Hans fährt *auch* nach Österreich.	*Hans* is going to Austria, *too*.

PRACTICE ONE

A. Restate the following sentences with the new subject given.

1. Ich werde morgen acht Jahre alt.   (du, er)
2. Hans ißt Brot und Wurst.   (ich, du)
3. Hast du auch Hunger?   (ihr, Erika)
4. Ich laufe heute vier Kilometer.   (er, Ingrid und Eva)
5. Wir fahren nach Zürich.   (der Zug, du)
6. Sie liest Thomas Mann.   (die Studenten, du)
7. Wissen Sie das?   (du, ihr)
8. Nehmen Sie ein Bier?   (du, er)
9. Ich arbeite in Bern.   (ihr, Petra)
10. Du heißt Müller, nicht wahr?   (er, ihr)

B. Fill in the correct form of **kennen** and **wissen**.

1. _____ du Klagenfurt?
2. Ich _____ Klagenfurt nicht, aber ich _____, es ist in Österreich.
3. _____ ihr auch, wo Basel ist?
4. Natürlich _____ wir, wo Basel ist.
5. Wir _____ Basel gut.
6. Mein Freund Philipp _____ nicht, wo die Schweiz[5] ist.

PATTERNS TWO

4/The Nominative and Accusative of Pronouns

Kennst du mich?	Do you know me?
Natürlich kenne ich dich. Du bist der Rolf Berger,[6] nicht wahr?	Of course I know you. You are Rolf Berger, aren't you?

Kennst du mich?
Natürlich kenne ich dich. Du bist der Rolf Berger,[6] nicht wahr?

Kennen Sie uns, Herr Schmidt?
Natürlich kenne ich euch. Ihr seid Hedi und Margret, nicht wahr?

Das ist Herr Lang. Kennen Sie ihn?
Nein, ich kenne ihn nicht, aber ich weiß, wer er ist.
Das ist Frau Holle. Kennst du sie?
Nein, aber ich weiß, wer sie ist.
Wer ist denn das Kind? Ich kenne es nicht.

Hier kommen Hans und Erika. Kennen Sie sie?
Ich kenne Sie. Sie sind Herr Schmidt, nicht wahr?

Ich sehe sie im Spiegel.
Ich sehe mich im Spiegel.
Sie sieht sich im Spiegel.

Edwin und Erich sind Brüder, aber sie verstehen sich nicht.

Do you know me?
Of course I know you. You are Rolf Berger, aren't you?

Do you know us, Mr. Schmidt?
Of course I know you. You are Hedi and Margret, aren't you?

That is Mr. Lang. Do you know him?
No, I don't know him, but I know who he is.
That is Mrs. Holle. Do you know her?
No, but I know who she is.
Who is that child? I don't know it.

Here come Hans and Erika. Do you know them?
I know you. You are Mr. Schmidt, aren't you?

I see her in the mirror.
I see myself in the mirror.
She sees herself in the mirror.

Edwin and Erich are brothers, but they don't understand each other (get along).

---

[5]Note that **Schweiz** must be used with the article.

[6]In colloquial German, the article is very frequently used with both first and last names, for example, **der Rolf, der Berger, der Rolf Berger**.

Kennen Sie sich?

Natürlich kennen wir uns; wir sind
Schwestern.

Ihr kennt euch nicht? Das ist Hans Müller
und das ist Erich Schmidt.

Do you know each other?

Of course we know each other; we are
sisters.

You don't know each other? That's Hans
Müller and that's Erich Schmidt.

5/The Nominative and Accusative of the Definite Article

Wer fragt wen?
    Was fragt die Frau den Mann?
    Was fragt der Mann die Frau?
    Was fragt der Junge das Mädchen?
    Was fragt das Mädchen den Jungen?

Who is asking whom?
    What is the woman asking the man?
    What is the man asking the woman?
    What is the boy asking the girl?
    What is the girl asking the boy?

Sehen Sie den Wagen?
Ja, der Wagen ist da drüben.
Seht ihr die Straßenbahn?
Ja, die Straßenbahn ist hier.
Siehst du das Motorrad?
Ja, das Motorrad ist da drüben.
Seht ihr die Fahrräder?
Ja, die Fahrräder sind da drüben.
Wo ist der Bus? Sehen Sie ihn?
Ja, er ist da drüben.
Wo ist die Straßenbahn? Sehen Sie sic?
Ja, sie ist hier.
Wo ist das Motorrad? Sehen Sie es?
Ja, es ist hier.
Wo sind die Fahrräder? Sehen Sie sie?
Ja, sie sind da drüben.

Do you see the car?
Yes, the car is over there.
Do you see the streetcar?
Yes, the streetcar is here.
Do you see the motorcycle?
Yes, the motorcycle is over there.
Do you see the bicycles?
Yes, the bicycles are over there.
Where is the bus? Do you see it?
Yes, it is over there.
Where is the streetcar? Do you see it?
Yes, it is here.
Where is the motorcycle? Do you see it?
Yes, it is here.
Where are the bicycles? Do you see them?
Yes, they are over there.

6/The Nominative and Accusative of the Indefinite Article

Ich brauche einen Löffel.
Hier ist ein Löffel.
Ich brauche eine Gabel.
Hier ist eine Gabel.
Ich brauche ein Messer.
Hier ist ein Messer.

I need a spoon.
Here is a spoon.
I need a fork.
Here is a fork.
I need a knife.
Here is a knife.

Haben Sie Kinder?
Ich habe einen Sohn.
       eine Tochter.
       ein Kind.

Do you have children?
I have a son.
    a daughter.
    a child.

Wen siehst du?	Whom do you see?
Ich sehe einen Herrn.	I see a gentleman.
Herrn Nagel.	Mr. Nagel.
eine Dame.	a lady.
Frau Engel.	Mrs. Engel.
ein Mädchen.	a girl.
Fräulein Hahn.	Miss Hahn.
Was liest er?	What is he reading?
Er liest einen Roman.	He is reading a novel.
eine Zeitung.	a newspaper.
ein Buch.	a book.

Hauptbahnhof in Bonn

Was lest ihr?	What are you reading?
Wir lesen Romane.	We are reading novels.
Zeitungen.	newspapers.
Bücher.	books.

Was ist das?	What is that?
Das ist ein Roman.	That's a novel.
Das sind Romane.[7]	Those are novels.
Das ist eine Zeitung.	That's a newspaper.
Das sind Zeitungen.	Those are newspapers.
Das ist ein Buch.	That's a book.
Das sind Bücher.	Those are books.

ANALYSIS TWO

18/The Nominative and Accusative Cases

The notion of "case" is used in grammar when speaking of the function of nouns or pronouns. Note how the function of *his father* changes in the following three sentences:

1. His father is a physician.
2. Erika knows his father.
3. Erika gives his father a book.

In the first sentence, *his father* precedes the verb and therefore must be the subject. In the second sentence, *his father* must be the direct object because it follows the verb, and in the third sentence, it must be the indirect object, because it in turn is followed by the direct

[7]Note that in this pattern the plural **sind** must be preceded by the singular **das** (see Anal. 50, p. 135).

object. In all three sentences, the phrase *his father* remains unchanged. In the first sentence, *a physician*, which follows the verb
and is identical with the subject, is a predicate noun.

As these three sentences show, English indicates function by position. The same is true of the personal pronoun *you*, which can function as subject or object. However, all other personal pronouns have
two different forms: *I-me, he-him*, etc.

German nouns can also indicate function by position, but like the
English pronouns, German pronouns as well as some articles and
some nouns have different forms for the subject and the object.

Sein Vater ist Arzt.　　　　**Er ist Arzt.**
Erika kennt seinen Vater.　**Erika kennt ihn.**

Because German indicates case much more frequently than English,
function is not necessarily tied to position. In the sentences **Inge
liebt Hans** and **Hans liebt Inge**, a role reversal takes place; but when
articles are added to the names, as is frequently done in colloquial
German, the two sentences

Die Inge liebt den Hans.

and

Den Hans liebt die Inge.

are identical and totally unambiguous: **den Hans** must be the object,
regardless of position.

In German, the subject and the predicate noun are in the nominative case. Direct objects are in the accusative case.

German has two more cases: the dative case for the indirect object,
introduced in Unit 5, and the genitive case, introduced in Unit 10.

19/The Nominative and Accusative of Pronouns

PERSONAL PRONOUNS

SINGULAR			PLURAL		
NOM.	ACC.		NOM.	ACC.	
ich	**mich**	(me)	**wir**	**uns**	(us)
du	**dich**	(you)	**ihr**	**euch**	(you)
er	**ihn**	(him, it)			
sie	**sie**	(her, it)	**sie**	**sie**	(them)
es	**es**	(it)			
Sie	**Sie**	(you)	**Sie**	**Sie**	(you)

AGREEMENT BETWEEN NOUNS AND PRONOUNS

If a noun is replaced by a personal pronoun, the pronoun must show
the same gender, case, and number as the noun it replaces. Thus,
what looks like "Where do you buy him?" really means "Where do
you buy it?" if *it* refers to coffee.

Er (der Kaffee) ist gut.	**Wo kaufst du ihn?**
Sie (die Milch) ist sauer.	**Ich trinke sie nicht.**
Es (das Buch) ist interessant.	**Ich lese es.**
Sie (die Mädchen) sind	**Kennst du sie?**
Studentinnen.	

REFLEXIVE PRONOUNS

Occasionally, the object of a verb is identical with the subject. Compare the following two pairs of sentences:

Susan sees Mary.	Susan sees her.
Susan sees Susan.	Susan sees herself.

Pronouns referring to an identical subject are called reflexive pronouns: *myself, herself, ourselves*, etc.

German has reflexive pronouns too, but in the first and second person they are identical with the personal pronouns:

Er sieht mich.	He sees me.
Ich sehe mich.	I see myself.

In the third person, use of the personal pronoun would be ambiguous. Therefore, German uses a special reflexive pronoun, **sich**, which
is used for all three genders, and in the singular as well as in the
plural; **sich** is never capitalized.

SINGULAR			PLURAL		
NOM.	ACC. REFL.		NOM.	ACC. REFL.	
ich	**mich**	(myself)	**wir**	**uns**	(ourselves)
du	**dich**	(yourself)	**ihr**	**euch**	(yourselves)
er	**sich**	(himself)			
sie	**sich**	(herself)	**sie**	**sich**	(themselves)
es	**sich**	(itself)			
Sie	**sich**	(yourself)	**Sie**	**sich**	(yourselves)

The plural reflexives are also used as reciprocal pronouns corresponding to English *each other*.

Kennen Sie sich?	Do you know each other?
Kennt ihr euch?	Do you know each other?
Ja, wir kennen uns.	Yes, we know each other.

20/The Nominative and Accusative of the Definite Article

In English the definite article *the* never changes its form. In German, however, the situation is quite different: the definite article changes its form to show the gender, case, and number (singular or plural) of the noun it goes with. You will need to learn not only the proper article for each noun, but also the appropriate forms for different cases in both singular and plural.

	MASC.	FEM.	NEUT.
NOM. SING. ACC. SING.	**der** Mann **den** Mann	**die Frau** **die Frau**	**das Kind** **das Kind**
NOM. & ACC. PLURAL	**die Männer** **die Frauen** **die Kinder**		

NOTE: Only the masculine singular definite article distinguishes the nominative from the accusative. The plural forms of the definite article in all three genders are identical in the nominative and accusative case.

Telefonbuch

Das Amtliche

Jeder hat's.
Jeder braucht's.

der-WORDS

There are several words which change their forms in the same way as the definite article and which are therefore called **der**-words. This group includes **dieser** (*this*), **jeder** (*each*), and **welcher** (*which*).

	MASC.	FEM.	NEUT.
NOM. SING. ACC. SING.	**dieser Mann** **diesen Mann**	**diese Frau** **diese Frau**	**dieses Kind** **dieses Kind**
NOM. & ACC. PLURAL	**diese Männer** **diese Frauen** **diese Kinder**		

INTERROGATIVES: **wer, was**

NOM.	**wer** who	**was** what
ACC.	**wen** whom	**was** what

Note that **wer, wen** are used for both masculine and feminine, singular and plural.

21/The Nominative and Accusative of the Indefinite Article

Unlike the English indefinite article *a*, *an*, the German indefinite article changes its form to show gender, case, and number (singular or plural).

	MASC.	FEM.	NEUT.
NOM. SING. ACC. SING.	**ein Mann** **einen Mann**	**eine Frau** **eine Frau**	**ein Kind** **ein Kind**
NOM. & ACC. PLURAL	**Männer** **Frauen** **Kinder**		

Again, only the masculine singular has a different form for the accusative. There is no plural of **ein**; for example, the plural of **ein Kind** is **Kinder**.

ein-WORDS

This group consists of **kein** (the negation of **ein**: *no, not a, not any,* to be introduced in Unit 3) and the possessive adjectives, which are presented in Part Three of this unit.

PRACTICE TWO

C. In the following sentences, replace the subject by a pronoun.

Der Mann heißt Meyer.	**Er heißt Meyer.**

1. Erika ist Studentin.
2. Dieses Buch ist interessant.
3. Der Zug fährt nach Dresden.
4. Der Kaffee ist gut.
5. Karl Meyer ist in Köln.
6. Herr und Frau May sind hier.

D. Replace the object by a pronoun.

Fragen Sie Hans Müller.	**Fragen Sie ihn.**

1. Ich kenne Helmut Lenz.
2. Er liest die Zeitung.
3. Siehst du Inge heute abend?
4. Ich kenne Hans und Erika gut.
5. Brauchen Sie diese Bücher?
6. Hast du das Buch?

E. Insert the correct form of the reflexive/reciprocal pronoun.

1. Siehst du *sich* im Spiegel?
2. Er sieht *sich* im Spiegel.
3. Seht ihr *euch* im Spiegel?
4. Natürlich kennen wir *uns*.
5. Kennen Sie *sich* ?

F. Insert the definite article; then replace each article plus noun with a pronoun.

1. Ich brauche _____ Teller.
2. Hier ist _____ Teller.
3. Ich brauche _____ Tasse.
4. Hier ist _____ Tasse.
5. Ich brauche _____ Glas.
6. Hier ist _____ Glas.

der Teller, - plate
die Tasse, -n cup
das Glas, ¨er glass

G. Complete the following sentences with the accusative form of the pronoun in parentheses.

1. Ich brauche _es_. (es)
2. Ich frage _dich_. (du)
3. Fragst du _mich_? (ich)
4. Versteht ihr _uns_? (wir)

5. Ja, wir verstehen _euch_. (ihr)
6. Ich brauche _ihn_. (er)
7. Wir kennen _sie_. (sie)
8. Ich sehe _ihn_ im Spiegel. (er)

German and English

German and English derive from a common Germanic ancestor two thousand years ago. Despite the obvious differences between modern English and modern German, their shared roots are still evident, for example, in such pairs of words as English *summer* and German **Sommer**, *winter* and **Winter**, *father* and **Vater**, *mother* and **Mutter**, *ship* and **Schiff**, *come* and **kommen**, and *green* and **grün**. Such pairs of words are called cognates.

If German and English had one common Germanic source, why are the two languages so different today? Passage of time and geographical separation have been major factors, of course, but in spite of the isolation of the British Isles, the English language has been much more strongly subjected to non-Germanic influences than the German language ever was. On a typical page of an English dictionary perhaps fifty percent of all words will be of French/Latin origin.

Much of the basic English vocabulary (the peasants' language of the Norman period) is still Germanic; among the most frequently used two or three hundred English words there are few of Romance origin. In some of them you can observe umlaut, that is, a vowel change from singular to plural, just as in many German words, for example, in *foot-feet* / **Fuß-Füße** or *mouse-mice* / **Maus-Mäuse**.

German, too, has borrowed from French and Latin, but to a much lesser degree, and many of the borrowings—for example, **Revolution** or **Sozialismus**—are still considered **Fremdwörter**, foreign words. Since World War II, there has been a veritable invasion of American words into German: words like **der Manager, der Computer, die Pipeline, der Trend, der Pop Star, der Top Hit** can be found in all German newspapers.

Americanisms in German.

PATTERNS THREE

7/The Nominative and Accusative of Possessive Adjectives

NOMINATIVE

MASC.

This is my husband.

Das ist mein Mann.
Ist das dein Sohn?
Peter ist sein Sohn.
Peter ist ihr Sohn.
Das ist unser Sohn.
Ist das euer Sohn?
Ihr Sohn heißt Peter.
Ist das Ihr Sohn, Herr
   Klein?

FEM.

This is my wife.

Das ist meine Frau.
Ist das deine Tochter?
Gabriele ist seine Tochter.
Gabriele ist ihre Tochter.
Das ist unsere Tochter.
Ist das eure Tochter?
Ihre Tochter heißt Gabriele.
Ist das Ihre Tochter, Herr
   Klein?

NEUT.

This is my child.

Das ist mein Kind.
Ist das dein Kind?
Das ist sein Kind.
Das ist ihr Kind.
Das ist unser Kind.
Ist das euer Kind?
Das ist ihr Kind.
Ist das Ihr Kind, Herr
   Klein?

PLURAL

My sons are living in Lübeck.

Meine Söhne wohnen in Lübeck.
Wo wohnen denn deine Töchter jetzt?
Seine Freundinnen wohnen jetzt alle in
   Wien.
Ihre Freundinnen wohnen auch alle in
   Wien.

Unsere Kinder wohnen in Mannheim.
Wo wohnen denn eure Eltern jetzt?
Jetzt wohnen ihre Eltern in Salzburg.
Wo wohnen Ihre Freunde denn jetzt,
   Herr Lehmann?

ACCUSATIVE

MASC.

I'm taking my car, and you take your car.

Ich nehme meinen Wagen, und ihr nehmt euren Wagen.
Du nimmst deinen Wagen, und wir nehmen unseren Wagen.
Er nimmt seinen Wagen, und sie nehmen ihren Wagen.

FEM.

Do you know my daughter?

Kennst du meine Tochter?
Ich kenne deine Tochter nicht.
Erika kennt seine Tochter.
Hans kennt ihre Tochter.

Kennst du unsere Tochter?
Natürlich kenne ich eure Tochter.
Wir kennen ihre Tochter nicht.

NEUT.

I read my book, and you read your book.

Ich lese mein Buch, und du liest dein Buch.
Du liest dein Buch, und er liest sein Buch.
Er liest sein Buch, und sie liest ihr Buch.
Sie liest ihr Buch, und wir lesen unsere Bücher.
Wir lesen unsere Bücher, und ihr lest eure Bücher.
Ihr lest eure Bücher, und sie lesen ihre Bücher.

PLURAL

I buy my books in Frankfurt.

Ich kaufe meine Bücher in Frankfurt.
Wo kaufst du deine Bücher?
Er kauft seine Bücher in Basel.
Sie kauft ihre Bücher in Salzburg.

Wir kaufen unsere Bücher in Bonn.
Wo kauft ihr eure Bücher?
Sie kaufen ihre Bücher in Leipzig.

8/Special Forms: n-nouns

Wer ist der Student?
Kennst du den Studenten?

Who is the student?
Do you know the student?

Wer ist der Junge?
Kennst du den Jungen?

Who is the boy?
Do you know the boy?

Wer ist der Herr?
Kennst du den Herrn?
Wer sind denn diese Herren?

Who is the gentleman?
Do you know the gentleman?
Who are these gentlemen?

9/Professional Status, Nationality, and Group Membership

Margret Baum und Kurt Schmitz studieren Medizin; sie sind Medizinstudenten. Margret wird Ärztin. Kurt wird Arzt.

Margret Baum and Kurt Schmitz are studying medicine; they are medical students. Margret is becoming (going to be) a doctor. Kurt will be a doctor.

Willi Baumgärtner ist Lehrling bei Braun und Co.; er wird Automechaniker.
Die Lehrlinge bei Braun und Co. werden alle Automechaniker.
Ursula Nagel wird Laborantin.
Und was wirst du, Lilo? —Ich werde Lehrerin.

Willi Baumgärtner is an apprentice with Braun and Co.; he'll be an auto mechanic.
All apprentices with Braun and Company are going to be auto mechanics.
Ursula Nagel is going to be a lab technician.
And what are you going to be Lilo? —I'll be a teacher.

Herr Straub ist Österreicher, aber seine Frau ist Engländerin. Sie kommt aus London, und er ist Salzburger.

John Ray ist Demokrat, und Jane Ray ist Republikanerin.

Mr. Straub is an Austrian, but his wife is an Englishwoman. She comes from London, and he is a native of Salzburg.

John Ray is a Democrat, and Jane Ray is a Republican.

10/Cardinal Numbers

Wo wohnst du?
Adenauerstraße 67 (siebenundsechzig).
Ist das das Studentenheim?
Ja, das ist das Adenauerhaus.
Wieviele Studenten wohnen dort?
80 (achtzig).
Habt ihr viele Ausländer?
Ja, 43 (dreiundvierzig). Das Heim ist sehr international. Wir sind 3 (drei) Amerikaner und 2 (zwei) Amerikanerinnen, und wir haben 5 (fünf) Engländer, 16 (sechzehn) Schweizer und 17 (siebzehn) Österreicher.
Du weißt wirklich alles.

Where do you live?
67 Adenauer Street.
Is that the student dormitory?
Yes, that's Adenauer House.
How many students live there?
Eighty.
Do you have many foreigners?
Yes, forty-three. The dorm is very international. We are three American men and two American women, and we have five English, sixteen Swiss, and seventeen Austrians.
You really do know everything.

ANALYSIS THREE

22 Possessive Adjectives

In both English and German, possessive adjectives indicate possession:

Das ist ein Buch.   That is a book.
Das ist mein Buch.   That is my book.

The possessive adjectives are:

mein	my	**unser**	our
dein	your	**euer**	your
sein	his		
ihr	her	**ihr**	their
sein	its		
Ihr	your	**Ihr**	your

All German possessive adjectives have the same endings as the indefinite article **ein** and are therefore called **ein**-words. Unlike **ein**, however, possessive adjectives have plural forms which are identical for all three genders.

	MASC.	FEM.	NEUT.
NOM. SING. ACC. SING.	**mein Roman** **meinen Roman**	**meine Zeitung** **meine Zeitung**	**mein Buch** **mein Buch**
NOM. & ACC. PLURAL	**meine Romane** **meine Zeitungen** **meine Bücher**		

Note that all possessive adjectives have the same endings, although only **mein, dein,** and **sein** "sound" like **ein**. Remember that only the masculine singular distinguishes the nominative from the accusative:

Das ist ihr Bruder.   That is her brother.
Ich kenne ihren Bruder.   I know her brother.

The **-er** in **unser** and **euer** is not an ending, but is part of the stem. When an ending is added to **unser** or **euer**, an **e** is frequently dropped: **unsern Sohn, unsre Tochter, eure Eltern.**

The word **ihr** may be confusing. You have learned it as the personal pronoun **ihr**, *you*, and now you will learn that **ihr** as a possessive adjective has no fewer than three meanings: *her, their, your.* Since the word **ihr** always appears in a context, however, you will not have any difficulty determining which **ihr** is meant. When **Ihr** means *your*, it must always be capitalized.

23/Time Expressions in the Accusative

Expressions indicating a stretch of time or a definite time are in the accusative. Note that in German these time expressions precede place phrases.

> **Ich bleibe einen Tag (eine Woche, einen Monat, ein Jahr) in Berlin.**
> **Sie fährt diesen Sonntag (nächsten Dienstag) nach Salzburg.**
> **Er läuft jeden Morgen in die Stadt.**

24 Special Forms: n-nouns

A few masculine nouns add **-(e)n** in all cases but the nominative singular; for example, **der Mensch** (*human being*), **der Student**, and **der Junge. Der Herr** adds an **-n** in all singular forms and an **-en** in all plural forms.

NOM. SING. ACC. SING.	der Mensch den Menschen	der Student den Studenten	der Junge den Jungen	der Herr den Herrn
NOM. PL. ACC. PL.	die Menschen die Menschen	die Studenten die Studenten	die Jungen die Jungen	die Herren die Herren

Note that in the vocabulary such nouns will be identified as n-nouns: **der Student,-en** (n-noun).

25/Professional Status, Nationality, and Group Membership

When nouns identifying professional status, nationality, citizenship, origin, and group membership are used after the verb **sein**, or occasionally after **werden**, they are not preceded by the indefinite article

ein. These nouns also have feminine forms in **-in,** some of which have an umlaut.

John Ray ist Amerikaner.	John Ray is an American.
Jane Ray ist Amerikanerin.	Jane Ray is an American.
Elke Winter ist Berlinerin.	Elke Winter is a Berliner.
Herr Meyer ist Rotarier.	Mr. Meyer is a Rotarian.

But:

Ich kenne den Österreicher.	I know the Austrian.
Wir brauchen einen Automechaniker.	We need an auto mechanic.

Some further examples:

der Arzt	**die Ärztin**
der Ausländer	**die Ausländerin**
der Biologe	**die Biologin**
der Professor	**die Professorin** (shift of stress)
der Sozialist	**die Sozialistin**

26/Cardinal Numbers

The cardinal numbers from 1 to 100 are:

1 **eins**	7 **sieben**	13 **dreizehn**	19 **neunzehn**	60 **sechzig**
2 **zwei**	8 **acht**	14 **vierzehn**	20 **zwanzig**	70 **siebzig**
3 **drei**	9 **neun**	15 **fünfzehn**	21 **einundzwanzig**	80 **achtzig**
4 **vier**	10 **zehn**	16 **sechzehn**	30 **dreißig**	90 **neunzig**
5 **fünf**	11 **elf**	17 **siebzehn**	40 **vierzig**	100 **hundert**
6 **sechs**	12 **zwölf**	18 **achtzehn**	50 **fünfzig**	

The uninflected numeral **eins** is used only for counting, for telephone numbers, in arithmetic, etc.; the inflected **ein** can be either the indefinite article or the numeral *one.*

Eins und eins ist zwei.	One and one is two.
Inge liest einen Roman.	Inge is reading a novel.
Er hat *ei*nen Sohn, nicht zwei.	He has one son, not two.

Only **ein** takes endings to indicate number, gender, and case. Other numbers have only one form.

Wir haben drei Kinder, zwei Töchter und einen Sohn.

Note also:

Es ist jetzt ein Uhr.   It is now one o'clock.

but:

Es ist jetzt eins.   It is now one (o'clock).

PRACTICE THREE

H. Insert the correct form of the possessive adjective which agrees with the italicized element(s).

1. *Hans* fährt nach Stuttgart. _Seinen_ Zug fährt um 11 Uhr.
2. *Ich* trinke _mein_ Bier, und *du* trinkst _dein_ Wein.
3. *Herr Anders* liest _sein_ Buch, und *Frau Anders* liest _ihre_ Zeitung.
4. So, *ihr* wohnt in England. Wohnen _eure_ Eltern auch in England?
5. Ist das _Ihren_ Sohn, *Herr Schmidt*?
6. Oh, Sie sind *Frau Meyer*. Ich kenne _ihren_ Sohn.
7. Heute abend nehmen *wir* _unsern_ Wagen.
8. Kennen Sie *Herrn und Frau Meyer*? Nein, aber ich kenne _ihre_ Tochter.
9. *Ich* bin 18 Jahre alt. _meine_ Schwester ist 26, und _meinen_ Bruder ist 23.
10. *Sie* heißt Erika, und _ihren_ Bruder heißt Max.

I. Provide the correct accusative form of the noun in the first sentence.

1. Das ist der Student.   Kennst du _ihn_ ?
2. Egon Braun ist mein Laborant.   Kennst du _ihn_ ?
3. Wer ist der Junge?   Kennst du _ihn_ ?
4. Das ist Herr Meyer.   Kennst du _ihn_ ?
5. Wer sind denn die Herren?   Kennst du _sie_ ?

J. Fill in the blank with the word indicating the correct nationality or place of origin.

1. Jane Ray kommt aus Amerika.   Sie ist _____.
2. Paul Stefanek kommt aus Wien.   Er ist _____.
3. Jutta Hartwig kommt aus Berlin.   Sie ist _____.
4. William Smith kommt aus England.   Er ist _____.
5. Hedi Strobl kommt aus Österreich.   Sie ist _____.

K. Count out loud from one to a hundred.

L. Write out the following equations and supply the missing part.

1. eins und eins ist zwei
2. 11 und _____ ist 22
3. 6 + 10 = _____
4. 16 + 14 = _____
5. 49 + _____ = 66
6. 30 + _____ = 100

CONVERSATIONS

I

HELMUT:	Was machst du dieses Wochenende? Fährst du nach Hause?	What are you doing this weekend? Are you going home?
HELGA:	Ja. Mein Vater hat Sonntag Geburtstag. Mein Bruder kommt aus Hamburg nach Hause, und meine Schwester kommt aus München. Und du? Fährst du auch nach Hause?	Yes. Sunday is my father's birthday. My brother is coming home from Hamburg, and my sister is coming from Munich. And you? Are you going home, too?
HELMUT:	Nein, ich bleibe hier und lese. Das heißt, heute abend gehe ich ins Theater.	No, I'll stay here and read. That is, tonight I'm going to the theater.
HELGA:	Was liest du denn?	What are you reading?
HELMUT:	Thomas Mann und James Joyce, für das Seminar nächste Woche.	Thomas Mann and James Joyce, for the seminar next week.

II

HELMUT:	Nimmst du den Bus oder den Zug?	Are you taking the bus or the train?
HELGA:	Ich glaube, ich nehme heute den Bus.	I think I'll take the bus today.
HELMUT:	Wann fährt denn der Bus?	When does the bus leave?[8]
HELGA:	Um sechs. Dann bin ich um acht zu Hause.	At six. Then I'll be home at eight.
HELMUT:	Also mach's gut. Schönes Wochenende.	Well, take care. Have a nice weekend.
HELGA:	Tschüß. Bis Montag.	Bye. See you Monday.

III

BIRGIT:	Hier kommt die Sylvia. Ihr kennt euch doch?	Here comes Sylvia. You know each other, don't you?
URSULA:	Natürlich kennen wir uns. Wir sehen uns doch jeden Tag im Labor.	Of course we know each other. We see each other every day in the lab.
BIRGIT:	Ach ja, ihr seid ja beide in Bio.	Oh, yes, you're both in bio.
SYLVIA:	Tag, Birgit. Tag, Ursula. Was macht ihr denn jetzt?	Hi, Birgit. Hi, Ursula. What are you going to do now?
URSULA:	Ich weiß nicht. Wieviel Uhr ist es denn?	I don't know. What time is it?
SYLVIA:	Zwölf. Ich gehe jetzt essen, ich habe Hunger.	Twelve. I'm going to go eat now; I'm hungry.

[8]Note that in this context **fahren** can mean *to go, leave, depart.*

BIRGIT:	Ich auch. Fährst du in die Stadt oder ißt du hier?	Me, too. Are you going downtown or are you going to eat here?
SYLVIA:	Ich glaube, ich bleibe heute hier.	I think I'll stay here today.
URSULA:	Dann essen wir doch zusammen.	Then why don't we eat together.

Fragen an Sie persönlich

1. Wo wohnen Sie hier auf dem Campus?
    in der Stadt?
2. Wo wohnen Ihre Eltern? (**die Eltern** *parents*)
    Was ist Ihr Vater (*What does your father do*)?
        Ihre Mutter?
3. Haben Sie Geschwister? (**die Geschwister** *brothers and sisters, siblings*)
        Brüder?
        Schwestern?
    Wie heißen Ihre Geschwister?
    Wie alt sind Ihre Brüder?
            Ihre Schwestern?
    Wo wohnen Ihre Geschwister?
4. Wen kennen Sie schon hier in der Klasse?
5. Was machen Sie heute abend?
    Bleiben Sie zu Hause?
    Arbeiten Sie?
    Gehen Sie ins Kino?
            ins Theater?
            in die Stadt?
6. Haben Sie einen Wagen?
        ein Fahrrad?
        ein Motorrad?
7. Wie ist das Wetter heute?
8. Was ist heute? Montag? Dienstag?

Now ask the same questions of other members of your class. Don't forget that you have to shift from **Sie** to **du**.

READING

In the following passage, you will find many words and grammatical features that are unfamiliar. But, with the aid of the parallel English translation, you will be able to "decode" the German text.

Read the text aloud several times to improve your pronunciation and sentence intonation; then compare the German text with the English translation; finally, read the German again for comprehension.

Mitteleuropa

Mitteleuropa ist das Gebiet „in der Mitte von Europa", aber „Mitteleuropa" ist nicht identisch mit „Deutschland". Es gibt heute kein Land mehr, das Deutschland heißt. Es gibt zwei Staaten, die das Wort „deutsch" in 5 ihrem Namen haben, die Bundesrepublik Deutschland (BRD) und die Deutsche Demokratische Republik (DDR). Aber nicht nur in der BRD und in der DDR spricht man Deutsch; die Republik Österreich ist ein 10 deutschsprachiges Land, und drei Viertel der Menschen in der Schweiz sprechen Deutsch.

Diese vier Länder sind ungefähr das, was wir Mitteleuropa nennen. Aber dieses Mittel- 15 europa ist keine politische Einheit: die Bundesrepublik gehört zum Westen, zur Europäischen Gemeinschaft (EG); die DDR gehört zum sozialistischen „Ostblock", und Österreich und die Schweiz sind politisch 20 neutral. „Mitteleuropa" ist eher ein kulturelles Konzept; seine historische Tradition basiert auf der Sprache, die alle Mitteleuropäer sprechen: der deutschen Sprache. Wenn also Mitteleuropa, so wie wir es definieren, 25 mit irgendetwas identisch ist, dann ist es identisch mit dem deutschen Sprachraum.

Central Europe

Central Europe is the area "in the middle of Europe," but "Central Europe" is not identical with "Germany." There is (*lit.* It gives) no country today that is called Germany anymore. There are two states which have the word "German" in their name, the Federal Republic of Germany (FRG) and the German Democratic Republic (GDR). But not only in the FRG and in the GDR is German spoken (*lit.* does one speak German); the Republic of Austria is a German-speaking country, and three-quarters of the people in Switzerland speak German.

These four countries are approximately what we call Central Europe. But this Central Europe is not a political entity: the Federal Republic belongs to the West, to the European Community (EC)[9]; the GDR belongs to the socialist "East Bloc," and Austria and Switzerland are politically neutral. "Central Europe" is, rather, a cultural concept; its historical tradition is based on the language which all Central Europeans speak: the German language. If, therefore, Central Europe, as we define it, is identical with anything, then it is identical with the German language area.

REVIEW EXERCISES

M. Restate the following sentences by starting with the element in italics.

1. Herr Schulte ist *morgen* in Mainz.
2. Natürlich ist *er* zu Hause.
3. Ich bleibe morgen abend *natürlich* zu Hause.
4. Übrigens gehen *wir* morgen ins Kino.
5. Morgen fährt *Sigrid* nach Graz.

[9]Also referred to as the "Common Market."

N. Form questions that could precede the following sentences. Note that news items are in italics.

1. Erika trinkt *Wein*.
2. *Erika* trinkt Wein.
3. Ich sehe *Erika* heute abend.
4. Der Mann heißt *Müller*.
5. Ernst Reuter wohnt in *Stuttgart*.
6. *Ernst Reuter* wohnt in Stuttgart.
7. Wir sind *um zwei Uhr* zu Hause.
8. Um zwei Uhr sind wir *zu Hause*.

O. Supply the correct plural form.

1. Ich bleibe ein Jahr in Deutschland. Fritz bleibt zwei _____ in Deutschland.
2. Herr Meyer hat ein Büro. Schmidt hat zwei _____.
3. Meyers Sohn heißt Peter. Meyers _____ heißen Peter und Paul.
4. Der Mann arbeitet in Bremen. Die _____ arbeiten alle in Bremen.
5. Frau Meyer und Frau Schmidt sind zu Hause. Die zwei _____ bleiben heute zu Hause.
6. Mein Bruder ist auch Arzt. Wir sind _____.
7. Hier ist nur ein Glas, aber wir brauchen doch drei _____.
8. Meyer hat nicht nur ein Haus, er hat drei _____.
9. Mein Fahrrad ist hier. Wo sind denn eure _____?
10. Herr Schobler und Herr Reinicke sind nicht hier, die _____ sind heute beide in Trier.

P. Insert the correct verb forms.

1. Ich fahre morgen nach Berlin. Wann <u>fährst</u> du nach Weimar?
2. Ich lese Günter Grass, und was <u>liest</u> du?
3. Ich esse ein Wiener Schnitzel. Was <u>ißt</u> du?

In München steht ein
HOFBRÄUHAUS
Herzlich willkommen!

4. Unser Fritz <u>hat</u> morgen fünf Jahre alt; wann <u>hast</u> du denn fünf, Rudi?
5. Wann kommt er denn?—Ich weiß es nicht; ~~recognise~~ <u>weiß</u> du es?
6. Ich kenne Frau Brandt nicht. <u>Kennst</u> du sie?
7. Ich nehme ein Bier. Was <u>nimmst</u> du?
8. Ich sitze zu Hause und arbeite, und du <u>sitzt</u> im Hofbräuhaus und trinkst Bier.
9. Ich heiße Susanne. Und wie <u>heißt</u> ihr?
10. Ich laufe jeden Tag fünf Kilometer. Hans <u>läuft</u> zehn Kilometer.
11. Ich habe Durst. <u>Hast</u> du auch Durst?
12. Ich sehe Peter heute abend. Wann <u>siehst</u> du ihn?

Zum guten Durst...
Ambrosius **Wurst**

Q. Formulate affirmative answers to the following questions, using personal pronouns.

Ist Karl zu Hause?	**Ja, er ist zu Hause.**

1. Kennen Sie Fritz Bertram?
2. Kennen Sie mich?
3. Kennst du die Frauen da?
4. Hast du meinen Roman?

5. Arbeitet dein Vater in Heidelberg?
6. Kennst du ihre Mutter?
7. Siehst du Sylvia?
8. Brauchst du den Wagen heute nachmittag?

R. Insert the possessive adjective which agrees with the noun or pronoun in the first sentence.

1. Das ist Frau Helbig. Kennen Sie _____ Mann?
2. Wo ist Herr Stickel? _____ Sohn ist hier.
3. Ich habe Durst. Wo ist _____ Bier?
4. So, ihr seid morgen in Kiel. Und wo sind _____ Eltern morgen?
5. Du gehst heute abend ins Kino. Geht _____ Schwester auch ins Kino?
6. Du wirst Automechaniker. _____ Bruder wird Laborant.
7. Sie fahren doch heute nach Hannover. Nehmen Sie _____ Wagen?
8. Da drüben sind Herr und Frau Ortmann. Kennen Sie _____ Söhne?
9. Das sind Herr und Frau Weydt, und das ist _____ Sohn Rolf.
10. Wir sind Hans und Hannelore König, und das ist _____ Tochter Birgit.

S. Form sentences from the following elements.

1. Fritz / morgen / fünf Jahre alt / werden.
2. Er / nicht / wissen // wo / wir / sein.
3. Er / um zwei Uhr / nach Hause / kommen.
4. Ich / natürlich / heute abend / zu Hause / bleiben.
5. Wohin / du / heute / fahren?
6. Er / Brot / essen / und / Milch / trinken.
7. Morgen / gut / bestimmt / Wetter / werden.
8. Inge / Fritz / heute abend / sehen.
9. Ich / 1 Löffel, 1 Messer und 1 Gabel / brauchen.
10. Mein / Freundin (pl.) / in Linz / wohnen.

T. Give the correct articles and plural forms of the following nouns.

1. Arzt	5. Kino	9. Sohn	13. Jahr
2. Lehrer	6. Herr	10. Kind	14. Tag
3. Haus	7. Frau	11. Tochter	15. Studentin
4. Schwester	8. Büro	12. Mädchen	16. Junge

Dr. Hubert FISCHER

FACHARZT
für
Ohren-Nasen-Halskrankheiten

1.Stock

ORDINATION:
MO.-DI.-DO.-FR. 10-11+17-18 UHR
MI.+SA. KEINE ORDINATION

U. Express in German. This is not a "translation exercise"; you should be able to produce the German equivalents of these short sentences quite spontaneously. If you have trouble, review the preceding pages once more.

1. He is hungry.
2. We are eating bread and cheese.
3. What is he eating?
4. They have children.
5. They have a son.
6. This is their son.
7. Is this their daughter?
8. They have one daughter.
9. This is my doctor.
10. He is a doctor.
11. Do you see the streetcar?
12. Do you see it (the streetcar)?
13. Do you see her?
14. I see you, Mr. Meyer.
15. I know this student (male).
16. I know this student (female).
17. Do you have our books?
18. We are reading a book.
19. It is a novel.
20. We are reading a novel.
21. Do you know Mr. Schmidt?
22. Mr. Schmidt is a Berliner.
23. His wife is Viennese.
24. She is Austrian.
25. Do you know their boy?
26. Do they know each other?
27. We understand each other.
28. Jane Ray is an American.

NOTE: Additional exercises can be found in the *Study Guide*.

VOCABULARY

Verbs

antworten	to answer	laufen (du läufst, er läuft)	to run, to walk
brauchen	to need	lesen (du liest, er liest)	to read
essen (du ißt, er ißt)	to eat	nehmen (du nimmst, er nimmt)	to take
essen gehen	to go to eat		
fahren (du fährst, er fährt)	to drive; to go (by train, boat, plane, car)	sehen (du siehst, er sieht)	to see
fragen	to ask	sitzen (du sitzt, er sitzt)	to sit
glauben	to believe	verstehen	to understand
haben	to have	werden (du wirst, er wird)	to become
kaufen	to buy		
kennen	to know, be acquainted with	wissen (du weißt, er weiß)	to know (facts)

Nouns

MASCULINE

der Ausländer, -	foreigner (m.)	der Mensch, -en (n-noun)	human being, person
die Ausländerin, -nen	foreigner (f.)	der Profes'sor, die Professo'ren	professor (m.)
der Bruder, ⸚	brother	die Professo'rin, -nen	professor (f.)
der Bus, -se	bus		
der Durst (no pl.)	thirst	der Roman', -e	novel
der Freund, -e	friend (m.)	der Sohn, ⸚e	son
die Freundin, -nen	friend (f.)	der Spiegel, -	mirror
der Geburtstag, -e	birthday	im Spiegel	in the mirror
der Hunger (no pl.)	hunger	der Staat, -en	state
der Junge, -n (n-noun)	boy	der Teller, -	plate
der Käse, -	cheese	der Vater, ⸚	father
der Lehrer, -	teacher (m.)	der Wagen, -	car
die Lehrerin, -nen	teacher (f.)	der Zug, ⸚e	train

FEMININE

die Bundesrepublik Deutschland (BRD)	Federal Republic of Germany (FRG)	die Deutsche Demokratische Republik (DDR)	German Democratic Republic (GDR)
die Dame, -n	lady	die Klasse, -n	class
		die Mutter, ⸚	mother

die Schweiz[1]	Switzerland	die Straße, -n	street
der Schweizer, -	Swiss (m.)	die Straßenbahn, -en	streetcar
die Schweizerin, -nen	Swiss (f.)	die Tasse, -n	cup
		die Tochter, ⸚	daughter
die Schwester, -n	sister	die Woche, -n	week
die Stadt, ⸚e	town, city	nächste Woche	next week
in die Stadt	to town	die Wurst, ⸚e	sausage
in der Stadt	in town	die Zeitung, -en	newspaper

NEUTER

das Brot, -e	bread, loaf	das Motorrad, ⸚er	motorcycle
(das) England[1]	England	(das) Österreich[1]	Austria
der Engländer, -	Englishman	der Österreicher, -	Austrian (m.)
die Engländerin, -nen	Englishwoman	die Österreicherin, -nen	Austrian (f.)
das Fahrrad, ⸚er[2]	bicycle	das Studentenheim, -e	student dormitory
das Glas, ⸚er	glass	das Theater, -	theater
das Jahr, -e	year	ins Theater	to the theater
das Mädchen, -	girl	das Wochenende, -n	weekend

PLURAL ONLY

die Eltern	parents	die Leute	people
die Geschwister	brothers and sisters, siblings		

Adjectives

alt	old
bestimmt	certain, certainly
interessant	interesting
kein, keine, kein, *pl.*: keine	no, (not any)
schön	pretty, beautiful
sicher	certain, certainly

Possessive Adjectives

mein	my
dein	your
sein	his; its
ihr	her; their
unser	our
euer	your

[1]Feminine and plural countries always use the definite article: **die Schweiz, die Vereinigten Staaten** (*United States*); neuter countries normally do not use the definite article, unless an adjective precedes.

[2]If an umlaut is indicated for the plural form of a compound noun, the umlaut is placed on the vowel in the last part of the compound. Thus, the plural of **Fahrrad** is **Fahrräder**.

Pronouns

dieser, diese, dieses, *pl.:* **diese**	this	**welcher, welche, welches,** *pl.:* **welche**	which
jeder, jede, jedes	each		
sich	*(third-person reflexive pronoun)*		

Interrogatives

wieviel	how much	**wieviele**	how many
wieviel Uhr	what time	**wohin (wo . . . hin)**	where (. . . to)

Adverbs

dann	then	**heute morgen**	this morning
doch = nicht wahr	that's true, isn't it? (see p. 88)	**heute nachmittag**	this afternoon
dort ‹da	there	**immer**	always
drüben	on the other side	**nicht**	not
da (dort) drüben	over there	**sehr**	very
		zusammen	together

Numbers

eins	one	**siebzehn**	seventeen
zwei	two	**achtzehn**	eighteen
drei	three	**neunzehn**	nineteen
vier	four	**zwanzig**	twenty
fünf	five	**einundzwanzig**	twenty-one
sechs	six	**zweiundzwanzig**	twenty-two
sieben	seven	**dreiundzwanzig**	twenty-three
acht	eight	**vierundzwanzig** *etc.*	twenty-four
neun	nine	**dreißig**	thirty
zehn	ten	**vierzig**	forty
elf	eleven	**fünfzig**	fifty
zwölf	twelve	**sechzig**	sixty
dreizehn	thirteen	**siebzig**	seventy
vierzehn	fourteen	**achtzig**	eighty
fünfzehn	fifteen	**neunzig**	ninety
sechzehn	sixteen	**hundert**	hundred

Other Words

ach ja	oh yes	**das heißt (d.h.)**	that is, i.e.
alle	all (of us/you/them)	**für**	for
alles	everything		

identisch – identical

ungefähr – approx.

(die) Einheit   entity

Unit 3

The Structure of German Sentences—
Verbal Complements—
Negation with *nicht* and *kein*

GDR
Facts and Figures*

The country, the state and its citizens

The German Democratic Republic was founded on 7 October 1949, Political power is in the hands of the working class allied with the class of cooperative farmers and the rest of the working people. The economy is characterized by socialist ownership of the means of production.

PANORAMA DDR
Auslandspresseagentur GmbH
Redaktion "DDR im Überblick"
DDR – 1054 Berlin, Wilhelm Pieck Strasse 49
Editing completed: February 1985
Translated by Intertext
Publishers: Zeit im Bild
DDR – 8012 Dresden, Julian Grimau Allee
Printed in the German Democratic Republic
by Grafischer Grossbetrieb Völkerfreundschaft Dresden
Berlin 1985
5051-2

Territory

Area: 108,333 sq.km.

Borders: Baltic Sea in the north, Poland in the east (length 460 km), Czechoslovakia in the southeast (454 km), and the Federal Republic of Germany in the southwest and west (1,378 km).

Capital: Berlin (1.2 million inhabitants).

Major cities: (population in '000)
Leipzig 556, Dresden 520, Karl Marx Stadt 317, Magdeburg 289, Rostock 242, Halle 236, Erfurt 215, Potsdam 138, Gera 131, Schwerin 126, Cottbus 123, Zwickau 120, Jena 107, Dessau 104.

Administrative structure: 15 counties, 191 rural and 36 urban districts.

Longest river: Elbe, a 566 km stretch of which runs through the GDR.

Largest lake: Müritz, 117 sq.km.

Largest island: Rügen, 926 sq.km.

Highest mountain: Fichtelberg, 1,214 m.

Breakdown of land use: 58 per cent farmland (arable land, meadows, pastures and gardens); 27 per cent forest, 15 per cent built-up areas, roads, rivers and lakes, and waste land.

Located in the midst of GDR territory is West Berlin, a city whose political status is defined in the Quadripartite Agreement signed by the Soviet Union, the United States, France and Great Britain.

Population

Inhabitants: 16.7 million; 53 per cent of the population is female, 47 per cent is male.

Population density: 154 inhabitants per sq.km.

Age structure: 64 per cent of the population is of working age (women between 15 and 60, and men between 15 and 65), 19 per cent are children, and 17 per cent of retirement age.

Live births: 227,440 (1985).

Life expectancy: 69 years for men and 75 years for women.

Population distribution: 75 per cent of the population live in towns and 25 per cent in rural communities.

Die Wappen unserer Bezirksstädte

PATTERNS ONE

1/Topic, Comment, and News Items

TOPIC		COMMENT
Hans	geht	heute ins The*a*ter.
Heute	geht	Hans ins The*a*ter.
Erika	kommt	um ein Uhr nach *Hau*se.
Um ein Uhr	kommt	Erika nach *Hau*se.
Gisela Müller	wohnt	jetzt in *Köln.*
Jetzt	wohnt	Gisela Müller in *Köln.*

2/The Two-Part Predicate

This section demonstrates the arrangement of elements in normal German sentences. Go through the model sentences carefully and note that the elements following the inflected verb often come in an order that is exactly the opposite of what you would expect in English.

FRONT FIELD	INFLECTED VERB	INNER FIELD	VERBAL COMPLEMENT	END FIELD
Das Bier	**ist**	**wirklich**	***gut***	**hier in München.**
Es	*re*gnet.			
Die *Sonne*	scheint.			
Karl	kommt	heute abend.		
Heute	ist	das Wetter	sehr *schlecht.*	
Ursula	ist	jetzt	*Lehr*erin.	
Margret	wird		*Ärzt*in.	
Frau Meyer	ist		zu *Hau*se.	
Er	wohnt		in Ber*lin.*	
Meine Freundin	geht	heute bestimmt	ins Mu*seum.*	
Der Zug	fährt	um 6 Uhr 5	*ab.*	
Hoffentlich	lernt	Otto jetzt	*fahren.*	
Wir	gehen	übrigens	ins *Kino*	heute abend.
Der Wein	ist	wirklich	*gut*	hier in Burgbach.
Wann	kommt	der Zug denn	*an?*	
	Fährt	der Zug jetzt	*ab?*	
	Fahren	Sie doch bitte jetzt	*ab.*	

*Text and illustrations on the facing page are taken from *GDR Facts and Figures* '85 published by Panorama DDR.

3/Coordinating Conjunctions: *aber, denn, oder, und*

Dieses Jahr bleiben wir zu Hause.	This year we'll stay at home.
Aber nächstes Jahr fahren wir nach Deutschland.	But next year we are going to Germany.
Nächstes Jahr fahren wir aber nach Deutschland.	
Meyer geht ins Büro, aber er arbeitet nicht.	Meyer goes to the office, but he doesn't do any work.
Tante Amalie geht schlafen, denn sie ist sehr müde.	Aunt Amalie is going to bed now, because she is very tired.
Ißt du Wurst oder[1] ißt du Käse?	Are you going to eat sausage, or are you going to eat cheese?
Ißt du Wurst oder Käse?	Do you eat sausage or cheese?
Ich esse den Käse, und du ißt die Wurst.	I'm going to eat the cheese, and you'll eat the sausage.
Er ißt Käse und Wurst und[1] trinkt eine Flasche Bier.[2]	He is eating cheese and sausage and drinking a bottle of beer.
Onkel Otto geht ins Büro und arbeitet.	Uncle Otto goes to the office and works.

ANALYSIS ONE

27/Topic, Comment, and News Items

Most sentences consist of a "topic" and some information or "comment" on that topic. Compare the following two sentences:

> Tonight John is going to the movies.
> John is going to the movies tonight.

While the two sentences contain the same information, they are focused in different ways: in the first one, the speaker is implying, "Now I am going to say something about tonight, and here is what is going to happen: John is going to the movies," whereas the implication of the second sentence is, "I'm going to talk about John, and here is what he is going to do: He is going to the movies tonight."

Topicalization, that is, choosing one element of the sentence as "the thing to talk about," accounts for the choice of a given element to

---

[1]If the subject of the two sentences is the same, there is no comma before **oder** and **und**.

[2]**eine Flasche Bier** corresponds to *a bottle of beer*; **eine Tasse Kaffee** to *a cup of coffee*; **ein Glas Wein** to *a glass of wine*.

occupy the German front field. Within the comment on this topic, there are usually one or more stressed elements, or stress points (see Anal. 10, p. 19), which contain the news the speaker wants to convey; these elements are referred to as "news items." In the above example, the news item is *to the movies*. The most usual topics are subjects or time phrases. Sentence adverbs like **leider** and **natürlich** do not function as topics in the same way (see Anal. 31, p. 77).

Remember that in German only one element can precede the inflected verb.

Examples:

> **Mein Bruder fährt morgen nach *Hamburg*.**
>   Topic: **Mein Bruder**
>   Comment: **fährt morgen nach *Hamburg***
>   News item: **nach *Hamburg***

> **Morgen kauft seine Schwester einen *Wagen*.**
>   Topic: **Morgen**
>   Comment: **kauft seine Schwester einen *Wagen***
>   News item: **einen *Wagen***

28/Verbal Complements

Consider the following English sentences:

> This bread is . . . really *good*.
> My father is . . . a *mechanic*.
> My parents are . . . *at home* tonight.
> They go . . . *to the movies* every Saturday night.
> My sister goes . . . *out* with her boyfriend every Friday night.
> Meyer drinks . . . *coffee* every morning.

If you end the sentence at the dots, you either get nonsense (*The bread is*) or you get statements that have a meaning completely different from the full sentence (*Meyer drinks* can only mean that he has an alcohol problem). The meaning of the verbs is completed only if something else is added. For example, in the first sentence above, you need the word *good*, a predicate adjective, and in the last sentence, you need the word *coffee*, a direct object. The words *good* and *coffee* are obligatory verbal complements. In all six sentences above, the verbal complements are printed in italics. Note that not all the words to the right of the dots are necessary to produce meaningful sentences. You can leave out such nonobligatory elements as time phrases without changing the basic meaning of the sentence.

> The verb and its obligatory complements together form the complete predicate of a sentence.

While most English verbs need a complement, there are some which have a complete meaning in themselves, as in the sentences *I understand* or *Susan smiled.*

German verbs function in exactly the same way. Some need no complement, as in the sentences **Susi kommt** or **es regnet**; but most verbs require complements to form a complete predicate. Some parts of speech are *always* verbal complements.

1. PREDICATE ADJECTIVES AND PREDICATE NOUNS

The verbs used most often with predicate adjectives and predicate nouns are **sein** and less frequently **werden** and **bleiben**. The verb **heißen** is always followed by a predicate noun.

Das Wetter ist schlecht.   **Das Wetter bleibt gut.**
Mein Vater ist Mechaniker.   **Ich werde Arzt.**
Meine Freundin heißt Brigitte.

2. Wo-COMPLEMENTS

Place phrases that answer the question **Wo?** (*Where?*) are obligatory complements when used with verbs that describe a state, such as **sein**,[3] **bleiben**, and **wohnen**, *to live, reside.*

Meine Eltern sind in Österreich.
Er wohnt in Rostock.
Wir bleiben heute abend zu Hause.

When used with other verbs, **wo**-phrases are not complements, that is, they are not obligatory.

Wir gehen (in Frankfurt) oft ins Kino.

3. Wohin-COMPLEMENTS

Place phrases that answer the question **Wohin?** (*Where to?*) are called directives; they are obligatory complements.

Wohin fährt er denn? —Er fährt nach Greifswald.

4. PREFIXED COMPLEMENTS

Another large group of obligatory verbal complements follows the pattern of *My sister goes out*; these one-word complements often look like prepositions.

Meine Schwester geht *aus*.
Der Zug fährt *ab*.
Der Zug kommt *an*.

---

[3]One exception is the use of *to be*, **sein**, as a complete verb, as in "*to be or not to be.*"

Short one-word complements like **ab, an, ein,** and **mit** are joined with their infinitives as one word; *these complements are always stressed*. When complement and verb are written as one word, they are listed in this form in the vocabulary of this book as well as in any German dictionary. In the vocabulary lists these verbs are indicated with a dot between the complement and the verb:

ab•fahren   to depart
an•kommen   to arrive

Other complements plus verb you will have to look up under their individual components.

5. INFINITIVE COMPLEMENTS

The verbs **gehen** and **lernen** occasionally have infinitives as complements. The translations are not always what you would expect:

schwimmen gehen	to go swimming	**fahren lernen**	to learn to drive
einkaufen gehen	to go shopping	**lesen lernen**	to learn to read
essen gehen	to go (somewhere) to eat	**kennenlernen**	to meet, become acquainted with
schlafen gehen	to go to bed		

— = conjugate (handwritten note)

Note that of all these combinations, **kennenlernen** is the only one that is written as one word in the infinitive.

6. OBJECT COMPLEMENTS

Objects are also verbal complements.

Meyer trinkt Kaffee.
Frau Meyer liest die Zeitung.

However, they function somewhat differently from the other complements and their syntax will be discussed in Part Two of this unit (see Anal. 36, p. 86).

SUMMARY: You can always identify verbal complements by a deletion test. The verbal complement is that element in the sentence that cannot be deleted without changing the meaning of the verb or making the sentence meaningless. For example, in the following sentence you can delete the time adverb and the sentence adverb. But if you delete the verbal complement **zu Hause**, the result is a meaningless **Ich bin**.

Ich bin heute abend bestimmt zu Hause.
Ich bin bestimmt zu Hause.
Ich bin zu Hause.
Ich bin.

SENTENCE STRESS

In all the examples above, sentence stress falls on the complement rather than on the inflected verb. This is the normal and most natural sentence intonation pattern in both English and German.

Morgen   fliegen   wir   nach *Mün*chen.
Wir   fliegen   morgen   nach *Mün*chen.

Any other intonation implies a contrast. The sentence

   Morgen fliegen *wir* nach München.

means "Tomorrow it's *our* turn to fly to Munich." The sentence

   Nein, wir fliegen *mor*gen nach München.

means "No, not next week! Tomorrow!" Without the preceding **Nein** the sentence could also be the answer to a **wann**-question. Finally

   Morgen *flie*gen wir nach München.

implies "Usually we take the train (bus, car, etc.)."

29/The Position of Verbal Complements

The structure of German assertions was discussed in Anal. 5, p. 12. As we now look at the position of verbal complements, we find the most basic difference between German and English.

> Whereas English complements usually follow the inflected verb immediately, German complements appear at or near the end of the sentence.

The area between the inflected verb and the complement is called the "inner field." The sentence

   Das Bier ist wirklich *gut* hier in München.

exemplifies the structure of all German assertions. This unvarying structure can be represented by the following schematic diagram:

FRONT FIELD	INFLECTED VERB	INNER FIELD	VERBAL COMPLEMENT	END FIELD
Das Bier	**ist**	**wirklich**	**gut**	**hier in München.**

Not all German assertions use this pattern in its entirety, but *no German assertion will disregard it.* The following patterns are possible:

FRONT FIELD	INFLECTED VERB	INNER FIELD	VERBAL COMPLEMENT	END FIELD

FRONT FIELD AND INFLECTED VERBS ONLY

Ich	**lese.**	
Es	**regnet.**	

FRONT FIELD, INFLECTED VERB, AND INNER FIELD

Da	**kommt**	**Frau Meyer.**
Das	**weiß**	**ich.**

FRONT FIELD, INFLECTED VERB, INNER FIELD, VERBAL COMPLEMENT

Heute	**ist**	**das Wetter**	**schlecht.**
Ursula	**wird**	**jetzt**	**Lehrerin.**
Meine Frau	**ist**	**heute leider**	**in Köln.**
Heute	**gehen**	**wir um 8**	**nach Hause.**
Der Zug	**fährt**	**um 6 Uhr**	**ab.**
Heute	**geht**	**er bestimmt**	**schwimmen.**

FRONT FIELD, INFLECTED VERB, INNER FIELD, VERBAL COMPLEMENT, END FIELD

Das Bier	**ist**	**wirklich**	**gut**	**hier in München.**
Es	**ist**	**wirklich**	**kalt**	**heute abend.**

In German sentences which do not use the end field (*and most of them don't*), the verbal complement is the last element of the sentence.

Das Bier ist wirklich gut hier in München.

A complement normally cannot be moved to the front field. Only inner field elements can appear in the front field as topics. Now you will understand the reason for the rule of thumb in Anal. 5, p. 12. Only those elements that can precede an *English* inflected verb can normally also precede a *German* inflected verb. None of the italicized complements in the English sentences at the beginning of Anal. 28, p. 71, can be moved in front of the subject.

The inner field need not be filled. Inner field elements, except for the subject, can be deleted without destroying the basic meaning of the sentence. If the only inner field element is the subject, it can be moved to the front field, thereby creating an empty inner field.

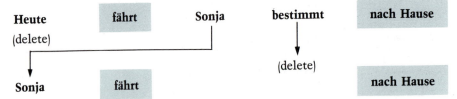

If there is an end field, it is frequently used for specification or amplification. These amplifications are always nonobligatory elements, especially time phrases; most of them are prepositional phrases.

Es ist *kalt* heute.   It's *cold* today.
Wir gehen doch nicht ins *Kino* bei   We're not going to the *movies* in this
  dem Regen.   rain.

German questions have the same basic structure as assertions. In word questions, the front field is *always* occupied by an interrogative, and personal pronoun subjects are always placed at the beginning of the inner field.

Warum **bleiben** **Sie heute abend** **zu Hause?**

In yes-or-no questions, the front field is empty, and again pronoun subjects are placed immediately after the inflected verb.

Bleiben   **Sie heute abend**   **zu Hause?**

Imperatives have the same structure as yes-or-no questions.

Bleiben   **Sie heute abend**   **zu Hause.**

The presence or absence of the question mark in the two sentences above is the difference between *Are you going to stay home tonight?* and *Stay home tonight.* In the spoken language, intonation distinguishes between these two sentences (see Anal. 11, p. 20).

30/Predicate Adjectives and Adverbs

In the English sentences

> He lived happily ever after.
> He was happy as long as he lived.

the word *happily* is an adverb and characterizes the verbal act, the mode of living. The word *happy* is a predicate adjective. It characterizes the subject, not the verbal act.

German normally makes no distinction in form between a predicate adjective and an adverb:

PREDICATE ADJECTIVE	**Der Kaffee ist gut.**	The coffee is good.
ADVERB	**Elke fährt gut.**	Elke drives well.

If the verb is a form of **sein, bleiben,** or **werden,** the complement is always a predicate adjective, never an adverb.

> **Heute ist das Wetter schlecht.**
> **Morgen wird das Wetter gut.**
> **Hoffentlich bleibt das Wetter gut.**

For the time being, do not use adjectives attributively—that is, in front of the noun to which they belong. Attributive adjectives require a special set of endings, which will be introduced later.

31/Sentence Adverbs

In most cases, adverbs modify

a verb:	He lived *happily* ever after.
an adjective:	She is *unusually* intelligent.
another adverb:	It happened *very* suddenly.

However, certain adverbs, called *sentence adverbs*, express the attitude of the speaker toward the content of the whole sentence.

Thus, *unfortunately* and *naturally* are used as sentence adverbs in

> Unfortunately, he died.
> (It is, in my opinion, unfortunate that he died.)

> Naturally, she was not at home.
> (As I had expected, she was not at home.)

Examples of German sentence adverbs are **bestimmt, hoffentlich, leider, natürlich,** and **übrigens.** In both English and German, these sentence adverbs count as *independent syntactical units* as far as word order is concerned. If a sentence adverb stands in the front field, nothing else can occupy the front field. Sentence adverbs are not set off by a comma.

Leider wohnt Tante Amalie wieder hier.
Tante Amalie wohnt leider wieder hier.

Particles like **denn** and **doch** are used as sentence adverbs. However, they can appear only in the inner field.

Sentence adverbs in the inner field: a) follow unstressed pronouns; b) precede stressed elements, that is, elements with news value; and c) precede the second prong, even if the second prong is unstressed.

Siehst	du	sie	**denn?**	
	Ist	sie	**denn**	zu *Hause?*
Ist deine Schwester			**denn**	zu *Hause?*
		Ist	**denn**	deine *Schwes*ter zu Hause?

Wir gehen doch *essen*.
Wir *ge*hen doch essen.

32/Coordinating Conjunctions

Coordinating conjunctions are used to connect two or more coordinate elements. The most commonly used coordinating conjunctions are:

aber	but, however	**oder**	or
denn	because, for	**und**	and

Coordinating conjunctions precede the front field and are not counted as a syntactical unit.

Monika studiert Psychologie.		Christa studiert Französisch.
Monika studiert Psychologie,	**und**	Christa studiert Französisch.
Monika studiert Psychologie,	**aber**	Christa studiert Französisch.

Of these four conjunctions, only **aber** does not have to precede the front field. It can stand between the front field and the inflected verb or in the inner field.

Erika studiert Englisch, Christa `aber` **studiert Französisch.**

Christa studiert `aber` **Französisch.**

When **aber** appears in the inner field, it can also be a particle meaning something like *ever* or *really*.

Das war aber heiß heute.   Was it ever hot today.
It was really hot today.

The conjunction **denn** never introduces the answer to a **warum**-question.

Remember that **denn** in the inner field is always a particle (see Anal. 12, p. 21, and Anal. 31, p. 77).

PRACTICE ONE

A. In the following sentences, identify the verbal complement. Then restate each sentence by moving another element into the front field. Remember that only one element can occupy the front field and that the verbal complement cannot be moved into the front field.

Heute ist es übrigens sehr kalt.   VERBAL COMPLEMENT: **sehr kalt**
Übrigens ist es heute sehr kalt.

1. Onkel Otto ist übrigens sehr alt. *Übrigens ist ...*
2. Dieser Wein ist leider sauer. *Leider ist ...*
3. Unser Sohn wird natürlich Lehrer. *Natürlich wird ...*
4. Wir essen heute Wiener Schnitzel. *Heute essen ...*
5. Unsere Tochter fährt nächsten Sommer nach Amerika.
6. Tante Amalie wohnt jetzt in Wuppertal.
7. Um ein Uhr gehen wir ins Museum.
8. Meine Eltern bleiben leider heute abend zu Hause.
9. Bernd und Bianca gehen heute abend aus.
10. Heute nachmittag gehen wir hoffentlich schwimmen. *hopefully*
11. Übrigens hat mein Bruder heute Geburtstag.
12. Der Zug nach Köln fährt um 3 Uhr 5 ab.
13. Thomas lernt dieses Wochenende fahren.
14. Es ist leider sehr kalt heute abend.
15. Meine Schwester kommt morgen früh an. *early*

B. For all the sentences in Exercise A, list the complete predicate in lexical (infinitive) form, with the verbal complement preceding the infinitive. Which are written as one word?

1. sehr alt sein
2. sauer sein
3. Lehrer werden
   etc.

PATTERNS TWO

4/Negation with *nicht*

		nicht	SECOND PRONG
Regnet es?	Nein, es regnet	nicht.	
Ist der Roman interessant?	Nein, er ist	nicht	interessant.
Ist die Milch sauer?	Nein, sie ist	nicht	sauer.
Bleibt das Wetter gut?	Nein, es bleibt bestimmt	nicht	gut.
Ist Herr Meyer heute in München?	Nein, er ist heute	nicht	in München.
Bleibst du heute zu Hause?	Nein, ich bleibe heute	nicht	zu Hause.
Wohnen Sie in Nürnberg?	Nein, ich wohne	nicht	in Nürnberg.
Fliegen Sie morgen nach München?	Nein, wir fliegen morgen	nicht	nach München.
Geht ihr heute abend ins Kino?	Nein, wir gehen heute abend	nicht	ins Kino.
Gehst du heute abend aus?	Nein, ich gehe heute abend	nicht	aus.
Gehen Sie jetzt einkaufen?	Nein, wir gehen jetzt	nicht	einkaufen.

5/Negation of Predicate Nouns

Ist das Ulrike?	Nein, das ist	nicht	Ulrike.
Ist das deine Freundin Erika?	Nein, das ist	nicht	meine Freundin Erika.
Ist das unser Bus?	Nein, das ist	nicht	unser Bus.
Heißt das Kind Fritz?	Nein, es heißt	nicht	Fritz.
Ist das ein Supermarkt?	Nein, das ist		kein Supermarkt.
Ist das eine Apotheke?	Nein, das ist		keine Apotheke.
Ist das Wein?	Nein, das ist		kein Wein.
Sind das Brötchen?	Nein, das sind		keine Brötchen.
Ist er Student?	Nein, er ist	nicht	Student.
	Nein, er ist		kein Student.
Ist Herr Strobl Österreicher?	Nein, er ist	nicht	Österreicher.
	Nein, er ist		kein Österreicher.

6/Negation of Objects

Siehst du den Jungen da drüben?	Nein, ich sehe den Jungen	nicht.	
	Nein, ich sehe ihn	nicht.	
	Nein, ich sehe keinen Jungen.		
Brauchst du deinen Wagen?	Nein, ich brauche meinen Wagen	nicht.	
	Nein, ich brauche ihn	nicht.	

Die Eule spricht:

Kein Feuer - Rauchen - offenes Licht...!

Württ. Gemeinde-Versicherungsverein a.G. Stuttgart

The owl says: No fire, no smoking, no open light . . . !

	nicht	SECOND PRONG
Kennen Sie meine Eltern?	Nein, ich kenne Ihre Eltern	nicht.	
	Nein, ich kenne sie	nicht.	
Kennst du Frau Schmidt?	Nein, ich kenne Frau Schmidt	nicht.	
	Nein, ich kenne sie	nicht.	
Trinkst du Milch?	Nein, ich trinke keine Milch.		
Trinken Sie Kaffee, Frau Meyer?	Nein, ich trinke keinen Kaffee.		
Ißt er Käse?	Nein, er ißt keinen Käse.		
Ißt sie Brötchen?	Nein, sie ißt keine Brötchen.		
Haben Sie einen Sohn?	Nein, wir haben keinen Sohn.		
Hat er eine Tochter?	Nein, er hat keine Tochter.		
Hat sie ein Kind?	Nein, sie hat kein Kind.		
Haben sie Kinder?	Nein, sie haben keine Kinder.		
Habt ihr ein Auto?	Nein, wir haben kein Auto.		
Fährt sie sein Auto?	Nein, sie fährt sein Auto	nicht.	
Fährt sie Auto?	Nein, sie fährt	nicht	Auto.

7/Negation of *schon* and *noch*

Ist er schon hier?
    Is he here already?
Ist er noch hier?
    Is he still here?

Nein, er ist noch nicht hier.
    No, he isn't here yet.
Nein, er ist nicht mehr hier.
    No, he isn't here anymore.

Ist es schon vier Uhr?
—Ja, es ist vier Uhr elf.

Ist er *im*mer noch hier?
   Is he *still* here?
Ist er noch Student?
   Is he still a student?
Habt ihr schon Hunger?
   Are you hungry already?
Habt ihr noch Hunger?
   Are you still hungry?
Trinkst du noch ein Bier?
   Would you like another beer?

Nein, er ist kein Student mehr.
   No, he isn't a student anymore.
Nein, wir haben noch keinen Hunger.
   No, we're not hungry yet.
Nein, wir haben keinen Hunger mehr.
   No, we're not hungry any more.
Nein danke, ich trinke jetzt kein Bier mehr.
   No thanks, I won't drink any more beer now.

8/mehr, mehr als, nicht mehr als

In the following sentences **mehr** refers to quantity and not to time, as in
[6] above.

Die Firma Braun braucht mehr Lehrlinge.
Auto-Braun hat mehr Mechaniker als Auto-
   Müller.
Sie arbeitet mehr als ich.
Sie weiß mehr, als sie sagt.
Sie hat mehr Geld, als sie braucht.
Ich habe nur zehn Mark; ich habe leider
   nicht mehr.
Das kostet nicht mehr als fünfzig Schilling.
Ich habe nicht mehr Geld als du.

The Braun firm needs more apprentices.
The Braun auto firm has more mechanics
   than Auto-Müller.
She works more than I do.
She knows more than she says.
She has more money than she needs.
I only have ten marks; unfortunately, I
   don't have any more.
That doesn't cost more than fifty schillings.
I don't have more money than you (have).

9/nicht, nicht wahr

Wohnen Sie in *Köln?*
Sie wohnen doch in *Köln,* nicht *wahr?*
Sie wohnen doch in *Köln, nicht?*

Do you live in Cologne?
You live in Cologne, don't you?
You live in Cologne, don't you?

10/*doch*

In the following sentences, **doch** is used as an unstressed or stressed particle.

Ist Ulrike heute nicht hier? —Nein, Ulrike ist doch heute in *Bremen*.

Isn't Ulrike here today? —No, Ulrike is in Bremen today, remember?

Du bist doch Erika *Müller*, nicht wahr?

You're Erika Müller, aren't you?

Hans sagt, er hat keinen Hunger, aber jetzt ißt er *doch*.

Hans says he isn't hungry, but now he's eating after all.

Das Wetter ist heute schlecht, aber wir gehen *doch* schwimmen.

The weather is bad today, but we're going swimming after all.

In the following sentences **doch** is used as an answer to a negative question or statement.

Trinken Sie *Tee*, Frau Schmidt?
Trinken Sie *keinen* Tee?

Nein, ich *trinke* keinen Tee.
Doch, natürlich trinke ich Tee.

Gehst du heute abend ins *Kino*?
Gehst du heute abend *nicht* ins Kino?

Ja, mit *Hans*.
Doch, aber nicht wieder mit *Hans*.

Es *regnet* noch.
Es *regnet* nicht mehr.

Nein, es regnet *nicht* mehr.
Doch, es *regnet* noch.

ANALYSIS TWO

33/Negation

German has two ways of negating, parallel to the following two English sentences:

(a) He is not at home tonight.
(b) He has no time today.

In sentence (a) *not* is placed behind the inflected verb; this *not* corresponds to German **nicht**:

(a) **Er ist heute abend nicht zu Hause.**

Sentence (b) is negated by placing *no* in front of the noun; this *no* corresponds to a form of German **kein**:

(b) **Er hat heute keine Zeit.**

German has no equivalent of the English pattern *He doesn't have any time today.*

German **nichts** means *nothing* or *not anything*; it is the antonym (opposite) of **etwas,** *something.*

Brauchst du etwas? —Nein, ich brauche nichts.

34/**Negation with** *nicht*

Negation with **nicht** is far more important than with **kein**.

> If there is no verbal complement, **nicht** stands at the end of the sentence. However, **nicht** *must precede* most verbal complements.

The inflected verb and the verbal complement at the end of the sentence embrace the inner field like parentheses or prongs. Since it is inconvenient to speak of "the first part of the predicate" and "the second part of the predicate," we call these two parts the *first prong* and the *second prong*. This two-prong structure is one of the most characteristic patterns of German.

Brigitte	geht	heute abend	ins Kino.
Brigitte	is going	to the movies	tonight.

1. **nicht** stands at the end of the sentence.

FRONT FIELD	1ST PRONG	INNER FIELD	nicht	2ND PRONG
Erika	arbeitet	heute	nicht.	
Hoffentlich	regnet	es morgen	nicht.	

2. **nicht** must always precede predicate adjectives.

Leider	ist	das Wetter heute	nicht	gut.
	Ist	sie wirklich	nicht	glücklich?

3. **nicht** must always precede **wo**-complements and **wohin**-complements.

Morgen abend	bleibe	ich natürlich	nicht	zu Hause.
Nächstes Jahr	fahren	wir	nicht	nach Deutschland.
Wir	gehen	sonntags	nicht	ins Kino.

4. **nicht** must always precede prefixed complements.

Heute abend	gehen	wir	nicht	aus.
Bianca	kommt	morgen früh	nicht	an.

5. **nicht** must always precede infinitive complements.

Warum	**lernst**	du denn	**nicht**	fahren?
Wir	**gehen**	heute nachmittag	**nicht**	schwimmen.

nicht, auch, beide, alle

Normally, **auch, beide,** and **alle** occupy the same position in the sentence as **nicht**.

If one of these words occurs together with **nicht** or **kein**, it precedes **nicht** or **kein**.

> **Wir sind heute abend beide nicht zu Hause.**
> **Die Studenten haben alle kein Geld.**

NOTE: When **auch** occurs in negated statements, it usually means *either*.

> **Erika ist auch nicht hier.**   Erika isn't here either.
> **Fritz hat auch kein Geld.**   Fritz doesn't have any money either.

35/Negation of Predicate Nouns

All predicate nouns are second-prong elements, but they are negated in two different ways.

1. Predicate nouns are negated by **nicht** if they are names or if they are preceded by a **der**-word or possessive adjective. Again, **nicht** must precede.

> **Das ist nicht Ilse.**
> **Er heißt nicht Müller.**
> **Das ist hoffentlich nicht der Fünf-Uhr-Zug.**
> **Silvia ist nicht seine Schwester.**

2. Predicate nouns are negated by a form of **kein** if they are preceded by the indefinite article **ein** or if they stand alone, that is, without a preceding article or possessive adjective.

> **Das ist ein Volkswagen.**   **Das ist kein Volkswagen.**
> **Das ist Wein.**   **Das ist kein Wein.**
> **Das ist Milch.**   **Das ist keine Milch.**
> **Das sind Brötchen.**[4]   **Das sind keine Brötchen.**

The word **kein** is an **ein**-word, that is, it has the same endings as the indefinite article **ein** (see Anal. 21, p. 48).

---

[4]Note that the verb form in sentences of this type is determined by the predicate noun; it is **sind** even though the subject **das** is singular.

Predicate nouns expressing professional status or group member-ship (see Anal. 25, p. 55) can be negated by either **kein** or **nicht**.

Ich bin Studentin.   **Ich bin keine Studentin.**
                                Ich bin nicht Studentin.

36/Negation of Objects

Objects are the one category of verbal complements that are not second-prong elements. *They appear in the inner field where their position is determined by news value* (see Anal. 54, p. 142). Like predicate nouns, they can be negated with either **nicht** or **kein**.

1. Objects are negated with **nicht** if they are a) pronouns, b) names, or c) nouns preceded by a **der**-word or a possessive adjective.

> Unlike second-prong elements, these objects are *followed, rather than preceded*, by **nicht**.

The **nicht** negating an object stands at the end of the inner field and does not necessarily follow the object immediately.

Ich kenne sie nicht.
Ich kenne die Dame nicht.
Wir brauchen unseren Wagen heute nicht.

2. Objects are negated by a form of **kein** if they are preceded by the indefinite article **ein**[5] or if they stand alone, that is, without a pre-ceding article or possessive adjective.

Meyers haben einen Sohn.   **Meyers haben keinen Sohn.**
Meyers haben Geld.   **Meyers haben kein Geld.**
Meyers haben Kinder.   **Meyers haben keine Kinder.**

37/Second-Prong Objects

There are certain combinations of verb plus accusative noun where the noun cannot be considered an object in the normal sense. Com-pare the following two English sentences:

He read her book.
He read her mind.

---

[5]The combination **nicht ein** occurs with the meaning *not one* or *not a single*; **ein** is then stressed.

Er hat nicht *einen* Freund hier.   He doesn't have a *single* friend here.

Only in the first sentence does the act of reading really occur. In the second, the "object," *the mind*, is so closely bound to the verb that the two together have become a unique phrase with a meaning of its own: he knew what she was thinking.

German, too, has some of these combinations. For example,

> **Sie fährt das Auto nicht.**

means that she does not drive a specific car; whereas

> **Sie fährt nicht Auto.**

means that she doesn't know how to drive.

In the first sentence **das Auto** is a normal object and is therefore followed by **nicht**. In the second sentence, **Auto** is a second-prong object and must be preceded by **nicht**.

Second-prong objects cannot be replaced by pronouns. The answer to **Fährt er Auto?** can only be either **Ja, er fährt Auto** or **Nein, er fährt nicht Auto**. It is best to learn verbs with second-prong objects as vocabulary items.

38/Negation of *schon* and *noch*

Consider the following pairs of English sentences:

> Is it raining already? —No, it isn't raining yet.
> Is it still raining? —No, it isn't raining anymore.

English *already* is negated by *not yet*, and *still* is negated by *not anymore*.

German expresses the same situations with the following pairs:

schon	noch nicht	**Regnet es schon? —Nein, es regnet noch nicht.**
	noch kein	**Hast du schon Hunger? —Nein, ich habe noch keinen Hunger.**
noch	nicht mehr	**Regnet es noch? —Nein, es regnet nicht mehr.**
	kein (*noun*) mehr	**Hast du noch Hunger? —Nein, ich habe keinen Hunger mehr.**

Note that when **noch** plus noun is negated, the noun is inserted between **kein** and **mehr**.

Keep in mind that **noch** and **noch nicht** are not opposites.

NOTE:

1. If **schon** is used in questions, it usually means *yet*.

Ist die Zeitung schon hier?   Is the newspaper here yet?
Haben Sie schon Freunde hier?   Do you have any friends here yet?

2. **schon** meaning *already* often implies an element of surprise, that is, something is happening sooner than expected.

> **Ist er denn schon hier?**   Is he here already?

3. The same surprise effect can be achieved with **noch** by adding **immer**; something is taking longer than expected. If **immer** is used, **noch** cannot be stressed. English achieves the same effect by strongly stressing *still*.

> **Er ist *immer* noch hier.**   He is *still* here.

4. Frequently, **noch ein** means *another* (additional):

> **Ich trinke noch eine Tasse Kaffee.**   I'll have another cup of coffee.

5. While **mehr** and *more* in the sentences above have a *temporal* meaning, they can also have a *quantitative* meaning, which always involves a comparison, even if only implied; *more than* is expressed by **mehr als**. If negated, **mehr als** becomes **nicht mehr als.**

> **Er arbeitet mehr als ich.**   He works more than I do.
> **Er hat mehr Geld (als ich).**   He has more money (than I do).
> **Er hat nicht mehr Geld als ich.**   He doesn't have any more money than I do.

39/ *nicht wahr?* and *nicht?*

Nicht wahr? (an abbreviation of **ist das nicht wahr?** — *isn't that true?*) corresponds to English *isn't that so?, don't you?, haven't you?, aren't you?*, etc. This **nicht wahr?** is frequently shortened to **nicht?**. Since **nicht?** or **nicht wahr?** ask for confirmation, the preceding sentence usually contains **doch** (see Anal. 40, p. 88).

> **Sie *kommen* doch heute abend, nicht**   You are coming tonight, aren't you?
> **wahr?**
> **Sie *kommen* doch heute abend, *nicht*?**

Frequently **oder?** is used in the same way as **nicht wahr?** or **nicht?**, especially after a negative statement.

> **Du fährst morgen *nicht* nach Frankfurt,**   You're not going to Frankfurt tomorrow,
> **oder?**   are you?

40/ *doch*

The word **doch** may be unstressed or stressed.

1. The unstressed particle **doch** is a sentence adverb. In assertions, it adds the note "Don't you know that . . .," "Don't forget that . . .," "Remember?" or "but."

Morgen fliegt sie doch nach *München*!   But she's flying to *Munich* tomorrow!

When assertions become questions, the unstressed **doch** expresses the speaker's hope that the opposite is not true.

**Sie *fliegen* doch morgen nach München,   You're *flying* to Munich tomorrow,
nicht wahr?**   aren't you?

Do not use the unstressed **doch** in regular questions.

In imperatives **doch** softens the request and frequently corresponds to English "Why don't you . . . ."

Gehen Sie doch heute abend ins Kino!   Why don't you go to the movies
                                                  tonight?

2. The stressed **doch** stands between inner field and second prong. It corresponds to English *after all* and expresses that the fact reported is contrary to expectations. This stressed **doch** is frequently preceded by **also**, which adds the flavor of *so* when used at the beginning of English sentences.

Es regnet also *doch*!   So it's raining *after all*!
                                          (I had hoped it wouldn't.)

Er fährt morgen *doch* nach München! He is going to Munich tomorrow *after all*!
                                          (He first said he wouldn't.)

Bleibst du *doch* hier?   Are you staying here *after all*?
                                          (I thought you were leaving.)

3. The stressed **doch** is used instead of **ja** if a negative question is answered in the affirmative.

Fährst du nicht nach Köln?   *Doch*, **natürlich fahre ich nach Köln.**
Fährst du nicht nach Köln?   *Doch*, **aber nicht *heute*.**

Doch is also used to contradict a negative statement with an affirmative statement. (Note that in the following examples all three types of **doch** are used.)

Es *regnet* doch nicht mehr.   *Doch*, **es regnet *doch* noch.**
  But it isn't raining anymore.   Oh, yes, it *is* still raining.

PRACTICE TWO

C. Negate the following sentences by using **nicht**.

1. Er arbeitet.
2. Das ist Ilse.
3. Siehst du sie heute abend?
4. Kennen Sie meine Schwester?
5. Er heißt Müller.

6. Sie wohnen in Düsseldorf.
7. Das Wetter ist gut.
8. Sie geht nach Hause.
9. Kennen Sie den Herrn?
10. Wir gehen heute abend aus.

D. Negate the following sentences by using **kein**. Do not stress **kein**.

1. Das ist Wasser.
2. Das ist ein Volkswagen.
3. Haben Sie einen Wagen?
4. Sie hat eine Tochter.

5. Brauchst du Geld?
6. Trinken Sie Kaffee, Frau Meyer?
7. Haben Meyers Kinder?
8. Sind das Weingläser?

E. Give appropriate answers to the following questions, using **noch, schon, noch nicht,** and **nicht mehr** as needed.

1. Gehst du schon schlafen?

Ja, ich _____.
Nein, ich _____.

2. Ist er noch nicht hier?

Doch, er _____.
Nein, er _____.

3. Ist er noch zu Hause?

Ja, _____.
Nein, _____.

4. Wie alt ist er denn?

Er ist _____ jung.

5. Regnet es noch?

Nein, _____.

6. Geht ihr schon essen?

Nein, _____.
Ja, _____.

7. Trinken Sie keinen Kaffee mehr?

Doch, _____.

8. Wohnt eure Tante Amalie noch in München?

Ja, _____.
Nein, _____.

F. Insert **nicht, auch, beide,** or **alle** into the following sentences as appropriate.

1. Meyer arbeitet.
2. Wir haben keine Zeit.
3. Trinkt ihr Bier?
4. Karen und Antonia gehen heute abend ins Kino.

CONVERSATIONS

I

When you arrive in Frankfurt or in Berlin or in Vienna, you will have to develop strategies for telling people that you are a foreigner and that your German is not perfect yet. When you ask a German for directions, you are apt to get a flood of words of which you can pick out only a few. The following conversation may provide some hints on how to deal with such a situation.

JOHN RAY:	Bitte, wie komme ich zum Hauptbahnhof?	Excuse me, how do I get to the main (railroad) station?
EINE FRAU:	Da gehen Sie gleich hier rechts um die Ecke, dann drei Straßen geradeaus, dann links immer die Theodor-Heuss-Allee runter, und dann sind Sie gleich da.	Go around the corner right here, then straight ahead three blocks, then turn left down Theodor-Heuss-Allee, then you'll be right there.
JOHN RAY:	Bitte, sprechen Sie etwas langsamer. Ich kann Sie nicht verstehen; ich bin Ausländer.[6]	Please speak a little more slowly. I can't understand you; I'm a foreigner.
FRAU:	Sind Sie Engländer?	You're an Englishman?
JOHN RAY:	Nein, Amerikaner. Ich bin erst eine Woche in Deutschland.	No, I'm an American. I've only been in Germany for a week.

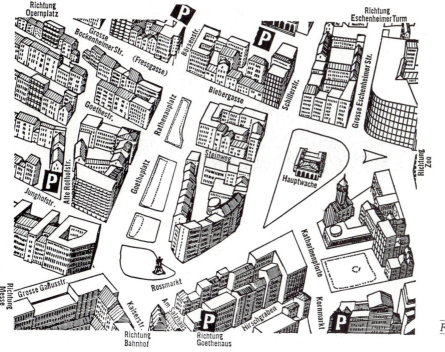

Frankfurt am Main

---

[6]Note that the words **Ausländer, Engländer, Amerikaner** are used here without the indefinite article (see Anal. 25, p. 55).

FRAU:	Also gut. Hier rechts, dann drei Straßen weiter, dann kommt die Theodor-Heuss-Allee. Gehen Sie links zum Bahnhof.	OK. (Turn) right here, then (go) three blocks, then comes Theodor-Heuss-Allee. You turn left to the station.
JOHN RAY:	Jetzt verstehe ich; jetzt sprechen Sie nicht so schnell. Vielen Dank.	Now I understand; now you're not speaking so quickly. Thank you.
FRAU:	OK. Wiedersehen.	OK. Good-bye.
JOHN RAY:	Auf Wiedersehen.	Good-bye.

II

Now let your teacher act as your "native informant" and ask him or her the questions that follow. Don't forget to be polite and say **Guten Tag** and **Entschuldigung**. Don't be surprised if at first your teacher uses all kinds of German you don't understand. Use whatever German you have learned to slow her or him down until you can understand the message. Remember to use **Sie** with your teacher.

Bitte, wo ist hier eine Bäckerei?	bakery
eine Metzgerei?	butcher's (shop)
ein Supermarkt?	supermarket
eine Drogerie?	drugstore
eine Apotheke?	pharmacy
eine Bank?	bank
ein Kaufhaus?	department store
ein Lebensmittelgeschäft?	grocery store

Sagen Sie, gibt es hier keine Apotheke? (*Tell me, is there no pharmacy here?*)
      kein Kaufhaus?
      keinen Supermarkt?
      etc.

Bitte, wie komme ich zum Bahnhof?
      zum Autobus?
      zum Flughafen?
      zur Bank?
      in die Bettinastraße?

Da gehen Sie hier rechts um die Ecke.
      zwei Straßen weiter und dann links.
Dort auf der anderen Seite. (*Over there on the other side.*)
Hier immer geradeaus (*always straight ahead*).
Das weiß ich nicht. Ich bin hier auch fremd (*I'm a stranger here, myself*).

Fragen an Sie persönlich

Geben Sie positive oder negative Antworten.

1. Haben Sie ein Fahrrad?
        ein Motorrad?
        einen Wagen?
        ein Segelboot? (**das Boot** *boat*, **das Segelboot** *sailboat*)
        ein Flugzeug? (**das Flugzeug** *airplane*)

2. Was machen Sie heute abend?
    Gehen Sie ins Kino?
        ins Theater?
        ins Konzert?
        in den Zirkus?
        ins Museum?
    Sind Sie heute abend zu Hause?
    Arbeiten[7] Sie heute abend?

3. Sind Sie aus (*Do you come from*) Neu-England?
                Idaho?
                Südamerika?
                Walla-Walla, Washington?

4. Gibt es in Ihrer Stadt ein Theater?
              ein Konzerthaus?
              einen Zirkus?
              ein Museum?
              Kinos?

5. Sind Sie schon zwanzig (20) Jahre alt?

6. Fahren Sie nächsten Sommer nach Europa?
                  nach Afrika?
                  nach Australien?
                  nach Asien?

7. Haben Sie (schon) einen Freund hier in der Klasse?
                    eine Freundin
    Haben Sie schon Freunde (Freundinnen) im College?
                          an der Universität?

8. Haben Sie einen Bruder?
        Brüder?
        eine Schwester?
        Schwestern?
        Geschwister?

---

[7]**arbeiten** is used here in the sense of *to study*: "Are you going to study tonight?"

Sind Ihre Brüder schon auf dem College?
Schwestern nicht mehr auf dem College?
auf der High School?
schon verheiratet (*married*)?
Haben sie schon Kinder?

9. Lesen Sie Romane?
Schreiben Sie viele Briefe (*many letters*)?
Trinken Sie Milch?
Kaffee?
Tee?
Orangensaft (*orange juice*)?
Trinken Sie keinen Wein?
kein Bier?
Ist das Bier gut hier?

10. Scheint heute die Sonne nicht?
Ist das Wetter nicht gut?
Regnet es heute?
Ist das Wetter schlecht?
Gehen Sie heute schwimmen?
schilaufen (*to ski*)?

11. Haben Sie Geld?
Brauchen Sie Geld?

Now ask the same questions of other members of your class and of your teacher. Don't forget to address your fellow students with **du** and your teacher with **Sie.**

READING

Instead of a translation, we have provided marginal glosses for this text; the glossed word or group of words, followed by the symbol °, is translated as it occurs in the text, not necessarily in basic form or with basic meaning. Read the German text aloud as many times as you can. Through this process you will gradually absorb words and structures in context, even if you don't actively control them yet.

Schweinefleisch

Ein Amerikaner, John Ray aus Detroit, zwanzig Jahre alt, College-student und neu in Deutschland, steht in einer Metzgerei° in Ulm (oder Stuttgart oder Sindelfingen) und wartet. Es ist zehn Uhr mor-   butcher shop

gens, und alle deutschen Hausfrauen kaufen ein. Vor ihm stehen
zehn Frauen und sprechen Dialekt. Er versteht kein Wort, denn er ⁵
ist ja noch nicht lange in Deutschland. Aber er liest: „Heute be-
sonders° billig° — Schweinefleisch, 500 g DM 5,80.“⁸   especially   cheap

Schweinefleisch, das versteht er nicht. Er nimmt sein Taschenwör-   pocket dictionary
terbuch° und sucht°: **das Schwein,-e**, *swine*, und **das Fleisch**, *flesh*.   searches
„Brrr“, denkt er, „und die Deutschen essen das?“   10

(Die Deutschen sagen aber nicht „brrr“, wenn° sie Schweinefleisch   when   **es gibt** there is
essen, denn für *pork* gibt es° im Deutschen kein anderes° Wort.)   other, different

Dann findet er, daß **Schwein** nicht nur *swine*, sondern° auch *pig*   but
und *pork* ist, und **Fleisch** ist auch *meat*. „Aha“, denkt er, „also *pork*
meat, oder einfach° *pork*.“ Aber er wartet immer noch, und vor ihm   15   simply
stehen noch immer fünf Hausfrauen und sprechen Schwäbisch°.   Swabian

„Ja, bitte°, der Herr“, sagt plötzlich° die Metzgersfrau°, „auch ein   (may I help you) please
Pfund° Schweinefleisch? Ganz frisch° — und sehr billig heute, nur   suddenly   butcher's wife
fünf Mark achtzig das Pfund. Oder lieber° ein Roastbeef oder ein   pound   very fresh
Steak?“ (Sie sagt „Rostbehf“ und „Schtehk“.)   20   rather

„Nein, danke“, sagt er, „kein Schweinefleisch, aber geben Sie mir
bitte 100 g Leberwurst°.“   liver sausage

„Gern°“, sagt die Metzgersfrau. — „So, das macht eine Mark achtzig.“   gladly

„Bitte“, sagt John jetzt, „sagen Sie, wo ist hier eine Bäckerei? Ich
brauche Brötchen. Ich habe heute noch nichts gegessen.“   25

„Brötchen kriegen Sie hier bei uns°, ganz frisch, von heute morgen.“   rolls you get right here
Jetzt versteht er sogar° ihren schwäbischen Dialekt.   from us   even

---

⁸Read as: **fünfhundert Gramm, fünf Mark achtzig** — 500 grams, five marks eighty.

Er bezahlt° und geht. Zehn Minuten später° sitzt er im Park auf einer   pays   later
Bank (gegenüber° ist ein Supermarkt), ißt seine Brötchen und seine   opposite
Wurst und trinkt eine Flasche Bier. Beim Essen° studiert er sein 30   while eating
Wörterbuch. Er sagt jetzt nicht mehr „brrr" (die Wurst ist sehr gut),
er sagt jetzt, „Aha: Ochsenfleisch ist nicht *ox flesh*, es ist *beef*, und
Kalbfleisch ist *veal*. Aha," denkt er wieder, „*pork, beef, veal*, diese
Wörter kommen aus dem Französischen, und *swine, ox* und *calf*
sind germanisch°."   35   Germanic

Vom Denken und vom Essen und Trinken wird er müde. Bald liegt
er auf der Bank, eine Zeitung über dem Gesicht°, und schläft ein°.   over his face   falls asleep
Dann träumt° er von dicken°, fetten, rosigen Schweinen auf einer   dreams   thick, fat
grünen Wiese°.   in a green meadow

The "Old" and the "New"

The pork story has perhaps given the impression that Germany is
a place with quaint and odd customs. But while it is true that this
scene is "typically German," it is also true that, since the end of
World War II, Germany has become a thoroughly modern, highly
industrialized, and very affluent country. Some West Germans will
tell you that their country has been "Americanized" beyond recognition, and many East Germans, officially referred to as "citizens of the
DDR," will say that their part of the country has been "Sovietized."
Advanced technology, tremendous industrial output, and gleaming
new high-rise buildings are part of the scene in both countries.

*Kölner Dom und
Museum Ludwig*

There is no doubt that all of Central Europe went through a quarter century of unprecedented economic growth, and it is understandable that the older generation regrets the passing of the good old ways, often forgetting that the Nazi period stands between the hectic present and those halcyon days they remember. To the uninitiated, however, to American students on their first trip to Europe, for example, the "old" Germany is still so apparent that they stumble across it with every step they take. They will notice the so-called Americanization, but it will also be obvious to them that West Germany, or Switzerland, or Austria, are not mirror images of the United States.

REVIEW EXERCISES

G. Express in German

1. He is intelligent, isn't he?
2. He lives in Vienna, doesn't he?
3. She has a house in Cologne, doesn't she?
4. You are a doctor, aren't you?
5. They have a daughter, don't they?
6. You're going to the movies, aren't you?

H. Insert first a stressed and then an unstressed **doch** into the following
sentences. Explain the difference in meaning.

1. Wir fahren nach München.
2. Meyer hat Geld.
3. Herr Lenz wohnt in Köln.
4. Sie ist zu Hause.

I. Insert the correct form of the possessive adjective.

Ich habe ein Buch; es ist mein Buch.

1. Der Mann heißt Müller; ich kenne _____ Sohn.
2. Rolf ist Erikas Sohn, und Else ist _____ Tochter.
3. Herr Graber, wo sind _____ Kinder?
4. Helmut und Wolfgang, wo sind _____ Bücher?
5. Wir wissen nicht, wo _____ Bücher sind.
6. Kennen Sie Herrn Müller?—Nein, aber ich kenne _____ Tochter.
7. Frau Schmidt, wo ist _____ Sohn?
8. Frau Schmidt, wo ist _____ Tochter?
9. Ja, das ist Herr Weber; aber ist das _____ Wagen?
10. Warum trinkt ihr _____ Kaffee nicht?

J. Give negative answers to the following questions.

1. Ist der Wein sauer? *Nein, er ist nicht sauer*
2. Habt ihr einen Wagen? *Nein, wir haben keinen Wagen.*
3. Haben wir noch Brötchen? *Nein, wir haben keine Br. mehr*
4. Regnet es schon? *Nein, es regnet noch nicht.*
5. Ist Ihre Tochter Ärztin? *Nein, sie ist keine Ärztin*
6. Arbeitet Herr Meyer noch in Hamburg? *N, er arb. nicht in Ham. mehr*
7. Fährt Angelika nächsten Sommer nach Italien? *N, sie fährt nä S. nicht nach It.*
8. Kennst du meinen Bruder? *Nein, ich kenne euren Bruder nicht*
9. Essen Sie Käse? *Nein, ich esse keinen Käse / oder Käse nicht*
10. Ist Bernd schon zu Hause? *Nein, Bernd ist noch nicht zu Hause*
11. Bist du immer noch unglücklich, Renate?
12. Habt ihr schon Hunger? *Wir haben noch nicht Hunger*
13. Kostet das mehr als zwanzig Mark? *Nein, es kostet nicht mehr als....*
14. Geht ihr heute nachmittag schwimmen? *Nein, wir gehen heute nachmittag nicht schwimmen*
15. Ist Heidi Schweizerin?

K. Form sentences from the elements given; supply articles where necessary. The double slash (//) indicates end of clause or sentence.

1. Ich / Sie / nicht verstehen // ich / Ausländerin / sein.
2. Bitte // wie / ich / zum Bahnhof / kommen?
3. Wir / in Deutschland / 12 Tage / bleiben.
4. Warum / du / denn / so schnell / laufen?
5. Heute abend / er / sein Wagen / nicht / nehmen.
6. Morgen / Sonne / hoffentlich / scheinen.
7. Ich / wissen // wer / er / sein // aber / ich / er / nicht / kennen.
8. Heute / wir / nicht / schwimmen gehen // denn / Wetter / schlecht / sein.

L. Express in German.

1. The train is leaving.
2. Is the beer good here?
3. I hope the milk isn't sour.
4. Do you have my novel?
5. She doesn't have a child.
6. She is not a doctor.
7. Is it raining yet?
8. Is it still raining?
9. He isn't here yet.
10. I'll drink another cup of coffee.
11. Bread doesn't cost much, and cheese doesn't cost much either.
12. We don't have any wine, and we don't have any beer either.

M. Supply the missing words.

1. Karin wohnt _____ Bonn, aber sie kommt _____ Hamburg.
2. Karin hat _____ Freund; ihr Freund _____ Richard.
3. Kennst _____ Richard? —Nein, ich kenne _____ nicht.
4. Wir sind heute abend _____ Hause. Wo _____ ihr heute abend?
5. Ich gehe jetzt _____ Hause.
6. Wann _____ der Zug ab? Um 6 _____ 5.
7. Er _____ Bier und _____ Brot und Käse.
8. Ich _____ nicht, wo sie wohnt.
9. Das ist Herr Meyer. Kennen Sie _____ Meyer?
10. Ja, ich kenne _____ und ich kenne auch _____ Sohn.

NOTE: Additional exercises can be found in the *Study Guide*.

VOCABULARY

Verbs

ab•fahren	to leave, depart	**finden**	to find
an•kommen	to arrive	**fliegen**	to fly
aus•gehen	to go out	**geben (du gibst,**	to give
denken	to think	**er gibt)**	
ein•kaufen	to shop	**es gibt**	there is, there are

kosten	to cost	**schreiben**	to write
liegen	to lie (flat); to be situated	**schwimmen**	to swim
		schwimmen gehen	to go swimming
sagen	to say; to tell	**sprechen (du sprichst, er spricht)**	to speak
schi•laufen	to ski		
schlafen (du schläfst, er schläft)	to sleep	**stehen**	to stand
		verheiratet sein	to be married
schlafen gehen	to go to bed	**warten**	to wait

Nouns

MASCULINE

der Bahnhof, ⸚e	train station	**der Markt, ⸚e**	market
der Hauptbahnhof, ⸚e	main train station	**der Supermarkt**	supermarket
		der Onkel, -	uncle
der Brief, -e	letter	**der Orangensaft**	orange juice
der Deutsche, -n	German (m.)	**der Park, -s**	park
die Deutsche, -n	German (f.)	**der Schilling, -e (öS)**	schilling (Austrian currency)
der Flughafen, ⸚	airport		

FEMININE

die Antwort, -en	answer	**die Mark** (no pl.)	mark (money)
die Apothe′ke, -n	pharmacy	**DM = die Deutsche Mark**	basic unit of German currency
die Bäckerei, -en	bakery		
die Bank, ⸚e	bench	**die Metzgerei, -n**	butcher shop
die Bank, -en	bank	**die Minu′te, -n**	minute
die Drogerie, -n	drugstore	**die Seite, -n**	page; side
die Ecke, -n	corner	**die Tante, -n**	aunt
um die Ecke	around the corner	**die Tasche, -n**	pocket
die Flasche, -n	bottle	**die Universität, -en**	university
die Hausfrau, -en	housewife	**die Zeit, -en**	time

NEUTER

das Boot, -e	boat	**das Kaufhaus, ⸚er**	department store
das Segelboot, -e	sailboat	**das Konzert′, -e**	concert
das Brötchen, -	(hard) roll	**das Muse′um, die Muse′en**	museum
das Fleisch (no pl.)	meat		
das Schweinefleisch	pork	**das Wasser, ⸚**	water
das Flugzeug, -e	airplane	**das Wort, ⸚er**	word
das Geld, -er	money	**das Wörterbuch, ⸚er**	dictionary

Adjectives

französisch	French	**müde**	tired
fremd	strange, foreign	**neu**	new
gleich	equal, same, like; right	**rechts**	to the right
		sauer	sour
gleich hier um die Ecke	right here around the corner	**schnell**	fast
		spät	late
intelligent	intelligent	**später**	later
lang	long	**viel**	much
lange	for a long time	**weit**	far
langsam	slow	**weiter**	further
links	to the left		

Prepositions

vor	in front of
vor ihm	in front of him

Adverbs

erst	only	**morgen früh**	tomorrow morning
geradeaus	straight, straight ahead	**nächstes Jahr**	next year
		noch	still
hoffentlich	I hope, hopefully	**noch ein**	another, one more
mehr	more	**noch nicht**	not yet
mehr als	more than	**noch kein**	no . . . yet
nicht mehr	no longer	**nur**	only
morgens	in the morning, mornings		

Other Words

denn (*conj.*)	because, for	**nichts**	nothing
etwas	something, somewhat	**oder**	or
etwas langsamer	somewhat slower	**vielen Dank**	thank you very much

Unit 4
Modal Auxiliaries—Contrast Intonation—Prepositions with Accusative

The Republic of Austria

The first Austrian Republic was created in the aftermath of World War I; it consisted of the German-speaking core of the old Austro-Hungarian Empire. The First Republic lasted until 1938, when it was absorbed into Hitler's Reich through what became known as the **Anschluß** (*joining, connecting*). After World War II, the Second Republic was born, but the country was occupied by the Allied Powers: there were British, French, Soviet, and U.S. zones of occupation. With the Austrian State Treaty of 1955, the occupation came to an end, and Austria regained its independence. The country is pledged to permanent neutrality.

Austria is a very small country, about the size of the state of Maine, with a population of about 7.5 million. One out of every five Austrians lives in the capital, Vienna (**Wien**). Vienna is also one of the nine federal states of Austria and the administrative center for the state of Lower Austria.

With a population of 1.5 million, Vienna is one of the world's great cities. It still reflects its former preeminence as the capital of a multinational empire; its museums and theaters, the Vienna State Opera, and the Vienna Philharmonic are world renowned. But Vienna is also a thoroughly modern city; it is the center of the Austrian economy and is also the site of the Vienna International Center (known as UNO-City), after New York City and Geneva the third location of the United Nations.

Republik Österreich

Oberösterreich   *Steiermark*

Kärnten   *Niederösterreich*

Wien   *Tirol*

Burgenland   *Salzburg*

Vorarlberg

BUNDESLAND (*state*)	POPULATION	HAUPTSTADT (*capital*)	POPULATION
Burgenland	269,000	Eisenstadt	10,000
Kärnten (Carinthia)	536,000	Klagenfurt	87,000
Niederösterreich (Lower Austria)	1,420,000	(Wien)	
Oberösterreich (Upper Austria)	1,269,000	Linz	200,000
Salzburg	442,000	Salzburg	139,000
Steiermark (Styria)	1,186,000	Graz	243,000
Tirol	586,000	Innsbruck	117,000
Vorarlberg	305,000	Bregenz	24,000
Wien (Vienna)	1,531,000		

PATTERNS ONE

Note that infinitives dependent on modals are second-prong elements and stand at the end of the sentence (see Anal. 43, pp. 113).

1/*können*

SONJA:	Du, Silke, wir machen heute abend eine Party. Kannst du kommen?	Silke, we're having a party tonight. Can you come?
SILKE:	Natürlich kann ich kommen. Kommt Jürgen auch?	Of course, I can come. Is Jürgen coming, too?
SONJA:	Nein, der Jürgen kann leider nicht kommen.	No, unfortunately, Jürgen can't come.
SILKE:	Und Thomas?	And Thomas?
SONJA:	Der[1] kann auch nicht.	He can't either.

Könnt ihr heute abend kommen?—Natürlich können wir heute abend kommen, und Hans und Therese können auch kommen.

Can you come tonight? Of course, we can come tonight, and Hans and Therese can come, too.

DR. SCHULTE:	Können Sie Deutsch, Frau Ray?	Do you know German, Ms. Ray?
JANE RAY:	Ja, ich kann Deutsch; ich kann auch Französisch.	Yes, I know German; I also know French.
DR. SCHULTE:	Und Ihr Bruder John, kann er auch Deutsch?	And your brother John, does he know German, too?
JANE RAY:	Nein, er kann leider kein Deutsch; aber ich weiß, er kann Spanisch und Italienisch.	No, he doesn't know German; but I know (that) he knows Spanish and Italian.

Jane Ray kann Deutsch sehr gut verstehen; sie kann Deutsch lesen und sprechen, aber sie kann es nicht sehr gut schreiben.

Jane Ray can understand German very well; she can read and speak German, but she can't write it very well.

2/*müssen*

HERR OTT:	Ich gehe jetzt schlafen. Ich muß morgen sehr früh aufstehen.	I have to go to bed now. I have to get up very early tomorrow.
FRAU OTT:	Wann mußt du denn aufstehen?	When do you have to get up?
HERR OTT:	Um halb sechs. Ich muß um acht in Augsburg sein, und bei dem Regen muß man langsam fahren.	At five-thirty. I have to be in Augsburg at eight, and you have to drive slowly in this rain.
FRAU OTT:	Aber gegen sechs mußt du zurück sein, denn morgen abend müssen wir ins Theater.	But you have to be back around six, because we have to go to the theater tomorrow night.

[1]In informal conversations, the pronouns **er** and **sie** are often replaced by **der** and **die**.

Ich muß leider draußen bleiben

Germans love their dogs, and they take them everywhere, even into restaurants. However, dogs are not permitted in grocery stores, and so you will see signs like this: Unfortunately, I have to stay outside.

3/*wollen*

| GISELA: | Wir wollen heute abend ins Kino gehen. Willst du mitgehen? | We want to go to the movies tonight. Do you want to go along? |
| INGRID: | Ich kann leider nicht, aber ich kann Andrea fragen. Vielleicht will *sie* mitgehen. | I can't (go), unfortunately, but I can ask Andrea. Perhaps she wants to go along. |

4/*sollen*

MÜLLER:	Herr Meyer, der Chef sagt, Sie sollen morgen nach Hannover fahren.	Mr. Meyer, the boss says (that) you're supposed to go to Hannover tomorrow.
MEYER:	Warum soll *ich* denn nach Hannover fahren? Warum fährt denn der Schmidt nicht?	Why am I supposed to go to Hannover? Why doesn't Schmidt go?
MÜLLER:	*Der* soll morgen nach *Lü*neburg.	He's supposed to go to Lüneburg tomorrow.

5/*möchte*

OBER:	Was möchten Sie trinken?	What would you like to drink?
HERR MEYER:	Ich möchte ein Bier. Und was möchtest du, Erna?	I would like a beer. And what would you like, Erna?
FRAU MEYER:	Ich möchte lieber ein Glas Wein.	I would prefer a glass of wine.

Wein der Könige   *König der Weine!*

Die geschützte Qualitätsmarke für geprüften Original

GUMPOLDSKIRCHNER
SPITZENWEIN

Gumpoldskirchner is a well-known Austrian wine.

| OBER: | Einen weißen oder einen roten, gnädige Frau?[2] | White or red, madam? |
| FRAU MEYER: | Haben Sie einen Gumpoldskirchner? | Do you have a Gumpoldskirchner? |

6/*dürfen*

FRAU MEYER:	Hier darfst du aber nicht parken, Hermann.	You are not allowed to park here, Hermann.
HERR MEYER:	Doch, Erna, ich glaube, ich darf hier parken.	Oh, yes, Erna, I think I can park here.
FRAU MEYER:	Ich weiß nicht. Du kannst ja mal den Polizisten fragen.	I don't know. You can ask the policeman.
HERR MEYER:	Entschuldigung. Darf man hier parken?	Excuse me. Can you park here?
POLIZIST:	Nein, aber fahren Sie doch um den Bahnhof. Da ist ein Parkplatz. Da dürfen Sie zwei Stunden parken.	No, but drive around the train station. There is a parking lot. There you can park for two hours.

Kurzparkzone

P

7-19

Höchstparkdauer
2 Stunden

[2]The term **gnädige Frau**, usually pronounced **gnä' Frau,** *madam,* is still used in Germany as an upper class form of address; in Austria, it is the standard way in which service personnel address female customers. Note that there is no male equivalent anymore.

And what would you like to drink?

Frau Meyer orders a "Gumpoldskirchner," a well-known Austrian wine from the town of Gumpoldskirchen at the foot of the famous Vienna woods (**Wienerwald**). Other Austrian wine regions include the Wachau in the Danube valley west of Vienna and the Burgenland area around Lake Neusiedl. Grapes have been grown here since Roman times around 2000 years ago. The Romans brought grape vines to Germany as well; all the famous German wine regions were once part of the Roman Empire: the Rhine and Moselle valleys, but also the upper Main valley and Swabia (see map on endpapers).

Wine making is serious business in Germany. The production is strictly controlled by government regulations, and one state, Rheinland-Pfalz, even has its own ministry of viticulture (wine-growing).

The stereotypical German, however, is not a wine drinker, but a beer quaffer, clad in **Lederhosen** and swinging a liter mug in the cavernous Hofbräuhaus in München during the **Oktoberfest**. This is obviously a caricature, but Germans do consume a lot of beer: the leading producer is not Bavaria, but the state of Nordrhein-Westfalen, where almost one third of all West German beer is brewed. (The United States puts out twice as much beer as the Federal Republic, but for four times as many people.)

The per capita consumption (FRG 1985) of wine was 21.2 liters, of beer 145.8 liters (38.5 gal.), but surprisingly the list was topped by coffee, of which the per capita consumption was 163.6 liters.

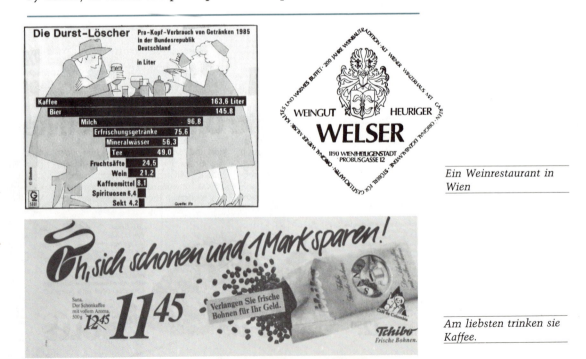

Ein Weinrestaurant in Wien

Am liebsten trinken sie Kaffee.

ANALYSIS ONE

41/Modal Auxiliaries: Forms and Meanings

Modal auxiliary verbs,[3] or simply modals, usually express not a specific action, but an attitude toward the action expressed by the infinitive. Thus in *I must go home, go home* expresses the action and *must* indicates that it is necessary that the speaker do this.

Such English modals as *must, can,* or *may* are incomplete: for example, they have only present tense forms (except for *can* which has the past tense *could*). To express the infinitive and all other tenses of modals, English uses alternate forms (*I can = I am able to;* infinitive *to be able to*). German modals are grammatically complete, that is, they have their own infinitives and can form all tenses. However, they have peculiarities of their own. The present tense singular, for example, has no endings in the first and third persons, and except for **sollen** and the **möchte**-forms, the German modals have different vowels in the singular and plural. When learning German modals, keep in mind the basic meaning of each modal because, except for *can* and *must*, there are no literal English equivalents.

können: to be able to (*expresses ability*)

ich kann	wir können	Ich kann bleiben.
du kannst	ihr könnt	I am able to (can) stay.
er/sie/es kann	sie können	

müssen: to have to (*expresses necessity*)

ich muß	wir müssen	Ich muß bleiben.
du mußt	ihr müßt	I have to (must) stay.
er/sie/es muß	sie müssen	

wollen: to want to (*expresses intention*)

ich will	wir wollen	Ich will bleiben.
du willst	ihr wollt	I want to stay.
er/sie/es will	sie wollen	

[3]Auxiliary verbs, or helping verbs, are verbs used with a following participle or infinitive. Examples: *has* arrived, *is* finished, *will* come, *must* go. The participle or infinitive always carries the main meaning.

sollen: to be (supposed) to (*expresses obligation*)

ich soll	wir sollen	Ich soll bleiben.
du sollst	ihr sollt	I am (supposed) to stay.
er/sie/es soll	sie sollen	

möchte-forms[4] (**mögen**): would like to (*expresses desire*)

ich möchte	wir möchten	Ich möchte bleiben.
du möchtest	ihr möchtet	I would like to stay.
er/sie/es möchte	sie möchten	

dürfen: to be allowed to (*expresses permission*)

ich darf	wir dürfen	Ich darf bleiben.
du darfst	ihr dürft	I am allowed (permitted)
er/sie/es darf	sie dürfen	to stay.

NOTE:

1. English *must not* (*mustn't*) is expressed by **nicht dürfen.**

   Das darfst du nicht tun,[5] Rudi.
   You mustn't do that, Rudi.

2. English *to know* corresponds to **kennen,** *to be acquainted with,* or **wissen,** *to know facts* (see Anal. 16, p. 39), *to know a language* is expressed by **können.**

   Er kann Deutsch (verstehen, lesen, sprechen, schreiben).
   Können Sie Englisch, Herr Braun?

3. An infinitive can be replaced by **das,** if the verb was mentioned in the sentence immediately preceding.

   Sie arbeiten sonntags? Müssen Sie das?

4. The infinitives **gehen, fahren,** and others, if clearly understood as complements, are frequently omitted. Compare English *The dog wants out.*

   Ich muß nach Hause.   (**gehen** omitted)
   Ich will heute nach Köln.   (**fahren** omitted)

5. To express polite requests, **möchte,** *would like* (and not a form of **wollen**), must be used.

---

[4]These **möchte**-forms are subjunctive forms of the modal **mögen** (see Anal. 110, p. 389) but are used like indicatives.

[5]Note that the infinitive as well as the first and third persons plural of **tun** do not have an **-e-** before the ending **-n.**

PRACTICE ONE

A. Vary the first sentence below by using the appropriate forms of **können**.

1. Ich kann heute kommen.
2. Er _____.
3. Er _____ nicht _____.
4. _____ Sie _____?
5. Warum _____ du denn _____ nicht _____?
6. Warum _____ ihr denn _____ nicht _____?
7. Wir _____ leider nicht _____.
8. Könnt _____ nicht _____?

B. Form the same variations as in Ex. A using (1) **das Haus kaufen** and (2) **morgen nach München fahren**. Watch the placement of **nicht**.

C. Vary each sentence with the new subjects indicated. Change possessive adjectives to agree with the subject.

1. Ich muß meinen Großvater besuchen.   (du, wir)
2. Sie muß ihren Freund fragen.   (er, ihr)
3. Ihr müßt eure Milch trinken.   (du, sie)

D. Vary the first sentence below by using the appropriate forms of **wollen**.

1. Hans und Erika wollen essen gehen.
2. Hans _____ essen gehen.
3. Ich _____ noch nicht _____.
4. Wir _____ erst um zwei Uhr _____.
5. Du _____ schon _____?
6. Wann _____ ihr denn _____?

E. Vary each sentence with the new subjects indicated.

1. Ich soll heute abend zu *Hau*se bleiben.   (wir, er)
2. Du *sollst* doch keinen Kaffee trinken.   (ihr)
3. Sie *soll* sonntags nicht mehr arbeiten.   (Gabriele und Sabine)
4. Wann soll sie denn *an*kommen?   (du, Meyers)
5. Sie sollen morgen nach Han*no*ver fahren.   (Meyer, ihr)

F. Restate each sentence by using the appropriate form of **möchte**.

1. Ich gehe essen.
2. Ich fahre nächstes Jahr nach Italien.
3. Morgen gehe ich nicht ins Kino.
4. Gehst du heute abend aus?
5. Meyer kauft unser Haus.
6. Wir essen heute abend mal im Regina.

Ob Osten, Westen, Süden, Norden – man ißt gern gut an allen Orten. Man findet uns an vielen Plätzen, um unsre Gastlichkeit zu schätzen.

Hier möchten wir nur noch hinzufügen, daß Sie immer bei uns willkommen sind. Wann dürfen wir Sie begrüßen?

Wienerwald

Das Gasthaus

G. Vary each sentence with the new subjects indicated.

1. Hier dürfen Sie nicht rauchen. (du, man)
2. Wir dürfen auch keinen Kaffee mehr trinken. (er, ihr, Erika)
3. Wann dürfen wir denn kommen? (ich)

PATTERNS TWO

7/Infinitives with and without *zu*

Es ist zehn Uhr, und die Sonne scheint, aber Hans scheint noch zu schlafen.

Warum? Braucht er heute nicht zu arbeiten?

Doch, aber erst heute nachmittag. Also braucht er heute nicht früh aufzustehen.

Ich muß immer früh aufstehen. Ich muß mehr arbeiten als Hans. Ich brauche das Geld.

It is ten o'clock, and the sun is shining, but Hans still seems to be asleep.

Why? Doesn't he have to work today?

Oh, yes, but only this afternoon. Therefore, he doesn't have to get up early today.

I always have to get up early. I have to work more than Hans. I need the money.

8/Second Prong after Modals

FRONT FIELD	1ST PRONG	INNER FIELD	NICHT	2ND PRONG	
				1ST BOX	2ND BOX
Er	muß				arbeiten.
Ich	möchte	das Buch			lesen.
Sie	darf	keinen Kaffee			trinken.
Er	kann		nicht		schlafen.
Sie	scheint	immer noch			zu schlafen.
Warum	brauchst	du morgen	nicht		zu arbeiten?
Meyer	muß	heute		nach Bonn	fahren.
Er	braucht	morgen	nicht	nach Bonn	zu fahren.
Das	kann	doch	nicht	seine Mutter	sein.
Wann	soll	Irene denn			an•kommen?
Ich	möchte	sie wirklich			kennen•lernen.
Sie	brauchen	nächsten Sonntag	nicht		zurück•zukommen.

9/Contrast Intonation

Du fährst morgen nach I*ta*lien? *Ich* kann *nicht* nach Italien fahren.

You are going to Italy tomorrow? I cannot go to Italy.

Hast *du Geld*? *Ich* habe *kein* Geld.

Do you have money? I don't have any money.

Trinken Meyers *Kaf*fee? — *Sie ja*, aber *er nicht*.

Do the Meyers drink coffee? — She does, but he does not.

Ist er intelli*gent* oder interes*sant*? — Intelli*gent ist* er, aber interes*sant* ist er *nicht*.

Is he intelligent or interesting? — He is intelligent all right. But interesting? No!

Kennen Sie Fritz *En*ders, Frau *Holl*mann? — Nein, seine *Mut*ter kenne ich *gut*, aber *ihn* kenne ich *nicht*.

Do you know Fritz Enders, Mrs. Hollmann? — No, I know his mother well, but I do not know him.

Ich höre, dein Bruder studiert Psycholo*gie*. Was studierst *du* denn? — *Ich* studiere Medi*zin*.

I hear your brother is majoring in psychology. What are you majoring in? — I am in med school.

Petra und Renate fahren nächsten Sommer nach Frankreich und Spanien. — Können sie denn Französisch und Spanisch? — *Pe*tra kann Französisch, und Re*na*te kann *Spa*nisch.

Petra and Renate are going to France and Spain next summer. — Do they know French and Spanish? — Petra knows French, and Renate knows Spanish.

10/Contradiction and Contrast

Das ist *Was*ser. Das ist *kein* Wasser. *Was*ser ist das *nicht*.

This is water. This is not water. This is no water.

Meyers haben einen *Sohn*. Meyers haben *kei*nen Sohn. Einen *Sohn* haben Meyers *nicht*.

The Meyers have a son. The Meyers do not have a son. The Meyers have no son.

Wir gehen ins *Ki*no. Nein, wir gehen *nicht* ins Kino. Ins *Ki*no gehen wir *nicht*.

We're going to the movies. No, we're not going to the movies. To the movies we won't go.

Du fährst morgen nach *Mün*chen? Nein, ich fahre morgen *nicht* nach München. Nein, *ich* fahre morgen *nicht* nach München. Nein, nach *Mün*chen fahre ich morgen *nicht*.

You are going to Munich tomorrow? No, I'm not going to Munich tomorrow. No, I am not going to Munich tomorrow. No, to Munich I am not going tomorrow.

11/Prepositions with the Accusative

Wir müssen	durch	die Stadt fahren.	We have to drive through the city.
Herr Lenz arbeitet	für	meinen Vater.	Mr. Lenz works for my father.
Hast du etwas	gegen	mich?	Do you have something against me?
Sie will	gegen	sechs zurückkommen.	She wants to return around six.
Ich muß	ohne	ihn fahren.	I have to go without him.
Ich komme	um	sechs Uhr.	I'm coming at six.
Ich wohne gleich hier	um	die Ecke.	I live right around the corner.

ANALYSIS TWO

42/Infinitives with and without *zu*

Both English and German modals are followed by infinitives.

Sie kann kommen.   She can come.

In sentences like *He is able to come* the infinitive is preceded by
to. English uses quite a few of these constructions because the
modals are incomplete, for example, *to have to*,[6] *to be supposed to*
(see Anal. 41, p. 107). Some German auxiliary verbs like **scheinen
zu**, *to seem to*, and **nicht brauchen zu**, *not to need to*, require a
following infinitive with **zu**.[7]

scheinen

As an independent verb, **scheinen** means *to shine*; as an auxiliary
verb, **scheinen** means *to seem*.

Die Sonne scheint.   The sun is shining.
Er scheint zu schlafen.   He seems to be asleep.

brauchen AND müssen

When **müssen** is negated, it is usually stressed and expresses the
absence of a compelling necessity.

Gute Bücher *müssen* nicht teuer sein.

means

Good books don't *have* to be expensive (though they usually are).

However, the far more common negation of **müssen** is with **nicht
brauchen zu**, which expresses the idea that there is no need to do
something. Compare the following two sentences:

Nein, ich *muß* heute nicht nach München fahren.
No, I don't *have* to go to Munich today (but I will).

Nein, ich brauche heute *nicht* nach München zu fahren.
No, I *don't* need to go to Munich today (and I won't).

---

[6]English *to have to* as in *I have to go now* (*I must go now*) cannot be expressed in
German by **haben zu**, but only by **müssen**; **haben zu** is used only in constructions
such as **Ich habe heute viel zu tun**, where **viel zu tun** is the object of **haben**.

[7]The basic meaning of **brauchen** is *to need*: **Ich brauche ein Buch (kein Buch)**. As
a modal, it can only be used in negative sentences, as above, whereas English *need*
can be used as a modal in positive sentences as well: *I need to go*, **Ich muß gehen**.

43/Position of Dependent Infinitives

When infinitives like **arbeiten** or **zu arbeiten** depend on modals or on auxiliary verbs like **brauchen**, they form a second prong, follow the inner field, and are preceded by **nicht**.

FRONT FIELD	1ST PRONG	INNER FIELD	NICHT	2ND PRONG
Sie	muß			arbeiten.
Sie	soll	heute		arbeiten.
Sie	scheint	heute		zu arbeiten.
	Kann	er heute		arbeiten?
Warum	willst	du heute	nicht	arbeiten?
Ich	möchte	heute	nicht	arbeiten.
Er	braucht	heute	nicht	zu arbeiten.

44/The Two-Box Second Prong

Verbal complements are always the second part of the predicate and form the second prong (see Anal. 28, p. 71). When modals are used and the infinitive becomes a second prong, this infinitive must follow its complement, thus forming a "two-box" second prong. The **zu** with verbs like **scheinen** and **brauchen** then appears between complement and infinitive.

FRONT FIELD	1ST PRONG	INNER FIELD		1ST BOX	2ND BOX
Sie	geht	heute		ins Kino.	
Sie	will	heute		ins Kino	gehen.
Er	scheint	heute	nicht	ins Kino	zu gehen.

Whenever complement and verb are written as one word, the two boxes are fused, as it were. If **zu** is required, it must still appear between complement and verb, and the whole thing is written as one word.

Sie	wollen	heute abend	nicht	aus•gehen.
Er	braucht	morgen	nicht	zurück•zugehen.

45/Contrast Intonation

In both English and German, statements are frequently made which contrast one fact with another:

He is intelligent all right, but . . .
Intelligent he's not, but . . .

The first sentence signals contrast by placing stress on *intelligent* and adding the phrase *all right, but* . . .

The second sentence, which is not used by all speakers of English, heightens the effect by placing the complement into first position. This second pattern is also possible in German, in both positive and negative statements.

Intelligent ist er (nicht), aber . . .

> A second-prong element can be moved into the front field only to signal contrast; contrast stress and intonation must then be used.

Contrast intonation is characterized by the fact that the first stressed syllable, usually in the front field, has rising pitch starting on level 1, and the second stressed syllable has falling pitch starting on level 3.

CONTRAST INTONATION   IMPLICATION

Geld hat er

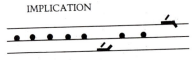

A-ber in-tel-li-gent ist er nicht
(contrast intonation)

or

A-ber er ist nicht in-tel-li-gent
(normal intonation)

Note that the following two sentences are not interchangeable. The first one is a remark of praise; the second is a sophisticated insult.

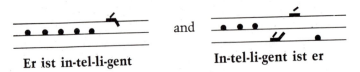

and

Er ist in-tel-li-gent   **In-tel-li-gent ist er**

With contrast intonation, **kein** is replaced by **(ein) . . . nicht** if the **kein**-noun is moved into the front field.

Meyer hat keinen *Sohn.*
Einen *Sohn* hat Meyer *nicht.*

Contrast intonation is not the same as contradiction intonation. The statement

Meyer ist intelligent.

can be contradicted by

Nein, er ist *nicht* intelligent. No, he's *not* intelligent.

or contrasted by

Ja, intelli*gent ist* er, . . . Yes, he's intelligent all right, (but . . .).

46/Prepositions with the Accusative

Some prepositions are always used with the accusative. This group includes: **durch** (*through*), **für** (*for*), **gegen** (*against*), and **ohne** (*without*). The preposition **um** also belongs in this group, but in its most frequent use in time phrases like **um sechs Uhr**, the accusative is not recognizable. In these time phrases, **um** means *exactly at;* in other cases, **um** means *around*. In time phrases, *around* or *at about* corresponds to German **gegen**.

Er kommt um sechs Uhr.	He is coming at six o'clock.
Er kommt gegen sechs Uhr.	He is coming around six o'clock.
Fahren Sie um den Bahnhof und dann immer geradeaus.	Drive around the train station and then continue straight ahead.

Only nouns referring to persons can be replaced by pronouns after these prepositions. Inanimate objects are replaced by **da**-compounds, which will be introduced in Unit 12.

Er arbeitet für mich.	He's working for me.
Wir gehen ohne sie (ohne meine Mutter).	We're going without her (without my mother).

47/The Impersonal Pronoun *man*

The impersonal third-person pronoun **man** is used very frequently in German. While it corresponds to the English impersonal pronoun *one*, its English equivalent is more often expressed by *you, we, people,* or *they*. Constructions with **man** are also frequently expressed by the English passive. The word **man** is always nominative; the accusative is **einen**.

Das macht man einfach nicht.	You simply don't do that.
Man sagt, hier ist das Wetter immer schlecht.	They say the weather is always bad here.
Hier spricht man Deutsch.	German is spoken here.

If you begin a German statement or question with **man**, you must continue to use **man** throughout (and not **er** or **sie**). The English shift from *one* to *he* or *she* is not possible in German.

Wenn man **krank ist, geht** man **zum Arzt.**

PRACTICE TWO

H. Restate the sentences by using the modal indicated in parentheses.

1. Ich verstehe Italienisch, aber ich spreche es nicht. (können)
2. Kommst du heute abend? (können)
3. Herr Rücker fliegt heute nach Düsseldorf. (müssen)
4. Tante Amalie ist nicht zu Hause. (scheinen)
5. Kurt und Rudi gehen jetzt schlafen. (sollen)
6. Gehst du heute schwimmen? (mögen)
7. Morgen stehe ich früh auf. (müssen)
8. Heute gehe ich nicht ins Kino. (wollen)
9. Was mache ich denn jetzt? (sollen)
10. Heute arbeitet Hans nicht. (brauchen)

I. Supply the appropriate form of **müssen** or **brauchen**.

1. Mußt du morgen arbeiten?   Nein, morgen _____ ich nicht zu arbeiten.

2. Ich hoffe, du brauchst morgen nicht zu arbeiten.   Doch, leider _____ ich auch *morgen* arbeiten.

3. Braucht er denn heute nicht zu arbeiten?   Nein, heute _____.

4. Müßt ihr heute arbeiten?   Ja, wir _____.

5. Muß Erika immer noch arbeiten?   Nein, sie _____ nicht mehr _____.

J. Form the same variations as in Ex. I, using (1) **nach Berlin fahren**, (2) **zu Hause bleiben**, and (3) **ins Museum gehen**.

K. Vary the following sentences as indicated.

Wir trinken *Wein.*   **Wir trinken** *keinen* **Wein.**   *Wein* **trinken wir** *nicht.*

1. Sie haben eine *Tochter.*   4. Wir gehen nach *Hause.*
2. Wir trinken *Bier.*   5. Er ist zu *Hause.*
3. Ich kenne hier einen *Arzt.*   6. Das ist *unser* Hund.

L. Express the following ideas by using sentences containing **man**.

1. English is spoken here.
2. No smoking here.   (Use **dürfen**)
3. You can't park here.   (Use **dürfen**)

M. Express in German.

1. I'm going out without him.
2. My friend Sonja is working for her father.
3. Go through the park and then always straight ahead.
4. The parking lot is around the corner.
5. Does she have something against him?
6. He has to be home at ten o'clock.
7. We want to come back around one.

ADAC-HOTEL UND SPEZIALITÄTENRESTAURANT

Bacher

A-3512 MAUTERN / DONAU
WACHAU · N.Ö.
TELEFON (0 27 32) 29 37

[handwritten:] Ich gehe ohne ihn aus. Meine Freundin Sonja arbeitet für ihren Vater. Gehen Sie durch den Park und dann immer geradeaus. Der Parkplatz ist gegen die Ecke. Hat sie etwas gegen ihn? Er muß um zehn Uhr zu Hause sein. Wir wollen um eins zurückkommen.

CONVERSATIONS

I

In a crowded restaurant. A student is looking for an empty chair.

STUDENT: Entschuldigung, ist der Platz hier noch frei? — Excuse me, is this seat taken (still free)?

MANN: Bitte nehmen Sie Platz. — Please, sit down.

STUDENT: Ist es hier immer so voll? — Is this place always so crowded?

MANN: Den ganzen Tag, aber besonders von zwölf bis zwei, zum Mittagessen. — All day, but especially from 12 to 2, for dinner.

STUDENT: Herr Ober,[8] kann ich bitte die Speisekarte haben. — Waiter, can I have the menu, please.

While the student studies the menu:

STUDENT: Sie scheinen hier Stammkunde zu sein. — You seem to be a regular customer here.

MANN: Ja, ich esse sehr oft hier. — Yes, I eat here quite often.

STUDENT: Können Sie etwas empfehlen? Was schmeckt am besten? — Can you recommend something? What tastes best?

[8] A waitress is addressed as **Fräulein**. Do not use **Frau Oberin**, which means *Mother Superior*.

MANN:	Ich nehme Menü⁹ Nummer eins. Das ist sehr gut und nicht sehr teuer.	I'm having dinner No. 1. That's good and not very expensive.
STUDENT:	Suppe, Schweinebraten, Rotkohl und Knödel. Und zum Nachtisch kriegt man Eis. Das klingt gut. Ich glaube, das nehme ich auch.	Soup, roast pork, red cabbage, and dumplings. And for dessert you get ice cream. Sounds good. I think I'll take that too.
OBER:	Bitte, der Herr, was darf ich Ihnen bringen?	Yes, sir, what can I bring you?
STUDENT:	Ich bekomme Menü eins.	I'd like dinner No. 1.
OBER:	Einmal Menü eins,—und was trinken Sie?	One number one—and what will you have to drink?
STUDENT:	Ein Glas Bier.	A glass of beer.
OBER:	Hell oder dunkel?	Light or dark?
STUDENT:	Hell, bitte.—Dauert es lange?	Light, please.—Will it take long?
OBER:	Nein, höchstens fünf Minuten.	No, five minutes at the most.

II

The following statements could be answers. Construct questions (usually more than one) that would fit them. Then write mini-conversations around these questions and answers and act them out in class.

1. Müller, Fritz Müller.
2. Es regnet schon wieder.
3. Für meinen Freund.
4. Nein, ich wohne jetzt in der Bettinastraße.
5. Mathematik.
6. Ich bleibe hier.
7. Nein, noch nicht.
8. Mein Vater ist Ingenieur.
9. Ins Theater.
10. Donnerstag.
11. Da rechts um die Ecke.
12. Das weiß ich nicht.

III

Plan a party with members of your class. When? Who can come? Who has to stay home and work? Who wants to bring sausage and cheese, something to drink? Can they bring friends? etc. Use as many modals as possible.

IV

Below you will find colloquial and mostly stereotypical phrases that are used with high frequency in everyday conversation. Most of these have been used in the first four units. Review these phrases and incorporate them into your conversations as much as possible.

bestimmt	certain(ly), I'm sure	**Er kommt bestimmt aus Österreich.**
hoffentlich	hopefully, I hope	**Hoffentlich regnet es morgen nicht.**
leider	unfortunately	**Tee haben wir leider nicht.**

⁹The word **das Menü** does not mean *menu*, but *complete dinner*; it usually includes soup, a main course, and dessert. English *menu* is expressed by **die Speisekarte.**

natürlich	naturally, of course	**Sie nimmt natürlich den Bus.**
übrigens	by the way	**Wir gehen übrigens ins Theater.**
guten Tag, Tag	hello	**Tag, Gabi.**
guten Morgen (Abend)	good morning (evening)	**Guten Morgen (Abend), Frau Meyer.**
gute Nacht	good night	**Gute Nacht, ich gehe jetzt schlafen.**
wie geht's?	how are you?	**Morgen, Ursula, wie geht's dir denn?**
danke	thank you	**Danke, gut.**

```
        Speiseplan - Mensa Wilhelmstraße - Mensa Morgenstelle
              Mensa Prinz Karl - Mensa Schlatterhaus
                   vom 15.12.86 - 20.12.86
      -------------------------------------------------------


Montag, 15.12.86
Stammessen              Jägerbraten, Kartoffelbrei (2), grüner Salat
Schlatterhaus           Sojagericht
Eintopf                 Reisbrei, Kompott
Mittag                  Salatbuffet
Abend                   Käsespätzle, grüner Salat in Joghurtdressing, Obst
Abend                   Salatbuffet

Dienstag, 16.12.86
Stammessen              Paniertes Schweineschnitzel, Zitrone, gemischter
                        Salat
Schlatterhaus           Vegetarisches Essen
Eintopf                 Laucheintopf
Mittag                  Salatbuffet
Abend                   Rindergulasch, Rösti (2), Salat
Abend                   Salatbuffet

Mittwoch, 17.12.86
Stammessen              Eingemachtes Kalbfleisch, Reis, grüner Salat
Vollwertgericht:        Tomatensuppe, Mex. Reisgericht, Kopfsalat in
                        Joghurt, Quarkspeise
Schlatterhaus           Eingemachtes Kalbfleisch, Reis, grüner Salat
Eintopf                 Linseneintopf
Mittag                  Salatbuffet
Abend                   Cevapcici, Pommes frites, Rohkostsalat
Abend                   Salatbuffet

Donnerstag, 18.12.86
Stammessen              Hackbraten in Sahne, Pommes frites, Rohkostsalat
Schlatterhaus           Sojagericht
Eintopf                 Hirsebrei, Kompott
Mittag                  Salatbuffet
Abend                   Gefülltes Pastetchen, Reis, grüner Salat
Abend                   Salatbuffet

Freitag, 19.12.86
Stammessen              Schollenfilet gebacken, Teufelsoße, gemischter
                        Gurkensalat, Joghurt
Schlatterhaus           Vollwertgericht
Eintopf                 Ital. Minestrone
Mittag                  Salatbuffet
Abend                   Kalbsbraten mit Spätzle, grüner Salat
Abend                   Salatbuffet

Samstag, 20.12.86
Stammessen              Gaisburger Marsch, 2 Brötchen, Joghurt


- Änderungen vorbehalten -

(2) geschwefelt

Zur Beachtung:  Abendessen nur Mensa Wilhelmstraße
```

vielen Dank, danke	thank you	**Vielen Dank für das Buch.**
(auf) Wiedersehen	good-bye	**Wiedersehen, Herr Meyer.**
tschüß	bye	**Tschüß, Hans.**
mach's gut	take care	**Mach's gut, Peter.**
bitte	please	**Bleiben Sie doch noch hier, bitte.**
Entschuldigung	excuse me	**Entschuldigung, sind Sie Engländerin?**
ich glaube	I think	**Ich glaube, ich gehe jetzt essen.**
Sagen Sie . . .	tell me, say	**Sagen Sie, wo ist hier ein Restaurant?**
ach ja	oh yes	**Ach ja, sie wohnt ja in Hamburg.**
also gut	OK then	**Also gut, wir sehen uns morgen.**
nicht wahr?	isn't that so, aren't you?	**Du _kommst_ doch, nicht wahr?**

Fragen an Sie persönlich

1. Sie lernen jetzt Deutsch. Können Sie auch andere Sprachen (_other languages_)?
   verstehen, lesen, sprechen, schreiben?
   Französisch? Spanisch? Italienisch? Russisch? Chinesisch? Japanisch?
   Arabisch?
2. Was essen Sie gern (_What do you like to eat_)?[10]
   Was trinken Sie gern (_What do you like to drink_)?

Fleisch oder Fisch?	meat or fish?
Suppe? Salat?	soup? salad?
Kartoffeln, Nudeln, Reis?	potatoes, noodles, rice?
Wurst, Käse?	sausage (cold cuts), cheese?
Obst? Kuchen? Eis? Pudding?	fruit? cake? ice cream? pudding?

Breakfast, Lunch, and Dinner

For breakfast, Germans have traditionally sat down to a couple of fresh **Brötchen** with butter and jam or jelly, and at midmorning, to a more substantial breakfast. Today there is not a great deal of difference between a German and an American breakfast.

However, while in America lunch is generally a light meal and the main meal is eaten in the evening, the German **Mittagessen**, eaten at midday, is the equivalent of the American dinner, and the **Abendessen** is normally a light, cold meal. A long **Mittagspause** used to be standard practice when businesses closed so that people could go home to eat. This custom is still so strongly ingrained that even today many people take a two-hour "lunch break," and many small shops still close from twelve to two. With urbanization, most people now eat their **Mittagessen** in a restaurant or in a company cafeteria called a **Kantine**.

---

[10]Note the difference between **gern** + verb, _to like to do something_, and **möchte**-forms, _would like something_.

Beim Mittagessen in der Küche.

Hier kann man siebzehn Salate essen.

READING

Wie ißt man als Student?

Samstag vormittag, elf Uhr. Bettina Hagen hat Hunger. Es ist bald Zeit zum Mittagessen, aber Bettina weiß nicht, soll sie zu Hause kochen°, soll sie in die Mensa° gehen, oder soll sie einmal in die Krone°? Sie muß heute allein° essen gehen, denn ihr Freund, Achim Steinle, ist in Stuttgart bei seinen Eltern. Sein Vater hat heute Geburtstag.

5

cook student cafeteria
Crown (name of
restaurant) alone

Bettina, Studentin der Germanistik im sechsten Semester, wohnt in einem Studentenheim in der Brentanostraße. Sie hat ein Zimmer im siebten Stock°, aber keine Küche°. (Für ein Zimmer mit Küche muß man etwas mehr bezahlen, aber Bettina will nicht so viel Geld ausgeben°.) Sie kann aber trotzdem° kochen, denn es gibt auf jedem Stock eine Küche, die alle Studenten benutzen° dürfen.

10

eighth floor kitchen

spend nevertheless

use

Ihr Frühstück—Joghurt, Brötchen, Butter und Marmelade—macht sie sich auf ihrem Zimmer; nur den Kaffee muß sie in der Küche kochen. Wenn° sie frische Brötchen essen will,[11] muß sie früh aufstehen. Die Brötchen holt° sie sich in einer Bäckerei gleich um die Ecke.

15

if

fetches

---

[11]In dependent clauses introduced by such subordinating conjunctions as **wenn** and **wo**, the inflected verb stands at the end. Dependent clauses are discussed in Unit 8.

Zum Mittagessen geht sie oft mit ihrem Freund Achim in die Mensa. Eine Mensa ist ein Studentenrestaurant. Jede Universität hat eine Mensa, wo man billig essen kann. Ein Mittagessen kostet nicht 20 mehr als DM 2,50; einen Eintopf° kann man schon für DM 1,40 bekommen. Wenn man etwas trinken will, zum Beispiel Bier, Saft°, Cola oder Kaffee, muß man extra bezahlen.

> one pot meal
> juice

Achim ißt oft Linsen°, Spätzle° und Würstchen°, eine schwäbische Spezialität. Bettina möchte lieber Schnitzel mit Pommes frites°. Sie 25 kommt aus Norddeutschland, und die norddeutsche Küche° kennt keine Spätzle.

> lentils   Swabian noodles
> frankfurters
> french fries   cuisine

Bettina kann natürlich auch im Studentenheim Mittagessen machen. Das ist billiger° als die Mensa, aber es braucht auch Zeit. Wenn sie in der Mensa ißt, braucht sie nicht einzukaufen und sie spart° Zeit. 30

> cheaper
> saves

Abends ißt man in Deutschland meistens° kalt. Bettina, Achim und noch ein paar° Freunde essen abends oft im Studentenheim. Zu einem normalen Abendessen ißt man Brot, Butter (oder Margarine), vielleicht eine Bauernwurst°, und Schweizerkäse oder Quark°, und man trinkt Tee oder Bier. Nach dem Abendessen gehen sie oft noch 35 „ein Bierchen trinken" (oder auch ein Glas Wein); ihr Lieblingslokal° ist eine Studentenkneipe° am Markt°. Dort bekommt man auch spät am Abend noch ein Schinkenbrot° oder einen Leberkäse° oder ein Paar° Würstchen.

> usually
> a few
> type of sausage   soft
>   curd cheese
> favorite hangout
> student pub
> market square   ham
>   sandwich   liver loaf
> couple

Am Wochenende sind keine Vorlesungen°. Sonntags ist die Mensa 40 zu°, und samstags ist sie nur von zwölf bis zwei auf°. Aber Bettina möchte heute nicht in die Mensa, denn es gibt nur „reduziertes Essen." Wenn sie im Studentenheim kochen will, muß sie noch in den Supermarkt. Aber es ist schon elf Uhr, und sie hat keine Lust° zum Kochen. Also geht sie heute in die Krone. 45

> lectures
> closed   open
> doesn't feel like

Das Lokal° ist voll, aber an einem Tisch in der Ecke ist ein Platz frei. An dem Tisch sitzt ein Ehepaar° mit einem Hund.° (In Deutschland darf man Hunde ins Restaurant mitbringen.) Bettina fragt: „Darf ich?" — „Aber natürlich. Nehmen Sie Platz." Bettina trinkt einen Apfelsaft und ißt Spinat° mit Spiegeleiern° und Salzkartoffeln°; zum 50 Nachtisch ißt sie einen Apfelstrudel. Das Ehepaar ist sehr nett, und sie bleiben alle drei nach dem Essen noch sitzen und reden° miteinander°.

> restaurant
> married couple   dog
> spinach   fried eggs
> boiled potatoes
> talk
> with one another

Am Samstag abend kommt Achim aus Stuttgart zurück, und am Sonntag kommen Bettinas Eltern zu Besuch. Sie möchten Achim 55 kennenlernen und laden ihn zum Mittagessen ins Hotel Vier Jahreszeiten° ein°. Dort ist das Essen ausgezeichnet° und teuer, aber wenn Eltern zu Besuch kommen, braucht man ja nicht zu bezahlen.

> Four Seasons Hotel
> **einladen** invite
> excellent

Am Montag ißt Bettina wieder in der Mensa.

TIMM (17): „Unsere große Pause ist um viertel vor zehn. Da habe ich meistens schon einen Heißhunger auf einen **Hamburger**. Oder **Pommes Frites** mit Ketchup. Dazu trinke ich fast immer eine **Cola**. Das bringt mich dann echt in Form. Und was **Süßes**, ein **Nuts** oder so für zwischendurch, muß sowieso sein!"

Was Schüler in
der Pause essen

REVIEW EXERCISES

N. Fill the blanks with appropriate forms of modals or with forms of **brauchen** or **scheinen**.

1. Danke, ich _____ jetzt keinen Wein.
2. Ich _____ heute leider nicht kommen; es geht mir nicht gut.
3. Hans studiert Medizin; er _____ Arzt werden.
4. Ich _____ sonntags nicht zu arbeiten, wenn ich nicht _____.
5. Was _____ Sie trinken, Fräulein Hannemann, — Kaffee oder Tee?
6. Für eine Mark _____ man nicht viel kaufen.
7. Italienisch _____ ich leider nicht, nur Spanisch.
8. Irmgard _____ noch zu schlafen.
9. Das Schwimmen ist hier verboten; hier _____ man nicht schwimmen.
10. Der Arzt sagt, ich _____ nicht mehr rauchen.
11. Das _____ du aber nicht tun, Rudi.
12. Wir _____ heute nicht früh aufzustehen.

O. Tell somebody:

> that you have to go home.   —   **Ich muß nach Hause gehen.**

1. that you would like a cup of coffee.
2. that she mustn't do that. (Use **du** and **Sie**.)
3. that she has to work on Sunday. (Use **du** and **Sie**.)
4. that he doesn't *have* to work on Sunday.
5. that he doesn't need to work on Sunday.
6. that you aren't able to come today.
7. that you know Japanese.
8. that he isn't permitted to smoke here. (Use **Sie**.)
9. that you don't want to eat anything now.
10. that you'd like to become an auto mechanic.
11. that she is supposed to come home soon. (Use **du**.)
12. that you (*plural*) want to stay home tonight.

P. Give negative answers to the following questions; use contrast intonation and move the second prong into the front field.

> **Ist sie zu *Hause*?**   **Nein, zu *Hause* ist sie *nicht*.**

1. Ist das Fritz *Schu*mann?
2. Können Sie Französisch, Herr Braun?
3. Ißt sie *Leber*wurst?
4. Will er nach *Ham*burg?
5. Fahrt ihr Sonntag in die *Stadt*?
6. Haben Schmidts einen *Sohn*?
7. Sie nehmen die *Straßen*bahn, nicht wahr?
8. Will sie heute *ar*beiten?

Q. For each of the following sentences, invent a preceding sentence with contrast intonation. Note that the elements to be contrasted are in italics.

> _____, und *ich* bleibe zu *Hause*.
> ***Du* kannst ins *Kino* gehen, und *ich* bleibe zu *Hause*.**

1. _____, und *ich* muß *ar*beiten.
2. _____, aber eine *Tochter* haben sie *nicht*.
3. _____, aber *ich* studiere *Deutsch*.
4. _____, aber *arbeiten will* er nicht.
5. _____, aber ihr *Freund* hat Geld.

R. Form sentences from the elements given; supply additional necessary elements.

1. Erich / nach Wien / morgen / wollen / fahren.
   Er / Wien / noch nicht / kennen.
   Sein Bruder / in Wien / jetzt / wohnen // ihn / besuchen wollen.
   Mit dem Wagen / fahren?
   Nein // fliegen.
   Wie lange / bleiben?
   Nicht wissen.
2. Herr Müller / jetzt / Französisch lernen.
   Nächstes Jahr / nach Paris / müssen.
   Dort / zwei Jahre / arbeiten / sollen.
   Er / allein / nach Frankreich / gehen?
   Nein // Frau und Kinder / auch.
   Kinder / wie alt?
   Sohn 12, Töchter 8, 6.

S. Form imperatives from the following verbs; use **doch** or **bitte** where indicated. Remember that the imperative of **sein** is **seien Sie**.

nach Österreich fahren (doch)	—	**Fahren Sie doch nach Österreich!**

1. Lehrer werden (doch)
2. den Bus nehmen (doch)
3. Philosophie studieren
4. Schweinefleisch kaufen
5. langsam fahren (bitte)

6. ein Steak essen (doch)
7. noch ein Glas Wein trinken (doch)
8. früh aufstehen (bitte)
9. schlafen gehen (doch)
10. glücklich sein

T. Develop the following sentences in stages, as indicated. Pay attention to the reminders in parentheses.

I have to get up early tomorrow, unfortunately.

(a)	I have to get up.	**Ich muß aufstehen.**
(b)	add: *early*	**Ich muß früh aufstehen.**
(c)	add: *tomorrow*	**Ich muß morgen früh aufstehen.**
(d)	start sentence with *Unfortunately*	**Leider muß ich morgen früh aufstehen.**

1. Next summer Aunt Amalie wants to go to Vienna again.
   (a) Aunt Amalie goes to Vienna. (**fahren**)
   (b) add: *wants to*
   (c) add: *already again*
   (d) start sentence with *Next summer . . .*
2. Hopefully, I don't have to go downtown today in this rain.
   (a) I go downtown. (**gehen**)
   (b) I have to go downtown.

    (c) negate (**brauchen** + **zu**)

    (d) add: *today*

    (e) add: *in this rain* (end field)

    (f) start sentence with *Hopefully* . . .

3. I believe their daughter Monika would like to become a doctor.

    (a) Monika becomes a doctor. (professional status, feminine)

    (b) change to *Monika would like to* . . .

    (c) add: *their daughter*

    (d) introduce sentence with *I believe* . . .

U. Express in German.

1. He is supposed to be home at six o'clock.
2. We want to eat around six-thirty.
3. Tonight we'd like to go to the movies.
4. Karl unfortunately can't go.
5. He still has to work.
6. But tomorrow he doesn't need to work.
7. Tomorrow we want to go to Garmisch.
8. Our train is going to leave at 8:10.
9. At ten o'clock we'll be there.
10. When are you going to come back?

VOCABULARY

abends	in the evening, evenings	**das Abendessen, -**	supper
auf•stehen	to get up (out of bed)	**das Mittagessen, -**	noon-day meal, dinner
bald	soon	**der Fisch, -e**	fish
bei	at; with; at the home of; near; while	**(das) Frankreich**	France
		frei	free
das Beispiel, -e	example	**früh**	early
zum Beispiel (z.B.)	for example	**das Frühstück, -e**	breakfast
bekommen	to get, receive	**ganz**	all of; entire; quite
besonders	especially	**ganz gut**	not bad
best- (*adj.* or *adv.*)	best	**gegen**	against; around
am besten (*adv.*)	best	**gegen neun**	around nine o'clock
besuchen	to visit	**gern**	gladly
der Besuch, -e	visit	**ich esse gern**	I like to eat
zu Besuch kommen	to come for a visit	**die Großeltern** (*pl. only*)	grandparents
bringen	to bring		
dauern	to last	**die Großmutter,** ⸚	grandmother
dunkel	dark	**der Großvater,** ⸚	grandfather
durch	through	**halb**	half
dürfen	to be permitted to	**hell**	light
das darfst du nicht	you mustn't do that	**hoffen**	to hope
einmal (mal)	once; for a change	**hören**	to hear
empfehlen (empfiehlst, empfiehlt)	to recommend	**das Hotel, -s**	hotel
		der Hund, -e	dog
das Essen, -	food; meal	**(das) Italien**	Italy

italienisch	Italian	der Regen	rain
die Kartoffel, -n	potato	das Restaurant', -s	restaurant
kennen•lernen	to get acquainted with	rot	red
klingen	to sound	(das) Rußland	Russia
können	to be able to; to	russisch	Russian
	know a language	der Salat, -e	salad
kriegen (colloq.)	to get, receive	sollen	to be supposed to
die Leberwurst, ⸚e	liver sausage	sonntags	on Sundays
lieber (adv.)	rather, preferably	(das) Spanien	Spain
man	you, we, people,	spanisch	Spanish
	they, one	die Speisekarte, -n	menu
die Mensa, Mensen	student cafeteria	die Sprache, -n	language
mit•bringen	to bring (along)	die Stunde, -n	hour
mit•gehen	to go with, come	die Suppe, -n	soup
	along	teuer	expensive
mögen	to like to	tun	to do
ich möchte	I would like (to)	verboten	forbidden, not
müssen	to have to		allowed, not
die Nacht, ⸚e	night		permitted,
gute Nacht	good night		prohibited
der Nachtisch, -e	dessert		
nett	nice	vielleicht	perhaps
die Nummer, -n	number	voll	full; crowded
der Ober, -	waiter	der Vormittag, -e	forenoon, morning
oft	often	weiß	white
ohne	without	wollen	to want to
parken	to park	das Zimmer, -	room
der Parkplatz, ⸚e	parking lot	zu	to; at; too
der Platz, ⸚e	place	zu (adj.)	closed
Platz nehmen	to sit down	die Tür ist zu	the door is closed
der Polizist, -en	policeman	zurück	back
(n-noun)		zurück•kommen	to return, come
rauchen	to smoke		back

Unit 5

The Dative—Prepositions with the Dative—Word Order within the Inner Field

Switzerland and Liechtenstein

Switzerland is one of the oldest democracies in the world. It is a federation of 26 states or cantons (**Kantone**) which exercise a considerable amount of autonomy; the three original cantons were Uri, Schwyz, and Unterwalden, which united in 1291 in opposition to the Habsburgs. The federal government is located in the capital Berne (**Bern**). Switzerland is dedicated to neutrality in international affairs. It was neutral in World War I and World War II; after the first war, it became the seat of the League of Nations, and it is now one of the three administrative centers of the United Nations (with New York and Vienna).

The population of Switzerland is just under 6.5 million, of whom about one million are foreigners.

The German spoken in Switzerland is often referred to as "Schwyzerdütsch." The original Swiss spoke German dialects, but as new cantons joined the confederation, speakers of French, Italian, and Romansh were added. Today there are four official languages, although Romansh is spoken by only one percent of the population:[1]

German	74.5%	Italian	4.0%
French	20.1%	Romansh	1.0%

The four language groups are reflected in the four names for Switzerland: Schweiz, Suisse, Svizzera, Svizzra; the official, language-neutral name is the Latin *Confoederatio Helvetica* (Helvetic Confederation).

The principality of Liechtenstein (Fürstentum Liechtenstein) is smaller than the District of Columbia. It has a population of about 26,000, of whom 5,000 live in the capital of Vaduz. Liechtenstein is a constitutional hereditary monarchy, independent since 1806, but has a customs and currency union with Switzerland.

Fürstentum Liechtenstein
die letzte Monarchie im Herzen der Alpen

[1]The figures do not include non-Swiss nationals.

APPENZELL (AR / AI)   AARGAU (AG)   BASLE (BL)

BASLE (BS)   BERNE (BE)   FRIBOURG (FR)

GENEVA (GE)   GLARUS (GL)   GRISONS (GR)

LUCERNE (LU)   NEUCHÂTEL (NE)   ST-GALLEN (SG)

SCHAFFHAUSEN (SH)   SCHWYZ (SZ)   SOLOTHURN (SO)

TICINO (TI)   THURGAU (TG)   UNTERWALDEN (NW)

UNTERWALDEN (OW)   URI (UR)   VALAIS (VS)

VAUD (VD)   ZUG (ZG)   ZÜRICH (ZH)

Swiss Cantons

PATTERNS ONE

1/The Dative of Pronouns

Guten Tag, Edgar. Wie geht's dir denn?
Danke, es geht mir gut.
   Danke, mir geht's gut.
   Danke, gut.
Und dir?

Hi, Edgar. How are you?
Thanks, I'm fine.

And you?

Wie geht's denn Schmidts?
Ihm geht's *gut*, aber *ihr* geht's *schlecht*.
   Sie hat die Grippe.

How are the Schmidts?
He's fine, but she isn't well.
   She has the flu.

Na, ihr beiden, wie geht's euch denn?
Uns geht's immer gut.

Well, you two, how are you?
We're always fine.

Und wie geht es Ihnen, Herr Doktor?

And how are you, Doctor?

2/Verbs with Accusative Objects

Bitte, was bekommen Sie heute, Herr Dr. Müller?

What can I do for you today, Dr. Müller?
(*lit.* What do you get today?)

Ich suche einen Roman von Schmidt-Ingelheim. Haben Sie den *Flamingo*?

I am looking for a novel by Schmidt-Ingelheim. Do you have *The Flamingo*?

Den Roman kenne ich leider nicht. Ist er neu?

I don't know that novel. Is it new?

Ja, ganz neu. Meine Frau will ihn lesen.
Brauchen Sie das Buch sofort, Herr Doktor?

Yes, quite new. My wife wants to read it.
Do you need the book immediately, Dr. Müller?

Ja, ich möchte es gern gleich mitnehmen.
Ich will mal sehen; vielleicht finde ich es doch.

Yes, I'd like to take it along right away.
Let me see; perhaps I'll find it after all.

Sie haben Glück, Herr Doktor. Hier ist es.
Und bezahlen Sie das Buch dann bitte dort an der Kasse.

You're in luck, Dr. Müller. Here it is.
And please pay for the book over there at the cashier's.

3/Verbs with Dative Objects

Sabine hilft ihrer Freundin.
Kannst du mir nicht auch mal helfen?
Ich danke dir für deine Hilfe.
Der Wagen gefällt mir. Ist das dein Wagen?
   —Nein, er gehört meinen Eltern.

Sabine helps her friend.
Can't you help me too (for a change)?
Thank you for your help.
I like that car. Is that your car?
   —No, it belongs to my parents.

4/Verbs with both Dative and Accusative Objects

Der Verkäufer zeigt dem Kunden einen Photoapparat.

The salesman is showing the customer a camera.

Ich möchte meinem Sohn eine Kamera zum Geburtstag schenken.

I'd like to give my son a camera for his birthday.

Geben Sie Ihrem Sohn doch eine Filmkamera.

Why don't you give your son a movie camera.

Nein, zum Geburtstag möchte ich ihm einen Photoapparat geben.

No, for his birthday I'd like to give him a still camera.

Eine Filmkamera will ich ihm zu Weihnachten kaufen.

I want to buy him a movie camera for Christmas.

Darf ich Ihnen diese 35 mm-Kamera anbieten? Ein Bestseller, und gar nicht teuer.

May I offer you this 35mm camera? A bestseller and not at all expensive.

Diesen Apparat empfehle ich vielen Kunden.

I recommend this camera to many customers.

Ich kann Ihnen den Apparat leihen, Herr Schulte, —zum Ausprobieren.

I can lend you the camera, Mr. Schulte, to try out.

Sie können ihn mir morgen zurückbringen.

You can return it to me tomorrow.

Ja, geben Sie mir die Kamera bis morgen. Vielen Dank.

Yes, give me the camera until tomorrow. Thank you very much.

Ich wünsche Ihnen viel Erfolg beim Fotografieren.

I wish you much success with your picture taking.

Ich kaufe mir einen Roman von Schmidt-Ingelheim.

I'll buy (myself) a novel by Schmidt-Ingelheim.

Meine Tochter kauft sich einen Roman von Schmidt-Ingelheim.

My daughter buys (herself) a novel by Schmidt-Ingelheim.

Zu Weihnachten wünsche ich mir einen Fernseher.

For Christmas I want (wish for myself) a television set.

Zu Weihnachten wünscht sich meine Frau einen Fernseher.

For Christmas my wife wants (wishes for herself) a television set.

Meyer sagt, er fährt nächste Woche nach Spanien, aber das glaube ich ihm nicht.

Meyer says that he's going to Spain next week, but I don't believe what he says.

Meyer sagt, morgen soll es regnen, aber das glaube ich nicht. Man kann ihm nie glauben.

Meyer says it's supposed to rain tomorrow, but I don't believe it. You can never believe him.

Sagen Sie ihm, er soll kommen.

Tell him to come.

Fragen Sie ihn doch; er antwortet Ihnen bestimmt.

Ask him; I'm sure he'll answer you.

ANALYSIS ONE

48/The Forms of the Dative Case

PERSONAL PRONOUNS

SINGULAR	NOM.	ich	du	er	sie	es	Sie
	ACC.	mich	dich	ihn	sie	es	Sie
	DAT.	*mir*	*dir*	*ihm*	*ihr*	*ihm*	*Ihnen*
PLURAL	NOM.	wir	ihr		sie		Sie
	ACC.	uns	euch		sie		Sie
	DAT.	*uns*	*euch*		*ihnen*		*Ihnen*

IMPERSONAL
PRONOUN

man
einen
einem

no pl.

REFLEXIVE PRONOUNS

Just as with the accusative reflexives, the first and second persons
of the dative reflexive are identical with the personal pronouns.
Again, all third-person forms are **sich**.

SINGULAR	ACC.	mich	dich	sich	sich	sich	sich
	DAT.	*mir*	*dir*	*sich*	*sich*	*sich*	*sich*
PLURAL	ACC.	uns	euch		sich		sich
	DAT.	*uns*	*euch*		*sich*		*sich*

der-WORDS

	MASC.	FEM.	NEUT.	PLURAL
NOM.	der	die	das	die
ACC.	den	die	das	die
DAT.	*dem*	*der*	*dem*	*den*

ein-WORDS

	MASC.	FEM.	NEUT.	PLURAL
NOM.	kein	keine	kein	keine
ACC.	keinen	keine	kein	keine
DAT.	*keinem*	*keiner*	*keinem*	*keinen*

NOTE: There is no difference between the dative endings of the **ein**-words and those of the **der**-words. The dative of **man** is **einem**.

INTERROGATIVE PRONOUNS

NOM.	**wer**	who
ACC.	**wen**	whom
DAT.	***wem***	to whom

NOUNS

In the singular, nouns have no special ending for the dative. Occasionally, masculine and neuter nouns of one syllable use **-e** (**dem Manne**), but this ending is obsolescent and no longer required, except in such idiomatic expressions as **zu Hause** or **nach Hause**.

In the dative plural, all German nouns must end in **-n**, except those foreign words the plural of which ends in **-s**. If the nominative plural already ends in **-n**, no additional **-n** is required.

NOM. SING.	NOM. PLURAL	DAT. PLURAL
der Mann	die Männer	den Männern
die Frau	die Frauen	den Frauen
die Freundin	die Freundinnen	den Freundinnen
das Auto	die Autos	den Autos

All **n**-nouns have the ending **-(e)n** in all cases except the nominative singular:

SING.	NOM.	**der Student**	**der Junge**	**der Herr**
	ACC.	**den Studenten**	**den Jungen**	**den Herrn**
	DAT.	**dem Studenten**	**dem Jungen**	**dem Herrn**
PL.	NOM.	**die Studenten**	**die Jungen**	**die Herren**
	ACC.	**die Studenten**	**die Jungen**	**die Herren**
	DAT.	**den Studenten**	**den Jungen**	**den Herren**

49/**Accusative and Dative Objects**

The only objects that have been used through Unit 4 have been direct objects in the accusative. German also has a few verbs with direct objects in the dative, and, like English, many verbs that take both direct and indirect objects. With these verbs, the direct object is always in the accusative, and the indirect object, usually a person, is always in the dative.

English differentiates between direct and indirect objects in two ways:

(1) by position: the indirect object *precedes* the direct object.

She gave her friend a book.

(2) by adding the preposition *to* to the indirect object when the indirect object *follows* the direct object.

She gave the book to her friend.

Whenever you have a genuine indirect object in English, you can, by rearranging the sentence, force the form with *to* to appear or to disappear.

She gave him the book.
She gave the book to him.

The *him* in *She gave him the book* is therefore syntactically not the same kind of *him* as that in

She loves him.

for only the first *him* can be changed into a *to him*. The *him* which can be replaced by *to him* corresponds to the German dative. Note also that the *to* in

He took Charlie to the station.

cannot be eliminated, since *to the station* is not an object but a directive.

The German indirect object never uses the preposition **zu**. Since the dative forms identify the indirect object, it may either precede or follow the direct object.

VERBS WITH ACCUSATIVE OBJECTS

bekommen	to receive	**kaufen**	to buy	**lesen**	to read
besuchen	to visit	**kennen**	to know [a	**lieben**	to love
brauchen	to need		person or	**nehmen**	to take
essen	to eat		thing]	**sehen**	to see
finden	to find	**kennenlernen**	to meet, get	**suchen**	to seek
heiraten	to marry		acquainted	**verstehen**	to understand
hören	to hear		with		

VERBS WITH DATIVE OBJECTS

danken	to thank	**gefallen**	to please	**helfen**	to help
folgen	to follow	**gehören**	to belong to		

Ich helfe meinem Vater.   I help my father.
Ich danke dir.   I thank you.

The verb **gehören** may express either ownership (with dative) or membership (with **zu** plus dative).

Das Haus gehört mir.	The house belongs to me.
Ernst gehört zu uns.	Ernst belongs to our group.

In contrast to German, English must use *to* with both meanings.

The verb **gefallen** (*to please, be pleasing to*) is often used as the equivalent of English *to like*. But the subject of *like* appears in German as a personal dative, and the object of *like* becomes the subject of **gefallen**.

I like your novel very much, Mr. Ingelheim.
= Your novel pleases me very much, Mr. Ingelheim.
  Ihr Roman gefällt mir sehr gut, Herr Ingelheim.

German also uses the personal dative in the construction **es geht ... gut** to express English phrases like *How are you?* and *I am fine.*

Wie geht es Ihnen, Herr Weber?	How are you, Mr. Weber?
Danke, es geht mir gut.	Thanks, I am fine.

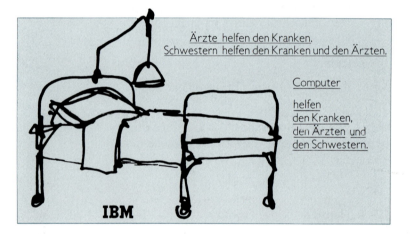

Ärzte helfen den Kranken.
Schwestern helfen den Kranken und den Ärzten.

Computer

helfen
den Kranken,
den Ärzten und
den Schwestern.

IBM

VERBS WITH BOTH ACCUSATIVE AND DATIVE OBJECTS

anbieten	to offer	**leihen**	to lend	**schreiben**	to write
bringen	to bring	**schenken**	to give (as a	**versprechen**	to promise
empfehlen	to recommend		present)	**wünschen**	to wish
geben	to give	**schicken**	to send	**zeigen**	to show
kaufen	to buy				

1. **Glauben** sometimes takes only a dative object and sometimes only an accusative object.

Ich glaube dir.	I believe you.
Das glaube ich nicht.	I don't believe that.

The dative object represents the person and the accusative object represents the facts.

Unlike English, German can combine these two sentences into one.

Das glaube ich dir nicht.	I don't believe what you say.

2. **Antworten** and **sagen** can also be used with two objects.

Was antwortest du ihm?	What are you answering him?
Was sagst du ihm?	What are you saying to him?

But **fragen** takes two accusatives.

Was fragst du ihn?	What are you asking him?

3. With some of these verbs, the dative object can be left out without changing the meaning of the verb. But it is normally not possible to leave out the accusative object and retain the dative object.

Er kauft seinem Sohn einen Wagen.	He buys his son a car.
Er kauft einen Wagen.	He buys a car.

But not:

[Er kauft seinem Sohn.]	[He buys his son.]

However, with the verb **schreiben**, either the dative or accusative object can be omitted.

Ich schreibe ihr einen Brief.	I write her a letter.
Ich schreibe einen Brief.	I write a letter.
Ich schreibe ihr.	I write her.

4. Depending on the speaker's perspective, **bringen** can mean both *to bring* and *to take* as in *to take something to somebody* and *to take somebody home.*

Er bringt mir eine Tasse Kaffee.	He is bringing me a cup of coffee.
Er bringt ihr eine Tasse Kaffee.	He is taking her a cup of coffee.
Er bringt sie nach Hause.	He is taking her home.

50/The Identifying *das* and *es*

A daughter pointing out that a woman in a group photograph is her mother can say:

　　That's my mother.

The same daughter, when asked with whom she is talking on the telephone, will say:

　　It's my mother.

This impersonal *that* or *it* is used in sentences identifying somebody or something for the first time. *She is my mother*, on the other hand, is used when *she* has already been talked about and a further statement is being made about her. German makes the same distinction.

Das (Es) ist meine Mutter.

But:

Wer ist denn das am Telefon? —Das ist Hannelore. Sie ist in Hamburg.

In contrast to English *that* or *it*, German **das** and **es** are followed by plural verb forms when the identifying nouns are in the plural.

Das sind die Kinder.	That's the children.
Es sind die Kinder.	It's the children.

51/Replacement of *er, sie, es* by *der, die, das*

In informal but perfectly acceptable German, nouns and names are frequently replaced by **der, die, das** instead of by **er, sie, es**. When used in this function, **der, die**, and **das** are not articles, but demonstrative pronouns, and the dative plural is **denen**, not **den**. These demonstrative pronouns may be stressed or unstressed.

Wem gehört denn der Wagen?	**Der Wagen gehört mir.**
	Er gehört mir.
	Der gehört mir.
Kennen Sie Frau Dr. Walter?	**Ja, die kenne ich sehr gut.**
	Ja, mit der gehe ich heute abend ins Theater.
Was hörst du denn von Schmidts?	**Oh, denen geht's gut.**

In the inner field, demonstrative pronouns follow personal pronouns.

Natürlich ist es ihr recht.
Natürlich ist ihr das recht.

For the time being, use the personal pronouns or the demonstrative pronouns after a preposition only when they refer to persons.

PRACTICE ONE

A. Express in German using the **es geht . . .** construction.

1. Good morning, Doris. How are you?
2. Good morning, Mr. Meyer. How are you?
3. I'm fine, thank you.
4. And how are your parents, Doris?
5. My grandfather is fine, but my grandmother is not well. She has the flu.

B. Replace the dative or accusative pronouns in italics by the proper form of the nouns in parentheses.

1. Ich will *es* nicht lesen. (Buch)
2. Kennst du *ihn*? (mein Vater)
3. Ich kann *ihn* schon sehen. (Zug)
4. Kennt er *sie*? (deine Freundin)
5. Tante Amalie will mit *ihr* nach Spanien fahren. (unsere Tochter)
6. Die Uhr gehört *ihr*. (meine Frau)
7. Liebt sie *ihn* denn nicht? (ihr Mann)
8. Liebt er *sie* denn nicht? (seine Frau)
9. Ich will nicht für *ihn* arbeiten. (Herr Meyer)
10. Bei *der* möchte ich nicht wohnen. (deine Tante)

C. Restate each sentence according to the example.

> **Das ist mein Wagen. —Der gehört mir.**

1. Das ist sein Auto.
2. Das ist unsere Zeitung.
3. Das sind meine Zeitungen.
4. Das sind eure Bücher.
5. Das ist Ihr Roman.

D. Restate each sentence according to the example.

> **Das Fahrrad gehört meinem Bruder. —Es gehört ihm.**
> **—Es ist sein Fahrrad. —Das ist sein Fahrrad.**

1. Das Haus gehört meinem Vater.
2. Der Wagen gehört meiner Tante.
3. Die Bücher gehören unseren Kindern.

E. Express in German using **gefallen**.

1. I like him.
2. I like her.
3. This car is beautiful. We like it.
4. My parents like the weather here.
5. You don't want this camera? Don't you like it?

F. Complete the following sentences by using first the appropriate form of **er**, then of **sie** (sing.), and then of **sie** (pl.).

1. Ich verstehe ____A____ .
2. Ich besuche ____A____ .
3. Ich danke ____D____ .
4. Ich helfe ____D____ .
5. Ich frage ____A____ .
6. Folgst du ____D____ ?
7. Liebst du ____A____ ?
8. Hörst du ____A____ ?
9. Antwortest du ____D A____ ?
10. Glaubst du ____D____ ?

Culture: Bits and Pieces

As you acquire the German language, you will also acquire a number of small bits of cultural information, much as you will encounter such phenomena when you first arrive in Europe. Most of them are in themselves insignificant, but the totality of culture is made up of a myriad of tiny bits of language and behavior patterns, of objects, and of facts which together create a mosaic unique to that culture.

Some examples: Germans invariably wish each other **Guten Appetit** at the beginning of a meal, and though this, of course, means *"good appetite,"* it is not part of American table manners and hence untranslatable. The same is true of the gesture of raising one's glass (but only with alcoholic beverages) toward one's companions and saying **Auf Ihr Wohl** or **Prosit**; this is a routine habit, not to be confused with an American toast. In this category we also find the German custom of saying **Gesundheit** (*health*) every time someone sneezes. When someone says *hello* to you, you cannot expect to hear **Guten Morgen, Guten Tag**, or **Guten Abend** everywhere in Central Europe. In Southern Germany and Austria, you are more apt to hear **Grüß Gott**, which, though it means *May God greet you*, means no more than *hello* or *hi*. In Switzerland, this turns into **Grüezi**. The farewell **Tschüß** derives from the French *adieu*, and Austrians are apt to use the Latin *Servus* instead of **Auf Wiedersehen** or **Auf Wiederschauen**.

If Germans tell you that they live **im ersten Stock** (*on the first floor*), beware, because they really live on the second floor. **Stock** docs not mean *"floor"* (though all dictionaries will lead you to believe that it does), but implies that something has been put on top of something else, hence it cannot refer to the first "floor."

PATTERNS TWO

5/Prepositions with the Dative

Wo kommst du her[2]? Woher kommst du?

  —Aus dem Kino.
  —Aus der Schweiz.
Wir sind alle hier außer meinem Vater.

Where do you come from? (Where are you coming from?)
  —From the movies.
  —From Switzerland.
We are all here except for my father.

[2]Both **woher**, *from where*, and **wohin**, *where to*, are frequently split into **wo . . . her** and **wo . . . hin**.

Hans ist heute bei seinen Großeltern. | Hans is at his grandparents today.
Bianca wohnt jetzt bei Tante Amalie. | Bianca is living with (at the home of) Aunt Amalie.

Tante Amalie wohnt in Bad Homburg bei Frankfurt. | Aunt Amalie lives in Bad Homburg near Frankfurt.
Frau Meyer ist nicht hier; sie ist beim Arzt. | Mrs. Meyer is not here; she's at the doctor's.
Um ein Uhr sind wir beim Essen. | At one o'clock we are at dinner.
Mit wem gehst du ins Kino? | With whom are you going to the movies?
—Mit Erika Hoffmann. | —With Erika Hoffmann.
—Mit ihr? —Mit der? | —With her? —With her?
Wo fährst du hin²? Wohin fährst du? | Where are you going?
—Nach Österreich. —Nach Lübeck. | —To Austria. —To Lübeck.
Nach diesem Semester geht er nach Frankreich. | After this semester he is going to France.

Wie spät ist es jetzt? —Es ist zehn nach sechs, und ich muß nach Hause. | What time is it now? —It is ten after six, and I have to go home.
Seit wann bist du denn hier? | Since when have you been here?
—Seit einer Stunde. —Seit einem Jahr. | —For an hour. —For a year.
Von wem hast du denn das Buch? | From whom do you have the book?
—Von meinem Bruder. —Von meiner Tante. | —From my brother. —From my aunt.
Ich gehe zu meinem Onkel. | I'm going to my uncle.
Diese Straßenbahn fährt zum Bahnhof. | This streetcar goes to the train station.
Um halb sieben gehen wir zum Essen. | At six-thirty we're going to dinner.
Jeden Sonntagabend ist er zu Hause. | Every Sunday evening he's at home.

6/Adjectives with the Dative

Ist Ihnen das recht, Frau Meyer? | Is that all right with you, Mrs. Meyer?
Natürlich ist mir das recht. | Of course that's all right with me.
Ist es Ihrem Mann recht? | Is it all right with your husband?
Natürlich ist es ihm recht. | Of course it's all right with him.

Das ist neu.
Das ist mir neu.

Die Blumen sind teuer.
Die Blumen sind zu teuer.
Die Blumen sind mir zu teuer.

That's new.
That's news to me.

The flowers are expensive.
The flowers are too expensive.
The flowers are too expensive for me.

7/Word Order in the Inner Field

Ich gebe meiner Freundin eine *Uhr*.
Ich gebe ihr eine *Uhr*.
Ich gebe die Uhr meiner *Freun*din.
Ich gebe sie meiner *Freun*din.
Ich gebe meiner Freundin die *Uhr*.
Ich gebe ihr die *Uhr*.
Ich *gebe* sie ihr.

Was willst du denn deiner Mutter *schicken*?
Ich glaube, ich schicke ihr *Blumen*.
Was willst du denn mit diesen *Blumen* hier machen?
Die schicke ich meiner *Mutter*.
Ich glaube, ich schicke sie meiner *Mut*ter.
Ich glaube, ich schicke diese Blumen meiner *Mut*ter.
Bringst du sie ihr?—Nein, ich *schicke* sie ihr.
Fritz möchte seiner Freundin ein *Buch* schicken.
Was will Fritz seiner Freundin schicken?
Ein *Buch*!
Er will ihr ein *Buch* schicken!
Wem will Fritz das Buch schicken?
Seiner *Freun*din!
Er will das Buch seiner *Freun*din schicken.
Er will es seiner *Freun*din schicken.

Freude schenken...

...per Telefon. Zum Beispiel mit einem
Telegramm: Zur Hochzeit, zum Geburtstag, zum Jubiläum. Zu Weihnachten und
zum Jahreswechsel, und, und, und...
ein Griff zum Telefon, ein Anruf bei der
Telegramm-Annahme, und Ihre guten
Wünsche sind unterwegs.

ANALYSIS TWO

52./Prepositions with the Dative

Unit 4 introduced prepositions that are *always* used with the accusative. This unit introduces prepositions that are *always* used with
the dative. Only nouns referring to persons can be replaced by pronouns after these prepositions. Inanimate objects are replaced by
da-compounds, which will be introduced in Unit 12.

ALWAYS ACCUSATIVE		ALWAYS DATIVE	
durch	through	**aus**	out of
für	for	**außer**	except
gegen	against; at about	**bei**	at; near *in the house of*
ohne	without	**mit**	with
um	around; exactly at	**nach**	after; to
		seit	since
		von	from
		zu	to

1. A third group of prepositions, which includes **in** and **vor**, is used with either dative or accusative. These prepositions will be introduced in Unit 10.

2. Some prepositions are normally contracted with the following article into a single word, as long as the article is not stressed.

von dem	Ich komme *vom* Bahnhof.	I am coming from the station.
zu dem	Ich gehe *zum* Bahnhof.	I am on my way to the station.
zu der	Ich gehe *zur* Universität.	I am on my way to the university.
durch das	Er geht *durchs* Haus.	He is going through the house.
für das	Er hat kein Geld *fürs* Kino.	He has no money for the movies.
bei dem	Meine Frau ist *beim* Arzt.	My wife is at the doctor's.

But:

Bei *dem* Regen kommt er nicht.   He won't come in *this* rain.

3. **Bei** does not normally correspond to English *by*; it expresses the idea of close proximity, and it may also mean *at the house of* or in the process of.

Er wohnt in Potsdam bei Berlin.   He lives in Potsdam near Berlin.
Er wohnt bei seiner Tante.   He is living with his aunt.
Wir sind gerade beim Essen.   We're just (in the process of) eating.

4. **Nach** has two basic meanings; it means

a. *after* with time expressions:

Nach dem Abendessen gehen wir ins Kino.   After supper, we'll go to the movies.
Er kommt nach acht Uhr.   He will arrive after eight o'clock.

b. *to* with a geographical proper name:

Sie geht nach Amerika	She is going to America
nach Deutschland	to Germany
nach Bayern	to Bavaria
nach Berlin	to Berlin

and in the idiom:

Sie geht nach Hause.

5. If no geographical proper name is used, **zu** is normally used to express direction.

Er geht zum Bahnhof.	He goes to the station.
Er geht zur Universität.	He is walking to the university.

Zu must be used with persons:

Er geht zu Karl.	He goes to Karl (to Karl's place).
Ich gehe zu meinem Vater.	I go to my father (to my father's place).

and in the idiom:

Er ist zu Hause.	He is at home.

Note the distinction between **bei** and **zu**:

Wir gehen heute zu Tante Amalie, und wir essen auch bei ihr.	We're going to Aunt Amalie's (house) today, and we'll eat at her house, too.

6. **Seit** means *since* if used with a definite point of time; it means *for* if it is used with a stretch of time. In both cases, it indicates that an action or state continues into the present time. *Note that German must use the present tense where English uses the present perfect.*

Karen ist seit September in Berlin.	Karen has been in Berlin since September.
Gisela ist seit drei Wochen in Wien.	Gisela has been in Vienna for three weeks.

53/Adjectives with the Dative

Certain adjectives like **neu** and **recht**, as well as most adjectives preceded by **zu**, can be used with a personal dative.

Das ist neu.	That's new.
Das ist mir neu.	That's news to me.

Der Wein ist zu teuer.	The wine is too expensive.
Der Wein ist ihm zu teuer.	The wine is too expensive for him.

54/Word Order within the Inner Field

Word order within the inner field is largely governed by *one* principle. The various elements are arranged in the order of *increasing news value.*

Because of this principle of increasing news value, two types of elements are logically position-fixed.

1. Personal pronouns have no news value and are therefore position-fixed *at the beginning of the inner field.*

2. Indefinite nouns, that is, nouns preceded by **ein** or not preceded by any article, always have news value and are therefore position-fixed *at the end of the inner field.*

Note that in the following diagram not all elements need be present, but their absence does not affect the relative position of the other elements.

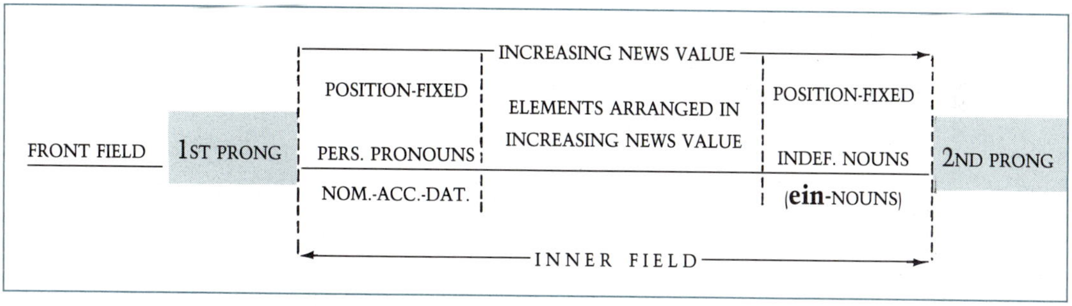

The following rules govern most normal situations.

POSITION OF THE SUBJECT

If the subject does not occupy the front field, it normally follows immediately after the first prong, but it may be preceded by pronoun objects. If a personal pronoun subject appears in the inner field, it *must* appear right after the first prong.

> **Morgen will meine Mutter zu Hause bleiben.**
> **Morgen will sie zu Hause bleiben.**

POSITION OF OBJECTS

Noun objects normally follow the subject. If there are two definite noun objects, that is, nouns preceded by a **der**-word or a possessive adjective, the dative object usually precedes the accusative object, because the "what" generally has more news value than the "to whom." However, the accusative object can precede if the dative object has more news value. The choice depends on the speaker's intention.

> **Er schenkt seinem Sohn den *Volks*wagen zum Geburtstag.**
> **Er schenkt den Volkswagen seinem *Sohn* zum Geburtstag.**

In the first sentence above, the accusative object **Volkswagen** has the most news value (What is he giving his son?). In the second sentence, the dative object **seinem Sohn** has the most news value (To whom is he giving the VW?).

Nouns preceded by definite articles or by possessive adjectives usually refer to something already known or mentioned before. Nouns preceded by indefinite articles (**ein Buch**, plural **Bücher**), on the other hand, usually introduce something not mentioned before — something, therefore, of news value.

Hence, if one of the two objects is an indefinite object (**ein**-noun), it will invariably come at the end of the inner field. The news value of **ein**-objects is so great that they are position-fixed at the end of the inner field and, like second-prong elements, can normally not be moved to the front field.

> **Er gibt seinem Freund einen Ro***man***.**
> **Er gibt den Roman einem *Freund*.**

> **Er will seiner Freundin *Blu*men schenken.**
> **Er will die Blumen einer *Freun*din schenken.**

Pronouns normally do not have news value because the noun they refer to has been mentioned previously; therefore, they are position-fixed at the beginning of the inner field.

Hence, if one of two objects is a pronoun, the pronoun object must precede the noun object. In fact, it may even precede a noun subject.

> **Ich muß es meinem Vater sagen.**
> **Ich kaufe mir morgen eine Uhr.**
> **Heute gehört ihm das Haus.**[3]

If there are two personal pronoun objects, the accusative pronoun object *always* precedes; both pronoun objects are preceded by a pronoun subject.

> **Warum will er es ihm nicht geben?**
> **Leider kann ich sie Ihnen nicht schenken.**

Demonstrative pronouns, however, usually follow personal pronouns.

> **Ist dir das recht?**

---

[3]However, **Heute gehört das Haus *ihm*** is also possible, if there is a strong stress on **ihm**.

TIME PHRASES

The position of time phrases in the inner field is again determined by news value, but they must precede **ein**-objects, which are position-fixed at the end of the inner field, and they must follow personal pronouns, which are position-fixed at the beginning of the inner field.

Ich soll ihm morgen das *Buch* geben.
Ich soll ihm das Buch *mor*gen geben.
Ich soll ihm *mor*gen ein Buch geben.

Several time phrases follow each other in the order of increasing specificity.

Sie will morgen abend um neun nach München fahren.

Tomorrow evening at nine she wants to go to Munich.

PLACE PHRASES

There are two types of place phrases: those that answer the question **wohin?** *whereto, to what place?* and those that answer the question **wo?** *where, at what place?*

All **wohin**-phrases are directives and are therefore position-fixed in the second prong.

Ich fahre morgen mit meinem Mann nach Frankfurt.

The position of **wo**-phrases is determined by news value, unless they are verbal complements as in **zu Hause sein** or **in Berlin wohnen.**

Ich will morgen in Frankfurt eine *Kam*era kaufen.
Ich will die Kamera morgen in *Frank*furt kaufen.

Place phrases normally follow time phrases and phrases answering *how?, with what?, with whom?* (manner-phrases).

Ich will | **morgen** | **mit der Kamera** | **im Zoo** | **Elefanten photografieren.**

(*time*)   (*manner*)   (*place*)

Wohin heute abend?

POSITION OF SENTENCE ADVERBS

Sentence adverbs like **leider, natürlich,** and **übrigens** (see Anal. 31, p. 77) in the inner field follow pronouns and precede elements with news value.

Morgen mußt du leider den Bus nehmen.

SUMMARY: The following variations show some of the possible positions of elements in the inner field. Note particularly how pronouns (no news value) are position-fixed at the beginning of the inner field and **ein**-nouns (always news value) are position-fixed at the end of the inner field. The elements in between are interchangeable; their sequence depends largely on increasing news value. Continue the table below by adding other possible arrangements of the same basic sentence.

FRONT FIELD	1ST PRONG	INNER FIELD			NICHT	2ND PRONG
		POS.-FIXED PRONOUNS	INTERCHANGEABLE ELEMENTS	POS.-FIXED **ein**-NOUNS		
Ich	will		meinem Sohn morgen in Frankfurt	eine Kamera		kaufen.
Ich	will		morgen meinem Sohn in Frankfurt	eine Kamera		kaufen.
Ich	will		morgen in Frankfurt meinem Sohn	eine Kamera		kaufen.
Ich	will		die Kamera meinem Sohn morgen in Frankfurt			kaufen.
Ich	will		meinem Sohn morgen in Frankfurt die Kamera			kaufen.
Ich	will	sie	meinem Sohn morgen in Frankfurt			kaufen.
Meinem Sohn	will	ich	morgen in Frankfurt	eine Kamera		kaufen.
Morgen	will	ich ihm	in Frankfurt	eine Kamera		kaufen.
Ich	will	ihm	dort morgen	eine Kamera		kaufen.
Morgen	will	ich sie ihm	dort			kaufen.
Ich	will		meinem Sohn die Kamera		nicht	kaufen.
Ich	will	sie ihm			nicht	kaufen.

PRACTICE TWO

G. Replace nouns and names by personal pronouns.

1. Sie wohnt bei ihrer Tante.
2. Er will zu seinem Vater.
3. Er hilft seiner Mutter.
4. Sie dankt ihrer Freundin.
5. Das gefällt meinem Onkel nicht.

6. Sie kommt von ihrem Freund Hans.
7. Er arbeitet für seinen Bruder.
8. Sie arbeitet heute ohne ihren Freund.
9. Außer Erika sind wir alle hier.
10. Bei meinen Großeltern bin ich gern.

H. Complete the following sentences by using **bei, nach,** or **zu.** Use contractions where possible.

1. Ich gehe _____ Bahnhof.
2. _____ dem Essen gehen wir schwimmen.

3. Wir gehen _____ Meyers.
4. Sie sind _____ Hans.
5. Wir fahren _____ Europa.

6. Wir fahren _____ Universität.
7. Er wohnt in Grafing _____ München.

8. Wir fahren _____ Wien.
9. Man spricht nicht _____ Essen.
10. Oskar wohnt _____ Schmidts.

I. In the following sentences, the inner field is left empty. Fill the inner field with each of the several series of words by rearranging them in correct word order. Note that in some cases you may have more than one possible arrangement.

1. Ich will _____ schenken.
   (a) es, morgen, ihm
   (b) das Buch, morgen, ihm
   (c) ein Buch, morgen, meinem Vater
   (d) es, morgen, meinem Vater

2. Willst du _____ zum Geburtstag schenken?
   (a) einen Roman, deiner Freundin
   (b) den Roman, deiner Freundin
   (c) deiner Freundin, ihn
   (d) einen Roman, ihr
   (e) ihn, ihr

3. Wollen Sie _____ schicken?
   (a) Ihrem Vater, das Buch
   (b) ein Buch, ihm (Ihrem Vater)
   (c) es, ihm
   (d) Ihrem Vater, es
   (e) das Buch, ihm

4. Ich will _____ mitbringen.
   (a) ein Buch, meiner Freundin, aus Berlin
   (b) aus Berlin, ein Buch, ihr
   (c) das Buch, ihr, aus Berlin
   (d) ihr, es, aus Berlin

5. Darf ich _____ ins Haus schicken, Herr Meyer?
   (a) morgen, Ihnen, den Wein
   (b) die Blumen, morgen, Ihrer Frau
   (c) sie (die Blumen), ihr (Ihrer Frau), morgen
   (d) sie (die Blumen), morgen, Ihrer Frau
   (e) Blumen, Ihrer Frau, morgen
   (f) Blumen, ihr, morgen
   (g) die Blumen, ihr, morgen

J. Express in German. Remember that the English present perfect in these sentences is expressed by the present tense plus the preposition **seit** in German.

1. Achim has been in Stuttgart since Wednesday. *Achim ist in St. seit der Mittwoch*
2. Bettina has been in Stuttgart for two weeks.
3. They have been living in Tübingen for three years. *Sie wohnen seit drei Jahren in Tübingen*
4. He has been working since eight o'clock.
5. They have been married for seven months.
6. Since Friday the weather has been bad.

Studying Abroad

Many colleges and universities have study abroad programs, but you can also attend a European university on your own. To enroll, you need to be at least a junior, and normally you must have completed two years of college German. All universities have a foreign student office (**Auslandsamt**), which handles inquiries and applications. Since all universities are state universities, tuition is minimal compared to U.S. institutions. Many universities have special summer courses for foreign students, which usually include language instruction. The University of Vienna, for example, has a summer program at the Wolfgangsee not far from Salzburg. German language courses are also offered at the many branches of the Goethe Institute, which is headquartered in Munich. Advanced undergraduates and graduate students can apply for fellowships through the German Academic Exchange Service (DAAD) or the Fulbright Program. Study in the German Democratic Republic can be arranged through the Liga für Völkerfreundschaft (*League for Friendship among Peoples*).

CONVERSATIONS

I

The student and the man in the restaurant (see Unit 4, p. 117) continue to talk while waiting for their meals:

STUDENT: Übrigens, ich heiße Ray, John Ray.   By the way, my name is Ray, John Ray.

MANN:	Jürgens. (Der Mann gibt dem Studenten die Hand.) Sie sind Ausländer, nicht wahr? Amerikaner?	Jürgens. (They shake hands.) You are a foreigner, aren't you? American?
STUDENT:	Ja, aber wie wissen Sie, . . . ?	Yes, but how do you know . . . ?
MANN:	Man hört es an Ihrem Akzent.	One can tell by your accent.
STUDENT:	Oh? —Aber Sie haben recht. Ich bin noch nicht lange in Deutschland.	Oh? But you are right. I haven't been in Germany very long.
MANN:	Sie sprechen aber sehr gut Deutsch.	But you speak German very well.

MANN:	Und was machen Sie in Deutschland, Herr Ray?	And what are you doing in Germany, Mr. Ray?
STUDENT:	Ich studiere hier an der Universität. Ich habe ein Stipendium für ein Jahr, vom DAAD.	I am studying at the university here. I have a fellowship for a year, from the DAAD.
MANN:	DAAD?	DAAD?
STUDENT:	Der Deutsche Akademische Austauschdienst. —Ich möchte natürlich auch reisen und Deutschland wirklich gut kennenlernen, aber nicht als Tourist.	The German Academic Exchange Service. —But I'd like to travel, too, of course, and really get to know Germany well, but not as a tourist.
MANN:	Sie müssen aber auch mal nach Österreich fahren, oder in die Schweiz.	Then you should go to Austria, too, some time, or to Switzerland.
STUDENT:	Das tue ich bestimmt. Ich habe eine Freundin in Wien. Sie studiert dort.	I'll certainly do that. I have a girlfriend in Vienna. She goes to the university there.

STUDENT:	Und Sie, Herr Jürgens, was sind Sie von Beruf?	And you, Mr. Jürgens, what is your profession?
MANN:	Ich bin Flugkapitän bei der Lufthansa.	I'm a pilot with Lufthansa.
STUDENT:	Wirklich? Das muß sehr interessant sein.	Really? That must be very interesting.

Flugkapitän Jürgens und Crew

MANN:	Ja, interessant ist es, aber auch anstrengend.	Yes, it's interesting all right, but also strenuous.
STUDENT:	Fliegen Sie auch manchmal nach Amerika?	Do you fly to America sometimes?
MANN:	Nein, hauptsächlich fliege ich in Europa, —Rom, Athen, Wien, Budapest, Belgrad.	No, I mainly fly in Europe, —Rome, Athens, Vienna, Budapest, Belgrade.
OBER:	So, die Herren, hier ist erst mal die Suppe. Vorsicht, sehr heiß. Und das Bier. Ich wünsche Ihnen guten Appetit.	There, gentlemen, here's your soup for a starter. Careful, very hot. And the beer. I wish you good appetite.
MANN:	(hebt sein Glas) Auf Ihr Wohl, Herr Ray, und ein gutes Studienjahr. (Sie trinken.) Also, guten Appetit.	(raises his glass) Here's to you, Mr. Ray, and to a good year of studies. (They drink.) Now then, good appetite.
STUDENT:	Danke, ebenfalls. —Die Suppe ist wirklich heiß.	Thanks, same to you. —This soup is really hot.

II

Review the two conversations between John Ray and Captain Jürgens (p. 148 and p. 149). Then let your teacher again play the role of the native German and initiate a similar conversation, but don't be surprised if your teacher turns out to be a social worker, computer expert, or kindergarten teacher. Use the following phrases in your part of the conversation.

Entschuldigung.
Ist der Platz noch frei?
Bitte die Speisekarte.
Was empfehlen Sie?
Menü eins oder zwei?
Dauert es lange?
Übrigens, ich heiße . . .
Ich bin Amerikaner.

Bitte sprechen Sie etwas langsamer.
Seit wann sind Sie . . .?
Was sind Sie von Beruf?
Ah, hier kommt die Suppe.

Fragen an Sie persönlich

1. Photografieren Sie gern?
    Was für eine Kamera (Filmkamera) haben Sie?
    Was photographieren Sie?
       Menschen, Landschaften, Sport, Blumen?

Was für What kind of

2. Machen Sie oft Reisen?
   (Reisen Sie oft, viel, selten, nie, gern?)
   Mit dem Flugzeug? dem Wagen?
3. Lesen Sie gern? Was lesen Sie am liebsten?
4. Kochen Sie gern? Was kochen Sie am liebsten?
5. Gehen Sie zum Essen oft aus? Wohin gehen Sie?

am liebsten like to . . . most

READING

Noch einmal Mitteleuropa

Mitteleuropa, wie wir es definieren, ist das Gebiet, in dem man Deutsch spricht, eine kulturell homogene Einheit mit gemeinsamer Tradition, mit gemeinsamen Sitten, sogar mit gemeinsamer Denkweise. Und doch ist dieses Mitteleuropa ein sehr komplexes Gebilde; es ist trotz seiner Homogenität auch heterogen, gegliedert in eine Reihe von Subkulturen, die man nur sehr schwierig begrenzen und definieren kann, und die zwischen Norden und Süden, zwischen Osten und Westen große Unterschiede aufweisen.

Diese Subkulturen sind nicht überall identisch mit den politischen Grenzen der Staaten Mitteleuropas, obwohl jeder dieser Staaten eine klare *politische* Identität hat. Ein Österreicher oder ein Schweizer ist *kein* Deutscher, auch wenn er Deutsch spricht, und die BRD und die DDR sind juristisch und politisch zwei separate Staaten.

Dennoch sind zum Beispiel die Menschen in Schleswig-Holstein (im Norden der Bundesrepublik) den Menschen in Mecklenburg (im Norden der DDR) ähnlicher als den Bundesbürgern in Baden-Württemberg (im Süden der BRD). Die Württemberger dagegen haben vieles gemeinsam mit den Schweizern, mit den Liechtensteinern und mit den Österreichern im österreichischen Bundesland

Central Europe Once Again

Central Europe, as we define it, is the area in which German is spoken, a culturally homogeneous unity with a common tradition, common customs, and even a common way of thinking. And yet this Central Europe is a very complex structure; in spite of its homogeneity it is heterogeneous, too, divided into a series of subcultures which are hard to delineate and to define, and which show great differences between north and south, east and west.

These subcultures are not everywhere identical with the political borders of the countries of Central Europe, although each of these countries has a clear *political* identity. An Austrian or a Swiss is *not* a German, even though he speaks German; and the FRG and the GDR are legally and politically two separate states.

Nevertheless, for example, the people in Schleswig-Holstein (in the north of the Federal Republic) are much more similar to the people in Mecklenburg (in the north of the GDR) than to the federal citizens in Baden-Württemberg (in the south of the FRG). The Württemberg people, on the other hand, have much in common with the Swiss, the Liechtensteiners, and the Austrians in the

Vorarlberg. Kompliziert? —Gewiß; aber so sieht die Wirklichkeit der „einheitlichen" Kultur Mitteleuropas aus.

Für Amerikaner ist es immer überraschend, wie klein Europa ist im Vergleich zu den Vereinigten Staaten, wie kurz die Entfernungen von Land zu Land. Wenn man in Europa so weit fliegen will wie von Los Angeles nach New York, muß man zum Beispiel von Gibraltar nach Leningrad fliegen, oder von Oslo nach Kairo, oder von London nach Teheran. Die Bundesrepublik, der größte Staat Mitteleuropas, ist genau so groß wie Oregon, und das Fürstentum Liechtenstein ist nicht ganz so groß wie der District of Columbia. Der Rhein ist 1320 km lang, die Ruhr—so wichtig für die deutsche Industrie—nur 235 km. Der Missouri-Mississippi ist dagegen ein Gigant von 6200 km.

Nicht viele Amerikaner wissen, wie weit im Norden Mitteleuropa liegt. Die Grenze zwischen den USA und Kanada ist 49° N (neunundvierzig Grad Nord), das ist genau die Breite von Stuttgart. New York liegt auf der Breite von Neapel, und Los Angeles ist so weit südlich wie Nordafrika. Die deutschdänische Grenze ist 55° N, das ist Labrador, Hudson Bay und fast so weit nördlich wie Juneau in Alaska. Dennoch ist Deutschland relativ warm, weil der Golfstrom die Westküste Europas erwärmt.

Austrian federal state of Vorarlberg. Complicated? —Certainly; but that's what the reality of the new "unified" culture of Central Europe looks like.

For Americans it is always surprising how small Europe is in comparison to the United States, how short the distances from country to country. If in Europe you want to fly as far as from Los Angeles to New York, you have to fly, for example, from Gibraltar to Leningrad, or from Oslo to Cairo, or from London to Teheran. The Federal Republic, the largest country of Central Europe, is exactly the size of Oregon, and the principality of Liechtenstein is not quite as large as the District of Columbia. The Rhine is 1,320 km long, the Ruhr—so important for German industry—only 235 km. The Missouri-Mississippi, on the other hand, is a giant of 6,200 km.

Not many Americans know how far north Central Europe is located. The border between the U.S. and Canada is the 49th parallel; that is exactly the latitude of Stuttgart. New York lies on the latitude of Naples, and Los Angeles is as far south as North Africa. The German-Danish border is 55° N, that is Labrador, Hudson Bay, and almost as far north as Juneau, Alaska. Nevertheless, Germany is relatively warm, because the Gulf Stream warms the west coast of Europe.

EINIGE STATISTISCHE DATEN ZUM VERGLEICH
SOME STATISTICAL DATA FOR COMPARISON

1 km (**der Kilometer,-**)　　= 0,621 mi. (**die Meile,-n**)
1 mi.　　　　　　　　　　= 1,609 km

1 km² (**der Quadratkilometer**) = 0,386 sq.mi. (**die Quadratmeile**)
1 sq.mi.　　　　　　　　 = 2,590 km²

FLÜSSE　　　　　　　　　　　　　　　　　　　　**der Fluß,⁺e** river

Ruhr	235 km	146 mi.
Rhein	1320 km	820 mi.
Donau	2850 km	1767 mi.
Missouri-Mississippi	6207 km	3860 mi.

FLÄCHEN　　　　　　　　　　　　　　　　　　　**die Fläche,-n** area

Bodensee	539 km²	208 sq.mi.
New York City	932 km²	360 sq.mi.
Los Angeles	1178 km²	455 sq.mi.
Lake Michigan	58016 km²	22400 sq.mi.

BRD	248 461 km²	95 931 sq.mi.	Oregon	96 315 sq.mi.
DDR	107 860 km²	41 645 sq.mi.	Ohio	41 000 sq.mi.
Österreich	83 848 km²	32 374 sq.mi.	Maine	31 040 sq.mi.
Schweiz	41 294 km²	15 944 sq.mi.	Mass. + N.H.	16 884 sq.mi.
Liechtenstein	157 km²	61 sq.mi.	D.C.	69 sq.mi.

Mitteleuropa	481 620 km²	185 955 sq.mi.	California	156 740 sq.mi.
			Texas	263 513 sq.mi.
			Alaska	571 065 sq.mi.
			USA	3,615 210 sq.mi.

REVIEW EXERCISES

K. Give negative answers to the following questions.

1. Bist du schon verheiratet?
2. Wohnt ihr noch in Freiburg?
3. Mußt du nach Augsburg fahren?
4. Hast du noch Geld?
5. Will Erika Ärztin werden?

6. Ist das Wetter heute schlecht?
7. Geht Fritz schon in die Schule?
8. Schläft deine Schwester noch?
9. Geht ihr heute ins Museum?
10. Haben Schmidts schon Kinder?

L. Express in German.

1. That is my house.
2. It (the house) belongs to me.
3. It (the house) belongs to you?
4. Yes, to me.
5. This house belongs to Hans.

6. It (the house) belongs to him.
7. It (the house) belongs to her.
8. The car belongs to her.
9. It (the car) belongs to her.
10. It is her car.

M. Form sentences from the elements given; supply additional necessary elements.

1. Hans / sein Vater / helfen.
2. Herr Müller / sein Sohn / Kamera / kaufen / wollen.
3. Erika / ein Roman / von Schmidt-Ingelheim / lesen.
4. Ich / sie (2 forms) / nicht glauben.
5. Buch / ich / nicht gehören // es / Freundin / gehören.
6. Wer / dieses Haus / gehören?
7. Wie / du / gehen? // Danke // gut / gehen.
8. Ich / Uhr / nicht kaufen // zu teuer.
9. Kurt / aus Stadt / kommen / und / Universität / gehen.
10. Wir / durch Stadt / fahren / müssen.

N. Construct sentences as indicated.

1. Mr. Meyer is not well today.
   (a) He is well. (Start with **Es**; use **gehen.**)
   (b) Start with *Mr. Meyer* (Watch dative; move **es.**)
   (c) add: *not*
   (d) add: *today*
2. The salesman always seems to recommend novels to his customers.
   (a) The salesman recommends novels.
   (b) add: *seems to*
   (c) add: *to his customers* (word order!)
   (d) insert *always* between objects
3. Mrs. Meyer would like to give (as a present) her husband 12 bottles of wine for his birthday.
   (a) *to give as a present* (not: **geben**)
   (b) Mrs. Meyer gives her husband wine.

(c) add: *12 bottles (of)*

(d) add: *would like to*

(e) add: *for his birthday* (second prong, first box)

(f) add: *This year* (Move subject!)

O. Express in German.

1. How are you? (3 sentences)
2. I give her the book for Christmas.
3. He gives it (the novel) to his father.
4. We give it (the newspaper) to them.
5. He is coming from the movies.
6. Inge is with us.
7. I'm going to the railroad station. *zum Bahnhof*
8. Drive around the corner and then always straight ahead.
9. I want to buy myself a car.

10. I've been working for him for seventeen years.
11. You have to go without me.
12. That's news to me.
13. Does this book belong to you, Hans?
14. Can you help him?
15. Please believe me. *Bitte glauben Sie mir*
16. Erika wants a camera for Christmas. (Use **wünschen** plus a reflexive.)
17. How do you like my motorcycle?
18. I'm tired; I've been driving for two days.

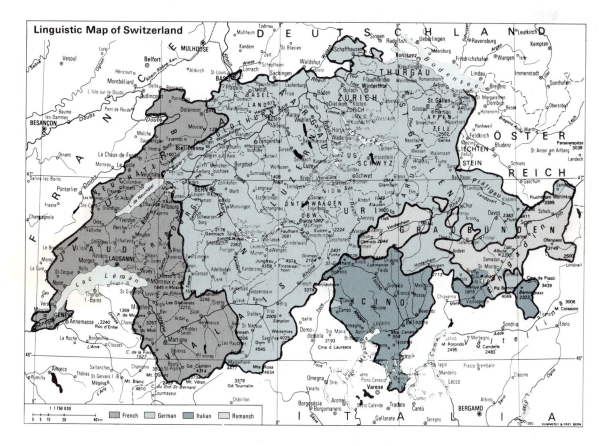

Linguistic Map of Switzerland

French   German   Italian   Romansh

VOCABULARY

ähnlich	similar	die Hauptstadt, ⸚e	capital (city)
als	as	heiraten	to marry; to get married
am liebsten (adv.)	(would like) most of all	helfen (hilfst, hilft) (dat.)	to give help to, to help
amerikanisch	American	die Hilfe	help, aid
der Apparat', -e	apparatus, instrument	die Industrie', die Industri'en	industry
der Photoapparat	camera	die Kamera, -s	camera
der Appetit' (no pl.)	appetite	klar	clear
Guten Appetit	(said at beginning of meal)	klein	small
		kochen	to cook
außer (dat.)	besides, except for	die Küche, -n	kitchen; cuisine
(das) Bayern	Bavaria	der Kunde, -n (n-noun)	customer (m.)
der Beruf, -e	job, profession	die Kundin, -nen	customer (f.)
Was sind Sie von Beruf?	What's your profession?	kurz	short
die Blume, -n	flower	lieben	to love
der Bundesbürger, -	citizen of Federal Republic	manchmal	sometimes
die Bundesbürgerin, -nen		das Menü, -s	complete dinner (i.e., not à la carte)
danken (dat.)	to thank	mit (dat.)	with
ebenfalls	likewise, too	mit•nehmen	to take along
der Erfolg, -e	success	der Monat, -e	month
etwa	about; by any chance	na	well
der Fluß, pl. die Flüsse	river	nie	never
folgen (dat.)	to follow	Nord	North
gar nicht	not at all	der Norden	north
gar kein	no . . . at all	nördlich	northern
gar nichts	nothing at all	Ost	East
gefallen (gefällst, gefällt) (dat.)	to be pleasing to	der Osten	east
		östlich	eastern
es gefällt mir	I like it	photographie'ren also: fotografieren	to photograph
gehören (dat.)	to belong to (possession)	Prost (Prosit)	cheers, here's to you
gehören zu (dat.)	to belong to, be a member of, be part of	recht-	right
		recht•haben	to be right
		reisen	to travel
genau	exact(ly)	die Reise, -n	trip
gerade	straight; just	schenken	to give (as a present)
die Gesundheit	health	schicken	to send
Gesundheit!	(said when someone sneezes)	die Schule, -n	school
		seit (dat.)	since
gewiß	certain(ly)	selten	rare(ly)
das Glück	luck, fortune	sofort	right away, immediately
groß	large, big		
Grüß Gott!	(lit. Greet God; Austrian greeting)	der Stock, pl. die Stockwerke	floor (of a building)
die Hand, ⸚e	hand		

im ersten Stock	on the second floor	**die Vorsicht** (*no pl.*)	caution
suchen	to look for, seek, search	**Vorsicht!**	Careful! Watch out!
		(die) Weihnachten (*pl.*)	Christmas
Süd	South		
der Süden	south	**West**	West
südlich	southern	**der Westen**	west
das Telefon, -e	telephone	**westlich**	western
vereinigen	to unify	**wichtig**	important
die Vereinigten Staaten	the United States	**das Wohl**	well-being, good health
der Verkäufer, -	salesman	**zum Wohl** *or* **auf Ihr Wohl**	to your health
die Verkäuferin, -nen	saleswoman	**wünschen**	to wish
der Volkswagen, - (der VW, die VWs)	Volkswagen (*lit.* people's car)	**zeigen**	to show
von (*dat.*)	from	**zurück•bringen**	to bring back, take back

Unit 6

The Perfect Tense—The Past of *sein, haben,* and the Modals—Time Phrases

Holidays (*Feiertage*)

Most official American holidays are secular in nature, for example, Presidents' Day, Memorial Day, the Fourth of July, and Labor Day. Christmas, Hanukkah, Easter, and Passover are religious holidays. In Central Europe, most holidays are religious holidays and still follow the Christian church calendar. Good Friday (**Karfreitag**) is an official holiday, and the celebration of Easter (**Ostern**) extends over two days (**Ostersonntag** and **Ostermontag**). Ascension Day (**Christi Himmelfahrt**) precedes Pentecost (**Pfingsten**), another official two-day holiday. All schools get at least a week's break at Easter and Pentecost.

The celebration of Christmas (**Weihnachten**) begins with the first Sunday in Advent. Santa Claus does not come at Christmas; his equivalent, Sankt Nikolaus, comes on December 6, St. Nicholas Day, and fills all good children's shoes with small presents. Christmas is also celebrated for two days (**erster und zweiter Weihnachtstag**). Among the other legal religious holidays are Epiphany (**Heilige Dreikönige**), Corpus Christi (**Fronleichnam**), All Saints' or All Hallows' Day (**Allerheiligen**), but no Halloween with witches and goblins. Some of these are celebrated only in predominantly Catholic areas, such as the Rhineland, Bavaria, and Austria. There is no Thanksgiving holiday with turkey and all the trimmings. The equivalent of Labor Day is celebrated on the first of May, an ancient holiday to welcome the arrival of spring, but now used as Workers' Day (**Tag der Arbeit**), especially in socialist countries. If you live in an area where all these holidays are celebrated, you will have as much as two weeks more vacation.

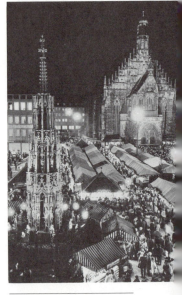

Weihnachtsmarkt in Nürnberg

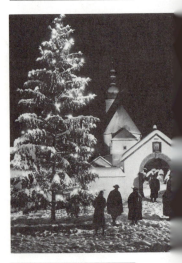

Ramsau (Oberbayern)

A Corpus Christi Sampler (1852)

PATTERNS ONE

1/Events in the Past: The Perfect Tense

The sentences in this section, although they are a continuous text of sorts, are not a "story"; they are written as if the young woman, Karin, were talking to a friend about a trip from Vienna to Burgbach, where she has just visited the Enderle family. Read and study the following sentences; note that the English translations must use the past tense and cannot use the present perfect.

Ich habe Frau Enderle letztes Jahr in Stuttgart kennengelernt.	I met Mrs. Enderle in Stuttgart last year.
Vor drei Wochen habe ich ihr von Wien aus[1] einen Brief geschrieben.	Three weeks ago I wrote her a letter from Vienna.
Sie hat mich zu einem Besuch in Burgbach eingeladen.	She invited me to visit her in Burgbach.
Gestern habe ich sie und ihre Familie besucht.	Yesterday I visited her and her family.
Ich habe den Nachtzug von Wien nach Stuttgart genommen.	I took the night train from Vienna to Stuttgart.
Dann bin ich gestern morgen mit dem Personenzug nach Burgbach gefahren.	Then I took a local train to Burgbach yesterday morning.
Frau Enderle hat mich mit dem Wagen am Bahnhof[2] abgeholt.	Mrs. Enderle picked me up at the station with her car.
Auf dem Weg zu ihrem Haus haben wir eingekauft.	On the way to her house we went shopping.
Das Haus haben Enderles erst vor vier Jahren gebaut.	The Enderles built the house only four years ago.
Vorher haben sie zwölf Jahre lang bei den Eltern von Herrn Enderle gewohnt.	Before that they lived with Mr. Enderle's parents for twelve years.
Frau Enderle hat mir das Haus gezeigt, und ich habe ihren Garten bewundert.	Mrs. Enderle showed me the house, and I admired her garden.
Dann habe ich ihr in der Küche geholfen.	Then I helped her in the kitchen.
Um ein Uhr sind die Kinder aus der Schule gekommen, und wir haben zu Mittag gegessen.	At one o'clock the children came home from school, and we ate dinner.
Nach dem Mittagessen haben wir lange im Wohnzimmer gesessen und haben geplaudert.	After dinner we sat in the living room for a long time and talked.
Die Kinder sind schwimmen gegangen.	The children went swimming.
Um halb fünf haben wir eine Tasse Kaffee getrunken und ein Stück Kuchen gegessen.	At 4:30 we had a cup of coffee and a piece of cake.

[1]Note that **von Wien aus** is one syntactical unit, meaning *from Vienna*.

[2]The prepositions **an, auf, in, über,** and **vor** can be used with either the dative or accusative. Do not worry about them until you get to Unit 10 (Anal. 90, p. 291).

Herr Enderle ist erst um Viertel nach sechs nach Hause gekommen, und um dreiviertel sieben haben wir zu Abend gegessen.	Mr. Enderle did not get home until 6:15, and at 6:45 we ate supper.
Nach dem Abendessen sind wir spazierengegangen.	After supper we went for a walk.
Auf einem Hügel über dem Dorf haben wir lange auf einer Bank gesessen, und Herr und Frau Enderle haben mir viel über das Leben in Burgbach erzählt.	On a hill above the village we sat on a bench for a long time, and Mr. and Mrs. Enderle told me a lot about life in Burgbach.

2/The Perfect Tense: Position of the Participle

FRONT FIELD	1ST PRONG	INNER FIELD	NICHT	2ND PRONG	
				1ST BOX	2ND BOX

A. Auxiliary: haben

WEAK VERBS

FRONT FIELD	1ST PRONG	INNER FIELD	NICHT	1ST BOX	2ND BOX
Wir	haben	ihn leider	nicht		gekannt.
Warum	hast	du ihn denn	nicht		besucht.
Wo	hast	du ihn		kennen•	gelernt?

STRONG VERBS

FRONT FIELD	1ST PRONG	INNER FIELD	NICHT	1ST BOX	2ND BOX
Wir	haben	sie leider	nicht		gesehen.
Wir	haben	schon		zu Mittag	gegessen.
	Haben	Sie mich	nicht		verstanden?

MODALS

FRONT FIELD	1ST PRONG	INNER FIELD	NICHT	1ST BOX	2ND BOX
Ich	habe	gestern			arbeiten müssen.
Ich	habe	gestern	nicht		zu arbeiten brauchen.
Er	hat	gestern	nicht	zu Hause	bleiben wollen.
Ich	habe	leider	nicht	mit•	gehen können.
Ich	habe	leider	nicht		gekonnt.

B. Auxiliary: sein

WEAK VERBS

FRONT FIELD	1ST PRONG	INNER FIELD	NICHT	1ST BOX	2ND BOX
Ich	bin	schnell		nach Hause	gerannt.
Er	ist	mir			gefolgt.
Wir	sind	lange		durch die Stadt	gewandert.

STRONG VERBS

	Ist	**Hans schon**				**gekommen?**
Der Zug	**ist**	**gerade**			**an•**	**gekommen.**
Warum	**seid**	**ihr denn**	**nicht**	**zu Hause**		**geblieben?**
Inge	**ist**	**schon oft**		**hier**		**gewesen.**
Er	**ist**	**erst um elf**			**auf•**	**gestanden.**

ANALYSIS ONE

55/The Perfect Tense: Events in the Past

When reading the following three sentences, you will discover that all verb forms look like the English present perfect (**ich habe besucht**, *I have visited*); the translations show, however, that these forms correspond to the English past tense.

Ich habe Frau Enderle letztes Jahr in Stutt-gart kennengelernt.	I met Mrs. Enderle in Stuttgart last year.
Gestern habe ich sie und ihre Familie be-sucht.	Yesterday I visited her and her family.
Ich bin gestern morgen mit dem Zug nach Burgbach gefahren.	I took the train to Burgbach yesterday morning.

German does have a past tense, but it is not always used in the same way as the English past tense. It will be introduced in Unit 7.

56/The Use of *haben* and *sein* as Auxiliaries

haben

Verbs that take an accusative object are called transitive verbs and take **haben** as an auxiliary.

Karin hat den Brief geschrieben.	Karin wrote the letter.

All other verbs are called intransitive. Most intransitive verbs also take **haben** as an auxiliary.

Karin hat gearbeitet.	Karin worked.

sein

However, a small number of very common intransitive verbs that indicate *a change in the position or the condition of the grammatical subject,* as well as the verbs **sein** and **bleiben,** *always* take **sein** as an auxiliary.

Karin ist gekommen.	Karin came.
Er ist Arzt geworden.	He became a doctor.

So far the following verbs using **sein** as an auxiliary have been introduced:

ankommen	to arrive	**folgen**	to follow
aufstehen	to get up	**gehen**	to go
bleiben	to remain	**kommen**	to come
einschlafen	to fall asleep	**laufen**	to run
fahren	to drive	**schwimmen**	to swim
fliegen	to fly	**sein**	to be
		werden	to become

57/The German Perfect: Formation of the Participle

The English present perfect (*I have seen*) consists of an auxiliary verb plus a participle; the German perfect likewise consists of an auxiliary plus a participle. German participles are formed in one of two ways which are traditionally referred to as *weak* and *strong.*

WEAK VERBS

Weak verbs form their participles by adding the prefix **ge-,** unless the verb already has a prefix (see Note 2 below), and by adding **-t** to the *unchanged* stem. Stems ending in **-t, -d,** or **-gn** insert **-e-** before the **-t.** The **ge-** prefix is never stressed.

INFINITIVE	STEM	AUX.	+	PARTICIPLE
machen	**mach-**	**hat**		**gemacht**
folgen	**folg-**	**ist**		**gefolgt**
arbeiten	**arbeit-**	**hat**		**gearbeitet**
baden	**bad-**	**hat**		**gebadet**
regnen	**regn-**	**hat**		**geregnet**
besuchen	**besuch-**	**hat**		**besucht**

IRREGULAR WEAK VERBS

A few weak verbs use a different stem in the participle, for example:

bringen — gebracht	**rennen — gerannt**
denken — gedacht	**wissen — gewußt**
kennen — gekannt	

Note that the participles of English *to bring* and *to think* are irregular in the same fashion: *brought, thought.*

Strong verbs form their participles by adding the prefix **ge-**, unless the verb already has a prefix (see Note 2 below), and by adding **-en** to the *changed* stem or even a *different* stem.

fahren	**fahr-**	ist	**gefahren**
finden	**find-**	hat	**gefunden**
gehen	**geh-**	ist	**gegangen**

NOTE:

1. Since the type of change in these strong and irregular weak verbs is as unpredictable as English *sing, sung* and *bring, brought* (**singen, gesungen** and **bringen, gebracht**), you will have to memorize their participles and auxiliaries (see list of strong and irregular verbs introduced in Units 1–6 at the end of this unit).

2. A participle cannot have more than one unstressed prefix. Therefore, all verbs formed with the unstressed prefixes **be-, emp-, ent-, er-, ge-, ver-,** and **zer-** form their participles without the **ge-** prefix. (Thus both **gehören** and **hören** have the participle **gehört**.) Weak verbs ending in **-ieren**, which always begin with at least one unstressed syllable, also form their participles without **ge-**.

beginnen — **begonnen**	**studieren**	— **studiert**
erzählen — **erzählt**	**telefonieren** — **telefoniert**

3. All verbs, weak or strong, with stressed complements like **ein-** or **auf-**, place the complement in front of the participle and form one word with it.

einkaufen — **ich kaufe ein** — **ich habe eingekauft**
aufstehen — **ich stehe auf** — **ich bin aufgestanden**

4. German has no progressive forms in any tense. Just as English *I write* and *I am writing* have only one equivalent in German, **ich schreibe**, so English *I have written* and *I have been writing* correspond formally to German **ich habe geschrieben**. But remember that normally the English equivalent of **ich habe geschrieben** is *I wrote*.

If the modals are used *without* a dependent infinitive, their participles are "normal"; that is, **gemußt, gewollt, gekonnt, gesollt, gedurft.**

However, these participles do not take an umlaut. When the modal auxiliaries and **brauchen** are used *with* a dependent infinitive, their participles are identical with their infinitives, that is, **müssen, wollen, können, sollen, dürfen,** and **brauchen.** These forms are often referred to as "double infinitives."

Er	hat	es	nicht	gewollt.
Er	hat	gestern		arbeiten müssen.
Er	hat	gestern	nicht	zu arbeiten brauchen.

58/Position of the Participle

Remember that dependent infinitives, like **kommen** in **er kann kommen,** have a reserved "slot": the second box of the second prong (see Anal. 44, p. 113). Participles are also placed in that box (**er ist gekommen**). Both infinitives and participles are preceded by verbal complements (if any) in the first box and by **nicht**. If a modal is used in the perfect tense, its participle (which looks like a modal infinitive) as well as the dependent infinitive appear in the second box, with the dependent infinitive preceding the modal participle (**er hat kommen können**).

FRONT FIELD	1ST PRONG	INNER FIELD	NICHT	2ND PRONG	
				1ST BOX	2ND BOX
Er	kommt	heute.			
Er	kann	heute			kommen.
Er	ist	gestern			gekommen.
Er	hat	gestern			kommen können.
Ich	fahre	morgen		nach Köln.	
Ich	muß	morgen		nach Köln	fahren.
Ich	bin	gestern	nicht	nach Köln	gefahren.
Ich	habe	gestern	nicht	nach Köln	fahren können.
Ich	habe	gestern	nicht	nach Köln	zu fahren brauchen.

59/The Use of the German Perfect

The German perfect is used to express what happened prior to the moment of speaking, that is, prior to the chronological present, the "here and now." It looks into the past from the point of view of the present and relates the past events to the present time. This normally occurs in conversational situations and also in letter-writing.

Note that in her story (Patterns 1, p. 159) Karin uses such time phrases as **gestern morgen** and **vor drei Jahren** which clearly relate events of the past to the moment she tells her story. The person she tells it to might interrupt her, also using the perfect tense, with such questions as:

Wann bist du in Wien abgefahren?   When did you leave Vienna?
Was habt ihr denn zu Mittag gegessen?   What did you have for dinner?

The German past tense, which will be introduced in Unit 7, does not establish the same psychological link to the moment of speaking.

PRACTICE ONE

Before attempting these exercises, memorize the auxiliary and participle of all strong and irregular weak verbs used so far. They are listed on p. 184.

A. Restate the following sentences in the perfect tense.

> **Karin schläft heute nicht lange.**
> **Karin hat heute nicht lange geschlafen.**

> **Karin steht um sieben Uhr auf.**
> **Karin ist um sieben Uhr aufgestanden.**

Ratskeller in Bremen

1. Sie trinkt eine Tasse Kaffee.
2. Sie ißt zwei Brötchen.
3. Dann geht sie einkaufen.
4. Um neun Uhr telefoniert[3] sie mit ihrem Freund Rolf.
5. Sie fährt mit dem Fahrrad zum Bahnhof.
6. Dort trifft sie ihren Freund.
7. Sie nehmen den 11-Uhr-Zug in die Stadt.
8. Der Zug fährt pünktlich ab.
9. Um elf Uhr dreißig kommen sie in der Stadt an.
10. Sie essen im Ratskeller zu Mittag.
11. Das Essen schmeckt gut.
12. Nach dem Mittagessen besuchen sie Freunde.
13. Sie gehen mit ihren Freunden ins Kino.
14. Der Film fängt um drei Uhr an.
15. Sie müssen fünfzehn Minuten warten.
16. Der Film dauert zwei Stunden.
17. Er gefällt ihnen gut.

[3]**telefonieren mit**   *to talk on the telephone with somebody = to call somebody.*

18. Um fünf Uhr kommen sie aus dem Kino.
19. Es regnet.
20. Im Regen wandern sie durch die Stadt.
21. Und dann suchen sie ein Weinrestaurant.
22. Nach dem Abendessen sitzen sie noch lange zusammen.
23. Sie bleiben bis zehn Uhr in der Stadt.
24. Dann fahren sie nach Burgbach zurück.
25. Rolf bringt Karin noch nach Hause.

B. Reread Patterns 1; then, without looking at the original sentences, use
the following elements to reconstruct the text. Use the perfect tense
and add whatever additional elements are necessary.

Frau Enderle / letztes Jahr / kennenlernen.
Karin hat Frau Enderle letztes Jahr kennengelernt.

1. Vor drei Wochen / Karin / Brief / schreiben.
2. Frau Enderle / Karin / einladen.
3. Gestern / Familie Enderle / besuchen.
4. Nachtzug / von Wien nach Stuttgart / nehmen.
5. Dann / mit / Personenzug / nach Burgbach / fahren.
6. Frau Enderle / am Bahnhof / abholen.
7. Karin und Frau Enderle / einkaufen gehen.
8. Enderles / Haus / vor einem Jahr / bauen.
9. Vorher / bei / Eltern / von Herrn Enderle / wohnen.
10. Frau Enderle / Haus / und / Garten / zeigen.
11. Karin / Frau Enderle / in der Küche / helfen.
12. ein Uhr / Kinder / aus / Schule / kommen.
13. Nach / Mittagessen / lange / im Wohnzimmer / sitzen.
14. Kinder / schwimmen / gehen.
15. sieben Uhr / zu Abend / essen.

C. Respond to the following imperatives with statements in the perfect.
Make structural changes as needed.

Laden Sie doch Herrn Meyer ein. —Aber ich habe ihn doch schon
eingeladen.

1. Fangen Sie doch an.
2. Kochen Sie doch Kaffee.
3. Schicken Sie ihr doch ein Buch.
4. Gehen Sie doch schwimmen.
5. Trinken Sie doch eine Tasse Tee.
6. Lesen Sie doch dieses Buch.
7. Sprechen Sie doch mal mit ihm.
8. Warten Sie doch eine Stunde.
9. Bringen Sie ihr doch diesen Roman.
10. Laufen Sie doch zwei Kilometer.

What is *Hochdeutsch?*

Over the last five hundred years, a common standard language has evolved as a means of communication within what used to be the Holy Roman Empire. This standard language is called **Hochdeutsch,** *High German*, and in its written form varies very little from the BRD to the DDR, to Austria and to Switzerland. However, if you talk with a native speaker of German, you can almost always tell where he or she is from. Genuine dialects—which are quite separate from High German—have largely vanished, but regional, and often local, intonation remains, such as the typical sing-song of Swabian, spoken in the southwest. There are a number of German terms that are expressed with different words in different parts of the country; for example, there are two words for *Saturday*: **Sonnabend** in the north, **Samstag** in the south; the word *butcher* has even more variations (see map below).

How do you say "butcher" in German?

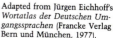

Adapted from Jürgen Eichhoff's *Wortatlas der Deutschen Umgangssprachen* (Francke Verlag Bern und München, 1977).

PATTERNS TWO

3/The Past Tense of *sein*

With **sein**, the past tense is used even in conversational situations
where other verbs demand the perfect; note the shift to the perfect
in the last sentence.

Herr Lenz ist heute in Saarbrücken.—Gestern war er in Trier.

Mr. Lenz is in Saarbrücken today.—Yesterday he was in Trier.

Wo warst du gestern, Inge?—Ich war in Frankfurt.

Where were you yesterday, Inge?—I was in Frankfurt.

Wir waren gestern auch in Frankfurt.—Wo wart ihr gestern?

We were in Frankfurt, too, yesterday.— Where were you yesterday?

Wo waren Sie denn, Herr Lenz?

Where were you, Mr. Lenz?

Ich war gestern krank und bin zu Hause geblieben.

I was sick yesterday and stayed at home.

Trier

4/The Past Tense of *haben*

The verb **haben** is frequently used in the past tense rather than in
the perfect, though not as regularly as **sein** and the modals.

Ich fahre heute nach Berchtesgaden; gestern hatte ich keine Zeit.

I am going to Berchtesgaden today; yesterday I didn't have time.

Warum hattest du denn keine Zeit?

Why didn't you have any time?

Herr Lenz hatte auch keine Zeit. Wir hatten alle zu viel zu tun.

Mr. Lenz had no time either. We all had too much to do.

Was, ihr hattet keine Zeit?

What, you had no time?

Sie hatten alle zu viel zu tun.

They all had too much to do.

5/The Past Tense of Modals

The modals are routinely used in the past tense where other verbs
require the perfect. Note the shift to the perfect in the last sentence.

Konntest du nicht ein bißchen früher nach Hause kommen?	Couldn't you come home a little earlier?
Ich wollte ja heute schon um zwei Uhr zu Hause sein.	Well, I wanted to be home at two o'clock today.
Aber wir mußten noch einen Bericht schreiben. Der sollte schon gestern fertig sein und durfte auf keinen Fall bis morgen liegen bleiben.	But we still had to write a report. It was supposed to be finished yesterday and couldn't under any circumstances wait (remain lying) until tomorrow.
Wir mußten sogar über die Mittagszeit im Büro bleiben, denn wir wollten um fünf Uhr fertig sein.	We even had to stay in the office over the noon hour, because we wanted to be finished by five o'clock.
Konntet ihr denn wenigstens im Büro etwas zu essen kriegen?	Could you at least get something to eat at the office?
Aber natürlich. Wir haben Wurst- und Käsebrote gegessen.	But of course. We ate meat and cheese sandwiches.

6/Point-in-Time Phrases

Frau Enderle habe ich vor einem Jahr in Stuttgart kennengelernt.	I became acquainted with Mrs. Enderle in Stuttgart a year ago.
Ich wollte sie letzten Winter besuchen, aber ich konnte nicht.	I wanted to visit her last winter, but I couldn't.
Im Frühling hat sie mir einen Brief geschrieben.	In the spring she wrote me a letter.
Gestern bin ich in Burgbach angekommen.	Yesterday I arrived in Burgbach.
Nächste Woche fahre ich nach Wien zurück, und im Herbst bin ich wieder in Amerika.	Next week I'm returning to Vienna, and in the fall I'll be in America again.

7/Frequency Phrases

Wie oft müssen Sie denn nach Wien fliegen, Herr Jürgens? — Dreimal im Monat.	How often do you have to fly to Vienna, Mr. Jürgens? — Three times a month.
Fliegen Sie auch manchmal nach Amerika? —Nein, nie.	Do you sometimes fly to America, too? —No, never.
Waren Sie schon einmal in Spanien? —Nein, noch nicht.	Have you ever been in Spain? —No, not yet.
Ich bin auch noch nie in Portugal gewesen.	I've not yet (never) been in Portugal either.
So, Sie haben zehn Jahre in Europa gelebt. Waren Sie auch einmal in Paris? —Ja, sehr oft.	So you lived in Europe for ten years. Did you ever go to Paris? —Yes, quite often.
Essen Sie oft Sauerkraut, Frau Enderle? —Nein, nur sehr selten.	Do you often eat sauerkraut, Mrs. Enderle? —No, only very rarely.

Haben Sie je Leberknödelsuppe gegessen? —In München sehr oft, aber in Hamburg nie.

Did you ever eat liver dumpling soup? —In Munich very frequently, but in Hamburg never.

Wie oft seid ihr denn in den Ferien schwimmen gegangen? —Leider nur zweimal.

How often did you go swimming during vacation? —Unfortunately only twice.

Wie oft seid ihr denn diesen Sommer schon schwimmen gegangen? —Mindestens schon zehnmal. —Leider erst zweimal.

How often have you been swimming this summer? —At least ten times. —Unfortunately only twice.

Fritz studiert jetzt Mathematik? Aber er wollte doch immer Arzt werden.

Fritz is studying mathematics now? But he always wanted to be a doctor.

Natürlich studiert Brigitte Medizin; sie hat doch schon immer Ärztin werden wollen.

Of course Brigitte is studying medicine; she has always wanted to be a doctor.

8/Stretch-of-Time Phrases

Ich habe zehn Jahre in Bern gewohnt.

I lived in Berne for ten years.

Müller hat jahrelang bei Mercedes-Benz gearbeitet.

Müller worked for Mercedes-Benz for years.

Wir haben lange im Garten auf einer Bank gesessen.

For a long time we sat on a bench in the garden.

So gut habe ich schon lange nicht gegessen, Frau Enderle.

I haven't eaten this well for a long time, Mrs. Enderle.

Gut, daß du endlich hier bist; ich habe seit zwei Stunden auf dich gewartet.

Good that you're here at last; I've been waiting for you for two hours.

Vielen Dank für die Kamera, Vater; du weißt ja, die habe ich mir schon lange gewünscht.

Thanks for the camera, Dad; you know I've wanted it for a long time.

Schmitz wohnt schon drei Jahre (seit drei Jahren, schon seit drei Jahren) in Düsseldorf.

Schmitz has been living in Düsseldorf for three years.

Ich warte seit fünf Uhr auf meinen Mann, aber das Flugzeug hat Verspätung, und er ist immer noch nicht hier.

I have been waiting for my husband since five o'clock, but his plane is late, and he still isn't here.

Jetzt stehe ich schon über eine Stunde hier, und Hans ist immer noch nicht gekommen.

I've been standing here for over an hour now, and Hans still hasn't come.

Tante Amalie bleibt sicher noch lange hier. —Ja, sie hat gesagt, sie will drei Wochen hierbleiben.

I'm sure Aunt Amalie is going to stay here for a long time. —Yes, she said she wants to stay for three weeks.

Wie lange bleibt Ihr Mann denn in Bremen, Frau König? —Drei Wochen.

How long is your husband going to stay in Bremen, Mrs. König? —For three weeks.

Er ist krank gewesen, und der Arzt hat ihm gesagt, er darf vier Wochen lang nicht schilaufen.

He has been ill, and the doctor told him not to go skiing for four weeks.

ANALYSIS TWO

60/The Past Tense of *sein, haben,* and the Modals

Although the past tense of German verbs will not be discussed until Unit 7, we introduce here the past of **sein, haben,** and the modals.[4] These past forms are usually preferred in conversational situations in which past events are described in the perfect.

Wo warst du denn gestern?—Ich wollte Tante Amalie besuchen, aber sie hatte keine Zeit. Dann bin ich ohne sie ins Kino gegangen.

Where were you yesterday?—I wanted to visit Aunt Amalie, but she didn't have any time. Then I went to the movies without her.

	sein	haben	dürfen	können	müssen	sollen	wollen
ich	war	hatte	durfte	konnte	mußte	sollte	wollte
du	warst	hattest	durftest	konntest	mußtest	solltest	wolltest
er	war	hatte	durfte	konnte	mußte	sollte	wollte
wir	waren	hatten	durften	konnten	mußten	sollten	wollten
ihr	wart	hattet	durftet	konntet	mußtet	solltet	wolltet
sie	waren	hatten	durften	konnten	mußten	sollten	wollten

NOTE: In the past tense the modals do not have an umlaut.

61/Time and Tense

Both English and German frequently use a combination of tense and time phrase to express certain time relationships. Unfortunately, the two languages sometimes use different combinations to express the same idea. One such difference was already introduced in Unit 5 in connection with the preposition **seit**.

Whereas in the sentence

Fritz has been living here since 1980.

English must use the present perfect progressive (*has been living*), German must use the present tense plus **seit** to express the same idea:

Fritz wohnt seit 1980 hier.

---

[4]The **möchte**-forms do not have a past; instead, the past of **wollen** is used.

Er möchte den Roman kaufen.	He would like to buy the novel.
Er wollte den Roman kaufen.	He wanted to buy the novel.

The present tense must be used in this sentence because there is no doubt that Fritz "is living here" at the moment of speaking. The sentence contains the notion that Fritz's living here has been going on since 1980, an action that continues into the present time.

The following examples show a different kind of divergence between English and German. The important difference in English between

> 1a. Last winter we went to the opera three times.   (past tense)

and

> 2a. This winter we have gone to the opera three times (so far). (present perfect)

cannot be expressed in German by changing tenses. In German both sentences have to be in the perfect, since the "going to the opera" occurred prior to the moment of speaking. The effect of the present perfect in sentence 2a is achieved in German by using the adverb **schon** with the perfect:

> 1b. Letzten Winter sind wir dreimal in die Oper gegangen. (English: *went*)
> 2b. Diesen Winter sind wir schon dreimal in die Oper gegangen. (English: *have gone*)

In other words:

> English uses *a single form of the adverb* (*three times*) and varies the *verb* (*went, have gone*).

> German uses *a single form of the verb* (**sind gegangen**) and varies the *adverb* (**dreimal, schon dreimal**).

You will gradually get used to such structural differences between the two languages. A brief overview of German time phrases follows.

Both English and German use three types of time phrases that are easy to distinguish by the question to which they are — or could be — the answers:

> 1. Point-in-time: **Wann** (*when?*)—**Um drei Uhr** (*at three o'clock*)
> 2. Frequency: **Wie oft** (*how often?*)—**Dreimal** (*three times*)
> 3. Stretch-of-time: **Wie lange** (*how long?*)—**Drei Jahre** (*for three years*)

POINT-IN-TIME PHRASES

Point-in-time phrases always answer the question **Wann?** *When?*

> **Wir sind gestern nach Freiberg gefahren.**
> **Nächste Woche wollen wir nach Basel fahren.**

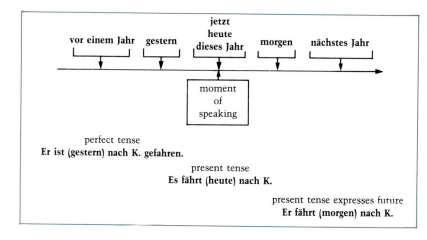

If the point-in-time occurs prior to the moment of speaking, the perfect tense must be used; if the point-in-time occurs at the moment of speaking or in the future, the present tense is used.

In time phrases, **vor** (plus dative) corresponds to English *ago*, but unlike *ago*, it precedes the noun: **vor einem Jahr**, *a year ago*.

FREQUENCY PHRASES

Frequency phrases always answer the question **Wie oft?** *How often?* Here you must distinguish between two types of situations. In sentence 1a above, the "going to the opera" is definitely over; in 2a, however, there may well be visits to the opera in the future. We refer to these two situations as closed-end and open-end. German uses the perfect tense for both, but uses **schon** and **noch nicht** or **noch nie** in open-end situations.

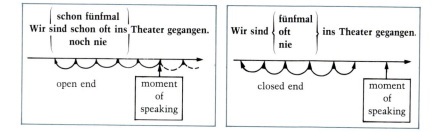

1. There is a neat difference between **nur dreimal, schon dreimal,** and **erst dreimal**. The **nur** adds to the simple **dreimal** the flavor "and that was all" (closed-end). The **schon** adds not only the open-end meaning but sometimes the notion "and that is more than expected." The **erst** adds the expectation "I hope that was merely the first three times."

2. German **(schon) immer** and **(noch) nie** like English *always* and *never* are usually used as frequency phrases (even though they seem to indicate "stretches" of time).

> **Sie hat mich nie besucht.**   She never visited me.

implies that she had frequent opportunities to visit me *but never did.*

> **Sie hat mich noch nie besucht.**   She has never visited me.

implies that she has had frequent opportunities to visit me, *but has not visited me yet.*

STRETCH-OF-TIME PHRASES

Stretch-of-time phrases always answer the question **Wie lange?** *(For) how long?*

There are four possible combinations of tense and time phrase to express:

    a. What was but is no longer.
    b. What just ended at the moment of speaking.
    c. What has been going on and still is.
    d. What will end in the future.

NOTE: The wavy line (⌇⌇⌇) in the chart below indicates the stretch of time during which the action was going on.

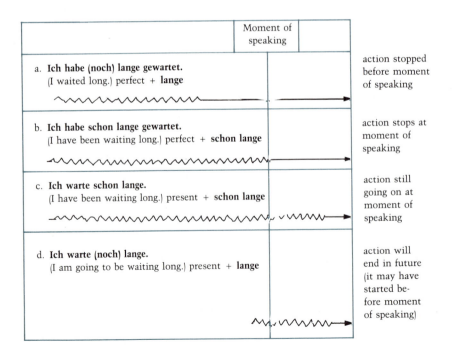

	Moment of speaking		
a. **Ich habe (noch) lange gewartet.** (I waited long.) perfect + **lange**			action stopped before moment of speaking
b. **Ich habe schon lange gewartet.** (I have been waiting long.) perfect + **schon lange**			action stops at moment of speaking
c. **Ich warte schon lange.** (I have been waiting long.) present + **schon lange**			action still going on at moment of speaking
d. **Ich warte (noch) lange.** (I am going to be waiting long.) present + **lange**			action will end in future (it may have started before moment of speaking)

Sentences of type **b** and **c** always contain **schon, seit,** or **schon seit**. Remember that the preposition **seit** must be followed by the dative, but **schon** alone is followed by the accusative. Hence, **seit drei Jahren** (dative) and **schon seit drei Jahren** (dative), but **schon drei Jahre** (accusative).

Sentences of type **a** and **d** may, but do not have to, contain **noch;** if **noch** is used with stretch-of-time phrases, it implies the continuation of an action or state beyond a certain point.

Sentences of type **b** are the least frequent of these. Remember that you must not use type **b** when you should be using type **c**, that is, when the action is still going on at the moment of speaking.

Darauf haben Sie schon lange gewartet: Eine Suppe für den großen Hunger.

Auf diese Suppe haben Sie schon lange gewartet.—You have been waiting for this soup a long time. (Now it is on the shelves.)

PRACTICE TWO

D. Restate the following sentences in the past tense.

Ich habe nicht nach Graz fahren können.	**Ich konnte nicht nach Graz fahren.**

1. Bettina hat allein essen müssen.
2. Achim ist in Stuttgart gewesen.
3. Sein Vater hat gestern Geburtstag gehabt.
4. Hast du gestern zu Hause bleiben können?
5. Wir sind oft in Nürnberg gewesen.

E. Express in German. Use the past tense of the modals.

1. She knew German and French.
2. They wanted to eat in the mensa.
3. She was supposed to come at eight o'clock.
4. Mr. Meyer was not permitted to drink wine.
5. Yesterday we had to get up early.

F. Express the following sentences in English. Be careful with your choice of English tenses.

1. Ich glaube, Hans wohnt in München.
2. Nein, er wohnt jetzt in Berlin.
3. Er hat noch nie in München gewohnt.
4. Sein Vater hat auch nie in München gewohnt.
5. Vor drei Jahren hat Hans noch in Bonn gewohnt.
6. Seit zwei Jahren wohnt er in Berlin.
7. In Bonn hat er drei Jahre gewohnt.
8. Seine Freundin Erika hat ihn letztes Jahr fünfmal besucht.
9. Dieses Jahr hat Erika ihn erst zweimal besucht.
10. Aber ich habe ihn schon dreimal besucht.

already

Mittagessen in der Mensa

BITTE GESCHIRR ZURÜCKBRINGEN

CONVERSATIONS

I

MÜLLER:	Waren Sie letzte Woche in Frankfurt?
SCHMIDT:	Nein, ich mußte nach Bonn.
MÜLLER:	Sind Sie mit dem Wagen gefahren?
SCHMIDT:	Nein, mit dem Zug. Auf der Autobahn war mir zu viel Verkehr, besonders am Wochenende. Außerdem konnte ich im Zug arbeiten.
MÜLLER:	Da haben Sie recht. Ich fahre auch lieber mit dem Zug. Wann sind Sie denn zurückgekommen?
SCHMIDT:	Ich bin nur fünf Tage geblieben; Freitag abend war ich wieder hier.

II

KARIN:	Wie lange wohnst du denn schon in der Goethestraße?	How long have you been living on Goethe Street?
BERND:	Erst drei Monate. Vorher habe ich lange in der Hölderlinstraße gewohnt. Und du? Wohnst du immer noch in der Schillerstraße?	Only three months. Before that I lived on Hölderlin Street for a long time. And you? Do you still live on Schiller Street?

| KARIN: | Nein, schon lange nicht mehr. Ich bin seitdem schon dreimal umgezogen. Jetzt wohne ich bei meiner Tante Amalie in der Eichendorffstraße. | No, not for a long time anymore. Since then I've moved three times. Now I'm living with my Aunt Amalie on Eichendorff Street. |
| BERND: | Oh, deine Tante Amalie. Wie geht's der denn? Die habe ich seit Jahren nicht mehr gesehen. | Oh, your Aunt Amalie. How is she? I haven't seen her for years. |

Street Names

The four streets mentioned in Conversation II are all named after famous German poets. There is nothing unusual about this; you are just as likely to find a Goethestraße in a small town or village as in a large city. The cultural past is reflected as well in streets named after composers (Mozartplatz, Beethovenstraße, Richard-Wagner-Allee) or after philosophers and theologians (Hegelweg, Kantstraße, Martin-Luther-Ring).

Johann Wolfgang von Goethe (1749–1832)

Ludwig van Beethoven (1770–1827)

Martin Luther (1483–1546)

Richard Wagner (1813–83)

Immanuel Kant (1724–1804)

III

Assume that late in the evening you meet a friend of yours who is interested in what you have been up to all day. Construct ten sentences in the perfect or, in the case of **sein, haben**, and the modals, in either the past or the perfect. When you read your sentences in class, have your classmates interrupt you with questions.

Ich habe heute lange geschlafen.
Ich habe erst um zehn gefrühstückt.
Dann bin ich mit dem Fahrrad in die Stadt gefahren.
Etc.

IV

Construct a conversation with a friend along the same lines and act it out in class.

A. Ich bin heute um sieben Uhr aufgestanden. Und du?
B. Ich bin erst um elf aufgestanden.
A. Warum so spät?
B. Ich mußte heute nacht[5] bis drei Uhr arbeiten. Aber warum bist du so früh aufgestanden?
   Etc.

Fragen an Sie persönlich

When you report on these questions in class, have your classmates interrupt you with follow-up questions.

1. Waren Sie schon einmal in Europa?
                              in Deutschland?
                              in Österreich?
                              in der Schweiz?
   Wenn ja, wann und wie oft? — Letzten Sommer?
                              Letztes Jahr?
                              1988?
2. Möchten Sie einmal nach Europa fahren, und warum?
              noch einmal
3. Sind Sie in Amerika (in den Vereinigten Staaten) schon viel gereist?
   Wann, und wohin?
   Mit wem? — Allein?
              Mit den Eltern?
              Mit Freunden?

[5]Note that **heute nacht** means *in the middle of the night;* only the tense indicates whether it is *last night* (past) or *tonight* (present or future).

4. Wie haben Sie den letzten Sommer verbracht?   **verbringen** to spend
5. Was haben Sie in den Ferien gemacht?
   letztes Wochenende
   gestern abend

READING

Familiengeschichten

Herr und Frau Enderle sitzen mit der Studentin Karin, ihrer amerikanischen Besucherin aus Wien, auf einer Bank. Die Bank steht
mitten° in den Weinbergen°, hoch über dem Ort Burgbach°. Es ist   in the middle of
neun Uhr abends an einem warmen Juliabend. Herr Enderle erzählt   vineyards   high above
von seiner Familie.   5   the town of Burgbach

„Sehen Sie, das Haus dort rechts von der Kirche° gehört schon seit   church
Generationen meiner Familie. Enderles hat es hier schon vor dem
30-jährigen Krieg° gegeben, —und sie haben alle Wein gemacht.   Thirty Years War
Mein Bruder wohnt immer noch dort, bei meinen Eltern."   (1618–48)

„Aber er macht sicher keinen Wein mehr", meint° Karin. „Sie haben 10   says
doch gesagt, daß er Apotheker° ist."   pharmacist

„Die Apotheke°, das ist sein Beruf°, aber seine heimliche° Liebe   pharmacy profession
ist immer noch der Weinbau°. Dort drüben, sehen Sie, unter der   secret wine-making
Burgruine°, dort ist unser Weinberg, —Burghalde° heißt die Lage°—,   castle ruin **Burghalde**
und wir machen einen prima Trollinger°. Wenn es da viel Arbeit 15   (castle slope) site
gibt, helfen wir immer noch alle mit.   first-rate Trollinger
                                                                       (type of red wine)

„Seit dem 30-jährigen Krieg", meint Karin, „das sind mindestens°   at least
zehn oder zwölf Generationen, die alle in einem Haus gewohnt
haben, —und *wir* wohnen erst° seit fünf Jahren in Seattle, und mein   only
Vater ist in New York geboren, und meine Mutter in Ohio."   20

„Ja, sehen Sie, wir wohnen ja auch nicht mehr alle zusammen. Früher
haben ganze Familien immer zusammen gewohnt, —Großeltern°,   grandparents
Eltern, Kinder und Enkelkinder°, und vielleicht noch ein unver-   grandchildren
heirateter° Onkel oder eine unverheiratete Tante; Großfamilien°   unmarried extended
nennen° die Anthropologen das, manchmal fünfzehn oder zwanzig 25   families call
Menschen unter einem Dach°. Aber nun haben wir das neue Haus   roof
gebaut und sind vor vier Jahren ausgezogen°. Meine Schwester   moved
wohnt seit acht Jahren in Schwäbisch-Gmünd; sie hat dort einen
Geschäftsmann° geheiratet."   businessman

Frau Enderle lacht°. „Und ich bin noch nicht einmal° eine Schwäbin." 30 laughs even a Swabian
„Ja", sagt Karin, „ich wollte gerade fragen: Sie sind doch nicht von
hier; man hört es an Ihrer Sprache."

„Nein, ich bin in Ostpreußen[6] geboren, in einem Dorf in der Nähe° near
von Königsberg. 1945 sind wir dann nach Berlin geflüchtet°; meine fled
Mutter wohnt immer noch dort. Mein Vater ist vor zehn Jahren 35
gestorben°." died

„Und wie haben Sie Ihren Mann kennengelernt?"

„Ach, das war '59, in den Ferien an der Ostsee°. Wir waren beide Baltic Sea
Studenten, er an der T.H. in Stuttgart, und ich in Hamburg."

„T.H.?" fragt Karin, „was heißt das?" 40

„Technische Hochschule°", sagt Herr Enderle, „das ist so etwas wie institute of technology
bei Ihnen zum Beispiel M.I.T. Sie wissen ja, ich bin Techniker°; technician
ich habe schon als Schüler° auf dem Gymnasium° Ingenieur° pupil German
secondary school
werden wollen, —und der Weinbau schien damals keine Zukunft° engineer future
zu haben." 45

„So!" Frau Enderle steht auf. „Jetzt gehen wir aber nach Hause. Die
Kinder müssen ins Bett°, und morgen müssen wir alle früh auf- to bed
stehen."

„Aber zuerst trinken wir noch[7] eine Flasche Wein", sagt Herr
Enderle. 50

„Einen Trollinger von der Burghalde?" möchte Karin wissen.

„Genau. Und Sie werden sehen: Der Wein ist wirklich gut hier in
Burgbach."

REVIEW EXERCISES

G. Express in German.

1. I met him in Graz.
2. We had to work last Sunday.
3. He never wanted to stay at home.
4. I hope you didn't invite Mr. Meyer.
5. We got up at six o'clock.
6. Monika has not come yet.
7. Why didn't you follow me?
8. Please visit us next summer.
9. I helped her yesterday.
10. At four o'clock we went swimming.

[6]The northern half of East Prussia is now part of the Soviet Union; the southern half
is part of Poland. Königsberg has been renamed Kaliningrad.

[7]This **noch** does not indicate that they will drink *another* bottle of wine, but that
before going to bed Mr. Enderle *still* wants them to drink some wine.

H. Construct sentences as indicated.

1. Sundays they often ate in the dorm.
   (a) They eat.
   (b) Change to the perfect.
   (c) add: **im Studentenheim**
   (d) add: *often*
   (e) Start the sentence with *Sundays . . .*
2. Her friend Achim went to Stuttgart by train last night.
   (a) Achim went. (Use the perfect of **fahren**)
   (b) add: *Her friend*
   (c) add: *to Stuttgart*
   (d) add: *last night*
   (e) add: *by train* (= with the train)
3. Erika has been living in Zurich for five years.
   (a) Erika has been living. (Watch tense!)
   (b) add: *in Zurich*
   (c) add: *for five years*

I. In order to test your understanding of time phrases, express the sentences below in English (watch your English tenses); then place each sentence into one of the following categories.

   a. having come to an end in the past
   b. ending at the moment of speaking
   c. reaching from the past into the moment of speaking and continuing
   d. definitely ending in the future

1. Wir bleiben *noch ein Jahr* in Köln.
2. Wir sind *noch ein Jahr* in Deutschland geblieben.
3. Sie hat *zwei Jahre* auf Hans gewartet.
4. Sie wartet *seit zwei Jahren* auf Hans.
5. Meine Mutter hat uns *nur zweimal* besucht.
6. Ich habe ihn *oft* besucht.
7. *Wie lange* wartest du denn *schon*?
8. *Wie lange* hast du denn *schon* gewartet?
9. *Wie lange* hast du denn gewartet?
10. Wir wollen ihn *schon lange* besuchen.
11. Das habe ich dir *schon lange* sagen wollen.
12. Er hat doch *immer* Arzt werden wollen.
13. Er hat doch *schon immer* Arzt werden wollen.
14. Ich kann *nur zwei Stunden* bleiben.
15. So eine Kamera habe ich mir *schon lange* gewünscht.
16. Hier hat George Washington *nie* geschlafen.

J. Express in German. Be sure you use the correct tenses and time phrases.

> Ask somebody how long she has been living here.
> **Wie lange wohnst du/wohnen Sie schon hier?**

Ask somebody:

1. how often he has been in Berlin this year.
2. how often he was in Berlin last year.
3. since when she has had her camera.
4. whether she went to the movies last night.
5. whether he has never been in Austria yet.
6. whether he has ever been in Zurich.
7. how long she has already been waiting for her friend.
8. how long she waited for her friend.

> Tell somebody that you've been sick for a long time.
> **Ich bin schon lange krank.**

Tell somebody:

1. that you were sick for a long time.
2. that you were not able to drive for two months.
3. that you won't be able to drive for two months.
4. that you haven't been able to drive since October.
5. that you've had that camera for five years.
6. that you want to stay with Aunt Amalie for four weeks.
7. that you've wanted that novel for a long time.

K. Supply the missing words.

1. Guten Tag, Frau Schmidt. Wie geht's _Ihnen_ denn?
2. So, du fährst _nach_ München. Ich war _noch_ nie in München.
3. Ich _war_ gestern bei Tante Amalie, aber ich _bin_ nicht lange geblieben.
4. Kaufmanns wohnen _seit_ drei Jahren in Innsbruck.
5. Sie haben Bier _getrunken_ und Brot und Käse _gegessen_
6. Diese Straßenbahn fährt _zum_ Bahnhof.
7. Ich kann jetzt nicht kommen. Wir sind gerade _beim_ Essen.
8. Ich kaufe den Wagen nicht. Der gefällt _mir_ nicht.
9. Wir _brauchen_ heute nicht zu arbeiten, wir können schwimmen _gehen_.
10. Kennt ihr euch? —Ja, wir haben _uns_ schon kennengelernt.

VOCABULARY

ab•holen	to pick up (at station, airport, etc.)
allein	alone
an•fangen (fängst an, fängt an)	to begin, start
auf	on
außerdem	moreover, in addition
die Autobahn, -en	superhighway, freeway, turnpike
bauen	to build
der Bericht, -e	report
der Besucher, -	visitor (m.)
die Besucherin, -nen	visitor (f.)
bewundern	to admire
bißchen	bit, little, little bit
das Dorf, -̈er	village
ein•laden (lädst ein, lädt ein)	to invite
einmal	once; some time
zweimal	twice
dreimal	three times
viermal	four times
nicht einmal	not once, not even
noch einmal	once more
nur einmal	just once
endlich	finally
erzählen	to tell (story)
essen (ißt, ißt)	to eat
zu Abend essen	to eat supper
zu Mittag essen	to eat dinner
der Fall, -̈e	case
auf jeden Fall	in any case
auf keinen Fall	in no case
die Fami'lie, -n	family
die Ferien (pl.)	vacation
fertig	ready, complete, finished
der Film, -e	film
früher	formerly
der Frühling, -e	spring
frühstücken	to (eat, have) breakfast
der Garten, -̈	garden
die Geschichte, -n	story; history
gestern	yesterday
gestern abend	last night
gestern morgen	yesterday morning
der Herbst, -e	autumn, fall
heute nacht	tonight; last night
jahrelang	for years
je	ever
krank	sick
der Kuchen, -	cake
leben	to be alive, live
das Leben, -	life
letzt-	last
letzten Sommer	last summer
letztes Jahr	last year
letzte Woche	last week
die Liebe, -n	love
der (or das) Meter, -	meter
der Kilome'ter, - (km)	kilometer
der Mittag, -e	noon
der Nachmittag, -e	afternoon
die Mittagszeit	noon hour, midday
der Personenzug, -̈e	local train
pünktlich	on time, punctually
rennen (sein)	to run
der Rotwein, -e	red wine
schmecken	to taste
das Schnitzel, -	cutlet
seitdem	since
sogar	even
spazieren•gehen (sein)	to go for a walk
das Stück, -e	piece; (theatrical) play
ein Stück Kuchen	a piece of cake
telefonieren	to talk on the telephone, to make a telephone call
treffen (triffst, trifft)	to meet; to hit
über	over
um•ziehen (sein)	to move (from one place to another
verbringen	to spend (time)
der Verkehr	traffic
die Verspätung, -en	delay
Verspätung haben	to be late (train, plane, etc.)
das Viertel, -	quarter
dreiviertel	three quarters
von . . . aus	from
vor	ago
vorher	before, earlier

ein Jahr vorher	a year earlier	**der Winter, -**	winter
wandern (sein)	to hike	**das Wohnzimmer, -**	living room
warten auf (*acc.*)	to wait for	**zahlen, bezahlen**	to pay
der Weg, -e	way, path		

Strong Verbs and Irregular Weak Verbs, Units 1–6

Before you will be able to use the German perfect, you will have to memorize the auxiliary and participle of all strong and irregular weak verbs. The table below will help you in this task.

INFINITIVE	PERFECT	
ab•fahren	ist **abgefahren**	to depart
an•fangen	hat **angefangen**	to begin, start
an•kommen	ist **angekommen**	to arrive
auf•stehen	ist **aufgestanden**	to get up (out of bed)
aus•gehen	ist **ausgegangen**	to go out
bekommen	hat **bekommen**	to get, receive
bleiben	ist **geblieben**	to stay, remain
bringen	hat **gebracht**	to bring
denken	hat **gedacht**	to think
dürfen	hat **gedurft**	to be allowed to
ein•laden	hat **eingeladen**	to invite
empfehlen	hat **empfohlen**	to recommend
essen	hat **gegessen**	to eat
fahren	ist **gefahren**	to drive; go (by train, boat, plane, car)
finden	hat **gefunden**	to find
fliegen	ist **geflogen**	to fly
geben	hat **gegeben**	to give
gefallen	hat **gefallen**	to please
gehen	ist **gegangen**	to go; walk
heißen	hat **geheißen**	to be called; to mean
helfen	hat **geholfen**	to help
kennen	hat **gekannt**	to know, be acquainted with
klingen	hat **geklungen**	to sound
kommen	ist **gekommen**	to come
können	hat **gekonnt**	to be able to
laufen	ist **gelaufen**	to run
lesen	hat **gelesen**	to read
liegen	hat **gelegen**	to lie (flat); to be situated
mögen	hat **gemocht**	to like to
müssen	hat **gemußt**	to have to
nehmen	hat **genommen**	to take
rennen	ist **gerannt**	to run
scheinen	hat **geschienen**	to seem; to shine
schlafen	hat **geschlafen**	to sleep
schreiben	hat **geschrieben**	to write
schwimmen	ist **geschwommen**	to swim
sehen	hat **gesehen**	to see

sein	ist gewesen	to be
sitzen	hat gesessen	to sit
sprechen	hat gesprochen	to speak, talk
stehen	hat gestanden	to stand
treffen	hat getroffen	to meet; to hit
trinken	hat getrunken	to drink
tun	hat getan	to do
um•ziehen	ist umgezogen	to move
verbringen	hat verbracht	to spend (time)
verstehen	hat verstanden	to understand
werden	ist geworden	to become
wissen	hat gewußt	to know (as a fact)

Unit 7

The Past—Past Perfect—Cardinal Numbers—Time—Word Formation

Shopping

A major American import into Western Europe after World War II was the supermarket, which Germans promptly called **der Supermarkt**. Especially in larger cities, the traditional corner grocery store (**Lebensmittelgeschäft**) has all but disappeared. However, other specialty shops, such as butcher shops and bakeries, continue to thrive. Butchers sell an incredible array of sausages and cold cuts. A type of bakery called **Konditorei** specializes in cakes and pastries; there you can sit down to have your **Apfelstrudel** or **Linzer Torte** with a cup of coffee or a glass of hot tea. Supermarkets have also invaded the traditional department stores (**Kaufhäuser**); one of the finest of these is on the top floor of the **Kaufhaus des Westens (KaDeWe)** in West Berlin. In recent years shopping centers (**Einkaufszentren**) have sprung up.

Many people still shop daily for fresh bread, meat, and produce, as they have done for generations. Almost all households have refrigerators, but these tend to be quite small.

If you look up the English word *drugstore* in a dictionary, you will find **die Drogerie**. However, that translation is somewhat misleading, since a **Drogerie** sells mainly health care items and over-the-counter drugs. Prescription drugs you can only buy in an **Apotheke**, and for fancy soaps and perfumes you go to a **Parfümerie**.

DORNBUSCH – APOTHEKE
FRITZ HERMENING
Eschersheimer Landstraße 240
6000 Frankfurt/Main 1

A **Tante Emma-Laden** is the equivalent of a "mom-and-pop store."

PATTERNS ONE

1/Past Tense of Weak Verbs

In Patterns 1 of Unit 6, Karin told her "story" in the perfect tense, thus relating past events to the moment of talking about them by using such time expressions as **gestern** and **vor drei Jahren**. In contrast, the first two pattern sections of this unit use the past tense and have a narrative rather than a conversational character. Here the two narrators do not relate their stories to the time of telling. These two sections are clearly not "conversation" and do not require a conversational partner.

Ich lebte[1] damals noch zu Hause und studierte in Stuttgart.

I was still living at home at that time and was studying in Stuttgart.

Meine Frau wohnte[1] seit 1958 in Hamburg und studierte dort an der Universität.

My wife had been living in Hamburg since 1958 and was studying at the university there.

In den Sommerferien arbeitete sie an der Ostsee, in einem Sportgeschäft in Travemünde.

During summer vacation, she worked at the Baltic Sea, in a sports shop in Travemünde.

Dort lernte ich sie kennen.

That's where I met her.

Jede Woche kaufte ich mindestens ein Paar Tennisschuhe.

Every week I bought at least one pair of tennis shoes.

Ich glaube, sie wußte, daß ich die Tennisschuhe nicht kaufte, weil ich sie brauchte.[2]

I think she knew that I didn't buy the tennis shoes because I needed them.

Aber sie sagte nichts; sie lachte nur.

But she didn't say anything; she only laughed.

Eines Tages brachte ich ihr eine Rose.

One day I took[3] a rose to her.

Ich dachte immer an sie.

I always thought of her.

Im Winter besuchte sie mich in Burgbach.

In the winter she visited me in Burgbach.

Wir heirateten ein Jahr später.

We got married a year later.

2/Past Tense of Strong Verbs

Es begann 1959 in Travemünde.

It began in Travemünde in 1959.

Er kam jeden Tag ins Sportgeschäft.

He came to the sports shop every day.

Zuerst fand ich ihn einfach sehr nett.

At first I just thought he was very nice.

---

[1] English *to live* can be expressed by either **leben** or **wohnen**; **leben** is the more inclusive term in the sense of *to spend one's life*; **wohnen** means *to reside, to have a residence.*

[2] Clauses beginning with such subordinating conjunctions as **daß**, **weil**, and **wenn** are dependent clauses with the inflected verb at the end; they will be discussed in Unit 8.

[3] Note that **bringen** can mean both *to bring* and *to take.*

Dann gefiel er mir immer besser.	Then I liked him better and better.[4]
Ich bekam Herzklopfen, wenn ich ihn sah.	My heart started thumping whenever I saw him.
Er schien Student zu sein, aber ich wußte zuerst nicht, wie er hieß.	He seemed to be a student, but at first I didn't know his name.
Er sprach mit einem Akzent,—Schwäbisch, fand ich später heraus—, und seine Stimme klang sehr sympathisch.	He talked with an accent—Swabian, I found out later—, and his voice sounded very attractive.
An einem Samstag bat[5] er mich, mit ihm auszugehen.	On a Saturday he asked me to go out with him.
In einem Fischlokal saß er mir gegenüber.[6]	In a fish restaurant, he sat across from me.
Wir aßen Flundern und tranken Moselwein, und er sprach von Burgbach und von seiner Familie.	We ate flounder and drank Moselle wine, and he talked about Burgbach and his family.
Er lud mich ein, ihn dort zu besuchen.	He invited me to visit him there.
Wir blieben beide bis Ende September in Travemünde.	We both stayed in Travemünde until the end of September.
Dann ging ich nach Hamburg zurück, und er fuhr nach Hause.	Then I went back to Hamburg, and he went home.
Ich versprach, ihm oft zu schreiben.	I promised to write him often.
Er schrieb mir jede Woche einen Brief und rief mich auch manchmal an.	He wrote me a letter every week and sometimes called me too.
Weihnachten sah ich ihn wieder.	At Christmas I saw him again.
Später wurde er Ingenieur, und ich wurde Studienrätin.	Later he became an engineer, and I became a teacher.

ANALYSIS ONE

62/Formation of the Past Tense

The past tense of **sein, haben,** and the modals was introduced in Unit 6. Unit 7 discusses the past tense of all verbs in greater detail.

In form the German past tense is analogous to the English past tense. Both languages have weak verbs and strong verbs.

---

[4]The English double comparative (*better and better*) is expressed in German by **immer** plus comparative (**immer besser**).

[5]Do not confuse **bitten**, *to ask, beg, request,* with **fragen**, *to ask, pose a question.*

[6]The preposition **gegenüber**, *opposite, across from,* takes the dative and usually follows the noun or pronoun.

	PRESENT	PAST
WEAK VERBS	*I learn* **ich lerne**	*learn-ed* **lern-te**
STRONG VERBS	*I find* **ich finde**	*found* **fand**

WEAK VERBS

While English marks the past tense of weak verbs with *-ed*, German does so with **-t-**. Except for the third person singular, German adds the same personal endings as in the present tense; because of the **-t-**, the **du-** and **ihr**-forms add an **-e-** (**-test, -tet**).

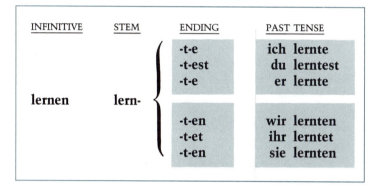

INFINITIVE	STEM	ENDING	PAST TENSE
lernen	**lern-**	**-t-e** **-t-est** **-t-e**	**ich lernte** **du lerntest** **er lernte**
		-t-en **-t-et** **-t-en**	**wir lernten** **ihr lerntet** **sie lernten**

German verbs with a stem ending in **-d** or **-t** must add an **-e-** before the **-t** to make the ending clearly audible.

ich redete	**ich arbeitete**
du redetest	**du arbeitetest**
er redete	**er arbeitete**
wir redeten	**wir arbeiteten**
ihr redetet	**ihr arbeitetet**
sie redeten	**sie arbeiteten**

An **-e-** must also be inserted before the **-te** in verbs like **regnen, atmen** (*to breathe*), and **rechnen** (*to figure, to calculate*):

   es regnete   **er atmete**   **er rechnete**

The modals (see Anal. 60, p. 171) are weak verbs, but they drop the umlaut in the past tense.

   er durfte   **konnte**   **mußte**   **sollte**   **wollte**

The verb **haben** (see Anal. 60, p. 171) is also a weak verb, but it changes the **-b-** of the stem to **-t-**:

ich hatte	wir hatten
du hattest	ihr hattet
er hatte	sie hatten

IRREGULAR WEAK VERBS

Some very common weak verbs change their stem in the past tense.

INFINITIVE	PAST TENSE
bringen	ich brachte
denken	ich dachte
nennen	ich nannte
kennen	ich kannte
werden	ich wurde
wissen	ich wußte

Note that the past forms of English *to bring* and *to think* are irregular in the same way: *brought, thought.*

The verb **werden** is an anomaly: it has a weak past **wurde** and a strong participle **geworden**.

ich wurde	wir wurden
du wurdest	ihr wurdet
er wurde	sie wurden

NOTE: In the past tense, the third person singular of a weak verb *never* ends in **-t**.

STRONG VERBS

While there are not many strong verbs in either English or German, they are used frequently. Both English and German mark the past tense of strong verbs not by adding *-ed* or **-te**, but by changing the stem.

The change in the stem is unpredictable, and the best way to master these forms is to memorize them as they appear in the tables of strong and irregular weak verbs at the end of each unit.

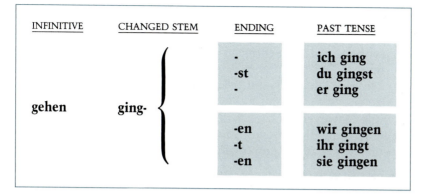

INFINITIVE	CHANGED STEM	ENDING	PAST TENSE
gehen	ging-	- -st -	ich ging du gingst er ging
		-en -t -en	wir gingen ihr gingt sie gingen

Like the weak verbs whose stems end in **-d** or **-t**, strong verbs ending in **-d** or **-t** insert an **-e-** between the stem and the ending in the **du**-form and the **ihr**-form.

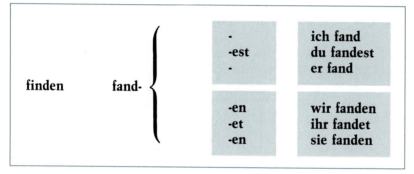

		ENDING	PAST TENSE
finden	fand-	- -est -	ich fand du fandest er fand
		-en -et -en	wir fanden ihr fandet sie fanden

NOTE: In the past tense, the first and third persons singular of a strong verb *never* have an ending. The past tense stem of the irregular verb **sein** is **war**.

63/Principal Parts of Strong and Irregular Weak Verbs

You can form all tenses of an English strong verb like *to sing* if you know the three forms

   sing   sang   sung

These three forms are called the principal parts of *to sing*.

With German verbs you must learn two additional forms:

1. The third-person singular present tense forms of verbs like **fahren**, that is, of strong verbs with a vowel change in the second and third persons singular. (Weak verbs never change their stem vowel in the present tense.)

2. The auxiliary (**haben** or **sein**) used to form the perfect. Thus the principal parts of **schreiben**, **fahren**, and **kennen** are:

schreiben	schreibt	schrieb	hat geschrieben
fahren	fährt	fuhr	ist gefahren
kennen	kennt	kannte	hat gekannt

The verb **kennen** is a weak verb. However, it changes the vowel in the past and in the perfect in an unpredictable way and therefore appears in the table of irregular verbs at the end of this unit.

By looking at the infinitive form of a verb, you can never tell whether it is weak or strong: **leben** is weak, but **geben** is strong. There is only one "rule": if a verb is not listed under the strong verbs, it must be weak.

64/The Difference in the Use of the Past and the Perfect

In conversational situations (see Anal. 59, p. 164), German uses the perfect to relate past events to the moment of speaking. The German past tense, however, does not establish such a psychological link to any given "here and now." Events related in the past tense stand on their own, as it were. Thus, if you start telling a real story, conversation changes to narration, and you must use the simple past to enumerate, step by step, those events, and *only* those events, which are part of the progressing story. It follows, therefore, that the past tense is the tense used in most German fiction.

You should have no trouble using the German past tense in storytelling; the real difficulty for an English learner of German is in using the German perfect correctly.

The modals, **sein**, and sometimes **haben** do not make this distinction in the use of the past and the perfect. They are normally used in the past, even when other verbs are used in the perfect: thus **ich war** rather than **ich bin gewesen**, and **er sollte kommen** rather than **er hat kommen sollen** (see Anal. 60, p. 171).

It is not exactly wrong to use these verbs in the perfect. One does hear it, especially in connection with such open-end phrases as **noch nie**, **schon oft**, or **erst zweimal**.

Ich bin noch nie in Paris gewesen.	Ich war noch nie in Paris.
Ich bin erst zweimal in Paris gewesen. or	Ich war erst zweimal in Paris.
Wir haben sonntags immer arbeiten müssen.	Wir mußten sonntags immer arbeiten.

PRACTICE ONE

A. Form the present, past, and perfect. This exercise is meant as a quick
drill of the forms of weak verbs.

> **antworten — er antwortet, er antwortete, er hat geantwortet**

arbeiten	— ich	heiraten	— wir
brauchen	— wir	hoffen	— ich
danken	— sie	kochen	— er
einkaufen	— er	leben	— wir
fragen	— sie	lernen	— ihr
gehören	— es	lieben	— ich
glauben	— du	machen	— sie

B. Restate the following sentences in the past tense. In each sentence, add
damals.

> **Erika studiert in München.**
> **Erika studierte damals in München.**

1. Hans hat nie Zeit.
2. Er besucht seinen Vater in Nürnberg.
3. Wir wohnen in Bayreuth.
4. Dieses Haus gehört meinem Vater.
5. Sie antwortet mir nicht.
6. Ist deine Mutter in Dortmund?
7. Wir können leider nicht kommen.
8. Ich will ihm die Stadt zeigen.
9. Er soll zu Hause bleiben.
10. Ich darf es ihm nicht sagen.
11. Ihr müßt leider nach Hause fahren.
12. Sie braucht nicht zu arbeiten.

C. Form the present, past, and perfect. All verbs in this exercise are strong
or irregular weak verbs.

> **bleiben — wir bleiben, wir blieben, wir sind geblieben**

anfangen	— ich	kennen	— ich	sein	— ihr
bringen	— er	kommen	— wir	sitzen	— wir
denken	— sie	lassen	— er	sprechen	— ich
essen	— er	laufen	— sie	stehen	— er
fahren	— du	lesen	— du	tragen	— sie
geben	— er	nehmen	— er	trinken	— wir
gehen	— wir	schlafen	— er	verstehen	— er
helfen	— er	schreiben	— ich	werden	— er
heißen	— sie	sehen	— er	wissen	— du

D. Restate the following sentences in the past tense.

1. Kurt geht zum Bahnhof.
2. Sie verstehen mich sehr gut.
3. Georg kauft ein Paar Tennisschuhe.
4. Jutta hilft mir bei der Arbeit.
5. Sie arbeitet in Travemünde.
6. Wir kommen um 9 Uhr aus dem Kino.
7. Achim fährt nach Stuttgart.
8. Sie sieht ihre Mutter in Freiburg.
9. Er trinkt keinen Wein.
10. Ich hole ihn in Tübingen ab.
11. Er bekommt jeden Tag einen Brief von ihr.
12. Hans lädt mich oft zum Essen ein.
13. Sie denkt oft an ihn.
14. Er bringt mich nach Hause.
15. Hans und Inge stehen vor dem Theater.

Stiegl
seit 1492
und dennoch:
DAS BIER VON HEUTE

PATTERNS TWO

3/The Past Perfect

Als ich ihn kennenlernte, war er gerade aus Hamburg gekommen.[7]	When I met him, he had just come from Hamburg.
Wir wußten nicht, daß sie Ärztin geworden war.	We didn't know that she had become a doctor.
Er war zwei Jahre lang in Berlin gewesen, bevor er nach Stuttgart zurückkam.	He had been in Berlin for two years before he returned to Stuttgart.
Ich hatte Hunger, denn ich hatte lange nichts gegessen.	I was hungry, for I hadn't eaten anything for a long time.
Sie war den ganzen Tag müde, denn sie hatte schlecht geschlafen.	She was tired all day, for she had slept badly.

4/um . . . zu

Inge fuhr nach Salzburg, um ins Theater zu gehen.
Er fuhr nach Rom, um dort einen Roman zu schreiben.
Er studiert Englisch, um Shakespeare lesen zu können.
Frau Lenz ging zum Telefon, um ihren Mann anzurufen.

[7]Clauses beginning with such subordinating conjunctions as **als**, **daß**, and **bevor** are dependent clauses with the inflected verb at the end. On the other hand, **denn** is a coordinating conjunction introducing clauses with verb second position.

5/Cardinal Numbers

null, eins, zwei, drei, vier, fünf, sechs, sieben, acht, neun, zehn, elf,
zwölf, dreizehn, vierzehn, fünfzehn, sechzehn, siebzehn, achtzehn,
neunzehn, zwanzig

eins und eins ist zwei
eins und zwei ist . . .
eins . . .

eins plus eins ist zwei
eins plus zwei ist . . .
eins . . .

zwanzig weniger eins ist neunzehn
neunzehn weniger eins . . .
achtzehn . . .

zwanzig minus eins ist neunzehn
zwanzig minus zwei ist . . .
zwanzig . . .

zwanzig, einundzwanzig, zweiundzwanzig, dreiundzwanzig, vier-
undzwanzig, fünfundzwanzig, sechsundzwanzig, siebenundzwanzig,
achtundzwanzig, neunundzwanzig, dreißig, einunddreißig, zweiund-
dreißig, vierzig, dreiundvierzig, vierundvierzig, fünfundvierzig, fünfzig, fünfundfünfzig, sechsundfünfzig, sechzig, sechsundsechzig,
siebenundsechzig, siebzig, siebenundsiebzig, achtundsiebzig, achtzig, achtundachtzig, neunundachtzig, neunzig, hundert (einhundert)

ein mal zwei ist zwei
zwei mal zwei ist vier
drei mal zwei ist sechs
vier mal zwei ist acht
fünf mal zwei ist zehn

hundert (geteilt) durch zehn ist zehn
neunzig (geteilt) durch zehn ist neun
achtzig (geteilt) durch zehn ist acht
siebzig (geteilt) durch zehn ist sieben
sechzig (geteilt) durch zehn ist sechs

100 *hundert*
101 hundert*eins*
102 hundert*zwei*
110 hundert*zehn*
120 hundert*zwanzig*
121 hundert*einundzwanzig*
122 hundert*zweiundzwanzig*
198 hundert*achtundneunzig*
199 hundert*neunundneunzig*
200 *zweihundert*

100 *ein*hundert
200 *zwei*hundert
300 *drei*hundert
900 *neun*hundert
1.000 *tausend*

7.839 *sieben*tausend*acht*hundert*neun*und*dreiß*ig
1.000.000 eine Milli*on*
2.000.000 zwei Millionen
1.000.000.000 eine Milli*arde* (one billion)

Geld aus der Deutschen Demokratischen Republik

Geld aus der Bundesrepublik Deutschland

Ich brauche zweihundert*ein*undvierzig *Mark*.
In unserer Stadt wohnen jetzt über *drei*hunderttausend *Men*schen.
Unsere Bibliothek hat drei Millionen *Mark* gekostet.

0,7   *null* Komma *sie*ben
0,17   *null* Komma *siebzehn* (*null* Komma *eins sie*ben)
3,14159 *drei* Komma *eins vier eins fünf neun*

  DM 4,20   vier Mark zwanzig (West) — 4,20 M vier Mark zwanzig (Ost)
  DM 0,75   fünfundsiebzig Pfennig
  öS 121,00 hunderteinundzwanzig Schilling (Österreich)
  öS 0,50 fünfzig Groschen
sFr 100,21 hundert Franken einundzwanzig (Schweiz)
sFr   0,60 sechzig Rappen
 $1.477,00 vierzehnhundertsiebenundsiebzig Dollar
          eintausendvierhundertsiebenundsiebzig Dollar
    $18,37 achtzehn Dollar siebenunddreißig

6/Time

Wieviel Uhr ist es?   Es ist zehn Uhr dreizehn.
Wie spät ist es?[8]   Es ist zehn Uhr dreizehn.

Wann kommt der Zug an?   Um sechs Uhr siebzehn.
Um wieviel Uhr kommt der Zug an? Um sechs Uhr siebzehn.
Wann fährt der Zug ab?   Um siebzehn Uhr sechzehn.
Um wieviel Uhr fährt der Zug ab? Um siebzehn Uhr sechzehn.

Wann fängt das Theater an?   Um zwanzig Uhr fünfzehn.

[8]This does not normally mean "How late is it?" but "What time is it?"

11.00 Uhr elf Uhr	11.35 Uhr fünf nach halb zwölf
11.05 Uhr fünf (Minuten) nach elf	11.40 Uhr zehn nach halb zwölf
11.10 Uhr zehn nach elf	11.45 Uhr dreiviertel zwölf; Viertel vor zwölf
11.15 Uhr Viertel nach elf; Viertel zwölf	11.50 Uhr zehn vor zwölf
11.20 Uhr zwanzig nach elf	11.55 Uhr fünf vor zwölf
11.25 Uhr fünf vor halb zwölf	12.00 Uhr zwölf Uhr
11.30 Uhr halb zwölf	

„Abfahrt 16 Uhr . . . Gleis 10 . . ."

How much does it cost?

It takes a while to get used to the different monetary systems of European countries, none of which have a 1:1 parity. West Germans use deutsche mark (DM) and pfennigs (pennies); East Germans also use marks but without the "D," and they put the "M" behind the figure rather than in front. Thus, you can easily tell the difference between DM5 and 5M. Theoretically, West and East marks have the same value, but they are not freely and easily convertible. It is illegal, for example, to take any East marks out of the DDR. The Swiss use francs, like the French and the Belgians, but the schweizer franken (sFr) is worth considerably more than either of the other two. The German pfennig corresponds to the Swiss rappen. The Austrian schilling (1öS = 100 groschen) is worth about one-sixth of the DM; thus, if you have to pay DM10 for a German meal, or about sFr10 for a Swiss meal, you will have to expect a bill for about öS60. And then try to convert all that into what some tourists still like to refer to as "real money," namely U.S. dollars!

ANALYSIS TWO

65/Formation and Use of the Past Perfect

The German past perfect is formed by combining the simple past
of **haben** or **sein** with the participle of the main verb.

schreiben	**ich hatte geschrieben**	I had written
bleiben	**ich war geblieben**	I had stayed

Like the English past perfect, the German past perfect is the tense
used to describe events or situations which precede events or situations that occurred in the past.

Er war den ganzen Tag müde, denn er hatte schlecht geschlafen.	He was tired all day, for he had slept badly.
Es war Abend geworden, und es regnete.	Evening had come, and it was raining.

When the sentence

1. **Erich wohnt jetzt schon drei Jahre in München, ist aber noch nie ins Theater gegangen.**   Erich has been living in Munich for three years, but has never gone to the theater.

becomes part of a narrative, it will appear as

2. **Erich wohnte damals schon drei Jahre in München, war aber noch nie ins Theater gegangen.**   Erich had been living in Munich for three years at that time, but had never gone to the theater.

The up-to-now situation in sentence 1 becomes an up-to-then situation in sentence 2. Therefore, the **jetzt** of sentence 1 must become
damals in sentence 2 (see Anal. 61, p. 171).

66/Summary of the Use of Tenses

Note the difference in the use of the terms *time* and *tense* in the
table.

	present TIME	past TIME	pre-past TIME
Conversational	**er geht** present TENSE	**er ist gegangen** perfect TENSE	**er war gegangen** past perfect TENSE
Narrative	**er ging** past TENSE	**er war gegangen** past perfect TENSE	**er war gegangen** past perfect TENSE

Remember that the German past and perfect are not identical with the English past and present perfect.

Conversational tenses relate to the chronological present. *Narrative tenses* relate to some time other than the chronological present, usually to some time in the past, but also, for example, to some future time, like 2001 or 2025. Within the framework of the narrative, the past tense represents the narrative present time. In the example

Am 15. Juli 1962 kam Klaus abends ins Hotel Regina; er war heute weit gefahren.

heute refers to a time in the chronological past (1962), but it could also refer to, say, 2062, as in a science fiction novel.

> **Sein**, **haben**, and the modals are usually used in the past tense rather than in the perfect.

67/um . . . zu

Some English infinitive phrases with *to* can be expanded by *in order*:

I have to take the night train (in order) to be in Stuttgart tomorrow morning.

Whenever this English expansion is possible, German must introduce the infinitive phrase with the preposition **um**:

Ich muß den Nachtzug nehmen, um morgen früh in Stuttgart zu sein.

Um morgen früh in Stuttgart zu sein, muß ich den Nachtzug nehmen.

The construction with **um . . . zu** must be separated from the main clause by a comma, and **um** must stand at the beginning and **zu** + infinitive at the end of the phrase. The **um . . . zu** phrase has no front field and first prong, but has an inner field and a second prong. If the **um . . . zu** phrase begins the sentence, it occupies the front field and is followed by the inflected verb.

68/*mit* as a Verbal Complement

The preposition **mit** is frequently used as a verbal complement, meaning *along*. It forms the second prong of the predicate.

Rosemarie geht *auch* mit.   Rosemarie is coming along too.

If the sentence is negated, **mit** is preceded by **nicht**.

Rosemarie geht diesmal leider nicht mit.

Mit is often used with, and always precedes, directives.

Sie geht wieder mit nach Deutschland.

If used with an infinitive, **mit** and the infinitive are written as one word.

Sie möchte wieder mitgehen.

If the sentence contains a prepositional phrase with **mit**, the verbal complement **mit** is not used.

Ich gehe mit ihr nach Deutschland.

Mit alone can never occupy the front field.

69/Cardinal Numbers

The German system is quite similar to English. From 0 to 12, each number has its own name; from 13 on, and with the exception of 100, the numbers are either compounded or are derived from the basic set 1–9. Note that from 21 to 29, 31 to 39, and so on, German reverses the English pattern: *twenty-one* becomes **einundzwanzig**.

null	zehn	zwanzig	
eins	elf	einundzwanzig	
zwei	zwölf	zweiundzwanzig	*zwanzig*
drei	dreizehn	dreiundzwanzig	*dreißig*
vier	vierzehn	vierundzwanzig	vierzig
fünf	fünfzehn	fünfundzwanzig	fünfzig
sechs	sechzehn	sechsundzwanzig	*sechzig*
sieben	siebzehn	siebenundzwanzig	*siebzig*
acht	achtzehn	achtundzwanzig	achtzig
neun	neunzehn	neunundzwanzig	neunzig
			(ein)hundert

Particular attention must be paid to the spelling and pronunciation of the italicized numbers in the table.

100 hundert (einhundert)	600 sechshundert
101 hunderteins	1.000 tausend (eintausend)
102 hundertzwei	7.625 siebentausendsechshundertfünfundzwanzig
110 hundertzehn	1.000.000 eine Million
121 hunderteinundzwanzig	2.000.000 zwei Millionen
200 zweihundert	1.000.000.000 eine Milliarde (one billion)[9]

[9]The German **eine Billion** corresponds to English *trillion*.

Note that German uses periods where English uses commas: 2.325.641. Conversely, in *decimal numbers*, German uses commas where English uses periods.

0,3	null Komma drei
12,17	zwölf Komma siebzehn
6,5342	sechs Komma fünf drei vier zwei
2.051,23	zweitausendeinundfünfzig Komma dreiundzwanzig

One can say either

zwei und zwei ist vier   or   **zwei plus zwei ist vier**

and

vier weniger zwei ist zwei   or   **vier minus zwei ist zwei**

Plus and **minus** are mathematical terms; **und** and **weniger** are used in nonmathematical everyday language.

Multiplication and division are expressed as follows:

zwei mal zwei ist vier
vier (geteilt) durch zwei ist zwei

70/Time

In colloquial German, the following terms are used to tell time:

8.00 Uhr	acht Uhr	8.30 Uhr	halb neun
8.05 Uhr	fünf nach acht	8.35 Uhr	fünf nach halb neun
8.10 Uhr	zehn nach acht	8.40 Uhr	zehn nach halb neun
8.15 Uhr	Viertel nach acht; Viertel neun	8.45 Uhr	dreiviertel neun; Viertel vor neun
8.20 Uhr	zwanzig nach acht	8.50 Uhr	zehn vor neun
8.25 Uhr	fünf vor halb neun	8.55 Uhr	fünf vor neun

For official purposes (transportation, radio, etc.), the following pattern is used:

0.10 Uhr	null Uhr zehn (12:10 A.M.)	20.05 Uhr	zwanzig Uhr fünf (8:05 P.M.)
8.05 Uhr	acht Uhr fünf (8:05 A.M.)	24.00 Uhr	vierundzwanzig Uhr (midnight)

71/Word Formation

Native speakers of any language not only have an active and a passive vocabulary at their disposal, but also know how to construct new words from known stems. Thus, by adding the suffix *-ing* to the stem of *love*, English derives the form *loving*; by adding the suffix *-er*, English forms the agent noun *lover*, and by adding the prefix *be-* plus the suffix *-ed*, the adjective *beloved* is formed. The suffix *-er* can not only be added to the stem *lov-*; it also appears in *worker*, *reader*, *listener*, *drinker*, *driver*, and many other agent nouns. The suffix *-er* is a very important part of our active vocabulary.

In German, even more frequently than in English, prefixes and suffixes are used to form derivatives. It is therefore important to learn when and how to apply the German prefixes and suffixes.

THE SUFFIXES **-chen** AND **-lein**

The suffix **-chen** is normally used to form diminutive nouns, all of which are neuter. All diminutives have the same ending in the singular and plural, and most have an umlaut. Nouns ending in **-e** and **-en** drop these endings before ending **-chen**. The endings **-el** and **-er** are retained.

das Brot	das Brötchen	das Glas	das Gläschen
der Bruder	das Brüderchen	das Kind	das Kindchen
der Garten	das Gärtchen	die Tasse	das Täßchen

If the stem of the noun ends in an **-s**, the **-ch-** of **-chen** is pronounced almost like an English *y* or German **j** (**Täß-jen; Gläs-jen**).

The noun **das Mädchen** is derived from the obsolete **die Magd** and no longer has a diminutive meaning.

The suffix **-lein** is used infrequently. It still occurs in **das Fräulein**, also no longer a diminutive, and with nouns ending in **-ch**: **das Buch, das Büchlein**.

In Southern Germany, **-lein** has become **-le** or **-el** and is preferred over **-chen**: **das Haus, das Häusle, das Häusel**. The Swiss use **-li, das Häusli**, and the Viennese use **-erl, das Häuserl**.

THE SUFFIX **-er**

The German suffix **-er** corresponds to the English suffixes *-er* and *-or*. It is added to verb stems to form agent nouns, which denote the person that performs the action implied. Some of these agent nouns add an umlaut.

backen	der Bäcker	the baker
denken	der Denker	the thinker
lesen	der Leser	the reader

Not all agent nouns are derived from verbs:

die Kunst	art	**der Künstler**	the artist
die Physik	physics	**der Physiker**	the physicist

The suffix **-in** is added to the suffix **-er** to form feminine agent nouns (see Anal. 13, p. 21 and Anal. 14, p. 22).

lesen   **der Leser, -**   **die Leserin, -nen**

INFINITIVES AS NEUTER NOUNS

German infinitives can be used as neuter nouns denoting the activity expressed by the verb. (English forms its verbal nouns by adding *-ing* to the verb.)

Hier ist das Parken leider verboten.
Das Essen und das Trinken haben ihn müde gemacht.

If such a verbal noun is preceded by **beim (bei dem)**, it means "in the process (or act) of" or "while."

beim Fahren	while driving
beim Essen	while eating
beim Trinken	while drinking

COMPOUND NOUNS

Both in English and in German two nouns can be combined to form a compound noun. For example, *house* and *dog* can form two combinations—*house dog* and *doghouse,* a house dog being a kind of dog and a doghouse being a kind of house. The second part of the compound is always the basic form, which is modified by the first part. For this reason, German compounds derive their gender and plural form from the second part. Thus:

das Haus	**der Hund**	**der Haushund, die Haushunde**
der Hund	**das Haus**	**das Hundehaus, die Hundehäuser**

Other examples:

der Sport	**das Geschäft**	**das Sportgeschäft**
der Sommer	**die Ferien**	**die Sommerferien**
(das) Tennis	**die Schuhe**	**die Tennisschuhe**
der Käse	**das Brot**	**das Käsebrot**
der Abend	**das Essen**	**das Abendessen**

In many such compounds, a letter is inserted between the two parts —for example, **Mittagszeit, Damenhut, Liebesbrief**. Since there are no general rules, it is best to memorize these compounds as they occur.

PRACTICE TWO

E. Add the correct past tense form of **sein** or **haben**; then express in English.

1. Als sie gerade eingeschlafen _____, klingelte das Telefon.
2. Er _____ in Göttingen studiert und wurde dann Arzt in München.
3. Weil es die ganze Nacht geregnet _____, blieben wir zu Hause.
4. Er _____ nach Wien gefahren, weil er Karin wiedersehen wollte.

F. Of the following pairs of sentences, change the second to an infinitive with **um . . . zu**. Note that in the second sentence of each pair both the subject (**Er** or **Sie**) and the modal (**wollte**) must be dropped.

Inge fuhr nach Frankfurt. Sie wollte ins Theater gehen.
Inge fuhr nach Frankfurt, um ins Theater zu gehen.

1. John fuhr nach Deutschland. Er wollte Deutsch lernen.
2. Seine Tochter ging nach Mainz. Sie wollte Archäologie studieren.
3. Achim kam nach Stuttgart. Er wollte seine Eltern besuchen.
4. Sein Vater fuhr zum Bahnhof. Er wollte Achim abholen.
5. Inge ging zum Telefon. Sie wollte Hans anrufen.

G. Read the following problems.

$2 + 4 = 6$	$1 + 14 = 15$	$19 - 12 = 7$
$12 + 4 = 16$	$9 + 11 = 20$	$16 - 10 = 6$
$7 + 3 = 10$	$18 + 1 = 19$	$8 - 5 = 3$
$7 + 10 = 17$	$16 + 2 = 18$	$20 - 3 = 17$
$5 + 8 = 13$	$17 + 2 = 19$	$11 - 11 = 0$

Solve the following problems.

$10 \times 6 =$	$212 - 32 =$
$77 : 7 =$	$180 : 9 =$
$6 \times 9 =$	$20 \times 5 =$
$144 : 12 =$	$0,9 + 1,8 =$

Read aloud.

21 32 34 54 65 76 87 98 109 120 213 324 435 546 657
768 879 987 1.003 1.011 1.248 1.376 1.492 2.549 14.395
27.603 849.527 3.492.716 0,3 7,45 421,7 3.054,25
DM 10,25 7,50 M öS 300,00 sFr 16.500,00 DM 0,75 öS 0,50 sFr 0,60

H. Read aloud and, where possible, in several ways:

9.05 (Uhr)	4.25 (Uhr)	12.45 (Uhr)
9.15	7.45	1.30
10.30	7.57	21.45

What are the equivalents?

18.45 Uhr   (achtzehn Uhr fünfundvierzig) = sechs Uhr fünfundvierzig
dreiviertel sieben
Viertel vor sieben

15.10 Uhr =
21.30 Uhr =
13.55 Uhr =

I. Form diminutives with **-chen** with the following nouns.

1. das Rad	5. das Bier	9. die Stadt
2. das Glas	6. das Bild	10. der Garten
3. der Hund	7. der Brief	11. die Tante (no umlaut)
4. die Tasse	8. die Schwester	12. der Onkel (no umlaut)

J. Try to guess the meaning of the following nouns in **-er.**

1. der Fahrer	6. der Läufer	11. der Lügner
2. der Erzähler	7. der Arbeiter	12. der Hörer
3. der Weinkenner	8. der Anfänger	13. der Nichtraucher
4. der Käufer	9. der Korkzieher	14. der Fernsprecher
5. der Uhrmacher	10. der Rechner	15. der Fernseher

CONVERSATIONS

I

ULRICH M.:	Darf ich mich zu dir setzen?	May I sit down by you?
LIESELOTTE A.:	Aber gerne; hier ist ja Platz.	Sure; there's enough room.
ULRICH:	Übrigens, ich heiße Markwardt, Ulrich Markwardt, aber man nennt mich Uli.	Incidentally, my name is Markwardt, Ulrich Markwardt, but they call me Uli.
LIESELOTTE:	Ich bin Lieselotte Aumüller, aber du darfst mich ruhig Lilo nennen.	I am Lieselotte Aumüller, but you may call me Lilo.

II

LIESELOTTE:	Wie lange bist du schon hier an der Uni?	How long have you been here at the university?

ULRICH:	Zwei Semester. Vorher war ich drei Semester in Tübingen, und im letzten Sommersemester habe ich gearbeitet. Mir war nämlich das Geld ausgegangen.	Two semesters. Before that I was in Tübingen for three semesters, and during the last summer semester I worked. I'd run out of money.
LIESELOTTE:	Das kann ich gut verstehen. Ich bin auch immer knapp bei Kasse. Aber ich arbeite jetzt an den Wochenenden als Kellnerin. Kennst du den „Grünen Baum"?	I can understand that very well. I am always short of cash, too. But I work on weekends now, as a waitress. Do you know the "Green Tree"?
ULRICH:	Das ist doch das Lokal in der Hohen Straße, nicht wahr? Da komme ich nächsten Sonntag hin.	That's the restaurant on High Street, isn't it? I'll be going there next Sunday.

III

LIESELOTTE:	Im Wintersemester gehe ich nach Paris. Ich bin nämlich Romanistin, aber ich war bis jetzt nur in den Ferien ein paar Mal in Frankreich.	In the winter semester I'll be going to Paris. I'm studying Romance languages, you see, but so far I've only been in France a few times during vacations.
ULRICH:	Ja, jeder sollte eigentlich ein oder zwei Semester im Ausland studieren; sonst bleibt man ewig provinziell.	Yes, everybody really ought to study abroad for a semester or two; otherwise you stay provincial forever.
LIESELOTTE:	Warst du schon mal im Ausland an einer Uni?	Have you ever studied at a foreign university?
ULRICH:	Ja. Ich wollte eigentlich Germanist werden. Aber dann war ich ein Jahr in den USA und jetzt mache ich Anglistik und Amerikanistik.	Yes. Actually, I wanted to study German. But then I was in America for a year, and now I'm in English and American studies.

IV

ULRICH:	Warst du schon mal in der Diskothek am Alten Markt?	Have you ever been in the discotheque at the Old Market Square?
LIESELOTTE:	Meinst du den „Hot Spot"? Ja, die kenne ich; da ist immer was[10] los.	You mean the "Hot Spot"? Yes, I know it; there is always something going on there.
ULRICH:	Ich kenne ein paar Amerikaner. Die treffe ich heute abend dort. Möchtest du nicht mit?	I know some Americans whom I'm going to meet there tonight. Wouldn't you like to come along?
LIESELOTTE:	Gern. Aber ich muß nach dem Abendessen noch einen Brief an meine Eltern schreiben. Meine Mutter hat nämlich am Sonntag Geburtstag.	I'd be glad to. But first I have to write a letter to my parents after dinner. My mother's birthday is next Sunday.

[10]**was = etwas.**

V

Assume that you are John Ray or Jane Ray and that you are talking to a German student who has become a friend of yours. Tell him or her about the two students, Uli and Lilo, whom you met in the Mensa today.

1. Their names.
2. That you like them.
3. How long they have been in Tübingen.
4. What are they studying?
5. What is their financial situation?
6. Have they studied abroad?
7. They have invited you to a disco.
8. Ask your friend whether he or she would like to go along too.

*Im „Grünen Baum"
trinkt man viel Bier.*

VI

Using the following German, Austrian, and Swiss menus, construct and memorize some mini-conversations. The prices on the German menu are in marks and in schillings on the Austrian menu, and in Switzerland you will have to pay in Swiss francs. Note that the Swiss menu is partly in German and partly in French. When you want to pay your bill, the following exchange might take place:

Herr Ober (or: Fräulein), ich möchte zahlen.
Bitte, die Damen. Zweimal Menü eins, ein Rotwein, ein Bier, zwei Kaffee,—hundertvierzig Schilling, bitte.

VII

Since there are lots of dishes on these menus whose names you can't figure out—which is, of course, exactly what happens when you first look at the menu, **die Speisenkarte**, in a German restaurant—get your teacher into the

Waldheimathof

ALPENGASTHOF BRUGGRABER · 8671 ALPL : TEL. 03855/26115 · STEIERMARK

Alpl, am *15. Mai 1987*

Speisen vom Grill

Filetbeefsteak garniert	*122,–*
Filets Mignons garniert	
Pfeffersteak garniert	*117,–*
Bernerwürstel mit Pommes frites	*45,–*
Cevapcici garniert	*62,–*

Fischgerichte

Forelle blau oder gebraten 1 dkg	*6,20*
Geb. Seefisch mit Mayonnaisesalat	*57,–*

Salate

Salatplatte	*35,–*
Gemischter Salat	*24,–*
Kraut-, Bohnen-, roter Rübensalat	*15,–*

Mehlspeisen

Sachertorte mit Schlagobers	*36,–*
Zwetschkenkuchen, Marillenkuchen	*18,–*
Topfenknödel kl. mit Kompott	*20,–*
Salzburger Nockerl	*56,–*

Suppen

Backerbsensuppe, klare Reissuppe	*21,–*
Leberknödelsuppe, Nudelsuppe	*23,–*
Bouillon mit Ei	*18,–*
Gemüsesuppe, Geflügelsuppe	*22,–*
Serbische Bohnensuppe	*28,–*
Ochsenschwanzsuppe	*25,–*

Fertige Speisen

vom Schwein

Schweinebraten mit 2 Beilagen	*68,–*
Geselchtes mit Semmelknödel u. Kraut	*60,–*
Bauernschmaus	*74,–*

vom Rind

Gekochtes Rindfleisch mit 2 Beilagen	*72,–*
Gedünsteter Rostbraten mit 2 Beilagen	*69,–*
Ungarisches Rindsgulyas	*48,–*

vom Kalb

Kalbsnierenbraten mit 2 Beilagen	*82,–*
Gebratene Kalbsschulter mit 2 Beilagen	*92,–*
Gefüllte Kalbsbrust mit 2 Beilagen	*75,–*

vom Huhn

¼ Brathuhn mit 2 Beilagen	*55,–*

Frischgemachte Speisen

vom Schwein

Geb. Schweinsschnitzel mit 2 Beilagen	*65,–*
Schweinskotelette geb. od. nat. 2 Beil.	*71,–*
Jägerschnitzel garniert	*68,–*
Bratwurst mit 2 Beilagen	*24,–*

vom Rind

Zwiebelrostbraten mit Kart. u. Gurkerl	*80,–*

vom Kalb

Wienerschnitzel mit 2 Beilagen	*71,–*
Naturschnitzel mit 2 Beilagen	*85,–*
Schnitzerl à la Holstein garniert	*89,–*

vom Huhn

1 ganzes Backhuhn mit 2 Beilagen	*135,–*

Wünschen Sie einen guten Tropfen, dann bitten wir Sie, die Weinkarte zu verlangen.
Einen guten Appetit und Aufenthalt wünscht Ihnen **das Haus Bruggraber.**

10% BEDIENUNGSZUSCHLAG

Reininghaus Bier

'Speisen · Getränke   inkl. 8%   inkl. 18%'

32,–
26,–
36,–

94

TEILSUMMEN ink. MWSt

FIRMENSTEMPEL
DAT...'74

ENDBETRAG

STEIRISCH PILS

Winzerkeller Wiesloch

**Die Pflegestätte Badischer Qualitätsw...
Bergstrasse · Kraichg...**

6908 Wiesloch · Postfach 1604 · Telefon 06222/8...

Filettopf	*20.5*
Pecces	*19.5*
Bier 1	*2.5*
WBS	*4.5*
1 Keffee 11	*24.–*

510
1

act. You be the guest, and let your teacher be the waiter or waitress. Ask questions like the following:

Bitte, was ist ein „Zwiebelrostbraten"?
Was bekommt man auf der „großen Salatplatte"?
Ist das Schnitzel vom Schwein oder vom Kalb?

RESTAURANT BÄRENSTUBE
SCHAUPLATZGASSE 4
3011 BERN

TEL. 22 33 67

DE LA POELE

TOURNEDOS ROSSINI   22.--
Rindsfilet mit Gänseleber

FILET DE BOEUF STROGANOFF   20.--
Rindsfiletwürfel an feuriger
Paprika-Rahmsauce, mit Pilzen
und Gurkenstreifchen

EMINCE DE FOIE DE VEAU
AU MADERE   17.50
Geschnetzelte Kalbsleber an
Madeira-Sauce

ESCALOPE DE VEAU CORDON BLEU   16.50
Kalbsschnitzel mit Schinken
und zartschmelzendem Käse

SALTIMBOCCA ALLA ROMANA
TAGLIATELLE VERDI   17.50
Kalbsschnitzel mit Rohschinken
und Salbei, dazu grüne Nudeln

ESCALOPE DE VEAU VIENNOISE   16.50

NOS SPECIALITES

MEDAILLONS DE VEAU VALDOSTANE 20.--
Kalbsfilets garniert mit Niere,
Milken und Morchel-Rahmsauce

ENTRECOTE DOUBLE AUX
HERBES DE PROVENCE   39.--
Zartes Entrecôte mit feinen Kräutern
aus der Provence (2 personnes)

CARRE D'AGNEAU A LA MODE
DU CHEF   40.--
Lammrücken pikant zubereitet -
eine wahre Gaumenfreude (2 personnes)

Burgrestaurant Staufeneck Tagesspezialitäten

Hauptspeisen

493	*Französische Bouchet-Muscheln im Wurzelsud, Stangenbrot*	17,50
570	*Schweinelendchen in der Senfkräuterkruste, Gemüseteller und Kartoffelplätzchen*	24,00
539	*Kalbsbries, gebraten, auf Blattspinat, mit Steinpilzen und Tomatenwürfeln, Kartoffelbeilage*	27,00
561	*Rinderfiletscheiben auf Paprikarahm, mit Pfifferlingen Nudeln und Blattsalaten in Vinaigrette*	33,00
555	*Kalbsmedaillons auf Steinpilzen, Weckknödel und Blattsalat in Vinaigrette*	33,00
517	*Wildente, auf zweimal serviert,(Brust, auf Pilzen mit Nudeln, Keule mit Gemüsen und Plätzchen)*	32,00
513	*Limousin Lammnüßchen auf geschmolzenen Tomaten mit Thymian, Paprika-Zwiebelgemüse, Keniaböhnchen und Kartoffelplätzchen*	38,00
482	*Rotzungenfilets (Limandes), gebraten, mit Gurken, auf Dill-Zitronenbutter und Kartoffelbeilage*	26,00
494	*Seeteufelmedaillons und Shrimps in Orangen-Basilikumsoße und Nudeln*	35,00
485	*Norweger Salmschnitte und Babysteinbutt, gebraten, auf Spinat mit roter und weißer Buttersoße,Kartoffelbeilage*	36,50

Ab 2 Personen

500	*Rehrückenfilet mit Pilzen, auf Preiselbeersoße, Bubenspitzle, Spätzle vom Brett, Blattsalate pro Pers.*	38,00

Warme Küche von 12.00 bis 14.00 Uhr und 18.00 bis 21.45 Uhr
Sonntags bis 21.30 Uhr
Donnerstag Ruhetag

Familie Erich Straubinger
7335 Salach
Telefon (0 71 62) 50 28

Fragen an Sie persönlich

1. Erzählen Sie, wie Sie einen Freund (eine Freundin) kennengelernt haben. (Watch your use of tenses: use either the past or the perfect, but don't mix the two; remember **haben, sein,** and the modals.)

2. Erzählen Sie, wie Sie einen Tag verbracht haben.

> gestern
> letzten Sonntag
> einen Tag im Sommer
> Ihren Geburtstag

      verbringen to spend

3. Wie lange leben Sie (lebt Ihre Familie) schon im gleichen Ort (*in the same place*)? Erzählen Sie, wo Sie und Ihre Eltern früher gewohnt haben.

To slur or not to slur

Very few Germans speak as slowly and deliberately as the speakers on our tapes. In real situations, speech is compressed and often slurred. Just as *Are you going to go?* frequently turns into *Gonna go?*, **Wo ist er denn?** will sound like **Wo isser denn?, Willst du . . . ?** becomes **Willste?**, and a question starting with **Haben wir . . .** with increasingly casual intonation turns into **Hab'm wer, Ham wer,** and **Hammer.** This kind of abbreviation is by no means substandard, but an accepted part of everyday speech.

READING

Beim Kölner Karneval[11]

This reading selection serves as a review of dative and accusative forms in context. Identify the case of each noun and pronoun and give the reason for the use of each given case.

Es regnet. Beim Wirtshaus° „Zum Löwen", steht ein Wagen. Bei dem Wagen steht mein Freund Fridolin Pechhammer mit seiner Freundin Brunhilde. Er scheint traurig° zu sein. Wo kommen die beiden her? Aus dem Kino? Aus der Kirche? Aus dem Wirtshaus?

      inn

      sad

[11]**Karneval** is the season before Lent. It is celebrated mainly in the Catholic regions of Germany—the Rhineland and Bavaria (where it is known as **Fasching**) and is a period of public merriment and of costume parties.

Karneval in Köln

Ich gehe zu ihnen und sage „Guten Tag" und ich sage zu[12] meinem 5
Freund: „Frido, was ist mit dir los? Geht es dir nicht gut? Bist du
krank?"

Aber Fridolin antwortet mir nicht. Er schüttelt° nur den Kopf°.   shakes   head

„Frido", sage ich, „was kann ich für euch tun? Kann ich euch helfen?"

„Nein", sagt er, „ja, —doch, vielleicht. Das Auto ist nämlich kaputt; 10
es läuft nicht mehr."

„Sei mir nicht böse°, Frido, aber das glaube ich dir nicht. Ich glaube,   Don't get mad at me
du hast zu viel getrunken. Ihr kommt doch gerade aus dem Wirts-
haus."

„Na ja°", sagt Frido, „wir sitzen seit dem Mittagessen hier im Löwen 15   Well, OK
und trinken Bier. Bei dem Wetter kann man doch sonst nichts
machen. Und jetzt kommen wir gerade aus dem Löwen und wollen
mit dem Wagen nach Hause fahren und . . ."

„Und was, Frido?"

„Pechhammer", sagt er.   20

„Natürlich", sage ich, „ich weiß, wie du heißt."

„Nein", sagt er, „mit dem Wagen hammer° Pech. Und dabei° ist es   **hammer = haben wir**
nicht einmal mein Wagen. Der gehört meinem Bruder. Aber der   besides
Schlüssel° funktioniert nicht. Hier, willste° mal sehen?"   key   **willste = willst du**

Jetzt verstehe ich: „Pech° haben wir." Und Frido gibt mir den 25   bad luck
Schlüssel, und ich muß lachen.

„Natürlich kannst du mit dem Schlüssel den Wagen nicht starten.
Das ist doch dein Hausschlüssel."

„Ja so was", sagt Frido, und schüttelt wieder den Kopf. Brunhilde
kichert°.   30   giggles

---

[12]Do not use **zu** after forms of **sagen** except in this pattern introducing a direct
statement.

„Frido, mein Freund, am besten fahrt ihr mit mir nach Hause zum
Abendessen. Bratwurst, Sauerkraut und Kartoffelpüree°. Wie klingt
das?"   mashed potatoes

„Das klingt gut", sagt Brunhilde. „Natürlich kommen wir. Und für
den Fridolin hast du doch sicher einen sauren Hering."   35

„O.K.", sagt Fridolin, „du fährst mit deinem Auto voraus°, und ich   ahead
folge dir mit meinem Auto."

„Nein, Frido, du folgst mir nicht, sonst folgt uns nämlich bald die   police
Polizei°. Ihr fahrt beide mit mir; ich habe Platz° für uns alle."   **Platz haben** have room

The following two reading selections are meant to introduce numbers and
letters of the alphabet in context. It is important that you read these passages
aloud several times.

Maße°, Gewichte° und das Dezimalsystem   measures   weights

Überall° in Europa gebraucht° man das Dezimalsystem; es gibt   everywhere   uses
keine Anachronismen wie *inches, feet* und *yards*, oder *quarts* und
gallons, und man mißt° die Temperatur nach Celsius und nicht   measures
nach Fahrenheit. Das System ist sehr einfach und leicht° zu ver-   easy
stehen, aber Amerikaner können es oft erst nach viel Übung° be-   5   practice
nutzen°. Wenn man Sie fragt: „Wie groß sind Sie?", dann denken   use
Sie instinktiv „Fünf Fuß vier" oder „Sechs Fuß", aber der Deutsche
erwartet° „Ein Meter zweiundsechzig" oder „Eins dreiundachtzig".   expects
An einer Straße sehen Sie ein Schild° „Höchstgeschwindigkeit° 80",   sign   speed limit
und Sie denken vielleicht: „So schnell fahre ich nie", aber 80 Kilo- 10
meter sind nur 50 Meilen.

Beim Einkaufen verlangen° Sie zum Beispiel ein Kilo Ochsenfleisch   ask
(1 Kilogramm = 1000 Gramm) oder ein Pfund Butter. Ein Pfund hat
500 Gramm (das amerikanische Pfund hat nur 454 Gramm), und
Sie können auch zum Beispiel 200 Gramm Leberwurst verlangen, 15

oder in Österreich 20 Deka (1 Deka = 10 Gramm). Getränke° wie   beverages
Wein, Bier und Milch kauft man in Literflaschen (1 l) oder Halbliter-
flaschen (0,5 l) oder Viertelliterflaschen (0,25 l).

„Wie kalt ist es denn?" fragt jemand°. „Fünf Grad unter Null." Min-   somebody
nesota im Januar? Nein, so kalt ist es nicht; fünf Grad° unter Null 20   degrees
ist 23 Grad Fahrenheit, denn Null Grad Celsius ist ja 32 Grad Fahrenheit. Wie rechnet man das um°? Nehmen wir ein Beispiel: Wasser   **umrechnen** convert
kocht bei 100°C oder 212°F.

$$212 - 32 = 180$$
$$180 : 9 = 20$$
$$20 \times 5 = 100$$

25

Oder umgekehrt°:   vice versa, conversely

$$100 : 5 = 20$$
$$20 \times 9 = 180$$
$$180 + 32 = 212$$

30

Hier sind die Formeln:

°F→°C: minus 32, geteilt durch 9, mal fünf

°C→°F: geteilt durch 5, mal neun, plus 32

$$(°F - 32) \times \frac{5}{9} = °C$$

$$\left(°C \times \frac{9}{5}\right) + 32 = °F$$

35

Nummernschilder° und das deutsche Alphabet   license plates

Das Alphabet hat 26 Buchstaben°. Man spricht sie aus wie folgt:[13]   letters

A (ah)	J (jott)	S (ess)
B (beh)	K (kah)	T (teh)
C (zeh)	L (ell)	U (uh)
D (deh)	M (emm)	V (fau)
E (eh)	N (enn)	W (weh)
F (eff)	O (oh)	X (iks)
G (geh)	P (peh)	Y (üpsilon)
H (hah)	Q (kuh)	Z (zett)
I (ih)	R (err)	

5

10

Jedes Auto hat ein Nummernschild (oder Kraftfahrzeugkennzei-
chen°); diese Schilder sind rechteckig°. Außerdem sieht man in   motor vehicle
Europa viele internationale Kennzeichen°. Diese internationalen   identification sign
Schilder sind oval und zeigen die Abkürzung° für das Land, aus dem   rectangular plates
sie kommen; also   abbreviation

15

---

[13]To pronounce the German letters, read the transcriptions in parentheses as *German* words with *German* pronunciation.

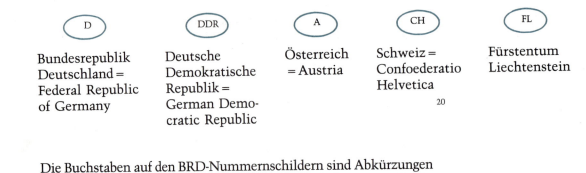

D

Bundesrepublik
Deutschland =
Federal Republic
of Germany

DDR

Deutsche
Demokratische
Republik =
German Demo-
cratic Republic

A

Österreich
= Austria

CH

Schweiz =
Confoederatio
Helvetica

20

FL

Fürstentum
Liechtenstein

Die Buchstaben auf den BRD-Nummernschildern sind Abkürzungen
für die Stadt oder für den Kreis°. Großstädte haben einen Buch- | county
staben, Kleinstädte oder Landkreise° haben zwei oder drei Buch- | rural counties
staben; dann kommen noch zwei Buchstaben und zwei oder drei 25
Zahlen°; zum Beispiel: M = München, MZ = Mainz, MOS = Mos- | numbers Federal
bach/Baden. BD steht für „Bundestag°, Bundesrat° oder Bundesre- | Parliament Federal
gierung°", BP für „Bundespost°", O für „Diplomatisches Corps" und | council Federal
Y für „Bundeswehr°". Ausländer, die ihre Wagen exportieren wollen, | government Federal
bekommen in der BRD eine ovale Zollnummer°. 30 | Post Office Federal
| Army customs plate

Die DDR benutzt für jeden Verwaltungsbezirk° einen oder zwei | administrative district
Buchstaben, z.B. I für Berlin (Ost), T oder X für Karl-Marx-Stadt. In
Österreich erkennt man die Bundesländer°, z.B. OÖ = Oberöster- | federal states
reich, K = Kärnten, oder die Großstädte: W = Wien, L = Linz. Die
Schweizer Schilder zeigen Abkürzungen für den Kanton°, z.B. ZH 35 | canton
für Zürich.

Lesen Sie die folgenden° Kennzeichen als Ausspracheübung° für | following
Buchstaben und Zahlen: | pronunciation exercise

D: B - CV 593   (Berlin)
        F - DA 13   (Frankfurt)   40
        K - RS 259   (Köln)
        HX - WP 517   (Höxter)
        JEV - HD 67   (Jever)

DDR: IA   08   93   (Berlin)
        RE   97   13   (Dresden)   45
        AO   04   59   (Greifswald)
        SM   43   59   (Leipzig)

A: W   352.751   (Wien)
        T   64.321   (Tirol)
        NÖ   610.389   (Niederösterreich)   50

CH: ZH   182 369   (Zürich)
        LU   98 054   (Luzern)
        VD   651 317   (Vaud)

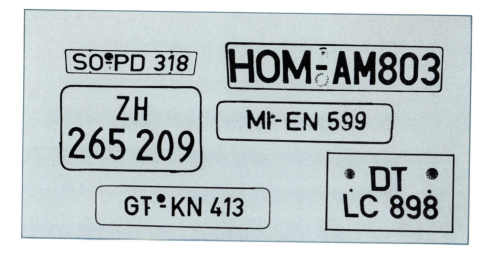

REVIEW EXERCISES

K. Read the following numbers.

758   75,8   7,58   2,718282   232.493,00   232,493

L. The following is an excerpt from a railroad timetable. Form questions and statements using the information given.

> **Wann fährt der Zug nach München in Köln ab?—Um 2 Uhr.**
> **Der Zug kommt um 8 Uhr 16 in Ulm an.**
> **Wie lange hält der Zug in Frankfurt?—12 Minuten.**

Köln	ab	2.00		München	ab	13.20
Bonn	an	2.18		Ulm	an	16.04
	ab	2.20			ab	16.05
Frankfurt	an	4.15		Stuttgart	an	17.08
	ab	4.20			ab	17.14
Heidelberg	an	5.12		Heidelberg	an	20.02
	ab	5.17			ab	20.06
Stuttgart	an	7.01		Frankfurt	an	21.08
	ab	7.06			ab	21.20
Ulm	an	8.16		Bonn	an	23.17
	ab	8.17			ab	23.20
München	an	10.03		Köln	an	24.00

M. Form sentences from the elements given. In each case, the clause in italics should be in the past tense and the other in the past perfect.

> *Ich / müde / sein //* denn / ganze Nacht / nicht schlafen.
> **Ich war müde, denn ich hatte die ganze Nacht nicht geschlafen.**

1. *Herr Enderle / Hamburg / gut kennen //* denn / dort / studieren.
2. *Ich / 10 Stunden / fahren //* und / um 8 Uhr abends / in Köln / ankommen.
3. Dr. Schmidt / in Wien / studieren // *und / dann / Arzt / in Salzburg / werden.*
4. *Herr Müller / uns / nicht anrufen //* denn / unsere Telefonnummer / verlieren.
5. *Inge / sofort / nach Hause / fahren //* denn / Großvater / sterben.

N. Construct sentences as indicated.

1. Unfortunately, Mr. Schmidt had gone to Berlin with his wife at that time.
   (a) Mr. Schmidt goes to Berlin.
   (b) change to past perfect (use correct auxiliary!)
   (c) add: *at that time*
   (d) add: *with his wife* (sequence of adverbs!)
   (e) start with *Unfortunately* (move subject!)
2. I simply haven't wanted to drive home in this rain.
   (a) I drive home.
   (b) I want to drive home.
   (c) I have wanted to drive home.
   ("double infinitive")

Parkplatz am Dom in Osnabrück

   (d) negate
   (e) add: *simply*
   (f) add: *in this rain* (end field!)
3. She asked me yesterday to call her tomorrow.
   (a) to call
   (b) add (insert): **zu**
   (c) add: *her*
   (d) add: *tomorrow*

   (e) precede infinitive phrase by: *She asks me* (use **bitten**)
   (f) change to perfect
   (g) add: *yesterday*

O. Express in German.

1. He gave his girlfriend a watch.
2. He gave the watch to his girlfriend.
3. He gave it (the watch) to her.
4. He was coming from the movies.
5. Were you living with your aunt at that time?
6. Why did you come home so late?
7. Meyer bought a car in Stuttgart.
8. For a long time I did not know that.
9. I did not drink coffee for two years.
10. Two years ago I drank too much coffee.
11. You are still drinking too much coffee.
12. Her grandfather died three years ago.
13. I wanted to call you, but I had forgotten your telephone number.
14. They went to Paris to learn French.

P. Review the menus on p. 208 and p. 209; find out from newspapers or from a local bank what the current exchange rate is and determine how much your meal costs in American dollars. Figure out also how much an Austrian meal would cost in marks and a German meal in schillings.

Q. Composition. Write a short conversation between two students, based on the conversations in this and previous units. Use the following outline:

A says hello to B and wonders whether B has time for a beer, but B has to go to work and has no time. A is surprised and wonders if B is still at the university. The answer is yes, but B is short of cash. B needs money because he or she wants to go to London for a semester. B is an English major and feels that one must go to England in order to really learn English.

VOCABULARY

der Akzent', -e	accent
der Anfang, -̈e	beginning
der Anfänger, -	beginner
an•rufen	to call (on the telephone)
die Arbeit, -en	work
der Arbeiter, -	worker (m.)
die Arbeiterin, -nen	worker (f.)
das Ausland (no pl.)	foreign countries
im Ausland	abroad
der Baum, -̈e	tree
beginnen	to start, begin
besser	better
die Bibliothek', -en	library
das Bild, -er	picture
bitten	to beg, to request
damals	at that time, then
der Dollar, -s	dollar
eigentlich	actually
einfach	easy, simple
ein•schlafen (sein)	to fall asleep
das Ende, -n	end

der Erzähler, -	narrator
ewig	eternal, forever
der Fahrer, -	driver
der Franken, - (sFr)	franc (Swiss)
das Geschäft, -e	business, store
das Sportgeschäft, -e	sporting goods store
der Groschen, -	(smallest unit of Austrian currency
grün	green
halten (hältst, hält)	to hold; to stop, halt
heraus•finden	to find out
kaputt'	busted, broken
der Kellner, -	waiter
die Kellnerin, -nen	waitress
klingeln	to ring (the bell)
lachen	to laugh
lassen (läßt, läßt)	to leave; let, allow
das Lokal, -e	restaurant
das Fischlokal, -e	fish restaurant
los	loose; going on
was ist hier los?	what's going on here?

was ist mit dir los?	what's the matter with you?
mal	once; times
meinen	to think, express an opinion; to say
die Milliar′de, -n	billion
die Million′, -en	million
minus	minus, less
nämlich	to be specific; you see; namely
nennen	to call; to name
null	zero
der Ort, -e	town; place
die Ostsee	Baltic Sea
das Paar, -e	pair
ein Paar Schuhe	pair of shoes
ein paar	a few
ein paar Mal	a few times
der Pfennig, -e	penny
plus	plus
das Rad, ¨er	wheel; bicycle
der Rappen, -	(smallest unit of Swiss currency)
die Rose, -n	rose
ruhig	quiet, restful; (sent. adv.) it won't bother me, I'll stay calm about it
der Schuh, -e	shoe
singen	to sing
sonst	otherwise
sonst nichts	nothing else
sterben (stirbst, stirbt) (sein)	to die
die Stimme, -n	voice
sympathisch	likeable
tausend	thousand
teilen	to divide
geteilt durch	divided by
tragen (trägst, trägt)	to carry; to wear (clothes)
um . . . zu	in order to . . .
verlieren	to lose
versprechen (versprichst, verspricht)	to promise
wenig	little
weniger	less; minus
weniger als	less than; fewer than
wieder•sehen	to see again
zuerst′ (erst)	at first

Strong Verbs and Irregular Weak Verbs

The following verbs have occurred in Units 1–7.

INFINITIVE	PRESENT	PAST TENSE	PERFECT	
ab•fahren	**fährt ab**	**fuhr ab**	**ist abgefahren**	to depart
an•fangen	**fängt an**	**fing an**	**angefangen**	to begin, start
an•kommen		**kam an**	**ist angekommen**	to arrive
an•rufen		**rief an**	**angerufen**	to call (on the telephone)
auf•stehen		**stand auf**	**ist aufgestanden**	to get up (out of bed)
aus•gehen		**ging aus**	**ist ausgegangen**	to go out
beginnen		**begann**	**begonnen**	to begin, start
bekommen		**bekam**	**bekommen**	to receive
bitten		**bat**	**gebeten**	to request
bleiben		**blieb**	**ist geblieben**	to stay, remain
bringen		**brachte**	**gebracht**	to bring
denken		**dachte**	**gedacht**	to think
dürfen	**darf**	**durfte**	**gedurft**	to be allowed to
ein•laden	**lädt ein**	**lud ein**	**eingeladen**	to invite
ein•schlafen	**schläft ein**	**schlief ein**	**ist eingeschlafen**	to fall asleep

INFINITIVE	PRESENT	PAST TENSE	PERFECT	
empfehlen	empfiehlt	empfahl	empfohlen	to recommend
essen	ißt	aß	gegessen	to eat
fahren	fährt	fuhr	ist gefahren	to drive
finden		fand	gefunden	to find
fliegen		flog	ist geflogen	to fly
geben	gibt	gab	gegeben	to give
gefallen	gefällt	gefiel	gefallen	to please
gehen		ging	ist gegangen	to go
halten	hält	hielt	gehalten	to hold; to stop
heißen		hieß	geheißen	to be called; to mean
helfen	hilft	half	geholfen	to help
kennen		kannte	gekannt	to know, to be acquainted with
klingen		klang	geklungen	to sound
kommen		kam	ist gekommen	to come
können	kann	konnte	gekonnt	to be able to
lassen	läßt	ließ	gelassen	to leave
laufen	läuft	lief	ist gelaufen	to run
lesen	liest	las	gelesen	to read
liegen		lag	gelegen	to lie (flat), to be situated
mögen	mag	mochte	gemocht	to like to
müssen	muß	mußte	gemußt	to have to
nehmen	nimmt	nahm	genommen	to take
nennen		nannte	genannt	to name
rennen		rannte	ist gerannt	to run
scheinen		schien	geschienen	to seem; to shine
schlafen	schläft	schlief	geschlafen	to sleep
schreiben		schrieb	geschrieben	to write
schwimmen		schwamm	ist geschwommen	to swim
sehen	sieht	sah	gesehen	to see
sein	ist	war	ist gewesen	to be
singen		sang	gesungen	to sing
sitzen		saß	gesessen	to sit
sprechen	spricht	sprach	gesprochen	to speak
stehen		stand	gestanden	to stand
sterben	stirbt	starb	ist gestorben	to die
tragen	trägt	trug	getragen	to carry
treffen	trifft	traf	getroffen	to meet; to hit
trinken		trank	getrunken	to drink
tun		tat	getan	to do
um•ziehen		zog um	ist umgezogen	to move
verbringen		verbrachte	verbracht	to spend (time)
verlieren		verlor	verloren	to lose
versprechen	verspricht	versprach	versprochen	to promise
verstehen		verstand	verstanden	to understand
werden	wird	wurde	ist geworden	to become
wissen	weiß	wußte	gewußt	to know

Unit 8

Dependent Clauses—The Imperative—
Open Conditions—The Future Tense

Past and Present

Wherever you go in Central Europe, you will be reminded of the past. You will constantly experience flashbacks into history—through talking to local people, looking at the architecture, visiting museums, and studying place names. The central square in the old city of Frankfurt is called the *Römerberg*, Hill of the Romans, because a Roman settlement was located there to protect the ford across the Main River, which later gave the town its name: Frankfurt means "the ford of the Franks." You will encounter history if you listen to Bach in the Thomaskirche in Leipzig or to Mozart in the palace at Brühl, once the summer residence of the archbishops of Cologne, or if you watch *Jedermann*, Hugo von Hofmannsthal's 1911 re-creation of the fifteenth-century *Everyman* play, during the summer festival in Salzburg. High culture and popular culture feed on the same tradition.

Berlin (Ost)

Thomaskirche in Leipzig
(1623)

Mainz

Römerberg

PATTERNS ONE

1/Unintroduced and Introduced Dependent Clauses

Ich glaube,	Er kommt heute erst spät nach Hause.			
	er kommt heute erst spät nach Hause.			

Ich glaube,	**daß**	er	heute erst spät nach Hause	**kommt.**
Ich glaube nicht,	**daß**	er	heute erst spät nach Hause	**kommt.**

Meinst du,	Hat Frau Enderle den Brief schon bekommen?		
	Frau Enderle hat den Brief schon bekommen?		

Meinst du,	**daß**	Frau Enderle	den Brief schon bekommen	**hat?**
Meinst du nicht,	**daß**	Frau Enderle	den Brief schon bekommen	**hat?**

2/Verb-Last Position in Introduced Dependent Clauses

Ich weiß, daß er Geld **hat.**
Ich weiß, daß er Geld **hatte.**
Ich weiß, daß er Geld **gehabt hat.**

Ich weiß nicht, ob Fritz mit dem Auto zum Bahnhof **fährt.**
Ich wußte, daß er immer mit dem Auto zum Bahnhof **fuhr.**
Ich glaube nicht, daß er mit dem Auto zum Bahnhof **gefahren ist.**

Wissen Sie, ob Meyers hier **wohnen?**
Wir wußten, daß Meyers da **wohnten.**
Wie soll ich wissen, wo Meyers **gewohnt haben?**

Nachbarn schützen Nachbarn

Wir wollen, daß Sie sicher wohnen. Ihre Polizei.

3/Word Order in Sentences with Introduced Dependent Clauses

Ich war müde. Ich ging ins Bett.
Ich ging ins Bett, weil ich müde war.
Weil ich müde war, ging ich ins Bett.

I was tired. I went to bed.
I went to bed because I was tired.
Because I was tired, I went to bed.

Wenn er kommt, gehen wir sofort.
Wir gehen sofort, wenn er kommt.
Wenn er bis sieben Uhr nicht hier ist, dann
gehen wir ohne ihn.

When he comes, we'll leave immediately.
We'll leave immediately when he comes.
If he isn't here by seven o'clock, we'll leave
without him.

4/Subordinating Conjunctions

Als ich meinen Mann kennenlernte, waren wir noch Studenten.

Bevor Frau Enderle nach Burgbach kam, hatte sie lange in Berlin gelebt.

Wir saßen im Wohnzimmer und plauderten, bis Herr Enderle aus Stuttgart zurückkam.

Da das Haus zu klein für uns alle geworden war, bin ich vor drei Jahren mit meiner Familie ausgezogen.

Nachdem er weggegangen war, schrieb er mir jede Woche einen Brief.

Obwohl mein Betrieb in Stuttgart ist, sind wir doch in Burgbach geblieben.

Meine Schwester kommt nur noch selten nach Hause, seit sie geheiratet hat.

Während die Kinder schwimmen gingen, saßen wir im Garten.

Wir rannten den ganzen Weg ins Dorf, weil wir nicht zu spät zum Essen kommen wollten.

Wenn wir gegessen haben, gehen wir ins Wohnzimmer und sehen fern.

Daß ihr nur zwei Tage hierbleiben könnt, tut mir leid.

Es tut mir leid, daß ihr nur zwei Tage hierbleiben könnt.

Ich wußte nicht, daß er nach dem Studium nach Amerika gehen will.

Daß er nach dem Studium nach Amerika gehen will, wußte ich nicht.

When I met my husband, we were still students.

Before Mrs. Enderle came to Burgbach, she had lived in Berlin for a long time.

We sat in the living room and talked until Mr. Enderle returned from Stuttgart.

Since the house had become too small for all of us, I moved out three years ago with my family.

After he had left, he wrote me a letter every week.

Although my place of work is in Stuttgart, we continued to live in Burgbach.

My sister rarely comes home anymore since she got married.

While the children went swimming, we sat in the garden.

We ran all the way to the village because we didn't want to be late for dinner.

When we have eaten, we'll go into the living room and watch TV.

I'm sorry that you can only stay for two days.

I didn't know that he wants to go to America after he graduates (after his studies).

5/Direct and Indirect Questions

Denkt er noch an dich?
Ich möchte wissen, ob er noch an dich denkt.

Möchtest du denn lieber hierbleiben, Fritz?
Ich habe Fritz gefragt, ob er lieber hierbleiben möchte.

Wer ist das denn?
Weißt du, wer das ist?

Wen haben Sie denn in der Stadt getroffen?
Können Sie mir bitte sagen, wen Sie in der Stadt getroffen haben?

Wie heißen Sie denn?
Darf ich Sie fragen, wie Sie heißen?

ANALYSIS ONE

72/Dependent Clauses: Definition

Consider the following sentences:

1. **Ich gehe ins Bett. Ich bin müde.**
   I am going to bed. I am tired.
2. **Ich gehe ins Bett, weil ich müde bin.**
   I am going to bed, because I am tired.
3. **Weil ich müde bin, gehe ich ins Bett.**
   Because I am tired, I am going to bed.

Sentence 1 contains two independent (main) clauses. In (2), the second clause is joined to the first with the conjunction **weil** (*because*) and the inflected verb **bin** appears at the end of the clause. In (3), the two clauses are reversed, and the subject of the second clause, **ich**, now appears after the inflected verb **gehe** because the preceding dependent clause constitutes the front field.

All clauses introduced by subordinating conjunctions like **weil** (see Anal. 74, p. 227) are called dependent (or subordinate) clauses. They do not convey a complete message unless accompanied by a "main" clause: *although he was tired* does not make sense without a statement like *he didn't go to bed* preceding or following:

> **Obwohl er müde war, ging er nicht ins Bett.**
> **Er ging nicht ins Bett, obwohl er müde war.**

Every dependent clause, including its verb, functions as one single syntactical unit of the main clause. For example, dependent clauses can function as:

SUBJECT	*The winner* gets the prize. *Whoever wins* gets the prize.
PREDICATE NOUN	This is not *the expected result.* This is not *what I had expected.*
OBJECT	I'll never know *your thoughts.* I'll never know *what you think.*
ADVERB	She met John *during his stay in New York.* She met John *while he was staying in New York.*

73/Word Order in Unintroduced and in Introduced Dependent Clauses

1. Most dependent clauses are introduced by such connecting words as *that, because, although,* but in both English and German there is a type of dependent clause that does not require such a connect-

ing word and is thus "unintroduced." English phrases of the type *I believe* and *I don't believe* can be followed by either kind of dependent clause.

> I believe (don't believe) she is in Cologne.
>   that she is in Cologne.

In German, *only positive introductory statements* using verbs like **denken, glauben, wissen** can be followed by both.

> **Ich glaube, sie ist in Köln.**
> **daß sie in Köln ist.**

Negative introductory statements must be followed by introduced dependent clauses.

> **Ich glaube nicht, daß sie in Köln ist.**

We have used many unintroduced dependent clauses in the preceding units; they have posed no problems because their word order is the same as that of main clauses. Introduced dependent clauses, however, show a new syntactic principle referred to as verb-last position.

> In all introduced dependent clauses, the finite verb (i.e., the first prong) appears behind the second prong at the very end of the clause.

	FRONT FIELD	1ST PRONG	INNER FIELD	2ND PRONG	
MAIN CLAUSE	Er	ist	heute	hier.	
UNINTRODUCED DEPENDENT CLAUSE	Ich glaube, er	ist	heute	hier.	
INTRODUCED DEPENDENT CLAUSE	Ich glaube, daß er		heute	hier	ist.

2. The sequence of elements following the subject **er** is a mirror image of the sequence of elements in the corresponding English sentence; that is, if the German sequence is 1–2–3, the English sequence will be 3–2–1.

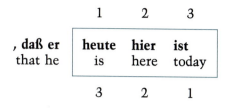

	1	2	3
, daß er that he	**heute** is	**hier** here	**ist** today

3   2   1

This mirror image principle holds for a great many English and German sentences and explains, for example, why the German sequence time-place corresponds to the English sequence of place-time.

Find other examples for this mirror image principle in the patterns and exercises.

3. In example 3 in Anal. 72 above,

Weil ich müde bin, gehe ich ins Bett.

the dependent clause precedes the main clause. Since each dependent clause represents one syntactic element of the main clause, it follows that the first prong of the main clause, **gehe**, must come immediately after the dependent clause, according to the principle of verb-second position. Thus, if a dependent clause precedes a main clause, their two finite verb forms always stand next to one another, and are *always* separated by a comma: . . . **bin, gehe** . . .

In Hamburg	**bin**	ich jeden Abend	**ins Kino**	**gegangen.**

Als ich in Hamburg **war,**	**bin**	ich jeden Abend	**ins Kino**	**gegangen.**

NOTE: While a **weil**-clause can follow or precede a main clause, clauses introduced by the coordinating conjunction **denn** must always follow.

Ich gehe jetzt ins Bett, denn ich bin müde.

4. Frequently, especially after **wenn**-clauses (English *if*-clauses), the dependent clause—that is, the first element of the main clause—is repeated and summed up at the beginning of the main clause by either **dann** or **so**. This **dann** or **so** immediately precedes the first prong—that is, the second element of the main clause.

Wenn er nicht bald kommt,

1

dann | *müssen* wir halt ohne ihn gehen.

1a | 2

If he doesn't come soon, then we'll just have to go without him.

5. Verbal complements like **ab-**, **an-**, **aus-**, and any others that are written as one word with an infinitive, must also be connected in verb-last position.

Er geht mit mir aus. —Wenn er mit mir ausgeht, . . .
Sie kommt bald zurück. —Daß sie bald zurückkommt, . . .
Er lernte sie in Bonn kennen. —Als er sie in Bonn kennenlernte, . . .

6. It was pointed out in Anal. 57, p. 162, that when modals and **brauchen** are used in the perfect with a dependent infinitive, their participles look like infinitives.

Ich habe sie noch nicht zu Hause besuchen können.

As a result, **besuchen können** looks like a double infinitive. If such double infinitives occur in dependent clauses, the inflected verb follows **nicht** and *precedes* the entire second prong; in this one case the principle of verb-last position does not apply.

Es tut mir leid, daß ich sie noch nicht habe zu Hause besuchen können.
I am sorry that I haven't been able to visit them at home yet.

However, as a rule, the past tense of the modals is used rather than the perfect, and thus the double infinitive construction is avoided.

Es tut mir leid, daß ich sie noch nicht zu Hause besuchen konnte.

7. In most dependent clauses, the subject follows the connecting word. However, a noun subject may be preceded by pronoun objects.

Ich weiß, daß *Herr Meyer seiner Frau* einen Sportwagen geschenkt hat.
Ich weiß, daß *Herr Meyer ihr* einen Sportwagen geschenkt hat.
Ich weiß, daß *ihr Herr Meyer* einen Sportwagen geschenkt hat.

In order to increase the news value of a noun subject, it may be moved toward the end of the inner field. Thus, in the following sentences, the news value is shifted from the time element to the subject:

Ich kann nicht glauben, daß *der Winter* hier schon im Oktober beginnt.
Ich kann nicht glauben, daß hier schon im Oktober *der Winter* beginnt.

If the subject of the dependent clause is a pronoun without news value, it must follow the connecting word immediately.

Morgen kommt   sie   wieder zu uns.

Ich weiß nicht, ob   sie   morgen wieder zu uns kommt.

/Subordinating Conjunctions

In Anal. 32, p. 78, we introduced the coordinating conjunctions **aber, denn, oder**, and **und**. These coordinating conjunctions connect either two or more main clauses or two or more dependent clauses; they do not influence the word order of either.

> **Hans wollte schon gehen, und Otto wollte noch hierbleiben.**
> **Ich gehe ins Bett, weil ich müde bin, und weil es schon elf Uhr ist.**

Subordinating conjunctions always introduce dependent clauses and require verb-last position. There are several types of subordinating conjunctions:

1. Subordinating conjunctions introducing adverbial clauses:

als	when (refers to a single event in the past)	**obwohl**	although
bevor	before	**seit(dem)**	since (temporal)
bis	until	**während**	while
da	because, since (causal)	**weil**	because
nachdem	after	**wenn**	if; when; whenever

> **Sie bleibt heute zu Hause. *Warum*? Es ist zu heiß.**
> **Sie bleibt heute zu Hause, weil es zu heiß ist.**

Adverbial clauses introduced by these conjunctions frequently have verbs in the past tense, even if the verb of the main clause is in the perfect. The past tense is virtually obligatory in **als**-clauses, unless the **als**-clause contains a past perfect.

> **Ich habe bis elf gewartet. Aber als er dann immer noch nicht kam, bin ich ins Bett gegangen.**
> I waited until eleven. But when he still did not come, I went to bed.

2. The subordinating conjunction **daß** introduces subject and object clauses.

> SUBJECT **Daß du das für mich getan hast, war sehr nett von dir.**
> OBJECT **Ich wußte nicht, daß er damals in Freiburg wohnte.**

If a subject clause follows the main clause, the "dummy subject" **es** occupies the front field to anticipate the subject clause:

> **Es war sehr nett von dir, daß du das für mich getan hast.**

3. The subordinating conjunction **ob** introduces indirect yes-or-no questions:

If the question

Does he live in Berlin?   **Wohnt er in Berlin?**

is preceded by clauses like *Do you know*, **Wissen Sie** or *Ask him*, **Fragen Sie ihn**, it becomes an indirect question. Indirect questions are always introduced dependent clauses and require verb-last position.

Indirect yes-or-no questions are introduced by *whether* or *if* in English and by **ob** in German. English *if* is the equivalent of **ob** only if it can be replaced by *whether*.

Do you know if he lives in Berlin?   **Wissen Sie, ob er in Berlin wohnt?**
         whether he lives in Berlin?

4. Interrogatives as subordinating conjunctions:

If word questions are preceded by an introductory clause, they retain their question word and require verb-last position.

Where does he live?   **Wo wohnt er?**
Do you know where he lives?   **Weißt du, wo er wohnt?**
I don't know where he lives.   **Ich weiß nicht, wo er wohnt.**

5. Relative pronouns also introduce dependent clauses; they will be discussed in Unit 12.

PRACTICE ONE

A. Restate the following sentences as indicated.

1. Sie hat dich nach Burgbach eingeladen.
   (a) Ich höre, _____.
   (b) Ich höre, daß _____.
2. Er hatte noch lange bei seinen Eltern gewohnt.
   (a) Ich wußte, _____.
   (b) Ich wußte, daß _____.
   (c) Ich wußte nicht, daß _____.
3. Ich gehe jetzt nach Hause. Ich bin müde.
   (a) Ich gehe jetzt nach Hause, denn _____.
   (b) Ich gehe jetzt nach Hause, weil _____.

B. Change the following direct questions to indirect questions, starting with **Weißt du. . . .** Be sure to leave out **denn** in the indirect questions.

1. Wie weit sind wir denn heute gefahren?
2. Was kostet ein Pfund Kalbfleisch?

3. Wieviel Gramm hat ein amerikanisches Pfund?
4. Wo ist Frau Enderle denn geboren?
5. Wie rechnet man Fahrenheit in Celsius um?
6. Wem gehört der Wagen mit der Zollnummer?
7. Wann fährt unser Zug denn ab?
8. Wie lange dauert der Film denn?

C. Combine the following sentences by making the first one into a dependent clause, starting with the conjunction in parentheses; then express the combined sentences in English.

> **(als) Ich kam an. Sie war schon da.**
> **Als ich ankam, war sie schon da.**

1. (als) Ich lernte meinen Mann kennen. Wir waren noch Studenten.
2. (bevor) Sie fährt nach München. Sie muß viel arbeiten.
3. (bis) Frau Enderle kam nach Burgbach. Sie hatte in Berlin gewohnt.
4. (da) Meine Schwester wohnt in Hamburg. Wir sehen sie nicht oft.
5. (wenn) Es gibt viel Arbeit. Wir helfen alle mit.
6. (obwohl) Er ist Ausländer. Er kennt Österreich sehr gut.
7. (während) Sie studierte in England. Sie hat mir jede Woche einen Brief geschrieben.
8. (seit) Sie reist so viel. Ich sehe sie selten.
9. (weil) Er lief so schnell. Ich konnte ihm nicht folgen.
10. (nachdem) Wir waren zurückgekommen. Wir haben noch eine Flasche Wein getrunken.

PATTERNS TWO

6/Imperative, *du*-Form

Ruf mich bitte nicht vor acht an.
Bitte ruf mich nicht vor acht an.
Aber ruf mich nicht vor acht an, bitte.
Ruf sie doch noch einmal an. Vielleicht
  ist sie jetzt zu Hause.
Ruf sie doch noch mal an, bitte.

Bitte sei doch so gut und fahr mich
  mal eben in die Stadt.
Entschuldige mich bitte; ich muß
  arbeiten gehen.
Bitte gib mir doch mal die Butter, Hans.
Sieh mal, da kommt die Erika.
Lauf doch nicht so schnell.
Bleib gesund.

7/Imperative, *ihr*-Form

Vergeßt nicht, uns aus Italien eine Postkarte zu schicken.
Es war schön, daß ihr kommen konntet; besucht uns bald mal wieder.
Seid so nett und wartet, bis Tante Amalie kommt.
Also auf Wiedersehen. Und ruft uns an, wenn ihr nach Hause kommt.

8/Imperative, *wir*-Form

Wo sollen wir denn essen, Rosemarie? — Gehen wir doch mal ins
  Regina, Klaus, da waren wir schon so lange nicht mehr.
Müssen wir denn heute schon wieder zu Müllers? — Natürlich müssen
  wir. — Also schön, fahren wir wieder zu Müllers.

9/Imperative, *Sie*-Form

Bitte geben Sie mir Zimmer 641.
Seien Sie herzlich gegrüßt von Ihrem Hans Meyer.
Entschuldigen Sie bitte, gnädige Frau; Ihr Mann ist am Telefon.
Bitte geben Sie mir ein Zimmer mit Bad.
Lassen Sie Ihren Wagen doch mal zu Hause: Fahren Sie mit der Bahn!

10/Impersonal Imperative

Einsteigen bitte.	Please board (train or streetcar).
Langsam fahren.	Drive slowly.
Nicht rauchen.	Don't smoke.
Nicht öffnen, bevor der Zug hält.	Don't open before the train stops.
Nicht benutzen, während der Zug hält.	Don't use while the train is stopped.
Bitte anschnallen.	Please fasten your seat belt.
Nicht mit dem Fahrer sprechen.	Don't speak with the driver.
Nicht stören.	Do not disturb.
Bitte an der Kasse zahlen.	Please pay at the cashier.

Rezepte für Feinschmecker aus bekannten Interhotels *

Schweinshaxe in Biersoße

4 Schweinshaxen (je 400 g) 1 Flasche Vollbier
3 Zwiebeln   20 g Stärkemehl
½ l Brauner Grundfond Salz, Pfeffer und Knoblauch

Haxen mit Salz, Pfeffer und zerdrücktem Knoblauch gut einreiben und mit Wasser in einer Röhre ansetzen. Regelmäßig mit dem Bratensaft übergießen, grobe Zwiebelwürfel zugeben und nach dem Einkochen mit Bier danach mit dem braunen Grundfond auffüllen. Bis zum Garwerden glacieren, Haxen ausstechen, die Soße binden und passieren.
Vor dem Servieren auslösen und gegebenenfalls in Scheiben schneiden, auf Apfel-Wein-Kraut anrichten.

*Interhotels: GDR hotels for foreigners.

Knuckles of pork in beer sauce

4 pork knuckles   1 bottle of beer
(400 g each)   (not lager or light beer)
3 onions   20 g starch-flour
Half a litre of brown salt, pepper, garlic
sauce base

Roll the knuckles well with salt, pepper and crushed garlic and roast them in water in a hot oven. Baste frequently with the dripping, add the coarsely chopped onions, and after the juice has been absorbed add the beer and the brown sauce base. Glaze until the meat is done, carve out the knuckles, thicken and strain the sauce. Bone the meat before serving and slice it if you so wish. Serve on a base of apple-and-wine cabbage.

11/Open Conditions

Wenn ich kann, komme ich.

Ich fahre nach Zürich, wenn du auch fährst.

Wenn du bei diesem Regen auf der Autobahn fährst, mußt du aber sehr vorsichtig sein.

Wenn du kein Geld hast, helfe ich dir gerne.

Wenn Paul hier ist, können wir ihn fragen.

If I can, I'll come.

I'll go to Zurich, if you'll go too.

If you drive on the autobahn in this rain, you've got to be very careful.

If you don't have money, I'll be glad to help you.

If Paul is here, we can ask him.

12/The Future Tense

Ich glaube, ich werde sie nie wiedersehen.

Diesen Sonntag werde ich nie vergessen.

Diesen Sonntag werde ich leider nie vergessen können.

Nein, Herr Harms, ich werde es nicht vergessen. Ich rufe Sie morgen um 9 Uhr an.

I believe I will never see them (her) again.

I shall never forget this Sunday.

Unfortunately, I shall never be able to forget this Sunday.

No, Mr. Harms, I shall not forget it. I'll give you a ring at 9:00 tomorrow.

13/The Future Tense to Express Present Probability

Gertrud ist schon vor einer Stunde abgefahren, also wird sie jetzt (sicher) schon lange zu Hause sein.

Ich möchte wissen, warum Peter mich immer noch nicht angerufen hat. — Er wird (wohl) noch schlafen.

Den Helmut habe ich schon wochenlang nicht gesehen. Wo kann der denn nur sein? — Er wird (wahrscheinlich) wieder in Essen arbeiten müssen.

Gertrude left an hour ago, so she has probably been home for a long time now.

I'd like to know why Peter still hasn't called me up yet. — He's probably still asleep.

I haven't seen Helmut in weeks. Where could he be? — He probably has to work in Essen again.

ANALYSIS TWO

75/The Imperative: Definition and Forms

Imperative forms are used to ask someone to do, or not to do, something. This can take the form of a polite request (*Hand me that corkscrew, dear, would you, please?*), of a cookbook instruction (*Sift the flour*), of an impatient shout (*Shut up! Get out!*), or of an order or command (*Stop! Drop that gun!*). Imperatives are used in the most varied situations, from religious services (*Let us pray*) to advertising (*Be a needlepointer!*), from child rearing (*Eat your spinach!*) to language instruction (*Change the following statements to imperatives*).

In German, you must use the form of the imperative that corresponds to the pronoun of address used in a given situation: **du, ihr, wir**, or **Sie**. There is also a widely used impersonal form of the imperative which is identical with the infinitive.

The **Sie**-form was introduced in Unit 1; remember that it corresponds to the third-person plural. The **ihr**- and **wir**-forms are identical with the corresponding forms of the present indicative. The **du**-form, however, drops the indicative ending **-(e)st**.

In principle, the ending **-e** of the **du**-form is optional. However, verbs whose stems end in **-d** (**reden**) or **-t** (**antworten**) or **-ig** (**entschuldigen**) are usually used with the **-e** ending.

Weak Verbs				
du-FORM	sag(e)	rede	antworte	entschuldige
ihr-FORM	sagt	redet	antwortet	entschuldigt
wir-FORM	sagen wir	reden wir	antworten wir	entschuldigen wir
Sie-FORM	sagen Sie	reden Sie	antworten Sie	entschuldigen Sie

Strong Verbs					
du-FORM	geh(e)	finde	fahr(e)	fang(e) an	lauf(e)
ihr-FORM	geht	findet	fahrt	fangt an	lauft
wir-FORM	gehen wir	finden wir	fahren wir	fangen wir an	laufen wir
Sie-FORM	gehen Sie	finden Sie	fahren Sie	fangen Sie an	laufen Sie
du-FORM	sieh	gib	nimm	werde	sei
ihr-FORM	seht	gebt	nehmt	werdet	seid
wir-FORM	sehen wir	geben wir	nehmen wir	werden wir	seien wir
Sie-FORM	sehen Sie	geben Sie	nehmen Sie	werden Sie	seien Sie

The change of vowel from **a** to **ä** (**ich fahre, du fährst**), from **au** to **äu** (**ich laufe, du läufst**), and from **o** to **ö** (**stoßen, du stößt**) does not occur in the imperative.

The change from **e** to **ie** or **i** (**ich gebe, du gibst; ich sehe, du siehst**) must be observed. These changed-vowel forms never show the ending **-e** in the **du**-form.

The **du**-form **werde** is irregular, as are the forms of **sein**.

Modals do not have imperative forms.

IMPERSONAL IMPERATIVE

With some verbs, the infinitive is used as an impersonal imperative when no one in particular is addressed, for example, **Nicht öffnen, Bitte einsteigen.**

76/The Use of the Imperative

1. The **du**-form is used when the persons involved say **du** to each other. It may also be used in advertisements.

Bring mir bitte die Zeitung mit,
Bring mir doch bitte die Zeitung mit, } **wenn du in die Stadt fährst.**
Bitte bring mir die Zeitung mit,

Mach mal Pause, trink Coca-Cola!

2. Like the **du**-form, the **ihr**-form is used between persons who say **du** to each other.

Kinder, vergeßt nicht,
Kinder, bitte vergeßt nicht, } **daß ihr um zehn zu Hause sein sollt.**
Kinder, vergeßt bitte nicht,

3. The **wir**-form can only be used if the speaker includes himself or herself among the persons addressed; the pronoun **wir** is always used.

Wo willst du denn essen? Im Grünen Baum? Also gut, gehen wir in den Grünen Baum.

The English equivalent is *Let's (go)*.

In contemporary German, this **wir**-form, as in **Gehen wir essen**, is frequently replaced by the rhetorical question **Sollen wir essen gehen?**

4. The **Sie**-form is used (with or without **bitte**) between persons who say **Sie** to each other.

(Bitte) bringen Sie mir noch ein Glas Wein.

**Schütze Deinen Kopf -
Du hast nur einen.**

In advertising it is used without **bitte.**

> **Fahren Sie doch mal einen BMW.**
> **Kommen Sie zu uns, wenn Sie Geld brauchen.**

5. The impersonal form is the infinitive used to express requests. It is used to give instructions to the public and is found on traffic signs, at airports, in planes, in railroad stations, and so on. It is also used in advertising and in cookbooks, without exclamation point.

> **Aussteigen bitte.**
> **Nicht öffnen, bevor der Zug hält.**
> **Nicht rauchen.**
> **Karotten, Sellerie und Bohnen in Salzwasser weich kochen, Parmesan daruntermischen.**

**ERST
DENKEN
DANN
HANDELN**

Bitte nicht stören!
Do not disturb please!
Ne pas déranger s.v.p.!

Fußgänger
bitte andere
Gehsteigseite
benutzen

NOTE: Imperatives range from polite requests (without exclamation point) to real commands (always with exclamation point).

<u>WORD ORDER IN IMPERATIVE CLAUSES</u>

The personal forms of the imperative normally begin the sentence, but they are frequently preceded by **bitte**.

> **Bring mir etwas zu lesen mit.**
> **Bitte bring mir etwas zu lesen mit.**

Since the impersonal imperatives are infinitives, they stand at the end of the imperative phrase.

> **Langsam fahren!**
> **Bitte die Türen schließen!**

When imperatives are negated, **nicht** stands, as usual, at the end of the inner field and precedes the second prong.

> **Bitte fahr morgen nicht nach Berlin.**
> **Sei doch nicht so ungeduldig!**
> **Nicht stören!**

The word **bitte** may appear at the beginning, in the middle, and at the end of imperative clauses. In the middle, it precedes items of news value. At the beginning and at the end, **bitte** may or may not be set off by commas.

77/Open Conditions

A condition is an event or a situation without which another event or situation cannot take place. Thus, in the statement *If the weather is good tomorrow, we can go to the beach*, good weather is the prerequisite for the trip to the beach. The *if*-clause (the grammatical "condition") does not indicate whether or not the weather will be good; it simply states that unless the weather is good, the second part of the statement (the grammatical "conclusion") will not become a reality.

If someone says, *I haven't seen my old teacher for years. If she is still alive, she was eighty years old last Monday*, this means that the speaker does not know whether the teacher is still alive, and consequently whether the teacher was able to celebrate her eightieth birthday. *The question as to the reality of the facts is left open.* However, this question *is not left open* if someone says, *If my teacher were still alive, she would have turned eighty last Monday*. The speaker now implies that the teacher is dead. In other words: The situation described in the condition is known to be unreal and to exist only in the speaker's thought and imagination.

The difference in meaning between *if she is alive* and *if she were alive* depends entirely on verb forms. The *is* leaves the question of the actual facts open; the *were* expresses the unreality of the situation imagined.

We use the term "open condition" to indicate that the question of the facts is open, and we use the term "contrary-to-fact condition" to indicate that these facts are contrary to reality and merely assumed in imagination.

In Unit 8, only open conditions are introduced. Contrary-to-fact conditions, which require the use of the subjunctive, will be discussed in Unit 9.

German *if*-clauses are introduced by the subordinating conjunction **wenn**. As dependent clauses, they require verb-last position.

> **Wenn Else kommt, gehe ich mit ihr ins Museum.**
> **Wenn er den 12-Uhr-Zug genommen hat, muß er schon zu Hause sein.**
> **Ich schenke dir den Roman gern, wenn du ihn haben möchtest.**

Without context, some **wenn**-clauses are ambiguous, since **wenn** means both *when* and *if*. Thus the **wenn**-clause of the first sentence above may mean *If Else comes* or *When Else comes*.

NOTE: Some **um . . . zu** clauses can be replaced by an open condition:

> **Um nach Berlin fahren zu können, braucht man Geld.**
> **Wenn man nach Berlin fahren will, braucht man Geld.**

Both **wenn** and **wann** frequently correspond to English *when*. But German **wann** *is an interrogative and means only "at what time"*; therefore, only an English *when* which can be replaced by *at what time* can be expressed by German **wann**.

> **So viel wie gestern abend redet Meyer nur, wenn er zuviel getrunken hat.**
> **Weißt du, wann Meyer gestern nach Hause gegangen ist?**

78/The Future Tense

FORMATION

The German future is formed by using **werden** as an auxiliary in the first prong and any infinitive in the second prong.

ich werde fahren	wir werden fahren
du wirst fahren	ihr werdet fahren
er wird fahren	sie werden fahren

USE

Since the present tense can refer to future time, the future tense is comparatively rare. One usually hears

Ich fahre morgen nach Berlin.

but it is also perfectly acceptable to say

Ich werde morgen nach Berlin fahren.

If a sentence contains no time phrase, the future is used more frequently in order to avoid ambiguity.

Ich werde euch besuchen.   I'll visit you.

Very frequently, future forms express not futurity, but present probability. Such a probability statement often contains adverbs such as **wohl** (*probably*), **sicher** (*certainly*), **vielleicht** (*perhaps*), and **wahrscheinlich** (*probably*).

Es ist jetzt sieben. Inge wird wohl (sicher, wahrscheinlich) schon zu Hause sein.   It's seven o'clock now. Inge is probably at home by now. (I bet she's home by now.)

79/einmal, mal

When **einmal** or the shorter **mal** is used in assertions and requests, it may mean *once, for once,* or *for a change.*

Ich will dieses Jahr nicht an die Nordsee. Ich möchte mal in die Berge fahren.
I don't want to go to the North Sea this year. I'd like to go to the mountains for a change.

Very often, however, the short **mal** loses its literal meaning ("*one time*") and expresses simply a note of casualness.

Ich geh' mal in die Stadt.
Ich muß mal telefonieren.

In requests, this casual **mal** is usually preceded by an unstressed **doch.**

Mach uns doch mal eine Tasse Kaffee.   How about fixing us a cup of coffee?

Noch (ein)mal and **doch noch (ein)mal** always mean *once more* or *again.*

Ruf sie doch noch mal an.   (Why don't you) call her up again?

80/Word Formation: Groups of Derivatives

As was pointed out in Anal. 71, p. 202, both English and German use prefixes and suffixes to create new words based on a common stem (or root). Note, however, that German derivatives often do not have an exact English equivalent and that it is not always possible to guess the meaning of the derived word. Also, sometimes the stem vowel is changed in some derivatives.

Here are some groups of words based on the same stem, to which you can add others as they occur. In addition to derivatives, some compound nouns are given.

arbeiten	to work	**kaufen**	to buy, purchase
die Arbeit,-en	work, task	**der Kauf,-̈e**	purchase
der Arbeiter,-	workman, (blue-collar) worker	**der Käufer,-**	buyer
		das Kaufhaus,-̈er	department store
arbeitslos	unemployed		
verarbeiten	to process	**verkaufen**	to sell
die Verarbeitung	processing	**der Verkauf,-̈e**	sale
die Datenverarbeitung	data processing	**der Verkäufer,-**	salesman
		die Verkäuferin,-nen	saleswoman
die Bahn,-en	track; railroad; streetcar	**kochen**	to cook, to boil
		der Koch,-̈e	cook
die Autobahn,-en	superhighway, freeway	**die Köchin,-nen**	cook
		die Küche,-n	kitchen
die Eisenbahn-en	railroad		
die Straßenbahn,-en	streetcar	**lehren**	to teach
der Bahnhof,-̈e	railroad station	**der Lehrer,-**	teacher
		die Lehrerin,-nen	teacher
fahren	to drive	**der Lehrling,-e**	apprentice
der Fahrer,-	driver		
die Fahrt,-en	drive; trip	**reisen**	to travel
der Fahrgast,-̈e	passenger	**die Reise,-n**	trip
abfahren	to leave, depart	**abreisen**	to leave (for a trip), depart
die Abfahrt,-en	departure		
die Einfahrt,-en	entrance (for vehicles)	**verreisen**	to go on a trip, travel
die Ausfahrt,-en	exit (for vehicles)	**verreist sein**	to be on a trip
fliegen	to fly	**zahlen**	to pay
der Flieger,-	flier, pilot	**bezahlen**	to pay
der Flug,-̈e	flight	**die Zahl,-en**	number, figure
der Fluggast,-̈e	(airline) passenger	**zählen**	to count
das Flugzeug,-e	airplane		

Housing

In the U.S., the decades after World War II were characterized by the development of suburbia, made possible largely by the automobile. In Central Europe, urban sprawl has been much more limited. Traditionally, Europeans have been apartment dwellers; only the wealthy could afford single-family houses. Farmhouses (**Bauernhäuser**) tended to be multipurpose, housing not only extended families and workers, but also farm animals.

Despite increasing affluence, this pattern has not changed as much as one might expect. Large populations and lack of space have led to building up instead of out. The Central European landscape is still characterized by lots of open space. Whereas Americans have built large housing developments on the outskirts of cities, Germans turned villages surrounding urban centers into satellite towns and bedroom communities. Centuries-old villages surrounded by modern high-rise apartment buildings have become a familiar sight. While most young people dream of a freestanding **Einfamilienhaus**, many end up in a **Reihenhaus** (*row house*) or, more likely, in an **Apartmenthaus.**

Einfamilienhaus

Reihenhäuser

PRACTICE TWO

D. Change the following sentences into **du**-form imperatives; use **doch, doch mal**, or **mal** where appropriate. Make other changes as necessary.

| **Ich rufe dich morgen an.** | **Ruf mich doch morgen an.** |

1. Ich bringe dir ein Glas Wasser.
2. Ich gehe in den Garten.
3. Ich besuche euch in München.
4. Ich laufe jeden Tag fünf Kilometer.

5. Ich gebe dir das Buch morgen.
6. Ich nehme mir ein Taxi.
7. Ich sehe nach, ob Meyer schon da ist.
8. Ich fahre diesen Sommer nach Österreich.

E. Change to **ihr**-form imperatives.

1. Wir kommen bald wieder.
2. Wir trinken nicht so viel Kaffee.
3. Wir sind um halb vier am Flughafen.

4. Wir bringen euch ein paar Blumen mit.
5. Wir bleiben noch ein bißchen hier.
6. Wir nehmen den Bus.

F. Change to the **wir**-form, starting with **Schön, . . .**

| **Ich möchte nach München fahren.** |
| **Schön, fahren wir nach München.** |

1. Ich möchte zu Hause bleiben.
2. Ich möchte heute im Hotel Berlin essen.
3. Ich möchte heute schwimmen gehen.

G. Join the following pairs of sentences to form open conditions. The first sentence should always become the **wenn**-clause.

| **Es regnet morgen. Wir gehen ins Kino.** |
| **Wenn es morgen regnet, gehen wir ins Kino.** |

1. Du hast Geld. Du kannst ein Haus kaufen.
2. Du hast kein Geld. Du kannst das Haus nicht kaufen.
3. Maria studiert Mathematik. Sie muß intelligent sein.
4. Morgen regnet es nicht. Wir besuchen euch.
5. Ihr wollt ins Kino gehen. Wir gehen mit.
6. Herr Meyer wohnt in Berlin. Ich kann ihn besuchen.
7. Er ist dein Freund. Er hilft dir bestimmt.

H. Rewrite the following sentences in the future tense. Leave out the time phrases.

1. Wir gehen morgen ins Theater.
2. Ich besuche Sie nächste Woche, Herr Schulte.
3. Für die Reise nächsten Sommer brauchen wir viel Geld.
4. Hilfst du mir morgen bei der Arbeit?
5. Das Wetter ist morgen bestimmt gut.

CONVERSATIONS

Zwei Studentinnen sprechen nach einer Vorlesung miteinander:

I

GERDA WOLLNER:	Sag mal, wo wohnst du eigentlich dieses Semester? Immer noch im Studentenheim?	Say, where are you living this semester? Still in the dorm?
LOTTE VOGT:	Nein, ich wohne jetzt privat. Ich habe ein möbliertes Zimmer gefunden, ganz prima, in einem Einfamilienhaus direkt am Fluß.	No, I live in town now. I've found a furnished room, really first-class, in a one-family house right by the river.
G.W.:	Na, da mußt du aber sicher ganz schön bezahlen.	Well, I guess you have to pay a steep price for it.
L.V.:	Nein, gar nicht. Die Leute sind viel weg und sind froh, wenn sie jemand im Hause haben.	No, not at all. The people are away a lot and are glad if they have someone in the house.

II

LOTTE VOGT:	Und du, Gerda?	And you, Gerda?
GERDA WOLLNER:	Ich wohne jetzt auch möbliert, in der Altstadt, in der Nähe vom Dom.	I'm renting a room too, now (I live in a furnished room), in the old city, near the cathedral.

L.V.:	Wirklich? Stören dich denn da die Domglocken nicht?	Really? Don't the cathedral bells bother you?
G.W.:	Zuerst ja, aber jetzt gar nicht mehr. Außerdem bin ich sowieso fast immer in der Bibliothek.	At first they did, but now not at all anymore. Besides, I'm almost always in the library anyway.
L.V.:	Richtig, du hast ja dieses Semester Examen. Und wie ist dein Zimmer sonst?	That's right, you have your exams this semester. And how's your room otherwise?
G.W.:	Klein, aber sehr gemütlich, direkt unterm Dach. Du mußt mich bald mal besuchen.	Small, but very cozy and comfortable, right under the roof. You've got to come and see me soon.

III

GERDA WOLLNER:	Übrigens macht der Karlheinz am Samstag wieder 'ne Party.	Incidentally, Karlheinz is going to have another party on Saturday.
LOTTE VOGT:	Ja, ich weiß; er hat mich auch eingeladen. Gehst du hin?	Yes, I know; he's invited me too. Are you going?
G.W.:	Klar. Ich habe zwar ziemlich wenig Zeit, aber die Partys bei Karlheinz sind ja immer toll.	Sure. I haven't got much time, but those parties at Karlheinz's are always great.
L.V.:	Er hat mir gesagt, daß er eine Menge neue Kassetten hat, und seine Eltern haben ihm zu Weihnachten eine neue Stereoanlage geschenkt.	He told me that he has a lot of new cassettes, and his parents gave him a new stereo for Christmas.

IV

LOTTE VOGT:	Am Sonntag wollen wir alle eine Wanderung machen.	On Sunday we all want to go for a hike.
GERDA WOLLNER:	Wo wollt ihr denn hin?	Where do you want to go?
L.V.:	Wir fahren mit dem Wagen in den Auwald, und dann wollen wir auf den Donnersberg.	We'll drive to the Au Forest, and then we want to hike up Thunder Mountain.
G.W.:	Das ist aber ganz schön weit. —Und der Willi bringt seine Gitarre mit?	That's quite a distance. —And Willi is going to bring his guitar?
L.V.:	Aber sicher. Und der Werner will das Bier mitbringen.	Sure. And Werner wants to bring the beer.
G.W.:	Das klingt ja sehr romantisch, —wie bei den Wandervögeln.[1]	Sounds very romantic—just like the *Wandervögel*.
L.V.:	Sei nicht so sarkastisch. Das macht doch Spaß bei dem Wetter.	Don't be so sarcastic. It's fun in weather like this.

[1]**Wandervögel**, literally, *migratory birds*, a reference to the nationalistic youth movement of the early twentieth century.

V

The following colloquial phrases were introduced in Units 5 to 8. Review
them and incorporate them into your conversations as much as possible.
Also review the list of phrases in Unit 4, pp. 118–120.

Schönes Wochenende.	(Have a) nice weekend!
Danke, ebenfalls.	Thanks, same to you.
Entschuldigung/entschuldigen Sie.	Excuse me, pardon me, I'm sorry.

Ist dir/Ihnen das recht?	Is that OK with you?
Da hast du/haben Sie recht.	You're right.

Guten Appetit.	(said at the beginning of a meal)
Prost/Prosit.	Cheers, here's to you (said when raising glasses, but only with alcoholic beverages).

gern(e)	I'll be glad to
(aber) natürlich	but of course

Was ist denn los?	What's going on, what's the matter?

Es tut mir leid.	(I'm) sorry.

Ich möchte wissen, ob . . .	I'd like to know if . . .

Wie spät ist es?	What time is it?
Wieviel Uhr ist es?	What time is it?

Es ist schön, daß . . .	It's nice/good that . . .
Sei/seien Sie so gut/nett und . . .	Would you please . . .; please do . . .
Sag mal/sagen Sie mal . . .	Say/tell me . . .

klar	sure
sicher	sure
wirklich	really

Fragen an Sie persönlich

1. Wohnen Sie in einem Studentenheim oder privat?
   bei einer Familie?
   in einem möblierten Zimmer?

2. Wohnen Sie allein oder mit anderen Studenten zusammen?
   Warum in einem Studentenheim? Weil . . .
   Warum allein? Weil . . .

3. Gehen Sie früh ins Bett oder bleiben Sie gern lange auf? Bis wann?
   Werktags? Am Wochenende? Sonntags?

4. Arbeiten Sie (*do you study*) lieber am Tag oder abends?

5. Gehen Sie oft auf Partys?

6. Gehen Sie gern zu Fuß, oder fahren Sie lieber
   mit dem Rad?
   mit dem Auto?

7. Wandern Sie gern? (**wandern** *to go for a hike*)
   Gehen Sie campen?
   das Zelt *tent*
   der Rucksack *backpack*

8. Warum, glauben Sie, kann man in Amerika nicht so gut wandern wie in Deutschland?

READING

Die deutsche Küche°
cuisine

This reading selection on German cuisine contains three recipes from a Viennese, a Bavarian, and a Berlin cookbook. They have been included here to demonstrate the use of the impersonal imperative (that is, the infinitive form) in cooking instructions.

Die deutsche Küche, die österreichische Küche und die schweizer Küche sind nicht so weltbekannt° wie etwa die französische oder die chinesische. Aber trotzdem° hat man in Mitteleuropa schon immer gut gekocht, und nicht nur Sauerkraut und Kartoffeln. Bis zum zweiten Weltkrieg° waren die deutschen Hausfrauen vielleicht ein bißchen provinziell in ihrem Geschmack°, —man aß zum Beispiel kaum Reis, und viele Gemüse, wie Zucchini oder Auberginen°, waren fast unbekannt°. Aber heute kaufen die deutschen Frauen im Supermarkt Schafskäse° aus Bulgarien, Spaghetti aus Italien, Aprikosen aus Griechenland, Orangen aus Israel und Ananas° aus China, und ihre Männer kochen ungarische Gulaschsuppe und

world famous
nevertheless

5 world war
taste

eggplant unknown
sheep's cheese
10 pineapple

Bayerische Spezialitäten

serbische Bohnensuppe°, sie grillen jugoslawischen Schaschlik im   bean soup
Garten hinter dem Haus und machen um Mitternacht schnell noch
einen „Toast Hawaii.“

Obwohl die deutsche Küche ziemlich international geworden ist, 15
ißt man doch noch viele traditionelle Gerichte°. Diese Gerichte sind   dishes
oft von Gebiet° zu Gebiet verschieden°: die Österreicher haben ihre   area different
Mehlspeisen[2] und die Schwaben ihre Spätzle°; die Hessen, und be-   a kind of noodle
sonders die Frankfurter, essen Rippchen° mit Sauerkraut, und an   cured and smoked pork
der Nordseeküste° ißt man Fisch, gekocht, gebraten°, gebacken, ge- 20   chop   North Sea
grillt, geräuchert°.   coast   fried   smoked

Es folgen drei typische Rezepte°:   recipes

Wiener Tafelspitz

1,5 kg Rindfleisch und 0,5 kg Kalbsknochen
mit Karotten, Petersilie, Sellerie[3] und Zwie- 25
beln anbraten. Das Fleisch gut salzen und
pfeffern. Wasser zugießen, Tomaten, Pfeffer-
körner und ein Lorbeerblatt dazugeben,
sowie etwas Madeirawein. Gut zudecken
und weich dünsten.   30

Wiener Boiled Beef

Brown 3 lbs. beef and 1 lb. veal bones with
carrots, parsley, celery, and onions. Salt and
pepper the meat well. Cover with water, add
tomatoes, pepper corns, and a bay leaf, as
well as some Madeira wine. Cover tightly
and simmer until soft.

Bayerische Leberknödel

5 alte Semmeln klein schneiden, salzen und
mit ½ l lauwarmer Milch übergießen. 500 g
Rindsleber mit einer Zwiebel durch die
Fleischmaschine geben, dann mit den Sem- 35
meln und mit drei Eiern und Majoran zu
einem Teig verarbeiten. Knödel formen und
in kochendem Salzwasser ½ Stunde leise
kochen.

Bavarian Liver Dumplings

Cut 5 day-old hard rolls in small pieces, salt
them, and cover with ½ liter lukewarm
milk. Run 1 lb. beef liver and an onion
through the meat grinder, then make into
a dough together with the rolls, three eggs,
and marjoram. Form dumplings and simmer
(cook softly) in boiling salted water for half
an hour.

[2]**Mehlspeise**, literally "a dish made with flour," Austrian term for desserts made with
flour, such as pancakes, but also for desserts and sweets in a more general sense.
(See the Austrian menu in Unit 7, p. 208.)

[3]**Sellerie**, though translated as *celery*, in Central Europe always means *celery root*
(*celeriac*); the celery-stalks you are used to are virtually unknown.

Weißwurst

Berliner Buletten[4]

2 Schrippen[5] von vorgestern in Wasser aufweichen. Dann mit 500 g Gehacktem vom Schwein gut durchkneten, ein Ei und eine feingeschnittene Zwiebel untermischen und mit Salz und Pfeffer würzen. Die Fleischmasse zu mehreren Buletten formen und in heißem Schmalz in der Pfanne knusprig braten.

40 Berlin Meat Patties

Soften two old rolls in water. Knead together well with 500 g. of ground pork, mix with an egg and a finely chopped onion, and season with salt and pepper. Form the meat-mass 45 into several patties and fry in hot lard in a pan until crisp.

Gastarbeiter

During the economic expansion of the 1950s and 1960s, there was an acute labor shortage in the Federal Republic, despite the influx of over 10 million refugees and expellees from Eastern Germany. This led to the arrival of the first foreign workers (**Gastarbeiter**) from the Mediterranean area, and by 1966 their number had reached 1.3 million. The first foreign workers were Italians, who were followed by Yugoslavs, Greeks, and Spaniards. Smaller groups came from Portugal, Morocco, and Tunisia. The largest group of foreign workers are the Turks, who now number about 1.6 million. Most of the Turkish workers live in enclaves in large cities, for example, in the Berlin district of Kreuzberg. Subject to religious and cultural discrimination as Moslems many of whom are illiterate, they constitute what may become a permanent underclass.

Today there are about 4.5 million foreign workers and their dependents in the Federal Republic, half of whom have lived there for over 10 years.

[4]The standard term for **Bulette** is **Frikadelle**.

[5]The standard term **das Brötchen**, (*hard*) *roll*, has several regional variants: in Bavaria and Austria, **die Semmel** is used (cf. the **Leberknödel** recipe above); in Berlin, it is **die Schrippe**, and in Southwest Germany, the term **der Weck** (also **die Wecke**) is commonly used.

Türken in der Bundesrepublik

Burgbach, zum Beispiel[6]

Ein Samstagvormittag im Juni. Die Glocken läuten°. Eine Taufe° in   ring baptism
der katholischen Kirche. Die Eltern sind jugoslawische Gastarbeiter°,   foreign workers
oder „ausländische Arbeitnehmer"°, wie man sie offiziell nennt; der   foreign employees
Vater arbeitet in einer Fabrik im „Industriegebiet" von Burgbach, die
Mutter war bis vor ein paar Wochen Kellnerin in einem Restaurant   5
in Stuttgart. Er ist seit fünf Jahren in Deutschland, sie seit drei Jahren;
er hat sie in Stuttgart kennengelernt, aber geheiratet haben sie zu
Hause, in Jugoslawien. Nun lassen sie ihr Kind hier in Burgbach
taufen°, denn hier sind sie ja nun sozusagen auch zu Hause, obwohl   have . . . baptized
sie in ein paar Jahren nach Jugoslawien zurückwollen. Nach der   10
Taufe feiern° sie mit ihren jugoslawischen Freunden, die,[7] wie sie,   celebrate
in einem alten Fachwerkhaus° wohnen. Das Haus gehört einem   half-timbered house
Burgbacher Bauer, der plötzlich reich geworden ist, weil er einen
Teil° seines Landes an eine Baufirma° verkauft hat, die dort ein   piece, part construc-
achtstöckiges° Apartmenthaus gebaut hat. Mit dem Geld hat er ein   15   tion firm eight-story
modernes Einfamilienhaus gekauft, oben am Hang° über dem Dorf,   slope
weil ihm das 300 Jahre alte Fachwerkhaus auf einmal zu primitiv
geworden war.

Eine Stunde später. Die Glocken läuten wieder, aber diesmal in der
alten protestantischen Kirche; sie läuten zur Hochzeit° von zwei   20   wedding

[6]For some details in this reading selection, we are indebted to our colleague George
D. Spindler and his book *Burgbach: Urbanization and Identity in a German Village*
(with Stanford student collaborators) (New York: Holt, Rinehart and Winston, 1973).

[7]This text contains a number of relative clauses. All relative clauses are dependent
clauses and therefore have verb-last position. They will be introduced systematically
in Unit 12.

jungen Burgbachern. Der Bräutigam° ist Lehrer an der Grundschule°, gleich hinter der Kirche und gegenüber vom Friedhof°; er stammt° aus einer alten Weinbauernfamilie, die seit Generationen in einem großen Haus am Markt wohnt. Sein älterer Bruder macht jetzt, zusammen mit dem Vater, den Weinbau°; er selbst hat an der Pädagogischen Hochschule° studiert, —er ist der erste Akademiker° in seiner Familie—, und ist Lehrer geworden. Bis jetzt hat auch er im alten Haus gewohnt, aber nun zieht° er mit seiner jungen Frau in eine Zweizimmerwohnung in der neuen Siedlung° am Ortsrand°. Die Braut° ist auch in Burgbach geboren und spricht Schwäbisch wie er, aber ihre Eltern waren als Flüchtlinge° 1945 aus Schlesien° ins Dorf gekommen. Ihr Vater war Beamter° in Breslau[8] gewesen und arbeitet jetzt in der Stadtverwaltung° in Stuttgart.

(margin, lines 22–33): groom elementary school cemetery, graveyard comes | 25 grows the wine teacher training institution university graduate moves development edge of town bride refugees Silesia (now part of Poland) civil servant city administration

Nach der Trauung° geht die ganze Hochzeitsgesellschaft° über den Marktplatz und die Marktstraße hinunter zum Gasthof „Krone". Während man dort Rehrücken° und Spätzle ißt, läuten die Glocken noch einmal. Viele Leute, vor allem ältere, bäuerlich gekleidete° Leute, die alten Frauen mit langen schwarzen Röcken° und schwarzen Kopftüchern°, gehen an der Kirche vorbei° zum Friedhof, wo um ein Uhr eine Beerdigung° stattfindet°. Die Tote, eine 86-jährige ungarndeutsche Bäuerin aus Siebenbürgen°, war am Ende des Krieges mit ihrer Familie nach Burgbach gekommen, Flüchtlinge wie so viele, und hatte hier eine neue Heimat° gefunden. Ihre letzten Jahre hatte sie in einem Altenheim° verbracht, wo sie sehr beliebt° gewesen war. Kaum jemand° ist mit dem Auto zur Beerdigung gekommen, während am Samstag vorher°, als ein junger Mann beerdigt wurde, der bei einem Autounfall° ums Leben gekommen war°, auf der Straße am Friedhof ein Mercedes hinter dem anderen stand.

(margin, lines 33–48): marriage ceremony wedding party | saddle of venison | dressed | skirts | kerchief past the church funeral takes place (part of Romania) | 40 | home old-age home well-liked | hardly anyone 45 on the Saturday before car accident had lost his life

Während der Pfarrer spricht, donnert eine Boeing 727 der Pan Am über das Dorf, auf dem Weg vom 15 km entfernten° Stuttgarter Flughafen nach Berlin, und ab und zu hört man Schallplattenmusik aus dem nahen Jugendzentrum°, dem Treffpunkt° für die Burgbacher Teenager. Sie kommen fast° alle mit dem Motorrad, sie sind laut, und am liebsten hören sie amerikanische Rockmusik.

(margin, lines 50–52): 50 distant | youth center meeting place almost

Die Zeit ist etwa 1980. Fünfzig Jahre vorher, in der Zeit vor dem zweiten Weltkrieg, hätten zwar auch die Glocken geläutet°, aber nicht in der katholischen Kirche, denn die gab es damals noch nicht. Gastarbeiterkinder wären in Burgbach nicht getauft worden°, Töchter von schlesischen Beamten hätten nicht in Burgbach geheiratet, und ungarische Bäuerinnen wären nicht einmal bis an die österreichische Grenze° gekommen, geschweige denn° in ein schwäbisches Dorf.

(margin, lines 55–61): 55 | would have rung | would not have been baptized | 60 border let alone

---

[8]The city of Breslau, former capital of Silesia, is now known as Wroclaw.

REVIEW EXERCISES

I. Transform the ten sentences of this exercise according to the following pattern.

> **Sie wohnt in Weimar.**
> **a. Ich glaube, sie wohnt in Weimar.**
> **b. Ich glaube nicht, daß sie in Weimar wohnt.**
> **c. Ich möchte wissen, ob sie in Weimar wohnt.**

1. Maria Eisler studiert Mathematik.
2. Der Wagen gehört Frau Körner.
3. Sie kann sie sehen.
4. Er will mir die Stadt zeigen.
5. Erich Hartwich spricht gut Französisch.

6. Sie muß heute nach Düsseldorf.
7. Hans will ohne Inge ins Theater gehen.
8. Herr Meyer hat zu viel Wein getrunken.
9. Sie sind gestern in Berlin gewesen.
10. Sie hat in Innsbruck eine Freundin besucht.

J. Ask correct questions for the following answers. Your questions should ask for the italicized parts of the answers.

> **Er geht *heute abend* ins Kino.**
> **Wann geht er ins Kino?**

Then restate the question, starting with **Ich möchte wissen.**

> **Ich möchte wissen, wann er ins Kino geht.**

1. Ihr Mann ist *gestern* nach Wien gefahren.
2. Erika war gestern *in Berlin.*
3. Das Buch gehört *meinem Vater.*
4. Er hat ihr *ein Buch* geschenkt.

5. Er heißt *Fritz.*
6. *Mein Vater* hat das gesagt.
7. Er geht *mit Inge* ins Kino.
8. Karin war *vierzehn Tage* in Burgbach.

K. Change the following sentences to dependent clauses as indicated. Note that in each case you will have to relocate the subject, and, in some cases, other elements as well.

> **Gestern abend ist er sehr früh ins Bett gegangen.**
> **Ich hoffe, daß er gestern abend sehr früh ins Bett gegangen ist.**

1. Seit ihrem Besuch in München hatte ich Charlotte nicht mehr gesehen.
   Ich war unglücklich, weil _____.
2. Von Wien aus habe ich Charlotte einen Brief geschrieben.
   Ich habe nichts von Charlotte gehört, obwohl _____.
3. Leider war sie schon nach Graz gefahren.
   Sie hat nicht geschrieben, da _____.
4. In Graz hat sie unser Freund Gerhard am Bahnhof abgeholt.
   Heute weiß ich, daß _____.

L. In the following sentences, change the **wenn-** and **weil**-clauses to **um . . . zu**-clauses.

1. Wenn Gudrun ins Theater gehen wollte, mußte sie immer nach Salzburg fahren.
   Um _____ zu können, mußte _____.
2. Wenn man in Baden-Baden wohnen will, muß man viel Geld haben.
   Um _____ zu können, muß _____.
3. Er lernt Deutsch, weil er Nietzsche lesen will.
   Er lernt Deutsch, um _____ zu können.
4. Herr Köhler ist in die Stadt gefahren, weil er seiner Frau ein Buch kaufen will.
   Herr Köhler ist in die Stadt gefahren, um _____ zu kaufen.

M. Repeat the following sentences three times, with **bitte** in the front field, the inner field, and the end field.

> **Seien Sie vorsichtig.   Bitte seien Sie vorsichtig.**
> **Seien Sie bitte vorsichtig.**
> **Seien Sie vorsichtig, bitte.**

1. Schreib ihr doch einen Brief.
2. Laden Sie ihn doch auch ein.
3. Bleibt noch ein bißchen hier.

4. Geh ins Bett.
5. Kommt nicht zu spät zum Essen.

N. Change the following questions to imperatives; use **doch mal** in the inner field.

1. Kannst du uns eine Tasse Kaffee machen?
2. Könnt ihr uns in Basel besuchen?
3. Kannst du mir ein bißchen in der Küche helfen?
4. Kannst du einen Moment ruhig sein, bitte?
5. Können Sie mit uns in die Schweiz fahren?

O. Change the following imperatives to the **du**-form and the **ihr**-form.

1. Seien Sie doch nicht so sarkastisch.
2. Stehen Sie doch morgen etwas früher auf.
3. Bringen Sie mir ruhig noch eine Tasse Kaffee.
4. Gehen Sie doch mal mit Tante Amalie ins Museum.
5. Sprechen Sie ruhig lauter.
6. Gute Nacht, schlafen Sie gut.
7. Denken Sie mal, wo ich gestern war.
8. Fahren Sie doch mal eben zur Post.
9. Bringen Sie die Bücher bitte in die Bibliothek zurück.
10. Nehmen Sie uns doch bitte mit.

P. Change the following complaints into imperatives. Use **doch bitte** in the inner field.

1. Du rauchst zuviel.
2. Du gibst zuviel Geld aus.
3. Du bist immer so unfreundlich.
4. Können Sie mir kein Zimmer mit Bad geben?
5. Kannst du nicht mal zu Hause bleiben?

Q. Express in German. All German sentences should be imperatives; use the imperative form indicated by the pronoun following the English sentence.

1. Be good to him. (Sie)
2. Don't forget me. (du)
3. Please be here at nine o'clock. (ihr)
4. Take me along, please. (du)
5. Why don't you call her up? (du)
6. Sleep well. (Sie)
7. Stay healthy. (Sie)
8. Read the *Spiegel*. (du)
9. Don't talk with the driver. (impersonal)
10. Drive slowly. (impersonal)

R. Rewrite the following sentences, using the future tense to express present probability; use **sicher, vielleicht, wahrscheinlich,** or **wohl** where appropriate.

> **Ich glaube, er ist noch hier.**
> **Er wird (wohl) noch hier sein.**

1. Ich glaube, Kurt arbeitet noch.
2. Ich glaube, er will ihn nicht einladen.
3. Ich glaube, es ist zu warm zum Schilaufen.
4. Ich glaube, Katharina wartet schon auf uns.
5. Ich glaube, er muß wieder nach Zürich fahren.

VOCABULARY

als (*conj.*)	when
auf•bleiben (**sein**)	to stay up
aus•geben	to give out, to spend
aus•ziehen (**sein**)	to move
das Bad, ⸚er	bath(room)
die Bahn, -en	track; railroad; street car
der Bauer, -n	farmer
die Bäuerin, -nen	farmer's wife
benutzen	to use
der Betrieb, -e	place of work; plant, factory
das Bett, -en	bed
bevor (*conj.*)	before
die Butter (*no pl.*)	butter
Celsius	centigrade
da (*conj.*)	since, because
das Dach, ⸚er	roof
daß (*conj.*)	that
direkt	direct(ly)
eben	just
einander	each other
ein•steigen (**sein**)	to get on (a train, etc.), board
entschuldigen	to excuse
entschuldigen Sie	excuse me
falsch	false, wrong
fast	almost
fern•sehen	to watch TV
freundlich	friendly
unfreundlich	unfriendly
der Fuß, ⸚e	foot

der Gast, ⸚e	guest
der Gastarbeiter, -	foreign worker
der Gasthof, ⸚e	inn; restaurant
geboren	born
das Gemüse	vegetables
gemütlich	cozy
gesund	healthy
gnädig	gracious
gnädige Frau	Madam (formal address)
das Gramm (*no pl.*)	(metric) gram
grüßen	to greet, say hello
herzlich	cordial
hin	there, away from the speaker
jemand	somebody, someone
laut	loud
leid tun	to be sorry
es tut mir leid	I'm sorry
er tut mir leid	I feel sorry for him
die Menge, -n	quantity, lot; crowd
miteinander	with one another
die Mitternacht	midnight
möblieren	to furnish (a room)
möbliert	furnished
der Moment', -e	moment, instant
nachdem (*conj.*)	after
die Nähe	vicinity, proximity, closeness
in der Nähe	nearby
ob (*conj.*)	whether; if

obwohl (*conj.*)	although	**toll** (*colloq.*)	crazy, great
öffnen	to open	**um•rechnen**	to convert (currency, etc.)
das Pfund, -e	pound		
die Post	mail; post office	**vergessen**	to forget
die Postkarte, -n	postcard	**die Vorlesung, -en**	lecture (university)
prima (*colloq.*)	excellent, tops, first-rate	**vorsichtig**	careful
		während (*conj.*)	while
richtig	correct, right	**wahrscheinlich**	probably
der Rucksack, ⸚e	backpack	**die Wanderung, -en**	hike
die Schallplatte, -n	record	**weg**	away
schwarz	black	**weg•gehen (sein)**	to go away
seit (*conj.*)	since	**weil** (*conj.*)	because
der Spaß, ⸚e	fun; joke	**werktags**	weekdays
Spaß haben	to have fun	**wochenlang**	for weeks
das macht Spaß	that is fun	**wohl** (*sent. adv.*)	probably
er macht Spaß	he is joking	**das Zelt, -e**	tent
stören	to disturb	**ziemlich**	rather
Nicht stören!	Do not disturb!	**zwar**	indeed, to be sure
das Studium, die Studien	(period of) study		

Strong Verbs

INFINITIVE	PRESENT	PAST TENSE	PERFECT	
auf•bleiben		**blieb auf**	**ist aufgeblieben**	to stay up
aus•geben	**gibt aus**	**gab aus**	**ausgegeben**	to give out, spend
aus•ziehen		**zog aus**	**ist ausgezogen**	to move out
ein•steigen		**stieg ein**	**ist eingestiegen**	to get on (a train, etc.), board
fern•sehen	**sieht fern**	**sah fern**	**ferngesehen**	to watch TV
vergessen	**vergißt**	**vergaß**	**vergessen**	to forget
weg•gehen		**ging weg**	**ist weggegangen**	to go away, leave

Unit 9
The Subjunctive

Highways and Byways

All of Central Europe is crisscrossed by a network of four- or six-lane superhighways (**Autobahnen**). There is no speed limit on the **Autobahn**, and you will encounter cars zipping past you at 180 km (112.5 mph). The speed limit on all other highways is 100 km (62 mph).

Although some federal highways (**Bundesstraßen**) are still only two-lane roads, most have been improved and bypass small towns and villages. They are referred to by their numbers, for example, B 14.

If you are not in a hurry, you can still enjoy the countryside by traveling narrow and often winding backroads. City traffic is often congested, especially in city centers which may be centuries old. Ironically, those cities that were most heavily bombed during World War II today have the best traffic flow.

In recent years, more and more cities have removed all vehicular traffic from large parts of their downtown areas, particularly where the core of medieval towns is still intact. Usually, this includes the area around the city hall (**Rathaus**) and the cathedral (**Dom**).

Berlin (Ost)

Wet pavement: more distance

Die wichtigsten Verkehrszeichen aus der neuen Straßenverkehrsordnung

PATTERNS ONE

1/The Future Subjunctive: *würde*-Forms

Ich wollte, du würdest mitgehen.	I wish you would come along.
Ich wünschte, du würdest mitgehen.	I wish you would come along.
Es wäre schön, wenn du mitfahren würdest.	It would be nice if you came along.
Wie wäre es, wenn er mitfahren würde?	How would it be if he came along?
Wenn er doch nur mitfahren würde.	If only he would come along.
Es wäre gut, wenn wir einmal früher in die Stadt fahren würden. Dann würden wir bestimmt noch einen Parkplatz finden.	It would be good if we drove to town earlier for a change. Then we would still find a placc to park, I'm sure.
Wenn wir vor dem Berufsverkehr fahren würden, würden wir im Parkhaus am Markt noch Platz finden.	If we went before the commuter traffic, we would still find a space in the parking garage at the Market Square.
Wir würden schneller hinkommen, wenn wir die Autobahn nehmen würden.	We would get there faster if we took the Autobahn.
Ich würde gern mitten in der Stadt wohnen. Dann würde ich nur noch zu Fuß gehen.	I would like to live in the middle of the city. Then I would only walk.
An deiner Stelle würde ich die Bundesstraße nehmen. Auf der Autobahn sind um diese Zeit doch immer Stauungen.	If I were you (in your place) I would take the Bundesstraße. There are always slowdowns on the autobahn at this hour.
Ich würde lieber hier draußen einkaufen gehen. Dann würden wir viel Zeit sparen.	I would rather go shopping out here. Then we would save a lot of time.
Am liebsten würde ich heute zu Hause bleiben.	I would like best to stay at home today.

2/The Present Subjunctive of Weak and Strong Verbs

Ich wünschte, wir wohnten nicht so weit draußen vor der Stadt.	I wish we didn't live so far outside the city.
Ich wünschte, wir würden nicht so weit draußen wohnen.	I wish we wouldn't live so far out.
Wie wäre es, wenn wir zum Mittagessen in der Stadt blieben (bleiben würden)?	How would it be if we stayed in town for lunch? (How about staying in town for lunch?)
Ich ginge eigentlich gern mal wieder in den Ratskeller.	I would like to go to the Ratskeller again for a change.
Wenn er den Wagen in einer Seitenstraße parken würde, brauchte er nicht ins Parkhaus zu fahren.	If he parked the car in a side street, he wouldn't have to go to the parking garage.

Wenn er sehr früh führe, bekäme er auch direkt am Dom noch einen Platz zum Parken.

If he left very early, he would of course find a place to park, even right by the cathedral.

Wenn es doch nur nicht schon wieder regnete (regnen würde). Ich wollte, die Sonne schiene endlich wieder.

If only it weren't raining again. I wish the sun would finally shine again.

Ja, wenn die Sonne wieder schiene, gäbe es auch nicht mehr so viele Unfälle auf der Autobahn.

Yes, if the sun were out again, there also wouldn't be so many accidents on the autobahn anymore.

Und wenn die Leute vernünftiger führen, würde auch nicht so viel passieren.

And if people drove more reasonably, not as much would happen either (there wouldn't be so many accidents).

Frankfurt Innenstadt

3/The Present Subjunctive of *haben*, *sein*, and the Modals

Ich wollte, wir hätten in Amerika so viele Fußgängerzonen wie in Deutschland.

I wish we had as many pedestrian zones in America as (they have) in Germany.

Dann wäre es ein Vergnügen, in der Innenstadt einkaufen zu gehen.

Then it would be a pleasure to go shopping downtown.

Wenn die Straßen um den Dom herum nicht so eng wären, hätten wir sicher keine Fußgängerzone.

If the streets around the cathedral weren't so narrow, we probably wouldn't have a pedestrian zone.

Der Verkehr wäre noch viel schlimmer, wenn es keine U-Bahn gäbe.

The traffic would be much worse if there were no subway.

Ich wollte, ich könnte mit der Straßenbahn fahren; aber da müßte ich dreimal umsteigen, und das dauert mir zu lange.

I wish I could take the streetcar; but then I would have to change three times, and that takes too long for me.

Wenn du doch nur nicht immer mit dem Wagen fahren wolltest!

If only you didn't always want to take the car!

Wir sollten eigentlich mal versuchen, die U-Bahn zu nehmen.

We really ought to try taking the subway sometime.

U-Bahn? Das wäre eine Idee. Wir könnten am Markt aussteigen und dann zu Fuß gehen. Dann wären wir in fünf Minuten im Kaufhof.[1] Das würde Benzin, Zeit und Nerven sparen.

Subway? That would be an idea. We could get out at the Market Square and then walk. We'd be at the Kaufhof in five minutes. That would save gasoline, time, and nerves.

ANALYSIS ONE

81/The Subjunctive Mood

All verb forms used in Units 1 to 8 refer to facts and real events or to open conditions which may turn out to be real events. All these forms belong to the *indicative mood* (reality). In contrast, all verb forms which refer to situations that do not actually exist or to events that are only hypothetical or imagined belong to the *subjunctive mood* (irreality).

In English, only a few constructions are left where subjunctive forms still *must* be used;[2] in German, on the other hand, the subjunctive is very common, and you will have to get used to using a new set of forms that is distinctly different from indicative forms.

Leaving the few true subjunctive forms aside, English has a normal way of expressing by verb forms alone that a situation does not (or did not) actually exist. Consider the following three pairs of sentences:

PAST TIME	1a. We were in Berlin yesterday.	1b. I wish we had been in Berlin yesterday (but we weren't).
PRESENT TIME	2a. We are in Berne today.	2b. I wish we were in Berne today (but we aren't).
FUTURE TIME	3a. We will be in Vienna tomorrow.	3b. I wish we would be in Vienna tomorrow (but we will not be).

---

[1]Name of a department store chain.

[2]Some English subjunctive forms still occur in formulaic phrases such as *Be that as it may, God bless you* (not *"blesses"*), and in biblical quotations such as *The Lord be gracious unto you and give you peace* (not *"is"* and *"gives"*). Subjunctives are also found in legal language, *Judge Brown ruled that bail be lowered* (not *"is"*) and in formal motions, *I move that the President appoint an ad hoc committee* (not *"appoints"*).

Sentences 1a, 2a, and 3a are in the indicative; they refer to actual
and real events in the past, present, and future and are expressed
respectively with the past indicative, present indicative, and future
indicative. Sentences 1b, 2b, and 3b seem paradoxical in their use
of tenses: they express past time by using the past perfect, present
time by using the past, and future time by using *would* plus infinitive. Actually, though these verb forms look like indicatives, they
function as subjunctives, and the sentences in which they occur are
"irreal." The parenthetical remarks at the end of 1b, 2b, and 3b,
however, are in the indicative; they describe the "real" facts and have
the same verb forms as sentences 1a, 2a, and 3a. Thus, English is
capable of expressing irreal (subjunctive) situations without resort-
ing to special verb forms by simply using what at first glance appears
to be "wrong" tenses (an exception is the form *would* in 3b).

	INDICATIVE	SUBJUNCTIVE
PRE-PAST TIME	We had been in Bonn the day be-fore vesterday.	I wish we had been in Bonn be-fore we went to Munich.
PAST TIME	We were in Bonn yesterday.	I wish we had been in Bonn yes-terday.
PRESENT TIME	We are in Bonn today.	I wish we were in Bonn today.
FUTURE TIME	We will be in Bonn tomorrow.	I wish we would be in Bonn to-morrow.

NOTE:

1. The forms *I were* and *he* or *she were* are clearly subjunctive.
However, *was* is often substituted for *were*, for example, *I wish I
was home* or *If I was you, I wouldn't do that.*

2. The constructions with *would* are frequently reduced to *'d*. These
forms are also often used to express present time subjunctive (*I'd
rather be sailing now*).

Both English and German use the subjunctive mood to express unfulfilled wishes as in sentences 1b, 2b, and 3b above and in contrary-
to-fact conditions as in 4b below.

In Unit 8, open conditions were introduced. These refer to events
or situations that may come about if the condition is fulfilled. For
example,

4a. If the weather is good tomorrow, we'll go to the beach.

Contrary-to-fact conditions, on the other hand, indicate that the facts are contrary to reality and are merely assumed or imagined.

4b. If the weather were good today, we'd go to the beach.

clearly indicates that the weather is not good and that we are not going to the beach.

82/Forms of the Future and Present Subjunctive

FUTURE SUBJUNCTIVE

The *will/would* distinction has an exact parallel in German:

1a. **Wir werden nach Wien gehen.**   We will go to Vienna.
1b. **Wir würden nach Wien gehen, wenn**   We would go to Vienna if . . .
. . .

Whereas the future indicative is formed by **werde** plus infinitive, the future subjunctive is formed by **würde** plus infinitive:

FUTURE INDICATIVE	FUTURE SUBJUNCTIVE
ich werde gehen	ich würde gehen
du wirst gehen	du würdest gehen
er wird gehen	er würde gehen
wir werden gehen	wir würden gehen
ihr werdet gehen	ihr würdet gehen
sie werden gehen	sie würden gehen

Like the English *would*-forms, **würde**-forms originally implied a time reference to the future, but are frequently used now, especially in contrary-to-fact conclusions with a clear reference to the present time.

Ich würde auch gern im Hotel Vier Jahres-zeiten wohnen, wenn ich genug Geld hätte.   I would also like to stay at the Hotel Four Seasons if I had enough money.[3]

The conclusion of this sentence contains the future subjunctive form **würde wohnen**, but the **wenn**-clause (the condition) contains the form **hätte**, which is a present subjunctive.

There is no difference in meaning between the **würde**-forms and their corresponding present subjunctive forms; these forms are often interchangeable.

[3]The German equivalent of *to stay at a hotel* is **im Hotel wohnen**.

PRESENT SUBJUNCTIVE

1. WEAK VERBS

The present subjunctive forms of weak verbs are identical with the past indicative forms just as in English (see Anal. 81, p. 257).

PAST INDICATIVE		PRESENT SUBJUNCTIVE	
ich wohn-te	I lived	wenn ich wohn-te	if I lived
du wohn-test		wenn du wohn-test	
er wohn-te		wenn er wohn-te	
wir wohn-ten		wenn wir wohn-ten	
ihr wohn-tet		wenn ihr wohn-tet	
sie wohn-ten		wenn sie wohn-ten	

2. STRONG VERBS

The present subjunctive forms of strong verbs use the same endings as weak verbs, but minus the **-t-**. If the past indicative stem has an **a**, **o**, or **u**, it receives an umlaut. The endings **-est** and **-et** are usually shortened to **-st** and **-t** when spoken.

PAST INDICATIVE		PRESENT SUBJUNCTIVE	
ich ging	I went	wenn ich ging-e	if I went
du ging-st		wenn du ging-est, ging-st	
er ging		wenn er ging-e	
wir ging-en		wenn wir ging-en	
ihr ging-t		wenn ihr ging-et, ging-t	
sie ging-en		wenn sie ging-en	
ich fuhr	I went	wenn ich führ-e	if I went
du fuhr-st		wenn du führ-est, führ-st	
er fuhr		wenn er führ-e	
wir fuhr-en		wenn wir führ-en	
ihr fuhr-t		wenn ihr führ-et, führ-t	
sie fuhr-en		wenn sie führ-en	

3. **haben, sein, werden,** AND THE MODALS

With the exception of **wollen** and **sollen**, all these verbs clearly distinguish between the past indicative and the present subjunctive by adding an umlaut; **war** also adds an **-e** to the first and third persons singular and usually drops the **-e-** before **-st** and **-t** (**du wärst, ihr wärt**). The **würde** used to form the future subjunctive (see above) is the present subjunctive of **werden,** *to become.*

INFINITIVE	PAST INDICATIVE	PRESENT SUBJUNCTIVE
haben	ich hatte	ich hätte
sein	ich war	ich wäre
werden	ich wurde	ich würde
dürfen	ich durfte	ich dürfte
können	ich konnte	ich könnte
müssen	ich mußte	ich müßte
sollen	ich sollte	ich sollte
wollen	ich wollte	ich wollte

4. IRREGULAR SUBJUNCTIVE FORMS

A few verbs form the present subjunctive in an irregular way; however, in most cases, **würde**-forms are substituted.

PAST INDICATIVE	PRESENT SUBJUNCTIVE
ich brachte	ich brächte
ich dachte	ich dächte
ich kannte	ich kennte
ich half	ich hülfe
ich starb	ich stürbe
ich wußte	ich wüßte

Note that there is only a single set of subjunctive endings for all verbs:

	SING.	PL.
	e	en
	(e)st	(e)t
	e	en

83/Uses of the Subjunctive

1. WISHES

The English *I wish* has two interchangeable equivalents in German: **ich wünschte, ich wollte**.[4] They are used with either **würde**-forms or the present subjunctive:

Ich wünschte, du würdest mitgehen.	I wish you would go along.
Ich wünschte, du gingst mit.	
Ich wollte, er würde noch bleiben.	I wish he would stay yet.
Ich wollte, er bliebe noch.	

[4]Whereas *I wish* is indicative, **ich wünschte** and **ich wollte** are subjunctive.

These stereotypical constructions have such a strong flavor of irreality that even ambiguous forms like **wir wohnten** (which could
be a past tense indicative) automatically are considered to be
subjunctives.

Ich wünschte, wir wohnten in München.   I wish we lived in Munich.

2. POLITE REQUESTS

Some polite requests are introduced with such fixed phrases as **Es
wäre nett, wenn . . .**, *It would be nice if . . .*, and **Wie wäre es, wenn
. . .**, *How would it be if . . .* Such polite requests may, of course,
turn out to be unfulfilled wishes.

> **Es wäre nett, wenn du mitgehen würdest.**
> **Es wäre nett, wenn du mitgingst.**
>
> **Wie wäre es, wenn du mitgehen würdest?**
> **Wie wäre es, wenn du mitgingst?**

Other polite requests with the subjunctive are used in social situations, in hotels, in stores, and so forth:

> **Hätten Sie vielleicht noch ein Zimmer frei?**
> **Ich hätte gerne ein Zimmer mit Bad.**
> **Könnte ich noch eine Tasse Kaffee haben?**
> **Würden Sie mir vielleicht noch eine Tasse Kaffee bringen?**

In wishes and polite requests, **haben, sein,** and the modals almost
always use the present subjunctive, whereas with all other verbs
either the present subjunctive or the **würde**-forms are used.

3. CONTRARY-TO-FACT CONDITIONS

Contrary-to-fact conditional sentences consist of an irreal **wenn**-
clause followed or preceded by an irreal conclusion. These sentences
relate facts that are contrary to reality and are merely assumed or
imagined.

The following example demonstrates that both the **würde**-forms and
the present subjunctive of some verbs can be used in either **wenn**-
clauses or the conclusion or both.

> **Ich würde gerne mitgehen, wenn Hans auch mitgehen würde.**
> **Ich würde gerne mitgehen, wenn Hans auch mitginge.**
> **Ich ginge gerne mit, wenn Hans auch mitgehen würde.**
> **Ich ginge gerne mit, wenn Hans auch mitginge.**
>
> **Wenn Hans auch mitgehen würde, würde ich gerne mitgehen.**
> **Wenn Hans auch mitginge, würde ich gerne mitgehen.**
> **Wenn Hans auch mitgehen würde, ginge ich gerne mit.**
> **Wenn Hans auch mitginge, ginge ich gerne mit.**

wenn-CLAUSES ALONE

Sometimes **wenn**-clauses can stand alone with a conclusion understood. Such clauses often express wishes, especially when they contain **doch nur** or **nur:**

> **Wenn du doch nur mitgehen würdest (mitgingst).**

CONCLUSIONS ALONE

Conclusions can sometimes stand alone too; frequently they occur
as speculations using **gern** (*like to*), **lieber** (*prefer to, rather*), **am
liebsten** (*like best to*).

Natürlich würde ich gern in München wohnen.	Of course I'd like to live in Munich.
Ich würde lieber in Salzburg wohnen.	I would prefer to live (would rather live) in Salzburg.
Aber am liebsten würde ich in Wien wohnen.	But I would like best to live in Vienna.

PRESENT SUBJUNCTIVE OR würde-FORM?

The sentence

> **Wir wohnten natürlich lieber in Wien.**

is ambiguous without a context; it could be part of a narrative and
would then, of course, have a past indicative meaning.

> We preferred living in Vienna, of course.

Given the right context, the present subjunctive meaning is clear.

Leider wohnen wir in Linz; wir wohnten natürlich lieber in Wien.	Unfortunately, we live in Linz; we would rather live in Vienna, of course.

But even if the context makes it clear that it is an irreal present
time statement, many Germans would say:

Wir würden natürlich lieber in Wien wohnen.	We would rather live in Vienna, of course.

In contrary-to-fact statements, the conclusions more often than not
contain **würde**-forms, and in many cases, especially in spoken German, **würde**-forms are used in the **wenn**-clause (the condition) as
well. Unfortunately, there is no hard and fast rule for when to use
the present subjunctive and when to use **würde**-forms.

In English, the present subjunctive or *would*-forms are interchangeable in *if*-clauses; in English conclusions, however, *would*-forms are
mandatory.

84/*sollte*

German **sollte** is one of the ambiguous forms which can be used either as a past indicative or as a present subjunctive. If the context refers to past time, **sollte** is past indicative and means *was supposed to*. If the context refers to present or future time, **sollte** is present subjunctive and means *should* or *ought to*.

PAST INDICATIVE

Jedesmal, wenn du mit mir ins Theater gehen solltest, hattest du Kopfschmerzen.

Every time you were supposed (Every time I wanted you) to go to the theater with me, you had a headache.

Wir sollten schon um acht in Köln sein. Jetzt ist es neun, und wir sind immer noch in Bonn.

We were supposed to be in Cologne at eight. Now it is nine, and we are still in Bonn.

PRESENT SUBJUNCTIVE

In an *if*-clause, the present subjunctive **sollte** denotes a future possibility which the speaker does not expect to materialize. The conclusion shows the indicative.

Wenn es morgen regnen sollte, bleiben wir zu Hause.

If it should rain tomorrow, we'll stay at home.

In a conclusion, the present subjunctive **sollte** denotes a strong suggestion. The *if*-clause shows the indicative.

Wenn du kannst, solltest du ihm helfen.

If you can, you should (ought to) help him.

Frequently, these sentences are polite substitutes for an imperative.

Du solltest nicht soviel essen.

You should (ought) not eat so much.

PRACTICE ONE

A. Complete the following sentences with the correct subjunctive form of the verb in parentheses; then repeat the sentence, replacing the subjunctive with a **würde**-form.

Ich wollte, er _____ nicht immer mit dem Wagen.   (fahren)
Ich wollte, er führe nicht immer mit dem Wagen.
Ich wollte, er würde nicht immer mit dem Wagen fahren.

1. Ich wollte, er _____ bald aus der Stadt zurück.   (kommen)
2. Ich wollte, der Wagen _____ mir.   (gehören)
3. Ich wollte, es _____ nicht so lange, einen Parkplatz zu finden.   (dauern)
4. Wenn er nur nicht immer so lange in der Stadt *bliebe* _____.   (bleiben)
5. An deiner Stelle *ließe* ich den Wagen zu Hause (lassen) und *führe* _____ mit der Bahn.   (fahren)
6. Den Wagen zu Hause lassen? Das *täte* _____ ich nie.   (tun)

B. Complete the following sentences with proper subjunctive forms. In several sentences, more than one verb is possible.

1. Ich wollte, das Benzin _____ nicht so teuer.
2. Wie _____ es, wenn du mal mit der Straßenbahn fahren _____.
3. Du _____ auch mal mit der U-Bahn fahren.
4. Dann _____ du aber ein bißchen früher aufstehen.
5. Wenn ich genug Geld _____, _____ ich mir einen neuen Diesel kaufen.
6. Ja, wenn das Wörtchen „wenn" nicht wäre, dann _____ du schon lange ein Millionär.

C. Change the following factual statements to irreal wishes, starting with **ich wollte (wünschte), . . . , es wäre nett, wenn . . . , wie wäre es, wenn . . . , or wenn . . . doch nur . . . .** Be sure to change from affirmative to negative and vice versa. Use either present subjunctive or **würde**-forms.

Du gehst nicht mit.
Es wäre nett, wenn du mitgehen würdest.

1. Du redest zu oft von deinem Hobby. (Change **zu** to **nicht so**.)
2. Wir fahren dieses Wochenende nicht in die Berge.
3. Wir fahren heute in die Stadt.
4. Du gehst nie zu Fuß. (Change **nie** to **einmal**.)
5. Du bleibst heute nicht zu Hause.

D. Replacing **leider** by **gerne, lieber,** or **am liebsten**, change the following factual statements to preferential statements using only **würde**-forms. Change from negative to affirmative.

> **Wir fahren leider nicht nach Deutschland.**
> **Wir würden am liebsten nach Deutschland fahren.**

1. Ich gehe heute abend leider nicht ins Kino.
2. Wir wohnen ja leider nicht im Vienna-Hilton.
3. Er kauft leider keinen Mercedes.
4. Er nimmt leider nie die Bundesstraße.
5. Wir bleiben dieses Wochenende leider nicht zu Hause.

E. The following sentences contain a dependent clause introduced by **weil.** Changing the **weil**-clause into a **wenn**-clause, transform the sentences into irreal conditions. Use both short forms and **würde**-forms as appropriate. Change from affirmative to negative and vice versa.

> **Wir wohnen in der Stadt, weil wir keine Kinder haben.**
> **Wenn wir Kinder hätten, wohnten wir nicht in der Stadt.**
> **Wenn wir Kinder hätten, würden wir nicht in der Stadt wohnen.**

1. Weil ich nicht in München wohne, gehe ich nicht jeden Tag ins Theater.
2. Meyer fährt immer mit dem Zug in die Stadt, weil er nicht Auto fahren will. (Place **nicht** in front of **immer**.)
3. Weil wir einen Hund haben, finden wir keine Wohnung.
4. Weil er nicht früh in die Stadt fährt, findet er bestimmt keinen Parkplatz.
5. Wir fahren wieder nach Hause, weil es jeden Tag regnet.

F. Change the following factual statements to irreal statements about what should or could be, but is not. Use the verb in parentheses. Change from affirmative to negative and vice versa.

> **Ich trinke zu viel. (sollen)**
> **Ich sollte nicht so viel trinken.**

1. Wir haben kein Auto.   (müssen)
2. Wir fahren Sonntag nicht in die Berge.   (können)
3. Wir schwimmen nicht jeden Tag eine halbe Stunde.   (sollen)
4. Morgen abend gehen wir nicht ins Theater.   (können)

PATTERNS TWO

4/The Past Subjunctive

Ich wollte, wir wären nicht am Wochenende in die Berge gefahren. Der Wochenendverkehr war wieder mal unmöglich.

I wish we hadn't gone to the mountains over the weekend. The weekend traffic was impossible again.

Ich wollte, die[5] hätten nicht überall Stopschilder hingestellt; dann käme man viel schneller vorwärts.

I wish they hadn't put up stop signs everywhere; then you could move along much faster.

Wenn nur das Benzin nicht so teuer geworden wäre.

If only gasoline hadn't become so expensive.

Ja, wir hätten einen Diesel kaufen sollen; dann könnten wir heute viel billiger fahren.

Yes, we should have bought a diesel; then we could drive much more cheaply today.

Wenn nicht alle Ampeln rot gewesen wären, wäre ich bestimmt rechtzeitig hier gewesen.

If all traffic lights hadn't been red, I'm sure I would have gotten here on time.

Wenn du nicht so schnell gefahren wärst, hättest du keinen Strafzettel bekommen. Aber du mußt ja immer rasen wie ein Irrer.

If you hadn't driven so fast, you wouldn't have gotten a ticket. But you've always got to race like an idiot.

Wenn es nicht so neblig gewesen wäre, hätte es auf der Autobahn nicht so viele Unfälle gegeben.

If it hadn't been so foggy, there wouldn't have been so many accidents on the autobahn.

Aber wenn es nicht geschneit hätte, hätten wir nicht schilaufen können.

But if it hadn't snowed, we could not have gone skiing.

Lotti wäre letztes Wochenende eigentlich gern mitgefahren, aber sie hatte zu viel zu tun.

Lotti would actually have liked to come along last weekend, but she had too much to do.

Ich wäre eigentlich lieber zu Hause geblieben. Dann wäre ich am Montag nicht so müde gewesen.

I would really rather have stayed at home. Then I wouldn't have been so tired on Monday.

Der Verkehr war so stark, daß mein Mann am liebsten den Wagen verkauft hätte und mit der Bahn nach Hause gefahren wäre.

The traffic was so heavy that my husband would have liked nothing better than to sell the car and to take the train home.

---

[5]In colloquial German, **die** is used as the plural of the impersonal **man** and corresponds to *they* as used above.

5/*hätte* in Dependent Clauses with "Double Infinitive"

Wenn Dora nicht hätte nach München fahren müssen, hätte Schulz sie nie kennengelernt.[6]	If Dora hadn't had to go to Munich, Schulz would never have met her.
Wenn du nicht hättest kommen können, wäre ich sehr unglücklich gewesen.	If you had not been able to come, I would have been very unhappy.
Wenn er gestern abend nicht hätte zu Hause bleiben müssen, hätte er mit uns ins Kino gehen können.	If he had not had to stay home last night, he could have gone to the movies with us.

6/Polite Requests

Guten Abend. Hätten Sie vielleicht noch ein Zimmer frei?	Good evening. Would you by any chance still have a room available?
Ich hätte gern ein Zimmer mit Bad oder Dusche, —und mit WC.	I'd like a room with bath or shower—and with a toilet.
Könnten (Würden) Sie mich bitte um sieben Uhr wecken?	Could (Would) you please wake me at seven o'clock?
Dürfte ich um das Telefonbuch bitten?	Could I ask you for the telephone book?
Ich hätte gerne Weinstadt bei Stuttgart, —Vorwahl 07151, und die Nummer ist 6 38 20.	I'd like to have Weinstadt near Stuttgart —area code 07151, and the number is 6 38 20.

[6]In unreal **wenn**-clauses, **nicht müssen** is used rather than **nicht brauchen zu**.

The Landscape

The physical features of Central Europe are extremely varied. The coastal areas along the North Sea (**Nordsee**) and the Baltic (**Ostsee**) are flat and rather monotonous. The central area is characterized by heavily forested rolling hills and low mountains (highest elevation about 1000 m). To the south, the Alps, the third major geographical feature, stretch from west to east across Switzerland and Austria and are a formidable barrier between northern and southern Europe. The Alps extend into the Federal Republic only in the southernmost part of Bavaria. Among the highest mountains are the Matterhorn (4477 m) in Switzerland, the Großglockner (3797 m) in Austria, and the Zugspitze (2963 m) in West Germany.

All but one of the major rivers flow from south to north. The Rhine, the Elbe, and the Weser empty into the North Sea and the Oder into the Baltic. The Danube originates in the Black Forest (**Schwarzwald**) and flows through the Federal Republic, Austria, and six eastern European countries before emptying into the Black Sea.

Use of Space in the Federal Republic

Agriculture	55%
Forests	30%
Buildings, roads, etc.	15%

sel Langenes (Schleswig-Holstein)

Leukerbad (1401 m) im Wallis (Schweiz)

ANALYSIS TWO

85/Forms and Uses of the Past Subjunctive

> To express past time, three tenses are available in the indicative: past, perfect, and past perfect. But for all three of these tenses, there is only one subjunctive to express past time.

ich war
ich bin gewesen   } **Wenn ich gewesen wäre, . . .**   If I had been, . . .
ich war gewesen

ich hatte
ich habe gehabt   } **Wenn ich gehabt hätte, . . .**   If I had had, . . .
ich hatte gehabt

The past subjunctive is derived from the past perfect. If the auxiliary in the indicative is **hatte** in the past perfect, it is **hätte** in the past subjunctive, and the indicative **war** is changed to **wäre**; thus there are never any ambiguous forms.

PAST PERFECT INDICATIVE	PAST SUBJUNCTIVE	
ich hatte gekauft	**ich hätte gekauft**	I had bought/would have bought
ich war gegangen	**ich wäre gegangen**	I had gone/would have gone
ich hatte arbeiten müssen	**ich hätte arbeiten müssen**	I had had to work/would have had to work
ich hatte nicht zu arbeiten brauchen	**ich hätte nicht zu arbeiten brauchen**	I had not had to work/ would not have had to work

Forms like **hätte können, hätte müssen,** or **hätte brauchen** are structured like **hätte gekauft.** The participles of the modals look like infinitives as long as they follow another infinitive; hence the term "double infinitive," which, strictly speaking, is incorrect because the second infinitive is really a past participle (see Anal. 57, p. 162). The English forms *could have* and *should have* always begin with **hätte** in German; *would have* begins with either **hätte** or **wäre** in German, never with **würde.** Note the difference in the following pairs of sentences.

Ich wollte, du könntest kommen.   I wish you could come.

Ich wollte, du hättest kommen können.   I wish you could have come.

Du solltest einen VW kaufen.	You should buy a VW.
Du **hättest** einen VW **kaufen sollen.**	You **should have bought** a VW.
Sie würde natürlich kommen.	Of course, she would come.
Sie **wäre** natürlich **gekommen.**	Of course, she **would have come.**

If subjunctive sentences like

Er hätte zu Hause bleiben können.

or

Er hätte nicht zu Hause bleiben müssen.

are changed into dependent clauses which should show verb-last position, the **hätte** does not go to the end, but follows **nicht** and precedes the second prong (see Anal. 72, p. 223).

Wenn ich doch nur hätte zu Hause bleiben können.
Es wäre schön gewesen, wenn ich gestern nicht hätte zu Hause bleiben müssen.

Like the future and present subjunctives, the past subjunctive is used to express unfulfilled wishes and contrary-to-fact conditions.

Ich wünschte (ich wollte), Hans wäre auch mitgegangen.	I wish Hans had gone along too.
Es wäre schön gewesen, wenn du hättest mitgehen können.	It would have been nice if you could have gone along.
Wenn er nicht gekommen wäre, wäre ich ohne ihn gefahren.	If he had not come, I would have gone without him.
Ich wäre ohne ihn gefahren, wenn er nicht gekommen wäre.	I would have gone without him if he hadn't come.
Wenn es gestern nur nicht geregnet hätte.	If only it hadn't rained yesterday.
Am liebsten wäre ich heute gar nicht aufgestanden.	I would like best not to have gotten up today at all.
Ich hätte natürlich auch zu Hause arbeiten können.	I could have worked at home too, of course.

Note that in English the past subjunctive and *would have*-forms are frequently interchangeable in *if*-clauses, but the past subjunctive is preferred. In conclusions, the *would have*-forms are mandatory, unless *could have* is used.

86/*wirklich* and *eigentlich*

The sentence adverbs **wirklich** and **eigentlich** both mean *really*, but they are not interchangeable.

The adverb **wirklich** means *really, in truth, indeed*; it frequently
reinforces the veracity of a statement.

Das weiß ich wirklich nicht.	I really (in truth) don't know that.
Elisabeth ist wirklich nett.	Elisabeth is really nice.
Wohnt er wirklich in Bonn?	Is it really true that he lives in Bonn?
Ich brauche das Geld wirklich nicht.	I assure you that I don't need the money.

The adverb **eigentlich** has a much broader range of meaning and is
frequently used in idiomatic expressions.

It may mean *actually, to come right down to it.*

Das Wetter ist eigentlich ganz gut hier.	The weather is actually quite good here.

It often conveys the notion *"I ought to, but won't,"* usually together
with a verb in the subjunctive.

Ich müßte eigentlich gehen, aber ich bleibe noch.	I really ought to go, but I'll stay a bit.

Sometimes it corresponds to *"tell me"* and expresses interest or
impatience.

Wer war das eigentlich?	Tell me, who was that?

When so used, **eigentlich** may be the equivalent of **denn.**

87/The Position of *nicht* again

Irreal wishes and irreal **wenn**-clauses frequently follow the pattern:
I wish "the whole thing" hadn't happened. One such "whole thing"
is described within the brackets of the factual statement

Gestern abend hat Meyer [drei Stunden lang nur von seinem Hobby geredet].	Last night, Meyer [talked for three hours about nothing but his hobby].

The "whole thing" was unpleasant. It should not have happened. But
it did happen, and nobody can change it. But one can, at least in
thought, erase it from the realm of reality. This is done by using
a contrary-to-fact subjunctive and by placing a condemning **nicht**
right in front of the "whole thing."

**Ich wollte, Meyer hätte gestern abend nicht [drei Stunden
    lang nur von seinem Hobby geredet].**

The **nicht**, in such cases, does not precede the second prong (**geredet**),
but the complete description of whatever the speaker considers the
"whole thing."

88/Word Formation

THE PREFIX **un-**

The prefix **un-** is added to many adjectives and a few nouns to form antonyms.

glücklich	**unglücklich**
interessant	**uninteressant**
vernünftig	**unvernünftig**
das Wissen (knowledge)	**das Unwissen** (ignorance)
das Glück (happiness, good luck)	**das Unglück** (misfortune, accident)

THE SUFFIX **-lich** ADDED TO NOUNS

Like the English suffix -ly, the German suffix **-lich**, if added to nouns, forms adjectives with the meaning of "having the qualities one associates with things or people of such a nature." The stem vowel of the noun is usually umlauted.

der Freund	friend	**freundlich**	friendly
die Mutter	mother	**mütterlich**	motherly
das Kind	child	**kindlich**	childlike
die Welt	world	**weltlich**	worldly, secular
die Natur	nature	**natürlich**	naturally

THE SUFFIXES **-bar** AND **-lich** ADDED TO VERB STEMS

Added to verb stems, **-bar** and **-lich** form adjectives with a passive meaning and correspond to English adjectives in -able and -ible.

glauben	to believe	**unglaublich**	unbelievable
brauchen	to use	**brauchbar**	usable
vergessen	to forget	**unvergeßlich**	unforgettable

Some of the adjectives formed by **-lich** have an active meaning.

sterben	to die	**sterblich**	mortal
vergessen	to forget	**vergeßlich**	forgetful

Note that **unvergeßlich** is not the opposite of **vergeßlich**. If Professor Reichmann is **vergeßlich**, he tends to forget things. If he is **unvergeßlich**, we can't forget him (he is "not to be forgotten").

PRACTICE TWO

G. Change the following sentences into past subjunctive irreal **wenn**-clauses
with irreal conclusions. Change from negative to affirmative and vice
versa.

1. Es war neblig, und wir konnten die Berge nicht sehen.
   Wenn es nicht so neblig *gewesen wäre*, *hätten* wir die Berge
   _____ _____ .

2. Erika studierte *auch* Germanistik, und so haben wir uns kennengelernt.
   Wenn Erika nicht *auch* Germanistik _____ _____, _____ wir uns
   nicht _____ .

3. Ich hatte kein Geld. Ich konnte nicht nach Österreich fahren.
   Wenn ich Geld _____ _____, _____ ich nach Österreich
   _____ _____ .

4. Ich wußte seine Telefonnummer nicht. Ich konnte ihn nicht anrufen.
   Wenn ich seine Telefonnummer _____ _____, _____ ich ihn
   _____ _____ .

5. Tante Amalie hat uns besucht. Wir sind ins Museum gegangen.
   Wenn Tante Amalie uns nicht _____ _____, _____ wir nicht ins
   Museum _____ .

H. Restate as indicated, changing from affirmative to negative and vice
versa.

1. Wolfgang konnte nicht kommen. Es wäre nett gewesen, wenn _____.
2. Andrea durfte nicht mitgehen. Es wäre nett gewesen, wenn _____.
3. Bernhard mußte zu Hause bleiben. Es wäre nett gewesen, wenn _____.
4. Sie hat uns nie besuchen können. Es wäre nett gewesen, wenn _____.

I. Change the following factual statements to irreal wishes. Change from
negative to affirmative and vice versa. Start first with **ich wollte**, then
with **ich wünschte, es wäre besser gewesen, wenn . . . , wenn** (*subject*)
doch nur . . . .

> **Wir haben das Haus leider nicht gekauft.**
> **Wenn wir das Haus doch nur gekauft hätten.**

1. Sie hat mich nicht angerufen.
2. Wir sind in den Berufsverkehr gekommen.
3. Ich habe meinen Mantel zu Hause gelassen. (Place **nicht** in front of **zu Hause**.)
4. Wir konnten das Haus nicht kaufen. (Watch the position of **hätten**.)
5. Ich habe heute abend zuviel Kaffee getrunken. (Replace **zuviel** by **nicht so viel**.)

J. Change the following factual assertions to irreal preferential statements using first **gerne**, then **lieber**, and then **am liebsten**, all three of them replacing **leider**.

> **Wir haben das Haus in Köln leider nicht gekauft.**
> **Wir hätten lieber das Haus in Köln gekauft.**

1. Wir sind leider nicht in die Berge gefahren.
2. Wir sind leider nicht in den Zoo gegangen.
3. Ich habe heute morgen leider nicht bis neun geschlafen.
4. Ich bin gestern leider nicht mit meinem Freund ins Kino gegangen.

Public Transportation

Central Europe has a superb public transportation system. Even small villages can be reached by train or bus. This extensive and highly efficient network of railways and highways was developed to meet the needs of the nearly 90 million residents of an area about the size of the states of Washington and Oregon. All large cities are connected by express trains. Many of the West German **Inter-City-Züge** depart every 60 minutes, and some attain top speeds of 120 mph. Most commuters can reach their destinations by local train, streetcar, or bus, since there is little urban sprawl as in the U.S. More and more cities, such as Frankfurt, Munich, and Vienna, have built subways; the Berlin **Untergrundbahn (U-Bahn)** dates back to the turn of the century. Air travel in Central Europe, however, is far less common than in the U.S. With the steadily increasing affluence of the past decades, travel by automobile has greatly reduced the use of public transportation. Nevertheless, although there are about 30 million cars on the road in the Federal Republic, over 20 million people, roughly a third of the population, use some form of public transportation every day.

Vienna subway ticket

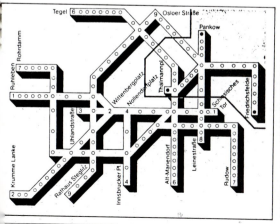

Berliner U-Bahn-Netz

U-Bahnhof Zoologischer Garten in Berlin (West)

CONVERSATIONS

I

Am Telefon:

KARLA B.:   Ich muß heute nachmittag in die Stadt. Wie wäre es, wenn du mitfahren würdest?

ELISABETH R.:   Gerne. Ich hätte zwar zu Hause viel zu tun, aber ich muß auch unbedingt in der Stadt ein paar Dinge erledigen. Nimmst du den Wagen?

K.B.:   Nein, ich wollte eigentlich mit der Bahn fahren. Mit dem Wagen kämen wir auf der Heimfahrt mitten in den Berufsverkehr.

E.R.:   Da hast du recht. Das letzte Mal habe ich vom Parkhaus am Dom bis zur Autobahn über eine halbe Stunde gebraucht.

II

Beim Verlassen des Hauptbahnhofs:

K.B.:   So, da sind wir.

E.R.:   Ja, und ich bin froh, daß wir den Wagen zu Hause gelassen haben.

Bonn → Frankfurt

ab	Zug	an	Bemerkungen
5.57	IC 565	8.10	-zuschlagfrei
6.17	IC 511	8.36	Ü Mainz S
6.26	E 2021	9.10	
7.07	IC 567	9.05	
7.23	IC 121	9.26	
7.49	FD 221	9.56	
8.17	IC 117	10.36	Ü Mainz S
8.23	IC 569	10.26	
8.36	E 2023	11.15	
8.38	FD 723	10.43	
9.01	E 2025	11.46	
9.23	IC 621	11.26	
9.56	D 721	12.07	
10.23	IC 125	12.26	
11.23	IC 521	13.26	
11.23	E 2425	14.07	
11.59	E 2027	14.47	
12.23	IC 525	14.26	
12.29	D 203	14.47	× Ü Mainz
13.17	IC 613	15.37	Ü Mainz
13.23	IC 527	15.26	
14.23	IC 529	16.26	
14.36	D 725	16.56	
15.17	IC 519	17.36	Ü Mainz S
15.23	IC 523	17.26	
15.30	E 2029	17.52	
16.23	IC 623	18.26	
17.05	E 2427	20.25	
17.23	IC 625	19.26	
17.53	IC 123	19.51	
18.23	IC 627	20.26	
19.23	IC 629	21.26	
19.43	E 2127	22.07	
20.17	IC 132	22.36	Ü Mainz S
20.23	E 542	22.26	
21.09	D 223	23.07	
21.23	IC 540	23.14	
21.57	D 225	24.00	
23.03	D 825	1.19	

2. Kl → 33,00 DM

Frankfurt → Bonn

ab	Zug	an	Bemerkungen
4.37	D 824	7.02	
6.00	E 2020	8.39	
6.25	D 224	8.22	
6.42	IC 545	8.29	
7.09	IC 122	9.07	
7.24	D 222	9.20	
7.29	IC 547	9.29	
7.53	S	10.14	Ü Mainz D
8.29	IC 628	10.29	
8.49	E 2028	11.11	Ü Mainz D
8.49	E 2028	11.30	
9.29	IC 626	11.29	
9.40	E 2424	12.18	
10.29	IC 520	12.29	
10.45	E 3354	13.13	Ü Mainz D
11.29	IC 522	13.29	
12.05	E 2024	14.21	Ü Wiesbaden D
12.05	E 2024	14.55	
12.29	IC 528	14.29	
13.19	E 2952	15.50	Ü Wiesbaden D
13.29	IC 526	15.29	
14.21	E 3294	16.35	Ü Mainz IC
14.29	IC 524	16.29	
15.21	D 720	17.30	
15.29	IC 124	17.29	
15.40	FD 722	18.04	
16.14	E 3360	18.47	Ü Mainz D ×
16.27	IC 566	18.23	
16.29	IC 620	18.29	
17.03	D 724	19.10	Ü Mainz
17.03	D 724	19.10	
17.29	IC 624	19.29	
18.11	D 220	20.14	
18.29	IC 120	20.29	
19.19	E 2120	22.06	(nicht 24., 31. XII.)
19.19	E 2120	22.12	Ü Koblenz
19.29	IC 568	21.29	
20.29	IC 622	22.29	
21.42	IC 564	23.58	-zuschlagfrei

1. Kl → 50,00 DM

9 nicht 24., 31. XII.
10 nicht 25. XII., 1. I.

15 ① bis ⑥
24 an bzw. ab Bonn-Beuel

| K.B.: | Genau. Mit dem Wagen wären wir noch gar nicht hier. |
| E.R.: | Der Verkehr ist wieder mal unmöglich. Heute hätten wir bestimmt keinen Platz zum Parken gefunden. |

III

Vor dem Kaufhof:

E.R.:	Gottseidank für die Fußgängerzone. Da braucht man wenigstens nicht immer Angst vor den Autos zu haben.
K.B.:	Hier in der Altstadt wäre es heute ja gar nicht mehr möglich, noch Autos reinzulassen. Da käme keiner mehr vorwärts, bei den engen Straßen.
E.R.:	Natürlich; wenn die Straßen nicht so eng wären, hätten wir sicher auch keine Fußgängerzone.
K.B.:	Genau. Dann hätte man mit dem Geld noch mehr Straßen gebaut, und der Verkehr wäre noch viel schlimmer.

In IV, V, and VI, construct a few exchanges according to the English outline. Use subjunctive constructions where possible.

IV

Nach dem Einkaufen:

K.B.:	How about a cup of coffee? (Wie wäre es, . . .)
E.R.:	That would be fine, but where?
K.B.:	We could go to the Dom Café.
E.R.:	I would rather go to the Café Schneider. OK with you?

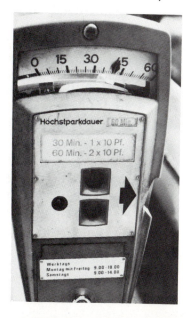

Wieviel Zeit haben wir noch?

V

Im Hauptbahnhof:

E. tells K. that they still have twenty minutes before their train
leaves; it is now 5:20 P.M. K. wishes they had a shopping center out
where they live. E. agrees that that would be very good. They could
then do all their shopping out there and wouldn't have to come into
town so often.

VI

Im Zug, kurz nach der Abfahrt:

From the train, they can see the *Bundesstraße*. Lots of cars, motorcycles, buses, even streetcars. K. wonders if something has happened,
but E. doesn't think there has been an accident; just the many traffic
lights—and they all seem to be always red. If there weren't so many
people living in the suburbs and working in the city, it wouldn't
be so bad. And if more people would take the bus or the train, that
would help too.

VII

Construct similar short exchanges, using the traffic vocabulary. Make your
sentences simple and straightforward, but try to use as many subjunctive
forms as you can.

Fragen an Sie persönlich

A

1. Wie ist der Verkehr in Ihrer Heimatstadt?[7]
2. Wie wäre es, wenn es in der Innenstadt keine Autos mehr gäbe? (Fußgängerzonen!)
3. Gibt es in Ihrem Heimatstaat[7] noch Personenzüge (*passenger trains*)?
4. Sind Sie schon einmal mit der Eisenbahn gefahren?
5. Gibt es eine U-Bahn in Ihrer Heimatstadt? Straßenbahn? Busse? andere öffentliche Verkehrsmittel (*public means of transportation*)?
6. Was würden Sie machen, wenn Sie der Verkehrsplaner in einer Großstadt wären? Was würden Sie zum Beispiel für den Berufsverkehr tun?

B

Was wurden Sie tun, wenn Sie Präsident(-in) der Vereinigten Staaten wären?
Präsident(-in) der Universität?
Bürgermeister(-in) von New York?
Berlin?
Burgbach?
Was möchten Sie sein, wenn Sie sein könnten, was Sie wollten?

READING

BARBARA BAYERSCHMIDT

Barbara Bayerschmidt (born in Geisenheim am Rhein) came to the U.S. with her parents at the age of 13. She studied art history, but later went to business school. Today she works as a financial analyst in New York City. She has written a number of short stories. The following text is from an unpublished manuscript.

Wie wäre es, wenn . . .

Ich hätte natürlich in Österreich bleiben können.

Wenn ich geblieben wäre, würden wir jetzt bald heiraten, aber nicht in Wien, sondern in seiner Heimat, im Süden, —von dort ist es nicht weit nach Jugoslawien. Es gäbe eine große Hochzeit° in der kleinen Kirche, zwei Stunden Gottesdienst°, das ganze Dorf wäre dabei°. Hochzeitsessen bis spät in die Nacht, es würde getanzt° und zuviel gegessen und getrunken,[8] und dann wäre ich seine Frau. Von jedem Fenster aus könnte ich die Alpen sehen, ich hätte Kühe und Schafe°, und Wald und Wiesen° und Obstbäume°. Das Leben wäre einfach und unkompliziert.

Oder wäre es wirklich so unkompliziert?

      *   *   *

Die Männer sitzen vorne° und die Frauen hinten°, in der Kirche. Jeden Sonntag zwei Stunden Gottesdienst. Zweihundert Menschen im Dorf, die meisten° sind irgendwie° mit ihm verwandt°, jeder kennt jeden. Wer weggeht, kommt fast nie wieder, aber wenn eine von draußen° hereinheiratet, bleibt sie eine Fremde ihr Leben lang. Er würde nach dem Studium zurückgehen müssen, er müßte den Hof° übernehmen°, wie sein Vater ihn vom Großvater übernommen

	wedding
5	church service there
	there would be dancing
	cows and sheep forest
	and meadows
10	fruit trees
	in front in the back
	most of them
15	somehow related
	from outside
	farm take over

---

[7]Note the difference between **die Stadt**, *town, city* and **der Staat**, *state.*
[8]These verb forms are in the passive voice, which will be introduced in Unit 18.

hatte. Drei- oder vierhundert Jahre Tradition und ein Familienwap-
pen° über der Haustür mit dem Datum A.D. 1603. Volkskunst° in   20   coat of arms   folk art
der Steiermark.[9]

Seit neun Semestern studiert er jetzt, und am liebsten bliebe er in
Wien. Aber eine Karriere in Wien käme nicht in Frage für ihn, das
habe ich immer gewußt. In Wien könnte ich leben, in Wien habe   25
ich gelebt, mit ihm, aber ich wußte, er würde den Hof nicht aufgeben, —und dann säße ich auf dem Lande, hätte einen Diplomland-
wirt[10] als Mann und wäre sehr einsam°: 120 Kilometer nach Graz,   lonely
120 Kilometer nach Klagenfurt, keine Konzerte, kein Museum, keine
Bibliothek, sogar der Fernsehempfang° ist schlecht, —zu viele Berge.   TV reception
Wien vielleicht drei- oder viermal im Jahr.   30

*   *   *

Südbahnhof. Abfahrt° 9 Uhr 48 nach Graz. Was wäre geworden,   departure
wenn er an dem Wochenende nicht nach Hause gefahren wäre?
Material sammeln° wollte ich, für meine Magisterarbeit°. „Das   collect   M.A. thesis
könntest du ja auch bei uns; wie wäre es, wenn du zu uns kämst?
Meine Eltern hätten nichts dagegen°".   35   against it

Sie hatten nichts dagegen, waren sehr freundlich, alle waren furcht-
bar° nett, kommen Sie wirklich aus Amerika, Sie sprechen so gut   terribly
Deutsch. Ja, aber keinen Dialekt. Wer von außen hineinheiratet,
bleibt sein Leben lang ein Fremder. Und die Frauen sitzen hinten,
und die Männer vorne. Das Dorf war eine Insel°.   40   island

Wien war auch eine Insel. Wir hatten uns ja vorher schon gekannt,
Grüß Gott auf der Treppe°, oder bei Partys im Studentenheim, oder   steps
mal ein paar Worte in der Straßenbahn auf dem Weg in die Uni. Aber
dann jede freie Minute, —zusammen gegessen, zusammen einkaufen
gegangen, zusammen durch die Stadt gebummelt°, zum Heurigen   45   strolled, wandered
nach Heiligenstadt,[11] Rosenkavalier[12] in der Staatsoper, ein Okto-
bertag im Prater,[13] „Wien, Wien, nur du allein, sollst stets die Stadt
meiner Träume sein",[14] Grillparzer im Burgtheater, „Der Traum ein
Leben".[15] Aber wir würden ja nicht in Wien leben.

*   *   *

[9]Styria, one of the Austrian states.

[10]Graduate of a school of agriculture.

[11]**der Heurige**, Austrian term for new wine (pressed the previous autumn); the term
is also used for many wine taverns, mostly in the wine-growing areas around Vienna. Heiligenstadt and Grinzing are the two best-known suburbs of Vienna where one
goes **zum Heurigen**.

[12]Opera (1911) by Richard Strauss (1864–1949).

[13]A large park on the outskirts of Vienna, along the Danube River.

[14]Well-known Viennese song.

[15]Play (1834) by the Austrian playwright Franz Grillparzer (1791–1872). The Burgtheater, formerly the imperial court theater, is one of Europe's leading theaters.

Ist es wirklich schon ein Jahr her, seit ich aus Österreich zurück- 50
gekommen bin? Wenn er nicht nach Amerika gekommen wäre, um
mich zu besuchen, wäre ich wahrscheinlich zurückgegangen. Aber
danach° wußte ich, es würde nicht gehen, ich würde mein eigenes°   after that own
Leben leben müssen.

Jetzt sitze ich in einem Büro in Manhattan. Es geht mir gut, und 55
ich verdiene° viel Geld.   earn, make

Aber in Manhattan gibt es keine Alpen.

Hochzeit in der Steiermark

REVIEW EXERCISES

K. Use the following elements to construct sentences in the past tense;
then rewrite these sentences in the perfect.

1. Fridolin / nach Hause / fahren // und / ich / er / folgen.
2. Ich / er / vor dem Bahnhof / sehen // aber / dann / er / plötzlich / weggehen.
3. Karin / mit / Bahn / nach Stuttgart / fahren // um / ihr Freund / besuchen.
4. Kinder / um eins / aus / Schule / kommen.
5. Im Sommer / wir / oft / schwimmen / gehen.
6. Am Abend / wir / noch lange / vor dem Haus / sitzen.
7. Robert Meyer / später / Arzt / werden.
8. Sommer 1986 / wochenlang / regnen.
9. Ich / gestern / arbeiten / müssen.
10. Ich / zu Hause / bleiben / wollen // aber / nicht / können.

L. Change the following factual statements to irreal wishes starting first with **ich wollte**, then with **ich wünschte**, then with **es wäre gut, wenn . . .** , and finally with **wenn wir (er) doch nur . . . .** Change from affirmative to negative and vice versa.

> **Mein Mann muß zu schwer arbeiten.**
> **Ich wollte, mein Mann brauchte nicht so schwer zu arbeiten.**
> **Ich wünschte, mein Mann brauchte nicht so schwer zu arbeiten.**
> **Es wäre gut, wenn mein Mann nicht so schwer zu arbeiten brauchte.**
> **Wenn mein Mann doch nur nicht so schwer zu arbeiten brauchte.**

1. Ich habe leider keinen Bruder.
2. Wir sind noch nicht zu Hause. (Replace **noch nicht** by **schon**.)
3. Du bist immer so pessimistisch. (Place **nicht** in front of **immer**.)
4. Wir dürfen ihn heute noch nicht besuchen. (Change **heute noch nicht** to **schon heute**.)
5. Wir können nicht jedes Wochenende in die Berge fahren.
6. Du fährst leider morgen schon wieder nach Hause. (Place **nicht** in front of **schon**.)
7. Ernst ruft mich heute abend nicht an.
8. Unser Sohn telefoniert jeden Abend zwei Stunden mit seiner Freundin. (Place **nicht** in front of **jeden Abend**.)

M. Formulate irreal preferential statements using only **am liebsten** this time. Place this **am liebsten** in the front field. Change from negative to affirmative and vice versa. Use both the present subjunctive and the **würde**-forms. Be sure to drop **leider**.

> **Wir fahren dieses Wochenende leider nicht in die Berge.**
> **Am liebsten führen wir dieses Wochenende in die Berge.**
> **Am liebsten würden wir dieses Wochenende in die Berge fahren.**

1. Ich sitze jetzt leider nicht im Hofbräuhaus.
2. Ich studiere leider nicht Medizin.
3. Ich bleibe nicht jeden Tag bis neun im Bett.
4. Wir wohnen leider nicht in München.
5. Wir gehen leider nicht zum Essen in den Ratskeller.

N. Combine the following pairs of sentences to form irreal **wenn**-clauses followed or preceded by an irreal conclusion. Change from affirmative to negative and vice versa.

> **Wir können nicht nach Italien fahren. Mein Mann ist nicht gesund.**
> **Wenn mein Mann gesund wäre, könnten wir nach Italien fahren.**

1. Ich bin kein Arzt. Ich kann Ihnen nicht helfen.
2. Wir haben kein Geld. Wir können nicht mit Meyers in die Schweiz fahren.
3. Wir können hier draußen nicht einkaufen. Es gibt kein Einkaufszentrum.
4. Wir müssen den Bus nehmen. Die U-Bahn fährt nicht nach Sondersbach.
5. Ich fahre mit der Bahn. Das Benzin ist zu teuer.
6. Ich komme erst um sieben. Ich muß dreimal umsteigen.

O. Combine the following pairs of sentences to form irreal **wenn**-clauses followed or preceded by an irreal conclusion. Change from affirmative to negative and vice versa.

> **Rosemarie studierte damals in München. Ich habe sie kennengelernt.**
> **Wenn Rosemarie damals nicht in München studiert hätte, hätte ich sie nie kennengelernt.**

1. Tante Amalie schickte mir jeden Monat fünfhundert Mark. Ich konnte Medizin studieren.
2. Auf der Autobahn war viel Verkehr. Wir kamen zu spät in die Oper.
3. Wir sind nicht in die Berge gefahren. Das Wetter war zu schlecht.
4. Tante Amalie kam. Ich mußte ins Museum gehen.
5. Wir saßen bis fünf im Café Schneider und kamen dann in den Berufsverkehr.

P. The following sentences contain a dependent clause introduced by **weil**. Changing the **weil**-clause into a **wenn**-clause, transform the sentences into irreal conditions. Change from affirmative to negative and vice versa.

> **Wir wohnten in der Stadt, weil wir keine Kinder hatten.**
> **Wenn wir Kinder gehabt hätten, hätten wir nicht in der Stadt gewohnt.**

1. Weil wir einen Hund hatten, haben wir keine Wohnung gefunden.
2. Er ist zu Hause geblieben, weil er krank war.
3. Wir sind nicht schwimmen gegangen, weil es geregnet hat.
4. Ich konnte nicht im Palast-Hotel wohnen, weil es zu teuer war.
5. Wir haben in Hamburg gewohnt, weil mein Mann dort gearbeitet hat.
6. Vorher hatten wir in München gewohnt, weil wir dort studiert haben.
7. Sie fuhren in die Berge, weil sie schilaufen wollten.

Q. Express in German.

1. It would be nice if we could go back to Lübeck.
2. If I had not been there twenty years ago, I would never have met him.
3. Frau Enderle would like to live there again.
4. But Herr Enderle prefers living in Burgbach. (Use **lieber**.)
5. I wish you would help me in the kitchen.
6. Then we could eat at six o'clock.
7. How would it be if we drank another bottle of wine?
8. We could have stayed here, but we didn't want to.
9. It would be nice if she would invite me.
10. I would like to visit her. (Use **gern**.)
11. If you'd go to bed early, you wouldn't always be tired.
12. If only the bus would come.
13. If it weren't raining, we could walk.
14. Would you like to have sauerkraut for lunch (**Mittagessen**) today?
15. I'd rather have cauliflower (**Blumenkohl**).

R. Composition.

Turn the conversations of Unit 9, p. 276, into a simple narrative, starting as follows. Number your sentences.

1. Frau B. telefoniert mit Frau R.   3. . . .
2. Sie will mit Frau R. in die Stadt fahren.

Then rewrite your sentences in the past tense.

1. Frau B. telefonierte mit Frau R.   2. Sie wollte . . .

Finally, have Frau B. tell the story to her family during **Abendessen** of the same day, using the perfect tense, but remember to use the past with **haben, sein**, and the modals.

1. Ich war den ganzen Tag mit Elisabeth in der Stadt.
2. Ich habe sie heute morgen angerufen.
3. Ich wollte mit ihr einkaufen gehen.

4. Wir sind mit der Bahn gefahren, weil . . .
5. . . .

VOCABULARY

die Ampel, -n	traffic light	die Ausfahrt, -en	exit, off-ramp
ander-	different, other	die Einfahrt, -en	entrance (way); driveway; on-ramp
die Angst, ⁻e	fear, anxiety, angst		
Angst haben vor (dat.)	to be afraid of	die Heimfahrt, -en	trip home
aus•steigen (sein)	to get off (a train, etc.)	froh	happy
das Benzin′	gasoline	der Fußgänger, -	pedestrian
der Berg, -e	mountain	die Fußgängerzone, -n	pedestrian zone
in die Berge	to the mountains	zu Fuß (gehen)	(to go) on foot
der Berufsverkehr	commuter traffic (rush hour)	genug	enough
		die Germanis′tik	study of German language and literature
billig	cheap		
die Bundesstraße, -n	federal highway		
der Bürgermeister, -	mayor	der Germanist, -en (n-noun)	Germanist (m.)
das Café, -s	café, coffeehouse		
das Ding, -e	thing	die Germanistin, -nen	Germanist (f.)
draußen	outside		
duschen	to shower	gottseidank	thank goodness
die Dusche, -n	shower	die Heimat	home, native land
das Einkaufszentrum, -zentren	shopping center	der Heimatstaat, -en	home state
die Eisenbahn, -en	railroad, train	die Heimatstadt, ⁻e	home town
eng	narrow	hin•kommen (sein)	to get there
erledigen.	to take care of	hin•stellen	to put, place
die Fahrt, -en	drive, trip	das Hobby, -s	hobby
die Abfahrt, -en	departure (by car, train, etc.)	die Idee′, die Ide′en	idea

die Innenstadt, ¨e	inner city, downtown
der (die) Irre, -n	insane person
irr(e)	insane
kaum	hardly
am liebsten (*adv.*)	(I would like) most of all
mal	once; times; for a change
jedesmal	every time
das letzte Mal	the last time
der Mantel, ¨	(over)coat
der Millionär', -e	millionaire
mit•fahren (sein)	to come along, to ride with
mitten in	in the middle of
möglich	possible
unmöglich	impossible
der Nebel, -	fog
neblig	foggy
öffentlich	public(ly)
die Oper, -n	opera
das Parkhaus, ¨er	parking garage
passieren (sein)	to happen
was ist passiert?	what has happened?
plötzlich	suddenly
der Präsident, -en (*n-noun*)	president (*m.*)
die Präsidentin, -nen	president (*f.*)
rasen (sein)	to race, to speed
der Ratskeller, -	restaurant in city hall basement
rechtzeitig	on time
reden	to talk, speak
rein•lassen (= herein• lassen)	to let in
das Schild, -er	sign
das Stopschild	stop sign
schlimm	bad
der Schmerz, -en	pain
die Kopfschmerzen (*pl.*)	headache
schneien	to snow
schwer	difficult; heavy
die Seitenstraße, -n	side street, side road
sparen	to save
die Stauung, -en	traffic jam, back-up
die Stelle, -n	spot, position
an deiner Stelle	in your place
das Telefonbuch, ¨er	telephone book
die U-Bahn, -en (= Untergrund- bahn)	subway
überall	everywhere
um•steigen (sein)	to change (trains, buses, etc.)
unbedingt	absolutely
der Unfall, ¨e	accident
unglaublich	unbelievable, incredible
das Unglück, -e	bad luck, misfortune; accident
unglücklich	unhappy
uninteressant	uninteresting
das Vergnügen, -	pleasure
verkaufen	to sell
verlassen (*with acc. obj.*)	to leave (someone or something)
vernünftig	reasonable
unvernünftig	unreasonable
versuchen	to try
vorwärts	forward
der Wald, ¨er	forest
der Schwarzwald	Black Forest
das WC, -s	(water closet), toilet
wecken	to awaken, wake (someone) up
die Welt, -en	world
die Wohnung, -en	apartment
der Zoo, -s	zoo

Strong Verbs

INFINITIVE	PRESENT	PAST TENSE	PERFECT	
aus•steigen		**stieg aus**	**ist ausgestiegen**	to get off (a train, etc.)
hin•kommen		**kam hin**	**ist hingekommen**	to get there
rein•lassen	**läßt rein**	**ließ rein**	**reingelassen**	to let in
schwimmen		**schwamm**	**ist geschwommen**	to swim
um•steigen		**stieg um**	**ist umgestiegen**	to change (trains, buses, etc.)

Unit 10

Prepositions with Dative or Accusative— The Genitive Case—*ein*-Words without Nouns

Note on the weather: don't leave your umbrella at home

Despite the northern latitude of Central Europe, the climate is surprisingly moderate. The northwest is affected by the mild Gulf Stream. With prevailing westerly winds, Atlantic low pressure systems bring frequent precipitation. In the northeast, the climate tends to be drier and colder, and in the southern highlands and in the Alps, summers are usually warmer and winters colder. The most significant aspect of the weather is that it is unpredictable; the phrase most often found in weather reports is **wechselnd bewölkt mit vereinzelten Niederschlägen** (*partly cloudy with occasional showers*).

WETTER: Es bleibt regnerisch

Lage: Die Ausläufer eines zur Nordsee ziehenden Tiefs beeinflussen mit einem breiten Niederschlagsgebiet weite Teile Deutschlands. Dabei verstärkt sich der Zustrom sehr kühler Meeresluft noch.

Vorhersage für Dienstag: Stark bewölkt mit länger andauernden Regenfällen. Nachmittags von Nordwesten her Bewölkungsauflockerungen, aber noch Schauer. Tages-höchsttemperaturen zwischen 10 und 14 Grad, im Bergland um 7 Grad. Tiefstwerte nachts um 4 Grad. Mäßiger, zeitweise böig auffrischender Wind um West.

Weitere Aussichten: Einzelne Schauer, sehr kühl.

Sonnenaufgang am Mittwoch: 5.35 Uhr*, Untergang: 21.02 Uhr; **Mondaufgang:** 21.39 Uhr, Untergang: 5.06 Uhr (* MESZ; zentraler Ort Kassel).

Vorhersagekarte für den 12. Mai, 8 Uhr

H Hochdruckzentrum
T Tiefdruckzentrum
○ wolkenlos
◔ heiter
◑ halb bedeckt
◕ wolkig
● bedeckt
( ) Windstille
⟋ Nordwind 10 km/h
⟋⟍ Ostwind 20 km/h
⟍ Sudwind 30 km/h
⟍⟍ Westwind 40 km/h
≡ Nebel
● Nieseln
● Regen
✳ Schnee
▼ Schauer
⟋⟍ Gewitter
▨ Niederschlagsgebiet
— Temperatur in °C
▲▲ Warmfront
▲▲ Okklusion
▲▲ Kaltfront am Boden
△△ Kaltfront in der Höhe
⟹ Luftstromung warm
⟹ Luftstromung kalt
— Isobaren

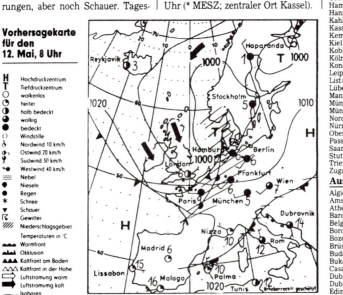

Temperaturen in Grad Celsius und Wetter vom Montag, 13 Uhr (MESZ):

Deutschland:		
Berlin	10	bw
Bielefeld	10	bd
Braunlage	5	bw
Bremen	8	R
Dortmund	9	bw
Dresden	10	bw
Düsseldorf	12	bw
Erfurt	8	bd
Essen	10	bw
Feldberg/S.	3	bw
Flensburg	6	R
Frankfurt/M.	10	bw
Freiburg	15	bw
Garmisch	8	R
Greifswald	9	bw
Hamburg	8	bw
Hannover	11	bw
Kahler Asten	6	bw
Kassel	9	bw
Kempten	11	bw
Kiel	7	R
Koblenz	12	bw
Köln-Bonn	11	bd
Konstanz	12	he
Leipzig	9	bw
List/Sylt	7	R
Lübeck	8	R
Mannheim	13	bw
München	12	he
Münster	10	bd
Norderney	10	bw
Nürnberg	11	bw
Oberstdorf	9	bd
Passau	13	bw
Saarbrücken	11	bw
Stuttgart	11	bw
Trier	11	bw
Zugspitze	-5	iW

Ausland:		
Algier	24	he
Amsterdam	12	bd
Athen	18	he
Barcelona	21	he
Belgrad	22	he
Bordeaux	19	he
Bozen	17	bw
Brüssel	13	bw
Budapest	15	bw
Bukarest	23	he
Casablanca	20	bw
Dublin	13	Sp
Dubrovnik	18	he
Edinburgh	11	bw

Faro	21	he
Florenz	17	bd
Genf	17	he
Helsinki	5	bd
Hongkong	29	bw
Innsbruck	12	he
Istanbul	14	he
Kairo	22	he
Klagenfurt	13	bd
Konstanza	21	he
Kopenhagen	10	he
Korfu	18	he
Las Palmas	21	bw
Leningrad	11	Rs
Lissabon	18	bw
Locarno	16	he
London	13	bd
Los Angeles	18	bd
Luxemburg	10	bw
Madrid	20	he
Mailand	20	he
Malaga	24	he
Mallorca	22	he
Moskau	16	he
Neapel	20	he
New York	28	he
Nizza	18	he
Oslo	11	bw
Ostende	13	bw
Palermo	22	bw
Paris	15	bw
Peking	25	he
Prag	11	bw
Rhodos	19	he
Rom	20	bw
Salzburg	10	bw
Singapur	31	bw
Split	18	bw
Stockholm	10	bw
Straßburg	15	bw
Tel Aviv	23	bw
Tokio	21	he
Tunis	25	bw
Valencia	26	he
Varna	24	he
Venedig	19	bw
Warschau	12	he
Wien	15	he
Zürich		

bd = bedeckt; bw = bewölkt; Gr = Graupel; Gw = Gewitter; he = heiter; iW = in Wolken; Ne = Nebel; R = Regen; Rs = Regenschauer; S = Schneefall o. Schneeschauer; Sp = Sprühregen, Sr = Schneeregen; wl = wolkenlos; - = keine Angabe

PATTERNS ONE

1/Review: Prepositions with the Accusative, Prepositions with the Dative

In einer halben Stunde fuhren wir durch ganz Liechtenstein.

In half an hour we drove through all of Liechtenstein

Was hast du denn für den Wein bezahlt?

What did you pay for the wine?

Ich habe gar nichts gegen deinen Bruder.

I have nothing at all against your brother.

Karla sagt, sie kommt gegen sechs.

Karla says she'll come around six o'clock.

Wenn ich nur nicht ohne meinen Regenmantel in die Berge gefahren wäre.

If only I hadn't gone to the mountains without my raincoat.

Der Zug aus Darmstadt kommt um sechs Uhr an.

The train from Darmstadt arrives at six o'clock.

Alle standen um den neuen Porsche herum.

They were all standing around the new Porsche.

Es wäre schön, wenn du um Weihnachten herum wieder hier wärst.

It would be nice if you would be back around Christmas.

Diskussion um Todesstrafe:

AUS DEM INHALT:

Von früh bis spät

Vom Keller bis zum Dach.

In Österreich auf dem ersten Platz.

Zu jeder Tageszeit

ganztägig geöffnet auch Samstag und Sonntag von 10 bis 19 Uhr

Wo kommst du denn her? —Aus dem Kino. Da komme ich auch her.

Where are you coming from? —From the movies. That's where I'm coming from, too.

Herr Enderle ist aus Stuttgart, aber seine Frau kommt aus Ostpreußen.

Mr. Enderle is from Stuttgart, but his wife comes from East Prussia.

Außer einem Kriminalroman habe ich leider nichts zu lesen mitgebracht.

Except for a detective novel, I unfortunately didn't bring anything to read.

Bei dem Regen hätten wir zu Hause bleiben sollen.

In this rain we should have stayed home.

Brötchen kriegen Sie hier bei uns.

Rolls you can get right here from us.

Burgbach liegt bei Stuttgart.

Burgbach is located near Stuttgart.

Bist du mit dem Wagen gefahren? —Nein, mit dem Zug.

Did you go by car? —No, by train.

Kirsten wohnt bei ihren Eltern.

Kirsten lives with her parents.

Ferien für Mutter

Liebe im Straßenverkehr

Flug über die Grenze

Nach dem Theater fuhr er noch nach Köln.	After the theater, he still drove to Cologne.
Seit dem Abitur[1] habe ich sie nicht mehr gesehen.	I haven't seen her since we got our *Abitur*.
Die Uhr habe ich von meinen Großeltern bekommen.	I received the watch from my grandparents.
Ich hätte gerne ein Pfund von dieser Leberwurst.	I'd like to have a pound of this liverwurst.
Ich wollte, ich könnte heute zum Mittagessen nach Hause fahren.	I wish I could go home for lunch today.
Hättest du was zu trinken im Hause? —Ja, was denn zum Beispiel?	Do you happen to have something to drink in the house? —Yes, what, for example?

topfit im Büro

Trotz Sturz erfolgreich

Gespräch zwischen zwei Schulen

Seit Jahren bewährt,

2/Prepositions with either Accusative or Dative

Wo seid ihr denn hingefahren? —Wir sind an den Rhein gefahren.	Where did you go? —We drove to the Rhine.
Ihr wart am Rhein? Da möchte ich auch mal hin.	You were at the Rhine? I'd like to go there, too, sometime.
Sie hat die Flasche Wein auf den Tisch gestellt.	She put the bottle of wine on the table.
Wo ist denn der Wein? —Er steht auf dem Tisch.	Where is the wine? —It's on the table.
Wo sind die Kinder denn hingelaufen? —Hinter das Haus.	Where did the children run to? —Behind the house.

[1]**Abitur**: final examinations after secondary school (**Gymnasium**).

Die Pfalz bei Kaub am Rhein

Sind sie immer noch hinter dem Haus?	Are they still behind the house?
Was habt ihr denn gestern gemacht? —Wir sind ins Theater gegangen.	What did you do yesterday? —We went to the theater.
Wo wart ihr denn gestern abend? —Im Theater.	Where were you last night? —At the theater.
Stellen[2] Sie Ihren Wagen doch neben die Kirche. Da steht[2] er gut.	Put your car next to the church. It's OK there.
Das Haus neben der Kirche gehört meinem Bruder.	The house next to the church belongs to my brother.
Wir sind über England und die Niederlande nach Deutschland geflogen.	We flew to Germany over England and the Netherlands.
Und über den Niederlanden haben wir gefrühstückt.	And over the Netherlands we had breakfast.
Es regnete, und wir hielten unter der Brücke.	It was raining, and we stopped under the bridge.
Es regnete, und wir liefen unter die Brücke.	It was raining, and we ran under the bridge.
Ich habe ihn bis vor den Bahnhof mitgenommen.	I took him as far as the station.
Vor dem Bahnhof hat Marina auf ihn gewartet.	Marina waited for him in front of the station.
Der Brief lag[2] zwischen den Zeitungen.	The letter lay between the newspapers.
Ich konnte ihn nicht finden, weil ich ihn zwischen die Zeitungen gelegt[2] hatte.	I could not find it because I had laid it between the papers.

[2]Note the difference: **legen, legte, gelegt** (weak), *to lay (flat), to put*
liegen, lag, gelegen (strong), *to lie (flat), to be*
stellen, stellte, gestellt (weak), *to place (upright), to put*
stehen, stand, gestanden (strong), *to stand (upright), to be*

ANALYSIS ONE

/Prepositions with the Accusative, Prepositions with the Dative

1. Nouns or pronouns following **durch, für, gegen, ohne, um** must always be in the accusative (see Anal. 46, p. 115).

> **Ich gehe ohne meinen Freund.**
> **Ich gehe ohne ihn.**

Remember that in time expressions **gegen** means *at about* or *around* and **um** means *at (exactly)*.

Er kam gegen halb neun.	He came around 8:30.
Sie kam um halb zehn.	She came at (exactly) 9:30.

When **um** is used in place phrases, it means *around* and is often followed by **herum** after the noun or pronoun.

Fahren Sie hier um die Ecke und dann um den Bahnhof herum.	Turn the corner here, and then drive around the station.

The preposition **bis** is also used with the accusative, but frequently the accusative is not readily recognizable. Occasionally **bis** is followed by another preposition, which then determines the case of the following noun or pronoun.

Also bis Donnerstag.	See you on Thursday.
Also bis nächsten Donnerstag.	See you next Thursday.
Sie nahm uns bis zum Bahnhof[3] mit.	She gave us a ride to the station.
Ich fahre bis nach Darmstadt mit.	I'll come along as far as Darmstadt.
Von März bis Oktober regnet es hier nie.	From March until October it never rains here.
Von Stuttgart bis München fährt der Zug etwa zwei Stunden.	The train takes about two hours from Stuttgart to Munich.

2. Nouns or pronouns following the prepositions **aus, außer, bei, mit, nach, seit, von, zu** must always be in the dative case (see Anal. 52, p. 140).

> **Ich komme von meiner Tante.**
> **Ich komme von ihr.**

In both groups, it is the preposition alone that determines the case of the following noun or pronoun.

---

[3]Dative case determined by **zu**, not by **bis**.

90/Prepositions with either Dative or Accusative

There is, however, a group of prepositions which can be used with either dative or accusative. When these prepositions are used to describe places, the case of the noun or pronoun following them depends on the particular situation.

Only nouns referring to persons can be replaced by pronouns after these prepositions. Inanimate objects are replaced by **da**-compounds, which will be introduced in Unit 12.

These "two-way" prepositions are:

an	at, next to, on	**über**	over
auf	on	**unter**	under
hinter	behind	**vor**	in front of
in	in	**zwischen**	between
neben	beside		

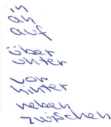

Both German and English distinguish between two kinds of place phrases:

<u>**wo?** = place at which</u>

zu Hause	at home
in Deutschland	in Germany

<u>**wohin?** = place to which</u>

nach Hause	home
nach Deutschland	to Germany

In these examples, you can turn one type of place phrase into another by changing prepositions.

In some instances, English does not use different prepositions, but speakers of English nevertheless have no difficulty distinguishing between the notions:

The dog slept *under the table*.	The dog ran *under the table*.
The cat was *behind the sofa*.	The cat ran *behind the sofa*.

The German equivalents of these sentences do distinguish, however, not by using different prepositions, but by using the dative for "place at which" and the accusative for "place to which."

Der Hund schlief unter dem Tisch.	**Der Hund lief unter den Tisch.**
Die Katze war hinter dem Sofa.	**Die Katze lief hinter das Sofa.**

All two-way prepositions function like this, that is, they answer **wo**-questions in the dative and **wohin**-questions in the accusative.

It is important to realize that the distinction between dative and accusative after these nine two-way prepositions is not one of rest versus motion. In both situations there may be motion (*He walked in the garden* and *He walked into the garden*). The determining factor is whether or not, in the course of the verbal action, a border line is crossed by either the subject or the object. If such a border line is crossed, the accusative must be used; if not, the dative must be used. This border line may be real or imagined. Thus, the area **vor dem Haus** does not have a clearly defined border, but there is nevertheless common consent as to the meaning of **vor dem Haus.** If this area **vor dem Haus** is entered in the course of the verbal action, the accusative must be used: **Er fuhr vor das Haus** (*He drove up to the house*). If the entire verbal action takes place within the area **vor dem Haus,** the dative must be used: **Er hielt vor dem Haus** (*He stopped in front of the house*).

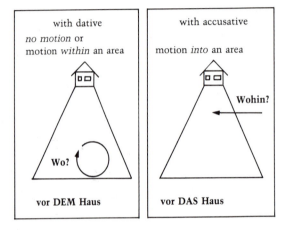

After verbs which cannot imply motion, such as **sein** and **bleiben,** the dative is always required with these nine prepositions.

> **Sie ist schon im Bett.**
> **Ich bleibe heute im Bett.**

The verbs **sitzen, stehen,** and **liegen** require the dative after two-way prepositions; **setzen, stellen,** and **legen** require the accusative.

NOTE:

1. Unless the article is stressed, the following contractions are customary: **an dem = am; an das = ans; in dem = im; in das = ins.** The contractions **aufs, hinterm, übers, unterm** also occur in colloquial German.

2. The preposition **an** describes an area "next to" the point of reference. Thus it is **Frankfurt am Main** and **Köln am Rhein.** One stands **am Fenster,** *at the window* (**an** plus dative), after having walked **an das Fenster,** *to the window* (**an** plus accusative). The preposition **auf** expresses the notion of "on top of a horizontal surface."

3. If used with the accusative, **über** means *over*, *across*, with the implication "to the other side," or it means *via* or *by way of*.

Er sprang über den Zaun.	He jumped over the fence.
Sie ist über die Schweiz nach Italien ge- **fahren.**	She went to Italy via Switzerland.

When **über** means *via*, the corresponding interrogative is **wie?**, not **wohin?**

Wie seid ihr nach Italien gefahren, über **Österreich oder über die Schweiz?**	How did you go to Italy, via Austria or via Switzerland?

4. As you already know, the preposition **vor** frequently means *ago*. If so used, it must be followed by the dative: **vor drei Jahren** (*three years ago*).

5. When **an** and **in** are used with a temporal meaning, they are followed by the dative: **am Sonntag, im Winter, in einem Jahr.**

91/Splitting *wohin*, *woher*, *dahin*, and *daher*

In spoken German, the interrogatives **wohin** (*to which place*) and **woher** (*from which place*) and the demonstratives **dahin** (*to that place*) and **daher** (*from that place*) are usually split in such a way that **hin** and **her** become part of the second prong. They are then treated as if they were complements like **ab** or **an** and thus join a following verb form. Thus, there are two distinct patterns of the types **Wohin...gehen** and **Wo...hingehen**. Note the shift in stress in the following pairs of sentences.

UNSPLIT POSITION	SPLIT POSITION
Wohin *gehst* du?	**Wo gehst du *hin*?**
Wohin willst du *gehen*?	**Wo willst du denn *hin*gehen?**
Woher *kommst* du?	**Wo kommst du *her*?**
Woher ist der Brief *gekommen*?	**Wo ist denn der Brief *her*gekommen?**
Dahin *will* ich nicht.	**Da will ich gar nicht *hin*.**
Daher komme ich *auch*.	**Da komme ich *auch* her.**

These "split" forms are very commonly used. When a German unexpectedly meets a friend, he is more apt to ask **Wo kommst du denn her?** than **Woher kommst du?**

92/Names of Countries

Most country names are neuter and are normally used without the article: **(das) Deutschland, (das) Frankreich.**

Wenn wir nur nach Italien fahren könnten.

A few country names are feminine: **die Schweiz, die Tschecho-slowakei, die Türkei**; a few others are plural: **die Niederlande, die Vereinigten Staaten (die USA)**. They must always be used with the article; in directives, the preposition **in** (and not **nach**) is used: **in die Schweiz** = to Switzerland.

> **Ali arbeitet in Berlin, aber er kommt aus der Türkei.**
> **Ich führe auch gerne einmal in die Vereinigten Staaten (in die USA).**
> **Jane Ray wohnt in den Vereinigten Staaten (in den USA).**

PRACTICE ONE

A. Fill the blanks with the correct definite article.

1. Nach _dem_ Frühstück sind wir schwimmen gegangen.
2. Nächstes Wochenende fahren wir zu _den_ Großeltern.
3. Was hast du für _das_ Motorrad bezahlt?
4. Ich hätte gerne Menü eins, aber ohne _den_ Nachtisch.
5. Ich komme gerade aus _der_ Stadt.
6. Bei _dem_ Regen fahre ich nicht in die Berge.
7. Letzten Frühling sind wir durch _die_ Schweiz gefahren.
8. Sprich mal mit _dem_ Arzt.
9. Was hast du denn gegen _den_ Professor Schmidt?
10. Gehen Sie um _den_ Bahnhof und dann gleich links.
11. Seit _dem_ Herbst raucht sie nicht mehr.
12. Könntest du mir von _der_ Bäckerei ein paar Brötchen mitbringen?

B. Fill the blanks with the correct definite article.

1. Sie stellte das Glas auf _den_ Tisch. Das Glas stand auf _dem_ Tisch.
2. Der Wagen steht hinter _dem_ Haus. Ich habe den Wagen hinter _das_ Haus gestellt.
3. Jutta fährt in _die_ Vereinigten Staaten. Sie wohnt in _den_ Vereinigten Staaten.
4. Wir brachten sie bis vor _die_ Haustür. Vor _der_ Tür sagten wir auf Wiedersehen.

C. Form questions for the following statements, using either **wo** or **wohin** (**wo . . . hin**).

1. Ich habe den Tisch an die Wand gestellt.
2. Gestern habe ich sie im Theater gesehen.
3. Ich wollte ihn am Bahnhof treffen.
4. Im Sommer war er mit Rosemarie an der Mosel.
5. Morgen fährt er mit Rosemarie nach Bonn.
6. Seine Tochter war in Mainz.
7. Bettina ißt heute in der Mensa.
8. Meyer hat uns zum Bahnhof gefahren.

D. Answer the following questions, using in your answers one of the prepositions that can take either the dative or the accusative.

1. Wo hast du denn die Zeitung hingelegt?
2. Wo hast du sie gesehen?
3. Wo steht denn euer Wagen?
4. Wie seid ihr denn nach Italien gefahren?
5. Wo geht ihr heute abend hin?
6. Wo ist denn Achim heute morgen?
7. Was hast du denn mit meinem Buch gemacht?
8. Wo hast du heute gefrühstückt?

E. Express in German.

1. Please wait at the corner.
2. Put the wine on the table, please.
3. Drive the car behind the hotel.
4. Shall we go into the house?
5. My uncle lives in Czechoslovakia.
6. I sat next to her.
7. She ran across the street.
8. He slept under the bridge.
9. She was standing in front of the church.
10. The hotel is between the station and the school.

Fußball

While the U.S. has two national sports, football and baseball, Central Europe has one, **Fußball**, which is soccer and not American football. Children learn to play **Fußball** at an early age; they play in the street or in backyards long before they compete on the playing field. Most people retain this interest as adults; in the Federal Republic alone there are 4.5 million members of **Fußballklubs**, and millions more enjoy soccer vicariously as spectators. Games in the national leagues are followed with avid interest on television, and this interest turns into an obsession when a German team competes in the **Weltmeisterschaft** (*world championship*).

Emblems of GDR soccer teams on beer coasters

Fußball in Österreich

FC Tirol - Eisenstadt		2:1
Austria - Grazer AK		1:1
Wiener SK - Linzer ASK		3:0
VOEST - Admira/W.		2:1
Sturm - Vienna		3:0
Klagenfurt - Rapid		1:0

1. Austria	16	47:21	25:7
2. Rapid	16	48:20	23:9
3. FC Tirol	16	36:23	21:11
4. Linzer ASK	16	23:26	18:14
5. Sturm	16	21:22	17:15
6. Admira/W.	16	29:26	15:17
7. Wiener SK	16	33:31	14:18
8. VOEST	16	26:29	14:18
9. Elsenstadt	16	22:32	14:18
10. Vienna	16	17:29	14:18
11. Grazer AK	16	21:32	12:20
12. Klagenfurt	16	12:44	5:27

Pokalspiele Schweiz Nationalliga A

Wettingen - Biehl	4:1
Sursee - Luzern	0:4
Kreuzlingen - GC Grasshoppers	0:5
Mondr. - Kriens (B)	2:3
Locarno - St. Gallen	2:1
Schallens - Martiny	3:2
FC Zug - Grenchen	0:5
Basel - Friebourg	3:1
Monthey - Xamax	0:3
Malley - Oldboys	2:3
Bellinzona - Youngboys	1:2
Aarau - Baden	3:0
CHDF - Colombier	1:1
Winthertur - Mury	5:0
Zerwitt - Lausanne	2:0
Sion - Meyrin	4:1

BUNDESLIGA TABELLE

1. München	6	5	0	22:10	+12	17:5
2. Leverkusen	7	1	3	25:10	+15	15:7
3. Hamburg	6	3	2	20:10	+10	15:7
4. Bremen	6	3	2	21:17	+ 4	15:7
5. Stuttgart	4	5	2	20:11	+ 9	13:9
6. Kaiserslautern	4	5	2	18:12	+ 6	13:9
7. Uerdingen	4	4	3	16:14	+ 2	12:10
8. Bochum	5	6	2	15:14	+ 1	12:10
9. Schalke	5	2	4	21:22	− 1	12:10
10. Dortmund	4	3	4	25:15	+10	11:11
11. Frankfurt	2	6	3	15:15	0	10:12
12. Köln	4	2	5	16:17	− 1	10:12
13. Mannheim	3	4	4	16:19	− 3	10:12
14. Gladbach	2	5	4	16:17	− 1	9:13
15. Nürnberg	1	5	5	14:21	− 1	7:15
16. Homburg	2	2	7	8:24	−16	6:16
17. BW Berlin	1	4	6	11:29	−18	6:16
18. Düsseldorf	2	1	8	11:33	−22	5:17

PATTERNS TWO

3/The Genitive Modifying Nouns

Werners Freundin kenne ich nicht.	I don't know Werner's girlfriend.
Schmidts Roman habe ich nicht gelesen.	I haven't read Schmidt's novel.
Herrn Bertrams Frau konnte leider nicht kommen.	Unfortunately, Mr. Bertram's wife could not come.
Hast du Mutters Hut gesehen?	Have you seen mother's hat?
Wie heißt denn die Freundin deiner Tochter?	What is the name of your daughter's friend?
Herr Harms ist ein Freund meines Mannes.	Mr. Harms is a friend of my husband.
Am Abend ihres Geburtstages ging er mit ihr ins Theater.	On the evening of her birthday he went to the theater with her.
Gegen Ende des Jahres kam er aus Afrika zurück.	Toward the end of the year he came back from Africa.

4/Genitive of Time

Eines Morgens mußte Gerda um fünf Uhr aufstehen.	One morning Gerda had to get up at five o'clock.
Eines Tages werde ich nach Kairo fahren.	Some day I'll go to Cairo.
Eines Nachts kam Horst erst um zwei Uhr nach Hause.	One night Horst did not come home until two o'clock.

5/Prepositions with the Genitive

Anstatt (Statt) des Rotweins hätte ich Orangensaft trinken sollen.	Instead of red wine, I should have drunk orange juice.
Wir haben trotz des Regens (trotz dem Regen) gestern gearbeitet.	We worked yesterday in spite of the rain.
Es hat geregnet, aber wir haben trotzdem gearbeitet.	It rained, but we worked in spite of that.
Während des Sommers war Schmidt in Tirol.	During the summer Schmidt was in the Tyrol.
Während der Woche kann ich dich leider nicht besuchen.	During the week I unfortunately can't visit you.
Sie können doch wegen des Regens (wegen dem Regen) nicht zu Hause bleiben.	You can't stay at home because of the rain.

6/Genitive Substitutes

Hannelore? Das ist doch die Freundin von Werner Schlosser, oder? (Werner Schlossers Freundin)	Hannelore? She's Werner Schlosser's friend, isn't she?

Das Haus meines Vaters steht neben der Kirche.

Onkel Harry ist der Bruder von meinem Vater. (der Bruder meines Vaters)	Uncle Harry is my father's brother.
Das Haus von meinem Vater steht neben der Kirche. (Das Haus meines Vaters)	My father's house is next to the church.
Der Marktplatz von diesem Dorf ist sehr alt. (Der Marktplatz dieses Dorfes)	The market square of this village is very old.
Dieser Parkplatz ist nur für Wagen von Studenten.	This parking lot is only for cars of students.
Frau Meyer ist die Mutter von drei Kindern.	Mrs. Meyer is the mother of three children.
Frau Meyer ist eine Freundin von Müllers Frau.	Mrs. Meyer is a friend of Müller's wife.
Renate ist eine Freundin von mir.	Renate is a friend of mine.
Renate ist eine Freundin von Dieter.	Renate is a friend of Dieter's.
Renate ist eine von Dieters Freundinnen.	Renate is one of Dieter's friends.
Dieter ist ein Freund von meiner Schwester. (ein Freund meiner Schwester)	Dieter is a friend of my sister's.
Dieter ist einer von den Freunden von meiner Schwester. (einer der Freunde meiner Schwester)	Dieter is one of the friends of my sister.
Möchten Sie noch eine Tasse Tee?	Would you like another cup of tea?
Und wie wäre es mit einem Stück Kuchen?	And how about a piece of cake?
Haben Sie schon gewählt? —Ja, ich hätte gerne ein Glas Mosel.	Have you decided yet? —Yes, I'd like a glass of Moselle.

So, die Herrschaften,[4] hier wären zwei Tassen Kaffee, zwei Flaschen Bier und drei Glas Rheinwein.

OK, ladies and gentlemen, here are two cups of coffee, two bottles of beer, and three glasses of Rhine wine.

7/ein-Words Used without Nouns

Ich habe leider kein Buch mitgebracht. Hast du eins bei dir?

Unfortunately, I didn't bring a book along. Do you have one with you?

Nimm doch deinen Regenmantel mit. —Ich habe leider keinen mitgebracht.

Take your raincoat with you. —Unfortunately I didn't bring one along.

Keiner von seinen Freunden hat ihn besucht.

None of his friends visited him.

Erika bekommt immer so viele Briefe, und ich bekomme nie welche.

Erika always gets so many letters, and I never get any.

Hier ist das Buch von Rolf. —Nein, das ist meins.

Here is Rolf's book. —No, that's mine.

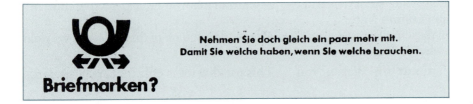

Briefmarken?

Nehmen Sie doch gleich ein paar mehr mit.
Damit Sie welche haben, wenn Sie welche brauchen.

Mir gehört das Buch nicht; es muß deins sein.

That book doesn't belong to me. It must be yours.

Wem gehört denn der Porsche? Ist das Ihrer, Frau Kröger?

Whose Porsche is that? Is it yours, Mrs. Kröger?

Eins ihrer Bücher habe ich gelesen. (Eins von ihren Büchern)

One of her books I have read.

Einer seiner Söhne studiert jetzt Medizin. (Einer von seinen Söhnen)

One of his sons is studying medicine now.

8/gar nicht, gar kein, gar nichts

Meyer ist gar nicht *dumm*; er weiß immer, was er will.

Meyer isn't at all stupid; he always knows what he wants.

Er spricht so leise, daß man ihn gar nicht ver*stehen* kann.

He speaks so softly that you can't understand him at all.

Hast du gut geschlafen? —Nein, ich habe *gar* nicht geschlafen.

Did you sleep well? —No, I didn't sleep at all.

Was habt ihr denn heute gelernt? —*Gar* nichts, wir haben nur gespielt.

What did you learn today? —Nothing at all; we only played.

Ich habe leider *gar* kein Geld bei mir.

Unfortunately, I have no money at all on me.

[4]The term **die Herrschaften,** *ladies and gentlemen,* is frequently used by waiters or waitresses.

ANALYSIS TWO

93/The Forms of the Genitive

In German, as in English, the genitive case expresses possession (*John's book*) or the dependent relationship of two nouns to one another (*the title of the book*).

das Haus meines Vaters	my father's house
Erikas Freundin	Erika's friend
das Ende des Semesters	the end of the semester

NOM.	**der Mann**	**die Frau**	**das Kind**	**die Leute**
ACC.	**den Mann**	**die Frau**	**das Kind**	**die Leute**
DAT.	**dem Mann**	**der Frau**	**dem Kind**	**den Leuten**
GEN.	**des Mannes**	**der Frau**	**des Kindes**	**der Leute**

All **ein**-words and **der**-words have the same genitive endings as the definite article.

GEN.	**eines Mannes**	**einer Frau**	**eines Kindes**	**—**
GEN.	**meines Mannes**	**meiner Frau**	**meines Kindes**	**meiner Leute**
GEN.	**dieses Mannes**	**dieser Frau**	**dieses Kindes**	**dieser Leute**

1. The majority of masculine and neuter nouns add the ending **-es** if their stem consists of one syllable and **-s** if their stem consists of two or more syllables: **des Mannes, des Kindes** but **des Vaters**.

2. Feminine nouns have the same form through the singular; there is no special ending for the genitive.

3. The genitive plural of all nouns has the same form as the nominative plural and the accusative plural. Remember that the dative plural of most German nouns ends in **-n** (see Anal. 48, p. 131).

NOM.	**die Männer**	**die Frauen**	**die Bücher**
ACC.	**die Männer**	**die Frauen**	**die Bücher**
DAT.	**den Männern**	**den Frauen**	**den Büchern**
GEN.	**der Männer**	**der Frauen**	**der Bücher**

4. N-nouns (see Anal. 24, p. 55), for example, **der Student, der Mensch, der Polizist**, end in **-en** in all forms but the nominative singular.

	SINGULAR	PLURAL
NOM.	der Student	die Studenten
ACC.	den Studenten	die Studenten
DAT.	dem Studenten	den Studenten
GEN.	des Studenten	der Studenten

There are a few n-nouns that are irregular in the singular.

NOM.	das Herz (*heart*)	der Gedanke (*thought*)	der Name (*name*)
ACC.	das Herz	den Gedanken	den Namen
DAT.	dem Herz(en)	dem Gedanken	dem Namen
GEN.	des Herzens	des Gedankens	des Namens

5. The genitive of all proper names ends in **-s**; German does not use an apostrophe with this personal genitive, unless the name ends in **-s** or **-z**. If **Mutter** is used as a name, it adds an **-s** in the genitive.

Anton Meyers Porsche
Doris' Bücher
Deutschlands Rolle in der Geschichte
Mutters Fahrrad

Note that the nominative **Herr Meyer** becomes **Herrn Meyers** in the genitive. Remember that the n-noun **der Herr** adds **-n** in the singular and **-en** in the plural.

INTERROGATIVE PRONOUNS

NOM.	wer	was
ACC.	wen	was
DAT.	wem	was
GEN.	wessen	(von was)

NOTE: **was** has no genitive of its own; to ask for inanimate genitives, **von was,** *of what,* is used, for example, **das Ende von was?** *the end of what?* The dative **was** can not be used alone, but only after prepositions, for example, **Zu was braucht man das?** *What do you need that for?*

94 /The Uses of the Genitive

There is a major difference between the use of the genitive and the use of the nominative, accusative, and dative: each of these three cases has a basic syntactical function:

nominative = subject or predicate noun
accusative = direct object
dative   = indirect object

The most common use of the genitive is as an attribute modifying a noun in any of the other three cases.

Subject: **Der Direktor** der Schule heißt Müller.

Predicate Noun: **Herr Müller ist** **der Direktor** **der Schule.**

Direct Object: **Kennen Sie** **den Direktor** **der Schule?**

Indirect Object: **Ich schreibe** **dem Direktor** **der Schule einen Brief.**

In each of these four sentences, **der Schule** is genitive.

THE GENITIVE MODIFYING NOUNS

English expresses the genitive relationship of two nouns in one of two ways: animates add *-'s* or only an apostrophe if the noun ends in *-s* (*Claudia's book, Doris' husband, my parents' apartment*). With inanimates, the two nouns are normally connected with *of* (*the history of the village*).

German also has two ways to express genitive relationships; it does not distinguish between animate and inanimate, but between proper names and *all other nouns*. Proper names add an **-s** (see Anal. 93, p. 299) and precede the noun they modify (**Claudias Buch, Doris' Mann**). All other genitives must follow the noun they modify (**die Wohnung meiner Eltern, die Geschichte des Dorfes**).

It is important to remember that *the girl's father* can only be rendered by **der Vater des Mädchens**.

NOTE: Remember that you have learned two other ways to express possession: the verb **gehören** and the possessive adjectives.

Das ist der Wagen meiner Freundin.
Der Wagen gehört meiner Freundin.
Das ist ihr Wagen.

THE GENITIVE OF TIME

Occasionally, the genitive is used to express indefinite time. In contrast to English *one day* (past) and *some day* (future), **eines Tages** can be used for both past and future. Similarly: **eines Morgens, eines Abends**, and, by analogy, **eines Nachts** (and not **einer Nacht**). Definite time is expressed in the accusative (see Anal. 23, p. 55): **nächsten Sonntag,** *next Sunday* (definite); **eines Sonntags,** *one (some) Sunday* (indefinite).

PREPOSITIONS WITH THE GENITIVE

There are a number of prepositions which must be used with the genitive, but only four of these are important at this stage of your study of German: **(an)statt** (*instead of*), **trotz** (*in spite of*), **während** (*during*), and **wegen** (*because of*).

> **Anstatt (Statt) des Motorrads hätte ich den Wagen nehmen sollen.**
> **Trotz des Regens sind wir nach Köln gefahren.**
> **Während des Sommers war Schmidt in Norwegen.**
> **Wegen des Regens bleiben wir zu Hause.**

With **trotz** and **wegen,** there is a tendency to replace the genitive with the dative, but this is still considered colloquial (**trotz dem Regen**). The adverb **trotzdem** (*in spite of that, nevertheless*) has become standard.

We have now introduced all the major German prepositions. Remember that they *must* be used with specific cases.

95/Genitive Substitutes

There is a growing tendency in German, especially in the spoken language, to avoid the genitive and to replace it with a prepositional phrase with **von** plus dative, especially if the genitive refers to a person. It is very important, therefore, that you memorize the patterns demonstrating these constructions and that you keep in mind the fact that quite often the same English phrase can be expressed in two different ways in German.

> **ein Freund meines Mannes** or **ein Freund von meinem Mann**   a friend of my husband
> **das Ende dieses Romans**   or **das Ende von diesem Roman**   the end of this novel

Note that **ein Freund meines Mannes** corresponds to *a friend of my husband* and **der Freund meines Mannes** to *my husband's friend*.

1. The construction with **von** is often used to avoid two genitives in a row; the **von**-phrase usually occurs first.

> **die Schwester der Frau meines Freundes** or **die Schwester von der Frau meines Freundes**

2. **von** plus dative *must* be used when the genitive would not be recognizable, that is, primarily in the absence of an article or of a **der-** or **ein-**word.

> **die Ankunft von Touristen**   the arrival of tourists
> **eine Freundin von Müllers Frau**   a friend of Müller's wife
> **ein Vater von zehn Kindern**   a father of ten children

but

der Vater der zehn Kinder	the father of the ten children

3. With **Freund** and other nouns expressing similar relationships, **von** plus dative is used as the equivalent of the English phrases:

He is a friend of mine.	**Er ist ein Freund von mir.**
He is a friend of Karl's.	**Er ist ein Freund von Karl.**

The idea *one of* in such sentences as *He is one of my friends* is expressed by **einer (eine, eins) von** (see Anal. 96, p. 303).

Er ist einer von meinen Freunden.
Sie ist eine von Karls Freundinnen.

4. In such phrases as *a cup of coffee, a glass of wine, a pound of butter*, where the first noun denotes a measure and the second something measured, the second German noun shows no case. If more than one measured unit is involved, only feminine nouns are used in the plural; masculine and neuter nouns retain the singular form.

eine Tasse Kaffee	**zwei Tassen Kaffee**
ein Glas Wein	**zwei Glas Wein**
ein Pfund Butter	**zwei Pfund Butter**
ein Stück Kuchen	**zwei Stück Kuchen**

but

eine Tasse von diesem Kaffee
ein Glas von diesem Wein

5. Compounding of nouns is another means by which German very frequently expresses the equivalent of English phrases with *of*, for example, *the production of leather goods:* **die Produktion von Lederwaren** or **die Lederwarenproduktion**. English, of course, uses the same device, but usually without spelling the compound as one word: *wheat production, book publishing*, and so forth.

96/*ein*-Words Used without Nouns

In both German and English, the indefinite articles and the possessive adjectives can be used as pronouns.

Ich habe einen Volkswagen, und Susanne hat auch einen.	I have a VW, and Susanne has one, too.

If the indefinite article **ein** and the **ein**-words (**kein** and the possessive adjectives, see Anal. 21, 22, pp. 48, 54) are used without a following noun, they take the same endings as the definite article **der**, even in the three cases where the indefinite article **ein** has no ending.

Thus the masculine **ein Wagen** becomes **einer**; the neuter forms, however, usually end in **-s** instead of **-es**: **ein Buch** becomes **eins**.

		MASCULINE		FEMININE		NEUTER	
NOM.		ein Freund	einer	eine Frau	eine	ein Kind	ein(e)s
ACC.		einen Freund	einen	eine Frau	eine	ein Kind	ein(e)s
DAT.		einem Freund	einem	einer Frau	einer	einem Kind	einem
GEN.		eines Freundes	—	einer Frau	—	eines Kindes	—

NOTE:

1. The genitive forms are replaced by **von** plus dative: **eines Freundes** = **von einem**.

2. Indefinite plural nouns, for example, **Bücher**, are replaced by **welche**, *some* or *any*.

Hier steht ein Mercedes, und dort steht auch einer.	Here is a Mercedes, and there is one, too.
Hier ist ein Restaurant, und dort ist auch eins	Here is a restaurant, and there is one, too.
Ich habe leider kein Buch. Hast du eins?	Unfortunately, I don't have a book. Do you have one?
Ich gebe Tanta Amalie Blumen zum Geburtstag. Gibst du ihr auch welche?	I'm giving Aunt Amalie flowers for her birthday. Are you giving her some, too?

When nouns following possessive adjectives are used as pronouns, English adds *-s* to the possessive adjective, except for *his* (which already ends in *-s*) and *my* which becomes *mine*.

German possessive adjectives without a following noun, like the indefinite article **ein** without a following noun, use the endings of the definite article **der**.

Das ist nicht ihr Buch; das ist meins. Oder ist es deins?	That's not her book; that's mine. Or is it yours?

97 /gar nicht, gar kein, gar nichts

The particle **gar** is used in connection with a following **nicht, kein,** or **nichts** either to add the idea "contrary to expectation" or to strengthen the negative particle in the same way in which *at all* strengthens the *not* in *not at all*.

Meyer ist gar nicht so dumm, wie du denkst.	Meyer isn't as stupid as you think.
Ich habe heute nacht gar nicht geschlafen.	I didn't sleep at all last night.
Er hat gar keinen Mercedes; er hat nur einen Volkswagen.	He doesn't have a Mercedes at all; he has only a VW.
Er hat mir gar nichts zum Geburtstag geschenkt.	He didn't give me anything at all for my birthday.

Nicht, kein, and **nichts** after **gar** are never stressed.

98 /Word Formation

THE SUFFIX **-ung**

The suffix **-ung** is added to many verb stems. It forms feminine nouns, the plural form being **-ungen,** and often corresponds to English *-tion.*

die Einladung	invitation
die Erwartung	expectation
die Erzählung	story, narration
die Hoffnung	hope
die Wohnung	living quarters, apartment

THE SUFFIX **-ig**

The suffix **-ig** may be added to nouns to form adjectives corresponding to English derivatives of the type *stone: stony, cat: catty,* which all express possession of the quality typical of the thing denoted by the noun.

der Stein	steinig	stony
der Hunger	hungrig	hungry
die Seite	einseitig	one-sided

THE SUFFIX **-los**

The suffix **-los** corresponds to English *-less.* It is added to nouns to form adjectives.

das Herz	herzlos	heartless
die Arbeit	arbeitslos	unemployed
die Zeit	zeitlos	timeless

PRACTICE TWO

F. Replace the phrases in italics by those that follow; use only the genitive.

1. Onkel Willi ist *der Bruder meines Mannes*.   (a professor's son, my mother's brother, Aunt Amalie's husband, the director of the museum, Mr. Meyer's friend)
2. Tante Amalie ging mit *der Schwester ihres Mannes* ins Museum.   (a friend of her daughter's, the daughter of a friend, Mrs. Schmidt's children, the wife of the director, her brother's daughters)
3. Hast du *Karls Wagen* gesehen?   (mother's hat, my mother's hat, my grandparents' apartment, my sister's boy, the end of the film)

G. Express in German.

1. Last summer we were in Austria.
2. One morning we had to get up at six.
3. We drank too much beer one evening.
4. One night we didn't go to bed until four o'clock. (use **erst**)
5. We stayed a month.
6. Some day we'll go to Austria again.
7. But next summer we'll go to the United States.

H. Express in German; then use each phrase in a complete sentence.

1. because of the weather
2. in spite of the rain
3. instead of a detective novel
4. during the semester

I. Give appropriate answers to the following questions, using either the genitive or **von** plus dative.

1. Wessen Buch ist das?
2. Mit wessen Wagen sind Sie denn nach Aachen gefahren?
3. Mit wessen Freundin warst du im Theater?
4. Von wessen Roman sprecht ihr denn?
5. Wessen Haus habt ihr gekauft?
6. Wessen Tochter hat er geheiratet?
7. Wessen Freundin ist das?
8. Wessen Vater hast du besucht?
9. Für wessen Haus willst du so viel Geld bezahlen?
10. Durch wessen Freundin hast du ihn kennengelernt?

J. Express in German.

1. Tell a waiter that you would like to have:
   a. a cup of tea
   b. two cups of tea

   c. three bottles of beer
   d. four bottles of this beer
   e. two glasses of white wine
   f. two pieces of cake
2. Tell a clerk in a grocery store that you would like:
   a. a pound of butter
   b. ten pounds of potatoes
   c. ten rolls
   d. 100 g of liver sausage
   e. 200 g of that liver sausage
   f. 1 kg of pork
   g. 2 bottles of milk
   h. 250 g of Swiss cheese

K. Fill the blanks with appropriate **ein**-words or forms of **welch**-.

1. Ich habe leider kein Buch. Hast du _____?
2. Ich habe meinen Wagen nicht hier, Herr Schnitzler. Wo ist denn _____?
3. Habt ihr schon ein Haus? Nein, wir haben noch _____.
4. Du sagst, hier gibt es so viele Segelboote. Ich habe noch nie _____ gesehen.
5. Das ist _____ von den Büchern, die mein Vater mir geschickt hat.
6. Ich habe nicht _____ von seinen Büchern gelesen.
7. _____ seiner Romane habe ich mir gekauft.
8. Mein Hut ist das nicht; es muß _____ sein, Frau Kästner.
9. Wir haben keine Eier mehr. Hast du _____?
10. Hast du Zeit? Ich habe _____.

Radio and TV

While public radio and television make up only a small percentage of the total number of stations in the U.S., radio and TV in Central Europe have always been public corporations, and, except in the GDR, operate independently of the government. These public corporations are funded in large part by monthly subscriber fees for each privately owned radio and TV set.

In the Federal Republic, there are a number of regional radio stations, such as **Bayrischer Rundfunk (BR), Hessischer Rundfunk (HR),** and **Süddeutscher Rundfunk (SDR).** There are three nationwide television networks: **das erste Programm (ARD, Arbeitsgemeinschaft der Rundfunkanstalten Deutschlands), das zweite Programm (ZDF, Zweites Deutsches Fernsehen),** and **das dritte Programm,** which broadcasts programs that originate from the regional radio and television stations. In West Berlin, there is **RIAS (Radio in the American Sector),** which was established by the American occupation forces after World War II.

Austrian Broadcasting Corporation (**ORF**) has two television channels; in Switzerland radio and television are more regionally oriented because of the multilingual character of the country.

The German Democratic Republic has two main radio stations (**DDR 1** and **DDR 2**) and two TV channels. Western radio and TV can be received in most of the GDR.

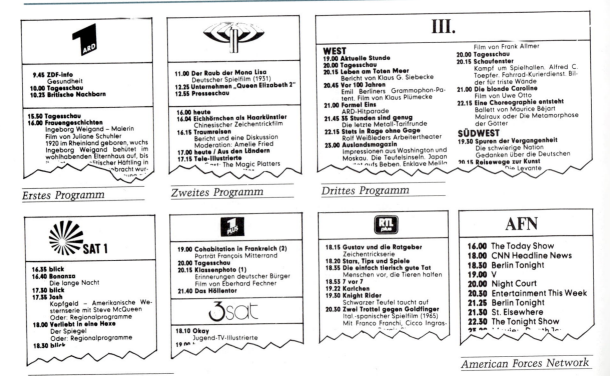

Erstes Programm

9.45 **ZDF-info**
    Gesundheit
10.00 **Tagesschau**
10.23 **Britische Nachbarn**

15.50 **Tagesschau**
16.00 **Frauengeschichten**
    Ingeborg Weigand – Malerin
    Film von Juliane Schuhler
    1920 im Rheinland geboren, wuchs
    Ingeborg Weigand behütet im
    wohlhabenden Elternhaus auf, bis
    ...litischer Häftling wur-
    ...bracht wur-

Zweites Programm

11.00 **Der Raub der Mona Lisa** (1931)
    Deutscher Spielfilm
12.25 **Unternehmen „Queen Elizabeth 2"**
12.55 **Pressschau**

16.00 **heute**
16.04 **Eichhörnchen als Haarkünstler**
    Chinesischer Zeichentrickfilm
16.15 **Traumreisen**
    Bericht und eine Diskussion
    Moderation: Amelie Fried
17.00 **heute / Aus den Ländern**
17.15 **Tele-Illustrierte**
    ...Gast: The Magic Platters

Drittes Programm

III.

WEST
19.00 **Aktuelle Stunde**
20.00 **Tagesschau**
20.15 **Leben am Toten Meer**
    Bericht von Klaus G. Siebecke
20.45 **Vor 100 Jahren**
    Emil Berliners Grammophon-Patent. Film von Klaus Plümecke
21.00 **Formel Eins**
    ARD-Hitparade
21.45 **35 Stunden sind genug**
    Die letzte Metall-Tarifrunde
22.15 **Stets in Rage ohne Gage**
    Rolf Weißleders Arbeitertheater
23.00 **Auslandsmagazin**
    Impressionen aus Washington und
    Moskau. Die Teufelsinseln. Japan
    ...aufs Beben. Enklave Melila...

    Film von Frank Allmer
20.00 **Tagesschau**
20.15 **Schaufenster**
    Kampf um Spielhallen. Alfred C.
    Toepfer. Fahrrad-Kurierdienst. Bilder für triste Wände
21.00 **Die blonde Caroline**
    Film von Uwe Otto
22.15 **Eine Choreographie entsteht**
    Ballett von Maurice Béjart
    Malraux oder Die Metamorphose der Götter

SÜDWEST
19.30 **Spuren der Vergangenheit**
    Die schwierige Nation
    Gedanken über die Deutschen
20.15 **Reisewege zur Kunst**
    Die Levante

Unabhängige (Independents)

SAT 1

16.35 **blick**
16.40 **Bonanza**
    Die lange Nacht
17.50 **blick**
17.55 **Josh**
    Kopfgeld – Amerikanische Westernserie mit Steve McQueen
    Oder: Regionalprogramme
18.00 **Verliebt in eine Hexe**
    Der Spiegel
    Oder: Regionalprogramme
18.30 **blick**

1 PLUS

19.00 **Cohabitation in Frankreich** (2)
    Porträt François Mitterrand
20.00 **Tagesschau**
20.15 **Klassenphoto** (1)
    Erinnerungen deutscher Bürger
    Film von Eberhard Fechner
21.40 **Das Höllentor**

3sat

18.10 **Okay**
    Jugend-TV-Illustrierte
19.00 ...

RTL

18.15 **Gustav und die Ratgeber**
    Zeichentrickserie
18.20 **Stars, Tips und Spiele**
18.35 **Die einfach tierisch gute Tat**
    Menschen vor, die Tieren halfen
18.53 **7 vor 7**
19.22 **Karlchen**
19.30 **Knight Rider**
    Schwarzer Teufel taucht auf
20.30 **Zwei Trottel gegen Goldfinger**
    Ital.-spanischer Spielfilm (1965)
    Mit Franco Franchi, Cicco Ingras...

AFN

16.00 The Today Show
18.00 CNN Headline News
18.30 Berlin Tonight
19.00 V
20.00 Night Court
20.30 Entertainment This Week
21.25 Berlin Tonight
21.30 St. Elsewhere
22.30 The Tonight Show
23.00 ...

American Forces Network

CONVERSATIONS

Ein junges Ehepaar°, Gerd und Sabine Mattes, nach dem Abendessen: married couple

I

SABINE: Mach doch mal den Fernseher° an; jetzt kommt gleich der Wetterbericht°.   TV / weather report

GERD: In welchem Programm?

SABINE: Im ersten.

GERD: Wahrscheinlich wird's morgen sowieso wieder regnen, aber wir können ja mal hören.

II

SABINE: Das sind noch die Nachrichten°, die habe ich vorhin° schon gehört.   news / a while ago

GERD: Ja, und dann kommt erst noch zehn Minuten Sport, und dann die Lotto-Zahlen,[5] und . . .

SABINE: Nein, die Lotto-Zahlen kommen doch erst nachher°, —nach dem Wetter.   afterwards

GERD: Ich dachte, die kämen immer vorher.

III

SABINE: Wenn's so bleibt, könnten wir morgen segeln° gehen.   sailing

GERD: Das wäre eine Idee, obwohl ich eigentlich lieber mit dem Motorboot rausfahren° würde, zum Fischen.   **= hinausfahren**

SABINE: Das kannst du doch auch mit dem Segelboot, —und außerdem sparst du dabei das Benzin.

GERD: Da hast du natürlich recht. —Sollen wir noch jemand mitnehmen?

SABINE: Ruf doch mal den Heinz an; der kommt sicher mit.

IV

SABINE: Na, was hat er gesagt?

GERD: Er sagt, er ist zwar zur Zeit sehr beschäftigt und müßte eigentlich auch am Sonntag in den Betrieb.

SABINE: Aber . . . ?

GERD: Aber er würde doch versuchen, mitzukommen.

SABINE: Dann sollten wir auch die Annemarie anrufen. Der würde das bestimmt Spaß machen°.   she would have fun

[5]**Lotto-Zahlen** refers to a weekly numbers game, played by millions of people. If you have correctly indicated six out of fifty numbers (from 1–50) on your entry blank, you can win several hundred thousand D-marks when the numbers are drawn on TV every Saturday night.

V

Construct a telephone conversation between Sabine and Annemarie, using the following elements:

SABINE: morgen, segeln, mitkommen?
ANNEMARIE: müde, lange Woche, schlafen wollen.
SABINE: früh ins Bett gehen, —übrigens: Heinz, mitgehen.
ANNEMARIE: nicht *so* müde, wann wegfahren?
SABINE: nicht sehr früh, neun Uhr.
ANNEMARIE: Heinz anrufen, fragen, ob abholen.

VI

Now produce a conversation between Annemarie and Heinz, as outlined. A. tells H. that she has just talked to S. He says that he has talked to Gerd and that Gerd and Sabine have asked him to go sailing tomorrow. A. tells him that they have asked her to go too. H. is delighted and asks A. if he can pick her up. A. says that she was about to ask him to pick her up. They agree that he will come at about 8:30.

VII

After reviewing the reading of Units 6, 8, and 10, let your teacher be a German from Burgbach and ask questions about the village and his or her background. Your teacher, playing the role of a native speaker, will, of course, speak much more involved German than you are capable of using. Slow him or her down (**"Bitte sprechen Sie langsamer"**), mention that you are a foreigner, that you haven't been in Germany very long, etc.

Fragen an Sie persönlich

1. Sehen Sie gern fern? (**fernsehen** *to watch TV*)
   Was für Programme sehen Sie am liebsten? (**was für** *what kinds of*)
      Sport?   Krimis? (**der Krimi** *cop show*)
      Spielfilme (*feature films*)?   Nachrichten?   Diskussionen?
   In Europa gibt es keine privaten (kommerziellen) Radio- und Fernsehstationen. Radio und Fernsehen werden vom Staat subventioniert, und kein Programm wird durch Reklame unterbrochen. Halten Sie das für gut oder schlecht? (**werden subventioniert** *are subsidized;* **wird unterbrochen** *is interrupted;* **die Reklame** *advertising*)

2. Treiben Sie Sport?
      Spielen Sie gern Fußball?
                     Golf?
                     Hockey?
                     Tennis?
      Können Sie schilaufen?
                     segeln?

Sport- und Erholungszentrum
BERLIN-HAUPTSTADT DER DDR

1017 Berlin, Leninallee 77

READING

Burgbach, zum Beispiel (Fortsetzung°)

continuation

1935 lebten in Burgbach 1600 Menschen, unter ihnen nur 16 Katholiken, alle anderen waren Protestanten. Die Bevölkerung° war homogen und konservativ; das Leben in Burgbach orientierte sich am Land; Weinberge, Getreidefelder°, Obst-° und Gemüsegärten waren der wichtigste Lebensinhalt°, und in den großen Bauernhäusern hielt ₅ man Kühe, Schweine, Gänse und Hühner. An Politik hatte man nicht viel Interesse.

population

grain fields   fruit

the most important content of life

Dann kam der Krieg, und 1945 war das Jahr Null. Von den Burgbachern, die Soldaten geworden waren, kamen über 100 nicht zurück. Und mit dem Krieg ging auch ein Zeitalter° zu Ende. Burgbach ₁₀ konnte nie mehr werden, was es einmal gewesen war. Es begann damals eine Entwicklung°, die bis heute nicht abgeschlossen° ist: rapider Bevölkerungszuwachs°, Veränderung° der sozialen Struktur, immer schnellere Urbanisierung.

epoch, age

development   concluded

population increase changing

Heute hat Burgbach eine Bevölkerung von fast 7000 Menschen, von ₁₅ denen° nur etwas mehr als die Hälfte in Burgbach und Umgebung° geboren sind. Fast ein Viertel sind Flüchtlinge und Vertriebene° aus dem Osten. Schon 1945 schickte die amerikanische Militärregierung° die ersten 500 Flüchtlinge, und die Burgbacher mußten ihre Häuser und ihre Lebensmittel° mit ihnen teilen°. Sie kamen aus Pommern°, ₂₀ aus Schlesien°, aus Ostpreußen°; andere aus Polen, aus der Tschechoslowakei, aus Ungarn, aus Rumänien, ja sogar aus der Ukraine. Später kamen Flüchtlinge aus der von Rußland besetzten° Zone, das heißt, aus dem Teil Deutschlands, der heute die Deutsche Demokratische Republik, die DDR, ist. Dieser Zustrom° hörte allerdings mit dem ₂₅ Bau der Berliner Mauer° im Jahre 1961 auf.

of whom
surrounding area
refugees and expellees
military government

food   share   Pomerania (now in Poland)
Silesia   East Prussia (now divided between the Soviet Union and Poland)   occupied

influx

wall

Das „Wirtschaftswunder"° der fünfziger und sechziger Jahre brachte neuen Wohlstand° nach Burgbach. In fast jedem Dorf entstand° ein Industriegebiet, und mit zunehmender° Industrialisierung nahm auch die Bevölkerung weiter zu. Fast 1000 der 7000 Burgbacher stammen ₃₀ aus anderen Teilen der Bundesrepublik, aber auch viele Stuttgarter haben hier draußen „auf dem Lande" Häuser gebaut, so daß Burgbach heute schon fast ein Vorort° von Stuttgart ist, oder das, was man in Amerika eine Schlafzimmer-Gemeinde° nennt.

economic miracle
wealth, affluence
originated, developed
increasing

suburb

bedroom community

Zuletzt° kamen die Gastarbeiter, die heute etwa 10% (zehn Prozent) ₃₅ der Bevölkerung von Burgbach ausmachen. In den ersten zehn oder fünfzehn Jahren nach dem zweiten Weltkrieg mußte man in der Bundesrepublik Arbeitsplätze für die Ostflüchtlinge° schaffen, aber dann gab es jahrelang mehr Arbeitsplätze als Arbeitsuchende, und so fing man an, ausländische Arbeiter zu beschäftigen°, zuerst meist ₄₀ Italiener, dann Jugoslawen, Spanier, Griechen, Türken. Viele von

last

refugees from the East (i.e., from the former German territories and from Eastern Europe)   employ

diesen Ausländern leben nun schon jahrelang in Burgbach, und ihre
Kinder sprechen nicht nur Türkisch oder Griechisch, sondern auch
fließend° Schwäbisch. Es ist ein interessantes Phänomen, daß auch   fluently
die Kinder der aus Ost- und Norddeutschland Zugewanderten° neben 45   immigrants
dem Hochdeutschen auch den Dialekt lernen, der ihren Eltern für
immer unzugänglich° bleibt.   impenetrable

Für die alten Weinbauern sind die „Neuen" immer noch „Fremde",
auch nach dreißig Jahren noch. Die mittlere Generation hat die neue
Zeit akzeptiert, und für die jungen Leute ist es ganz selbstverständ- 50
lich°, daß Burgbach kein Dorf mehr ist, sondern Teil eines städtischen   self-understood, a
Großraumes°, heterogen, zentrifugal und mit einer sehr komplexen   matter of course
Sozialstruktur. Burgbach ist immer noch ein „beliebter Weinort", wie   metropolitan urban area
es in den Broschüren für den Fremdenverkehr° heißt; zugleich° aber   foreign tourists
ist es ein moderner Industrieort, der ebensogut in der Nähe von jeder 55   at the same time
anderen Großstadt liegen könnte.

Dennoch lebt die Vergangenheit°. Auch die rapide Urbanisierung   past
kann eine Tradition von vielen hundert Jahren nicht einfach aus-
wischen°. Alte Sitten und Gebräuche° leben fort; die alten Bauwerke°   wipe out   ways and
erinnern an die Geschichte, und der Zement, sozusagen, ist der 60   customs   buildings
schwäbische Dialekt.

(Fortsetzung folgt—continued in *Study Guide*)

Wein- und
Ausflugsort

BEUTELSBACH

MATHIAS SCHREIBER

Demokratie

Ich will
du willst
er will
was wir wollen
geschieht   5
aber was geschieht
will keiner von uns

ARNFRID ASTEL

Ostkontakte°   contacts with the East

Als mein Freund kürzlich°   recently
wieder nach Weimar fuhr,
bat ich ihn,
mir den Baum zu fotografieren,
auf dem wir als Kinder   5
Burgen° gebaut hatten.   castles
Er brachte mir
eine Fotographie mit,
darauf waren Kinder zu sehen,
die auf unserem Baum   10
eine Burg bauten.

REVIEW EXERCISES

L. Fill the blanks with the correct preposition or article, or contracted
preposition plus article.

1. Wart ihr gestern __im__ Kino?
2. Ja, wir sind __ins__ Kino gegangen.
3. Helene wohnt immer noch __bei__ ihren Eltern.
4. Sie will __mit__ ihren Eltern __in__ die Türkei fahren.
5. Letzten Sommer sind sie __nach__ Frankreich gefahren.
6. Ich habe ihn __vor__ zehn Jahren kennengelernt.
7. __Seit__ fünf Jahren habe ich ihn nicht mehr gesehen.
8. Er ist durch __die__ Schweiz gefahren.
9. Christian wohnt in __der__ Altstadt.
10. Ich komme gerade aus __der__ Stadt.
11. Der Zug kam __um__ 10.37 Uhr an.
12. __Wegen__ des Regens gehen wir heute nicht segeln.

13. Die Maschine fliegt _____ London _____ Frankfurt.

14. Also auf Wiedersehen, _____ nächsten Sonntag.

15. Stellen Sie den Wagen doch bitte hinter _____ Hotel.

16. Bitte, kommt _____ Essen.

17. Wir waren gerade _____ Essen, als er kam.

18. Wir fuhren _____ die Stadt _____.

19. Köln liegt _____ Rhein.

20. Er rannte aus _____ Haus und auf _____ Straße.

M. Express the following sentences in English. (Watch apostrophes.) Determine when the **von**-phrase is obligatory in German.

1. Ingelheims Kinder sind noch klein.

2. Die Kinder von Ingelheim sind noch klein.

3. Die Kinder von Ingelheims sind noch sehr klein.

4. Ingrids Kinder sind noch sehr klein.

5. Die Kinder von Ingrid sind noch sehr klein.

6. Sie war eine Freundin von Overhoffs Frau.

7. Er war der Vater von dreizehn Kindern.

8. Ich bin kein Freund von Rheinwein.

9. Jeder Leser von Kriegsromanen weiß, wer Schmidt-Ingelheim ist.

N. Express in German.

1. He is my friend.
2. He is Karl's friend.
3. He is my sister's friend.
4. He is a friend of my sister's.
5. He is one of my sister's friends.
6. She is my mother.
7. She is Ursula's mother.
8. She is my wife's mother.
9. She is her daughter.
10. She is Jutta's daughter.
11. He is my brother's son.
12. Karl is one of my brother's sons.
13. Ernst is one of the sons of Mr. Bertram.
14. Fritz is her friend.
15. Fritz is a friend of hers.
16. Fritz is one of her friends.
17. Her daughters are very intelligent.
18. Ingrid's daughter is also very intelligent.
19. Ingelheim's daughters are intelligent.
20. The Ingelheims' daughters are intelligent.

O. Read the following sentences and supply either **nicht** or **nichts**, or the correct form of **kein**.

1. Ich habe seit gestern morgen gar _____ gegessen.

2. Daß du in Italien warst, habe ich gar _____ gewußt.

3. Hast du denn mit deiner neuen Kamera noch gar _____ Bilder gemacht?

4. Es ist doch dumm, daß er uns gar _____ geschrieben hat, wann er ankommt.

5. Aber sie ist doch gar _____ in Berlin gewesen.

P. Express in German.

1. We really ought to put (**stellen**) that (little) table between our beds.

2. Do you always have to put your books on the table?

3. Why can't they lie on the table?

4. During the autumn Meyer worked in the Netherlands.
5. At that time he was happy that he did not have to go to Africa.
6. It is cold tonight; I wish you hadn't forgotten your overcoat.
7. If only that policeman hadn't been so unfriendly.
8. If only I hadn't slept so long.
9. You should have given him more money.
10. I wish I hadn't gone to Switzerland last summer.

Q. Form derivatives as indicated and guess their meaning.

1. fahren — der Fahrer
   anfangen — *der anfänger*
   besuchen — *der besucher*
   helfen — *der helfer*
   kennen — *der Kenner*
   sprechen — *der sprecher*

2. glücklich — unglücklich
   bestimmt — *unbestimmt*
   ~ sympathisch —
   ~ modern —
   die Vernunft — die
   das Wetter — das *Unwetter - storm*

3. brauchen — brauchbar *usable*
   zahlen — *zahlbar - worth buying*
   erreichen — *der attainable*
   lesen — *legible*
   lernen — *learnable*
   denken — *thinkable*

4. der Berg — bergig *mountainous*
   die Ecke —
   das Glas —
   der Saft — *saftig · juicy*
   die Vernunft —
   die Vorsicht —
   caution/cautious

5. der Fluß — [das] Flüßchen
   der Wald —
   die Hand —
   das Messer —
   das Schild —
   die Bank —

6. der Freund — freundlich
   der Winter —
   das Wort — *wen - literal*
   das Bild —
   der Tag — *daily   real?*
   das Dorf —

7. wohnen — die Wohnung
   bewundern — *admiration*
   erzählen — *story*
   mischen — *mixture*
   rechnen — *bill*
   benutzen —

8. die Arbeit — arbeitslos
   das Beispiel —
   der Geschmack —   *tasteless*
   der Erfolg — *success*
   das Ende —
   die Zeit —

R. Try to guess the meaning of the following compounds and derivatives.

1. ein achtjähriges Mädchen
2. er ist ein Bergsteiger
3. das Alleinsein ist schwer
4. kinderlos
5. eine vielköpfige Familie
6. ich bin wunschlos glücklich
7. endlos
8. ein gleichseitiges Dreieck
9. ein vielseitiger Künstler
10. unfreundlich
11. ein Autounglück
12. Zigaretten sind ungesund
13. schlaflos
14. die Dinosaurier sind ausgestorben
15. eine ärztliche Untersuchung *medical exam.*
16. ein Mittagsschläfchen halten
17. ein Stückchen Kuchen
18. ein Menschenkenner
19. die Tänzerin
20. die Bahnhofshalle *concourse*

21. unhörbar
22. in unerreichbarer Ferne
23. unbrauchbar
24. eine winterliche Landschaft

25. du bist herzlich eingeladen
26. eine Kurzgeschichte
27. bildlich gesprochen
28. eine Nacherzählung

S. Write a brief paragraph in German containing the following ideas. Do *not* translate the passage; just use it as an outline. Use your own words, but do not attempt to use any construction or any vocabulary that you haven't had yet.

During her trip to Germany, Elisabeth Reichmann visited Mr. Schmid, the teacher in Burgbach. Mr. Schmid is a friend of Elisabeth's father, a native of Burgbach, who came to America only fifteen years ago. Elisabeth was born in Germany, too, and speaks German very well. She is studying psychology in America and wanted to learn (**erfahren**) something about life in the village, and especially about the schools. Mr. Schmid told her about the urbanization of the village. Before World War II, Burgbach had been way out in the country, and there had been only vintners. After the war came the refugees, then people from North Germany and from the city, and, finally, foreign workers. Today Burgbach, although it is still a "Weinort," has become a suburb of the city.

VOCABULARY

das Abitur'	final examination in secondary school
allerdings	however
die Ankunft, ⁻e	arrival
an•machen	to switch on, turn on (light, TV, etc.)
anstatt (statt) (*prep.* *with gen.*)	instead of
der Ball, ⁻e	ball
Fußball	soccer
das Fußballspiel, -e	soccer game
beschäftigt sein	to be busy; to be employed
die Brücke, -n	bridge
daher	therefore
daher (da . . . her)	from there
dahin (da . . . hin)	(to) there
der Direk'tor, die Direkto'ren	director (*m.*)
die Direkto'rin, -nen	director (*f.*)

dumm	dumb, stupid
das Ehepaar, -e	(married) couple
das Ei, -er	egg
die Einladung, -en	invitation
erreichen	to reach (a destination)
erst-	first
die Erzählung, -en	story; narration
der Gedanke, -n (*n-noun*) (*gen.* **des Gedankens**)	thought
das Gedicht, -e	poem
geschehen (sein)	to happen
der Geschmack (*no pl.*)	taste
das Gymnasium, die Gymnasien	German secondary school, grades 5–13
die Haustür, -en	front door
hinter	behind
der Hut, ⁻e	hat

jung	young	die Rekla'me	advertising
katho'lisch	Catholic	der Rhein	Rhine River
der Katholik', -en	Catholic (*m.*)	der Rheinwein, -e	Rhine wine
die Katholi'kin, -nen	Catholic (*f.*)	der Saft, ⸚e	juice
die Kirche, -n	church	segeln	to sail
der Krimi, -s	detective novel; TV cop show	der Soldat, -en (*n-noun*)	soldier
der Kriminalroman, -e	detective novel	sowieso	anyhow, in any case
die Lebensmittel (*pl.*)	groceries, food	spielen	to play
das Lebensmittel-geschäft, -e	grocery store	das Spiel, -e	game
legen	to lay (flat), place	Sport treiben	to exercise
leise	quiet(ly)	stellen	to put, place (upright)
der Leser, -	reader (*m.*)	trotz (*prep. with gen.*)	in spite of
die Leserin, -nen	reader (*f.*)	trotzdem	nevertheless
der Marktplatz, ⸚e	market square	die Tschechoslowakei	Czechoslovakia
die Maschine, -n	machine; airplane	die Türkei	Turkey
mit•kommen (sein)	to come along	türkisch	Turkish
modern'	modern	der Türke, -n (*n-noun*)	Turk (*m.*)
die Mosel	Moselle River		
der Moselwein, -e	Moselle wine	die Türkin, -nen	Turk (*f.*)
der Motor', -en	motor	um . . . herum	around
nachher	afterwards, later	unter	under
die Nachricht, -en	report, message	unterbrechen	to interrupt
die Nachrichten (*pl.*)	news (radio, TV, etc.)	die Vernunft (*no pl.*)	(power of) reason
		vorhin	a while ago
eines Nachts	one night, some night	wählen	to choose, decide; elect; dial (telephone)
neben	beside, next to		
die Niederlande (*pl.*)	Netherlands		
das Programm', -e	program	während (*prep. with gen.*)	during
protestan'tisch	Protestant		
der Protestant', -en (*n-noun*)	Protestant (*m.*)	die Wand, ⸚e	wall (of a room)
		wegen (*prep. with gen.*)	because of
die Protestan'tin, -nen	Protestant (*f.*)	wessen	whose
raus•fahren (= hinaus•fahren) (sein)	to go out	der Wetterbericht, -e	weather report
		die Zahl, -en	number, figure
		zur Zeit	at the moment, right now; for the time being
rechnen	to figure, to calculate		
der Regenmantel, ⸚	rain coat	zwischen	between

Strong Verbs

INFINITIVE	PRESENT	PAST TENSE	PERFECT	
geschehen	geschieht	geschah	ist geschehen	to happen
unterbrechen	unterbricht	unterbrach	unterbrochen	to interrupt

Unit 11

Indirect Discourse—*als, ob, wann, wenn*

Architecture

In some places in Central Europe, you can study the entire history of architecture. In the Cologne area, for example, you will find extensive Roman excavations, early medieval Romanesque churches, and a Gothic cathedral that was not finished until the late nineteenth century. There are Baroque palaces, nineteenth century neoclassical buildings as well as some superb examples of contemporary architecture. Over the next five units, we include drawings that illustrate some of the high points of the history of architecture.

Freiburger Münster

PATTERNS ONE

1/Indirect Discourse: Future and Present Time

Inge sagte: „Mein Vater fährt morgen nach Nürnberg."
   Inge sagte, ihr Vater würde morgen nach Nürnberg fahren.
   Inge sagte, ihr Vater führe morgen nach Nürnberg.
   Inge sagte, daß ihr Vater morgen nach Nürnberg führe.
   Inge sagte, daß ihr Vater morgen nach Nürnberg fahren würde.

Frau Dr. Naumann sagte: „Ich kann leider nicht nach Stuttgart kommen."
   Frau Dr. Naumann sagte, sie könnte leider nicht nach Stuttgart kommen.

2/Indirect Discourse: Past Time

Sie sagte: „Ich arbeitete gerade in Hamburg."
           „Ich habe gerade in Hamburg gearbeitet."
           „Ich hatte gerade in Hamburg gearbeitet."
   Sie sagte, sie hätte gerade in Hamburg gearbeitet.

Er sagte: „Ich fuhr dann nach Hamburg."
        „Ich bin dann nach Hamburg gefahren."
        „Ich war dann nach Hamburg gefahren."
   Er sagte, er wäre dann nach Hamburg gefahren.

Er sagte: „Ich wollte damals nach Hamburg fahren."
        „Ich habe damals nach Hamburg fahren wollen."
        „Ich hatte damals nach Hamburg fahren wollen."
   Er sagte, er hätte damals nach Hamburg fahren wollen.

3/Indirect Discourse: Introductory Verb in Present Tense

Herr Enderle sagt: „Ich komme heute erst spät nach Hause."
   Herr Enderle sagt, er kommt heute erst spät nach Hause.
   Herr Enderle sagt, er käme heute erst spät nach Hause.
   Herr Enderle sagt, daß er heute erst spät nach Hause kommt.
   Herr Enderle sagt, daß er heute erst spät nach Hause käme.

Christa sagt: „Ich bin die ganze Woche krank gewesen."
   Christa sagt, sie ist die ganze Woche krank gewesen.
   Christa sagt, sie wäre die ganze Woche krank gewesen.
   Christa sagt, daß sie die ganze Woche krank gewesen ist.
   Christa sagt, daß sie die ganze Woche krank gewesen wäre.

4/Indirect Discourse: The Alternate Subjunctive

Rosemarie sagte: „Ich bin nur zwei Tage in München."
  Rosemarie sagte, sie wäre nur zwei Tage in München.
  Rosemarie sagte, sie sei nur zwei Tage in München.

Sie sagte: „Ich habe ein Zimmer im Bayerischen Hof."
  Sie sagte, sie hätte ein Zimmer im Bayerischen Hof.
  Sie sagte, sie habe ein Zimmer im Bayerischen Hof.

Er erzählte: „Ich bin erst um elf Uhr nach Hause gekommen."
  Er erzählte, daß er erst um elf Uhr nach Hause gekommen wäre.
  Er erzählte, daß er erst um elf Uhr nach Hause gekommen sei.

Er sagte: „Ich mußte gestern nach Regensburg fahren."
  Er sagte, er hätte gestern nach Regensburg fahren müssen.
  Er sagte, er habe gestern nach Regensburg fahren müssen.

Er sagte: „Ihr braucht nicht auf mich zu warten; ich komme erst morgen früh."
  Er sagte, wir brauchten nicht auf ihn zu warten; er käme erst morgen früh.
  Er sagte, wir brauchten nicht auf ihn zu warten; er komme erst morgen früh.

Er sagte: „Dann können wir zusammen frühstücken."
  Er sagte, wir könnten dann zusammen frühstücken.

5/Indirect Discourse in Context

Meyer rief gestern abend an und erzählte, er hätte gerade mit seiner Frau telefoniert. Sie sei an der Nordsee; der Arzt hätte sie dort hingeschickt, weil sie krank gewesen wäre. Aber es gehe ihr sehr gut, das Wetter sei wunderschön, und sie würde bestimmt gesund zurückkommen.

Heute morgen um neun rief Meyer wieder an. Jetzt sei *er* krank. Es ginge ihm sehr schlecht, er hätte Kopfschmerzen, und er müßte unbedingt zum Arzt. Er meinte, es sei doch ungerecht, daß seine Frau jetzt an der Nordsee säße und gesund wäre, und er wäre hier und sei krank und könnte nicht arbeiten. Später würde er wieder anrufen.

Um zwölf telefonierte er wieder. Er sei beim Arzt gewesen. Der Arzt habe ihn gefragt, was er gestern abend gemacht hätte. Nichts, hätte er geantwortet; er hätte nur vor dem Fernseher gesessen und Bier und Schnaps getrunken. Er müßte nur zehn Stunden schlafen, hätte der Arzt gemeint, dann würde es ihm wieder gut gehen. Er sei gar nicht krank; er hätte nur zu viel getrunken.

ANALYSIS ONE

99/Direct and Indirect Discourse

If a speaker (or writer), Hans Müller, for example, wants to report to a second person what a third person has said or written, he can choose between several syntactical patterns.

DIRECT DISCOURSE

The speaker can repeat verbatim—in quotation marks, as it were— what he has been told. If his friend Gerda told him on the phone, *I have been sick all week*, he can report that Gerda called and said, *"I have been sick all week."* Gerda's original statement as well as the speaker's repetition of it are in "direct discourse." This reporting technique presents no grammatical problems in either English or German.

INDIRECT DISCOURSE

The speaker can also change the original message *I have been sick all week* into a dependent clause which functions as the direct object of some verb of reporting, such as *to say* or *to write*. He can use this introductory verb in the present tense or in a past tense form. This "secondhand" reporting technique is called "indirect discourse."

Introductory verb in the present tense:

"I have been sick all week."
She says she has been sick all week.
She says that she has been sick all week.

The *I* of the original statement is changed to *she*, but the tense of the original statement, the present perfect, remains the same. The object clause can be unintroduced or introduced by *that*.

Introductory verb in the past tense:

"I have been sick all week."
She wrote she had been sick all week.
She wrote that she had been sick all week.

Now not only is *I* changed to *she*, but the tense may be changed as well: *has been* becomes *had been*, though, strictly speaking, this is not a change of tense, but a change from the indicative to the subjunctive. (See Anal. 81, p. 257, on the subjunctive in English.) In the same way, a present tense in the original statement is changed to the past tense in the indirect statement. Again, these past tense forms are really subjunctives, though, interestingly, the *was/were* choice does not exist: *she were* is not possible in indirect discourse.

"I am sick."
She wrote that she *was* sick.

There are, however, situations in which English does not change from the indicative to the subjunctive even if the introductory verb is in the past tense. For example, if you have just talked to a friend on the phone and somebody asks you what she said, you might reply:

She said that she is sick.
She said that she has been sick all week.

100/Indirect Discourse in German

In German, the change from direct to indirect discourse frequently involves a change from the indicative to the subjunctive. This subjunctive can be either the "normal subjunctive" introduced in Unit 9 or a second set of subjunctive forms, introduced below in Anal. 101, which is used mainly in indirect discourse and cannot be used in any of the patterns of Unit 9. We call this second set the "alternate subjunctive."

The subjunctive tenses used are the same as those introduced in Unit 9: future, present, and past. The choice of tense for the indirect statement depends on the tense of the direct statement:

DIRECT STATEMENT	INDIRECT STATEMENT
1. Future Indicative ⟶	Future Subjunctive
2. Present Indicative ⟶	Present Subjunctive (or Future Subjunctive)[1]
3. Past Indicative Perfect Indicative Past Perfect Indicative ⟶	Past Subjunctive

[1]Use the future subjunctive (**würde**-forms) in indirect statements only if the present indicative in the direct statement has a clear future meaning.

Er sagte: „Ich fahre nächstes Jahr nach Salzburg."
Er sagte, er würde (nächstes Jahr) nach Salzburg fahren.

1. **Ich werde bald wiederkommen.**

Sie würde bald wiederkommen. (normal subjunctive)

Sie werde bald wiederkommen. (alternate subjunctive)

2. **Ich bin nur zwei Tage in München.**

Sie wäre nur zwei Tage in München. (normal subjunctive)

Sie sei nur zwei Tage in München. (alternate subjunctive)

3. **Ich war nur zwei Tage in München.**
Ich bin nur zwei Tage in München gewesen.
Ich war nur zwei Tage in München gewesen.

Sie wäre nur zwei Tage in München gewesen. (normal subjunctive)

Sie sei nur zwei Tage in München gewesen. (alternate subjunctive)

Indirect statements are normally introduced by such verbs as **sagen, meinen** (*to say, express an opinion*), and **denken**. The introductory verb can be in any tense and does not influence the tense of the indirect statement. The choice of tense in the direct or indirect statement depends on whether the events related take place a) later than the time of the introductory verb, b) at the same time as the introductory verb, or c) earlier than the time of the introductory verb.

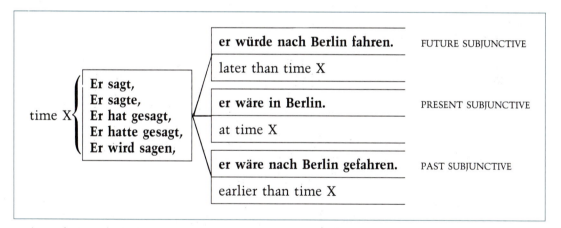

Rosemarie sagte (gestern), sie würde (heute) nach Salzburg fahren.
Rosemarie sagte (gestern), sie wäre (gestern) in München.
Rosemarie sagte (gestern), sie wäre (vorgestern) in Nürnberg gewesen.

1. All indirect statements are dependent clauses. All the examples above are unintroduced dependent clauses (see Anal. 73, p. 223), that is, they do not begin with a conjunction and have verb second position. All these indirect statements can also be introduced with the subordinating conjunction **daß**, *that*, with verb last position.

Indirect yes-or-no questions must be introduced by **ob,** *whether* (see Anal. 103, p. 332).

> **Rosemarie sagte, daß sie in München wäre.**
> **Ich fragte Rosemarie, ob sie in Salzburg gewesen wäre.**

2. Because the subjunctive clearly identifies indirect discourse, one introductory statement is sufficient for an entire narrated passage.

> **Rosemarie sagte, sie wäre in Nürnberg. Gestern hätte sie Gisela angerufen. Gisela wäre krank gewesen, aber es ginge ihr jetzt gut. Morgen abend kämen sie beide nach München.**

3. If the normal subjunctive is used in the direct statement, it must also be used in the indirect statement.

> **Ich würde gerne mitgehen, wenn ich könnte.**
> **Sie sagte, sie würde gerne mitgehen, wenn sie könnte.**

4. Just as the present indicative is frequently used to express future time, the present subjunctive is often used instead of the future subjunctive (**würde**-forms) in indirect discourse. The future subjunctive of **haben, sein,** and the modals is rarely used.

> **Ich komme nach München.**
> **Sie sagte, sie käme nach München.**
> **Sie sagte, sie würde nach München kommen.**

> **Ich bin nächste Woche in Zürich.**
> **Sie sagte, sie wäre nächste Woche in Zürich.**

5. The indicative is frequently used in indirect statements when the introductory verb is in the present tense. It is also occasionally used in the past tense to express indisputable facts. The use of the indicative for indirect discourse is more prevalent in the spoken language than in the written language.

> **Sie sagt, sie hat heute abend keine Zeit.**
> **Er hat gesagt, sein Zug fährt um elf Uhr.**

101/The Alternate Subjunctive

The "alternate subjunctive" is used mainly in indirect discourse. It cannot be used in any of the patterns introduced in Unit 9. It has a more "educated" flavor and is preferred by some and avoided by others. For all practical purposes, only the third-person singular forms are used, although some first-person singular forms also occur. As usual, **sein** is an exception. The first-person forms in parentheses are even less commonly used than those not in parentheses.

PRESENT TENSE									
	sein	**haben**	**werden**	**können**	**wollen**	**wissen**	**lieben**	**nehmen**	**fahren**
ich	sei	(habe)	(werde)	könne	wolle	wisse	(liebe)	(nehme)	(fahre)
du	—	—	—	—	—	—	—	—	—
er	sei	habe	werde	könne	wolle	wisse	liebe	nehme	fahre
wir	seien	—	—	—	—	—	—	—	—
ihr	—	—	—	—	—	—	—	—	—
sie	seien	—	—	—	—	—	—	—	—

The past forms of this subjunctive simply add the past participle to the correct forms of **sein** or **haben**. The future uses the present alternate subjunctive of **werden** plus an infinitive.

ich sei gefahren
sie habe gelesen
sie werde kommen

1. The forms in active use are the only ones which are clearly recognizable as subjunctives and distinguishable from the corresponding indicative forms. Hence a) the third-person singular forms of *all* verbs can be used because they end in **-e** and not in **-t** and b) the first-person singular forms of the modals and **wissen** can be used.

2. Other first-person forms can be used only if the context makes clear that they are indeed used as subjunctive forms.

3. When normal subjunctive forms are identical with the past indicative, the alternate subjunctive is often preferred.

Er sagte, er wohne jetzt in Berlin.
Er sagte, Meyer solle/wolle morgen nach Berlin fahren.

4. When the alternate subjunctive forms are identical with the indicative, the normal subjunctive is used. In fact, you will occasionally find forms of both subjunctives in the same sentence.

Hans sagte, er wisse nicht, ob Rosemarie heute käme.

5. If the normal subjunctive was used in the direct statement to express wishes, contrary-to-fact conditions, etc., this subjunctive cannot be replaced by the alternate subjunctive.

6. The alternate subjunctive is also used in sentences with **als ob**, *as if* (see Anal. 103, p. 331 below).

PRACTICE ONE

A. Restate as indirect discourse, using both present subjunctive and **würde**-forms. Change pronouns as appropriate.

1. Herr Meyer sagte: „Mein Sohn fährt morgen in die Schweiz."
2. Frau Schulz sagte: „Meine Tochter bleibt noch drei Wochen in den USA."
3. Hans sagte: „Ich gehe mit Inge ins Kino."
4. Silvia sagte: „Ich bringe dich zum Flughafen."
5. Mein Freund sagte: „Morgen bekommst du bestimmt einen Brief von ihr."
6. Carola sagte: „Wir rufen euch heute abend an."
7. Achim sagte: „Der Film fängt um sieben Uhr an."
8. Er sagte: „Der Film gefällt dir bestimmt."
9. Herr Enderle sagte: „Morgen nehme ich den Zug."
10. Sie sagten: „Wir treffen euch vor der Kirche."

B. Restate as indirect discourse, using the past subjunctive. Begin each sentence with **Sie sagte, . . .**

1. Ich habe meinen Regenmantel vergessen.
2. Ich habe die Nachrichten schon gehört.
3. Wegen des Regens bin ich zu spät gekommen.
4. Für den Wein hat er nur vier Mark bezahlt.
5. Ich habe meine Großeltern angerufen.
6. Außer mir war niemand da.
7. Johannes mußte nach Basel fahren.

C. Change the following sentences to indirect discourse, starting with an appropriate introductory verb. Use both forms of the subjunctive, if possible.

1. Meine Frau ist schon lange wieder zu Hause.
2. Morgen habe ich keine Zeit.
3. Ich kann Sie morgen leider nicht besuchen.
4. Leider muß ich morgen nach Wiesbaden fahren.
5. Ich darf meinen Mann noch nicht besuchen.
6. Ich will nicht studieren.
7. Der Mantel ist ganz neu.
8. Ich muß mal telefonieren.

Baden-Baden and similar places

The obligatory state health insurance (**Krankenkasse**) in the Federal Republic pays for a wide range of services, including medically prescribed stays at health resorts. Germans consider their vacation an **Erholung**, which can be roughly translated as *"recovery."* If it is medically prescribed, it is called a **Kur**, for which you go to a **Kurort**, a spa or health resort. Many of these are located at natural mineral springs or hot springs dating back to Roman times, and their names frequently contain **Bad** (*bath*), as in Wiesbaden, Schlangenbad, Bad Salzuflen, Bad Langensalza, Bad Boll, Baden bei Wien, and Baden-Baden.

KURHAUS BAD BOLL

Nordsee

PATTERNS TWO

6/Indirect Imperative

Mein Arzt hat gesagt: „Fahren Sie doch einmal an die Nordsee."
    Mein Arzt hat gesagt, ich sollte (solle) doch einmal an die Nordsee fahren.

Er sagte: „Bleiben Sie mindestens vierzehn Tage[2] dort."
    Er sagte, ich sollte (solle) mindestens vierzehn Tage dort bleiben.

Carola sagte: „Bring mir doch bitte etwas zu lesen mit."
    Carola sagte, ich sollte (solle) ihr doch bitte etwas zu lesen mitbringen.

Tante Amalie sagte: „Besucht mich bald wieder."
    Tante Amalie sagte, wir sollten sie bald wieder besuchen.

7/Indirect Questions

Sie fragte: „Ist dein Vater heute abend zu Hause?"
    Sie fragte, ob mein Vater heute abend zu Hause wäre.

Er fragte: „Wohin geht ihr heute abend zum Essen?"
    Er fragte, wohin wir heute abend zum Essen gingen.

Sie fragte: „Kommt Fritz morgen früh?"
    Sie wollte wissen, ob Fritz morgen früh käme.

Sie fragte, ob ich krank wäre.
Er fragte, ob wir das Haus in Wiesbaden kaufen wollten.
Sie fragte, ob sie mich zum Flughafen bringen dürfte.
Er fragte mich, warum ich denn nicht mit nach Bern führe.
Er wollte wissen, ob Maria zu Hause wäre.
Sie wollte wissen, warum Hans nicht mitgehen könnte.

Er fragte, warum ich denn gestern nicht nach Graz gefahren wäre.
Sie wollte wissen, mit wem ich gestern abend im Theater gewesen wäre.
Er wollte wissen, wieviel der Wein gekostet hätte.
Sie wollte wissen, wie lange ich für die Lufthansa gearbeitet hätte.

8/*als* with the Comparative

Du bist auch nicht besser als er.	You are no better than he is.
Das ist besser als nichts.	That is better than nothing.
In Berlin wohnen mehr Menschen als in Unterzwingenbach.	More people live in Berlin than in Unterzwingenbach.

[2]**vierzehn Tage** is commonly used to express *two weeks*; *one week*, oddly enough, turns out to be **acht Tage**. Count them: **Sonntag, Montag, Dienstag, Mittwoch, Donnerstag, Freitag, Samstag, Sonntag.**

| Meyer hat in Baden-Baden mehr Geld verloren, als er wollte. | Meyer lost more money in Baden-Baden than he intended to. |
| Er wußte bestimmt mehr, als er uns gesagt hat. | I'm sure he knew more than he told us. |

9/The Conjunction *als* Meaning *when*

Wenn wir in München sind, wohnen wir im Bayerischen Hof.
  When(ever) we are in Munich, we stay at the Bayerischer Hof.
Als wir in München waren, wohnten wir im Bayerischen Hof.
  When we were in Munich, we stayed at the Bayerischer Hof.
Wenn ich nach Freiburg komme, besuche ich ihn sofort.
  If (When) I get to Freiburg, I'll visit him immediately.
Als ich nach Freiburg kam, besuchte ich ihn sofort.
  When I got to Freiburg, I visited him immediately.

Als Rosemarie ins Hotel kam, wartete Erich schon auf sie.
Wir wollten gerade ins Haus gehen, als Meyers kamen.
Frau Enderle studierte in Hamburg, als sie ihren Mann kennenlernte.

10/*als ob, als wenn, als*

Er tut, als ob er schliefe (schlafe).	
Er tut, als schliefe (schlafe) er.	He acts as if he were asleep.
Er tat, als ob er schliefe (schlafe).	
Er tat, als schliefe (schlafe) er.	He acted as if he were asleep.
Er tut, als ob er geschlafen hätte (habe).	
Er tut, als hätte (habe) er geschlafen.	He acts as if he had been asleep.
Er tat, als ob er geschlafen hätte (habe).	
Er tat, als hätte (habe) er geschlafen.	He acted as if he had been asleep.
Er tat, als wenn er schliefe (schlafe).	He acted as if he were asleep.
Er tat, als wenn er geschlafen hätte (habe).	He acted as if he had been asleep.
Meyer sieht aus, als hätte (habe) er viel Geld.	Meyer looks as if he had a lot of money.
Gerda sah aus, als wäre (sei) sie krank.	Gerda looked as if she were sick.

11/*ob*

„Fährst du nach Bern?"
Mutter will wissen, ob du nach Bern fährst.

„War Erich wirklich in Garmisch-Partenkirchen?"
Ich weiß nicht, ob Erich wirklich in Garmisch-Partenkirchen war.

„Ist Erich hier?"
Sie fragte, ob Erich hier wäre.

„Warst du in Zürich?"
Er fragte mich, ob ich in Zürich gewesen wäre.

12/wann

„Wann will Heidi denn heiraten?"
Ich weiß nicht, wann sie heiraten will.
Ich wüßte auch gerne, wann sie heiraten will.

„Wann ist Wolfgang denn gestern abend nach Hause gekommen?"
Wolfgang, Vater möchte wissen, wann du gestern abend nach Hause gekommen bist.

13/wenn

Wenn es morgen regnet, bleiben wir zu Hause.
Wenn er schon hier wäre, könnten wir ihn besuchen.
Wenn er damals hier gewesen wäre, hätten wir ihn besuchen können.

Wenn der Sommer kam, fuhren unsere Eltern immer mit uns an die Nordsee.
Jedesmal, wenn Tante Amalie uns besuchte, mußte ich mit ihr ins Museum gehen.
Ich gehe abends immer ins Kino, wenn ich in München bin.

Wenn du in Frankfurt ankommst, fahren wir sofort zu Onkel Otto.
Ich muß noch zwei Stunden arbeiten, wenn ihr weggeht.

ANALYSIS TWO

102/Indirect Imperative and Indirect Questions

1. Any imperative constitutes direct discourse. In order to report,
by indirect discourse, that a request was made or a command given,
sollen is used.

IMPERATIVE

Fahren Sie doch einmal an die Nordsee.

INDIRECT DISCOURSE

Der Arzt meinte, ich solle (sollte) doch einmal an die Nordsee fahren.
Der Arzt meinte, er solle (sollte) doch einmal an die Nordsee fahren.
Der Arzt meinte, wir sollten doch einmal an die Nordsee fahren.

English usually expresses the indirect imperative by a form of *to
tell* plus infinitive.

Go to the North Sea.
The doctor told me to go to the North Sea.

But English also uses a construction that is exactly parallel to the German indirect imperative.

The doctor said I *should* go to the North Sea.

2. Any direct question can be turned into an indirect question following an introductory statement like **Sie fragte, . . .** or **Er wollte wissen, . . .** They are always dependent clauses and begin either with an interrogative conjunction like **wann** or **warum** or in the case of yes-or-no questions with the conjunction **ob,** *whether.*

> **Sie fragte mich, wann ich an die Nordsee fahren würde.**
> **Er wollte wissen, ob ich an die Nordsee führe.**

103/*als, ob, wann, wenn*

These words tend to be troublesome because their range of use does not correspond exactly to that of their English equivalents.

als

1. In comparisons, the conjunction **als** means *than* and is used only to compare what is *not* equal. Comparison of adjectives will be discussed in Unit 17.

> **Er trinkt mehr als du.**   He drinks more than you (drink).
> **Ich habe nicht mehr als hundert Mark.**   I don't have more than a hundred marks.

The phrase with **als** always stands in the end field.

> **Er hat mehr getrunken als ich.**
> **Ich glaube, daß er mehr getrunken hat als ich.**

If the **als**-phrase contains its own verb, it is a dependent clause and must be separated from the main clause by a comma.

> **Er hat mehr gewußt, als er uns sagen wollte.**

2. The conjunction **als** meaning *when* introduces dependent clauses referring to *one single event or situation in the past.* English *when* has a much wider usage: It corresponds to German **als** only if it can be replaced by *at the specific time when* followed by a past tense.

> **Als wir letzten Sonntag in München**   When (at the time when) we were in
> **waren, sind wir ins Theater gegangen.**   Munich last Sunday, we went to the
> theater.

3. **Als** may be the short version of **als ob** or **als wenn**, both meaning *as if.* When so used, **als** or **als ob** is followed either by the normal subjunctive or, less frequently, by the alternate subjunctive.

If **als** is equivalent to **als ob** (**als wenn**), the verb of the dependent
clause follows immediately after **als**.

Er tat, als ob er schliefe.	He acted as if he were asleep.
Er tat, als schliefe er.	
Er tat, als schlafe er.	
Er tat, als wenn er alles wüßte.	He acted as if he knew everything.
Er tat, als wüßte er alles.	
Er tat, als wisse er alles.	

If the introductory verb is in the present tense, the indicative can
also be used, especially in the spoken language, but only with **als
ob** and not with **als.**

Er tut, als schliefe er.
Er tut, als schlafe er.
Er tut, als ob er schläft.

ob

The conjunction **ob** means *whether* and is used to introduce indirect
yes-or-no questions. It must be used whenever *whether* can be substituted for *if* in English.

Kommst du nach Berlin?	
Mutter will wissen, ob du nach Berlin kommst.	Mother wants to know if (whether) you are coming to Berlin.
Mutter wollte wissen, ob du nach Berlin kämst.	Mother wanted to know if (whether) you were coming to Berlin.

wann

The interrogative **wann,** *when,* can only be used in situations where
English *when* can be replaced by *at what time* and is used to introduce both direct and indirect questions.

Wann fährst du nach Köln?	When (at what time) are you going to Cologne?
Mutter will wissen, wann du nach Köln fährst.	Mother wants to know when (at what time) you are going to Cologne.

wenn → not indirect (questions).

The conjunction **wenn** can mean *if, when,* or *whenever* and introduces both conditional and temporal clauses.

1. In conditional clauses, **wenn** always means *if* (see Anal. 77, p. 235,
open conditions, and Anal. 83, p. 261, contrary-to-fact conditions).
Remember that if you can replace *if* by *whether,* you must use **ob.**

Wenn Rosemarie heute abend kommt, gehen wir ins Theater.

If Rosemarie comes tonight, we'll go to the theater.

Wenn Rosemarie heute abend käme, würden wir ins Theater gehen.

If Rosemarie were to come tonight, we would go to the theater.

2. In temporal clauses, **wenn** is used in two ways:

(a) **Wenn** introduces clauses expressing repeated actions; in such clauses *when* can be replaced by *whenever*. The main clause frequently contains an adverb like **oft** or **immer** or the time phrase **jedesmal,** *every time.*

Wenn Rosemarie nach Wien kommt, geht sie sehr oft ins Theater.

When(ever) Rosemarie comes to Vienna, she goes to the theater very often.

Jedesmal, wenn Rosemarie nach Wien kam, ging sie ins Theater.[3]

Every time Rosemarie came to Vienna, she went to the theater.

(b) **Wenn** introduces clauses referring to present or future time in which English *when* can be replaced by *at the (specific) time when.* Remember that if the clause refers to one event in past time, **als** must be used.

Wenn Rosemarie heute abend kommt, gehen wir ins Theater.

When Rosemarie comes tonight, we'll go to the theater.

Since **wenn** also corresponds to English *if,* this last German sentence is ambiguous; only the context makes the meaning clear. There no linguistic means in German of distinguishing between *when* and *if* as long as **wenn** refers to the future. In the first sentence under 1 above, an open condition, **wenn** must mean *if.* (Note, however, that contrary-to-fact conditions are never ambiguous and **wenn** can only mean *if.*)

SUMMARY:

	IF (condition)	IF (whether)	WHEN-EVER	WHEN (interrog.) (at what time)	WHEN (conj.) (at the time when)
PAST	**wenn**	**ob**	**wenn**	**wann**	**als**
PRESENT	**wenn**	**ob**	**wenn**	**wann**	**wenn**
FUTURE	**wenn**	**ob**	**wenn**	**wann**	**wenn**

[3]Note that after **jedesmal, wenn** cannot be omitted.

PRACTICE TWO

D. Change the following imperatives to indirect discourse, starting with
Er sagte, . . . Use both forms of the subjunctive where possible.

1. Mach doch mal den Fernseher an.
2. Geht doch morgen mit uns segeln.
3. Sei morgen pünktlich.
4. Geh doch mal mit Tante Amalie ins Museum.
5. Holen Sie mich bitte ab.

E. Change the following questions to indirect yes-or-no questions. First start
with **Ich wüßte gerne, ob . . .** (indicative), and then with **Er fragte mich,
ob . . .** (subjunctive).

1. Fährt Erika übermorgen bestimmt nach Berlin?
2. Ist Fritz verheiratet?
3. Wohnt Doris immer noch in Innsbruck?
4. Arbeitet Meyer jetzt in Hamburg?
5. Hat Thomas wirklich Musik studiert?
6. Ist Frau Fischer schon angekommen?

F. Change to direct questions. Change pronouns
as appropriate.

1. Sie wollte wissen, ob ich nach Berlin kommen könnte.
2. Er wollte wissen, ob mein Vater Physiker wäre.
3. Sie wollte wissen, was sie mir schenken solle.
4. Er wollte wissen, wann mein Vater nach Hause käme.
5. Sie wollte wissen, ob ich ihm vielleicht zwanzig
   Mark geben könnte.

G. Change to indirect questions (past time). Start with **Sie fragte mich, . . .**

1. Wann kam Tante Amalie nach Hause?
2. Ist sie mit der Straßenbahn gefahren?
3. Wie lange war sie im Museum gewesen?
4. Mußte er sie am Museum abholen?
5. Hatte Tante Amalie gestern abend Besuch?

H. In the following sentences, supply **als, als ob, ob, wann,** or **wenn.**

1. Ich saß im Café Schneider, _als_ ich den Brief schrieb.
2. _Wenn_ ich gewußt hätte, daß sie nicht schwimmen konnte, wäre ich natürlich nicht mit ihr fischen gegangen.
3. Können Sie mir sagen, _wann_ der Zug aus Kiel ankommt?
4. Können Sie mir sagen, _ob_ der Zug aus Kiel schon angekommen ist.

SPIELPLAN
LEIPZIGER THEATER

OPERNHAUS
SCHAUSPIELHAUS
KAMMERSPIELE
MUSIKALISCHE KOMÖDIE
THEATER
DER JUNGEN WELT
KELLERTHEATER

AUGUST/SEPTEMBER

Berliner
Ensemble
2. Rang
Links VI
5-10
15. 4. 79

Berliner Ensemble
am Bertolt-Brecht-Platz

Reihe **5**   2. RANG   Sitz Nr.
LINKS VI   **10**

Bei Zuspätkommen Einlaß erst nach Bildschluß
Sonntag, 15. April

(87/72) BG 039

5. Ich wußte nicht, _____ob_____ Erich mich erkannt hatte; jedenfalls tat er, _____als_____ hätte er mich nicht gesehen.
6. Ich bin so müde. _____Wenn_____ ich nur endlich einmal lange schlafen könnte!
7. Ich bin nicht sicher, _____ob_____ ich das Geschenk annehmen soll oder nicht.
8. Was? Tante Amalie will uns schon wieder besuchen? _____Wann_____ kommt sie denn?
9. Aber Inge, du tust ja, _____als ob_____ *du* immer mit ihr ins Museum gehen müßtest.
10. Du weißt doch, ich komme erst um 7 Uhr nach Hause. _____Wann_____ soll ich denn essen, _____wenn_____ das Theater schon um 7 Uhr 30 anfängt?

The Arts

In the seventeenth and eighteenth centuries, many of the sovereign princes of Central Europe, then the Holy Roman Empire, established their own court theaters, operas, orchestras, and museums. With the rise of the bourgeoisie in the nineteenth century, municipalities also created such institutions. Because of the political and cultural diversity of the area, there are to this day an astoundingly large number of these cultural institutions. The vast majority are still heavily subsidized by state and municipal governments; and actors, singers, and musicians are civil servants.

Some of the most famous institutions are:

Operas: Hamburg (est. 1678), Berlin (West), Berlin (East), Cologne, Dresden, Frankfurt, Munich, Vienna

Orchestras: Berlin Philharmonic, Dresden Staatskapelle, Leipzig Gewandhaus, Vienna Philharmonic

Theaters: Vienna Burgtheater; major theaters in Federal Republic in Berlin, Bochum, Bremen, Düsseldorf, Frankfurt, Hamburg, Cologne, Munich, and Stuttgart; Brecht Theater in East Berlin

Berlin (West)

	Deutsche Oper Berlin
	Bismarckstraße 35
	Tel. 34 38–1
	(16)
1. *Fr*	20.00: Neueinstudierung: Wozzeck
2. *Sa*	18.00: Der Barbier v. Sevilla 23.00: Midnight-Medley
3. *So*	17.00: Götterdämmerung
4. *Mo*	20.00: Ballettabend: Der blaue Engel
5. *Di*	20.00: Wozzeck
6. *Mi*	19.30: Der Barbier von Sevilla
7. *Do*	19.30: Lucia di Lammermoor*
8. *Fr*	20.00: Wozzeck
9. *Sa*	20.00: Madame Butterfly* 23.00: Midnight-Medley
10. *So*	19.00: Wozzeck
11. *Mo*	19.30: Lucia di Lammermoor*
12. *Di*	20.00: Ballettabend: Giselle
13. *Mi*	19.30: Die lustigen Weiber von Windsor
14. *Do*	20.00: Die Weise von Liebe und Tod ...
15. *Fr*	19.00: Der Messias
16. *Sa*	19.00: Der Messias
17. *So*	19.30: Fidelio
18. *Mo*	19.00: Der Messias
19. *Di*	20.00: Der blaue Engel 23.00: Midnight-Medley
20. *Mi*	19.00: Der Messias
21. *Do*	19.30: La Bohème*
22. *Fr*	20.00: Der Wildschütz
23. *Sa*	20.00: Der Troubadour*
24. *So*	18.00: Don Carlos*
25. *Mo*	20.00: Salome
26. *Di*	19.30: Premiere Ballettabend
27. *Mi*	18.30: Tannhäuser
28. *Do*	20.00: Die Weise von Liebe und Tod ...
29. *Fr*	20.00: Ballettabend: Der blaue Engel
30. *Sa*	18.30: Tannhäuser

Deutsche Staatsoper in Berlin (Ost)

Konzert im Zwinger, Dresden

Cuvilliés-Theater, München

Festivals: Bayreuth, Lucerne, Salzburg

Ballet: Stuttgart

Museums: Kunsthistorisches Museum in Vienna; Alte und Neue Pinakothek and Deutsches Museum in Munich; Römisch-Germanisches Museum in Cologne; Pergamon in Berlin (East); Zwinger in Dresden

CONVERSATIONS

I

ERIKA:	Du Hans, Tante Amalie hat angerufen.
HANS:	Was wollte sie denn?
ERIKA:	Sie wollte wissen, ob du heute nachmittag mit ihr ins Museum gehen könntest.
HANS:	Du hast ihr doch hoffentlich gesagt, ich wäre heute nicht zu Hause.
ERIKA:	Nein, ich dachte, du würdest gerne mit ihr gehen.
HANS:	Das hättest du nicht tun sollen.
ERIKA:	Ja, wenn ich gewußt hätte, daß du nicht willst, dann hätte ich ihr natürlich gesagt, du könntest heute nicht. Aber ich dachte, . . .
HANS:	Du solltest nicht immer so viel denken.

II

TANTE AMALIE:	Das war wirklich nett von dir, daß du mit mir ins Museum gegangen bist. Und jetzt würde ich gerne noch eine Tasse Kaffee trinken.
HANS:	Das ist mir recht. Wo möchtest du denn hin?
TANTE AMALIE:	Ich ginge gerne mal ins Café Schneider; da war ich schon lange nicht mehr.
HANS:	Gut, und dann könnten wir Erika anrufen. Sie käme sicher auch gerne.
TANTE AMALIE:	Ja, und wie wäre es, wenn ihr dann zum Abendessen zu mir kommen würdet?
HANS:	Das wäre sehr nett, Tante Amalie, aber ich kann leider nicht; ich habe zu viel zu tun.
TANTE AMALIE:	Wenn du nur nicht immer so viel arbeiten müßtest!
HANS:	Ja, aber ohne meine Arbeit wäre das Leben nur halb so schön.

Willst du mit dem Taxi ins Museum, Tante Amalie?
Die Nummer ist sechs-sechs, null-null, zwo-zwo.

III

ERIKA:	Na, Hans, wie war's denn?
HANS:	Ach, weißt du, Tante Amalie ist ja eigentlich sehr nett. Wenn sie nur nicht immer so viel reden würde.
ERIKA:	Dann wäre sie nicht Tante Amalie.
HANS:	Weißt du, sie hat mir erzählt, daß sie gestern bei Overhoffs den Museumsdirektor kennengelernt hat. Sie sagte, er wäre sehr interessant und hätte ihr sehr viel über Picasso erzählt.
ERIKA:	Nun, wenn sie jetzt den Direktor kennt, brauchst du vielleicht nicht mehr so oft mit ihr ins Museum zu gehen.
HANS:	Ja, und wenn sie den Direktor heiraten würde, brauchte ich nie mehr mit ihr ins Museum zu gehen. Dann könnte sie im Museum wohnen.
ERIKA:	Hans, das ist nicht sehr nett von dir.

IV

The following brief exchanges contain characteristic conversational patterns, many using subjunctive forms. By recombining these phrases, construct similar exchanges.

A: Wer war denn das eben am Telefon?
B: Frau Schmidt.
A: Welche Frau Schmidt.
B: Die Mutter von Heinz.
A: Ach so. —Was wollte sie denn?

A: Herr Doktor, Frau Schulz ist am Apparat.°   **= Telefon**
B: Ja, was ist denn?°   What's the matter?
A: Sie sagt, ihrem Mann ginge es nicht gut.
B: Sagen Sie ihr, ich würde in ein paar Minuten zurückrufen.

A: Hast du nicht gesagt, du müßtest morgen in die Stadt?
B: Ja, ich muß zum Zahnarzt. —Warum fragst du?
A: Ich dachte, du könntest vielleicht etwas für mich erledigen.
B: Aber gerne. —Was denn?

A: Tante Amalie hat mich gefragt, wo du gestern gewesen wärst. Sie hätte den ganzen Nachmittag auf dich gewartet.
B: Ich hätte natürlich hingehen sollen, aber ich hatte tatsächlich°   indeed, really
   keine Zeit.
A: Dann hättest du sie aber wenigstens anrufen sollen.
B: Da hast du natürlich recht. Am besten ruf ich sie jetzt gleich mal an und bitte sie um Entschuldigung.

Fragen an Sie persönlich

1. Haben Sie gestern (oder heute) den Wetterbericht gehört oder gelesen?
   Wie soll das Wetter werden?
2. Haben Sie im Radio oder im Fernsehen die Nachrichten gehört?
   Erzählen Sie, was Sie gehört haben. (*indirect discourse*)
3. Haben Sie in den letzten Tagen interessante Post bekommen?
   Hat Sie jemand angerufen?
   Was hat er/sie gesagt?
   (Hier dürfen Sie auch erfinden.°)   invent

READING

E. Y. MEYER

E. Y. Meyer (born 1946 in Liestal, Switzerland) is a contemporary Swiss novelist, who now lives in Berne. The following selection is from his novel *Die Rückfahrt*, published in 1977. It is a slightly ironic description of the city of Lucerne written entirely in indirect discourse.

Luzern

Auf Bergers Frage, wie es sich in dieser Stadt leben lasse, antwortete ihm Santschi, daß es eigentlich zwei Luzern gebe: die »große« Stadt im Sommer, und die »kleine« im Winter. Luzern sei zwar kein Kurort, aber doch ein Fremdenzentrum, und wer die Schweiz sehen wolle, besuche bestimmt auch Luzern, finde er hier doch alles, was ⁵ für einen Ausländer zum Bild der Schweiz gehöre: Bergseen, Bergbahnen, Alphornbläser° und Fahnenschwinger°, Jodler, Uhren, Schokolade und ein gutes Hotel, das seine Gäste verwöhnen° wolle. Die Amerikaner, die Luzern besonders liebten, würden dann fragen, wo das Matterhorn sei, und nicht begreifen° können, daß die ¹⁰ Schweiz, die ihnen zu Hause auf der Landkarte so winzig° vorkam°, nun doch so groß war, daß man das Matterhorn nicht von überall erblicken° konnte. Sie würden fragen, ob man in den Gletschergarten° einen Eispickel° mitnehmen müsse, oder sie wollten, weil sie einen Dampfer° gesehen hätten der ITALIA heiße, per Schiff nach ¹⁵ Italien fahren, und fast alle würden sich natürlich nach *William Teall*[4] erkundigen°.

alpine horn players
flag wavers   spoil

comprehend
tiny   appeared

see
Glacier Garden (a park
   in Lucerne)   ice axe
steamer

inquire

[4]Ironic reference to Wilhelm Tell, the Swiss national hero.

Im Sommer finde hier das größte Seenachtsfest der Schweiz statt, es würden internationale Springkonkurrenzen° und Flachrennen° veranstaltet°, die Regatten auf dem Rotsee mit der Weltelite des Rudersports und die Musikfestwochen, die die Stadt, neben Salzburg, zum Treffpunkt der besten Dirigenten°, Sänger und Musiker gemacht hätten. Im Winter seien die Luzerner aber wieder unter sich, feierten ihre Fasnacht° und würden sich in den Restaurants, im Stadttheater oder beim Konzert treffen, wie das in den Schweizerstädten halt so sei°. Im Großen und Ganzen° lasse es sich hier ganz gut leben, sagte Santschi, wie das eben in den Schweizerstädten auch wiederum° so sei.

jumping contests
flat races   organized
rudern = to row
conductors

= **Karneval**

as is customary
on the whole
again

BERTOLT BRECHT

Bertolt Brecht (born 1898 in Augsburg) was one of the major figures in German literature during the first half of this century, and also one of the most controversial. Though best known in America for his plays, for example, *Mutter Courage, Der gute Mensch von Sezuan, Der kaukasische Kreidekreis,* he also produced poetry and prose. In 1933, he emigrated from National Socialist Germany, first to Denmark, then to Finland, and then, via Siberia, to the United States. He lived in California until 1948, then returned to East Berlin, where he died in 1956. The following story is from his *Geschichten vom Herrn Keuner.*

Bertolt Brecht

Wenn die Haifische Menschen wären

„Wenn die Haifische Menschen wären", fragte Herrn K. die kleine Tochter seiner Wirtin, „wären sie dann netter zu den kleinen Fischen?" „Sicher", sagte er. „Wenn die Haifische Menschen wären, würden sie im Meer für die kleinen Fische gewaltige Kästen bauen lassen, mit allerhand Nahrung drin, sowohl Pflanzen als auch Tierzeug. Sie würden sorgen, daß die Kästen immer frisches Wasser hätten, und sie würden überhaupt allerhand sanitäre Maßnahmen treffen. Wenn zum Beispiel ein Fischlein sich die Flosse verletzen würde, dann würde ihm sogleich ein Verband gemacht, damit es den Haifischen nicht wegstürbe vor der Zeit. Damit die Fischlein nicht trübsinnig würden, gäbe es ab und zu große Wasserfeste; denn lustige Fischlein schmecken besser als trübsinnige. Es gäbe natürlich auch Schulen in den großen Kästen. In diesen Schulen würden die Fischlein lernen, wie man in den Rachen der Haifische schwimmt. Sie würden zum Beispiel Geographie brauchen, damit sie die großen Haifische, die faul irgendwo liegen, finden könnten. Die Hauptsache wäre natürlich die moralische Ausbildung des Fischleins. Sie würden unterrichtet werden, daß es das Größte und Schönste sei, wenn ein Fischlein sich freudig aufopfert, und daß sie alle an die Haifische glauben müßten, vor allem, wenn sie sagten, sie würden für eine schöne Zukunft sorgen. Man würde den Fischlein beibringen, daß

If Sharks Were People

"If sharks were people," the landlady's little daughter asked Mr. K., "would they be nicer to the little fishes?"

"Certainly," he said. "If sharks were people, they would have enormous boxes built in the sea for the little fishes with all sorts of things to eat in them, plants as well as animal matter.

They would see to it that the boxes always had fresh water and, in general, take hygienic measures of all kinds. For instance, if a little fish injured one of its fins, it would be bandaged at once, so that the sharks should not be deprived of it by an untimely death. To prevent the little fishes from growing depressed there would be big water festivals from time to time, for happy little fishes taste better than miserable ones. Of course there would also be schools in the big boxes. In these schools the little fishes would learn how to swim into the sharks' jaws. They would need geography, for example, so that when the big sharks were lazing about somewhere they could find them.

The main thing, of course, would be the moral education of the little fishes. They would be taught that the greatest and finest thing is for a little fish to sacrifice its life gladly, and that they must all believe in the sharks, particularly when they promise a splendid future. They would impress upon the little fishes that this future could only be assured if they learned obedience. The little

diese Zukunft nur gesichert sei, wenn sie Gehorsam lernten. Vor allen niedrigen, materialistischen, egoistischen und marxistischen Neigungen müßten sich die Fischlein hüten und es sofort den Haifischen melden, wenn eines von ihnen solche Neigungen verriete. Wenn die Haifische Menschen wären, würden sie natürlich auch untereinander Kriege führen, um fremde Fischkästen und fremde Fischlein zu erobern. Die Kriege würden sie von ihren eigenen Fischlein führen lassen. Sie würden die Fischlein lehren, daß zwischen ihnen und den Fischlein der anderen Haifische ein riesiger Unterschied bestehe. Die Fischlein, würden sie verkünden, sind bekanntlich stumm, aber sie schweigen in ganz verschiedenen Sprachen und können einander daher unmöglich verstehen. Jedem Fischlein, das im Krieg ein paar andere Fischlein, feindliche, in anderer Sprache schweigende Fischlein tötete, würden sie einen kleinen Orden aus Seetang anheften und den Titel Held verleihen. Wenn die Haifische Menschen wären, gäbe es bei ihnen natürlich auch eine Kunst. Es gäbe schöne Bilder, auf denen die Zähne der Haifische in prächtigen Farben, ihre Rachen als reine Lustgärten, in denen es sich prächtig tummeln läßt, dargestellt wären. Die Theater auf dem Meeresgrund würden zeigen, wie heldenmütige Fischlein begeistert in die Haifischrachen schwimmen, und die Musik wäre so schön, daß die Fischlein unter ihren Klängen, die Kapelle voran, träumerisch, und in allerangenehmste Gedanken eingelullt, in die Haifischrachen strömten. Auch eine Religion gäbe es ja, wenn die Haifische Menschen wären. Sie würden lehren, daß die Fischlein erst im Bauche der Haifische richtig zu leben begännen. Übrigens würde es auch aufhören, wenn die Haifische Menschen wären, daß alle Fischlein, wie es jetzt ist, gleich sind. Einige von ihnen würden Ämter bekommen und über die anderen gesetzt werden. Die ein

fishes would have to guard against all base, materialistic, egotistic, and Marxist tendencies, reporting at once to the sharks if any of their number manifested such tendencies.

If sharks were people they would also, naturally, wage wars among themselves, to conquer foreign fish boxes and little foreign fishes. They would let their own little fishes fight these wars. They would teach the little fishes that there was a vast difference between themselves and the little fishes of other sharks.
Little fishes, they would proclaim, are well known to be dumb,[5] but they are silent in quite different languages and therefore cannot possibly understand each other. Each little fish which killed a few other little fishes in war—little enemy fishes, dumb in a different language—would have a little seaweed medal pinned on it and be awarded the title of Hero.
If sharks were people they would also have art, naturally. There would be lovely pictures representing sharks' teeth in glorious colors, their jaws as positive pleasure grounds in which it would be a joy to gambol.
The seabed theaters would show heroic little fishes swimming rapturously into sharks' jaws, and the music would be so beautiful that to its strains the little fishes, headed by the band, would pour dreamily into the sharks' jaws, lulled in the most delightful thoughts.
There would also be a religion if sharks were people. It would teach that little fishes only really start to live inside the bellies of sharks. Moreover, if sharks were people, not all little fishes would be equal anymore, as they are now. Some of them would be given positions and be set over the others. The slightly bigger ones would even be allowed to gobble the smaller ones. That would give nothing

[5]German distinguishes between **stumm**, *dumb* (incapable of speech) and **dumm,** *dumb* (stupid, simple-minded, lacking intelligence).

wenig größeren dürften sogar die kleineren auffressen. Das wäre für die Haifische nur 80 angenehm, da sie dann selber öfter größere Brocken zu fressen bekämen. Und die größern, Posten habenden Fischlein würden für die Ordnung unter den Fischlein sorgen, Lehrer, Offiziere, Ingenieure im Kastenbau 85 usw. werden. Kurz, es gäbe überhaupt erst eine Kultur im Meer, wenn die Haifische Menschen wären."

but pleasure to the sharks, since they would more often get larger morsels for themselves. And the bigger little fishes, those holding positions, would be responsible for keeping order among the little fishes, become teachers, officers, box-building engineers, and so on. In short, the sea would only start being civilized if sharks were people."

A German Tongue Twister

Fischers Fritz frißt[6] frische Fische; frische Fische frißt Fischers Fritz.
   The Fischers' (son) Fritz eats fresh fish; fresh fish does the Fischers' (son) Fritz eat (indeed).

REVIEW EXERCISES

I. Supply the missing words.

1. Ich habe heute morgen meine Frau _____ Bahnhof gebracht.
2. Ich habe gerade gelesen, daß Sie _____ drei Wochen in München wohnen.
3. Liegt er immer noch _____ Bett?
4. Ich weiß, daß Anton nach Berlin gefahren _____.
5. Kannst du mir sagen, _____ Ingelheims Kinder haben?
6. Er ist einer _____ Ingelheims Söhnen.
7. Können Sie mir sagen, _____ der Zug nach Bamberg fährt?
8. _____ der Krieg anfing, studierte Schmidt in Frankfurt Medizin.
9. Man kann doch nicht im Garten arbeiten, _____ es regnet.
10. Ich wollte, ich _____ dich nie gesehen.
11. Wenn er nicht an die Ostsee gefahren _____, hätte ich ihn nie kennengelernt.
12. Ich habe das Haus nicht kaufen _____.

J. Change the following sentences to indirect discourse, starting with **Sie sagte, daß . . . .** Change pronouns as appropriate. Use both normal and alternate subjunctives, if possible.

1. Meyer wohnt in Köln.
2. Ich brauche kein Geld.
3. Wir arbeiten heute nicht.
4. Ich brauche nicht nach Bonn zu fahren.
5. Ich bleibe heute abend zu Hause.
6. Das kann ich Ihnen nicht glauben.
7. Ich will ihn in Berlin besuchen.
8. Ich möchte mit dir ins Kino gehen.
9. Ich muß Ingelheims Roman lesen.
10. Ich darf mit meinem Vater nach Afrika fahren.

[6]The verb **fressen, fraß, hat gefressen** is normally used only with animals.

K. Change the following sentences to indirect discourse, starting with **Er sagte, ...** Change pronouns as appropriate.

1. Man hat ihn nach Bayern geschickt.
2. Achim ist mit ihr nach Berlin gefahren.
3. Ich mußte nach Zürich fliegen.
4. Wir konnten das Haus in Köln nicht kaufen.
5. Ich habe zuviel Kaffee getrunken.
6. Er konnte uns gestern nicht besuchen.
7. Den Roman von Ingelheim habe ich noch nicht gelesen.

L. Change to indirect questions (past time). Start with **Sie fragte mich, ...** Change pronouns as appropriate.

1. Waren Sie damals auch Student?
2. Warst du gestern in der Universität?
3. Hattest du kein Geld bei dir?
4. Stand da drüben nicht früher ein Hotel?
5. Warum hattest du keine Zeit?
6. Wie lange war Hans denn in Afrika?
7. Warum konntest du nicht kommen?
8. Warum ist Inge nicht mitgegangen?
9. Wen wolltest du denn besuchen?
10. Mußtest du am Sonntag arbeiten?

M. Change the following imperatives to indirect discourse, starting with **Er sagte, ...** Use both forms of the subjunctive where possible.

1. Fahren Sie doch mal an die See.
2. Sei nicht so unfreundlich.
3. Schicken Sie mir den Brief nach.
4. Geht doch mit ins Theater.
5. Nimm mich doch bitte mit.
6. Besuchen Sie uns doch mal.

N. Change to direct questions.

1. Sie fragte, ob viele Leute dagewesen wären.
2. Er fragte, ob ich gestern krank gewesen sei.
3. Sie fragte, ob es wahr wäre, daß es im Winter hier immer so kalt ist.
4. Er fragte, ob ich Irene gesehen hätte.
5. Sie fragte, wie lange ich in der Schweiz gewesen wäre.
6. Er fragte, warum ich um neun Uhr noch im Bett gelegen hätte.
7. Sie fragte, warum Inge nicht hätte mit nach Italien fahren können.
8. Er fragte, warum Erika gestern abend hätte zu Hause bleiben müssen.
9. Sie fragte, warum ich ihr nicht hätte schreiben können.
10. Er fragte, um wieviel Uhr Ernst hätte aufstehen müssen.

O. Restate the following sentences by starting with **Sie sah aus, als ob . . .** and **Sie sah aus, als . . . .**

1. Sie ist müde.
2. Sie hat nicht gut geschlafen.
3. Sie hat viel erlebt.
4. Sie ist unglücklich.
5. Sie war krank.

P. Restate the following sentences in the past tense. Note that with the change from present tense to past tense, **wenn** must be changed to **als** in some cases.

1. Wir können erst ins Theater gehen, wenn Else kommt.
2. Jedesmal, wenn Tante Amalie hier ist, muß ich mich zwingen, nett zu ihr zu sein.
3. Wenn mein Zug in München ankommt, bist du schon lange zu Hause.
4. Wenn meine Wohnung groß genug wäre, könnte ich auch fünfundzwanzig Leute einladen.
5. Wenn Hans geht, gehe ich auch.

Q. Express in German.

1. If it began to rain now, we wouldn't be able to work anymore.
2. If it begins to rain now, we can't work anymore.
3. When it began to rain, we couldn't work anymore.
4. I was often unhappy; but when I saw her, I was always happy.
5. I'd like to know whether he is really a doctor.
6. I wish he didn't always have so much to do.
7. I wish we could eat at home tonight.
8. It would have been nice if you had stayed at home.
9. I really should (ought to) invite him, but I have no time.
10. I really should have invited him, but I had no time.
11. She told me she would go to Bonn with me.
12. If only we could go to Bonn again!
13. He said he had never been in Berlin.
14. I'd like to have a cup of coffee.
15. You should have seen him three years ago.
16. If only she had learned to drive.
17. I wish he didn't always forget my birthday.
18. I wish you hadn't forgotten my birthday again.
19. He knows he should have stayed at home.
20. If he hadn't lived in Munich at that time, he would never have met her.

Abteikirche Maria-Laach

R. Supply the missing words.

1. Wir _____ gestern in die Stadt gefahren, _____ wir einkaufen wollten.
2. _____ habt ihr denn gekauft?
3. Was habt ihr denn _____ den Wein bezahlt?
4. Die Studenten standen alle _____ den Professor herum.
5. Sie wollten in _____ Schweiz fahren.
6. Weil er kein Geld _____, mußte er zu Hause bleiben.
7. Wenn er Geld gehabt _____, _____ er mit uns ins Theater gegangen.
8. Der Arzt sagte mir, ich _____ an die See fahren.
9. Wo waren Sie denn während _____ Sommers?
10. Herr Dr. Schmidt _____ leider verreist.
11. Ich habe Hans einen Brief _____, aber er hat _____ noch nicht geantwortet.
12. Sind Sie _____ einmal in Berlin gewesen? —Nein, noch nie.
13. Ich denke sehr oft _____ dich.
14. Hans lud mich ein, _____ in Köln zu besuchen.
15. Wußtest du, daß Erika Ärztin geworden _____?
16. Kann ich _____ helfen, Fridolin?
17. Nach dem Kino _____ er mich nach Hause.
18. Aber Fritz, _____ doch nicht so unfreundlich!
19. Wir sind gestern schwimmen gegangen, _____ es sehr kalt war.
20. _____ ist schön, _____ du noch eine Woche hierbleiben willst.

VOCABULARY

ach so	oh, I see	**die Farbe, -n**	color
acht Tage	a week; eight days	**feiern**	to celebrate
als ob	as if	**der Feiertag, -e**	holiday
als wenn		**das Fernsehen**	television
an•nehmen	to assume; to accept	(*no pl.*)	
der Apparat', -e	telephone; apparatus;	**der Fernseher, -**	television set
	instrument	**das Fest, -e**	celebration, party,
am Apparat	speaking (phone)		festivity
aus•sehen	to appear, look	**das Festspiel, -e**	festival
begreifen	to comprehend,	**fischen**	to fish
	understand	**fressen**	to eat (of animals), feed
damit'	so that, in order that	**frisch**	fresh
der Dampfer, -	steamer, steamship	**gerecht**	just
einige	some; few	**ungerecht**	unjust
um Entschuldigung	to apologize	**das Geschenk, -e**	present
bitten		**die Hauptsache, -n**	main thing
erfinden	to invent	**der Ingenieur', -e**	engineer (*m.*)
die Erholung	recreation; recupera-	**die Ingenieurin,**	engineer (*f.*)
	tion	**-nen**	
erkennen (an *dat.*)	to recognize (by)	**jedesmal, wenn**	whenever
erleben	to experience	**die Krankenkasse, -n**	health insurance,
			medical plan

der Krieg, -e	war
die Kultur', -en	culture
die Kunst, ⁻e	art
der Künstler, -	artist (m.)
die Künstlerin, -nen	artist (f.)
die Kur, -en	cure, medical treatment
der Kurort, -e	spa, health resort
die Landkarte, -n	map
das Meer, -e	ocean
die Musik'	music
der Nachmittag, -e	afternoon
nach•schicken	to forward
niemand	nobody
die Pflanze, -n	plant
das Radio, -s	radio
recht	right
das ist mir recht	that's alright with me
der Rundfunk (no pl.)	(radio) broadcasting
der Sänger, -	singer (m.)
die Sängerin, -nen	singer (f.)
das Schiff, -e	ship
der Schnaps, ⁻e	(hard) liquor, schnapps
die Schokolade	chocolate
schweigen	to be silent
der See, Se'en	lake
die See (no pl.)	sea, ocean

die Nordsee	North Sea
statt•finden	to take place, occur
die Tatsache, -n	fact
tatsächlich	in fact, indeed
das Tier, -e	animal
übermorgen	day after tomorrow
unterrichten	to instruct, teach
verreisen (sein)	to go on a trip
verreist sein	to be on a trip, out of town
verwöhnen	to spoil, pamper (someone); to take good care (of someone)
vierzehn Tage	two weeks; fourteen days
vor allem	above all, particularly
vorgestern	day before yesterday
vor•kommen (sein)	to appear; to occur
wieder•kommen (sein)	to return, come back
der Wirt, -e	innkeeper
die Wirtin, -nen	landlady; innkeeper
wunderschön	wonderful, very beautiful
der Zahn, ⁻e	tooth
der Zahnarzt, ⁻e	dentist (m.)
die Zahnärztin, -nen	dentist (f.)
zwingen	to force

Strong Verbs and Irregular Weak Verbs

INFINITIVE	PRESENT	PAST TENSE	PERFECT	
an•nehmen	nimmt an	nahm an	angenommen	to assume; to accept
aus•sehen	sieht aus	sah aus	ausgesehen	to appear, look
begreifen		begriff	begriffen	to comprehend, understand
erfinden		erfand	erfunden	to invent
erkennen		erkannte	erkannt	to recognize
fressen	frißt	fraß	gefressen	to eat (of animals)
schweigen		schwieg	geschwiegen	to be silent
statt•finden		fand statt	stattgefunden	to take place, occur
vor•kommen		kam vor	ist vorgekommen	to appear; to occur
wieder•kommen		kam wieder	ist wiedergekommen	to return, come back
zwingen		zwang	gezwungen	to force

Unit 12

Relative Pronouns—*da*-Compounds— *wo*-Compounds—Prepositional Objects

Political Parties

The American political system is based on two parties, one of which will always receive the absolute majority in elections. Both the Federal Republic of Germany and the Republic of Austria also have two major parties, but because of the presence of other, smaller parties, the major parties rarely have an absolute majority and must therefore form coalitions, even occasionally a grand coalition of the two major parties. The major parties left of center are the **Sozialdemokratische Partei Deutschlands (SPD)** and **Sozialistische Partei Österreichs (SPÖ)**. The right of center is represented in the Federal Republic by the **Christlich-Demokratische Union (CDU)** and its Bavarian sister party, the **Christlich-Soziale Union (CSU)**, and in Austria by the **Österreichische Volkspartei (ÖVP)**, which despite its name, Austrian Peoples' Party, is ideologically closer to the German **CDU/CSU**. Both countries have a small liberal party, the **Freie Demokratische Partei (FDP)** in the Federal Republic and the **Freiheitliche Partei Österreichs (FPÖ)** in Austria. In the early 1980s, a coalition of environmentalist groups formed a new party, **Die Grünen** (The Greens), which in the 1983 election in the Federal Republic received more than 5% of the vote and could therefore seat representatives in the Federal Parliament (**Bundestag**). The Austrian Greens entered Parliament (**Nationalrat**) in 1986. The Swiss party system by and large reflects the same political spectrum as that of the Federal Republic and Austria. The four largest parties form a governing coalition.

Soon after the end of World War II, political parties were reestablished in what was then the Soviet zone of occupation, the strongest of which was the Social Democratic Party. The **SPD** and the very small Communist Party (**KPD**) were merged into the Socialist Unity Party (**Sozialistische Einheitspartei Deutschlands, SED**), which has become the state party of the German Democratic Republic.

SED

Freier Deutscher Gewerkschaftsbund

Freie Deutsche Jugend

PATTERNS ONE

1/Definite Relative Pronouns

Much of the German used in this unit is more formal than in earlier units; that is, it is more highly structured and the syntax is more complex than in the simple drills you started out with. One reason for this is the use of nonrestrictive relative clauses, which occur with greater frequency in the written than in the spoken language. Thus, the pattern sections dealing with relative pronouns are as much a reading exercise as they are the basis for oral drills.

NOMINATIVE

Mein Vater hatte nicht studiert.
Er konnte nicht verstehen, warum ich Schriftsteller werden wollte.
Mein Vater, der nicht studiert hatte, konnte nicht verstehen, warum ich Schriftsteller werden wollte.
  My father, who had not gone to the university, could not understand why I wanted to be a writer.

Meine Mutter war Klavierlehrerin.
Sie wollte immer, daß ich Musik studieren sollte.
Meine Mutter, die Klavierlehrerin war, wollte immer, daß ich Musik studieren sollte.
  My mother, who was a piano teacher, always wanted me to study music.

Hier stand früher das Gymnasium.
Es stammte noch aus dem neunzehnten Jahrhundert.
Das Gymnasium, das früher hier stand, stammte noch aus dem neunzehnten Jahrhundert.
  The *Gymnasium* (secondary school) which once stood here dated from the nineteenth century.

Meyers Kinder gehen noch aufs Gymnasium.
Sie wollen später alle studieren.
Meyers Kinder, die noch aufs Gymnasium gehen, wollen später alle studieren.
  Meyer's children, who are still in secondary school, all want to go to the university later on.

ACCUSATIVE

Studienrat[1] Meinig war der Lehrer, den ich als Schüler[2] am meisten bewundert habe.
  Studienrat Meinig was the teacher I admired most when I was in school.
Die Schule, die ich neun Jahre lang besuchte, hieß Wöhler-Realgymnasium.[3]
  The school that I attended for nine years was called Wöhler-Realgymnasium.

[1]**Studienrat, Studienrätin** (literally, *studies counselor*) is the official title for tenured teachers in a **Gymnasium**.

[2]**Schüler, Schülerin**, student in a primary or secondary school; the term **Student, Studentin** is used only for university students.

[3]**Realgymnasium**, a type of secondary school oriented toward the sciences and modern languages, in contrast to the classical **Gymnasium**, which stressed Greek, Latin, and sometimes Hebrew.

Das Fach, das ich am liebsten hatte, war Chemie.
>   The subject I liked best was chemistry.
Viele von den Mädchen (Jungen), die ich auf der Schule kennengelernt habe, sind heute
>   noch meine Freundinnen (Freunde).
>   Many of the girls (boys) I met in school are still my friends.

DATIVE

Die Grundschule ist der Schultyp, von dem man mit zehn Jahren entweder auf die Haupt-
>   schule, auf die Realschule oder auf das Gymnasium geht.
>   The *Grundschule* (basic school) is the type of school from which, at age ten, one goes either to
>   the *Hauptschule* (main school), the *Realschule* (middle school), or the *Gymnasium*.
Die Prüfung, mit der das Gymnasium abschließt, ist das Abitur.
>   The examination with which the *Gymnasium* terminates is (called) the *Abitur*.
Das Abitur, mit dem man das Gymnasium abschließt, besteht aus einer Reihe von schrift-
>   lichen und mündlichen Prüfungen.
>   The *Abitur*, with which you finish the *Gymnasium*, consists of a series of written and oral tests.
Es gibt heute nur wenige Abiturienten, denen es gelingt, einen Studienplatz in der Medizin
>   zu bekommen.
>   There are only very few *Gymnasium* graduates who succeed in getting admitted to study medicine.

*Gesamtschule in Lud-
wigshafen am Rhein*

GENITIVE

Meyer, dessen Sohn ein sehr schlechtes Zeugnis bekam, hatte auch die achte Klasse wieder-
>   holen müssen.
>   Meyer, whose son got a very bad grade report, had had to repeat the eighth grade as well.
Anni Müller, in deren Klasse Fritz Meyer jetzt ist, erzählt immer, wie dumm Fritzchen ist.
>   Anni Müller, in whose class Fritz Meyer is now, always tells about how dumb Fritzchen is.
Dieses Mädchen Anni, dessen Eltern Herrn Meyer nicht leiden können, ist auch nicht gerade
>   intelligent.

This girl Anni, whose parents can't stand Mr. Meyer, is not exactly intelligent either.

Meyers, deren Kinder alle studieren wollen, haben sehr viel Geld.

The Meyers, whose children all want to go to the university, have loads of money.

2/Indefinite Relative Pronouns

Wer das Abitur hat, kann die Universität besuchen.

Wer das Abitur hat, der kann die Universität besuchen.

He who has (those who have, whoever has) the *Abitur*, can go to the university.

Wer mit 15 Jahren von der Hauptschule abgeht, (der) muß noch drei Jahre die Berufsschule besuchen.

Those who graduate from the *Hauptschule* at age fifteen have to attend a vocational school for another three years.

Was man in der Berufsschule lernt, kann man sofort praktisch im Betrieb verwenden.

What you learn in (the) vocational school you can put to use immediately in your place of work.

Unser Sohn will Automechaniker werden, was ich sehr vernünftig finde.

Our son wants to become an auto mechanic, which I think makes a lot of sense (is very reasonable).

Ich habe leider nicht alles verstanden, was Professor Kunz erklärt hat.

Unfortunately, I did not understand everything Professor Kunz explained.

Professor Bodenstein hat wirklich nichts gesagt, was ich nicht schon wußte.

Professor Bodenstein really didn't say anything that I didn't already know.

Aber Sabine, du mußt doch etwas gelernt haben, was neu für dich war.

But Sabine, you must have learned something that was new for you.

Was man gern macht, macht man gut.

Wieviel hast du dabei?
How much money do you have on you?

3/*da*-Compounds

Ich habe nichts dagegen.
I have nothing against it.

Wo ist denn mein Kugelschreiber?—Ich schreibe gerade damit.
 Where is my ballpoint pen?—I'm writing with it.

Wir haben ein Haus mit einer Garage dahinter.
 We have a house with a garage behind it.

Haben Sie Ingelheims Roman gelesen?—Nur den Anfang davon.
 Have you read Ingelheim's novel?—Only the beginning of it.

Den Kugelschreiber kannst du zurückbringen.
*Da*mit (mit *dem*) kann ich nicht schreiben.
Da kann ich nicht mit schreiben.
Der Kugelschreiber hier ist mir zu schwer. Darf ich mal *den* da versuchen?

den da...
... gibt es in allen Städten und Dörfern der Bundesrepublik • mindestens 1 Million mal • einer sogar ganz in Ihrer Nähe • er ist Tag und Nacht durchgehend geöffnet • niemals überfüllt • für Sie stets reserviert • darum auch die beste „Niederlassung" für uns • durch ihn bieten wir • besonders für Sie • den bequemsten, einfachsten und zugleich billigsten Weg, Bücher zu kaufen

From an ad for
MAIL ORDER KAISER
München 13.

4/*wo*-Compounds

Wofür brauchst du denn so viel Geld? Was willst du denn kaufen?
 What do you need so much money for? What do you want to buy?

Für was brauchst du denn das Geld?
 What do you need the money for?

Ich weiß nicht, wofür er das Geld ausgegeben hat.
 I don't know what he spent the money for.

War der Briefträger immer noch nicht da?—Warum fragst du denn schon wieder? Auf was (worauf) wartest du denn eigentlich, auf einen Brief von deiner Freundin?
 Hasn't the mailman been here yet?—Why are you asking again? What are you waiting for anyway, a letter from your girlfriend?

Ich weiß nicht, worauf er wartet.
 I don't know what he is waiting for.

ANALYSIS ONE

104/Relative Clauses

Relative clauses are dependent clauses that have an element in common with their main clause.

You want to buy the car ?   What does the car cost?

What does the car cost that you want to buy?

Du willst den Wagen kaufen?   Was kostet denn der Wagen?

Was kostet denn der Wagen, den du kaufen willst?

When the two questions are combined, the object of the first question, *the car*, becomes the object of the relative clause, the relative pronoun *that*. German forms relative clauses in the same way.

Kennst du den Mann ,   der gerade hier war ?

antecedent	function: subject
masc. sing.	nominative

The noun in the main clause to which the relative pronoun refers is called the *antecedent*. The relative clause modifies its antecedent the same way an adjective would.

Der neue Wagen gehört mir. —Welcher Wagen? —Der Wagen, der neu ist.

1. In English, the relative pronoun is often omitted.

   The man (whom) I saw yesterday was Mr. Meyer.

In German, the relative pronoun can never be omitted:

   Der Mann, den ich gestern gesehen habe, war Herr Meyer.

2. Relative pronouns function like subordinating conjunctions; relative clauses, therefore, are always dependent clauses with verb-last position.

3. German relative clauses must *always* be set off by commas.

4. Relative pronouns are frequently used with prepositions. In German these prepositions must always precede the relative pronoun. Placing the preposition at the end of the clause, as is often done in English, is not possible in German.

The woman (whom) I work for is Emma Meyer.
Die Frau, für die ich arbeite, heißt Emma Meyer.

5. Relative clauses do not always follow their antecedents immediately. If only the second prong is needed to complete the main clause, this clause is not normally interrupted by a relative clause.

Ich wollte Hermann Schneider besuchen, der jetzt in Hamburg wohnt.

Not

[Ich wollte Hermann Schneider, der jetzt in Hamburg wohnt, besuchen.]

THE DEFINITE RELATIVE PRONOUN

English has three relative pronouns: *who* (*whom, whose*) for persons; *which* for things; and *that* for either. German has only one relative pronoun, the forms of which are the same as those of the definite article **der, die, das**, except that the singular genitive and the plural genitive and dative add the ending **-en**. This **-en** necessitates doubling the **-s** in the masculine and neuter forms in order to keep the preceding **-e-** short.

	MASC.	FEM.	NEUT.	PLURAL
NOM.	der	die	das	die
ACC.	den	die	das	die
DAT.	dem	der	dem	denen
GEN.	dessen	deren	dessen	deren

These relative pronouns can refer either to persons or to things. They must agree in gender and number (singular or plural) with their antecedent, but their case depends on their function within the relative clause.

NOM. **Kennst du den Mann, der gestern hier war?**
Kennst du die Frau, die gestern hier war?
Kennst du das Mädchen, das gestern hier war?

ACC. **Der Junge, den du gestern gesehen hast, ist mein Sohn.**
Die Dame, die du gestern gesehen hast, ist meine Tante.
Das Mädchen, das du gestern gesehen hast, ist meine Schwester.

DAT.   **Wer war denn der Junge, mit dem ich dich gestern gesehen habe?**
         Wer war denn die Dame, mit der ich dich gestern gesehen habe?
         Wer war denn das Mädchen, mit dem ich dich gestern gesehen habe?

GEN.   **Ihr Vater, dessen Mutter aus Leningrad kam, sprach gut Russisch.**
         Seine Frau, deren Vater aus Leningrad kam, sprach gut Russisch.

PLURAL   **Kennst du die Leute, die gestern hier waren?**
         Die Mädchen, die du gesehen hast, waren meine Schwestern.
         Wer waren denn die Mädchen, mit denen ich dich gestern gesehen habe?

Like English *whose,* the genitives **dessen** and **deren** are followed by
a noun and frequently are preceded by a preposition (see Anal. 95,
p. 302). The choice of **dessen** or **deren** depends only on the antecedent.

Der Mann, dessen Sohn (*acc. obj.*) **ich kenne, . . .**	The man whose son I know . . .
Der Mann, dessen Sohn (*subject*) **hier war, . . .**	The man whose son was here . . .
Die Frau, mit deren Sohn ich in München war, . . .	The woman, with whose son I was in Munich, . . .
Die Frau, mit deren Tochter ich in Wien war, . . .	The woman, with whose daughter I was in Vienna, . . .

THE INDEFINITE RELATIVE PRONOUN

1. The German indefinite relative pronouns are **wer** and **was**. They
are always used if there is no antecedent.

Wer Geld hat, hat auch Freunde.
Whoever (He who) has money has friends, too.

Wer nicht für mich ist, ist gegen mich.
Whoever is not for me is against me.

Was er zu erzählen hatte, war nicht viel.
What he had to tell was not much.

2. Occasionally, the main clause following an indefinite relative
clause is introduced by a demonstrative pronoun that sums up the
relative clause. This demonstrative pronoun immediately precedes
the first prong, that is, the second element of the main clause (see
Anal. 73, p. 223).

Was er zu erzählen hatte, das war nicht viel.
Wer Geld hat, der hat auch Freunde.
Wer mich liebt, den liebe ich auch.

3. **Was** is also used to refer to an entire clause or to **alles, nichts,**
or **etwas.**

Hans hat mich zum Essen eingeladen, was ich sehr nett finde.
Ich habe nicht alles verstanden, was er gesagt hat.
Er hat nichts gesagt, was ich nicht schon wußte.
Er hat mir etwas geschenkt, was ich schon lange haben wollte.

105/*da*-Compounds

All personal pronouns (see Anal. 1, p. 3) can be used to replace any
noun, not just nouns referring to persons. If a masculine noun like
der Wagen is replaced, the pronoun is **er, ihn, ihm.**

Er (der Wagen) ist sechs Jahre alt.	It (the car) is six years old.
Ich habe ihn in München gekauft.	I bought it in Munich.

However, after prepositions, all pronouns are strictly *personal* pronouns, that is, they can only refer to persons and not to things. If
you want to say that you drove to Paris with *it* (the *car*), you cannot
say

Ich bin mit ihm nach Paris gefahren.

since **mit ihm** can only mean *with him* and not *with it*. To express
with it (the car) German uses **damit:**

Ich bin damit nach Paris gefahren.

This combination of **da** + preposition is used with most other prepo
sitions as well when referring to an inanimate object. With **da**-
compounds there is no longer any difference between masculine,
feminine, and neuter; no difference between dative and accusative;
and no difference between singular and plural.

Was hast du denn	**für diesen Wein** **für diese Uhr** **für dieses Haus** **für diese Blumen**	= **dafür**	be*zahlt*?

TABLE OF **da**-COMPOUNDS

If the preposition starts with a vowel, **dar-** is used instead of **da-.**

dadurch	daraus	daran	
dafür	dabei	darauf	
dagegen	damit	dahinter	
darum	danach	darin	darunter
	davon	daneben	davor
	dazu	darüber	dazwischen

Note that **ohne, außer, seit**, and the prepositions governing the genitive (**während, wegen, statt, trotz**) do not form **da**-compounds. **Außer** forms **außerdem** (*besides*), **seit** forms **seitdem** (*since then*; conj. *since*), and **trotz** forms **trotzdem** (*in spite of that, nevertheless*).

da-COMPOUNDS WITH STRESSED da-

As long as *unstressed* nouns and pronouns denoting things are replaced after prepositions, you have no choice but to replace them with a **da**-compound. However, if *stressed* nouns and pronouns denoting things and preceded by a preposition are to be replaced, you have a choice. You can use either the stressed demonstrative pronoun *after* the preposition or a stressed **da-** *preceding* the preposition.

> **Was hast du denn** | für *diesen* Wein | or | für diesen *Wein* | **bezahlt?**

becomes either

> **Was hast du denn** | für *den* | or | *da*für | **bezahlt?**

In assertions, **da**-compounds with a stressed **da-** usually occupy the front field and carry contrast intonation.

> *Da*für hast du zu*viel* bezahlt.

NOTE: Do not replace directives like **ins Haus, zum Bahnhof, nach Berlin** with **da**-compounds. Such directives are replaced by **hin** or **dahin** or **daher** (see Anal. 91, p. 293).

> **Mußt du zum Bahnhof? Ich bringe dich gerne hin.**
> **Ich soll nach Kairo fahren? Nein, dahin fahre ich nicht.**
> **Sie fahren nach Berlin? Da möchte ich auch gerne mal hinfahren.**
> **Sie kommen aus Berlin? Daher komme ich auch.**
> **Da komme ich auch her.**

SPLIT da-COMPOUNDS

In the spoken language, **da**-compounds are sometimes split. The **da-** (stressed or unstressed) then stands in the front field, and the preposition becomes the first part of the second prong. This pattern, however, is quite colloquial.

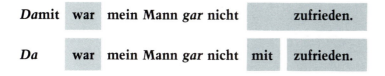

| *Da*mit | war | mein Mann *gar* nicht | | zufrieden. |
| *Da* | war | mein Mann *gar* nicht | mit | zufrieden. |

If the preposition begins with a vowel, **daraus** does not become
da . . . aus, but **da . . . draus; daran: da . . . dran; darauf: da . . . drauf;**
and so on.

der hier AND der da

In spoken German, the contrast *this one, that one* is expressed by
der hier (or **dieser hier**): **der da** (or **dieser da**).

> **Dieses Haus hier möchte ich nicht, aber das da hätte ich gerne.**
> **Die hier (diese Uhr hier) kostet mir zu viel. Darf ich die da mal sehen?**

106/*wo*-Compounds

If the question word **was** is preceded by a preposition, it may be replaced by **wo** (**wor-** in front of vowels) compounded with a preposition.

> **Ich möchte wissen,** auf was *or* worauf **du noch wartest.**

The indefinite relative pronoun **was** cannot be preceded by a preposition; instead a **wo**-compound is used.

> **Das ist etwas,** worüber **ich nicht gern spreche.**

In questions asking for directives, only the **wo**-compounds **wohin**
and **woher** can be used.

> **Wohin fährst du?**   **In die Stadt.**
> **Woher kommst du?**   **Aus der Stadt.**

PRACTICE ONE

A. Each of the following incomplete sentences contains a blank for a relative
pronoun. Fill in the correct forms.

1. das Haus, aus _____ er kam
2. die Betten, zwischen _____ der Tisch stand
3. das Brot, _____ wir hier essen
4. der Wagen, mit _____ er kam
5. die Blumen, _die_ ich von ihm bekommen habe
6. die Apotheke, in _____ ich gegangen bin
7. der Stuhl, _der_ hinter dem Tisch stand
8. seine Frau, _deren_ Vater in Berlin Architekt war
9. die Menschen, _denen_ man helfen muß

10. die Dame, nach _der_ Sie fragen
11. das Haus, vor _dem_ wir unseren Wagen stellten
12. die Leute, _die_ zu uns kamen
13. der Brief, _den_ sie mir geschrieben hat
14. die Frau, für _deren_ Mann mein Freund arbeitet
15. die Familie, bei _der_ du wohnst
16. das Theater, vor _dem_ ich sie treffen wollte
17. das Kind, _dessen_ Großeltern in Innsbruck wohnen
18. der Ingenieur, _____ wir gestern kennengelernt haben
19. meine Bücher, ohne _die_ ich nicht leben kann
20. der Zug, mit _____ du fahren willst
21. die Ecke, an _____ er stand
22. ihr Mann, _____ Vater Architekt war
23. die Familien, _deren_ Kinder hier zur Schule gehen
24. der Mann, mit _dessen_ Frau ich gesprochen habe
25. die Antwort, _____ sie mir gab

B. Determine the antecedent and the function and case of each relative
     pronoun; then insert the correct relative pronoun.

1. Ihr Mann, _dessen_ Mutter aus Moskau kam, sprach gut Russisch.
2. Seine Frau, _deren_ Vater aus Leningrad kam, sprach gut Russisch.
3. Kennen Sie meinen Freund Rombach?—Meinen Sie den Rombach, _____ das
     Corona-Hotel gehört?
4. Ist das der Wein, _____ Achim dir geschenkt hat?
5. Habe ich dir schon die Uhr gezeigt, _____ ich in Zürich gekauft habe?
6. Das Essen, _____ wir hier bekommen, ist sehr gut.
7. Ich wollte Gerd und Lotte wiedersehen, _deren_ Gast ich damals gewesen war.
8. Ist das der Wagen, mit _____ du nach Sylt gefahren bist?
9. Hermann, durch _____ ich meine Frau kennengelernt habe, ist jetzt Bankdirektor.
10. Wer waren denn die drei Herren, mit _denen_ ich Sie gesehen habe?
11. Wer sind eigentlich diese Schäufeles, von _denen_ du immer redest?
12. Ihre Kinder, für _____ sie so schwer gearbeitet hat, studieren jetzt alle.
13. Der Mann, ohne _dessen_ Hilfe ich heute nicht Arzt wäre, ist Professor Bornemann.
14. Studenten, _deren_ Eltern nicht genug Geld verdienen, bekommen ein Stipendium
     (*scholarship*) vom Staat.
15. Wo ist denn das Kaufhaus, in _dem_ du diese Teller gekauft hast?

C. In the following sentences, substitute a **da**-compound for the italicized
     prepositional phrases.

1. Der Garten *hinter dem Haus* braucht viel Wasser.
2. *Mit dem Boot* waren wir gestern segeln.
3. Und *vor dem Wohnzimmer* ist eine große Terrasse.
4. Er hat viel Geld *für das Haus* bezahlt.
5. Aber den Namen *unter dem Bild* kann ich nicht lesen.

D. Write down the questions to which the following sentences would be the answers. Start each question with (a) a **wo**-compound and (b) the preposition plus **was.**

> **Meine Tochter hat Angst vor der Schule.**
> **(a) Wovor hat sie denn Angst?**
> **(b) Vor was hat sie denn Angst?**

1. Wir warten auf schönes Wetter.
2. Ich brauche das Geld für meine Reise in die Schweiz.
3. Wir haben gerade von dem neuen Film gesprochen.
4. Ich denke gerade daran, daß Vater morgen Geburtstag hat.
5. Wir sprachen gerade über die Weihnachtsferien.

PATTERNS TWO

5/Prepositional Objects

Most of the verbs in this section are not new, and many have already been used with the prepositions introduced here. Therefore, use this section as a review of verbs and to learn some more school and university terminology in small contexts.

Angst haben vor (dat.)

Ich glaube, Franziska hat Angst vor dem Abitur. —Aber sie braucht doch wirklich keine Angst davor zu haben, daß sie durchfällt.
  I think Franziska is afraid of the *Abitur.* —But she really doesn't need to be afraid of flunking.

antworten auf (acc.)

Sie hat noch nicht auf meinen Brief geantwortet.
  She hasn't answered my letter yet.

bitten um (acc.)

Ich habe Frau Professor Baumgärtner um eine Empfehlung gebeten.
  I've asked Professor Baumgärtner for a recommendation.

danken für (acc.)

Herr Studienrat, ich möchte Ihnen noch einmal für alles danken, was Sie für unsere Tochter getan haben.
  Herr Studienrat, I'd like to thank you once more for all that you have done for our daughter.

denken an (*acc.*)

Ich denke oft und gern an meine Schulzeit in Frankfurt zurück.
I often think back with pleasure to my school years in Frankfurt.

nachdenken über (*acc.*)

Wir denken oft darüber nach, wie man den Fremdsprachenunterricht verbessern könnte.
We often think (meditate) about how one could improve foreign language instruction.

einladen zu (*dat.*)

Darf ich dich nach der Vorlesung[4] zu einer Tasse Kaffee einladen?
May I invite you to (have) a cup of coffee after class?

Wir haben Professor Müller zu einem Vortrag[4] in unserem Institut eingeladen.
We have invited Professor Müller to give a lecture in our Institute.

fragen nach (*dat.*)

Früher war Professor Meyer *der* Spezialist für Chirurgie; heute fragt kein Mensch mehr nach ihm.
Professor Meyer used to be *the* specialist in surgery; today nobody asks about him (mentions him) anymore.

Hast du auch danach gefragt, wann nächstes Jahr die Sommerferien anfangen?
Did you inquire when summer vacation begins next year?

gehören zu (*dat.*)

Fritzchen Meyer gehört sicher zu denen, die nie das Abitur machen werden.
Fritzchen Meyer, I'm sure, is one of those (belongs to those) who will never get their *Abitur*.

Unser Institut gehört zum Fachbereich Angewandte Physik.
Our Institute belongs to (is part of) the Department of Applied Physics.

Nein, das sind nicht meine Bücher; die gehören dem Institut.
No, those aren't my books; they belong to the Institute.

glauben an (*acc.*)

Viele Leute glauben nicht an den Erfolg der Universitätsreform. Glauben Sie daran?
Many people don't believe in the success of the university reform. Do you believe in it?

Ich glaube nicht daran, daß die Universitätsreform das Hochschulsystem[5] wirklich verbessern wird.
I don't believe that the university reform will really improve the system of higher education.

---

[4]The term **Vorlesung** is used in the sense of *class*, for daily lectures in a university course; **Vortrag** refers to individual public lectures.

[5]**Hochschule** does not mean *high school*, but is used for all institutions of higher learning, that is, for the university level. Secondary schools are referred to as **höhere Schulen**, but since they are not really the equivalent of secondary schools in the U.S., it is best to use the term *high school* when speaking of American schools. Also, since

halten von (*dat.*)

Was halten Sie von den höheren Schulen[5] in der Bundesrepublik, Mr. Ray? Sind sie besser
    als in Amerika?
    What do you think of the secondary schools in the Federal Republic, Mr. Ray? Are they better
    than in America?

halten für (*acc.*)

Ich halte sie für sehr gut, Herr Huber; aber man kann sie nicht gut mit der High School[5]
    in Amerika vergleichen.
    I consider them (to be) very good, Mr. Huber. But it is difficult to compare them with the high
    school in America.

hoffen auf (*acc.*)

Meyer hofft immer auf Wunder. Zur Zeit hofft er darauf, daß Fritzchen das Abitur bestehen
    wird.
    Meyer always hopes for miracles; right now he hopes that Fritzchen will pass the *Abitur.*

hören von (*dat.*)

Was hören Sie denn von Ihrem Sohn, Herr Schulze?
    What do you hear from your son, Mr. Schulze?

Ich hatte gar nichts davon gehört, daß er promoviert[6] hatte.
    I had heard nothing about his having gotten his Ph.D.

lachen über (*acc.*)

Fritzchen will Kernphysik studieren? Mit einer Fünf[7] in Mathematik? Darüber kann ich
    nur lachen.
    Fritzchen wants to study nuclear physics? With a D in math? That's ridiculous. (About that I can
    only laugh.)

Lacht doch nicht immer über Fritzchen.
    Don't always laugh about little Fritz.

reagieren auf (*acc.*)

Auf den Vorschlag der Fakultät haben die Studenten und Assistenten sehr positiv reagiert.
    Students and assistants reacted very positively to the proposal by the faculty.

---

there is no equivalent of the American college in Germany, the term *college* should
be used as well; thus:

> **Mein Bruder geht noch auf die High School, aber ich bin schon im College, —in
> Massachusetts.**

[6]**promovieren** is used only in the sense of *to receive the Ph.D.;* the noun **die Promotion** is also used only in this sense.

[7]German grades go from 1 (highest) to 6 (lowest).

sein für (*acc.*)/**sein gegen** (*acc.*)

Frau Doktor Schmidt, sind Sie *für* die Universitätsreform oder sind Sie da*gegen*?
  Doctor Schmidt, are you *for* university reform or are you *against* it?

sprechen von (*dat.*)

Von wem (von was; wovon) sprecht ihr denn?
  Whom (what) are you talking about?

Wir sprachen gerade davon, daß wir in den Semesterferien nach Schweden fahren wollen.
  We were just talking about going to Sweden during vacation (the semester break).

sprechen über (*acc.*)

In seinem Vortrag sprach Professor Schmidtke über die Verschmutzung unserer Flüsse durch
    die Industrie.
  In his lecture, Professor Schmidtke talked about the pollution of our rivers by industry.

stolz sein auf (*acc.*)

Natürlich sind wir stolz auf Fritz. Ich hätte nie gedacht, daß er einmal Arzt werden würde.
  Of course we are proud of Fritz. I would never have thought that he'd be a doctor some day.

verstehen von (*dat.*)

Wissen *Sie*, was Endokrinologie ist? —Nein, davon verstehe ich leider gar nichts.
  Do *you* know what endocrinology is? —No, unfortunately I know nothing about it.

warten auf (*acc.*)

Ich warte seit einer Stunde auf Joachim. Er wollte gleich nach dem Seminar hierher kommen.
  I've been waiting for Joachim for an hour. He wanted to come here right after his seminar.

wissen von (*dat.*)

Was wissen Sie vom Schulsystem in der Bundesrepublik? —Davon weiß ich leider nur sehr
    wenig.
  What do you know about the school system in the Federal Republic? —Unfortunately, I know
    very little about it.

zufrieden sein mit (*dat.*)

Carola Müller ist mit ihrem Zeugnis sehr zufrieden.
  Carola Müller is very satisfied with her report card.

> # Mit sich und der Welt zufrieden.

ANALYSIS TWO

107/Prepositional Objects

Verbs with accusative and dative objects were introduced in Anal. 49, p. 132. In this unit a third type is introduced, the prepositional object.

In sentences like

The bartender refused to wait on him.

the prepositional phrase *on him* functions just like the direct object *him* in

The bartender refused to serve him.

Therefore, *on him* is called a prepositional object. Prepositional objects always form one single unit of meaning with their verbs and are always verbal complements. If the preposition is changed, the meaning of the verb is also changed: *to wait on somebody* and *to wait for somebody* are two separate dictionary entries.

Questions asking for a prepositional object always use the preposition plus a form of **wer** or the preposition plus **was** (or a **wo**-compound):

Auf wen wartest du?	Whom are you waiting for?
Ich warte auf Erika.	I'm waiting for Erika.
Auf was (worauf) wartest du?	What are you waiting for?
Ich warte auf die Post.	I'm waiting for the mail.

Do not confuse prepositional objects with time phrases, place phrases, or directives:

vor einem Jahr	(question: **wann?**)
zu Hause	(question: **wo?**)
nach Leipzig	(question: **wohin?**)

Both English and German have hundreds of such fixed combinations of verbs plus prepositional objects. Unfortunately, however, the prepositions used with the German verbs hardly ever correspond to the prepositions used with the English verbs. Compare the following sentences:

Ich warte *auf* Meyer.	I'm waiting *for* Meyer.
Ich spreche *von* Meyer.	I'm talking *about* Meyer.
Ich bin *in* sie verliebt.	I'm in love *with* her.
Ich bin *mit* ihr verlobt.	I'm engaged *to* her.
Ich habe Angst *vor* ihr.	I'm afraid *of* her.
Ich bin stolz *auf* sie.	I'm proud *of* her.

Note that the prepositional objects sometimes go with such compound verbs as **Angst haben** or **stolz sein**.

Not all English prepositional objects can be expressed by prepositional objects in German, and vice versa:

He looked *at me*.	**Er sah *mich* an.**
Ich halte es *für* gut.	I consider it *good*.

FREQUENT PREPOSITIONAL OBJECTS

Memorize the following verbs with their prepositions:

Angst haben vor (*dat.*)	to be afraid of
antworten auf (*acc.*)	to reply to (something)
jemandem antworten	to answer somebody
bitten um (*acc.*)	to ask for (something)
danken für (*acc.*)	to thank (someone) for
denken an (*acc.*)	to think of, to remember
nachdenken über (*acc.*)	to think, meditate about
einladen zu (*dat.*)	to invite to
fragen nach (*dat.*)	to ask about, inquire about
gehören zu (*dat.*)	to be part or a member of, to belong to
glauben an (*acc.*)	to believe in
halten von (*dat.*)	to have an opinion about; to think (highly, a great deal, not much, etc.) of (somebody or something)
halten für (*acc.*)	to think that something (or somebody) is (something)
hoffen auf (*acc.*)	to hope for
hören von (*dat.*)	to hear from somebody or about something
lachen über (*acc.*)	to laugh about
jemanden auslachen	to laugh at (make fun of) somebody
reagieren auf (*acc.*)	to react to (something or somebody)
sein für or **sein gegen** (*acc.*)	to be for or against
sprechen von (*dat.*)	to talk of, to mention
sprechen über (*acc.*)	to talk in detail about a topic
stolz sein auf (*acc.*)	to be proud of
verstehen von (*dat.*)	to understand about
warten auf (*acc.*)	to wait for
wissen von (*dat.*)	to know about
zufrieden sein mit (*dat.*)	to be satisfied with

NOTE: A number of these prepositional objects use two-way prepositions. In all cases listed, **an**, **auf**, and **über** are used with the accusative, even though these phrases are not directives answering the question **wohin**. There are a few cases where the dative must be used—for example, with **Angst haben vor**. From now on, the correct case will be indicated in the vocabulary. The importance of using the correct case can be seen in the following.

Ich warte auf die Straßenbahn.

means

I am waiting for the streetcar.

whereas

Ich warte auf   der   Straßenbahn.

could only mean

I am waiting on top of the streetcar.

108/The Syntax of Prepositional Objects

PREPOSITION PLUS NOUN OR PERSONAL PRONOUN

The prepositional object constitutes the second prong and is preceded by **nicht**. With contrast intonation, it can be placed in the front field.

Ich warte auf meinen Mann.
Ich warte nicht auf sie.
Auf Fritz brauchst du heute abend nicht zu warten.

REPLACEMENT OF NOUNS AND PRONOUNS BY DEMONSTRATIVES

The stressed demonstratives used to replace nouns or names usually occur in the front field and produce contrast intonation.

Erika? Auf *die* brauchst du nicht zu warten.
Meyers? Von *denen* haben wir lange nichts gehört.

PREPOSITIONAL **da**-COMPOUNDS

The **da**-compounds with an unstressed **da**- appear in the first box of the second prong. The compounds with a stressed **da**- usually appear in the front field, with contrast intonation.

Ich *glaube* noch nicht daran.

Ich hoffe, ich brauche nicht darauf zu *warten*.

Daran *glaube* ich nicht.

Darauf kann ich nicht *warten*.

PREPOSITIONAL **wo**-COMPOUNDS

Like all questions, questions introduced by a **wo**-compound can be changed into dependent clauses.

Auf was wartet er denn?
Worauf wartet er denn?

Ich weiß nicht, auf was er wartet.
Ich weiß nicht, worauf er wartet.

da-COMPOUNDS WITH AN ANTICIPATORY FUNCTION

The prepositional object may be replaced by a dependent clause or
an infinitive phrase which can contain more information than the
prepositional object alone. If this is the case, a **da**-compound anticipating this dependent clause frequently appears in the main clause.

Ich warte auf einen Brief von ihm.	I'm waiting for a letter from him.
Ich warte darauf, daß er mir (einen Brief) schreibt.	I'm waiting for him to write me a letter.
Ich bat sie um Hilfe.	I asked her for help.
Ich bat sie (darum), mir zu helfen.	I asked her to help me.

Conversely, some clauses anticipated by a **da**-compound cannot be
reduced to a prepositional object.

Ich habe gar nicht daran gedacht, daß du ja auch in Köln wohnst.	It had slipped my mind that you too live in Cologne.

These anticipatory **da**-compounds are especially frequent if the ideas
contained in the dependent clause or in the infinitive phrase have
been expressed before in some form and are not news either for the
speaker or for the listener.

Governments

The U.S. is a presidential democracy in which the president serves
both as head of state and as head of government and is elected to
a set four-year term of office. The Federal Republic of Germany and
the Republic of Austria are parliamentary democracies with a president (**Bundespräsident**) who serves only as head of state for a fixed
term and a federal chancellor (**Bundeskanzler**) who serves as head
of government. The chancellor is always a member of the strongest
party in parliament; he can be dismissed by a vote of no confidence,
and he can call early elections.

Beim Wählen in der BRD

The parliaments of both countries have an upper house and a lower house. In the Federal Republic, the lower house (**Bundestag**) combines the functions of the American Senate and House; it is the only popularly elected body in the Federal Republic. The upper house (**Bundesrat**) represents the states (**Länder**) and is elected by the state governments. In Austria, the two houses are called the **Nationalrat** (lower house) and **Bundesrat** (upper house).

The federal government in Switzerland does not play as large a role as in the Federal Republic or Austria, and party politics are insignificant by comparison. The Swiss parliament also has two chambers which elect an executive council (**Bundesrat**) of seven members, one of whom serves as the federal president for a one-year term.

The German Democratic Republic is a socialist state based on "democratic centralism," a system in which all authority derives from the Socialist Unity Party (SED). The general secretary of the SED Central Committee serves also as head of state in his role as chairman of the Council of State. The government consists of the Council of Ministers (**Ministerrat**) and the People's Chamber (**Volkskammer**).

PRACTICE TWO

E. Read the following sentences aloud and supply the missing prepositions.

1. Ich glaube _____ Gott.
2. Wir haben _____ unserer Reise gesprochen.
3. Denkst du auch noch _____ mich?
4. Hast du schon _____ den Brief geantwortet?
5. Hast du auch nicht vergessen, ihn _____ seiner Frau zu fragen?
6. Ich danke Ihnen _____ Ihre Hilfe.
7. Meyer hat mich _____ einem Glas Wein eingeladen.
8. Dürfte ich _____ die Butter bitten?
9. Er spricht nie _____ seiner Frau.
10. _____ wen warten Sie denn?

F. Read the following sentences aloud and supply the missing articles or possessives.

1. Wir warten auf _____ Zug aus Hannover.
2. Wir warten auf _____ Bahnhof.
3. Fritzchen hat Angst vor _____ Abitur.
4. Er hat viel über _____ Krieg geschrieben.

5. Kurt stand an _____ Ecke und wartete auf _____ Freundin.
6. Gestern in _____ Schule haben wir über _____ Roman von Ingelheim gesprochen.
7. Ich halte nicht viel von _____ Film.
8. Meyer ist sehr stolz auf _____ Sohn.
9. Wie hat sie auf _____ Brief reagiert?
10. Frau Doktor, als Sie an die Tür kamen, habe ich Sie für _____ Tochter gehalten.

G. Join the following pairs of sentences by changing one of them into a relative clause.

1. Werners Vater sprach gut Englisch. Er hatte lange in Amerika gelebt.
2. Herr Schmitz sprach gut Englisch. Seine Frau kam aus London.
3. Ich habe dich im Theater mit einem jungen Mann gesehen. Wer war denn der junge Mann?
4. In Mainz besuchte ich meine Freundin Ingrid. Ich bin mit ihr in die Schule gegangen.
5. Ich wollte Hermann wiedersehen. Während des Krieges war ich mit ihm in Afrika.
6. Wer ist denn eigentlich dieser Schmitz? Du redest schon seit Tagen von ihm.
7. Der Brief lag vor ihr auf dem Tisch. Ihr Mann hatte ihn aus Rom geschickt.
8. Ich kann diese Postkarten doch nicht wegwerfen. Tante Amalie hat sie mir geschickt.

H. Fill in each blank by using a form of the demonstrative **der, die, das.**

1. Sollen Inge und Gerda auch kommen? — Nein, _____ brauchst du nicht einzuladen; _____ können zu Hause bleiben; mit _____ will ich nichts mehr zu tun haben.
2. Kennen Sie _____ Friedrich Bertram? — Aber natürlich; mit _____ war ich doch in Mainz auf der Schule.
3. Diese Tassen hier möchten Sie also doch nicht? — Nein, ich nehme lieber _____ da.
4. Nein, Maria; mit _____ Hut kannst du nicht nach Paris fahren. _____ läßt du besser zu Hause. — Aber Paul, _____ kommt doch aus Paris. _____ hast du mir doch letztes Jahr aus Paris mitgebracht.
5. Dieser Kaffee ist aber gut. Wo hast du _____ denn gekauft? — _____ hat mein Mann gekauft. — Dein Mann? Versteht _____ was von Kaffee?

CONVERSATIONS

The following is one continuous conversation in typical, everyday German, containing quite a few subjunctive constructions. Read it aloud several times; then follow the instructions under **II** below.

I

TELEFONISTIN: Hotel Bayerischer Hof, guten Morgen.
KLAUS: Guten Morgen. Ich hätte gerne Zimmer 641 (sechseinundvierzig).
TELEFONISTIN: Einen Augenblick, bitte.

ROSEMARIE:	Ja, bitte?
KLAUS:	Rosemarie? Guten Morgen.
ROSEMARIE:	Klaus? Guten Morgen. Du hättest aber wirklich nicht so früh anzurufen brauchen. Ich schlafe ja noch.
KLAUS:	Das höre ich.
ROSEMARIE:	Wieviel Uhr ist es denn? Sieben? Oder ist es schon acht?
KLAUS:	Acht? Es ist zwanzig nach zehn.
ROSEMARIE:	Nein, das ist nicht möglich—zwanzig nach zehn?
KLAUS:	Doch, das *ist* möglich. Wenn es *nicht* schon so spät wäre, hätte ich dich nicht angerufen.
ROSEMARIE:	Ja, und wenn wir gestern abend nicht so lange getanzt hätten, wäre ich auch schon lange auf.
KLAUS:	Aber wer wollte denn gestern so lange tanzen, du oder ich?
ROSEMARIE:	Ich, natürlich. Wenn ich nur zwei Tage in München bin, will ich doch auch etwas erleben.
KLAUS:	Na, *so* interessant ist diese Diskothek ja *auch* nicht!
ROSEMARIE:	Du, Klaus, wo bist du denn eigentlich? Hier im Hotel?
KLAUS:	Nein, ich bin noch zu Hause. Aber wenn du willst, komme ich um elf ins Hotel. Dann können wir zusammen frühstücken. Du könntest natürlich auch auf deinem Zimmer frühstücken, und ich komme erst um zwölf—wie du willst.
ROSEMARIE:	Nein, das möchte ich nicht. Wenn ich nur drei Nächte in München bin, will ich mit *dir* frühstücken.
KLAUS:	Gut, Rosemarie—ich bin um elf in der Hotelhalle—und es wäre schön, wenn du nicht erst um zwölf kämst: ich habe Hunger, ich bin schon seit acht Uhr auf.
ROSEMARIE:	Aber Klaus, du weißt doch, daß du nie auf mich zu warten brauchst. Gestern hast du auch gesagt, daß ich um acht Uhr da sein müßte odcr wir kämen nicht mehr in das Restaurant—wie hieß es doch?
KLAUS:	Feldherrnkeller.
ROSEMARIE:	Ja richtig—wir kämen nicht mehr in den Feldherrnkeller, weil dort immer so viele Leute seien. Na, und wann war ich da? Um zehn vor acht.—Übrigens,

München, Ludwigstraße von der Feldherrnhalle

Klaus, wie ist denn das Wetter? Ich habe noch nicht aus dem Fenster gesehen, aber es wäre schön, wenn heute die Sonne schiene.

KLAUS: Das Wetter könnte nicht besser sein. Heute morgen sah es ja aus, als ob es wieder regnen würde—und wenn du nicht hier wärst, hätte es heute bestimmt geregnet.

ROSEMARIE: Vielen Dank für das Kompliment, Klaus. Aber wenn es geregnet hätte, das hätte auch nichts gemacht. Wir hätten ja in ein Museum gehen können. Aber weißt du was? Ich ginge nach dem Frühstück gerne durch die Stadt; ich möchte mir doch einen Mantel kaufen, und es wäre nett, wenn wir das zusammen machen könnten.

KLAUS: Gut—und was machen wir, wenn wir den Mantel gekauft haben?

ROSEMARIE: Dann könnten wir eine Stunde auf einer Bank in der Sonne sitzen.

KLAUS: Im Hofgarten.[8] Das wäre prima. Wir gehen eine Stunde in den Hofgarten, und dann gehen wir essen.

ROSEMARIE: Du, aber bitte in ein Restaurant, wo keine Touristen sind, ja, Klaus? Ich wollte, in München wären nicht immer so viele Touristen.

KLAUS: Ja, was wäre München ohne die Touristen! Aber ich kenne ein Restaurant bei der Universität; da ist noch nie ein Tourist gewesen, nur Studenten. Wie wäre das, Rosemarie?

ROSEMARIE: Du, das wäre nett. Übrigens, hast du gestern nicht gesagt, daß es heute abend die *Fledermaus*[9] gibt°?   **es gibt** they are playing

KLAUS: Ja, im Theater am Gärtnerplatz. Das ist eine Idee. Wie wäre es, wenn wir heute abend ins Theater gingen?

ROSEMARIE: Gerne, ich habe die *Fledermaus* noch nie gesehen. Und dann könnten wir nach Schwabing[10] gehen und tanzen, ja?

KLAUS: Und ein Glas Wein trinken,—und jetzt ist es halb elf, und wenn ich jetzt nicht gehe, bist du um elf Uhr *doch* nicht in der Halle. Oder soll ich doch lieber erst um zwölf kommen?

ROSEMARIE: Nein, nein—ich bin bestimmt da.

II

Now construct some brief exchanges based on the conversation above; for example, arrange with a friend to meet at a certain time and place; discuss a proposed shopping expedition or a visit to a museum or theater; or recall something you did the day before.

III

Using the map and information below, talk about topics such as the following:

1. Why do you want to spend your vacation in Strümpfelbach?
2. Where is Strümpfelbach?
3. How does one get there?

[8]The Royal Gardens, a public park in the center of Munich.
[9]Operetta by Johann Strauss— (*lit.*) The Bat.
[10]Artists' and students' quarter near the University of Munich.

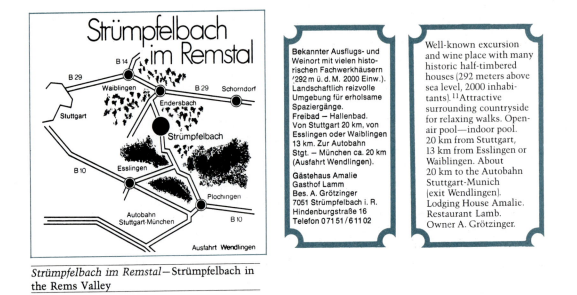

Strümpfelbach im Remstal:

Bekannter Ausflugs- und Weinort mit vielen historischen Fachwerkhäusern (292 m ü. d. M. 2000 Einw.). Landschaftlich reizvolle Umgebung für erholsame Spaziergänge. Freibad — Hallenbad. Von Stuttgart 20 km, von Esslingen oder Waiblingen 13 km. Zur Autobahn Stgt. — München ca. 20 km (Ausfahrt Wendlingen).

Gästehaus Amalie
Gasthof Lamm
Bes. A. Grötzinger
7051 Strümpfelbach i. R.
Hindenburgstraße 16
Telefon 07151 / 61102

Well-known excursion and wine place with many historic half-timbered houses (292 meters above sea level, 2000 inhabitants).[11] Attractive surrounding countryside for relaxing walks. Open-air pool—indoor pool. 20 km from Stuttgart, 13 km from Esslingen or Waiblingen. About 20 km to the Autobahn Stuttgart-Munich (exit Wendlingen). Lodging House Amalie. Restaurant Lamb. Owner A. Grötzinger.

Strümpfelbach im Remstal—Strümpfelbach in the Rems Valley

IV

1. Make a topical list of vocabulary on education; divide into three sections: (1) school, (2) university, (3) general educational terms, such as **lernen** or **die Prüfung**.

2. Ask your teacher to play the role of a "native informant" whom you can question about such topics as (1) his or her own education, (2) the education of his or her children, (3) education reform.

3. Prepare a report, to be given orally before your class, on some aspect of education in Germany. Use the lists you made, as well as the pattern sentences and the reading selections of Unit 12.

V

The following colloquial phrases were introduced in Units 9 to 12. Review them and incorporate them into your conversations as much as possible. Also review the list of phrases in Unit 8, p. 243.

Ich wollte/ich wünschte . . . (*with subj.*)	I wish . . .
Es wäre schön/nett/gut, wenn . . . (*with subj.*)	It would be nice if . . .
Wie wäre es, wenn . . . (*with subj.*)	How would it be if/how about . . .
Würdest du/würden Sie bitte . . .	Would you please . . .
Es sieht aus, als (ob) . . . (*with subj.*)	It looks as if . . .
aber gern(e)	(I'll) be glad to . . .
Ich hätte gern(e) . . .	I'd like to have . . .
lieber . . .	I'd prefer to/would rather . . .
am liebsten . . .	I'd like best to . . .
(Das ist/wäre eine) gute Idee.	(That is/would be a) good idea.
genau	exactly, that's right
gottseidank	thank goodness

[11]Above sea level: **ü. d. M. = über dem Meeresspiegel**; inhabitants: **Einw. = Einwohner**.

unbedingt	absolutely
Ich meine . . .	I mean/think . . .
Was meinst du/meinen Sie?	What do you mean/think?
Was hältst du/halten Sie davon?	What do you think of it?
Was ist denn?	What's the matter?
Ach so.	Oh (now I understand).
Einen Augenblick.	Just a moment.

Fragen an Sie persönlich

1. Welche Schulen haben Sie bisher besucht°?   attended
2. Was halten Sie vom amerikanischen Schulsystem?
            von der amerikanischen Grade School?
                        High School?
            vom amerikanischen College?
3. Was ist Ihr Hauptfach°?   major
    Warum haben Sie dieses Hauptfach gewählt°?   chosen
4. Wollen Sie auf die Graduate School?
    Wenn ja, auf welche?
            in welchem Fach?
5. Wollen Sie promovieren°?   get a doctorate (Ph.D., M.D., etc.)
6. Was sind Ihre Berufspläne°?   career plans
7. Wozu, meinen Sie, soll eine College-Ausbildung dienen, zur All-   general education
    gemeinbildung° oder zur Vorbereitung° auf einen Beruf?   preparation

READING

ERICH KÄSTNER

Erich Kästner (1899–1974) is best known in the United States for his children's story *Emil und die Detektive* (1929). He wrote, especially in the late 1920s and 30s, a large number of humorous and satirical poems, one of which is the following "Sachliche Romanze" (1929). Because of his bitter social criticism, much of which was directed against German militaristic tendencies, he was forbidden to write by the Nazis, and his books were burned in 1933. He stayed in Germany, however, and, after World War II, wrote for the American-sponsored *Neue Zeitung* in Munich from 1945–48. He refers to his poetry, most of which is written in the same matter-of-fact style as the "Sachliche Romanze," as *Gebrauchslyrik* ("utility poetry").

Erich Kästner

Sachliche° Romanze   matter-of-fact

Als sie einander acht Jahre kannten
(und man darf sagen: sie kannten sich gut),
kam° ihre Liebe plötzlich abhanden°.   got lost
Wie andern Leuten ein Stock° oder Hut.   walking stick, cane

Sie waren traurig°, betrugen sich heiter°,   5   sad   acted cheerful
versuchten Küsse°, als ob nichts sei,   kisses
und sahen sich° an und wußten nicht weiter.   each other
Da weinte° sie schließlich°. Und er stand dabei.   cried   at last

Vom Fenster aus konnte man Schiffen winken°.   wave at
Er sagte, es wäre schon Viertel nach Vier   10
und Zeit, irgendwo Kaffee zu trinken.
Nebenan° übte° ein Mensch Klavier.   next door   practiced

Sie gingen ins kleinste Café am Ort
und rührten° in ihren Tassen.   stirred
Am Abend saßen sie noch immer dort.   15
Sie saßen allein, und sie sprachen kein Wort
und konnten es einfach nicht fassen°.   comprehend

Schulen in Deutschland
oder
Wie real ist die Realschule?

„Meine Tochter geht seit fünf Jahren aufs Gymnasium", erklärt Herr
Hinz dem Besucher aus Amerika. „Oh", sagt der Besucher, „dann ist
sie wohl Sportlerin von Beruf°." „Nein, sie ist Schülerin, und in Sport   professional athlete
hat sie Vier plus." „Vier plus", denkt der Besucher, „das ist doch ein
A plus", und er sagt: „Dann ist sie sicher die beste in ihrer Klasse." 5
„Im Gegenteil°", sagt Herr Hinz, „sie ist sportlich ganz unbegabt°."   on the contrary
Als der Besucher mit Frau Kunz über ihre Kinder spricht, erfährt   untalented
er, daß der Sohn auf der Realschule ist, und er überlegt°, ob es in   wonders
Deutschland wohl auch „unreal schools" gibt. Die Tochter ist 24
Jahre alt und auf der Hochschule für Musik. „So alt", meint der 10
Besucher, „und immer noch auf der High School?" „Nein, nein", sagt
Frau Kunz, „,Hochschule' ist das gleiche° wie ,Universität'. Ihre High same
School in Amerika ist das gleiche wie unsere ,höhere Schule'." „Aber
das ist doch paradox, daß die höhere Schule nicht so hoch ist wie
die Hochschule!"   15

Und als Xaver Schreibmeyer ihm erklärt, in Deutschland gäbe es
kein College, aber zehn Minuten später beim Weggehen sagt, er
müsse jetzt ins Kolleg°, da ist der Besucher aus Amerika ganz ver-   lecture
zweifelt°.   in despair

Unser Besucher aus Amerika ist natürlich eine Fiktion. Aber 20
Amerikaner, die das deutsche Schulsystem kennenlernen wollen,

Johann Wolfgang Goethe-
Universität
Frankfurt am Main

haben am Anfang immer das gleiche Problem: sie begegnen einem
Begriff°, den sie zu verstehen glauben, aber der Begriff hat im
Deutschen eine ganz andere Bedeutung°. *Das Gymnasium* ist nicht
the gymnasium, obwohl es das gleiche Wort ist. Griechisch° *gym-* 25
nasion, von *gymnos, nackt*, war zuerst° der Ort, wo man Sport
trieb°, später auch der Platz, wo die Philosophen zusammenkamen.
Das Englische hat die erste Bedeutung beibehalten°, und im
Deutschen benutzt man seit dem sechzehnten Jahrhundert die
zweite Bedeutung für die höhere Schule, für die Akademie, die junge 30
Leute auf die Universität vorbereitet°.

Statt *höhere Schule* sagt man im Amerikanischen *high school*, aber
die Übersetzung° von *high school, Hochschule*, entspricht° im
Deutschen der *Universität*. Das deutsche Wort *Kolleg* und das
englisch-amerikanische *College* gehen beide zurück auf das latei- 35
nische *collegium*, aber im Deutschen ist ein *Kolleg* eine *Vorlesung,
a lecture*, das englische *College* ist Teil° einer Universität, und das
amerikanische *College* ist synonym mit *undergraduate school*.

Schließlich° hat *Real-* nichts mit *wirklich* zu tun, und die *Realschule* ist keine „real school". Das Wort bedeutet hier eine Orien- 40
tierung auf das Praktische und Technische, im Gegensatz° zum
Gymnasium, das mehr auf Theorie und Philosophie hin° orientiert
ist.

An die Bedeutung dieser Begriffe ist man bald gewöhnt°, aber es ist
nicht so leicht, das System der Schulen in der Bundesrepublik zu 45
verstehen, denn es basiert° auf einem ganz anderen Prinzip als die
Schulen in Amerika.

Die Tradition des Schulsystems in Deutschland ist elitär°. Früher
gab es° nur die Volksschule, das heißt, die Schule für das „Volk",
für den „gemeinen Mann"°, und daneben das Gymnasium, die 50
Akademie für die „Gebildeten"°. Bis lange nach dem zweiten Welt-

encounter a term	
meaning	
Greek	
at first	
exercised	
retained	
prepares	
translation	
corresponds to	
part of	
finally	
contrast	
auf . . . hin toward	
used to	
is based	
elitist	
there used to be	
common man	
educated and cultured	

krieg gingen nur wenige Kinder von Arbeitern aufs Gymnasium, und das, was man im Englischen „social mobility" nennt, gab es kaum. Nur wer das Abitur hatte, „war etwas", und wer die Universität besucht hat, den nennt man auch heute noch einen „Akademiker". Das 55 intellektuelle Niveau° der alten Gymnasien und Universitäten war sehr hoch, und die Zahl der Abiturienten° war sehr klein, die Zahl der Doktoranden° noch viel kleiner. Aber das System war auch sehr ungerecht°, denn die Entscheidung°, ob Gymnasium oder nicht, mußten Eltern schon treffen°, wenn ihre Kinder erst zehn Jahre alt 60 waren, das heißt, nach vier Jahren Volksschule.

In der Bundesrepublik, in der Schweiz und in Österreich stehen die Schulen auch heute noch vertikal nebeneinander. Neben dem Gymnasium gibt es die Realschule (oder Mittelschule) und die Volksschule, die in der Bundesrepublik jetzt Hauptschule heißt. Von der 65 ersten bis zur vierten Klasse gehen alle Kinder in die gleiche Schule, die Grundschule.

Im Gegensatz° dazu ist das amerikanische Schulsystem horizontal gegliedert° und deshalb° im Prinzip egalitär und nicht elitär. Nach der grade school gehen alle Kinder in die junior high school und 70 dann, bis zum Ende der Schulpflicht°, in die high school. Jeder, der will, kann auf ein College gehen, und braucht dazu keine Prüfung wie das Abitur abzulegen°.

Interessanterweise ist das Schulsystem in der DDR dem amerikanischen viel ähnlicher° als dem westdeutschen. Alle Kinder besuchen von sechs bis sechzehn Jahren eine „allgemeinbildende, polytechnische Oberschule"°, die Basis des sozialistischen Schulsystems.

	level
	Gymnasium graduates
	doctoral candidates
	unjust decision
	make
	contrast
	structured therefore
	compulsory schooling
	take, pass
	more similar
	general-education, poly-technic high school

Oberschule in Weimar

REVIEW EXERCISES

I. In the following sentences, substitute for the prepositional phrase in the front field (a) a stressed **da**-compound and (b) the preposition plus demonstrative article.

> **Für *den* Wein hast du zuviel bezahlt.**
> (a) ***Da*für hast du zuviel bezahlt.**
> (b) **Für *den* hast du zuviel bezahlt.**

1. Mit *dem* Wagen fahre ich nicht.
2. Von *die*sem Film halte ich nicht viel.
3. In *die*sem Bett kann ich nicht schlafen.
4. Für *den* Wagen bezahle ich keine zehntausend Mark.
5. Mit *mei*ner Kamera kann ich auch bei Nacht Aufnahmen machen.

J. Using the verbs in parentheses, form main clauses containing a **da**-compound anticipating the dependent clause.

> **(oft denken), daß du mich bald besuchen wirst.**
> **Ich denke oft daran, daß du mich bald besuchen wirst.**

1. (sehr hoffen), daß er morgen kommen kann.
2. (gerade sprechen), daß er im Sommer nach Italien fahren will.
3. (warten), daß mein Mann endlich nach Hause kommt.
4. (nicht viel halten), daß meine Tochter Psychologie studieren will.
5. (wohl bitten dürfen), daß Sie um acht Uhr im Büro sind.

K. Expand the prepositional objects in the following sentences into **daß**-clauses.

> **Ich warte auf einen Brief von ihr.**
> **Ich warte darauf, daß sie mir schreibt.**

1. Ich möchte Ihnen noch einmal für Ihre Hilfe danken.
2. An seinen Geburtstag gestern habe ich gar nicht gedacht.
3. Er war sehr glücklich über den Erfolg seines Buches.
4. Lacht sie immer noch über seinen Akzent?

L. Expand the prepositional objects in the following sentences into infinitive phrases.

> **Erika denkt gar nicht an eine Italienreise.**
> **Erika denkt gar nicht daran, nach Italien zu fahren.**

1. Darf ich Sie zu einem Glas Wein einladen, Herr Rohrmoser?
2. Ich habe meinen Freund um Ingelheims Romane gebeten.
3. Hoffst du immer noch auf ein Wiedersehen mit ihr?
4. Ich hoffe auf ein Wiedersehen mit Ihnen.
5. Ich habe wochenlang auf einen Brief von ihr gewartet.

M. Supply the missing words.

1. Es wäre nett, _____ du mit mir in das Restaurant gehen _____, von _____ du gestern abend gesprochen hast.
2. Ist das der Mantel, _____ du dir in München gekauft hast?
3. Hast du auch _____ gedacht, daß ich morgen Geburtstag _____?
4. Frau Meyer war sehr stolz _____ Fritz, _____ er hatte endlich das Abitur gemacht.
5. Wie lange wartest du schon auf _____ Bus, Karl?
6. _____ Inge kam, _____ wir sofort in die Stadt gefahren, _____ ins Kino zu gehen.
7. Wenn wir nicht ins Kino gegangen _____, _____ wir zu Hause ferngesehen.
8. Er fragte mich, _____ ich die Tochter von Direktor Helbig _____.
9. Das Buch kostet bestimmt nicht mehr _____ öS 200.
10. Möchtest du nicht mitfahren? — _____, aber nur _____ zum Bahnhof.

N. Construct sentences as indicated.

1. The woman I saw yesterday is a teacher at the Wöhler-Gymnasium.
   (a) The woman is a teacher. (professional status!)
   (b) add: *at the Wöhler-Gymnasium* (Use **am.**)
   (c) I saw her yesterday.
   (d) gender, case of *her*?

(e) change *her* to *whom* (You *must* use relative pronoun.)

(f) whom I saw yesterday (Don't forget commas.)

(g) insert relative clause after *The woman*

2. The trip I took was very interesting.
   (a) The trip was interesting.
   (b) I took a trip. (Use **machen**.)
   (c) case, gender, of *trip*?
   (d) which I took (commas!)
   (e) insert relative clause after *The trip*

3. This is Mrs. Meyer whose son you met last night.
   (a) This is Mrs. Meyer.
   (b) You met her son last night.
   (c) change *her son* to *whose son*
   (d) start (b) with *whose son* (verb-last position!)
   (e) add relative clause to (a)

4. Dr. Scholte is the man I have to fly to Berlin with tomorrow.
   (a) I have to fly to Berlin.
   (b) add: *with him*
   (c) add: *tomorrow*
   (d) change *with him* to *with whom*
   (e) with whom I have to fly to Berlin tomorrow
   (f) Dr. Scholte is the man
   (g) add relative clause

O. Express in German.

1. The man with whom Mrs. Ingelheim is talking is called Behrens.
2. Doris wanted to know whether I could pick her up at the station.
3. When did you pick her up?
4. Can you tell me when you picked her up? (indicative)
5. When I arrived, she was not there yet.
6. He acted as if the house belonged to him.
7. He looked as if he hadn't slept well.
8. You know him better than her, don't you?
9. That was more than I had expected.
10. That was a moment I will not forget.
11. The man I saw in front of the house was Erich.
12. He said that he had seen nothing at all.
13. If I'm not there at three o'clock, you'll simply have to wait for me.
14. And this is a picture of our house. —And where is the garage? —It's behind it.
15. In front of the house stood a Mercedes; next to it stood a Volkswagen.

P. Using the map above, write a letter to a friend or relative:

       Herrn/Frau

       X.Y.

       Bahnhofstr. 27

       D-0000 A-Stadt

You have just arrived for a two weeks' winter vacation at the Hirzingerhof, a resort hotel in Kitzbühel in the Austrian Tyrol. Describe how you got there, how you like the place, and what your plans are for the next two weeks.

Start your letter as follows:
    Lieber Fritz, (Liebe Tante Amalie, Liebe Frau Enderle)
and sign off with
    Mit herzlichen Grüßen
    Dein (Deine, Ihr, Ihre)

Herzlichen Gruß aus Dortmund.

VOCABULARY

allgemein	general	**entweder . . . oder**	either . . . or
im allgemeinen	generally	**erfahren**	to find out, learn; to experience
der Anfang, ⸚e	beginning		
die Aufnahme, -n	photograph, picture	**erklären**	to explain; to declare
der Augenblick, -e	moment, instant		
(einen) Augenblick, bitte	just a moment, please	**erwarten**	to expect
		das Fach, ⸚er	(academic) subject, discipline
die Bedeutung, -en	meaning, importance		
begegnen (*with dat.*)	to meet (by chance)	**die Fremdsprache, -n**	foreign language
bestehen	to pass (an examination)	**das Hauptfach, ⸚er**	(academic) major
		die Gara'ge, -n	garage
bestehen aus	to consist of	**das Gegenteil, -e**	opposite
bisher (*adv.*)	up to now, so far	**im Gegenteil**	on the contrary
der Briefträger, -	mailman	**gelingen (sein)**	to succeed
dienen (*with dat.*)	to serve, be used for	(*impers.*)	
durch•fallen (sein)	to flunk (an examination)	**es gelingt mir**	I succeed
		der Gott, ⸚er	god
die Empfehlung, -en	recommendation	**der Gruß, ⸚e**	greeting
die Entscheidung, -en	decision	**halten für**	to consider
eine Entscheidung treffen	to make a decision	**halten von**	to have an opinion about

irgendwo	somewhere; anywhere
das Jahrhun′dert, -e	century
das Klavier, -e	piano
der Kugelschreiber, -	ballpoint pen
meist	most
am meisten	most of all
mündlich	oral(ly)
nachdenken über (*acc.*)	to think about, meditate about
der Name, -n (*n-noun*) (*gen.* **Namens**)	name
nebenan	next door
nebeneinander	next to each other
die Prüfung, -en	examination
reagieren auf (*acc.*)	to react to
die Reihe, -n	row; series
schließlich	finally, after all
schriftlich	in writing
der Schriftsteller, -	writer, author
die Schule, -n	school
die höhere Schule, -n	secondary school, *Gymnasium*
die Hochschule, -n	university, institution of higher learning
der Schüler, - (*m.*) **die Schülerin, -nen** (*f.*)	pupil, (*Gymnasium*) student
das Semester, -	semester
stammen aus	to come from, be a native of
stolz sein auf (*acc.*)	to be proud of
tanzen	to dance
üben	to practice
überset′zen	to translate
die Übersetzung, -en	translation
der Unterricht	instruction
verbessern	to improve, to make better; to correct
verdienen	to earn
Geld verdienen	to make money
vergleichen mit	to compare with
verliebt sein in (*acc.*)	to be in love with, to be infatuated
verlobt sein mit	to be engaged to
die Verschmutzung	pollution
verwenden	to use, make use of, put to use
vor•schlagen	to suggest, propose
der Vorschlag, ⸚e	proposal
der Vortrag, ⸚e	(formal) lecture
die Weihnachtsferien (*pl.*)	Christmas vacation
werfen	to throw
weg•werfen	to throw away
wiederho′len	to repeat
das Wunder, -	miracle
das Zeugnis, -se	report card
zufrieden sein mit	to be satisfied with

Strong Verbs and Irregular Weak Verbs

INFINITIVE	PRESENT	PAST TENSE	PERFECT	
bestehen		**bestand**	**bestanden**	to pass (an examination)
durch•fallen	**fällt durch**	**fiel durch**	**ist durchgefallen**	to flunk (an examination)
erfahren	**erfährt**	**erfuhr**	**erfahren**	to find out, learn; to experience
gelingen		**gelang**	**ist gelungen**	to succeed
nach•denken		**dachte nach**	**nachgedacht**	to think, meditate
vergleichen		**verglich**	**verglichen**	to compare
verwenden		**verwandte (verwendete)**	**verwandt (verwendet)**	to use
vor•schlagen	**schlägt vor**	**schlug vor**	**vorgeschlagen**	to suggest, propose
werfen	**wirft**	**warf**	**geworfen**	to throw

Unit 13

Present and Past Infinitives—Objective and Subjective Use of Modals—Negation in the Inner Field—Contrary-to-Fact Conditions without *wenn*

Vacations

During the major vacation months of July and August, massive traffic jams occur on every autobahn leading south. Historically, the Germans have yearned for the sunny south, and as more and more families acquired automobiles, Mediterranean beaches were suddenly in easy reach. During the 1960s and 1970s, West Germans experienced a **Reisewelle** (*travel wave*); the most popular foreign destinations were Austria, Italy, Spain, Portugal, and France. Austria and Switzerland, of course, are typical tourist countries, and tourism is a major source of their income. In recent years, however, there has been a reverse trend to vacation in one's own country, especially on the coasts of the Baltic and North Sea.

In the German Democratic Republic, the state strongly supports recreational holiday travel, both within the country and in the East Bloc. The state maintains hundreds of vacation facilities, and the state travel office books more than 3 million trips per year.

Almost 90% of West German workers are contractually entitled to at least 5 weeks of vacation per year. Schools have shorter summer vacations than in the U.S., but there are vacations of seven to ten days at Christmas, Easter, Pentecost, and in the middle of the fall. University vacations (**Semesterferien**) come in two blocks between semesters, in the early spring and in the late summer.

Die beliebtesten Reiseziele
1985 unternahmen die Bundesbürger (über 14 Jahre) insgesamt 32,3 Millionen Urlaubsreisen

Innerhalb Deutschlands in Mio	Außerhalb Deutschlands in Mio	
3,5 Bayern	Italien	3,9
Schleswig-Holstein 2,0	Spanien	3,5
Baden-Württemberg 1,7	Österreich	3,2
Niedersachsen 1,4	1,8	Jugoslawien
Berlin, Hamburg, Bremen 0,8	1,7	Frankreich
Nordrhein-Westfalen 0,8	0,9	Griechenland
Rheinland-Pfalz Saarland 0,5	0,8	Schweiz
Hessen 0,5	0,7	Dänemark
DDR 0,2	0,6	Niederlande
	3,8	sonstige

Quelle: Studienkreis für Tourismus

© Globus

GÄSTEKARTE

Steirisches
Salzkammergut

Altaussee/Loser	Pichl-Kainisch
Bad Aussee	Bad Mitterndorf
Grundlsee	Tauplitz/Tauplitzalm

Lieber Gast!

Die Bürgermeister und Bewohner des steirischen Salzkammergutes heißen Sie herzlich willkommen und wünschen Ihnen schöne und frohe Urlaubstage.

Mit der Abgabe dieser Gästekarte nehmen Sie an der Verlosung eines Freiaufenthaltes in Ihrem Urlaubsort teil.

PATTERNS ONE

1/Past Infinitives

Sie scheint zu schlafen.
Sie scheint gut geschlafen zu haben.

Er schien zu schlafen.
Er schien gut geschlafen zu haben.

Christine schien sehr glücklich zu sein.
Christine scheint sehr glücklich gewesen zu sein.

Er muß schlafen.
Er muß geschlafen haben.

Tante Amalie muß schon wieder im Museum gewesen sein.

2/The Objective and Subjective Use of *müssen*

OBJECTIVE

Sie muß am Dienstag nach Heidelberg fahren.
   She has to go to Heidelberg on Tuesday.

Sie mußte oft Geschäftsreisen in die Schweiz machen.
   She often had to take business trips to Switzerland.

Er sagte, er müßte nächste Woche wieder nach Bern.
   He said he had to go to Berne again next week.

Wenn er nicht krank geworden wäre, hätte er nach Bern fahren müssen.
   If he hadn't gotten sick, he would have had to go to Berne.

SUBJECTIVE

Ich habe ihn schon lange nicht gesehen; er muß wieder in der Schweiz sein.
   I haven't seen him for a long time; he must be in Switzerland again.

Sie muß lange in England gelebt haben, denn sie spricht Englisch praktisch ohne Akzent.
   She must have lived in England for a long time, because she speaks English practically without
      an accent.

Heute ist Donnerstag. Andrea müßte heute eigentlich in Salzburg sein.
   Today is Thursday. Andrea ought to be in Salzburg today.

Ruf doch mal den Bahnhof an. Der Zug müßte doch schon lange angekommen sein.
   Why don't you call the station? That train ought to have arrived a long time ago.

3/*können*

OBJECTIVE

Klaus ist krank und kann leider nicht kommen.
> Klaus is sick and unfortunately can't come.

Seine Frau sagte, er sei krank und könne leider nicht kommen.
> His wife said he was sick and unfortunately wouldn't be able to come.

Könnte ich vielleicht ein Zimmer mit Bad haben?
> Could I have a room with bath?

SUBJECTIVE

Intelligent kann er nicht sein. Sonst würde er nicht für Meyer arbeiten.
> He can't be intelligent. Otherwise he wouldn't work for Meyer.

Der Junge konnte nicht älter sein als sechs.
> The boy couldn't be older than six.

Ich glaube, wir sollten heute im Garten arbeiten. Morgen könnte es regnen.
> I think we should work in the garden today. It could (might) rain tomorrow.

Ich weiß nicht, wer angerufen hat, aber es könnte Helga gewesen sein.
> I don't know who called, but it could have been Helga.

4/*wollen*

OBJECTIVE

Tante Amalie will die Osterferien bei uns verbringen.
> Aunt Amalie wants to spend Easter vacation with us.

Sie wollte auch an Weihnachten zu uns kommen, aber dann ist sie krank geworden.
> She wanted to come at Christmas too, but then she became sick.

SUBJECTIVE

Er will Ingenieur sein, aber das glaube ich nicht.
> He claims to be an engineer, but I don't believe it.

Er will in Rom studiert haben, aber er spricht kein Wort Italienisch.
> He claims to have studied in Rome, but he doesn't speak a word of Italian.

Er wollte ein Freund meines Großvaters gewesen sein.
> He claimed to have been a friend of my grandfather's.

5/*sollen*

OBJECTIVE

Wir sollen morgen um acht auf dem Bahnhof sein.
> We are supposed to be at the station at eight tomorrow.

Er sagte, wir sollten morgen um acht Uhr auf dem Bahnhof sein.
> He said we were to be at the station at eight tomorrow.

SUBJECTIVE

In Österreich sollen die Hotels viel billiger sein als in der Schweiz.
In Austria the hotels are supposed to be much cheaper than in Switzerland.

Hast du etwas von Dietlinde gehört?—Die soll im Juni geheiratet haben. Ihr Mann soll Ingenieur sein.
Have you heard anything about Dietlinde?—I've heard that she got married last June. I understand her husband is an engineer.

6/*mögen*

OBJECTIVE

Ingelheims Romane sind ja ganz gut, aber als Mensch mag ich ihn gar nicht.
Ingelheim's novels aren't bad, but as a person I don't care for him at all.

Ich mochte ihn schon nicht, als wir noch auf dem Gymnasium waren.
I disliked him already when we were still in the *Gymnasium.*

Meine Frau hat ihn auch nie gemocht.
My wife never liked him either.

Danke, Schweinefleisch mag ich nicht; ich esse lieber ein Steak.
Thanks, I don't care for pork; I'd rather have a steak.

SUBJECTIVE

Wie alt ist seine Tochter eigentlich?—Oh, ich weiß nicht. Sie mag achtzehn oder neunzehn sein.
How old is his daughter?—Oh, I don't know, maybe eighteen or nineteen.

Er mochte damals etwa dreißig sein.
> At that time, he was probably about thirty.

Er mag gedacht haben, ich hätte ihn nicht gesehen.
> He may have thought that I hadn't seen him.

7/*dürfen*

OBJECTIVE

Darf ich heute abend ins Kino gehen, Mutti?
Kann ich heute abend ins Kino gehen, Mutti?
> May I go to the movies tonight, Mom?

Ich fragte sie, ob ich sie nach Hause bringen dürfte.
> I asked her whether I could (might) take her home.

Rauchen darf man hier leider nicht.
> Unfortunately, smoking is not permitted here.

SUBJECTIVE

Wann ist er denn weggefahren? — Vor zwei Stunden. — Dann dürfte er jetzt schon in Frankfurt sein.
> When did he leave? — Two hours ago. — Then we can assume that he is in Frankfurt by now.

Ich möchte wissen, wer gestern abend um elf noch angerufen hat. — Das dürfte Erich gewesen sein; der ruft doch immer so spät an.
> I wonder who called last night at eleven. — I suppose that was Erich; he always calls that late, doesn't he?

8/**werden**

OBJECTIVE

Wir werden im Juni heiraten.
> We will get married in June.

Ich fahre morgen an die See, aber ich werde nicht lange bleiben.
> I'm going to the ocean tomorrow, but I won't stay long.

SUBJECTIVE

Wenn diese Perlen so teuer sind, werden sie wohl echt sein.
> If these pearls are that expensive, then I guess they are genuine.

Er wird Schwierigkeiten mit seinem Wagen gehabt haben; sonst hätte er von hier bis nach Mailand keine drei Tage gebraucht.
> He's probably had trouble with his car; otherwise he wouldn't have taken three days (to get) from here to Milan.

ANALYSIS ONE

109/Present and Past Infinitives

The infinitives we have used up to now have all been present infinitives; they are called "present" because they refer to the same time as the inflected verb of the sentence, regardless of the tense of the inflected verb.

Er scheint zu schlafen.	He seems to be asleep.
Er schien zu schlafen.	He seemed to be asleep.

The action described by the infinitive **schlafen** and the action described by the inflected verb **scheint** or **schien** occur at the same time.

If the action described by the infinitive occurs earlier than the action described by the inflected verb, a "past" infinitive construction must be used. The past infinitive consists of a past participle followed by the infinitive of the auxiliary, either **haben** or **sein**, and **zu** stands between the participle and the infinitive. After modals, **zu** is not used.

Er scheint geschlafen zu haben.	He seems to have been asleep.
Er schien geschlafen zu haben.	He seemed to have been asleep.
Er muß schlafen.	He has to sleep.
Er muß geschlafen haben.	He must have slept.

110/Objective and Subjective Use of Modals

Consider the use of *must* in the following two sentences:

Schmidt says: 1. Meyer must be at the office by eight every morning.
2. It is now nine. He surely must be there by now.

In sentence 1, Schmidt says that the subject, Meyer, is compelled to be at the office at a certain time. He reports this as a fact. In sentence 2, however, the speaker is not describing Meyer's obligation to be at the office, but reports his own conclusion that Meyer indeed is there, given the fact that he has to report for work by eight.

In sentence 1, the modal *must* is used *objectively*, and in sentence 2, it is used *subjectively*.

Since subjective conclusions can also be drawn about past actions or events, *must* can be used with a past infinitive.

At nine Meyer must have been at the office.

Like English *must*, German modals can also be used objectively or
subjectively. The subjective use of modals is restricted to the present
and past tense indicative and to the present subjunctive.

müssen

OBJ.	**Meyer muß jeden Morgen um acht Uhr im Büro sein.**	Meyer must be (has to be) at the office every morning at eight.
SUBJ.	**Jetzt ist es neun Uhr. Meyer muß also jetzt schon im Büro sein.**	It's now nine o'clock. Meyer must be at the office by now.
	Meyer muß heute im Büro gewesen sein.	Meyer must have been at the office today.

The objective sentence implies that Meyer's job requires him to be
at the office at a certain time. The subjective sentences convey someone else's assumption about Meyer's whereabouts. They can be
restated as

Ich bin sicher, daß Meyer jetzt im Büro ist.	I'm sure that Meyer is at the office now.
Ich bin sicher, daß Meyer heute im Büro war.	I'm sure that Meyer was at the office today.

können

OBJ.	**Meyers können jeden Sommer nach Italien fahren.**	The Meyers can go to Italy every summer.
SUBJ.	**Meyers können schon in Italien sein; es ist doch schon Ende Juni.**	The Meyers might (*lit.* can) already be in Italy; it's the end of June already.
	Meyers können nicht in Italien gewesen sein; sie waren doch den ganzen Sommer hier.	The Meyers cannot have been in Italy; they were here the whole summer.

The objective sentence implies that the Meyers are able to go to
Italy every summer. The subjective sentences express possibilities
inferred by someone else on the basis of observable facts. They can
be restated as

Es ist möglich, daß Meyers in Italien sind.
Es ist möglich, daß Meyers in Italien waren.

wollen

OBJ.	**Sie will Ärztin werden.**	She wants to become a doctor.
SUBJ.	**Sie will Ärztin sein.**	She claims to be a doctor.
	Sie will in München studiert haben.	She claims to have studied in Munich.

The objective sentence implies that the subject intends to do something in the future. The subjective sentences express a claim made by the subject about herself or himself which the speaker reports with suspicion.

Er behauptet, Arzt zu sein.	He claims to be a doctor.
Er behauptet, in München studiert zu haben.	He claims to have studied in Munich.

sollen

OBJ.	**Sie soll morgen um neun am Bahnhof sein.**	She is supposed to be at the train station at nine tomorrow.
SUBJ.	**Sie soll schon wieder in Wien sein.**	She is said to be in Vienna again.
	Sie soll schon wieder in Zürich gewesen sein.	She is said to have been in Zurich again.

The objective sentence implies that the subject is obligated to do something. The subjective sentences express hearsay; the speaker reports something he has heard about the subject.

Ich höre, sie ist schon wieder in Wien.	I hear that she is in Vienna again.
Ich höre, sie war schon wieder in Zürich.	I hear that she was in Zurich again.

mögen

Up to this point, we have used only the **möchte**-forms. Although these forms are the ones used most frequently, **mögen**, like the other modals, has a complete set of forms.

PRESENT INDICATIVE	PRESENT SUBJUNCTIVE
ich mag	**ich möchte**
du magst	**du möchtest**
er mag	**er möchte**
wir mögen	**wir möchten**
ihr mögt	**ihr möchtet**
sie mögen	**sie möchten**

PAST INDICATIVE	PAST SUBJUNCTIVE
ich mochte	**ich hätte . . .** (infinitive) **mögen**
du mochtest	**du hättest . . .** (infinitive) **mögen**
etc.	*etc.*

PERFECT WITH DEPENDENT INFINITIVE	PERFECT WITHOUT INFINITIVE
ich habe . . . mögen	**ich habe gemocht**
du hast . . . mögen	**du hast gemocht**
etc.	*etc.*

The verb **mögen** can be used without a following infinitive. If so used, it is not a modal; it means *to like*, takes an accusative object, and is usually used in negative statements.

Sie mag ihn nicht.	She doesn't like him.
Wir mögen kein Schweinefleisch.	We don't like pork.
Wir mochten ihn nicht.	We did not like him.
Ich habe sie nie gemocht.	I never liked her.

When used as a modal—that is, with a dependent infinitive, **mögen** has an objective and a subjective meaning.

OBJ.	**Fritzchen möchte Ingenieur werden.**	Fritzchen would like to become an engineer.
SUBJ.	**Sie mag schon zu Hause sein.**	She may be at home already.
	Sie mag im Theater gewesen sein.	She may have been to the theater.

Used objectively, **mögen** implies desire on the part of the subject. This use, for all practical purposes, is restricted to the **möchte**-forms. When used subjectively, as in **Das mag sein, mögen** expresses what the speaker reports "may be" the case. The subjective use of **mögen** does not occur very often.

Es ist möglich, daß sie schon zu Hause ist.	It is possible that she is at home already.
Es ist möglich, daß sie im Theater war.	It is possible that she was at the theater.

dürfen

OBJ.	**Hier dürfen wir nicht parken.**	We cannot (mustn't) park here.
SUBJ.	**Erika dürfte jetzt schon in Frankfurt sein.**	Erika is probably already in Frankfurt by now.

Of the six modals, **dürfen** has the lowest frequency. When used objectively, **dürfen** means *may* or *to be permitted*. The subjective use of **dürfen** is rare and is limited to the present subjunctive, which expresses a tentative assumption.

USE OF THE SUBJUNCTIVE

When used subjectively, **müssen** and **können** can also occur in the present subjunctive and are frequently followed by **eigentlich**. The subjunctive of subjectively used modals does not express irreality, but only states an assumption more tentatively.

Meyer müßte jetzt (eigentlich) im Büro sein.	Meyer ought to be at the office now.
Meyers könnten (eigentlich) schon in Italien sein.	It is entirely possible that the Meyers are in Italy already.

111 /*scheinen* and *werden*

scheinen

When **scheinen** is used with the meaning *to seem*, it is followed by an infinitive with **zu**. We mention it here because it behaves like a subjective modal and can be used only in the present and past. It can be followed by either a present or a past infinitive.

> **Er scheint zu schlafen.**
> **Er scheint gut geschlafen zu haben.**
> **Er schien zu schlafen.**
> **Er schien gut geschlafen zu haben.**

werden

As was pointed out in Anal. 78, p. 236, the German future tense (**werden** plus infinitive) can also be used to express present probability.

> **Er wird schon zu Hause sein.**

He is probably at home by now.
I am sure (I guess; I think) he's at home by now.

This subjective use of **werden** expresses a subjective judgment by the speaker.

Past probability is expressed by a form of **werden** plus a past infinitive:

> **Er wird schon nach Hause gegangen sein.**

He has probably gone home already.
I assume he's gone home already.

The *objective* use of this construction is the German future perfect.

> **Weil unser Bus erst um 12.15 Uhr am Bahnhof ankommt, wird der 12-Uhr-Zug schon abgefahren sein.**

Because our bus won't arrive at the station until 12:15, the twelve-o'clock train will already have left.

NOTE: Just as the future is usually expressed by the present tense, the future perfect is usually expressed by the present perfect:

> **Ich fahre morgen nach München.**
> **Bis wir zum Bahnhof kommen, ist der Zug bestimmt schon abgefahren.**

Fahren Sie doch mit der Bahn!

PRACTICE ONE

A. In the following sentences, change the present infinitives to past infinitives; then express in English.

1. Meyer muß nach Berlin fahren.
2. Er scheint sehr freundlich zu sein.
3. Er wird wohl nicht zu Hause sein.
4. Sie kann doch nicht schon wieder spazierengehen.
5. Ihr Mann muß sehr viel Geld haben.

B. Restate the following sentences by using **müssen** subjectively.

> **Ich bin sicher, daß sie schon zu Hause ist.**
> **Sie muß schon zu Hause sein.**

1. Ich bin sicher, daß sie in München ist.
2. Ich bin sicher, daß er hier war.
3. Ich bin sicher, daß Meyer im Hilton gewohnt hat.
4. Ich bin sicher, daß Christine schon angekommen ist.

C. Supply appropriate statements using **können** subjectively.

> **Ist er schon hier?**
> **Nein, er kann noch nicht hier sein. Es ist doch erst acht.**

1. Ist das Herr Meyer dort drüben?
   Nein, _____. Der ist doch heute in München.
2. War er gestern abend im Kino?
   Nein, _____. Er war gestern abend bei Meyers.
3. Bist du sicher, daß es Erich war?
   Nein, sicher bin ich nicht, aber _____.

D. Restate the following sentences using **wollen** subjectively.

> **Er behauptet, ein Freund des Direktors zu sein.**
> **Er will ein Freund des Direktors sein.**

1. Er behauptet, ein Freund des Direktors gewesen zu sein.
2. Er behauptete, ein Freund des Direktors zu sein.
3. Er behauptete, ein Freund des Direktors gewesen zu sein.
4. Er behauptet, ein Haus an der Riviera zu haben.
5. Er behauptet, ein Haus an der Riviera gehabt zu haben.
6. Er behauptete, ein Haus an der Riviera zu haben.
7. Er behauptete, ein Haus an der Riviera gehabt zu haben.

E. Restate the following sentences using **sollen** subjectively.

> **Ich höre, Meyer wohnt in Berlin.—Meyer soll in Berlin wohnen.**

1. Ich höre, er ist schon wieder in Tirol.
2. Ich höre, sie ist noch nie in Afrika gewesen.
3. Ich höre, seine Frau war krank.
4. Ich höre, Hans hat geheiratet.
5. Ich höre, er muß schon wieder nach Amerika fahren.

F. Restate the following sentences using **mögen** subjectively.

> **Ich glaube, sie ist etwa zwanzig.—Sie mag etwa zwanzig sein.**

1. Ich glaube, sie war damals etwa zwanzig.
2. Ich glaube, er hat mich nicht gesehen.
3. Ich glaube, das ist Zufall.
4. Ich glaube, das war Zufall.

G. Express the following sentences in English and determine whether
   werden is used to express futurity or probability.

1. Sei nur ruhig; er wird bald kommen.
2. Versuchen Sie unseren Moselwein; Sie werden damit zufrieden sein.
3. Meyer wird wohl in Berlin gewesen sein.
4. Er sagte, er werde wahrscheinlich nicht mitgehen können.
5. Hans wird wohl noch schlafen.

PATTERNS TWO

9/Negation in the Inner Field

Determine how much of each sentence is negated by **nicht**.

Aber du kannst doch nicht den ganzen Tag schlafen!
   But you can't sleep all day!
   (Question: Was kannst du nicht tun? Answer: Den ganzen Tag schlafen.)

Warum denn nicht? Ich habe die ganze Nacht nicht geschlafen.
   Why not? I didn't sleep all night.
   (Question: Was hast du die ganze Nacht nicht getan? Answer: Geschlafen.)

Meyer war krank und hat lange nicht arbeiten können.
   Meyer was sick, and for a long time he couldn't work.

Heute haben wir nicht lange arbeiten können.
Today we couldn't work very long.

Du brauchst nicht auf dem Sofa zu schlafen. Wir haben ein Bett für dich.
You don't have to sleep on the sofa. We have a bed for you.

Ich kann in diesem Bett einfach nicht schlafen. Es ist zu kurz.
I simply can't sleep in this bed. It's too short.

Geschlafen habe ich. Aber ich habe nicht gut geschlafen.
I slept all right, but I didn't sleep well.

Nicht alle Urlaubsländer sind Käseländer. Und nicht alle Käseländer sind Urlaubsländer. Aber Bayern ist Urlaubsland und Käseland.

10/nicht A, sondern B

Ich wartete nicht auf Inge. Ich wartete auf Erika.
Ich wartete damals nicht auf Inge, sondern auf Erika.
Ich habe nicht auf Inge, sondern auf Erika gewartet.
Ich habe nicht auf Inge gewartet, sondern auf Erika.
Nicht auf Inge, sondern auf Erika habe ich gewartet.
Du weißt doch, daß ich nicht auf Inge, sondern auf Erika gewartet habe.
Du weißt doch, daß ich nicht auf Inge gewartet habe, sondern auf Erika.
Er ist gestern nicht nach Berlin, sondern nach Hamburg gefahren.
Er ist nicht gestern, sondern erst heute nach Berlin gefahren.
Er ist nicht gestern nach Berlin gefahren, sondern erst heute.
Er ist gestern nicht nach Berlin gefahren, sondern nach Hamburg.
Wir sind gestern nicht nach Hamburg geflogen, sondern gefahren.

11/entweder . . . oder; weder . . . noch

Wer mag das wohl gewesen sein? Es könnte entweder Liselotte oder Hannelore gewesen sein.
Sie kommt entweder überhaupt nicht, oder ihr Zug hat Verspätung.
Entweder fahren wir in die Berge, oder wir fahren an die See. Wir wissen es noch nicht.
Frau Meyer trinkt weder Kaffee noch Tee.
Ich habe sie weder besuchen können, noch hatte ich Zeit, sie anzurufen.
Weder Meyer noch Kunz konnte damals nach Berlin fahren.

12/Conditional Clauses without wenn

Ist sie nach Wien gefahren, dann hat sie bestimmt auch die Hedi besucht.
If she has gone to Vienna, then I'm sure she visited Hedi.

Hätten wir uns dieses Wochenendhaus nicht gekauft, dann könnten wir jetzt jeden Sommer nach Italien fahren.
> If we hadn't bought this weekend house, we could go to Italy every summer now.

Hätte ich doch nur gewußt, daß Monika krank war! Ich hätte sie gerne besucht.
> Had I only known that Monika was sick! I would have been glad to visit her.

13/*sonst*

Wir waren ja sonst immer in Italien, aber dieses Mal wollen wir in den Ferien an die Nordsee.
> We've always gone to Italy (in the past), but this time we want to go to the North Sea for our vacation.

Was ist nur mit Hans los? Der ist doch sonst nicht so unhöflich.
> What's the matter with Hans? He isn't usually so impolite.

Herr Hanfstängl ist noch im Büro, aber sonst ist niemand mchr da.
> Mr. Hanfstängl is still in the office, but nobody else is here anymore.

Hat sonst noch jemand angerufen?
> Has anybody else called?

Erika muß mitgehen, sonst bleibe ich zu Hause.
> Erika has to come along, otherwise I'll stay home.

Sie sind leider umsonst gekommen; der Herr Doktor ist heute nicht da.
> Unfortunately you've come for nothing (in vain); the doctor is not in today.

Wenn das Kind noch keine zwei Jahre alt ist, fährt es umsonst.
> If the child isn't two yet, he travels free.

Religion

While the U.S. has a large number of religious denominations, most Central Europeans tend to be either Catholic or Protestant. The population of the Federal Republic and Switzerland is almost evenly divided between the two mainstream churches; Austria is nearly 100% Catholic. Protestants are the largest religious group in the German Democratic Republic, but they make up less than half of the population.

When the National Socialists came to power, there were more than half a million Jews in Germany and about 200,000 in Austria. After the Holocaust, there are today only 30,000 Jews in the Federal Republic, 600 in the GDR, and 7500 in Austria.

Because of the presence of foreign workers, especially of Turks, there are now almost 2 million Moslems in the Federal Republic.

The geographical distribution of Catholics and Protestants goes back to Martin Luther and the Protestant Reformation and the subsequent religious Treaty of Augsburg (1555), which allowed each ruler to determine the religion of his territories.

The separation between church and state is not as clear cut as in the U.S. In the Federal Republic the state partly supports such church institutions as hospitals and schools, and it collects the taxes

(**Kirchensteuer**) levied by the churches. In order to leave a church, a person must make a formal declaration to the state. The state does not recognize a marriage performed by the church unless it is also performed before a magistrate.

ANALYSIS TWO

112/Negation in the Inner Field

In Anal. 35, p. 85, we pointed out that **nicht** follows the inner field and precedes the second prong. In Anal. 87, p. 272, we showed that **nicht** can negate "the whole thing."

> **Ich wollte, er hätte nicht wieder den ganzen Abend nur von seinem Hobby geredet.**

This sentence does not deny that he talked, but only bemoans the fact that he talked so long and only about his hobby. In other words, **nicht** negates only elements in what we normally consider the inner field. Now consider the following two sentences:

> **Ich bin oft nicht zu Hause.**
> **Ich bin nicht oft zu Hause.**

The first sentence negates the verbal idea **zu Hause sein** for many instances (**oft**); the second sentence states that I can indeed be found at home, though not very often. If someone says

>**Ich habe die ganze Nacht nicht geschlafen.**

she didn't sleep at all, but if she says

>**Ich habe nicht die ganze Nacht geschlafen.**

then she did sleep, but not all night.

Thus, we can say that as **nicht** moves forward in the sentence, it loses some of its negative force upon the verb and its complement, and it restricts rather than totally negates the verbal idea.

113 /*nicht . . . , sondern . . .*

The English pattern "not A, but B," which occurs in such sentences as

>She is not in Vienna, but in Salzburg.

is expressed in German by **nicht A, sondern B:**

>**Sie ist nicht in Wien, sondern in Salzburg.**

Usually such sentences use contrast intonation. The element introduced by **nicht** (or **kein**) has a rising stress (⟋), and the element introduced by **sondern** has a falling stress (⟍). The **nicht** (or **kein**) and the **sondern** are normally unstressed.

The element introduced by **sondern** can either stand behind the second prong in the end field, or it can follow immediately upon the **nicht A**-element.

>**Ich war nicht gestern in Berlin, sondern vorgestern.**
>**Ich war nicht gestern, sondern vorgestern in Berlin.**

Like **aber, sondern** is a coordinating conjunction, but sentences introduced by **sondern** normally do not repeat information already contained in the first sentence.

>**Ich war nicht gestern in Berlin, sondern (ich war) vorgestern (in Berlin).**

114 /**Review of Conjunctions**

1. Coordinating conjunctions (see Anal. 32, p. 78) connect two or more main clauses or two or more dependent clauses without influencing the word order.

>**aber, denn, oder, sondern, und**

2. Subordinating conjunctions (see Anal. 74, p. 227) always introduce dependent clauses and require verb-last position.

als	when	**ob**	whether, if
bevor	before	**obwohl**	although
bis	until	**seit**	since (temporal)
da	since (causal)	**während**	while
daß	that	**weil**	because
nachdem	after	**wenn**	when; if

Remember that interrogatives in indirect questions and relative pronouns also require verb-last position.

> **Sie kann nicht kommen, weil sie krank ist.**
> **Ich weiß nicht, wann sie zurückkommen kann.**
> **Ist das der Roman, den du gekauft hast?**

3. Conjunctive adverbs, that is, adverbs that join two sentences, often occupy the front field and are followed immediately by the first prong. Some of the most common of these are:

daher (and **deshalb**)	therefore, for that reason, that's why
dann	then
darum	therefore, for that reason
seitdem	since then
trotzdem	nevertheless

> **Im Sommer war ich mit ihr in Paris, seitdem habe ich sie nicht mehr gesehen.**

Unlike conjunctions, these adverbs can also appear in the inner field.

> **Im Sommer war ich mit ihr in Paris. Ich habe sie seitdem nicht mehr gesehen.**

4. Another way of connecting clauses is the 1-1a-2 pattern (first introduced in Anal. 72, p. 223), by which dependent clauses are summed up at the beginning of the following main clause.

> **Wenn du nicht mitgehen willst, dann gehe ich allein.**
> **Daß es heute so regnen würde, das hätte ich nie gedacht.**
> **Daß du heute kommen würdest, damit habe ich nicht gerechnet.**

115/*entweder . . . oder; weder . . . noch*

The pairs of conjunctions **entweder . . . oder,** *either . . . or* and **weder . . . noch,** *neither . . . nor* can connect either two elements in the same sentence or two sentences. Unlike **oder,** which has no influence on word order, **entweder, weder,** and **noch** can occupy the front field and then are followed immediately by the first prong.

FRONT FIELD	1ST PRONG	
Ich	gehe	entweder nach Hause oder ins Kino.
Er	ging	weder ins Kino noch ins Theater.
Ich	gehe	entweder ins Theater,
oder ich	gehe	ins Kino.
Sie	ging	weder ins Kino,
noch	ging	sie ins Theater.
Entweder	gehe	ich ins Theater,
oder ich	gehe	ins Kino.
Weder	ging	er ins Kino,
noch	ging	er ins Theater.

116/Conditional Clauses without *wenn*

In both open conditions and contrary-to-fact conditions, the conjunction **wenn** may be omitted. In contemporary German, and particularly in the spoken language, this pattern occurs almost exclusively in past time.

> **Wenn sie nach Wien gefahren ist, hat sie bestimmt auch die Hedi besucht.**
> **Ist sie nach Wien gefahren, dann hat sie bestimmt auch die Hedi besucht.**

> **Wenn sie nicht in Bonn gewesen wäre, hätte sie ihn nicht kennengelernt.**
> **Wäre sie nicht in Bonn gewesen, dann hätte sie ihn nicht kennengelernt.**

The clause with the omitted **wenn** always shows verb-first position and usually precedes the conclusion. The conclusion is usually introduced by **dann** or **so**.

If the contrary-to-fact condition stands alone to express a wish or desire, **wenn** can also be omitted, but again primarily in past time.

> **Wenn er mir nur geschrieben hätte!**
> **Hätte er mir doch nur geschrieben!**

These clauses almost always contain the sentence adverbs **nur, doch nur**, or **wenigstens**. Like all sentence adverbs, they follow unstressed pronouns and nouns and precede items of news value.

> **Ich wollte ja studieren. Wenn ich nur das Geld dazu gehabt hätte!**
> **Jetzt habe ich das Geld. Wenn ich das Geld nur früher gehabt hätte!**

117 /sonst

The word **sonst** is very versatile. It is used in a variety of ways:

1. as an adverb meaning *in other times, formerly, in other cases.*

   Sonst war er immer so fröhlich, aber jetzt lacht er kaum mehr.
   He always used to be so cheerful, but now he rarely laughs anymore.

2. as an adverb meaning *else, besides, otherwise.*

   Sonst noch etwas?
   Anything else?

   Das Essen ist nicht besonders gut, aber sonst gefällt es mir hier.
   The food is not particularly good, but otherwise I like it here.

3. as a conjunctive adverb (which occupies the front field), meaning *otherwise, or else.* In this case, **sonst** substitutes for a **wenn**-
clause, usually negative.

   Du mußt deine Medizin nehmen,   sonst   wirst du nicht gesund.

   Wenn du deine Medizin nicht nimmst,   wirst du nicht gesund.

   You must take your medicine, or else you won't get well.

   **Hat es dir in Salzburg gefallen? —Natürlich, sonst wäre ich doch
   nicht so lange geblieben.**
   Did you like it in Salzburg? —Of course, otherwise I wouldn't
   have stayed so long.

The adverb **umsonst** means *in vain;* or *free, without charge, for
nothing.*

   **Ich bin umsonst zu ihm in die Wohnung gefahren; er war gar
   nicht da.**
   **Was hast du denn dafür bezahlt? —Gar nichts, ich habe es um-
   sonst bekommen.**

118 /ja

The most obvious use of **ja**, of course, is to answer a question. Frequently, however, it is used in the same position and with the same
affirmative function, even if there is no question or previous conversation. Similar to English *well*, this **ja** can precede any reaction.

Ja, das ist aber schön, daß ihr da seid.   Well, how nice that you are here.
Ja, was machen wir denn jetzt?   Well, what are we going to do now?

It also occurs very frequently as an unstressed sentence adverb in two functions:

1. The speaker wants to express the idea that the facts asserted are well known and accepted by both speaker and listener.

> **Hier regnet es im Sommer ja sehr oft.**   As you know, it rains a lot here in the summer.

2. In sentences spoken with emphatic stress, **ja** heightens the emotional flavor.

> **Das ist ja *wunderbar.***
> **Ich *komm*e ja schon.**
> **Ich bin ja *so* glücklich.**
> **Das ist ja nicht *möglich.***

When used as a sentence adverb, **ja** follows items of no news value and precedes items with news value, unless the verb itself is stressed.

119/Word Formation

ADVERBS IN **-erweise**

These sentence adverbs are formed from adjectives and express a judgment.

glücklicherweise	fortunately, it is fortunate that
möglicherweise	possibly, it is possible that
normalerweise	normally, as a rule, it is normal that

ADVERBS IN **-ens**

The following derivatives are frequently used:

frühestens	at the earliest	**nächstens**	in the near future
spätestens	at the latest	**mindestens**	at least
höchstens	at most	**wenigstens**	at least
meistens	in most cases, mostly		

PRACTICE TWO

H. Without changing word order, negate the following sentences by using **nicht** in two different positions. How does the different position of **nicht** change the meaning of the sentence?

1. Ich möchte mit Rosemarie ins Theater gehen.
2. Meyer hat lange arbeiten können.
3. Ich bin oft ins Kino gegangen.
4. Ich kann aber auf dem Sofa schlafen.
5. Er wollte aber die Julia heiraten.

I. Using the **nicht A, sondern B** pattern, combine the following pairs of
sentences.

> **Wir fahren nicht im Juli nach Berlin. Wir fahren im August.**
> (a) **Wir fahren nicht im Juli, sondern im August nach Berlin.**
> (b) **Wir fahren nicht im Juli nach Berlin, sondern im August.**

1. Ich habe nicht meine Mutter besucht. Ich habe meinen Vater besucht.
2. Sie hat nicht acht Stunden gearbeitet. Sie hat nur zwei Stunden gearbeitet.
3. Gestern abend hat Erich keinen Wein getrunken. Er hat nur Bier getrunken.
4. Sie hat mir kein Buch geschenkt. Sie hat mir eine Uhr geschenkt.

J. Connect the following pairs of sentences by means of the words in parentheses. Which of the connecting words are conjunctive adverbs, which
are coordinating conjunctions, and which are subordinating conjunctions?

1. Ich habe nichts davon gewußt. Er hat mir nicht geschrieben. (weil)
2. Er stand lange vor der Tür. Er klopfte endlich an. (dann)
3. Er wollte nicht mit Professor Müller sprechen. Er hatte Angst vor ihm. (denn)
4. Sie war krank. Ich konnte sie nicht besuchen. (daher)
5. Ich konnte sie nicht besuchen. Sie war krank. (da)
6. Ich rief von Paris aus an. Mein Flugzeug hatte Verspätung. (weil)
7. Er fuhr sofort nach Hamburg. Er hatte meinen Brief bekommen. (nachdem)
8. Sollen wir ins Kino gehen? Sollen wir zu Hause bleiben? (oder)
9. Tante Amalie kommt morgen. Wir gehen bestimmt wieder ins Museum. (Wenn . . . , dann)
10. Fritzchen ist Arzt geworden. Ich kann es nicht glauben. (Daß . . . , das)
11. Ich habe Erika nicht mehr gesehen. Wir haben das Abitur gemacht. (seit)
12. Ich war mit Erika zusammen auf der Schule. Ich habe sie nicht mehr gesehen. (seitdem)
13. Er ist nicht mit ins Kino gegangen. Er hat seiner Freundin einen Brief geschrieben. (sondern)
14. Der Meyer will mich heiraten. Ich kann nur lachen. (Daß . . . , darüber)
15. Er hätte eigentlich um zehn nach Hause gehen sollen. Er blieb bis elf. (trotzdem)
16. Er blieb bis elf. Er sollte um zehn zu Hause sein. (obwohl)
17. Ich habe sie lange gesucht. Ich habe sie nicht finden können. (aber)
18. Er hat mir nicht geschrieben. Ich habe ihm auch nicht mehr geschrieben. (darum)
19. Ich kenne Erich nicht. Ich kenne Hans nicht. (weder . . . noch)
20. Wir wollen meine Mutter in Hamburg besuchen. Sie kommt zu uns nach München. (entweder . . . oder)

K. The following sentences contain a dependent clause introduced by **weil**.
By changing the **weil**-clause, first into a conditional clause with **wenn**
and then without **wenn**, transform the sentences into contrary-to-fact
conditions. Start all sentences with the conditional clause, and change
from affirmative to negative and vice versa.

> **Weil er krank war, konnte er nicht arbeiten.**
> (a) **Wenn er nicht krank gewesen wäre, hätte er arbeiten können.**
> (b) **Wäre er nicht krank gewesen, dann hätte er arbeiten können.**

1. Weil ich nicht so viel Geld hatte wie Meyer, konnte ich nicht an der Riviera wohnen.
2. Weil es mir in Hamburg zu kalt war, bin ich nach Afrika gefahren.
3. Sie kam spät nach Hause, weil sie ins Kino gegangen war.
4. Wir mußten zu Hause bleiben, weil es so stark regnete.
5. Weil das Essen so schlecht war, fuhren wir nach Hause.

Wir machen
Ferien vom
7.Aug. bis 26.Aug.

CONVERSATIONS

I

HERR STRAUSS: Wann nimmst du denn dieses Jahr deinen Urlaub,[1] Kurt?

HERR GSCHEIDLE: Früher als sonst. Unsere Firma macht dieses Jahr schon im Juni Betriebs-ferien,[1] und da müssen wir, ob wir wollen oder nicht.

HERR STRAUSS: Na ja, das muß nicht unbedingt ein Nachteil sein. Im Juni haben doch die Schulferien[1] noch nicht angefangen.

HERR GSCHEIDLE: Da hast du natürlich recht; aber wir wollten eigentlich wieder an die Ost-see, an den Ort, wo wir letztes Jahr waren, und da ist es um die Zeit noch zu kalt.

II

An einer Tankstelle:

TANKWART: Voll machen?

HERR GSCHEIDLE: Ja, bitte, mit Super.

TANKWART: Soll ich auch das Öl und das Wasser nachsehen?

HERR GSCHEIDLE: Ja, und sehen Sie doch auch mal nach den Reifen.

[1]The words **der Urlaub** and **die Ferien** (pl. only) both mean *vacation*; generally, **Urlaub** is used in the case of white- or blue-collar workers, and **Ferien** is always used for school vacations. The term **Betriebsferien** is used when an entire firm, whether corner grocery store or industrial plant, shuts down for two or three weeks and all employees have to take their vacation at the same time.

Selbstbedienung beim Tanken

```
SHELL SB-STATION
   HEINZ KERN
OFFENBACHER LDSTR.
TEL.06181/659810
   6450 HANAU 7

SCHNELLWASCHANLAGE
AUTOLACKIEREREI
KAROSSERIEARBEITEN

  14-11-86 R9956

 BENZIN  19,63l
     DM     18,24 I
Ust 14,00%       I
     DM      2,24
 TOTAL
     DM     18,24
 BAR
     DM     18,24

   543 1111
```

TANKWART (beim Scheibenwaschen°):	Das ist ja direkt ein Insektenfriedhof.

while washing the windshield

TANKWART (beim Scheibenwaschen°): Das ist ja direkt ein Insektenfriedhof.

HERR GSCHEIDLE: Ja, wir sind gerade zwei Stunden am Fluß entlanggefahren.

TANKWART: Ah, *daher.*

TANKWART: Öl ist O.K., und das Wasser ist auch in Ordnung, aber die Vorderreifen sind ein bißchen niedrig, —nur 1,9.[2] Die Hinterreifen haben 2,5.

HERR GSCHEIDLE: Dann machen Sie es vorne doch 2,1, ja?

HERR GSCHEIDLE: So, was bekommen Sie jetzt von mir?

TANKWART: 118 Schilling. Brauchen Sie eine Quittung?

HERR GSCHEIDLE: Nein, danke. —Sagen Sie, wie weit ist es noch nach Innsbruck?

TANKWART: 38 Kilometer. In einer halben Stunde sind Sie garantiert da.

HERR GSCHEIDLE: Na, ich weiß nicht; bei *dem* Verkehr. —Also, Wiedersehen.

TANKWART: Auf Wiederschaun, —und gute Fahrt.

III

Paßkontrolle und Zoll:

ZOLLBEAMTER: Darf ich mal Ihren Ausweis sehen?

JOHN RAY: Ja bitte, —hier ist mein Paß.

ZOLLBEAMTER: Ah, Sie sind Amerikaner. Und wie lange wollen Sie in Österreich bleiben?

JOHN RAY: Nur ein, zwei Tage. Ich bin auf der Durchreise nach Italien.

ZOLLBEAMTER: Haben Sie etwas zu verzollen? Zigaretten? Alkohol?

JOHN RAY: Nein, gar nichts. So viel Platz habe ich gar nicht in meinem Rucksack.

ZOLLBEAMTER: Vielen Dank, —und gute Reise.

---

[2]In Europe, tire pressure is measured in **atü; 1,9 atü** stands for **1,9 Atmosphären Überdruck** or 1.9 times normal atmospheric pressure. This corresponds to 27 psi (pounds per square inch).

IV

FRAU SCHUSTER: Wir fahren diesen Sommer überhaupt nicht weg.
FRAU VOGT: Warum denn nicht? Ihr seid doch sonst immer nach Jugoslawien gefahren.
FRAU SCHUSTER: Ja, aber diesmal wollen wir lieber im Winter Urlaub machen.
FRAU VOGT: Aha, zum Schilaufen.
FRAU SCHUSTER: Na klar. Und zwar wollen wir entweder in den Harz oder ins Allgäu.

V

Make another topical vocabulary list, this time on vacation, travel, tourism, etc. Then have your teacher act the role of a policeman, travel agent, customs officer, ticket agent, or just an ordinary Central European with whom you want to talk about traveling.

Fragen an Sie persönlich

1. Wo und wie haben Sie die Sommerferien verbracht?
     Winterferien
     Osterferien
     Weihnachtsferien

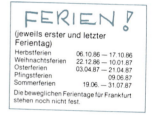

FERIEN!
(jeweils erster und letzter Ferientag)

Herbstferien	06.10.86 — 17.10.86
Weihnachtsferien	22.12.86 — 10.01.87
Osterferien	03.04.87 — 21.04.87
Pfingstferien	09.06.87
Sommerferien	19.06. — 31.07.87

Die beweglichen Ferientage für Frankfurt stehen noch nicht fest.

2. Wie würden Sie gern Ihre nächsten Ferien verbringen?
     Wo würden Sie hinfahren, wenn Sie viel Zeit und viel Geld hätten? Und warum? (Use subjunctives.)
3. Was wissen Sie über Urlaub, Ferien und Tourismus in Deutschland, Österreich, in der Schweiz, in Europa?
4. Was halten Sie von den Eisenbahnen in Amerika?
     Wie wäre es, wenn die Eisenbahnen in Amerika so gut wären wie in Europa?
5. Wie, meinen Sie, könnte man das Energieproblem im Verkehr lösen?

ZOLL
DOUANE

READING

Franz Kafka

FRANZ KAFKA

Franz Kafka (born 1883 in Prague), though most of his works were published posthumously, was one of the most influential prose writers of this century. Among his best-known works are the novels *Der Prozeß* (The Trial) and *Das Schloß* (The Castle) and such stories as *Das Urteil* (The Judgment), *Die Verwandlung* (Metamorphosis), and *Der Landarzt* (The Country Doctor). He died in 1924. The short piece below was written around 1920–22.

Heimkehr

Ich bin zurückgekehrt, ich habe den Flur durchschritten und blicke mich um. Es ist meines Vaters alter Hof. Die Pfütze in der Mitte. Altes, unbrauchbares Gerät, ineinanderverfahren, verstellt den Weg zur Bodentreppe. Die Katze lauert auf dem Geländer. Ein zerrissenes Tuch, einmal im Spiel um eine Stange gewunden, hebt sich im Wind. Ich bin angekommen. Wer wird mich empfangen? Wer wartet hinter der Tür der Küche? Rauch kommt aus dem Schornstein, der Kaffee zum Abendessen wird gekocht. Ist dir heimlich, fühlst du dich zu Hause? Ich weiß es nicht, ich bin sehr unsicher. Meines Vaters Haus ist es, aber kalt steht Stück neben Stück, als wäre jedes mit seinen eigenen Angelegenheiten beschäftigt, die ich teils vergessen habe, teils niemals kannte.

Homecoming

I have returned. I have crossed the entrance-way and am looking around. It is my father's old place. The puddle in the middle. Old, unusable equipment, shoved into a heap, bars the way to the stairway to the loft. The cat lies in wait on the railing. A torn cloth, wound around a stake once at play, rises in the wind. I have arrived. Who will receive me? Who is waiting behind the kitchen door? Smoke comes from the chimney, coffee for supper is being made. Do you feel at home? I don't know, I am very unsure. My father's house it is, but coldly piece stands by piece, as if each were occupied with its own affairs, which partly I have forgotten, partly never knew. Of what use can I be to them, what am I to them, even if I am my father's, the old farmer's, son. And I dare not knock at

Was kann ich ihnen nützen, was bin ich ihnen und sei ich auch des Vaters, des alten Landwirts Sohn. Und ich wage nicht, an der Küchentür zu klopfen, nur von der Ferne horche ich, nur von der Ferne horche ich stehend, nicht so, daß ich als Horcher überrascht werden könnte. Und weil ich von der Ferne horche, erhorche ich nichts, nur einen leichten Uhrenschlag höre ich oder glaube ihn vielleicht nur zu hören, herüber aus den Kindertagen. Was sonst in der Küche geschieht, ist das Geheimnis der dort Sitzenden, das sie vor mir wahren. Je länger man vor der Tür zögert, desto fremder wird man. Wie wäre es, wenn jetzt jemand die Tür öffnete und mich etwas fragte. Wäre ich dann nicht selbst wie einer, der sein Geheimnis wahren will.

the kitchen door, only from the distance I listen, only from the distance I listen, standing, not in such a way that I could be surprised as an eavesdropper. And because I listen from a distance, I hear nothing, only the soft ring of a clock do I hear, or perhaps I only imagine hearing it, from the days of my childhood.

What else happens in the kitchen is the secret of those sitting there, which they keep from me. The longer you hesitate in front of the door, the more of a stranger you become. How would it be if someone opened the door now and asked me something. Would I then myself not be like one who wants to keep his secret.

AUS DER BIBEL

Das Gleichnis vom verlornen Sohn

Aus dem Evangelium nach Lukas 15:11–32

¹¹Er sprach aber: Ein Mann hatte zwei Söhne. ¹²Und der jüngere von ihnen sagte zum Vater: Vater, gib mir den Teil des Vermögens, der mir zukommt! Der aber verteilte seine Habe unter sie. ¹³Und nicht viele Tage darnach nahm der jüngere Sohn alles mit sich und zog hinweg in ein fernes Land, und dort vergeudete er sein Vermögen durch ein zügelloses Leben. ¹⁴Nachdem er aber alles durchgebracht hatte, kam eine gewaltige Hungersnot über jenes Land, und er fing an, Mangel zu leiden. ¹⁵Und er ging hin und hängte sich an einen der Bürger jenes Landes; der schickte ihn auf seine Felder, Schweine zu hüten. ¹⁶Und er begehrte, seinen Bauch mit den Schoten zu füllen, die die Schweine fraßen: und niemand gab sie ihm. ¹⁷Da ging er in sich und sprach: Wie viele Tagelöhner meines Vaters haben Brot im Überfluß, ich aber komme hier vor Hunger um! ¹⁸Ich will mich aufmachen und zu

The Parable of the Prodigal Son

From The Gospel According to Luke 15: 11–32

¹¹Again he said: There was once a man who had two sons; ¹²and the younger said to his father, "Father, give me my share of the property." So he divided his estate between them. ¹³A few days later the younger son turned the whole of his share into cash and left home for a distant country, where he squandered it in reckless living. ¹⁴He had spent it all, when a severe famine fell upon that country and he began to feel the pinch. ¹⁵So he went and attached himself to one of the local landowners, who sent him on to his farm to mind the pigs. ¹⁶He would have been glad to fill his belly with the pods that the pigs were eating; and no one gave him anything. ¹⁷Then he came to his senses and said, "How many of my father's paid servants have more food than they can eat, and here am I, starving to death! ¹⁸I will set off and go to my father, and say to him, 'Father, I have sinned against God and against you; ¹⁹I am

meinem Vater gehen und zu ihm sagen: Vater, ich habe gesündigt gegen den Himmel und vor dir; [19]ich bin nicht mehr wert, dein Sohn zu heißen; stelle mich wie einen deiner Tagelöhner! [20]Und er machte sich auf und ging zu seinem Vater. Als er aber noch fern war, sah ihn sein Vater und fühlte Erbarmen, lief hin, fiel ihm um den Hals und küßte ihn. [21]Der Sohn aber sprach zu ihm: Vater, ich habe gesündigt gegen den Himmel und vor dir; ich bin nicht mehr wert, dein Sohn zu heißen. [22]Doch der Vater sagte zu seinen Knechten: Bringet schnell das beste Kleid heraus und ziehet es ihm an und gebet ihm einen Ring an die Hand und Schuhe an die Füße, [23]und holet das gemästete Kalb, schlachtet es und lasset uns essen und fröhlich sein! [24]Denn dieser mein Sohn war tot und ist wieder lebendig geworden, er war verloren und ist wiedergefunden worden. Und sie fingen an, fröhlich zu sein.

[25]Sein älterer Sohn aber war auf dem Felde; und als er kam und sich dem Hause näherte, hörte er Musik und Reigentanz. [26]Und er rief einen der Knechte herbei und erkundigte sich, was das sei. [27]Der aber sagte ihm: Dein Bruder ist gekommen, und dein Vater hat das gemästete Kalb geschlachtet, weil er ihn gesund wiedererhalten hat. [28]Da wurde er zornig und wollte nicht hineingehen. Doch sein Vater kam heraus und redete ihm zu. [29]Er aber antwortete und sagte zum Vater: Siehe, so viele Jahre diene ich dir und habe nie ein Gebot von dir übertreten; und mir hast du nie einen Bock gegeben, damit ich mit meinen Freunden fröhlich wäre. [30]Nun aber dieser dein Sohn gekommen ist, der deine Habe mit Dirnen aufgezehrt hat, hast du ihm das gemästete Kalb geschlachtet. [31]Da sagte er zu ihm: Kind, du bist allezeit bei mir, und alles, was mein ist, ist dein. [32]Du solltest aber fröhlich sein und dich freuen; denn dieser dein Bruder war tot und ist lebendig geworden, und war verloren und ist wiedergefunden worden.

no longer fit to be called your son; treat me as one of your paid servants.'" [20]So he set out for his father's house. But while he was still a long way off his father saw him, and his heart went out to him. He ran to meet him, flung his arms round him, and kissed him. [21]The son said, "Father, I have sinned, against God and against you; I am no longer fit to be called your son." [22]But the father said to his servants, "Quick! fetch a robe, my best one, and put it on him; put a ring on his finger and shoes on his feet. [23]Bring the fatted calf and kill it, and let us have a feast to celebrate the day. [24]For this son of mine was dead and has come back to life; he was lost and is found." And the festivities began.

[25]Now the elder son was out on the farm; and on his way back, as he approached the house, he heard music and dancing. [26]He called one of the servants and asked what it meant. [27]The servant told him, "Your brother has come home, and your father has killed the fatted calf because he has him back safe and sound." [28]But he was angry and refused to go in. His father came out and pleaded with him; [29]but he retorted, "You know how I have slaved for you all these years; I never once disobeyed your orders; and you never gave me so much as a kid, for a feast with my friends. [30]But now that this son of yours turns up, after running through your money with his women, you kill the fatted calf for him." [31]"My boy," said the father, "you are always with me, and everything I have is yours. [32]How could we help celebrating this happy day? Your brother here was dead and has come back to life, was lost and is found."

REVIEW EXERCISES

L. Change the following sentences, all containing objective modals, from present indicative to present subjunctive and add **eigentlich** in the place indicated by /. Then translate these sentences into English.

1. Hans muß / hierbleiben.
2. Wir müssen heute abend / schon wieder ausgehen.
3. Wir können / auch einmal ins Theater gehen.
4. Ich kann ja / auch mit *Inge* spazierengehen.
5. Ich soll / um sechs Uhr zu Hause sein.

M. Change the following sentence in two ways: (a) Change the modal to the perfect; (b) keep the modal in the present and change the infinitive to a past infinitive. Then translate the two resulting sentences so as to show the difference in meaning.

Sie soll um acht Uhr zu Hause sein.
(a) **Sie hat um acht Uhr zu Hause sein sollen.**   She had to be home at eight.
(b) **Sie soll um acht Uhr zu Hause gewesen sein.**   She is said to have been at home at eight.

1. Er kann nicht in Berlin arbeiten.
2. Sie muß in die Stadt fahren.
3. Meyer will ein Haus in Tirol kaufen.
4. Ingelheim soll Arabisch lernen.

N. Following the pattern of the examples below, answer the questions by using a subjective form of **müssen**; try to support your conclusion with a sentence starting with **denn**.

(a) **Ist sie wirklich schon achtzehn?**
Sie muß achtzehn sein, denn sie hat einen Führerschein (*driver's license*).
(b) **Waren Meyers wirklich im Ausland?**
Sie müssen im Ausland gewesen sein, denn sie reden dauernd über Spanien und Portugal.

1. Hat Meyer wirklich so viel Geld?
2. War Ingelheim schon oft in Frankreich?
3. Hat sie wirklich bis zehn Uhr geschlafen?

O. Change the following sentences from the past indicative to the past subjunctive. Add **eigentlich** in the place indicated by /.

> **Ich mußte gestern nach Berlin fahren.**
> **Ich hätte gestern eigentlich nach Berlin fahren müssen.**

1. Ich sollte gestern / meine Mutter besuchen.
2. Ich durfte es Ihnen / nicht sagen.
3. Ich brauchte / gar nichts zu sagen.
4. Ich konnte damals / auch nach Rom fliegen.
5. Mir konntest du das ja / erzählen.

P. In the following sentences, change the modals from indicative to subjunctive. Then translate each pair of sentences into English.

1. Er kann, wenn er will.
2. Ich konnte auch mitgehen.
3. Ich muß auch einmal nach Italien fahren.
4. Ich mußte gestern zu Hause bleiben.
5. Sie sollen nicht so viel rauchen.
6. Sein Sohn sollte in Heidelberg studieren.

Q. By using the proper forms of modals, express in one sentence each of the following ideas.

1. There is a rumor that he has been sick.
2. Meyer claims that he was in Africa again.
3. It is possible that he was living in Berlin.
4. I have arrived at the conclusion that he had been in America.
5. You should have gone to Berlin two years ago.
6. There is a rumor that she had gone to Berlin.
7. It is possible that he is still here.
8. It is not possible that he was in Berlin.
9. It has never been possible for him to go to Berlin.
10. He tries to give the impression that he was a friend of my father's.

R. Change the following statements to wishes contrary to fact, using either **doch nur** or **doch nur nicht** and starting with **wenn** and then without **wenn**. (Like **eigentlich, doch nur** follows the pronouns and elements of no news value.) Change from affirmative to negative and vice versa.

> **Er ist nach Italien gefahren.**
> (a) **Wenn er doch nur nicht nach Italien gefahren wäre.**
> (b) **Wäre er doch nur nicht nach Italien gefahren.**

1. Er kam so oft.
2. Er hat mir nicht geschrieben, daß er Geld braucht.
3. Sie hat mir gesagt, daß sie Thusnelda heißt.
4. Vor den Sommerferien ist sie krank geworden.
5. Ich habe nicht gewußt, daß du auch in Berlin warst.

S. In the following sentences, change the first clause into a real or irreal **wenn**-clause; leave out **sonst**.

> **Der Wein ist gut. Sonst wäre ich nicht mehr hier.**
> **Wenn der Wein nicht so gut wäre, wäre ich nicht mehr hier.**

1. Du mußt die Medizin regelmäßig nehmen, sonst wirst du nicht gesund.
2. Er ist krank. Sonst wäre er bestimmt gekommen.
3. Du mußt schnell fahren, sonst kommen wir zu spät.
4. Du darfst nicht so spät ins Bett gehen, sonst bist du morgen den ganzen Tag müde.
5. Er fuhr mit dem Wagen, denn sonst hätte er dreimal umsteigen müssen.

T. Express in German.

1. She must have waited for me for three hours.
2. She had to wait for me for three hours.
3. He can't have slept long. I called him up at seven o'clock, but I couldn't reach him anymore.
4. Had she sent the letter to me, I could have answered her immediately.
5. Her letter must have arrived when I had already gone to Munich.
6. The man you claim to have seen cannot have been von Hollenbeck.
7. He has always wanted to go to Rome.
8. He cannot have been in Rome.
9. Erich has probably already been here.
10. Erika seems to have arrived already.
11. I don't think much of him.
12. I often think of you.
13. She ought to have arrived an hour ago.
14. Dr. Schmidt was at the Meyers' too; you must have met him there.
15. It cannot have been Erich, for I know that Erich has gone to the airport to pick up Hans.
16. Could I have another cup of coffee, please?
17. Could you work in the garden yesterday?
18. Of course we could have gone to the movies, but we didn't want to.
19. He is said to be seventy years old, but he looks as though he were only fifty.
20. She may have thought that Erich wanted to help her.

U. Composition. Write on the following topic, using as many modals as possible.

Yesterday you saw your friend Fridolin whom you hadn't seen in a long time. Fridolin claims to have become a writer, and that he travels to all sorts of countries. Since you don't believe that, list a number of reasons why it cannot be true.

VOCABULARY

an•klopfen — to knock (on a door)
der Ausweis, -e — identification paper, I.D. card
behaupten — to claim, maintain, assert
brauchbar — usable
  unbrauchbar — unusable
darum (adv.) — therefore; for that reason
deshalb (adv.) — because of that
diesmal (dieses Mal) — this time
echt — genuine
empfangen — to receive
die Energie', -n — energy
entlang — along
  am Fluß entlang — along the river
fern — far, distant
  die Ferne — distance
fröhlich — cheerful
frühestens — at the earliest
führen — to lead, take
der Führerschein, -e — driver's license
garantiert — guaranteed; I guarantee you
die Geschäftsreise, -n — business trip
glücklicherweise — fortunately
hängen — to hang (something)
hinten (adv.) — in the back
höchstens — at most
der Hof, ⸚e — court(yard); farm
  der Bauernhof, ⸚e — farm
höflich — polite
  unhöflich — impolite
(das) Jugoslawien — Yugoslavia
klopfen — to knock, to pound; to beat
kurz — short
  kürzlich — recently
küssen — to kiss
  der Kuß, die Küsse — kiss
lösen — to solve
meistens — in most cases, mostly
mindestens — at least
die Mitte — middle, center
möglicherweise — possibly

na ja — oh well
nach•sehen — to check
nächstens — in the near future
der Nachteil, -e — disadvantage
niedrig — low
normalerweise — normally, as a rule
das Öl, -e — oil
die Ordnung, -en — order
  in Ordnung — all right, O.K.
die Osterferien — Easter vacation
der Paß, die Pässe — passport
  die Paßkontrolle, -n — passport control
praktisch — practical(ly)
das Problem', -e — problem
regelmäßig — regular
der Reifen, - — tire
die Schwierigkeit, -en — difficulty
sondern — but (on the contrary)
spätestens — at the latest
stark — strong
tanken — to get gas
  die Tankstelle, -n — gas station
der Teil, -e — part, piece
  verteilen — to distribute
überhaupt — in general; altogether
  überhaupt nicht — not at all
umsonst — in vain; for nothing
der Urlaub — leave; vacation
verzollen — to declare; to pay duty on
voll machen — to fill up
vorne (adv.) — in front
der Vorteil, -e — advantage
waschen — to wash
weder . . . noch — neither . . . nor
wenigstens — at least
(auf) Wiederschau(e)n — Austrian for auf Wiedersehen
der Wind, -e — wind
wunderbar — marvelous, wonderful
die Zigaret'te, -n — cigarette
der Zoll, ⸚e — customs; duty
der Zufall, ⸚e — chance, accident
  durch Zufall — by chance, accident
  zufällig — accidentally

Strong Verbs

INFINITIVE	PRESENT	PAST TENSE	PERFECT	
empfangen	empfängt	empfing	empfangen	to receive
nach•sehen	sieht nach	sah nach	nachgesehen	to check
waschen	wäscht	wusch	gewaschen	to wash

Unit 14

Reflexive Verbs

Life behind closed doors

Privacy is very important to Germans. When they come home, they unlock and lock the garden gate as well as the front door. All rooms in the apartment or house have doors, which are always left closed. There are not only curtains on the windows but also heavy drapes and shutters. Office doors are routinely kept closed, and visitors often find a sign asking them to knock: **Bitte anklopfen**. University dormitories have mostly single rooms, and their doors tend to be closed. The ultimate in the quest for privacy is the staking out of one's turf at the beach in the form of a **Strandburg** (*beach castle*).

PATTERNS ONE

1/Reflexive Pronouns

Ich dachte, ich hätte dich gesehen; aber du warst es nicht. Ich habe mich im Spiegel gesehen.

I thought that I had seen you, but it wasn't you. I saw myself in the mirror.

Warum hast du die Tante Amalie eingeladen? —Die hat sich selber eingeladen.

Why did you invite Aunt Amalie? —She invited herself.

Und dann hat er gesagt: „Ich hoffe, ich langweile Sie nicht."

And then he said: "I hope I'm not boring you."

Wenn der nur gewußt hätte, wie sehr ich mich gelangweilt habe.

If he had only known how bored I was.

Ich halte ihn für dumm, aber er hält sich für sehr intelligent.

I think he's stupid, but he thinks he's very intelligent.

Du brauchst mir nicht zu helfen. Ich kann mir selber helfen.[1]

You don't have to help me. I can help myself.

Darf ich mich vorstellen? Ich bin Dr. Ingelheim.

May I introduce myself? I'm Dr. Ingelheim.

Frau Steinmetz, darf ich Ihnen Herrn Dr. Ingelheim vorstellen?

Mrs. Steinmetz, may I introduce Dr. Ingelheim (to you)?

Ich habe mich gestern dem Direktor vorgestellt.

I introduced myself to the director yesterday.

Ich koche mir gerade eine Suppe.

I'm just making some soup (for myself).

Mach dir ruhig noch eine Tasse Kaffee; wir brauchen noch nicht zu gehen.

Go ahead and make yourself a cup of coffee; we don't have to go yet.

Wir haben uns gerade ein Haus gekauft.

We just bought a house.

Brigitte will sich eine Wohnung in der Nähe der Uni suchen.

Brigitte wants to look for an apartment near the university.

Zu Weihnachten wünscht sich unsere Tochter einen Fernseher.

For Christmas our daughter wants a TV.

Haben Sie einen Hotelführer? Ich möchte mir in Badgastein ein Hotel aussuchen.

Do you have a hotel guide? I'd like to select a hotel in Badgastein.

Ich kann mir nicht erklären, warum er nicht gekommen ist.

I can't figure out (explain to myself) why he didn't come.

(Daß er nicht gekommen ist,) das kann ich mir nicht erklären.

(That he didn't come,) that I can't figure out.

Ich spreche von Tante Amalie, nicht von mir.

I'm talking about Aunt Amalie, not about myself.

Sie war sehr stolz auf sich, weil sie die Goldmedaille gewonnen hatte.

She was very proud of herself because she had won the gold medal.

[1]Of the verbs with only dative objects introduced in this book (see Anal. 49, p. 132), only **helfen** is used reflexively.

Hat er den Porsche für sich gekauft oder für seinen Sohn?	Did he buy the Porsche for himself or for his son?
Tante Amalie hat uns zu sich eingeladen.	Aunt Amalie has invited us to her house.

2/Reciprocal Pronouns

Wo haben Sie einander denn kennengelernt? — Bei Tante Amalie. Vorher hatten wir uns noch nie gesehen.

Im Sommer hat er ihr das erste Mal geschrieben, und seitdem schreiben sie sich jede Woche zweimal, und mindestens einmal im Monat rufen sie sich an.

Heute abend gehe ich mit ihr ins Theater. — Wo triffst du sie denn? — Wir treffen uns am Bahnhof.

3/Mandatory Reflexive Verbs

REFLEXIVE PRONOUNS IN THE ACCUSATIVE

sich ärgern über (acc.), *to be annoyed with (by)*

Der Meyer ist wirklich ein Dummkopf. Ich habe mich gestern abend furchtbar über ihn geärgert.

Ich ärgere mich immer darüber, daß er so spät kommt. Gestern abend kam er erst um halb neun.

sich beeilen, *to hurry (up)*

Kannst du dich nicht mal ein bißchen beeilen? Wir müssen in zehn Minuten hier wegfahren, sonst verpassen wir den Zug.

Ich beeile mich doch. Ich muß nur eben noch eine Postkarte an Tante Amalie schreiben.

sich freuen auf (acc.), *to look forward to*

Ich freue mich auf eure Party am nächsten Sonntag.

sich freuen über (acc.), *to be happy (glad) about*

Ich habe mich wirklich darüber gefreut, daß du an meinen Geburtstag gedacht hast.

sich irren, *to be mistaken, to err*

Was, Meyer soll Generaldirektor geworden sein? Bist du sicher, daß du dich da nicht irrst?
Ich weiß, Irren ist menschlich, aber ich irre mich bestimmt nicht; ich habe nämlich gerade einen Brief von ihm bekommen.

sich wundern über (acc.), *to be amazed (surprised) at*

Ich habe mich doch gestern abend über den Fritz gewundert. Daß der gar nichts gesagt hat! Früher hat er immer zu viel geredet.
Ich würde mich nicht wundern, wenn er überhaupt nicht mehr zu unserem Stammtisch käme.

REFLEXIVE PRONOUNS IN THE DATIVE

sich etwas ansehen, *to look at something*

Ich wollte mir den Hitchcock Film eigentlich gar nicht ansehen; aber du kennst ja Tante Amalie. Sie interessiert sich nur noch für Hitchcock und Picasso.
Sieh dir das an! Da kommt Edith Maschke mit ihrem neuen Freund.

sich etwas überlegen, *to meditate about something*

Ich überlege mir oft, ob es nicht besser wäre, wenn wir nach Heidelberg zögen.
Wie wäre es, wenn Sie auch in die Stadt zögen? —Das muß ich mir erst noch überlegen.

sich etwas vorstellen, *to imagine something*[2]

Ich kann mir nicht vorstellen, daß Meyer in Südamerika war.
Ich hatte mir das alles viel leichter vorgestellt.

---

[2]Do not confuse this use of **vorstellen,** *to imagine* (with a dative reflexive), with **vorstellen,** *to introduce* (with an accusative reflexive), as used in [1] above.

4/*selbst* **and** *selber*

Das weiß ich *selbst.*
Ihrer Frau geht es also wieder gut—und wie geht es Ihnen *selbst?*
Ich habe nicht mit Meyers Frau gesprochen; ich habe mit ihm *selbst* gesprochen.
Meine Frau hat nicht mit ihm gesprochen; ich habe *selbst* mit ihm gesprochen.

Kaufen Sie Ihr Fleisch doch im Supermarkt; da können Sie sich *selbst* bedienen.
*Da*bei brauchst du mir nicht zu helfen; das kann ich *sel*ber machen.
Er *selbst* ist ja ganz *nett*; aber mit seiner *Mut*ter könnte ich nicht *le*ben.

Ich habe *sel*ber kein Geld.
Ich habe *auch* kein Geld.
Ich kann dir nicht helfen; ich habe *sel*ber viel zu tun.

5/*selbst, sogar, auch* **meaning** *even*

Selbst (sogar, auch) *das* ist ihm zu viel.
Selbst (sogar, auch) Herrn Dr. Müller, der sonst immer da ist, konnte ich diesmal nicht
    sprechen.
In Berlin sprechen selbst (sogar, auch) kleine Kinder Deutsch.
Selbst (sogar, auch) von seiner Frau läßt er sich nichts sagen.

Ein Selbstbedienungs-
laden

ANALYSIS ONE

120/Reflexive Pronouns

Reflexive pronouns were introduced in Units 2 and 5; they can be
in the accusative (see Anal. 19, p. 45) or in the dative (see Anal. 48,
p. 131).

	SINGULAR				PLURAL		
NOM.	ACC. REFL.	DAT. REFL.		NOM.	ACC. REFL.	DAT. REFL.	
ich	mich	mir	(myself)	wir	uns	uns	(ourselves)
du	dich	dir	(yourself)	ihr	euch	euch	(yourselves)
er	sich	sich	(himself)				
sie	sich	sich	(herself)	sie	sich	sich	(themselves)
es	sich	sich	(itself)				
Sie	sich	sich	(yourself)	Sie	sich	sich	(yourselves)

In the first and second person the reflexive pronoun is identical with the personal pronoun. All third-person reflexives are **sich**.

These reflexive pronouns are either accusative or dative objects (see Anal. 49, p. 132); they are used when the object is identical with the subject.

Many verbs that take an object can also be used with a reflexive pronoun object.

VERBS WITH ACCUSATIVE OBJECTS

Sie hat mich beruhigt.	She calmed me down.
Ich habe mich beruhigt.	I calmed down.
Er hat sich beruhigt.	He calmed down.

VERBS WITH DATIVE OBJECTS

Er konnte mir nicht helfen.	He couldn't help me.
Ich konnte mir nicht helfen.	I couldn't help myself.
Sie konnte sich nicht helfen.	She couldn't help herself.

VERBS WITH BOTH DATIVE AND ACCUSATIVE OBJECTS

Ich kaufe ihm ein Auto.	I buy him a car.
Ich kaufe mir ein Auto.	I buy (myself) a car.
Er kauft sich ein Auto.	He buys (himself) a car.

In the first two sets of examples above, the verbs **beruhigen** and **helfen** can only take one object. When this mandatory object is identical with the subject, German must use a reflexive pronoun.

In the third set of examples above, the verb **kaufen** takes both a dative and an accusative object, but only the accusative object must always be expressed. If the dative object is identical with the subject, English normally does not use a reflexive pronoun, but German frequently does. In fact, German uses reflexive constructions much more often than English.[3]

Like **beruhigen** in the first set of examples above, the following German verbs can all take a reflexive object, but none of their English equivalents are used with reflexive pronouns.

sich anziehen	to get dressed
sich ausziehen	to undress
sich umziehen	to change (clothes)
sich rasieren	to shave
sich verändern	to change

Some prepositional objects can be reflexive if the object of the preposition is identical with the subject. These pose no problem because their English equivalents are also reflexive.

Er denkt immer nur an sich.   He only thinks of himself.

Plural reflexive pronouns can also be used as reciprocal pronouns meaning *each other* (see Anal. 19, p. 45). **Wir küßten uns** can only mean *We kissed (each other)* and not *We kissed ourselves*.

Occasionally, the reciprocal **sich** is used with the singular pronoun **man**, as in

Wo trifft man sich?   Where do people meet?

In addition to the plural reflexives, **einander** can also express reciprocity; **einander** is more elevated.

Haben sie einander in Rom   Did they meet (each other) in
kennengelernt?   Rome?

121/Mandatory Reflexive Verbs

Some German verbs are always used with a reflexive pronoun which can neither be left out nor be replaced by a noun or another pronoun. Unlike the reflexive pronouns introduced before, these mandatory reflexive pronouns are not true objects.

English has only a few such verbs, for example, *to enjoy oneself*, which, when meaning "to have fun," forms one inseparable unit. If the reflexive *oneself* is replaced by a nonreflexive pronoun or a noun

---

[3]With a small group of verbs that take both a dative and an accusative object, for example, **vorstellen**, *to introduce*, the accusative rather than the dative can be reflexive: **Ich habe mich ihm vorgestellt**, *I introduced myself to him.*

(*I enjoyed them and their hospitality*), *to enjoy* changes its meaning to "to derive pleasure from." These two meanings of *to enjoy* cannot even be accommodated in one and the same sentence without repeating the verb. You cannot say [*Thanks; I enjoyed myself and that good dinner.*].

German, on the other hand, has a number of such mandatory reflexives. Some verbs take only an accusative reflexive, for example, **sich erkälten,** *to catch a cold*, or an accusative reflexive plus a prepositional object, for example, **sich ärgern über** (acc.), *to be annoyed with*. Other verbs take a dative reflexive followed by an accusative object, for example, **sich** (dat.) **etwas ansehen,** *to take a look at something*; these are structurally parallel to **Ich kaufe mir ein Auto** except that the reflexive is mandatory and cannot be replaced by a pronoun or noun.

ACC. REFL.

Ich habe mich erkältet.
Du hast dich erkältet.
Sie hat sich erkältet.
Wir haben uns erkältet.
Ihr habt euch erkältet.
Sie haben sich erkältet.

ACC. REFL. + PREP. OBJ.

Ich ärgere mich immer über ihn.
Du ärgerst dich immer über ihn.
Er ärgert sich immer über ihn.
Wir ärgern uns immer über ihn.
Ihr ärgert euch immer über ihn.
Sie ärgern sich immer über ihn.

DAT. REFL. + ACC. OBJ.

Ich will mir den Film ansehen.
Du willst dir den Film ansehen.
Sie will sich den Film ansehen.
Wir wollen uns den Film ansehen.
Ihr wollt euch den Film ansehen.
Sie wollen sich den Film ansehen.

All reflexive verbs form the perfect tense with **haben**. In the vocabulary, they will be indicated by **sich** before the infinitive.

122/*selbst* and *selber*

1. The English reflexive pronouns *myself, yourself, himself,* and so on, sometimes merely repeat, for emphasis, a preceding noun or pronoun. When so used, they carry the main syntactical stress, but they cannot function independently as subjects or objects.

He said it him*self.*
They did it them*selves.*

German cannot repeat a preceding noun or pronoun. Instead, German uses the strongly stressed particles **selbst** or **selber** to emphasize these nouns or pronouns. **Selbst** and **selber** are interchangeable. They always immediately follow the word to be emphasized or stand at the end of the inner field.

Das weiß ich *selbst*.	I know that my*self*.
Das war der Direktor *sel*ber.	That was the boss him*self*.
Ich fahre morgen *selbst* nach Berlin.	I am going to Berlin my*self* tomorrow.

Note that the use of **selbst** is not determined by the presence or absence of a reflexive pronoun, and that **selbst** does not replace the reflexive pronoun when the reflexive is required.

Er sollte auch einmal an *sich* denken.
Er sollte auch einmal an sich *selbst* denken.
He ought to think of himself, too, for a change.

2. When **selbst** (or **selber**) is used at the end of the inner field, it frequently assumes the meaning *without help* or *others don't have to*.

Das kann ich doch *sel*ber machen.	I can do that my*self*.
Hänschen kann sich *sel*ber anziehen; er	
ist doch schon drei.	

3. If **selbst** (or **selber**) appears in the front field, contrast intonation is used, and a contrast with others, of whom the opposite statement is true, is implied.

Sie *selbst hat* kein Geld; aber ihre *Mut*ter hat *viel* Geld.
Er *sel*ber bleibt zu *Hause*; *uns* schickt er in die *Kirche*.

4. If **selbst** (or **selber**) appears in the inner field, it may also be a substitute for **auch** and express the notion *just like others*.

Ich bin *sel*ber arm, so arm wie du.
Ich bin *selbst* nicht glücklich, ich bin so unglücklich wie ihr.

5. **Selbst, sogar**, and **auch**, without stress, may form a syntactical unit with an immediately following stressed word. If so used, they mean *even*.

Selbst (sogar, auch) *das* ist ihm zu viel.
**Er *will* einfach nicht, und solange jemand nicht *will*, kann ihm selbst (sogar, auch) *Gott*
nicht helfen.**

PRACTICE ONE

A. Replace the words in italics by reflexive pronouns corresponding with the subject of each sentence.

> **Hast du *ihn* im Spiegel gesehen?**   **Hast du dich im Spiegel gesehen?**

1. Ich hoffe, ich werde *Sie* nicht langweilen.
2. Wolfgang hält *Brigitte* für sehr intelligent.
3. Ich will *meiner Tochter* ein Haus bauen.
4. Wir wünschen *euch* gutes Wetter in den Ferien.
5. Hast du *deinen Freund* schon vorgestellt?
6. Ich mache *ihr* gerade ein Steak zum Abendessen.
7. Warum denkst du nicht auch mal an *Tante Amalie*?

B. Replace the object in the following sentences with a reciprocal pronoun; change the subject from singular to plural. Then give the English equivalent of both sentences.

> **Ich habe Karin kennengelernt.**   **Wir haben uns kennengelernt.**

1. Er hat sie in Travemünde kennengelernt.
2. In den Sommerferien habe ich sie oft besucht.
3. Wie oft hast du ihm denn geschrieben?
4. Ich habe ihn immer gut verstanden.
5. Er hat sie immer in der Mensa getroffen.
6. Wie oft rufst du ihn denn an?

C. Express in German, using reflexive verbs.

1. Hurry up. (Express three ways.)
2. I'm looking forward to my birthday.
3. We were very happy about your visit.
4. You shouldn't always be annoyed with him.
5. Unfortunately, I was mistaken.
6. Can you imagine how it would be if you lived in Switzerland?
7. You must look at my apartment tomorrow evening.

D. In the following sentences, insert **selbst** or **selber** in as many places as possible and translate the resulting sentences into English. The number of possibilities is indicated in parentheses.

1. Erika fährt nicht. (4)
2. Ich wollte, ich könnte einmal mit Meyer reden. (4)
3. Warum denkst du eigentlich nie an dich? (1)
4. Meyer geht jeden Sonntag in die Kirche. (3)
5. Ich habe Angst gehabt. (3)
6. Mit Tante Amalie könnte ich, wenn nötig, ins Museum gehen. (5)

PATTERNS TWO

6/Replacement of Possessive Adjectives

Ich wasche mich.	I wash myself.
Ich wasche das Kind.	I wash the child.
Ich wasche dem Kind die Hände.	I wash the child's hands.
Ich wasche ihm die Hände.	I wash his hands.
Ich wasche mir die Hände.	I wash my hands.

Hast du dir schon die Zähne geputzt?	Have you brushed your teeth yet?
Erika schneidet sich die Haare selber.	Erika cuts her own hair.
Er hat sich den Arm gebrochen.	He broke his arm.
Zieh dir doch die Jacke aus.	Why don't you take off your jacket.
Sie hat sich den Mantel angezogen.	She put on her coat.
Ich muß mir schnell die Schuhe putzen.	I have to polish my shoes quickly.

7/Action and State

anziehen; sich anziehen; angezogen sein
to dress (somebody); to get dressed; to be dressed

Hast du den Kleinen schon angezogen?
Der kann sich doch jetzt schon selbst anziehen; den brauche ich nicht mehr anzuziehen.
Ich *bin* schon angezogen, Mutti; ich habe mich *sel*ber angezogen.

ausziehen; sich ausziehen; ausgezogen sein
to undress (somebody); to get undressed; to be undressed

Als er nach Hause kam, zog er sich schnell aus und legte sich ins Bett.
Heute abend bin ich zu müde, um noch ins Kino zu gehen. Ich bin schon ausgezogen und
    möchte mich nicht noch einmal anziehen.

aufregen; sich aufregen über (acc.)**; aufgeregt sein**
to upset (somebody); to be upset about; to be upset

Ich fahre lieber später in die Stadt. Der Berufsverkehr regt mich zu sehr auf.
Reg dich doch nicht immer so über den Meyer auf.
Aber ich bin doch gar nicht aufgeregt.

beruhigen; sich beruhigen; beruhigt sein
to calm (somebody) down; to calm down; to be calmed down

Beruhigen Sie sich, Frau Meyer, Ihrem Mann ist nichts passiert. Ich habe gerade eben mit
    ihm telefoniert.
Gottseidank; ich war ja so beunruhigt.

Na, sehen Sie, es ist ja alles in Ordnung, und Sie können ganz beruhigt sein.
Daß Sie mit ihm telefoniert haben, beruhigt mich sehr.

entschuldigen; sich entschuldigen; entschuldigt sein
to excuse; to excuse oneself, to apologize; to be excused

Ich glaube, Sie sitzen auf meinem Platz.
    Oh, entschuldigen Sie, Sie haben recht.
    Oh, Entschuldigung, Sie haben recht.
    Oh, ich bitte um Entschuldigung.
Entschuldigen Sie, daß ich so spät komme.
Sie brauchen sich gar nicht zu entschuldigen, bei dem Regen ist das ja kein Wunder. — Aber
    wo ist denn Herr Schneider?
Schneider kommt nicht; er ist entschuldigt; er mußte nach Berlin.
Entschuldigen Sie mich bitte noch einen Augenblick, bevor wir anfangen, ich muß eben
    noch mal telefonieren.

gewöhnen an (acc.)**; sich gewöhnen an** (acc.)**; gewöhnt sein an** (acc.)
to get (somebody) used to (something); to get used to (something); to be used to

Ich kann den Jungen einfach nicht an Pünktlichkeit gewöhnen.
Ich dachte, ich könnte mich nie an dieses Klima gewöhnen, aber jetzt bin ich doch daran
    gewöhnt.

rasieren; sich rasieren; rasiert sein
to shave (somebody); to shave; to be shaved

Ich muß mich noch rasieren, bevor wir zu Erdmanns gehen; wenn ich nicht gut rasiert bin,
    fühle ich mich einfach nicht wohl.

verändern; sich verändern; verändert sein
to change (something); to undergo a change; to be changed

Die Möbel im Wohnzimmer sind neu, aber im Schlafzimmer haben wir nichts verändert.
Ich habe ihn fast nicht erkannt, so sehr hat er sich verändert.
Das stimmt. Seit dem Tod seiner Frau ist er ganz verändert.

vorbereiten; sich vorbereiten; vorbereitet sein
to prepare (something); to prepare; to be prepared

Wir haben alles gut vorbereitet.
Haben Sie sich auch gut vorbereitet?
Ja, Herr Professor, ich glaube, ich bin gut vorbereitet.

MANDATORY REFLEXIVE VERBS

sich ausruhen; ausgeruht sein
to rest; to be rested

*Gerd Weber ruht sich
heute aus.*

Du solltest dich wirklich einmal gut ausruhen.
Aber ich habe doch heute morgen bis zehn geschlafen und bin ganz
ausgeruht.

sich erholen; erholt sein
to get a rest; to be well rested

Na, hast du dich gut erholt?
Ich bin so gut erholt wie noch nie.

sich erkälten; erkältet sein
to catch cold; to have a cold

Bei Schmidts war es gestern abend so kalt, daß ich mich erkältet
habe.
Hannelore ist auch erkältet. War die auch bei Schmidts?

sich verlieben in (acc.)**; verliebt sein in** (acc.)
to fall in love with; to be in love with

Fridolin ist schon wieder verliebt.
In wen hat er sich denn diesmal verliebt? — In eine Studentin.

sich verloben mit; verlobt sein mit
to become engaged to; to be engaged to

Weißt du, daß die Emma sich mit einem Zahnarzt verlobt hat?
Ich dachte, die wäre schon lange verlobt. Wie heißt denn ihr
Verlobter? — Klaus, — Meyer oder Müller oder so irgendetwas. Und
nächsten Sonntag sollen wir zu ihr kommen und Verlobung
feiern.

sich scheiden lassen von; geschieden sein
to get a divorce from; to be divorced

Seit ich von Hans geschieden bin, habe ich viel mehr Zeit für mich
selbst und für die Kinder.

Aber damals sagtest du doch immer, du wolltest dich auf keinen
Fall scheiden lassen, gerade wegen der Kinder.
Das stimmt; aber nach der Scheidung wußte ich plötzlich, daß es
so doch besser war.

8/*sich setzen, sich stellen, sich legen*

sitzen; setzen; sich setzen

Wer sitzt denn da bei euch am Tisch? — Den kenne ich auch nicht. Der hat sich einfach
an unseren Tisch gesetzt.
Nein, unter *die*sen Brief setze ich meinen Namen *nicht.*
Als ich mich an den Frühstückstisch setzte, saß Erika schon da und trank Kaffee.

stehen; stellen; sich stellen

Wer steht denn da bei Frau Schmidt? Ist das nicht Dr. Gerhardt?
Diese Cocktailpartys machen mich wirklich müde. Ich habe stundenlang stehen müssen
und war froh, als ich mich endlich setzen konnte.
Ich habe den Wein auf den Tisch gestellt.
Bitte, gnädige Frau, wie wäre es, wenn Sie sich hier auf diesen Stuhl setzten? Und Sie stellen
sich links neben Ihre Frau, Herr Doktor. Und der Kleine kann rechts von Ihrer Frau
stehen. — So, und jetzt bitte recht freundlich!
In der Zeitung steht, daß Carola van Dongen wieder geheiratet hat. — So? Auf welcher Seite
steht das denn?

liegen; legen; sich legen

Ich hatte mich gerade ins Bett gelegt, als Erich anrief. „Liegst du etwa schon im Bett?" sagte er.
Ich lag noch nicht lange im Bett, als Erich anrief. „Hast du dich etwa schon ins Bett gelegt?"
sagte er.
Wo hast du denn mein Buch hingelegt? — Ich habe es auf deinen Schreibtisch gelegt. Liegt
es denn nicht mehr dort?
Köln liegt am Rhein. Wolframs-Eschenbach liegt in der Nähe von Nürnberg.

ANALYSIS TWO

123/Replacement of Possessive Adjectives by Pronouns plus Article

To identify parts of the body and items of clothing, German, unlike
English, does not use possessive adjectives, but usually uses a dative
pronoun plus an article.

Ich wasche mir die Hände.	I wash my hands.
Ich ziehe mir den Mantel an.	I put on my coat.

The most frequent use of this construction is with dative reflexive pronouns, but, if the part of the body or the item of clothing is not the speaker's, a dative personal pronoun or a dative noun is used.

Ich wasche dem Kind die Hände.	I wash the child's hands.
Ich wasche ihm die Hände.	I wash his/her hands.
Ich ziehe ihm den Mantel an.	I put his/her coat on for him/her.

124/**Action and State**

Some verbs denote a transition of the subject from one condition or state to another, for example, **sich verlieben in** (acc.), *to fall in love with.*

Er hat sich in sie verliebt.   He has fallen in love with her.

These two sentences represent the action of "falling in love" and result in the state of "being in love"; the state is expressed by a form of **sein** plus participle.

Er ist in sie verliebt.   He's in love with her.

A number of reflexive verbs show this pattern, though they are not all mandatory reflexives.

Ich habe mich entschuldigt.	I excused myself; I apologized.
Ich bin entschuldigt.	I am excused.
Ich habe ihn entschuldigt.	I excused him.
Er ist entschuldigt.	He is excused.

sich setzen, sich stellen, sich legen

The weak transitive verbs **setzen**, **stellen**, and **legen** describe the action leading to the state expressed by the strong intransitive verbs **sitzen**, **stehen**, and **liegen**.

Er hat das Kind auf die Bank gesetzt; jetzt sitzt das Kind auf der Bank.	He set the child on the bench; now the child is sitting on the bench.
Sie hat die Flasche auf den Tisch gestellt; jetzt steht die Flasche auf dem Tisch.	She put the bottle on the table; now the bottle is (standing) on the table.
Sie hat das Buch auf den Tisch gelegt; jetzt liegt das Buch auf dem Tisch.	She laid the book on the table; now the book is lying on the table.

The verbs **setzen**, **stellen**, and **legen** are also used with reflexive pronouns. When so used, they normally do not have a literal English equivalent.

Sie hat sich auf die Bank gesetzt.	She sat down on the bench (*lit.* She set herself on the bench).
Er hat sich vor die Haustür gestellt.	He went and stood in front of the door (*lit.* He placed himself in front of the door).

| **Sie hat sich ins Bett gelegt; jetzt liegt sie im Bett.** | She went to bed (*lit.* She laid herself into bed); now she is (lying) in bed. |

Use two-way prepositions (see Anal. 90, p. 291) with the *accusative* after **(sich) setzen, (sich) stellen,** and **(sich) legen;** use the *dative* after the verbs **sitzen, stehen,** and **liegen.**

Note the principal parts of the verbs and their English equivalents:

INTRANSITIVE STRONG VERBS

sitzen, saß, hat gesessen, er sitzt	sit, sat, sat, he sits
stehen, stand, hat gestanden, er steht	stand, stood, stood, he stands
liegen, lag, hat gelegen, er liegt	lie, lay, lain, he lies

TRANSITIVE WEAK VERBS

setzen, setzte, hat gesetzt, er setzt	set, set, set, he sets
stellen, stellte, hat gestellt, er stellt	(no literal English equivalent)
legen, legte, hat gelegt, er legt	lay, laid, laid, he lays

FREQUENT MANDATORY REFLEXIVE VERBS

REFLEXIVE PRONOUN IN THE ACCUSATIVE

sich ärgern über (*acc.*)	to be annoyed with (by)
sich ausruhen	to rest
sich ausschlafen	to get enough sleep
sich beeilen	to hurry (up)
sich erholen	to get a rest
sich entschließen	to make up one's mind
sich erkälten	to catch cold
sich freuen auf (*acc.*)	to look forward to
sich freuen über (*acc.*)	to be happy (glad) about
sich fürchten vor (*dat.*)	to be afraid of
sich irren	to be mistaken, to err
sich scheiden lassen von	to get a divorce from
sich verfahren	to lose one's way driving
sich verlassen auf (*acc.*)	to rely on
sich verlaufen	to lose one's way walking
sich verlieben in (*acc.*)	to fall in love with
sich verloben mit	to become engaged to
sich wundern über (*acc.*)	to be amazed (surprised) at

REFLEXIVE PRONOUN IN THE DATIVE

sich etwas ansehen	to look at something
sich etwas denken	to imagine something
sich etwas überlegen	to meditate about something
sich etwas vorstellen	to imagine something

125/*eben* and *gerade*

If **eben** is used with a full lexical meaning, it means either *flat, even,* or *just (a while ago).*

Das Land ist eben (flach).	The land is flat.
die Ebene, -n	the plain
die Norddeutsche Tiefebene	the North German Plain
Er ist eben gekommen.	He just came.

Eben can also be used as a sentence adverb meaning "it won't take long; I hope you won't mind the interruption." In this function, it minimizes the significance of the action, and for this reason is frequently used in connection with the casual **mal**. As a sentence adverb, **eben** is never stressed.

Ich muß mal eben in die Stadt.
I've got to run downtown for a minute. (Nothing important; I'll be right back.)

Entschuldigst du mich einen Augenblick? Ich muß mal eben telefonieren.
Will you excuse me for a minute? I just want to make a quick phone call.

If **gerade** is used with full lexical meaning, it means *straight.*

Die Linie ist gerade.	The line is straight.

In connection with numbers, one speaks of **gerade Zahlen** and **ungerade Zahlen** (*even* and *odd numbers*).

Gerade can also mean *just then* or *just now*; it is then a synonym of **eben.**

Er ist gerade (eben) gekommen.	He just came.

Ich war gerade (eben) nach Hause gekommen, als das Telefon klingelte.

126/*ruhig*

German **ruhig** can be used either as an adjective or as a sentence adverb. As an adjective, it means *calm, quiet.*

Seid ruhig, Kinder.	Be quiet, children.

If used as a sentence adverb, **ruhig** denotes that the speaker will remain "quiet" and has no objections.

Bleib ruhig im Bett; ich frühstücke im Flughafen.
Don't bother to get up for me; I'll have breakfast at the airport.

Ihr könnt ruhig laut sein, Kinder, ich will jetzt *doch* nicht schlafen.
I won't mind your being loud; I don't want to sleep now anyway.

PRACTICE TWO

E. Supply an appropriate reflexive pronoun or an article.

1. Putz _____ bitte die Schuhe.
2. Ich habe _____ schon gewaschen.
3. Hast du _____ Kind die Hände gewaschen?
4. Wann hast du _____ denn den Arm gebrochen?
5. Habt ihr _____ schon die Zähne geputzt, Kinder?
6. Sie hat sich _____ Mantel angezogen.

F. Restate the following sentences using the perfect of the corresponding reflexive verb.

1. Ich bin gut ausgeruht.
2. Er ist schon rasiert.
3. Sie ist in Christian verliebt.
4. Ich bin schwer erkältet.
5. Sie ist seit einer Woche mit meinem Bruder verlobt.

G. Restate the following sentences by replacing the reflexives with a form of **sein** plus participle.

1. Mit wem hat er sich denn verlobt?
2. Warum hat sie sich denn so aufgeregt?
3. Hat Andrea sich vorbereitet?
4. Hast du dich schon wieder erkältet?
5. Ich habe mich entschlossen, das Haus zu kaufen.

H. Fill in the blanks by using the correct form of **setzen, sitzen; stellen, stehen; legen, liegen**.

1. Ich habe den Wein auf den Tisch _____.
2. Der Wein _____ auf dem Tisch.
3. Ich habe die Kleine schon in ihren Stuhl _____.
4. Die Kleine _____ schon in ihrem Stuhl.
5. Ich habe den Kleinen schon ins Bett _____.
6. Der Kleine _____ schon im Bett.
7. Warum hast du dich noch nicht ins Bett _____?
8. Warum _____ du noch nicht im Bett?
9. Warum hast du dich denn an Meyers Tisch _____?
10. Warum _____ du an Meyers Tisch?

Don't forget the flowers

Europeans are generally more formal in their social interactions. If you are invited into someone's home, it is usually for the evening, which means that you will likely be served a **kaltes Abendessen** accompanied by wine or beer. The custom of serving cocktails before dinner is almost unknown. If you are invited for 7 o'clock, it is considered polite to arrive at 7:15 with a bouquet of flowers for your hostess. Flowers are available at numerous florists (**Blumenläden**) and flower stands. In fact, in a pinch you can even purchase flowers from a vending machine. You always give flowers in odd numbers, for example, five, nine, or eleven, but never thirteen, and red roses only "for the woman you love." On the way to the front door, you take the wrapping paper off the flowers and discreetly put it into your coat pocket. Of course, among students many of these formalities tend to be dispensed with.

CONVERSATIONS

Instead of the usual type of conversations, we introduce here another group of reflexive verbs; each verb is presented within a mini-conversation. By using the situations suggested, enlarge these conversations (though not necessarily with the same verbs) until you have four or more exchanges for each. The first set below can serve as a model. Many of the pattern sentences can be used in the same way.

I

A: Guten Morgen, Hans. Bist du endlich ausgeschlafen?

B: Mein Gott, es ist ja schon zehn Uhr. Aber so gut habe ich schon lange nicht mehr geschlafen.

A: Kein Wunder. Du warst ja wochenlang jede Nacht bis eins oder zwei im Labor.

B: Ja, ich mußte mich wirklich mal ausschlafen.

A: Bist du denn jetzt fertig mit dem Experiment?

B: Noch nicht ganz; aber in zwei, drei Tagen bin ich so weit.

A: Das beruhigt mich. Dann können wir ja über das Wochenende wegfahren.

B: Ja,—und darauf freue ich mich jetzt schon.

A: So, jetzt wollen wir aber erst mal frühstücken.

sich ausschlafen (*mandatory refl.*)**; ausgeschlafen sein** to get enough sleep; to have had enough sleep

II

Könntest du dich nicht doch noch dazu entschließen, am Sonntag
   mit nach Heidelberg zu fahren, Irene?
Ja, weißt du, Jürgen, gestern abend war ich ja fast dazu entschlossen,
   aber heute morgen habe ich an meine Prüfung gedacht, — na ja,
   ich bleibe doch besser hier.

sich entschließen zu
(*mandatory refl.*);
entschlossen sein zu
to make up one's
mind to; to have
made up one's mind,
to be determined

III

Ich möchte dich nur daran erinnern, daß wir heute abend bei Gerda
   eingeladen sind. Sie hat gerade angerufen, — Hannelore Ebert
   kommt auch, mit ihrem Mann.
Hannelore Ebert?
Ja, erinnerst du dich nicht? Die war doch damals mit Gerda zusam-
   men in England.
Natürlich, ich erinnere mich sehr gut an sie; ich hatte nur den
   Namen nicht mehr in Erinnerung.

jemanden erinnern an
(*acc.*); **sich erinnern
an** (*acc.*) to remind
somebody; to remember

IV

Ist Professor von Embden wirklich Leiter der Prüfungskomission?
Ich fürchte, ja. Weißt du, der ist immer so ironisch, — ich habe direkt
   Angst vor ihm.
Bis jetzt habe ich mich vor dem Examen ja gar nicht gefürchet, aber
   mit von Embden . . . ?
Na, wir wollen mal sehen. Vielleicht ist er gar nicht so.

sich fürchten vor (*dat.*)
(*mandatory refl.*);
fürchten to be
afraid of; to fear

V

Meinen Glückwunsch, Herr Maurer, das war wirklich eine sehr gute
   Prüfung. — Sie interessieren sich also besonders für den Impres-
   sionismus in Frankreich.
Ja, Frau Professor, — und das Thema, das Sie mir für die Disserta-
   tion vorgeschlagen haben, interessiert mich sehr.
Das freut mich. Ich bin gerne bereit, Ihnen dabei zu helfen. — Übrigens, wären Sie an einer Assistentenstelle in meinem Institut
   interessiert?

**jemanden interessieren;
sich interessieren für;
interessiert sein an**
(*dat.*) to interest
somebody; to be
interested in; to be
interested in (acquir-
ing or doing)

VI

Ich muß mich noch umziehen, bevor wir ins Theater gehen.
Oh, ich dachte, du wärst schon umgezogen.

Meyers sind umgezogen.
Wirklich? Wo sind sie denn hingezogen?
Nach Wiesbaden.

**sich umziehen; umge-
zogen sein** to change
(clothes); to have
changed (clothes)
umziehen; ziehen to
move (one's residence)

VII

Gib mir doch mal die Straßenkarte. Ich glaube, wir haben uns verfahren.
Was heißt „wir"! Wer verfährt sich denn immer, du oder ich?

In München kann man sich leicht verlaufen.
Wieso denn? Ich habe mich in München noch nie verlaufen.

sich verfahren; sich verlaufen (*mandatory refl.*) to lose one's way driving; to lose one's way walking

NOTE: Do not use **sich vergehen**, which means *to commit a crime*.

VIII

Wenn du den Mercedes nimmst, kannst du beruhigt sein. Auf den
  kann man sich verlassen.
Ja, aber aufs Wetter kann man sich nicht verlassen, nicht um diese
  Jahreszeit.

sich verlassen auf (*acc.*) (*mandatory refl.*) to rely on

Ich muß Sie leider schon verlassen, Frau Vogt, aber der Abend war
  wirklich nett.
Schade, daß Sie schon gehen müssen, Herr Burckhardt.

verlassen (*acc. object*) to leave (a place or person)

Fragen an Sie persönlich

1. Interessieren Sie sich für Politik?
                              Sport?
                              Musik?
                              Literatur?
   Wofür interessieren Sie sich sonst?
   Was interessiert Sie an der Politik?
                      am Sport?
                      usw. (= **und so weiter** etc.)

2. Langweilen Sie sich oft?
   Ärgern   selten?
                     nie?
   Was langweilt Sie am meisten?
   Worüber ärgern Sie sich am meisten?

3. Worauf freuen Sie sich am meisten, wenn das Semester zu Ende ist?
                                       die Schule aus ist?
                                       die Ferien beginnen?

4. Sind Sie verlobt?
            verheiratet?
            verliebt?

5. Fürchten Sie sich vor irgendjemand?
                     vor irgendetwas?
                     vor der nächsten Prüfung?
   (Oder sind Sie sehr gut vorbereitet?)

READING

Kurt Held

Das Märchen° vom Spiegel

<small>° fairy tale</small>

In einem Restaurant hing ein Spiegel. Es gingen° viele Menschen an ihm vorbei° und spiegelten sich. Sie wollten alle wissen, wie sie aussahen. Der Spiegel nahm° ihre Gesichter in sich auf° und schluckte° sie hinunter°. Er sagte kein Wort. Er dachte aber sehr viel und ärgerte sich oft.   5

<small>° passed by   ° took up, received   ° swallowed</small>

Er konnte auch ihre Gedanken lesen, er war ein ganz besonderer Spiegel. „Die Menschen irren sich alle", dachte er. „Die einen bilden sich ein°, schön zu sein, und dabei sind sie häßlich°, und die anderen glauben, häßlich zu sein, und dabei sind sie oft recht hübsch. Keiner sieht sich richtig. Aber wozu soll ich ihnen das sagen und zu sprechen 10 anfangen. Sie würden mir doch nicht glauben."

<small>° imagine   ° ugly</small>

Wenn sie Hüte und Kleider° vor ihm ausprobierten°, so fragten sie ihn unaufhörlich°: „Was steht mir am besten? Wie bin ich am schönsten?" Der Spiegel war geduldig° und schwieg°, aber er dachte: „Wie eitel° sie alle sind. Es ist nicht gut, daß ich da bin." Schließlich 15 bekam der Spiegel Magenweh° von den vielen gespiegelten Menschen, er konnte sie nicht mehr verdauen°. Er geriet immer mehr in Zorn° über ihre Eitelkeit, und zuletzt wurde er trübe° und blind. Die Leute putzten und polierten mit Tüchern° an ihm herum. „Was hat er nur?" fragten sie. „Er spiegelt nicht mehr gut. Er taugt° nichts 20 mehr. Er ist alt." Sie nahmen ihn ab und stellten ihn in eine Ecke. Da dachte der Spiegel: „Ich will ein wenig an die frische Luft° gehen. Vielleicht wird mir dann besser." Er lief auf die Straße und ging an den Häusern entlang. Die Autos, die an ihm vorbeifuhren, spiegelten sich und sagten: „Seht, jetzt fahren die Autos schon auf dem Bürger- 25 steig°. Wir vermehren° uns immer mehr." Die Firmen- und Reklameschilder nickten° erfreut°, als sie sich in dem Spiegel sahen: „Überall steht schon unser Name." Auch die kleinen Bäume, die an den Straßenecken standen, winkten° übermütig° ihren Spiegelbildern zu°: „Wir sind bald ein richtiger Wald." —Und die vielen, vielen Men- 30 schen, die vorüberkamen? Kein einziger° sah den Spiegel, sie sahen alle nur sich selbst und riefen: „Ei seht, da kommt ein Mensch, und der gleicht mir aufs Haar°." Dem Spiegel wurde immer schlechter. „Ich will nicht länger spiegeln", sagte er zu sich, „es ist besser für die Menschen und die Dinge. Wenn sie sich selber nicht mehr sehen 35 können, schauen sie sich vielleicht gegenseitig° genauer an und werden gütiger° zueinander."

<small>° clothes   ° tried on   ° incessantly   ° patient   ° was silent   ° vain   ° stomachache   ° digest, take   ° became more and more angry   ° gloomy, sad   ° cloths   ° is of use   ° air   ° sidewalk   ° multiply   ° nodded   ° pleased   **° zuwinken** to wave playfully   ° single one   ° he looks exactly like me   ° each other   ° kinder</small>

Der Spiegel ging aus der Stadt hinaus. Er ging in den Wald und kam auf ein große Sandhalde°. Dort blieb er stehen. „Hier werde ich

<small>° sandy slope</small>

bleiben", sagte er und spie° alles aus°, was er jemals° gesehen hatte, 40
und dann zerplatzte° er. Keiner konnte mehr erkennen, daß er
jemals ein Spiegel gewesen war. Er war wieder Sand geworden, denn
daraus hatte man ihn gemacht.

Aber die Menschen hängten sich einen neuen Spiegel auf. Es hat
nichts genützt°, daß der alte geplatzt ist.   45

ausspeien to spit out   ever
burst, shattered

it was of no use

BERTOLT BRECHT

Freundschaftsdienste°

Good Turns

Als Beispiel für die richtige Art°, Freunden einen Dienst zu er-
weisen°, gab Herr K. folgende Geschichte zum besten°. „Zu einem
alten Araber kamen drei junge Leute und sagten ihm: ‚Unser Vater
ist gestorben. Er hat uns siebzehn Kamele hinterlassen und im Testament verfügt°, daß der Älteste die Hälfte, der zweite ein Drittel und   5
der Jüngste ein Neuntel der Kamele bekommen soll. Jetzt können
wir uns über die Teilung° nicht einigen°; übernimm° du die Entscheidung!' Der Araber dachte nach und sagte: ‚Wie ich es sehe, habt
ihr, um gut teilen zu können, ein Kamel zu wenig. Ich habe selbst
nur ein einziges Kamel, aber es steht euch zur Verfügung°. Nehmt   10
es und teilt dann, und bringt mir nur, was übrigbleibt°.' Sie bedank-
ten sich für diesen Freundschaftsdienst, nahmen das Kamel mit und
teilten die achtzehn Kamele nun so, daß der Älteste die Hälfte, das
sind neun, der Zweite ein Drittel, das sind sechs, und der Jüngste
ein Neuntel, das sind zwei Kamele bekam. Zu ihrem Erstaunen°   15
blieb, als sie ihre Kamele zur Seite geführt hatten, ein Kamel übrig.
Dieses brachten sie, ihren Dank erneuernd°, ihrem alten Freund
zurück."

Herr K. nannte diesen Freundschaftsdienst richtig, weil er keine be-
sonderen Opfer° verlangte°.   20

way   do
zum besten geben
to tell

stipulated

division   agree
undertake

zur Verfügung stehen
to be available
remains

amazement

renewing

sacrifice
demanded, required

FRANZ KAFKA

Gibs auf!

Es war sehr früh am Morgen, die Straßen rein und leer°, ich ging zum
Bahnhof. Als ich eine Turmuhr° mit meiner Uhr verglich, sah ich,
daß es schon viel später war, als ich geglaubt hatte, ich mußte mich
sehr beeilen, der Schrecken° über diese Entdeckung° ließ mich im
Weg unsicher werden, ich kannte mich in dieser Stadt noch nicht   5
sehr gut aus°, glücklicherweise war ein Schutzmann° in der Nähe,
ich lief zu ihm und fragte ihn atemlos° nach dem Weg. Er lächelte
und sagte: „Von mir willst du den Weg erfahren?" „Ja", sagte ich,
„da ich ihn selbst nicht finden kann." „Gibs auf, gibs auf", sagte er
und wandte sich mit einem großen Schwunge ab°, so wie Leute,   10
die mit ihrem Lachen allein sein wollen.

clean and empty
tower clock

fright, panic   discovery

sich auskennen to
know one's way
around   policeman
breathlessly   find out
turned away from me
with a big swinging
motion

REVIEW EXERCISES

I. Restate the following sentences by using the subjects indicated in parentheses. Be sure to distinguish between dative and accusative reflexives.

1. Natürlich haben sie sich schon einmal geküßt. (wir)
2. Kann er sich schon selber anziehen? (du)
3. Und dann sah er sich im Spiegel. (ich)
4. Ich muß mir morgen eine Wohnung suchen. (wir) (ihr)
5. Das können sie sich nicht kaufen. (ich) (du) (er) (Erika)
6. Sie trafen sich am Bahnhof. (wir)
7. Du mußt auch einmal an dich selbst denken. (Sie)
8. Kannst du dir das Frühstück nicht einmal selber machen? (er)
9. Sie hat sich in ihn verliebt. (er)
10. Hat er sich schon umgezogen? (du)

J. Complete the following sentences.

sich ärgern

Hast du _____ heute im Büro wieder _____ müssen?
Über _____ hast du _____ denn heute _____?
Ja, heute habe ich _____ über Meyer geärgert.
Ich glaube, du bist nicht glücklich, wenn du dich nicht _____ kannst.

sich freuen

Ich habe mich sehr _____ gefreut, daß sie gekommen ist. (Use **da**-compound.)
Ich freue mich sehr _____, daß sie morgen kommt. (Use **da**-compound.)

sich verfahren

Wo bleibt er denn? Ob er sich schon wieder _____ hat?
Ich brauche keine Straßenkarte; ich verfahre _____ nie.

K. Complete the following sentences.

1. Petra freut sich _____ Weihnachten.
2. Das kann ich _____ nicht vorstellen.
3. Ich habe _____ noch nicht vorgestellt; ich bin Hans Ingelheim.
4. Das solltest du _____ gut überlegen.
5. Habt ihr _____ schon überlegt, welchen Film ihr _____ anschauen wollt?
6. _____ Herrn Müller kann ich _____ nur wundern.
7. Ich habe mich sehr _____ sie gewöhnt.
8. Hast du _____ schon ein Zimmer gesucht?

L. Express in German by using reflexive verbs.

1. Why don't you go to bed?
2. Did you shave this morning?
3. They got engaged.
4. They got a divorce.
5. Can Fritzchen get dressed by himself now?
6. You ought to change before Aunt Amalie comes.
7. I broke my arm and I can't undress myself.
8. Have you had enough sleep?
9. Did you have a good rest?
10. He always gets so upset.
11. Did she finally calm down?

M. Change the following actions into states.

1. Sie hat sich in ihren Lehrer verliebt.
2. Sie hat sich mit ihm verlobt.
3. Sie soll ihn geheiratet haben.
4. Hast du dich schon angezogen?
5. Meyer soll sich furchtbar darüber aufgeregt haben.
6. Ich hoffe, du hast dich gut ausgeruht.

N. Change the following states into action; use the perfect.

1. An das Klima bin ich schon gewöhnt.
2. Ich bin davon überzeugt, daß sie gut Englisch spricht.
3. Meine Frau ist wirklich überarbeitet.
4. Ist er schon wieder nicht rasiert?

O. In the following sentences, fill in the blanks by using the correct form of **setzen, sitzen; stellen, stehen; legen, liegen.**

1. Als ich nach Hause kam, _____ meine Frau schon im Bett.
2. Als ich nach Hause kam, hatte meine Frau sich schon ins Bett _____.
3. Hast du die Weinflasche auf den Tisch _____?
4. Meine Frau geht nur dann ins Theater, wenn sie in der ersten Reihe _____ kann.
5. Ich hatte einen guten Platz. Aber dann _____ sich der dicke Meyer vor mich, und ich konnte nichts mehr sehen.
6. Gestern im Theater habe ich neben Rosemarie _____.
7. Heute möchte ich eigentlich gern im Garten _____.
8. Ich habe deinen Mantel aufs Bett _____.
9. Der Zug war so voll, daß ich keinen Sitzplatz finden konnte, und ich mußte von Köln bis nach Frankfurt _____.
10. Wir haben den Tisch jetzt an die Wand _____.

P. In the following sentences, replace the transitives **setzen, stellen, legen** or the reflexives **sich setzen, sich stellen, sich legen** with the intransitives **sitzen, stehen, liegen,** or vice versa. Observe the difference in tense and, in some cases, the change of subject; remember also that you have to change case in the prepositional phrase.

Sie liegt schon im Bett.   **Sie hat sich schon ins Bett gelegt.**

1. Er hat sich neben sie gesetzt.
2. Wir saßen am Tisch.
3. Sie sitzen alle im Garten.
4. Warum hast du dich denn noch nicht ins Bett gelegt?
5. Er muß sich schon ins Bett gelegt haben.
6. Sie hatte sich direkt neben die Tür gestellt.
7. Er stand am Fenster.
8. Er hat das Buch auf den Nachttisch gelegt.
9. Ich habe die Flasche auf den Tisch gestellt.
10. Er saß schon am Frühstückstisch.
11. Vor ihm stand eine Tasse Kaffee. (New subject: Ingrid)
12. Er legte die Bibel vor sich auf den Tisch.
13. Wo hast du denn meinen Hut hingelegt?
14. Wo sitzt denn deine Frau? (Start new question with **Wo** and use **sich hinsetzen.**)
15. Wo steht denn mein Wagen? (Start question with **Wohin**; new subject: **du.**)

Q. Express the following sentences in German. These sentences all contain reflexives. Do not use **sein** plus participle.

1. Are you still interested in her?
2. Think of yourself for a change.
3. I was really mad at him last night.
4. She fell in love with her teacher.
5. We have never been so bored.
6. I've bought myself a coat.
7. They want to get a divorce.
8. May I introduce myself?
9. Just imagine: after twenty years he still remembered me.
10. I am looking forward to seeing her again.
11. We want to have a look at Meyer's house.
12. I haven't changed yet, and I still have to shave.
13. Don't get so upset.
14. Has she calmed down again?
15. I simply can't get used to his accent.
16. Did you lose your way again? (hiking) (driving)

Bürgerhaus aus dem 16. Jahrhundert

VOCABULARY

sich (dat.)[4] etwas an•schauen	to look at
sich (dat.) etwas an•sehen	to look at
sich (acc.) an•ziehen	to get dressed
sich (acc.) ärgern über (acc.)	to be annoyed by
der Arm, -e	arm
sich (acc.) auf•regen	to get upset
sich (acc.) aus•ruhen	to rest
sich (acc.) aus•schlafen	to get enough sleep
sich (dat.) etwas aus•suchen	to select, pick out
sich (acc.) aus•ziehen	to undress
sich (acc.) bedienen	to serve (oneself)
der Selbstbedie-nungsladen, ⸚	self-service store
sich (acc.) beeilen	to hurry
bereit sein zu	be ready for
sich (acc.) beruhigen	to calm down
beunruhigt sein	to be worried
brechen	to break
sich (dat.) den Arm brechen	to break one's arm
sich (dat.) denken	to imagine
ich denke mir etwas	I imagine
dick	thick, fat
der Dummkopf, ⸚e	stupid person, block-head, dumbbell
eben	flat, even; just
sich (acc.) ent-schließen	to decide, to make up one's mind
entschlossen sein	to be determined
sich (acc.) entschul-digen	to excuse (oneself), to apologize
sich (acc.) erholen	to get a rest
erholt sein	to be well rested
erinnern an (acc.)	to remind of
sich (acc.) erinnern an (acc.)	to remember
die Erinnerung, -en	remembrance, memory
sich (acc.) erkälten	to catch a cold

erkältet sein	to have a cold
sich (acc.) freuen auf (acc.)	to look forward to
sich (acc.) freuen über (acc.)	to be happy (glad) about
die Freundschaft, -en	friendship
furchtbar	terrible
sich (acc.) fürchten vor (dat.)	to be afraid of
gerade	straight; just
gerade Zahlen	even numbers
ungerade Zahlen	odd numbers
gewinnen	to win
sich (acc.) gewöhnen an (acc.)	to get used to
gewöhnt sein an (acc.)	to be used to
der Glückwunsch, ⸚e	congratulation
das Haar, -e	hair
sich (dat.) die Haare schneiden lassen	to get a haircut
häßlich	ugly
hübsch	pretty
sich (acc.) interes-sieren für	to be interested in
interessiert sein an (dat.)	to be interested in
irgendetwas	anything; something
irgendjemand	anybody; somebody
sich (acc.) irren	to err, be in error
die Jacke, -n	jacket
die Jahreszeit, -en	season
jemals	ever
die Karte, -n	card; map
die Straßenkarte, -n	road map
das Klima	climate
sich (acc.) langweilen	to be bored
sich (acc.) legen	to lie down
leicht	easy; light
die Literatur', -en	literature
menschlich	human
die Möbel (pl.)	furniture
niemals	never
nötig	necessary

[4]Since **sich** can be either dative or accusative, the case of the reflexive pronoun is indicated in parentheses.

die Politik′	politics; policy	sich (dat.) überlegen	to think (meditate); to wonder
poli′tisch	political	sich (acc.) um•ziehen	to change (clothes)
putzen	to clean	usw. (und so weiter)	and so on
sich (acc.) rasieren	to shave	sich (acc.) verändern	to change
rufen	to shout, call out	sich (acc.) verfahren	to get lost (driving)
schade	too bad	sich (acc.) verlassen	to rely on
scheiden	to separate, divide	auf (acc.)	
sich (acc.) scheiden lassen	to get a divorce	sich (acc.) verlaufen	to get lost (walking)
die Scheidung, -en	divorce	sich (acc.) verlieben in (acc.)	to fall in love with
das Schlafzimmer, -	bedroom	sich (acc.) verloben mit	to get engaged to
schneiden	to cut	verpassen	to miss
der Schreibtisch, -e	desk	vorbei•gehen an	to pass by
selbst	-self; even	(dat.) (sein)	
selber	-self	sich (acc.) vor•be-	to prepare for
setzen	to set, put, place	reiten auf (acc.)	
sich (acc.) setzen	to sit down	sich (acc. or dat.)	to introduce; to
sich (acc.) stellen	to place oneself; to stand (up)	vorstellen	imagine
		ich stelle mich vor	I introduce myself
stimmen (impers.)	to be correct	ich stelle mir vor	I imagine
das stimmt	that is correct	sich (acc.) wohl•fühlen	to feel well
stundenlang	for hours	sich (acc.) wundern	to be amazed
das Thema, die Themen	topic; theme	ziehen (sein)	to move (from one place to another)
der Tod	death		
sich (acc.) treffen	to meet		

Strong Verbs

INFINITIVE	PRESENT	PAST TENSE	PERFECT	
sich an•sehen	sieht an	sah an	angesehen	to look at
sich an•ziehen		zog an	angezogen	to dress
sich aus•schlafen	schläft aus	schlief aus	ausgeschlafen	to sleep one's fill
sich aus•ziehen		zog aus	ausgezogen	to undress
brechen	bricht	brach	(ist) gebrochen	to break
sich entschließen		entschloß	entschlossen	to make up one's mind
gewinnen		gewann	gewonnen	to win
rufen		rief	gerufen	to shout, call out
scheiden		schied	geschieden	to separate, divide
schneiden		schnitt	geschnitten	to cut
sich treffen	trifft	traf	getroffen	to meet
sich um•ziehen		zog um	umgezogen	to change clothes
sich verfahren	verfährt	verfuhr	verfahren	to lose one's way
sich verlassen	verläßt	verließ	verlassen	to depend
sich verlaufen	verläuft	verlief	verlaufen	to lose one's way

Unit 15
Adjectives

The Press

Germans have always been avid newspaper readers, and in spite of television, the sale of newspapers has continued to rise. In the Federal Republic alone over 20 million copies of local, regional, and national newspapers are sold daily. Some of the major and most influential dailies in the Federal Republic range from the conservative *Die Welt* and the middle-of-the-road *Frankfurter Allgemeine* to the liberal *Süddeutsche Zeitung* and the left-leaning *Frankfurter Rundschau*. Another internationally known daily is the Swiss *Neue Zürcher Zeitung*. These major papers have a low circulation compared to the street tabloid *Bild-Zeitung* with 5 million copies sold daily. The Federal Republic also has a weekly news magazine, *Der Spiegel* (circulation about 1 million), comparable to *Time* or *Newsweek*, but somewhat more aggressive and controversial in its reporting. The only major paper in the German Democratic Republic is the official party newspaper, *Neues Deutschland — Zentralorgan der SED*, comparable to *Pravda* in the Soviet Union.

Zeitungen aus Österreich

Zeitungen aus der Bundesrepublik

Ein Zeitungsstand

PATTERNS ONE

1/Attributive Adjectives: Nominative Singular

Der neue Direktor hieß Bodenstein.	The name of the new director was Bodenstein.
Ein junger Mann wartete auf ihn.	A young man was waiting for him.
Die junge Frau hieß Petra.	The young woman's name was Petra.
Eine junge Frau stand neben ihm.	A young woman was standing next to him.
Das kleine Mädchen hieß auch Petra.	The little girl's name was also Petra.
Damals war sie noch ein kleines Mädchen.	She was still a little girl then.
Mein lieber Vater,	My dear Father,
Meine liebe Mutter,	My dear Mother,
Mein liebes Kind,	My dear Child,
Lieber Vater,	Dear Father,
Liebe Mutter,	Dear Mother,
Liebes Kind,	Dear Child,
Das ist wirklich ein guter Wein!	That is really a good wine!
Guter Wein ist teuer.	Good wine is expensive.
Italienische Gemüsesuppe ist eine Spezialität unseres Hauses.	Italian vegetable soup is a speciality of the house.
Eine gute Suppe gehört zu jeder Mahlzeit.	A good soup belongs with every meal.
Frisches Obst ist immer gut.	Fresh fruit is always good.
Das italienische Obst ist gar nicht teuer.	Italian fruit is not expensive at all.
Ich empfehle Ihnen Dortmunder Union; das ist ein gutes Bier.	I recommend Dortmunder Union; that's a good beer.

2/Attributive Adjectives: Accusative Singular

Hast du den alten Mann gesehen?	Did you see the old man?
Ich habe einen alten Mann gesehen.	I saw an old man.
Ich kenne die junge Dame leider nicht.	I don't know the young lady, unfortunately.

Ich habe das junge Mädchen nicht gesehen.	I haven't seen the young girl.
Schmidts haben ein kleines Mädchen.	Schmidts have a little girl.
Wie heißt das kleine Mädchen?	What's the little girl's name?

3/Attributive Adjectives: Dative Singular

Mit dem alten Wagen fahre ich nicht.	I won't drive that old car.
Was soll ich denn mit einem alten Wagen?	What am I supposed to do with an old car?
Wir wohnten damals in einer kleinen Stadt.	At that time we lived in a small town.
Wir wohnten in einem kleinen Städtchen.	We lived in a small town.
Bei schlechtem Wetter fahren wir mit dem Bus.	In bad weather we take the bus.

4/Attributive Adjectives: Genitive Singular

Ingrid war die Tochter eines bekannten Architekten in Berlin.	Ingrid was the daughter of a well-known architect in Berlin.
Der Besuch der alten Dame ist ein Stück von Dürrenmatt.	*The Visit of the Old Lady* is a play by Dürrenmatt.
Wegen des schlechten Wetters konnten wir in Frankfurt nicht landen.	Because of the bad weather we couldn't land in Frankfurt.
Innerhalb[1] eines einzigen Tages verkauft unsere Firma oft zwanzig bis fünfundzwanzig Wagen.	Within a single day our firm often sells twenty to twenty-five cars.
Außerhalb[1] der inneren Stadt gibt es noch viel offenes Land.	Outside (of) the inner city there is still much open space.

5/Attributive Adjectives: Plural

Die jungen Leute gehen ins Kino.	The young people go to the movies.
Unsere deutschen Freunde wohnen in Bonn.	Our German friends live in Bonn.
Gute Bücher müssen nicht teuer sein.	Good books don't have to be expensive.
Petra ist die Mutter der beiden[2] Kinder.	Petra is the mother of the two children.

KALTE SPEISEN
WARME SPEISEN

[1]The prepositions **innerhalb** (*within, inside of*) and **außerhalb** (*outside of*) take the genitive, like **statt, trotz, während, wegen.**

[2]When preceded by a definite article or possessive adjective, **beid-** is the equivalent of *two*.

Für diese alten Bücher habe ich viel Geld bezahlt.	I paid a lot of money for these old books.
Niemand liest seine letzten Romane.	Nobody reads his last novels.
Er brachte ihr rote Rosen.	He brought her red roses.
Sie hat zwei intelligente Kinder.	She has two intelligent children.

6/Series of Attributive Adjectives

Der blonde junge Mann da drüben heißt Kleinholz.	The name of the blond young man over there is Kleinholz.
Ein blonder junger Mann kam aus dem Haus.	A blond young man came out of the house.
Die blonde junge Dame ist seine Frau.	The blond young lady is his wife.
Eine blonde junge Frau kam aus dem Haus.	A blond young woman came out of the house.
Das kleine blonde Mädchen hieß Petra.	The name of the blond little girl was Petra.
Vor dem Haus saß ein blondes kleines Mädchen.	A blond little girl was sitting in front of the house.
Die Eltern des netten jungen Mannes kamen aus Leipzig.	The parents of the nice young man came from Leipzig.
Der Wagen gehört der netten jungen Frau.	The car belongs to the nice young woman.
Kennen Sie den netten jungen Mann?	Do you know the nice young man?
Diese schönen alten Bücher habe ich in Heidelberg gekauft.	I bought these beautiful old books in Heidelberg.
Schöne alte Bücher sind oft sehr teuer.	Beautiful old books are often very expensive.

ANALYSIS ONE

127/Attributive Adjectives

In both English and German, adjectives can be used in two ways:
as predicate adjectives and as attributive adjectives.

Predicate adjectives, that is, adjectives following **sein** or **werden**, are second-prong elements and never have an ending (see Anal. 30, p. 77).

Sein Sohn war leider nicht intelligent.

Attributive adjectives precede the nouns they modify and always have an ending; they are usually preceded by an article.

Unser Sohn ist intelligent.	**Wir haben einen intelligenten Sohn.**
Unsere Tochter ist intelligent.	**Wir haben eine intelligente Tochter.**
Unser Kind ist intelligent.	**Wir haben ein intelligentes Kind.**
Unsere Kinder sind intelligent.	**Wir haben intelligente Kinder.**

Attributive adjectives always have an ending; this ending depends on the gender, case, and number of the noun and on whether or not a **der**-word or an **ein**-word precedes (see Anal. 20–21, pp. 47–48).

There are two sets of adjective endings: strong (or primary) and weak (or secondary) endings. Their distribution may at first seem confusing, but once you grasp the principle, using correct endings should become quite easy.

You have already learned the forms of **der**-words (**der, dieser, jeder, welcher**) and **ein**-words (**ein, kein, mein,** etc.).

	der-WORDS				**ein**-WORDS			
	MASC.	FEM.	NEUT.	PL.	MASC.	FEM.	NEUT.	PL.
NOM.	der	die	das	die	ein	eine	ein	keine
ACC.	den	die	das	die	einen	eine	ein	keine
DAT.	dem	der	dem	den	einem	einer	einem	keinen
GEN.	des	der	des	der	eines	einer	eines	keiner

Remember that the endings of **der**-words and **ein**-words are identical except for the nominative masculine singular and the nominative and accusative neuter singular, where the **ein**-words have no ending.

STRONG ENDINGS (PRIMARY ENDINGS)

The strong adjective endings are identical with the endings of the **der**-words except in the genitive case, where the masculine and neuter singular are both **-en** rather than **-es**. These forms do not occur frequently.

STRONG ADJECTIVE ENDINGS			
	MASC.	FEM.	NEUT.	PL.

	MASC.	FEM.	NEUT.	PL.
NOM.	**-er**	**-e**	**-es**	**-e**
ACC.	**-en**	**-e**	**-es**	**-e**
DAT.	**-em**	**-er**	**-em**	**-en**
GEN.	**-en**	**-er**	**-en**	**-er**

WEAK ENDINGS (SECONDARY ENDINGS)

There are only two weak adjective endings, **-e** and **-en**. Note that only the masculine singular distinguishes between nominative and accusative.

WEAK ADJECTIVE ENDINGS			
	MASC.	FEM.	NEUT.	PL.

	MASC.	FEM.	NEUT.	PL.
NOM.	**-e**	**-e**	**-e**	**-en**
ACC.	**-en**	**-e**	**-e**	**-en**
DAT.	**-en**	**-en**	**-en**	**-en**
GEN.	**-en**	**-en**	**-en**	**-en**

USE OF STRONG AND WEAK ENDINGS

Noun phrases usually begin with some kind of "identifier" to indicate gender, case, and number. The strong endings of **der**-words and **ein**-words are such identifiers (except for the three forms of **ein** without endings). If adjectives follow these strong **der**-words or **ein**-words, the adjective takes weak endings.

If the noun phrase begins with an **ein**-word without ending, the adjective takes over the function of identifier and takes a strong ending.

By the same logic, if the noun phrase begins with an adjective, that is, if there is no **der**-word or **ein**-word preceding the adjective, the adjective must take a strong ending.

The table illustrates the distribution of adjective endings.

		SLOT 0 NO ENDING	SLOT 1 STRONG ENDING	SLOT 2 WEAK ENDING	SLOT 3 NOUN	
1		Dies (das) ist	guter		Kaffee.	
2	NOM. SING.	Dies (das) ist	gute		Butter.	
3		Dies (das) ist	gutes		Bier.	
4		Das (dies) ist	ein	guter		Kaffee.	
5	NOM. SING.	Das (dies) ist	eine	gute	Suppe.	
6		Das (dies) ist	ein	gutes		Bier.	
7				Der	junge	Mann	blieb zu Hause.
8	NOM. SING.		Die	junge	Dame	bleib zu Hause.
9			Das	kleine	Kind	blieb zu Hause.
10		Gegen	hohen		Blutdruck	nehmen Sie Vitalin.
11	ACC. SING.	Gegen	große		Nervosität	nehmen Sie Vitalin.
12		Gegen	hohes		Fieber	nehmen Sie Vitalin.
13		Siehst du	den	jungen	Mann	da drüben?
14		Ich sehe	keinen	jungen	Mann.	
15	ACC. SING.	Siehst du	die	junge	Frau	da drüben?
16		Ich sehe	keine	junge	Frau.	
17		Siehst du	das	kleine	Mädchen	da drüben?
18		Ich sehe	kein	kleines		Mädchen.	
19		Bei	dichtem		Nebel	bleiben wir zu Hause.
20	DAT. SING.	Bei	großer		Hitze	bleiben wir zu Hause.
21		Bei	schlechtem		Wetter	bleiben wir zu Hause.
22		Mit	dem	alten	Wagen	fahre ich nicht.
23	DAT. SING.	Mit	der	alten	Kutsche	fahre ich nicht.
24		Mit	dem	alten	Auto	fahre ich nicht.
25		Ich bin die Frau	eines	intelligenten	Mannes.	
26	GEN. SING.	Ich bin der Mann	einer	intelligenten	Frau.	
27		Sie ist die Mutter	eines	intelligenten	Kindes.	
28	NOM. PL.		Gute		Menschen	lügen nicht.
29	ALL GENDERS		Die	guten	Menschen	lügen nicht.
30	ACC. PL.	Wir haben	gute		Kinder.	
31		Wir haben	unsere	guten	Kinder.	
32	DAT. PL.	Die Eltern von	intelligenten		Kindern	sind meistens auch intelligent.
33		Die Eltern von	diesen	intelligenten	Kindern	sind auch intelligent.
34	GEN. PL.	Die Eltern	intelligenter		Kinder	sind meistens auch intelligent.
35		Die Eltern	dieser	intelligenten	Kinder	sind auch intelligent.

The table has four slots, marked 0, 1, 2, and 3, respectively. The zero-slot is reserved for the three forms of **ein**-words without endings; slot 1 contains words with strong endings; slot 2 words with weak endings; and slot 3 the nouns that follow.

Additional adjectives can be added to each sentence in the table, and they will take the same ending as the first. For example:

dieser intelligente junge Mann
dieses intelligente junge Mädchen
ein intelligenter junger Mann
ein intelligentes junges Mädchen

To sum up: Slot 1 *must be filled* as long as there is a word that can take a strong ending. If there is no word that *has* a fixed strong ending (like **der**), the adjective "moves forward" and takes strong endings.

128/Adjective Endings: Variants

1. In the dative masculine and neuter, the sequence **-em -en** is so ingrained that of two or more adjectives not preceded by an **ein**-word or **der**-word only the first tends to take the strong ending **-em**.

	SLOT 0	SLOT 1	SLOT 2	SLOT 3
Bei		**diesem**	**nebligen kalten**	**Wetter**
Bei		**nebligem**	**kalten**	**Wetter**

2. In the genitive masculine and neuter, with adjectives not preceded by a **der**-word or an **ein**-word, the strong endings have been replaced by weak endings.

	SLOT 0	SLOT 1	SLOT 2	SLOT 3
Trotz			**starken**	**Nebels**
Trotz			**schlechten**	**Wetters**

These forms, however, do not, as a rule, occur in the spoken language, which prefers the regular pattern with the dative.

	SLOT 0	SLOT 1	SLOT 2	SLOT 3
Trotz		**starkem**		**Nebel**
Trotz		**schlechtem**		**Wetter**

3. Adjectives ending in **-el** and **-er** drop the **-e-** if an attributive ending is added.

Das Zimmer war dunkel.	The room was dark.
Sie saßen in einem dunklen Zimmer.	They sat in a dark room.
Die Zimmer hier sind aber sehr teuer.	The rooms here are very expensive.
Wir wohnten in einem teuren Zimmer.	We stayed in an expensive room.

4. The adjective **hoch** drops the **-ch**-sound if an ending is added and substitutes a silent **-h-**.

Der Baum war sehr hoch.	The tree was very tall.
Vor dem Haus stand ein hoher Baum.	A tall tree stood in front of the house.

PRACTICE ONE

A. Fill in the blanks with an adjective in the nominative singular.

1. Der Mann war sehr alt. Er war ein sehr _alter_ Mann.
2. Sie ist intelligent. Sie ist ein _intelligentes_ Mädchen.
3. Der Wein ist wirklich gut. Das ist wirklich ein _gutes_ Wein.
4. Sie ist immer noch schön. Sie ist immer noch eine _schöne_ Frau.
5. Das Wasser ist aber kalt. Das ist aber _kaltes_ Wasser.
6. Das Bier hier ist gut. Das ist wirklich ein _gutes_ Bier.
7. So klein ist eure Barbara nicht mehr. Sie ist kein _kleines_ Kind mehr.
8. Gestern war es kalt. Gestern war ein _kalter_ Tag.

B. Fill in the blanks with an adjective in the accusative singular.

1. Gestern war das Wetter schlecht. Gestern hatten wir _schlechtes_ Wetter.
2. Gestern war es kalt. Gestern hatten wir einen _kalten_ Tag.
3. Der Wein war gut. Wir haben einen _guten_ Wein getrunken.
4. Das Bier ist wirklich gut. Wo habt ihr denn dieses _gutes_ Bier gekauft.
5. Diese Suppe ist wirklich gut. Heute gibt es _gute_ Suppe.

C. Fill in the blanks with an adjective in the dative singular.

1. Das Haus ist alt. Wir wohnen in einem _alten_ Haus.
2. Die Stadt ist klein. Wir wohnen in einer _kleinen_ Stadt.
3. Das Wetter ist schlecht. Bei dem _schlecht_ Wetter bleibe ich zu Hause.
4. Das ist französischer Wein. Bei _französischen_ Wein sage ich nie nein.

D. Fill in the blanks with an adjective in the genitive singular.

1. Die Reise war lang, aber trotz der _____ Reise war ich gar nicht müde.
2. Ihr neuer Roman heißt *Schwestern*. Der Titel ihres _neuen_ Romans ist *Schwestern*.
3. Das Museum ist ganz neu. Wer ist denn der Direktor des _neuen_ Museums?

E. Fill in the blanks with an adjective in the plural.

1. Meyers Kinder sind intelligent. Meyer hat _intelligente_ Kinder.
2. Rot ist meine Lieblingsfarbe; daher bringt er mir immer _rote_ Rosen.
3. Ich habe Freunde in Amerika. Ich fliege morgen zu meinen _amerikanischen_ Freunden.
4. Sie kennen doch Amerika, nicht wahr? Was halten Sie denn von den _amerikanischen_ Schulen?

F. Insert the adjectives **neu** and **automatisch** in the following sentences.

1. Ich wollte, ich hätte eine Waschmaschine. _neue automatische_
2. Der Preis einer Waschmaschine ist gar nicht so hoch. _neuen automatischen_
3. Die Preise unserer Waschmaschinen sind gar nicht so hoch.
4. Mit dieser Waschmaschine sind Sie bestimmt zufrieden.
5. Ist das eure Waschmaschine?
6. Diese Waschmaschinen sind gar nicht teuer.
7. Waschmaschinen sind gar nicht teuer.
8. Wir können nur noch Waschmaschinen verkaufen.

Cash or credit

It used to be that if you wanted to make a major purchase, you saved the money until you could afford it. This kind of cash economy existed throughout Central Europe until well after World War II. Installment buying became more popular when people started purchasing automobiles and their own homes. Only recently has "plastic money" made inroads. The major credit cards used today are American Express, Diners Club, Visa, and Eurocard, which has joined forces with Master Card. But as late as 1983, the total number of credit cards in circulation in the Federal Republic was only about 800,000. Checking accounts are also not as common as in the U.S., but the number of savings accounts is still very large. One unusual feature is that you can have a savings account at the post office, and you use your **Postsparbuch** to make deposits or withdrawals at any post office.

PATTERNS TWO

7/der-Words

Bei diesem schlechten Wetter bleibe ich zu Hause.

In this bad weather I'll stay home.

Welche deutschen Städte haben Sie denn gesehen?

Which German cities did you see?

Jeder junge Mensch sollte einmal ein Jahr lang im Ausland leben.

Every young person ought to live abroad for a year.

Von hier aus fährt jede halbe Stunde ein Zug nach Stuttgart.

From here, a train goes to Stuttgart every half hour.

Dort haben wir schon manchen schönen Tag verbracht.

We've spent many a beautiful day there.

Manche von meinen alten Freunden wohnen nicht mehr hier.

Some of my old friends no longer live here.

8/so, solch, solcher

So einen guten Freund finde ich so bald nicht wieder.

Such a good friend I will not find again soon.

Wie kann ein so intelligenter Mensch nur so blöd sein!

How can a person who is that intelligent be so stupid!

Für einen so alten Wagen bekommst du bestimmt keine tausend Mark.

I'm sure you won't get a thousand marks for a car as old as that.

Für solch einen Wagen muß man mindestens zwanzigtausend Mark bezahlen.

For such a car you'll have to pay at least twenty thousand marks.

Ich wußte gar nicht, daß er noch so kleine Kinder hat.

I didn't know that his children are still that little.

Solche Kinder wie die möchte ich auch haben.

I'd like to have children like that too.

Das Bier, das unsere Sprache spricht

So ein Bier...

So ein Bier, so wunderschön wie Hofbräu!

9/Ordinal Numbers; Dates; Fractions

Am wievielten Februar wart ihr in Hamburg?

When (on what day) in February were you in Hamburg?

Am ersten und zweiten März waren wir in Berlin, am dritten und vierten in Hamburg und vom fünften bis zum zehnten in Bonn.

On the first and second of March we were in Berlin, on the third and fourth in Hamburg, and from the fifth to the tenth in Bonn.

Der wievielte ist heute? —Heute ist der siebte Mai.

What is today's date? —Today is the seventh of May.

Den wievielten haben wir heute? —Den siebzehnten.

What is today's date? —The seventeenth.

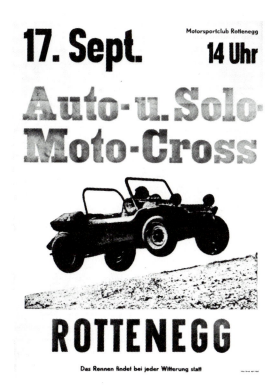

Motorsportclub Rottenegg

17. Sept. **14 Uhr**

Auto- u. Solo-Moto-Cross

ROTTENEGG

Das Rennen findet bei jeder Witterung statt

Rottenegg in Österreich

In letters, dates are expressed as follows:

Berlin, den 1.12.1987 (den ersten Dezember 1987)
Hamburg, 8.9.1988 (den achten September 1988)

Elisabeth II. (Elisabeth die Zweite)
Friedrich Wilhelm IV. (Friedrich Wilhelm der Vierte)
Er war ein Sohn Friedrichs II. (Er war ein Sohn Friedrichs des Zweiten.)

Und hier, meine Damen und Herren, sehen Sie ein Bild von Herzog August III., der, wie
Sie wissen, der Vater Sigismunds II. war. Seine Frau Mechthild, eine Tochter Augusts
V. von Niederlohe-Schroffenstein, soll die schönste Frau ihrer Zeit gewesen sein.

Nein, nach Italien fahren will ich nicht. Erstens habe ich kein Geld, zweitens habe ich keine
Lust, drittens mag ich Meyers nicht und viertens ist meine Frau dagegen.

Nein, soviel kann ich nicht essen. Die Hälfte davon ist mehr als genug.

Hat Tante Amalie schon ihr Testament gemacht? — Ja, und ein Drittel von ihrem Geld bekommt das Museum.

Seine Frau erhielt zwei Drittel seines Vermögens, und das dritte Drittel ging an seine beiden
Söhne.

Ich hätte gerne ein halbes Pfund Butter.
Geben Sie mir bitte ein viertel Pfund Schinken.

10/The Rhetorical *nicht*

Haben Sie einen *Bru*der?	Do you have a brother?
Haben Sie keinen *Bru*der?	Don't you have a brother?
Haben Sie nicht *ei*nen *Bru*der?	Don't you have a single brother?
Haben Sie nicht einen *Bru*der?	You have a brother, haven't you?

Ist Manfred Schmidtke nicht ein netter junger Mann?

Warst du nicht gestern abend mit Inge im Kino?
Haben Sie nicht früher bei der Hansa-Bank gearbeitet?
Hat nicht unsere Partei seit Jahren immer wieder bewiesen, daß sie allein den Weg weiß
in eine bessere Zukunft?

11/*hin* and *her*

Wohin gehst du denn?	Wo gehst du denn hin?
Woher kommst du denn?	Wo kommst du denn her?
Wohin ist er denn gegangen?	Wo ist er denn hingegangen?
Woher ist er denn gekommen?	Wo ist er denn hergekommen?
Dahin gehe ich auch.	Da gehe ich auch hin.
Daher komme ich auch.	Da komme ich auch her.
Ich fahre sofort hin.	Er kommt sofort her.
Kannst du hinfahren?	Kannst du herkommen?
Ich bin sofort hingefahren.	Er ist sofort hergekommen.
Ich brauche nicht hinzufahren.	Er braucht nicht herzukommen.
Wer hat dich denn dahingebracht?	Wer hat dich denn hierhergebracht?
Wie bist du denn dahingekommen?	Wie bist du denn hierhergekommen?
Sie fahren nach Tirol? Dahin fahre ich auch.	Sie kommen aus Tirol? Daher komme ich auch.
Ich gehe ins Eßzimmer hinunter.	I'm going down to the dining room.
Er kommt sofort herunter.	He'll be down in a minute.

Ist er schon heruntergekommen?	Has he come down yet?
Sie ist gerade hinausgegangen.	She just went out.
Sie ist schon hinaufgegangen.	She has already gone up.
Hast du die Zeitung schon hereingeholt?	Have you brought the paper in yet?
Ich habe sie noch nicht herauskommen sehen.	I haven't seem them come out yet.
Herein.	Come in.

ANALYSIS TWO

129/der-Words

The following are declined like the definite article; that is, they always take strong endings:

dieser	this
jeder	each, every
mancher	many a; *plural*, some
welcher	which, what

(a) The neuter singular **dieses** may be used without an ending (**dies**) in the nominative and accusative.

Dies Buch hier ist wirklich gut.

In sentences identifying or introducing persons or objects, **dies** (or **das**) must be used.

Gerda, dies (das) ist mein Freund Hans.
Und dies (das), meine Damen und Herren, war das Schlafzimmer des Königs.

(b) The plural of **jeder** is **alle: jeder Mensch, alle Menschen.**

(c) **Welcher** is normally used as an interrogative: **in welcher Stadt?** *in which (what) city?*

130/so, solch, solcher

In the singular, **so ein** may be and **ein so** must be followed by adjectives.

| **Sie ist doch so (solch) eine intelligente Frau.** | She is such an intelligent woman. |
| **Eine so intelligente Frau findet sicher eine gute Stellung.** | A woman who is that intelligent will certainly find a good job. |

In the plural, **so** is immediately followed by an adjective.

Ich wußte gar nicht, daß er noch so kleine Kinder hat.	I didn't know that his children are still so little.

The word **solcher**, *such*, is also a **der**-word, but it is frequently replaced in the spoken language by **so** or **solch** without an ending. With endings, **solch-** is usually followed immediately by a noun.

Warum hast du denn immer solche Angst? (so große Angst?)	Why are you always so afraid?
Mit solchen Menschen will ich nichts zu tun haben.	I don't want to have anything to do with such people.

131/Ordinal Numbers; Dates; Fractions

German ordinal numbers (*first, second, third,* etc.) are attributive adjectives. With the exception of **der erste** and **der dritte**, they are formed by adding **-t-** plus ending to the cardinal number. From **zwanzig** on **-st-** plus ending are added.

der *erste*	der **neunzehnte**
der **zweite**	der **zwanzigs***te*
der *dritte*	der **einundzwanzigs***te*
der **vierte**	der **dreißigs***te*
der **fünfte**	*etc.*
der **sechste**	
der *siebte*	
etc.	

To indicate that a number is an ordinal, German places a period after the number. Ordinals *must* always be used with dates.

der 4. Juli (der vierte Juli)	the Fourth of July or July 4

There are two ways to ask for or give a date:

Der wievielte ist heute? **Den wievielten haben wir heute?**	What's today's date (*lit.* the "how-manyeth" is today)?
Heute ist der achte. **Heute haben wir den achten.**	Today is the eighth.

To refer to a date on which something happens, **am** + date is used.

Washington ist am 22. (am zweiundzwanzigsten) Februar geboren.	Washington was born on the twenty-second of February (on February 22).

After the names of sovereigns, roman numerals are used.

Elisabeth II. (Elisabeth die Zweite)
Friedrich Wilhelm IV. (Friedrich Wilhelm der Vierte)
Er war ein Sohn Friedrichs II. (Friedrichs des Zweiten)

Series are also indicated by adding a period to a cardinal number or, if written out, by adding **-ens**.

1. **erstens**	*first(ly), in the first place*	5. **fünftens**	
2. **zweitens**		6. **sechstens**	
3. **drittens**		7. **siebtens**	
4. **viertens**		*etc.*	

Do not confuse **erstens,** *first(ly),* with **erst,** *only, not until,* and **(zu)erst,** *(at) first.*

> **Erstens bin ich zu alt und zweitens bin ich zu müde.**
> **Er ist erst acht Jahre alt.**
> **Sie kommt erst um zehn nach Hause.**
> **Zuerst gehen wir ins Kino und dann fahren wir nach Hause.**

Fractions, except for **die Hälfte,** are neuter and are formed by adding **-el** to the stem of the ordinal; they have no plural endings.

die *Hälfte,-n*	das Sechstel,-
das *Drittel,-*	das Siebtel,-
das Viertel,-	*etc.*
das Fünftel,-	

All fractions are uninflected, except for **halb,** which is usually used with endings.

⅓	**ein drittel**
¾	**drei viertel**
⅞	**sieben achtel**
1/20	**ein zwanzigstel**

> **Ich hätte gerne ein viertel Pfund Butter.**
> **Ich hätte gerne ein halbes Pfund Butter.**

But

um halb neun	at eight-thirty
eineinhalb Pfund Butter	one and a half pounds of butter

132/The Rhetorical *nicht*

If a speaker asks for a positive confirmation of a statement he makes, he adds *don't you?, aren't you?, haven't you?* and so on in English and **nicht?** or **nicht wahr?** in German.

> **Du warst doch gestern abend mit Inge im Kino, nicht?**
> You and Inge were at the movies last night, weren't you?

This rhetorical **nicht** can be moved forward, usually behind the last pronoun, if the statement is transformed into a rhetorical question. The normal question

> **Warst du gestern abend mit Inge im Kino?**

thus becomes the rhetorical

Warst du nicht gestern abend mit Inge im Kino?

This rhetorical **nicht** appears only in yes-or-no questions. It is never stressed; it is always followed by the stress point of the sentence; and if followed by **ein**, it cannot be replaced by **kein**. An affirmative answer to such rhetorical questions can be either **Ja** or **Doch**. However, even though the speaker always expects a confirmation, the answer can, of course, also be **Nein.**

Haben Sie nicht einen Bruder? Answer: **Ja, Doch,** or **Nein.**	You have a brother, don't you?
*Ha*ben Sie keinen Bruder? Answer: **Doch** or **Nein,** but never **Ja.**	Don't you *have* a brother?
Haben Sie einen Bruder? Answer: **Ja** or **Nein,** but never **Doch.**	Do you have a brother?

Further examples:

Warum hast du denn den *Mey*er nicht besucht?
(Real question; stress point precedes **nicht**.)

Hast du den Meyer letzte Woche *nicht* besucht?
(Real question; **nicht** is stressed.)

Hast du nicht letzte Woche den *Mey*er besucht?
(Rhetorical question; stress point follows unstressed **nicht**.)

133/*hin* and *her*

Hin and **her** are both directional adverbs denoting motion. **Hin** generally indicates motion away from the speaker; **her** refers to motion toward the speaker. They are always verbal complements, sometimes in combination with other complements, for example:

Wo gehst du denn hin? **Wohin gehst du denn?**	Where are you going?
Wo kommst du denn her? **Woher kommst du denn?**	Where are you (coming) from?
Fahr doch mal hin? **Komm doch mal her?**	Why don't you go there (sometime)? Why don't you come here (sometime)?
Kommen Sie bitte herein. **Gehen Sie doch bitte hinein?**	Please come in. Why don't you go on in?
Kommt doch bitte herunter. **Geht doch bitte hinunter.**	Please come down. Please go down.

PRACTICE TWO

G. Express in German.

1. Who is this young man?
2. Which young man? (nom.)
3. Who are these young women?
4. Which young women?

5. In which hotel do they live?
6. They always live in this old hotel.
7. These old hotels are not expensive.
8. Every good hotel should have a garage.

H. Reply to the following questions with the dates given:

Wann kommen Sie uns besuchen? —Ich komme am . . .

1. 1. Dezember
2. 7. Juli
3. 16. März

4. Montag, 17. Januar
5. Mittwoch, 25. April
6. Freitag, 3. Mai

Der wievielte ist heute? —Heute ist . . .

1. 8. Februar
2. 18. Juni

3. 20. 8.
4. 31. 10.

Den wievielten haben wir heute? —Heute haben wir . . .

1. 9. Nov.
2. 2. Sept.

3. 25. 12.
4. 11. 3.

I. Read the following:

13.1.27	7.7.42	18.6.1962
8.2.25	20.8.54	22.2.1732
25.10.04	1.9.39	7.12.1941

Benedikt XV. (1914–1922) (1914 bis 1922)
Pius XI. (1922–1939)
Pius XII. (1939–1958)
Johannes XXIII. (1958–1963)
Paul VI. (1963–1978)
Johannes Paul I. (1978)
Johannes Paul II. (1978–)

½   ⅓   2/7   6/8   5/12

J. Change the following statements into questions with a rhetorical **nicht**.

1. Sie haben ihn schon vor dem Krieg kennengelernt, nicht wahr?
2. Seine Tochter hat den Fritz Müller geheiratet, nicht wahr?
3. Sie haben schon immer einmal nach Amerika fahren wollen, nicht wahr?

Suffragette Congress (1901)

Premier issue of Emma, *founded by the influential feminist, Alice Schwarzer* (second from left)

Women in Central Europe

The status of women used to be defined by "Kinder, Küche, Kirche," but the women's movement (**Frauenbewegung**) has sought to change this attitude by working for equality in all spheres of life. Politically, women have come far since first winning the right to vote after World War I: in the U.S. women received the vote in 1920, in Germany in 1918, and in Austria in 1920. Swiss women first voted in national elections in 1971. Now, 10% of the members of the West German Bundestag are women, and one or two women regularly serve as cabinet ministers. The number of professional women has increased considerably, though as yet few women occupy top management positions. In education, the number of women students in the universities has increased to about 40%; however, only 5% of university professors are female.

These figures show a changing role for women in Central Europe, with complete equality not fully achieved. Still, equality of status and opportunity is the law in all German-speaking countries. The Federal Republic, for example, legally recognizes equality in marriage; married couples can use the last name of either husband or wife; there is a generous maternity leave (up to a year in Austria); and there is a no-fault divorce law. The constitution of the GDR views the professional training and advancement of women as the duty of the state. In 1980, the European Community passed an anti-discrimination law that is binding to all member countries.

CONVERSATIONS

The following exchanges could take place as you arrive in Germany after an overnight flight from the United States.

I

STEWARDESS:	(Vor der Landung): Meine Damen und Herren, wir werden in wenigen Minuten in Frankfurt landen und möchten Sie bitten, sich nun wieder anzuschnallen° und das Rauchen einzustellen°.

     fasten seat belt   stop

(Nach der Landung): Wir sind soeben° in Frankfurt gelandet. Die Ortszeit° ist 7 Uhr 35. Wir bitten Sie, sitzenzubleiben, bis die Maschine völlig zum Stillstand gekommen ist. Flugkapitän Bauer und seine Besatzung° wünschen Ihnen einen angenehmen° Aufenthalt° in der Bundesrepublik Deutschland.

     just

     local time

     crew   pleasant

     stay

„Lufthansa kann sich sehen lassen.“

II

SCHLÄFRIGER FLUGGAST:°	Wieviel Uhr, sagten Sie, ist es jetzt hier in Frankfurt?
STEWARDESS:	Sieben Uhr fünfunddreißig, mitteleuropäische Zeit. Sie müssen Ihre Uhr sechs Stunden vorausstellen°.
FLUGGAST:	Sechs? Ich dachte, der Zeitunterschied wäre fünf Stunden. Wir haben doch jetzt Daylight Saving Time in Amerika.
STEWARDESS:	Das stimmt. Aber wir haben auch in Deutschland Sommerzeit; das heißt, so lange Amerika und Deutschland beide Sommerzeit haben, ist der Unterschied sechs Stunden. In New York ist es kurz nach halb zwei nachts.
FLUGGAST:	(sieht auf die Uhr.) Stimmt. Mein Gott, bin ich müde.

     sleepy passenger

     set ahead

III

Bei der Bank[3] im Flughafen:

STUDENTIN:	Würden Sie mir bitte einen Reisescheck wechseln°?	change
DER JUNGE MANN HINTER DEM SCHALTER°:	(sagt nichts.)	counter
STUDENTIN:	Bitte, was ist heute der Wechselkurs° für den Dollar?[4]	exchange rate
DER JUNGE MANN:	Zwei elf.	
STUDENTIN:	Zwei Mark elf für den Dollar?	
DER JUNGE MANN:	(sagt nichts.)	
STUDENTIN:	Dann wechseln Sie mir bitte 20 Dollar.	
DER JUNGE MANN:	(sagt nichts, füllt ein Formular° aus und gibt der Studentin DM 40,70.)	form
STUDENTIN:	Wieso°? Zwanzig mal zwei Mark elf ist zweiundvierzig Mark zwanzig.	How come?
DER JUNGE MANN:	Eins fünfzig Spesen°.	service charge
STUDENTIN:	Das hätten Sie mir aber vorher sagen sollen!	
DER JUNGE MANN:	Der nächste°!	Next

IV

Am Zeitungstand°:   newsstand

STUDENT:	Haben Sie den *Spiegel*?[5]
VERKÄUFER:	Nur den von der letzten Woche; der neue ist noch nicht da.
STUDENT:	Dann geben Sie mir den alten, — und die *Herald Tribune* von heute.
VERKÄUFER:	Tut mir leid, aber ich habe gerade die letzte verkauft.
STUDENT:	Dann nehme ich die *Frankfurter Rundschau* und die *Süddeutsche Zeitung* und dann möchte ich noch einen guten Kriminalroman.
VERKÄUFER:	Bitte hier drüben. Suchen Sie sich doch etwas aus, — vielleicht den ganz neuen von Schmidt-Ingelheim, *Der Spion° im Rosengarten*?

spy

[3]Note: **die Bank,** *pl.* **die Banken,** *bank*
         die Bank, *pl.* **die Bänke,** *bench*

[4]The dollar value of foreign currencies fluctuates; you can look up the exchange rates in a newspaper or call a bank to find out today's rates.

[5]**Der Spiegel** is a West German news magazine like *Time* or *Newsweek*; the **Frankfurter Rundschau** and the **Süddeutsche Zeitung** are daily papers.

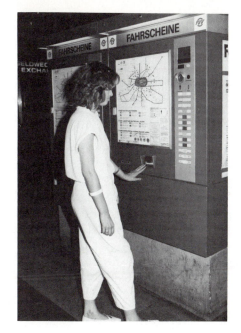

V

Bei der Auskunft°:   information

STUDENTIN: Bitte, würden Sie mir wohl sagen, wie ich am besten in die Innenstadt komme?

BEAMTER: Wie wollen Sie fahren, schnell oder billig?

STUDENTIN: Wie teuer ist schnell?

BEAMTER: Ein Taxi kostet Sie zwischen zwanzig und fünfundzwanzig Mark, und für Ihren Rucksack bezahlen Sie auch noch mal 'ne Mark, und dann noch zwei oder drei Mark Trinkgeld. Aber in zwanzig Minuten sind Sie da.

STUDENTIN: Danke, dann fahre ich lieber billig und langsam.

BEAMTER: Nehmen Sie die Bahn für eine Mark zehn. Hier vorne die linke Treppe° hinunter und dann durch den langen   stairs
Tunnel. Die Bahn fährt alle halbe Stunde, —und hier rechts ist der Fahrkartenautomat.

STUDENTIN: Vielen Dank.

VI

As in previous units, let your teacher play the role of a native German. Have him/her be the friendly person behind an information counter at the airport in Frankfurt with whom you have struck up a conversation. You have just arrived from the United States and are insatiably curious: where do you change money; what is the dollar worth today; how do you get downtown; where should you go to buy (soap, shoes, a dictionary, —what else?); how has the weather been (is it always so hot?), etc.

Or have your teacher be your Kusine[6] Emma or your Vetter[6] Fritz who has come to pick you up. Report about the trip, about your parents and your brothers and sisters; ask about their family, their new house, etc.

---

[6]**die Kusine,** *female cousin;* **der Vetter,** *male cousin.*

Fragen an Sie persönlich

1. Halten Sie es für wichtig, daß man als Student nach Europa fährt?
2. Was würden Sie von Europa (von Deutschland) erwarten? Oder, wenn Sie schon einmal dort waren, was hatten Sie vor ihrer Reise erwartet, und wie war die Wirklichkeit?
3. Glauben Sie, daß es für einen Amerikaner wichtiger ist, nach Europa zu fahren (wegen der „westlichen Tradition" Amerikas), als etwa nach Afrika oder Asien?
4. Woher kamen Ihre eigenen Vorfahren°? Seit wievielen Generationen ist Ihre Familie in Amerika? Betrachten° Sie sich als Mitglied° einer ethnischen Gruppe oder einfach als Amerikaner oder Amerikanerin?   ancestors / consider / member
5. Halten Sie „ethnisches Bewußtsein°" für besser oder schlechter als die alte Idee von den USA als „Schmelztiegel°"?   consciousness / melting pot
6. Glauben Sie, daß alle Amerikaner zweisprachig° sein sollten, und wenn ja, warum?   bilingual

READING

ANGELIKA MECHTEL

Angelika Mechtel (born in 1943 in Dresden) today lives in Munich and is the author of stories, novels, radio plays, poems, and film scripts.

Netter Nachmittag

Ich gehe hin, und er steht schon an der Tür; nachmittags um fünf zum Tee.

Gnädige Frau, sagt er und küßt mir mit feuchten° Lippen die Hand.   moist
Ich habe Ihren Artikel gelesen, sagt er. Er findet ihn exzellent. Ich mache eine Handbewegung° und stimme° ihm zu°.   5 hand motion / **zustimmen** to agree

Dann hilft er mir aus dem Mantel, hängt ihn auf und geht voraus zu Torte und Tee, dickbäuchig°, aber in guter Position. Alt, aber noch frisch wie ein Junger, meint er und setzt sich neben mich auf die Couch.   potbellied

Er könne was für mich tun, sagt er und legt mir die Hand auf die 10 Schulter. So hingelehnt° ans Sofa, den Oberkörper° schräg° zum Unterkörper, lächelt er mir zu.   leaning / **der Körper** body / at an angle

Er schätzt° mich, sagt er.   has high regard for

Mit seiner Vergangenheit ist er zufrieden, auch mit seiner Zukunft. Zwei Weltkriege hat er überstanden° und eine Ehe, sagt er. Er ser- 15   survived
viert immer den gleichen Kuchen, wenn er einlädt. Er hat drei Woh-
nungen: eine in der Stadt, eine auf dem Land und eine am Lago
Maggiore°.   lake in Italy

Er hat das Leben gemeistert°.   mastered

Artig° trinke ich meinen Tee und nehme die Zigarette, die er mir 20   politely
anbietet°; gehe auf das Gespräch ein, das er führen will°.   offers   join the conversation he initiates

So ist eben einer, der groß geworden ist. Unverbraucht°, denkt er,   not used up
anders als unser Jahrhundert.

Er vergißt nicht, höflich zu sein.

Das gehört dazu.   25

Beim Abschied° der Griff° zum Mantel und zu den Haaren: Die ge-   departure   reach
hören doch raus aus dem Mantelkragen°, sagt er. Und zur Hand,   coat collar
um die feuchten Lippen zu postieren°. Das tut er alles mit der   place
Selbstverständlichkeit° derer, die was besitzen°.   self-evidence, matter-of-
factness   own

Du solltest nicht diese Handbewegung machen, wenn er sagt, er 30
fände ihn exzellent. Anstelle° der Hand zum Handkuß gibst du ihm   instead
einen Schlag°, nicht übertrieben° scharf, nur ganz leicht, und dann   slap   excessively
dein Gelächter°.   laughter

Den Artikel findest du schlecht.

Torte, sagst du, ißt du grundsätzlich° nicht und statt Tee verlangst 35   in principle
du Kaffee.

Er stellt° dir heißes Wasser und Nescafé zur Verfügung°. Du nimmst   **zur Verfügung stellen**
nicht nur einen Löffel Kaffeepulver° in die Tasse, du nimmst zwei,   to provide
schraubst° das Glas wieder fest zu° und stellst es mitten auf den   **das Pulver** powder
Tisch, so, daß er sich aufrichten° muß, wenn er es mit seinen 40   **fest zuschrauben**
Händen erreichen will.   to close tightly
   sit up straight

Noch hockt° er schräg auf der Couch, den Oberkörper schräg abge-   sits
winkelt°. Du läßt ihn fallen, wenn er deine Schulter fassen will. Du   angled
machst ihm Platz.

Weiche° Landung, sagst du: Glückauf°, und greifst° nach der vollen 45   soft   good luck   reach
Packung Zigaretten mit der Sicherheit jener, die nichts besitzen.

Er besitzt Einfluß°, das weißt du.   influence

Ich könnte was für Sie tun, sagt er, und du lachst. Du hörst nicht
mehr auf zu lachen. Vor Vergnügen schlägst du mit der flachen°   flat
Hand auf den Tisch; die Füße könntest du drauflegen.   50

Oder ihn durchs Dachfenster auf die Straße transportieren; sieben
Etagen° abwärts° ohne Lift; unten die Feldherrnhalle.[7] Von der ent-   floors   down

---

[7]During the attempted putsch on November 9, 1933, Hitler and the Nazis marched
through Munich to the **Feldherrnhalle**, a monument honoring Bavarian generals.

gegengesetzten° Seite marschierte Hitler mal an. Glückab°. Den
kannte er, und nachher war er auch gleich wieder da.

opposite (pun on the
word **Glückauf** in
line 45)

Zwei Weltkriege? fragst du ihn.   55

Kein Schrapnell hat ihn erwischt°.

hit

Glück muß der Mensch haben.

Ich bin Augenzeuge° unsres Jahrhunderts, sagt er.

eyewitness

Unser? sagst du, nimmst deinen Mantel, gehst und denkst: Den habe
ich fertiggemacht°, dem habe ich seine Heuchelei vor den Latz   60
geknallt°, der ist erledigt.

finished off
threw his hypocrisy at
  him

Aber er steht frisch an der Tür und hat ein verbindliches° Lächeln im
Gesicht.

obliging

Jetzt beklatscht° er noch deinen Abgang°.

applauds   departure

Bravo, sagt er: Ein ganz neuer Stil°.   65

style

Du bist verblüfft°, weil du kein Kraut mehr weißt, das gegen ihn
wächst°, nimmst den Aufzug° ins Parterre°, gehst Richtung° Feldherrnhalle und fragst dich, warum du Angst hast.

taken aback
because you can't think
  of any other way of
  getting at him
elevator   ground floor
direction

Du hast dir in den Mantel helfen lassen, hast ihm das Glas Nescafé
zugeschoben°, das heiße Wasser gereicht°, hast um eine Zigarette   70
gebeten und dir Feuer° geben lassen. Du hast dich angepaßt°, warst
empfänglich°.

pushed toward   handed
a light   adapted
receptive

Du fragst dich, warum du Angst hast?

Abends rufe ich ihn an und danke für den netten Nachmittag.

REVIEW EXERCISES

K. Insert the adjectives given in parentheses into the following sentences.

1. Meyer ist mit einer Frau verheiratet. (sehr intelligent)
2. Eine Frau ist sie *nicht*. (intelligent)
3. Er ist dumm, aber er hat eine Frau geheiratet. (intelligent)
4. Sie ist dumm, aber sie hat einen Mann geheiratet. (intelligent)
5. Er ist ein Mensch. (intelligent)
6. Wer *ist* denn der Mann, von dem ihr da sprecht? (intelligent)
7. Sie ist ein Kind. (intelligent)
8. Wer *ist* denn das Mädchen, von dem ihr da sprecht? (intelligent)
9. Mein Sohn hat ein Mädchen geheiratet. (intelligent)
10. Meyers haben drei Kinder. (intelligent)
11. Frauen wissen immer, was sie wollen. (intelligent)
12. Mit Studenten kann man gut arbeiten. (intelligent)

L. Restate the following sentences, leaving out the italicized **der-** or **ein**-words.

1. *Jeder* gute Wein ist teuer.
2. *Dieses* deutsche Bier ist sehr gut.
3. *Mein* lieber Vater!
4. *Das* frische Obst ist jetzt zu teuer.
5. Bei *dem* starken Regen fahre ich nicht in die Stadt.

M. Place the word in parentheses in front of the adjective.

1. Für intelligente Kinder tun wir viel zu wenig. (unsere)
2. Automatische Uhren sind teuer. (diese)
3. Nach kurzer Pause fuhren wir weiter. (einer)
4. Beide Kinder gingen damals schon in die Schule. (seine)
5. Westfälischer Schinken ist eine Spezialität unseres Hauses. (dieser)

N. Restate the following sentences by changing the italicized nouns to the singular and by making the corresponding changes in the **der**-words and adjectives.

1. Siehst du *die jungen Mädchen* da drüben?
2. Woher hast du denn *die schönen Bücher*?
3. *Diese neuen Maschinen* fliegen tausend Kilometer in der Stunde.
4. Wir fragten *die jungen Männer*, wo sie herkämen.
5. *Die kleinen Dörfer* lagen im Schwarzwald.

O. Restate the following sentences by changing the nouns to the singular. Change the adjective ending as required and place an **ein**-word before the adjective.

1. Ich habe gute Freundinnen in Frankfurt.
2. Bei uns wohnen jetzt amerikanische Studenten.
3. Vor ihm saßen zwei blonde Mädchen.
4. Er rauchte österreichische Zigaretten.
5. Meyers sind gute Freunde von mir.

P. In the following sentences, insert an appropriate **der-** or **ein**-word (if necessary) and the correct form of the adjective in parentheses.

1. Mit _____ _____ Roman hat er viel Geld verdient. (letzt)
2. Wir wohnen in _____ _____ Haus. (neu)
3. Gestern abend habe ich _____ _____ Professor kennengelernt. (deutsch)
4. Ich freue mich auf _____ Sonntag. (nächst)
5. Mein Mann ist gerade von _____ _____ Reise zurückgekommen. (lang)
6. Mit _____ _____ Schreibmaschine kann ich nicht schreiben. (alt)
7. Wann soll _____ _____ Brücke denn fertig sein? (neu)
8. Mit _____ _____ Wagen kannst du nicht nach Paris fahren. (alt)
9. Bist du mit _____ _____ Schreibmaschine zufrieden? (neu)

10. Die Mutter _____ _____ Kinder hieß Alexandra. (beide)
11. Bei _____ Wetter bleiben wir zu Hause. (schlecht)
12. Er hat zwei _____ Romane geschrieben. (gut)

Q. Insert the adjectives in parentheses in the appropriate place in each sentence.

1. Wir sehen einen Mann. (jung)
2. Er ist ein Amerikaner. (jung)
3. Er kommt aus einer Stadt im Nordosten. (groß)
4. Nach dem Flug ist er müde. (lang)
5. Er wartet auf seine Kusine. (deutsch)
6. Ein Mädchen kommt auf ihn zu. (hübsch, jung)
7. Er erkennt sie an ihrem Haar. (lang, blond)
8. Sie hat ihren Vetter gefunden. (amerikanisch)
9. Er erzählt von seinem Großvater. (alt)
10. Sie erzählt von ihrer Tante Amalie. (komisch)
11. Tante Amalie ist eine Köchin. (gut)
12. Am besten ist ihr Schweinebraten. (bayrisch)
13. Er freut sich auf Tante Amalies Essen. (gut)
14. Die Kusine heißt Emma. (deutsch)
15. Der Vetter heißt Jimmy. (amerikanisch)
16. Emma wohnt in einem Dorf. (klein)
17. Dort lebt man besser als in einer Stadt. (groß)
18. Sie fahren in Emmas Wagen nach Oberroden. (alt)
19. So ein Wagen ist gar nicht schlecht. (alt)
20. Emma will kein Auto kaufen. (neu, teuer)
21. Oberroden ist ein Dorf. (ruhig)
22. Es hat eine Kirche. (schön, alt)
23. Tante Amalie wohnt neben der Kirche. (alt)
24. Jimmy hat ihr eine Flasche Wein mitgebracht. (amerikanisch)
25. Sie freut sich sehr über den Wein. (amerikanisch)

R. Supply the missing words.

1. Er sagte, seine Frau _____ gestern nach Hamburg gefahren.
2. Er konnte leider nicht kommen _____ des Regens.
3. Er wollte wissen, mit _____ ich telefoniert hätte.
4. Er sagte mir, ich _____ ihn in Berlin besuchen.
5. Es kostet viel weniger, _____ ich dachte.
6. _____ Andreas mitgeht, gehe ich auch mit.
7. Sie sah aus, _____ hätte sie nicht geschlafen.
8. Ich habe _____ ganzen Nachmittag auf dich gewartet.
9. Die Dame, _____ gestern hier war, ist Amerikanerin.
10. Meyer, _____ Frau aus New York kam, sprach gut Englisch.
11. Fritzchen Meyer hat Angst _____ dem Abitur.
12. Wenn Ihnen dieser Wein zu sauer ist, versuchen Sie doch mal _____ da.

13. Ich möchte Ihnen noch einmal _____ danken, daß Sie mir geholfen haben.
14. Kann ich _____ helfen, Herr Schmitz?
15. Ja, danke; ich trinke gerne _____ eine Tasse Kaffee.
16. Wann fangen denn dieses Jahr die Ferien _____?
17. Fridolin, wir sind alle sehr stolz _____ dich.
18. Sie scheint schon wieder in England _____ zu sein.
19. Er _____ Schriftsteller sein, aber das glaube ich ihm nicht.
20. Das war nicht meine Freundin, _____ meine Schwester.

S. Construct a conversation between yourself and your cousin Uta, who has come to pick you up at the Frankfurt Airport. This is not an exercise in translation, but you should nevertheless follow the English outline. Use your imagination, but avoid using patterns that you are not thoroughly familiar with. Be prepared to produce a similar conversation orally in class.

Uta, of course, wants to know how you are, how the flight was, whether you are tired, and whether you would like to have breakfast before driving into town. You try to figure out what time it is in New York and you talk a bit about time differences. When Uta mentions MEZ°, you are puzzled because you've never heard the term. Uta explains. Then you decide that you are really tired and ought to get to your hotel. She wants to know whether you have ordered a room, which, of course, you have done. Uta thinks it might be a good idea to call the hotel to be sure that you have the room. Since you have never made a phone call in Germany, you ask her whether she would please do that for you. While she telephones, you want to get some German money. She asks you to come to the exit in ten minutes, and she will get her car in the meantime.

          mitteleuropäische Zeit

Now, here is your first sentence: Uta: „Da bist du ja endlich."

VOCABULARY

angenehm	pleasant
der Aufenthalt, -e	stay, residence
auf•hängen	to hang up
auf•hören	to stop, cease
die Auskunft, ⸚e	information
außerhalb (*prep. with gen.*)	outside of
der Beamte, -n	civil servant (*m.*)
die Beamtin, -nen	civil servant (*f.*)
bekannt	(well) known
unbekannt	unknown
best-	best
betrachten	to regard, to look at
betrachten als	to consider as
beweisen	to prove
blöd	stupid, dumb
blond	blond
dritt-	third
das Drittel, -	third
drittens	third(ly)
eigen-	own
eineinhalb	one and a half
einzig	single, sole; solitary
erhalten	to receive; to preserve
erst-	first
erstens	first(ly)
das Eßzimmer, -	dining room
die Fahrkarte, -n	ticket (train, etc.)
fallen (sein)	to fall
flach	flat
der Flug, ⸚e	flight
die Frauenbewegung, -en	women's movement
die Gegenwart	present
die Hälfte, -n	half
herein!	come in, enter!
die Hitze	heat
hoch	high
holen	to get, fetch
innerhalb (*prep. with gen.*)	inside of
der Koch, ⸚e	cook (*m.*)
die Köchin, -nen	cook (*f.*)
komisch	funny; odd; comical
die Kusine, -n	(female) cousin
landen (sein)	to land
die Landung, -en	landing

Wallfahrtskirche Vierzehn-heiligen

lieb	dear
Lieblings-	favorite
die Lust	desire
ich habe keine Lust	I don't feel like it
die Mahlzeit, -en	meal
mancher, manche, manches	many a
nachmittags	afternoons, in the afternoon
nachts	at night
das Obst (*no pl.*)	fruit
offen	open
die Pause, -n	pause, stop, break, intermission
der Preis, -e	price; prize
der Reisescheck, -s	traveler's check
der Schinken, -	ham
schlagen	to hit, strike, beat
die Schreibmaschine, -n	typewriter
der Schweinebraten, -	roast pork

die Sicherheit	safety, security, certainty	völlig	completely
solcher, solche, solches	such	wechseln	to change (money)
		wenige	few, a few
solch ein, so ein	such a	wieso	why, how come
die Sommerzeit	daylight saving time	wieviel	how much
die Stellung, -en	position	Der wievielte ist heute?	What is today's date?
das Stück, -e	(theatrical) play; piece	Den wievielten haben wir heute?	What is today's date?
die Treppe, -n	stairs; staircase		
das Trinkgeld, -er	tip	die Wirklichkeit	reality
der Unterschied, -e	difference	die Zukunft	future
die Vergangenheit	past	zweit-	second
der Vetter, -n	(male) cousin	zweitens	second(ly)

Strong Verbs

INFINITIVE	PRESENT	PAST TENSE	PERFECT	
beweisen		bewies	bewiesen	to prove
erhalten	erhält	erhielt	erhalten	to receive; to preserve
fallen	fällt	fiel	ist gefallen	to fall
schlagen	schlägt	schlug	geschlagen	to hit, strike, beat

Unit 16
Dependent Infinitives—
Comparison of Adjectives

Air Travel

If you fly to German-speaking Europe, chances are that you will arrive at the Rhein-Main Airport in Frankfurt, after Heathrow the second busiest airport in Europe and also a major U.S. airbase. In addition to Frankfurt, West Germany has only a few other airports, including Munich, Düsseldorf, Hamburg, and Cologne-Bonn. The other German-speaking countries have only one major airport each: Zurich, Vienna, and East Berlin. Intra-German air travel is not as common as air travel in the U.S. Since distances are so short, it is often more convenient to go by car or train. Passengers arriving in Frankfurt from abroad can take a special express train which takes them directly from the airport to Bonn, Cologne, and Düsseldorf faster than they can go by connecting flight.

All four countries have national carriers; the West German Lufthansa is one of the major airlines of the world. Lufthansa and Swissair are the only two of the four national airlines that fly to North America. Austrian Airlines (AUA) operates only in Europe, and the East German Interflug only in the East Block. There are also two charter airlines that provide inexpensive service between North America and Germany: Lufthansa's Condor and LTU (Lufttransportunternehmen).

West Berlin has a special status; scheduled air service is provided only by British Airways, Air France, and Pan Am; Lufthansa is prohibited from flying to West Berlin. This peculiar arrangement dates back to an agreement among the four occupying powers after World War II. This same agreement specifies that planes may not fly higher than 10,000 ft. over the territory of the GDR. This frequently makes for bumpy flights, since the cloud cover is usually between 8,000 and 10,000 ft.

Flugkapitän Bauer und seine Besatzung wünschen Ihnen einen angenehmen Aufenthalt in der Bundesrepublik Deutschland.

PATTERNS ONE

1/*bleiben, gehen, lernen* plus Infinitive

Bitte bleiben Sie doch sitzen, Frau Schmidt.
> Please stay seated (don't get up), Ms. Schmidt.

Ich glaube, Fritzchen Meyer bleibt wieder sitzen.[1] —Wirklich? Er ist doch vor zwei Jahren erst sitzengeblieben.
> I think Fritzchen Meyer is going to be kept behind again. —Really? He just repeated a grade two years ago, didn't he?

Du brauchst noch nicht aufzustehen; du kannst noch liegen bleiben.
> You don't have to get up yet; you can still stay in bed.

Wem gehört denn das Buch da? —Das weiß ich nicht; es ist gestern abend hier liegengeblieben.
> To whom does that book belong? —I don't know; it was left here last night.

Meine Uhr ist heute nacht plötzlich stehengeblieben.
> My watch suddenly stopped last night.

Bitte gehen Sie weiter; Sie dürfen hier nicht stehen bleiben.
> Please go on, you mustn't stop here.

Wie wäre es, wenn wir jetzt essen gingen?
Andreas ist auch schon essen gegangen.
Können wir bald essen gehen?
Du brauchst doch nicht schon wieder essen zu gehen; du hast doch gerade erst gefrühstückt.
Wie wär's denn, wenn wir Sonntag baden gingen?

Ingelheim kannte ich schon vor dem Kriege, aber seine Frau lernte ich erst kennen, als er mit ihr nach München zog.
Ingelheim kenne ich schon lange, aber seine Frau habe ich leider noch nicht kennengelernt. Ich möchte sie gerne kennenlernen.

Sein Urgroßvater war sehr intelligent, aber er hatte nie lesen gelernt.
Viele Kinder lernen schon mit fünf Jahren lesen.
Bevor Sie nach Kalifornien gehen, müssen Sie unbedingt Auto fahren lernen.
Es wäre besser, wenn Sie Auto fahren gelernt hätten.

2/*hören* and *sehen* plus Infinitive

Ich hörte ihn heute nacht nach Hause kommen.

Ich habe ihn heute nacht nach Hause kommen hören.

> I heard him come home last night.

---

[1]It is not unusual for German students, from grade school through the *Gymnasium*, to have to repeat a grade if they fail in a certain number of subjects. Thus **sitzenbleiben**, quite literally, means "to remain seated" in your classroom while your classmates move up to the next grade.

Ich habe ihn gehört, als er heute nacht nach
    Hause kam.
Wir sahen sie in Berlin die Desdemona   We saw her play Desdemona in Berlin.
    spielen.
Wir haben sie die Desdemona spielen sehen.

3/*lassen*

lassen: *to leave (behind)*

Bitte lassen Sie mich jetzt allein.
    Please leave me alone now.

Ich wollte, er ließe mich in Ruhe.
    I wish he'd leave me alone (in peace).

Heute regnet es bestimmt nicht. Deinen Regenmantel kannst du zu Hause lassen.
    I'm sure it won't rain today. You can leave your raincoat at home.

Heute regnet es bestimmt nicht. Du hättest deinen Mantel zu Hause lassen können.
    I'm sure it won't rain today. You could have left your raincoat at home.

Jetzt habe ich schon wieder meinen Mantel im Hotel hängenlassen.
    Now I've left my coat at the hotel again.

Und wo ist deine Aktentasche?—Die habe ich bei Tante Amalie auf dem Tisch stehenlassen.
    Where is your briefcase?—I left it on the table at Aunt Amalie's.

Und deine Handschuhe hast du wohl auch irgendwo liegenlassen?
    And I suppose you left your gloves somewhere too?

lassen: *to let, to permit; to cause somebody to do something*

Ich lasse dich nicht allein nach Berlin fahren.
    I will not let you go to Berlin alone.
Ich wollte, ich hätte ihn nicht nach Berlin fahren lassen.
    I wish I had not let him go to Berlin.

Du kannst mich doch nicht ohne Geld nach Berlin fahren lassen.
    You certainly cannot let me go to Berlin without money.

Wir ließen den Arzt kommen.
    (*lit.* We let the doctor come *or* caused the doctor to come.)
    We had the doctor come.
    We called (for) the doctor.

Lassen Sie mich das mal sehen!
    Let me see that!

Lassen Sie mich doch erst meinen Kaffee trinken!
    Let me first drink my coffee!

Lassen Sie den Meyer diese Arbeit machen.
    Let Meyer do that job.

Wir lassen gerade unser Dach reparieren.
    (*lit.* We are just letting [somebody] repair our roof.)
    We are just having our roof repaired.

Wir müssen unser Auto reparieren lassen.
> We have to have our car repaired.

Wir haben den Motor noch nie reparieren lassen müssen.
> We've never yet had to have the motor repaired.

Ich habe ihm ein Telegramm schicken lassen.
> (I had [somebody] send him a telegram.)
> I had a telegram sent to him.

Ich habe ihm sagen lassen, daß er mich morgen anrufen soll.
> (I had [somebody] tell him that he should give me a ring tomorrow.)
> I sent word to him to give me a ring tomorrow.

Ich lasse mir immer das Frühstück aufs Zimmer bringen.
> (I always request [somebody] bring me breakfast to my room.)
> I always have breakfast brought to my room.

Wo hast du dir die Haare schneiden lassen?
> Where did you get your hair cut?

Wir lassen unseren Kindern von Overhoff ein Haus bauen.
> We are having Overhoff build a house for our children.

Wir lassen uns von Overhoff ein Haus bauen.
> We are having Overhoff build us a house.

ENGLISH *leave*: GERMAN **verlassen** OR **gehen**

Jeden Abend verließ Meyer sein Büro um 5 Uhr 30.	Every evening Meyer left his office at 5:30.
Ich muß euch jetzt leider verlassen.	Unfortunately, I have to leave you now.
Ich kann nur bis acht Uhr bleiben; dann muß ich gehen.	I can only stay until eight o'clock; then I'll have to leave.
Fritz ist nicht mehr hier; er ist schon gegangen.	Fritz isn't here anymore; he has already left.

4/End-Field Infinitives

Es fing an zu regnen.
Als es anfing zu regnen, gingen wir nach Hause.
Es hat angefangen zu regnen.
Es fing an, sehr stark zu regnen.
Als es anfing, sehr stark zu regnen, gingen wir nach Hause.
Kannst du nicht endlich aufhören zu arbeiten?
Weil ich vergessen hatte, ihm zu schreiben, kam er nicht zum Bahnhof.
Hast du denn nicht versucht, sie anzurufen?

Er schlug mir vor, an die Nordsee zu fahren.
> He suggested that I go to the North Sea.

Ich rate dir, nicht mehr so viel zu rauchen.
> I advise you not to smoke so much anymore.

Bei uns hat jeder die Freiheit, seine Lektüre selbst zu wählen

z.B. DIE ZEIT

Mein Arzt hat mir verboten zu rauchen.
> My doctor has forbidden me to smoke.

Wir erlauben unseren Kindern nicht, jede Woche zweimal ins Kino zu gehen.
> We don't allow our children to go to the movies twice a week.

Niemand kann mir befehlen, am Wochenende zu arbeiten.
> Nobody can order me to work on weekends.

Darf ich Ihnen empfehlen, einmal einen Mosel zu versuchen?
> May I recommend that you try a Moselle?

Vielen Dank, daß Sie mir geholfen haben, die Sachen ins Haus zu bringen.
> Thank you for helping me bring the things into the house.

5/End-Field Infinitives after Predicate Adjectives

Inge war froh, ihre Mutter wiederzusehen.
> Inge was glad to see her mother again.

Ich bin immer bereit gewesen, ihm zu helfen.
> I have always been ready to help him.

Ich war sehr erstaunt, Erich so bald wiederzusehen.
> I was very astonished to see Erich again so soon.

6/End-Field Infinitives after *da*-Compounds

Ich denke nicht daran, mit Inge schwimmen zu gehen.
Ich hoffe immer noch darauf, ihn eines Tages kennenzulernen.
Ich habe Angst davor, bei Nacht nach München fahren zu müssen.
Ich habe sie darum gebeten, mir aus der Schweiz Schokolade mitzubringen.

7/End-Field Infinitives with *um ... zu, ohne ... zu, statt ... zu*

Wir bleiben heute zu Hause, um uns endlich einmal ausruhen zu können.
> We're going to stay at home today in order to get some rest finally.

Wir bleiben heute zu Hause, damit wir uns endlich einmal ausruhen können.
> We're going to stay home today in order that we can finally get some rest.

Ohne auch nur einen Augenblick nachzudenken, gab er die richtige Antwort.

   Without a moment's thought, he gave the right answer.

Mit Meyer kann man nie sprechen, ohne daß Müller dabei ist.

   You can never talk to Meyer without Müller being there too.

Hast du schon wieder die ganze Nacht gelesen, statt zu schlafen?

   Have you read all night again instead of sleeping?

Statt daß man *Mey*er nach Berlin geschickt hätte, muß *ich* schon wieder fahren.

   Instead of their having sent Meyer to Berlin (which they should have done and didn't), I have to go again.

ANALYSIS ONE

134/Dependent Infinitives

The two-pronged predicate is the most characteristic feature of German syntax. The first prong is always an inflected verb form, and the second prong contains verbal complements and infinitives or participles.

In the "two-box" second prong, the complement or the dependent infinitive precedes the infinitive or participle of the main verb. Examples:

FRONT FIELD	1ST PRONG	INNER FIELD	2ND PRONG	
Ich	gehe	jetzt	nach Hause.	
Ich	bin	bald	nach Hause	gegangen.
Er	fährt	bald	ab.	
Er	ist	sofort	ab-	gefahren.
Er	will	morgen		arbeiten.
Er	hat	nie	arbeiten	wollen.[2]
Er	hat	nie	zu arbeiten	brauchen.[2]

[2]Remember that the "infinitive" forms **wollen** and **brauchen** in these sentences are really participles; the participles **gewollt** and **gebraucht** are used when there is no dependent infinitive.

FRONT FIELD	1ST PRONG	INNER FIELD	2ND PRONG		
Er	hat	es nie			gewollt.[2]
Er	hat	es nicht			gebraucht.[2]
Er	scheint	heute	nach Berlin		zu fliegen.
Er	scheint	gestern	nach Berlin		geflogen zu sein.
Er	soll	gestern	nach Berlin		geflogen sein.
Er	hat	leider	nach Berlin	fliegen	müssen.[3]
Er	scheint	heute	nach Berlin	fliegen	zu müssen.[3]
Er	hat	heute nicht	nach Berlin	zu fliegen	brauchen.[3]

Since dependent infinitives with modals (without **zu**) and with **brauchen** or **scheinen** (with **zu**) always appear in the second prong, we can refer to them as *second-prong infinitives*. A number of other German verbs also take such second-prong infinitives, without **zu** (see Anal. 135, p. 478). Many other verbs can be followed by infinitives in the end field, with **zu** (see Anal. 136, p. 481).

135/Second-Prong Infinitives

bleiben, gehen, lernen

These verbs often appear with dependent infinitives, but since they are not modals, they use the regular participles **geblieben, gegangen,** and **gelernt**. Only a few of these constructions have literal equivalents in English.

1. **bleiben** is most frequently used with **sitzen, stehen,** and **liegen**.

Sie dürfen ruhig sitzen bleiben.	You may remain seated.
Nur ein Haus ist stehen geblieben.	Only one house remained standing.
Er wollte noch eine Weile liegen bleiben.	He wanted to stay in bed a while longer.

[3]If a dependent infinitive with a complement precedes a modal, then the first box in turn contains two boxes.

When used with nonliteral meanings, these combinations are written as one word. For example:

sitzenbleiben	not to be promoted to the next higher class in school
stehenbleiben	to stop (of a watch or clock)
liegenbleiben	to be left behind (of an object)

2. **gehen** is used with such common verbs as **essen, schlafen,** and **baden.**

Wir wollen um zwölf essen gehen.	We want to go to lunch at twelve.
Hans ist schon schlafen gegangen.	Hans has already gone to bed.
Sollen wir morgen baden gehen?	Shall we go swimming tomorrow?

3. With the exception of the nonliteral **kennenlernen**, combinations with **lernen** (*to learn to do something*) are written as two words.

Erika lernt jetzt fahren.	Erika is learning to drive now.
Wann haben Sie denn fahren gelernt?	When did you learn to drive?

hören AND sehen

In contrast to **bleiben, gehen,** and **lernen, hören** and **sehen** behave like modals when used with dependent infinitives and replace the participles **gehört** and **gesehen** with the infinitive form. In these sentences, the direct object is also the subject of the dependent infinitive.

Er sang. Wir hörten ihn.
   Wir hörten ihn singen.
   Wir haben ihn singen hören.
   Wir haben ihn   gehört; er sang.
Er kam. Ich sah ihn.
   Ich sah ihn kommen.
   Ich habe ihn kommen sehen.
   Ich habe ihn   gesehen; er kam.

lassen

Lassen is one of the verbs frequently used with a second-prong infinitive. Like the modals, it uses the infinitive form as a participle when there is a dependent infinitive in "double infinitive" constructions.

The verb **lassen** is used in many constructions that have no literal English equivalent; **lassen** may correspond to English *let* and *leave*, but *let* and *leave* cannot always be expressed by **lassen.**

Lassen has two quite separate meanings:

1. **lassen,** *to leave (behind).* When used with this meaning, **lassen** is an independent verb that can be used without a dependent infinitive. When there is a dependent infinitive, the "double infinitive" is frequently written as one word.

Hast du deinen Mantel zu Hause gelassen?	Did you leave your coat at home?
Nein, ich habe ihn im Café hängenlassen.	No, I left it (hanging) in the café.

2. **lassen,** *to let, to permit somebody to do something* or *to have somebody do something (to cause something to be done by somebody).* When used with this meaning, **lassen** is a causative auxiliary that must be used with a dependent infinitive. Some of these **lassen**-constructions are exactly parallel to English, while others are not.

Wir lassen ihn fahren.	We let him drive.
Wir lassen ihn den Wagen fahren.	We let him (permit him to) drive the car.

In these sentences, the accusative object **ihn** also expresses the subject of the infinitive **fahren: er fährt (den Wagen).** When there is an accusative object, the English equivalent of **lassen** is normally *let*.

However, if there is no accusative object which also serves as the subject of the infinitive, English and German use different constructions, and the English equivalent of **lassen** is normally *have*.

Wir lassen unseren Wagen waschen.	We're having our car washed. (*lit.* We let [someone] wash our car.)

The dative is used to indicate the person for whose benefit an action is performed. If this person is identical with the subject, a dative reflexive pronoun is used.

Ich lasse meinem Sohn ein Haus bauen.	I'm having a house built for my son.
Ich lasse mir ein Haus bauen.	I'm having a house built for myself.

To express the person of whom an action is requested, **von** + dative is used:

Ich lasse mir das Haus von ihm (dem Architekten) bauen.	I'm having him (the architect) build the house for me. (I'm having the house built for myself by him [the architect.])

ENGLISH *to leave*: GERMAN **verlassen, (weg)gehen**

English *to leave* is also used with the meaning *to depart (from).*

He left the city in 1980.
I have to leave now.

In neither of these cases can German use **lassen**. If there is a direct object, **verlassen** must be used:

Es verließ die Stadt im Jahre 1980.

If there is no direct object, neither **lassen** nor **verlassen** can be used:

Ich muß jetzt gehen.
Ich muß jetzt weg.
Ich muß jetzt nach Hause.

136/End-Field Infinitives

In all the constructions in Anal. 135, the dependent infinitive is a second-prong element. Many German verbs, however, require infinitive phrases (always with **zu**) in the end field. We have already used a number of such end-field infinitives, for example, in connection with prepositional objects.

Ich hoffe nicht mehr darauf, daß er wiederkommt.
Ich hoffe nicht mehr darauf, ihn wiederzusehen.

The infinitive phrase **ihn wiederzusehen** has the same syntactic function as the **daß**-clause, but in the first sentence, the subject of the two clauses is not the same, and in the second it is.

The following verbs are frequently used with end-field infinitives. The subject of the main clause and the understood subject of the infinitive phrase are then identical.

anfangen	to begin	**vergessen**	to forget
aufhören	to stop, cease	**versprechen**	to promise
behaupten	to claim	**versuchen**	to try

Ich habe ihr gestern versprochen, sie heute anzurufen.

NOTE:
1. The word order in these infinitive phrases is the same as in normal sentences, that is, the infinitive stands in second-prong position at the end of the phrase.

2. If infinitives with verbal complements are written as one word, the **zu** must be inserted between the complement and the infinitive.

3. End-field infinitives must be separated by a comma unless preceded only by **zu**.

Es hat angefangen, sehr stark zu regnen.
Es hat angefangen zu regnen.

The following verbs can also be used with end-field infinitives. With these verbs, however, the *dative object* of the main clause is identical with the understood subject of the infinitive phrase.

befehlen	to give an order to somebody
empfehlen	to make a recommendation to somebody
erlauben	to give permission to somebody
helfen	to give help to someone in doing something
raten	to give somebody advice
verbieten	to forbid someone to do something
vorschlagen	to make a suggestion to somebody

Mein Arzt hat mir geraten, einmal an die See zu fahren.

END-FIELD INFINITIVES AFTER PREDICATE ADJECTIVES

The following predicate adjectives are frequently used with end-field infinitives:

bereit	ready	**glücklich**	happy
erstaunt	astonished	**schön**	nice
froh	glad		

Ich war so froh, dich endlich wiederzusehen.
Warum sind Sie denn so erstaunt, mich hier zu sehen?
Ich war immer bereit, ihm zu helfen.

REPLACEMENT OF PREPOSITIONAL OBJECTS

Verbs which take a prepositional object frequently replace this complement with a **da**-compound which anticipates an infinitive phrase in the end field (see Anal. 108, p. 366).

Ich denke ja gar nicht daran,
Du weißt doch, daß ich gar nicht daran denke,
Ich habe ja nie daran gedacht,
Du weißt doch, daß ich nie daran gedacht habe,
} **nach Rom zu fahren.**

137/um . . . zu, ohne . . . zu, statt . . . zu

We have already used infinitives with **um . . . zu** in the end-field position. The same construction is possible with **ohne . . . zu** and **statt (anstatt) . . . zu**. All of these infinitives appear most frequently in either end-field or front-field position.

Sie fuhr nach Afrika, um dort einen Roman zu schreiben.
Sie fuhr nach München, ohne ihre Familie mitzunehmen.
Sie fuhr nach Afrika, statt zu Hause zu bleiben.
Statt zu Hause zu bleiben, fuhr sie nach Afrika.

English uses an infinitive as the equivalent of the **um . . . zu** forms (*in order to write a novel*), but for the **ohne . . . zu** and **statt . . . zu** forms, English must use the gerund (*without taking her family along; instead of staying at home*).

In the above examples, the subject of the infinitive phrase is the same as the subject of the main clause. If there is a different subject, the infinitive construction must be replaced by dependent clauses, but dependent clauses are sometimes used even when the subject is the same.

um . . . zu	**damit**
ohne . . . zu	**ohne daß**
statt . . . zu	**statt daß**

Wir gingen nach Paris, um Französisch zu lernen.
Wir gingen nach Paris, damit unsere Kinder Französisch lernen konnten.

PRACTICE ONE

A. Complete the following sentences with the verbs in parentheses, using modals, the subjunctive, and various tenses; then give the English equivalents.

1. Bitte _____, Herr Vollmer (sitzen bleiben).
2. Ich hoffe, meine Uhr _____ (nicht stehenbleiben).
3. Ich glaube, meine Uhr _____ (stehenbleiben).
4. Ich dachte, meine Uhr _____ (stehenbleiben).
5. Er kommt heute nicht zum Frühstück. Er _____ (noch liegen bleiben).
6. Es wäre nett, wenn wir morgen _____ (schwimmen gehen).
7. Er soll jeden Tag mit Erika _____ (schwimmen gehen).
8. Ist Hans schon im Bett? — Ja, er _____ (schlafen gehen).
9. Ich wollte, wir _____ (schlafen gehen).
10. Es wäre besser, wenn er _____ (kochen lernen).
11. Ich möchte wissen, ob er _____ (kochen lernen).
12. Ich dachte, du _____ (schwimmen lernen).
13. Er soll tatsächlich _____ (Auto fahren lernen).
14. Ich hoffe, daß er hier jemanden _____ (kennenlernen).

B. Form sentences with the following phrases, using various tenses.

1. Emma einmal (noch nie) lachen sehen
2. den Kleinen schreien hören
3. die Maria nach Hause kommen hören

C. Express in German (note that the infinitives **hängen, liegen, stehen** behave like prefixes and do not change).

1. I hope you won't leave your coat in the hotel again.
2. I have left my gloves at Aunt Amalie's.
3. You can't leave your car in front of the hotel.

D. Express in German, using **lassen**.

1. Why don't you let me study medicine?
2. I wish you would let me study medicine.
3. I wish we had let him study medicine.
4. We can't let him study medicine.
5. We shall let her study medicine.

E. Change the following sentences to infinitive phrases and use the verbs in parentheses to form introductory clauses. In some cases, you will have to make additional changes.

> **Es regnet nicht mehr. (aufhören)**
> **Es hat aufgehört zu regnen.**

1. Er will in Davos gewesen sein. (behaupten)
2. Ich habe ihr nicht geschrieben. (vergessen)
3. Meyer will seiner Frau ein Auto schenken. (versprechen)
4. Ich möchte sie bald wiedersehen. (hoffen)
5. Ich wollte dich gestern abend anrufen. (versuchen)

F. Change the following sentences to infinitive phrases and use the verbs in parentheses to form introductory clauses. Use **Er** and the perfect tense.

> **Fahren Sie doch mal an die See. (raten)**
> **Er hat mir geraten, einmal an die See zu fahren.**

1. Trinken Sie jeden Abend vor dem Schlafengehen ein Glas Wein. (empfehlen)
2. Bleiben Sie morgen zu Hause. (erlauben)
3. Fahren Sie doch mit mir nach München. (vorschlagen)

G. Change the following sentences to infinitive phrases. Use the subjects of these sentences and the adjectives in parentheses to form introductory clauses.

> **Inge sah ihren Onkel wieder. (froh)**
> **Inge war froh, ihren Onkel wiederzusehen.**

1. Gottseidank sind wir wieder zu Hause. (glücklich)
2. Erich half uns immer. (bereit)
3. Ich sah ihn letztes Wochenende in Hamburg wieder. (erstaunt)

H. Expand the prepositional object in the following sentences into infinitive
phrases. Remember to use anticipatory **da**-compounds.

Ingeborg denkt gar nicht an eine Berlinreise.
Ingeborg denkt gar nicht daran, nach Berlin zu fahren.

1. Wir hoffen immer noch auf ein Wiedersehen mit Tante Amalie.
2. Wir warten schon wochenlang auf einen Brief von ihr.
3. Darf ich Sie um baldige Antwort bitten?

PATTERNS TWO

8/Comparative Forms of Adjectives

Sie ist so alt wie ich.
Hier ist es so kalt wie in Hamburg.
Leider ist sie nicht so jung wie er.
Hier ist es nicht so warm wie bei euch.
Die Alpen sind nicht so hoch wie die Sierras.
Ingelheim ist nicht ganz so interessant wie Thomas Mann.
Du bist doch nicht so groß wie ich.
Das Bier hier ist wirklich gut.
Tante Dorothea redet genau so viel wie Tante Amalie.
Hier ist das frische Obst nicht so teuer wie bei uns.
Inges Haar war schon immer so dunkel wie meins.
Möchtest du dir gern den Faustfilm ansehen?

Sie ist älter als ich.
Hier ist es kälter als in Hamburg.
Leider ist er jünger als sie.
Bei euch ist es viel wärmer als bei uns.
Die Sierras sind höher als die Alpen.
Thomas Mann ist etwas interessanter als Ingelheim.
Doch, ich bin größer als du.
Ja, aber das Bier in München ist noch besser.
Nee, nee, die redet noch mehr als Tante Amalie, noch viel mehr.
Bei uns ist das Obst viel teurer als bei euch.

Aber seit sie vierzig ist, wird es immer dunkler.
Nein, ich ginge viel lieber in einen Wildwestfilm.

9/Superlative Form of Adjectives

Die Frau mit dem Flamingo ist sein bester Roman.
Ich halte *Die Frau mit dem Flamingo* für seinen besten Roman.

Monika ist die interessanteste Frau, die ich kenne.
Von allen Frauen, die ich kenne, ist sie die interessanteste.

Im Dezember sind die Tage am kürzesten.
Der 21. Dezember ist der kürzeste Tag des Jahres.

In dieser Show sehen Sie Giganto, den stärksten Mann der Welt.
Giganto ist von allen Männern der stärkste.

Was ist Ingelheims bester Roman?
Mir gefällt *Die Frau mit dem Flamingo* am besten.[4]

Hier ist es ja das ganze Jahr sehr schön, aber im Mai ist es hier doch am schönsten.
Die meisten Studenten essen in der Mensa.

Der schnellste Weg zum Erfolg ist eine Anzeige in der SZ,
denn die meistgelesene Tageszeitung
in der Stadtregion München ist die   SüddeutscheZeitung

10/Comparatives and Superlatives in Advertising

Sie können natürlich mehr Geld ausgeben, aber es ist nicht sicher,
  ob Sie einen besseren Waschautomaten bekommen.
Gesünder und darum besser ist ein Cottona-Hemd°.   shirt
Sie solltcn nicht weniger für ihr Geld verlangen. Sie sollten mehr
  verlangen. Ein VW ist der beste Kauf.
Cinzano on the rocks: der beste Anfang einer guten Sache.
Was trinken Sie am liebsten, wenn Sie abends fernsehen? Natürlich
  Löwenbräu.
Wie gern essen wir ein Steak. Noch lieber ist es uns mit einem
  Schuß° Ketchup. Am liebsten essen wir es aber mit Thomy's   shot
  Tomaten-Ketchup.
Statt für jeden etwas, etwas Besonderes für alle: Triumpf, die beste
  Schreibmaschine.
Für Ihre höchsten Ansprüche°—Unser Bester von Nescafé.   expectations

[4]With **gefallen,** degrees are expressed by **gut, besser, am besten**
and not **gern, lieber, am liebsten:**

  Der Film hat mir gut (besser, am besten) gefallen.
  Ich esse gern (lieber, am liebsten) Apfelstrudel.

European Community (EC)

In 1957, the Federal Republic of Germany together with France, Italy, and the Benelux countries (Belgium, the Netherlands, Luxembourg) founded the European Economic Community (EEC), **Europäische Wirtschaftsgemeinschaft (EWG)**. By 1986, the community had grown to 12 members, including Great Britain, Denmark, Ireland, Greece, Spain, and Portugal. Within the European Community, all trade barriers and tariffs were gradually removed, so that today, with over 300 million people, the EC represents the largest economic bloc in the world. But the aim of the community goes beyond economic cooperation; there is freedom of movement for the entire population of the community, and passports are no longer required for travel within the EC. There is frequent political consultation among the EC governments, especially with regard to foreign policy vis-à-vis nonmembers. From their inception, the Council of Europe and the European Parliament in Strasbourg, though without much power, have represented the hope for a united Europe.

Because of their neutral status, Switzerland and Austria do not belong to the European Community. The German Democratic Republic has been a member since 1950 of COMECON (Council for Mutual Economic Assistance), an economic alliance of east bloc countries.

West-Europas Einigung

Westeuropa unter einem Dach

Mit dem Beitritt Spaniens und Portugals zur EG ist das erreicht, was den Gründern der Gemeinschaft vor vielen Jahren als Hoffnung vorgeschwebt hat: Der Zusammenschluß der großen Mehrheit der westeuropäischen Staaten unter einem gemeinsamen Dach. 91 Prozent der Bevölkerung Westeuropas sind jetzt EG-Bürger. Der Weg zu ihrer Einigung verlief in vier Etappen, 1957 wurde der Anfang gemacht.

ANALYSIS TWO

138/Comparison of Adjectives and Adverbs

FORMS OF THE COMPARATIVE AND THE SUPERLATIVE

English has two ways of forming the comparative and superlative of adjectives and adverbs:

1. by adding *-er* for the comparative and *-est* for the superlative: *fast, fast-er, fast-est* (both adjective and adverb).

2. by using *more* for the comparative and *most* for the superlative: *interesting(ly), more interesting(ly), most interesting(ly)* (adjective and adverb) or *quickly, more quickly, most quickly* (adverb).

German, however, has only one way of forming comparatives and superlatives. All German adjectives and adverbs follow the first English example above and add **-er** and **-(e)st** to the stem; you cannot use **mehr** and **meist-** to form comparatives and superlatives in German.

schnell, schneller, schnellst-
{ fast, faster, fastest
quick, quicker, quickest
quickly, more quickly, most quickly

interessant, interessanter, interessantest-
{ interesting, more interesting, most interesting

To indicate that superlatives cannot be used without an ending, the superlative forms above are followed by hyphens.

The **-e-** in the superlative forms is added whenever the **-st-** ending alone would be hard to pronounce—for example, **weitest-, ältest-, kürzest-**. An exception is the superlative form of **groß.**

groß, größer, größt-

Many monosyllable adjectives add an umlaut in both the comparative and superlative.

alt, älter, ältest-	old
arm, ärmer, ärmst-	poor
hart, härter, härtest-	hard
jung, jünger, jüngst-	young
kalt, kälter, kältest-	cold
kurz, kürzer, kürzest-	short
lang, länger, längst-	long
oft, öfter, öftest-	often
schwarz, schwärzer, schwärzest-	black
stark, stärker, stärkst-	strong

Adjectives ending in **-el** and **-er** lose the **-e-** in the comparative.

> **dunkel, dunkler, dunkelst-**
> **teuer, teurer, teuerst-**

The adjective **hoch** replaces the **-ch** by a silent **-h-** in the comparative:

> **hoch, höher, höchst-**

and the adjective **nah** changes the silent **-h** to a **-ch** in the superlative.

> **nah, näher, nächst-**

Gut, viel, and **gern** have irregular forms:

> **gut, besser, best-**
> **viel, mehr, meist-**[5]
> **gern, lieber, liebst-**

Note that **gern, lieber, liebst-** can only be used as adverbs.

USE OF COMPARISONS

1. In comparisons implying equality, **so . . . wie** is used.

> **Sie ist so alt wie ich.**
> **Sie ist nicht so alt wie ich.**
> **Sie ist nicht so alt, wie ich dachte.**

If the comparison expresses inequality, the comparative form of the adjective is used, followed by **als.**

> **Sie ist älter als ich.**
> **Sie kann nicht älter sein als ich.**
> **Sie ist älter, als ich dachte.**

2. As *attributive adjectives*, comparative and superlative forms are treated like any other adjective; that is, they add normal adjective endings to the **-er** and **-(e)st** suffixes:

> **Einen interessanteren Roman habe ich nie gelesen.**
> **Ein interessanteres Buch habe ich nie gelesen.**
> **Das ist die interessanteste Geschichte, die ich kenne.**

---

[5]All forms of **meist-** must be preceded by a definite article: **das meiste Geld, die meisten Leute.**

Nouns preceded by comparative and superlative forms of attributive adjectives can be omitted if they are clearly understood or implied. In English such omitted predicate nouns can be replaced by *one* or *ones.*

Der Wagen ist groß, aber wir brauchen einen größeren.	The car is large, but we need a larger (one).
Welcher von den drei Wagen ist der teuerste?	Which of the three cars is the most expensive (one)?
Von seinen Romanen sind die beiden letzten die interessantesten.	Of his novels the last two are the most interesting (ones).

3. When used as predicate adjectives and as adverbs, comparative forms do not take endings; superlative forms always use the pattern **am** (adjective)**-sten.**

PREDICATE ADJECTIVES

Meyers finde ich ja ganz nett, aber Schmidts sind doch netter.	I find the Meyers rather nice, but the Schmidts are really nicer.
Im Juni sind die Tage am längsten.	In June the days are longest.
Ich reise ja sehr gerne, aber zu Hause ist es doch am schönsten.	I do like to travel, but I still like it best at home.

ADVERBS

Mit deinem Mercedes kommen wir bestimmt schneller nach München als mit meinem VW-Bus.	We'll certainly get to Munich faster with your Mercedes than with my VW bus.
Können Sie mir sagen, wie ich am schnellsten zum Flughafen komme?	Can you tell me how I can get to the airport fastest?
Da nehmen Sie am besten ein Taxi.	Then you best take a taxi.

SOME SPECIAL FORMS

1. A few comparatives are used as "absolute comparatives," that is, without an explicit comparison. For example

Wir haben längere Zeit in Berlin gewohnt.

means we lived there for a rather long time. Similarly, **ein älterer Herr** (*elderly gentleman*) means a somewhat older man.

2. To express a high degree of a certain quality, German can use **höchst** as the equivalent of English *most*. Observe the degrees:

Das war ganz interessant.	(quite interesting)
Das war interessant.	(interesting)
Das war sehr interessant.	(very interesting)
Das war aber höchst interessant.	(most interesting)

3. German uses **immer** with the comparative where English repeats the comparative to indicate an increase in degree.

Es wurde immer wärmer.   It was getting warmer and warmer.

139/Word Formation: Nouns Derived from Adjectives

German, like English, has a number of suffixes which can be used to derive nouns from adjectives.

THE SUFFIX **-e**

A number of adjectives may be changed into feminine nouns by adding the suffix **-e** and by umlauting when possible. These nouns correspond in meaning to English nouns in *-th* (*strong, strength; long, length*), *-ness* (*weak, weakness; great, greatness*), or *-ity* (*brief, brevity*).

breit	**die Breite**	breadth
groß	**die Größe**	greatness; size
hart	**die Härte**	hardness
heiß	**die Hitze**	heat
hoch	**die Höhe**	height
kalt	**die Kälte**	cold(ness)[6]
kurz	**die Kürze**	shortness, brevity
lang	**die Länge**	length
nah	**die Nähe**	nearness, proximity
schwach	**die Schwäche**	weakness
stark	**die Stärke**	strength
still	**die Stille**	peacefulness, calm, quiet
warm	**die Wärme**	warmth

[6]But *cold* in the medical sense: **die Erkältung**.

THE SUFFIXES -heit, -keit

Many feminine abstract nouns can be formed by adding one of these suffixes to the adjective; they form their plurals by adding **-en**. Feel free to use the nouns listed, but do not try to invent your own: they may not exist.

	dunkel	die Dunkelheit	darkness
	frei	die Freiheit	freedom
	gesund	die Gesundheit	health
	krank	die Krankheit	sickness
	möglich	die Möglichkeit	possibility
	müde	die Müdigkeit	tiredness
	neu	die Neuheit	newness, novelty
		die Neuigkeit	news
	schön	die Schönheit	beauty
	sicher	die Sicherheit	security
	vergangen	die Vergangenheit	past
	wahr	die Wahrheit	truth
	wirklich	die Wirklichkeit	reality
	zufrieden	die Zufriedenheit	contentment
der Freund,-e	freundlich	die Freundlichkeit	friendliness
der Hof,-e (court)	höflich	die Höflichkeit	politeness (courtliness)
der Mensch,-en	menschlich	die Menschlichkeit	humaneness
die Hoffnung	hoffnungslos	die Hoffnungslosigkeit	hopelessness
der Dank	dankbar	die Dankbarkeit	gratitude

The following compounds are all derived from the stem **ein**:

die Einheit	unit, unity
einig	in agreement, in accord
vereinigt	united
die Vereinigten Staaten	the United States
die Einsamkeit	loneliness, solitude
einzeln	single (apart from the rest)
einzig	single, unique, sole
einfach	simple, simply

How to get around

Backpack travelers, many of them American students, are a common sight during the summer in Central Europe. Even when the dollar is weak, students can travel economically in Europe. There are almost 600 youth hostels (**Jugendherbergen**) in the Federal Republic (100 in Austria, 90 in Switzerland) that offer inexpensive dormitory-style room and board. Membership in the American Youth Hostels (AYH, Inc., 1332 I Street, N.W., Washington, D.C. 20005) allows you to use these hostels. Before leaving for Europe, you should also get an International Student I.D., and if you want to travel by train, a Eurail Pass. In Europe, you can purchase an Inter-Rail Pass, which, however, gives you only a 50% discount in the country in which it is purchased. (That's why really clever people buy them in Luxembourg or Liechtenstein.) Neither rail pass is valid in the German Democratic Republic. Another moderately priced type of lodging is the traditional European **Pension** providing bed and breakfast. City hotels tend to be quite expensive, but you can still find clean and comfortable rooms at a reasonable price in small town hotels or village inns.

PRACTICE TWO

I. Form pairs of sentences with the following adjectives.

Sie ist (nicht) so alt wie ich.	**Sie ist älter als ich.**

1. schnell, schneller
2. freundlich, freundlicher
3. arm, ärmer
4. hart, härter
5. kurz, kürzer
6. lang, länger
7. oft, öfter
8. stark, stärker
9. nah, näher

J. Fill the blanks with the comparative form of the adjective in the first sentence.

1. Das Bier hier ist gut, aber in München gibt es noch _____ Bier.
2. Der Wagen ist wirklich nicht sehr groß. Wir brauchen einen _____ Wagen.
3. Diese Wohnung ist ja ganz billig, aber vielleicht können wir eine _____ finden.
4. Schmidts sind wirklich nette Leute; ich kenne keine _____ Leute.

K. Express in German.

1. The third of January was the coldest day of the winter.
2. Of their daughters Erica is the youngest one.
3. In June the nights are shortest.
4. Of my friends Meyer drives fastest.
5. Which car cost the most?
6. I like his first novel the best. (use **gefallen**)

CONVERSATIONS

I

How to Express What?

The following groups of expressions are arranged topically. Each group lists characteristic reactions in conversational situations. You are familiar with most of them; some others we have translated into near English equivalents. In your conversations from now on, use as many of these expressions as possible and try to develop a feeling for the "social register" for which each expression is adequate and acceptable.

AGREEMENT

Ja.
Natürlich.
Aber natürlich.
Gern(e).
Richtig.
Genau.
Da haben Sie recht.
   hast du
Stimmt.
Sicher.
Na klar.
O.K.
Ach so! (reconfirmation: *"Now I get it."*)

DISAGREEMENT

Nein. (Nee.)
Leider nein.
     nicht.
Das glaube ich dir nicht.
       Ihnen
Das stimmt nicht.
Da haben Sie (aber) nicht recht.
   hast du
Mensch, hör auf. (*"Come off it."*)
Rede doch nicht so'n Unsinn.
Quatsch. (*Nonsense.*)

REQUESTS

Bitte.
Ich bitte sehr.
Darf (dürfte) ich um X bitten?

THANKS

Danke (sehr).
Vielen Dank.
Dankeschön.

Bitte, geben Sie mir X.   Herzlichen Dank.

Gib mir doch mal X.   Ich bedanke mich.

Ich hätte gerne X.   Das ist (war) sehr nett von dir.

Wie wär's mit X?   Ich bin Ihnen sehr dankbar dafür, daß . . .

Ich möchte (gerne) X.   Das war aber nicht nötig.

Könnte (dürfte) ich wohl mal . . .   Das hätten Sie aber nicht zu tun brauchen.

Es wäre nett, wenn . . .

Bitte, seien Sie so gut und . . .

Würdest du bitte mal . . .

II

Construct conversations around the topics below; as before, your teacher can play the role of the native speaker of German.

AUF DER POST

das Postamt post office

die Post post office; mail

der Postbeamte,-n postal clerk

    die Postbeamtin,-nen

der Brief,-e letter

    einen Brief aufgeben to post (mail) a letter.

    der Luftpostbrief[7] airmail letter

    der Eilbrief special-delivery letter

die Postkarte,-n postcard

der Einschreibebrief; das Einschreiben registered letter

die Briefmarke,-n stamp

das Paket,-e package

das Telegramm,-e telegram, cable

    ein Telegramm (nach Übersee) aufgeben

das Telefongespräch,-e phone call

    das Ferngespräch long-distance call

die Auskunft information

selbst wählen to dial direct

    das Selbstwählferngespräch direct-dial long-distance call

die Postleitzahl zip code

die Vorwahlnummer area code

[7]The Austrian term for airmail is **Flugpost**.

	VORWAHL[8]	POSTLEITZAHL[9]
Frankfurt	069	6000
Wiesbaden	06121	6200
Berlin	030	1000
München	089	8000
Augsburg	0821	8900
Wasserburg am Inn	08071	8090
Weil über Landsberg am Lech	08195	8911

KINO, THEATER, OPER, KONZERT

das Kino,-s
das Theater,-
die Oper,-n
das Konzert,-e
die Vorstellung,-en; die Aufführung,-en
  performance

der Akt,-e act
die Szene,-n scene
die Pause,-n intermission
der Beifall; der Applaus applause

die Karte,-n ticket
die Kinokarte
Theaterkarte
Opernkarte
Konzertkarte
Karten bestellen to order tickets

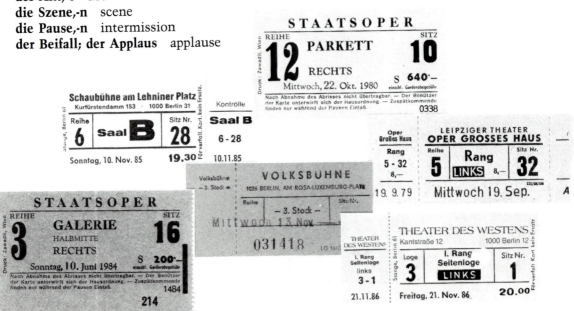

[8]To dial outside of Germany, an additional area code is used; for example, Austria's code is 0043, and to get Vienna (0222), you dial 0043-222- and the local number. To dial Europe from the U.S., you dial 011, then the country code (Austria 43, FRG 49, GDR 37, and Liechtenstein and Switzerland 41), then the city code, and finally the number.

[9]All zeros at the end of the zip code can be left out; thus **6 Frankfurt**, or **809 Wasserburg**.

III

Berichten° Sie über einen Film (ein Theaterstück, eine Oper, ein Konzert).   report
Was hat Ihnen gut (schlecht) gefallen?

READING

Peter Handke

Peter Handke

Peter Handke (born 1942 in Kärnten) is probably the best-known contemporary Austrian author. He has written numerous novels, poems, plays,
and essays.

Zugauskunft

»Ich möchte nach Stock.«

Sie fahren mit dem Fernschnellzug° um 6 Uhr 2.   long-distance express
Der Zug ist in Alst um 8 Uhr 51.   train
Sie steigen um in den Schnellzug nach Teist.
Der Zug fährt von Alst ab um 9 Uhr 17.   5
Sie fahren nicht bis nach Teist, sondern steigen aus° in Benz.   **aussteigen** to get off
Der Zug ist in Benz um 10 Uhr 33.
Sie steigen in Benz um in den Schnellzug nach Eifa mit dem Kurs-
wagen° nach Wössen.   through-car
Der Schnellzug nach Eifa fährt ab um 10 Uhr 38.   10
Der Kurswagen wird in Aprath abgehängt° und an den Schnellzug   uncoupled
Uchte-Alsenz gekoppelt.
Der Zug fährt in Aprath ab um 12 Uhr 12.
Ab Emmen fährt der Zug als Eilzug°.   local express
Sie fahren nicht bis nach Wössen, sondern steigen um in Bleckmar. 15
Der Zug ist in Bleckmar um 13 Uhr 14.

In Bleckmar können Sie sich umsehen° bis 15 Uhr 23. — *look around*

Um 15 Uhr 23 fährt von Bleckmar ein Eilzug ab nach Schee.

(Dieser Zug verkehrt° nicht am 24. und 25. 12. und führt nur sonntags 1. Klasse.) — *runs (of trains, buses, etc.)* [20]

Sie kommen in Schee-Süd an um 16 Uhr 59.

Die Fähre° nach Schee-Nord geht ab um 17 Uhr 5. — *ferry*

(Bei Sturm, Nebel und unvorhergesehenen Ereignissen° kann der — *events*

Fährverkehr ausfallen°.) — *be canceled*

Sie sind in Schee-Nord um 17 Uhr 20. [25]

Um 17 Uhr 24 fährt vom Bahnhof Schee-Nord der Personenzug° — *local train*

ab nach Sandplacken.

(Dieser Zug führt nur 2. Klasse und verkehrt nur an Werktagen und

verkaufsoffenen Samstagen.)[10]

Sie steigen aus in Murnau. [30]

Der Zug ist in Murnau ungefähr° um 19 Uhr 30. — *approximately*

Vom gleichen Bahnsteig fährt um 21 Uhr 12 ein Personen- und

Güterzug° weiter nach Hützel. — *freight train*

(In Murnau gibt es einen Warteraum.)

Sie sind in Hützel um 22 Uhr 33. *(Diese Zeiten sind ohne Gewähr°.)* [35] — *not guaranteed*

Da der Personenverkehr von Hützel nach Krün eingestellt° ist, neh- — *discontinued*

men Sie den am Bahnhofsvorplatz wartenden Bahnbus *(ohne Ge-*

währ).

Sie steigen aus in Vach gegen 1 Uhr.

Der erste Straßenbus von Vach geht ab um 6 Uhr 15. [40]

(In Vach gibt es keinen Mietwagen°.) — *rental car*

Sie sind in Eisal um 8 Uhr 9.

Der Bus um 8 Uhr 10 von Eisal nach Weiden verkehrt nicht in den

Schulferien.

Sie sind in Weiden um 8 Uhr 50. [45]

Um 13 Uhr geht der Bus eines Privatunternehmens° von Weiden — **das Unternehmen** *firm*

über Möllen-Forst-Ohle nach Schray.

(Nach Schray und Ohle fährt der Bus weiter nur nach Bedarf°.) — *if needed*

Sie sind in Schray um 14 Uhr 50.

Zwischen Schray und Trompet verkehrt um diese Zeit ein Milch- [50]

wagen, der bei Bedarf auch Personen befördert°. — *transports*

In Trompet können Sie gegen 16 Uhr sein.

Zwischen Trompet und Stock gibt es keine Kraftverkehrslinie°. — *bus line*

Zu Fuß können Sie gegen 17 Uhr 30 in Stock sein.

»Im Winter ist es dann schon wieder dunkel?« [55]

»Im Winter ist es dann schon wieder dunkel.«

(1967)

GEÖFFNET:
MONTAG - FREITA
8 30 - 18
SAMSTAG   8 30 - 14
jeden 1. Samstag des Mona
8 30 - 18

---

[10]On Saturdays, stores normally close at 1:00 or 2:00 P.M., but are open in the afternoon of the first Saturday of every month.

ERICH KÄSTNER

Das Eisenbahngleichnis°

Wir sitzen alle im gleichen Zug
und reisen quer durch° die Zeit.
Wir sehen hinaus. Wir sahen genug.
Wir fahren alle im gleichen Zug.
Und keiner weiß, wie weit.

Ein Nachbar° schläft, ein andrer klagt°,
ein dritter redet viel.
Stationen werden angesagt°.
Der Zug, der durch die Jahre jagt°,
kommt niemals an sein Ziel°.

Wir packen aus°. Wir packen ein°.
Wir finden keinen Sinn°.
Wo werden wir wohl morgen sein?
Der Schaffner° schaut zur Tür herein
und lächelt vor sich hin.

Auch er weiß nicht, wohin er will.
Er schweigt und geht hinaus.
Da heult° die Zugsirene schrill!
Der Zug fährt langsam und hält still.
Die Toten steigen aus.

Ein Kind steigt aus. Die Mutter schreit.
Die Toten stehen stumm°
am Bahnsteig° der Vergangenheit.
Der Zug fährt weiter, er jagt durch die Zeit,
und niemand weiß, warum.

Die 1. Klasse ist fast leer.
Ein feister° Herr sitzt stolz
im roten Plüsch und atmet° schwer.
Er ist allein und spürt° das sehr.
Die Mehrheit° sitzt auf Holz°.

Wir reisen alle im gleichen Zug
zur Gegenwart in spe°.
Wir sehen hinaus. Wir sahen genug.
Wir sitzen alle im gleichen Zug
und viele im falschen Coupé°.

(1932)

Glossary (right column):

das Gleichnis,-se
parable

straight across

neighbor   complains

are announced
rushes
destination

auspacken   to unpack
einpacken   to pack
sense

conductor

howls

silent
platform

fat
breathes
feels
majority   wood

present-in-the-future

train compartment

REVIEW EXERCISES

L. Express in German. All sentences must contain a form of **lassen**.

1. That leaves me cold.
2. Why didn't you leave your books at home?
3. You shouldn't let him go to Hamburg.
4. I must get myself a haircut.
5. Why don't you have your hair cut?
6. He went downtown to get a haircut.
7. She has left her coat here again.
8. You should leave her in peace.
9. We are having a house built in Cologne.
10. We want to have Overbeck build us a house.
11. I wish we had had Overbeck build us a house.

M. Restate the following sentences in the perfect.

1. Ich blieb oft vor Erikas Haus stehen.
2. Er riet mir, an die Nordsee zu fahren.
3. Wir ließen gestern abend den Arzt kommen.
4. Sie braucht *doch* nicht nach Berlin zu fahren.
5. Wir dachten damals daran, nach Köln zu ziehen.
6. Um sechs Uhr gingen wir essen.
7. Der Müller war einfach nicht zu verstehen.
8. Gegen Abend fing es dann an zu regnen.
9. Er lief aus dem Haus, ohne ein Wort zu sagen.

N. Transform the following pairs of sentences into sentences with **ohne**
    . . . zu or **statt . . . zu**. Note that the negation disappears in the infinitive
    phrase.

> **Sie fuhr in die Schweiz. Sie nahm die Kinder nicht mit. —ohne**
> **Sie fuhr in die Schweiz, ohne die Kinder mitzunehmen.**

1. Er fuhr nach Afrika. Er blieb nicht zu Hause. —statt
2. Sie schrieb ihm einen Brief. Sie rief ihn nicht an. —statt
3. Sie war in Berlin. Sie hat mich nicht besucht. —ohne
4. Er kauft sich einen Wagen. Er hatte nicht das Geld dafür. —ohne

O. Express in German.

1. Where is your coat?—Oh, I left it (hanging) at the Meyers.
2. Perhaps you should try once more to call her.
3. This chair you must leave (standing) in the living room.
4. He forgot to put the chairs back into the living room.
5. He promised his wife to be back at nine o'clock.
6. He suggested that my wife should go to the North Sea this year.

P. Change to comparatives.

> **Ich bin nicht so alt wie er. Er ist älter als ich.**

1. Unser Haus ist nicht so groß wie eures.
2. Bei uns ist es nicht so kalt wie bei euch.
3. Glas ist nicht so hart wie ein Diamant.
4. Der Weg war nicht so lang wie ich dachte. (Use **kurz**.)
5. Ich gehe nicht so oft ins Theater wie du.
6. Amerikanisches Bier ist nicht so stark wie deutsches Bier.
7. Von Köln bis Bonn ist es nicht so weit wie von Frankfurt bis Bonn.
8. Ich kann nicht so viel essen wie du.
9. Bier trinke ich nicht so gerne wie Wein.
10. Ich finde ihn nicht so interessant wie seine Frau.

Q. Change the adjectives to superlatives. Make other changes where necessary.

1. Hans hat viel getrunken.
2. München ist eine schöne Stadt.
3. In München gibt es gutes Bier.
4. Im Dezember sind die Tage kurz.
5. Im Juni sind die Tage lang.
6. Der 21. Juni ist ein langer Tag.
7. Giganto ist ein starker Mann.
8. Ich wäre jetzt gern in Deutschland.
9. In Alaska ist das Obst teuer.
10. Dieser Film hat mir gut gefallen.

R. Imagine that you have a cousin, Hildegard, who lives in Munich and knows no English. You want to visit her during your stay in Germany, so you decide to write her a letter after you arrive in Frankfurt. For lack of anything profound to say (owing to your lack of that kind of German), you tell her about your adventures at the Frankfurt airport. Address her as "Liebe Hildegard" and sign off with "Viele herzliche Grüße."

The envelope would be addressed as follows: Frau
Hildegard Pfeilguth
Tengstraße 40
8 München 13

VOCABULARY

die Alpen (*pl.*)	Alps
arm	poor
baden	to bathe, swim
sich (*acc.*) **bedanken**	to thank
befehlen	to command, order
der Beifall	applause
berichten	to report
bestellen	to (place an) order
breit	broad
der Brief, -e	letter
einen Brief auf•geben	to post (mail) a letter
der Eilbrief, -e	special-delivery letter
der Einschreibebrief, -e	registered letter
der Luftpostbrief, -e	airmail letter
die Briefmarke, -n	stamp
dankbar	grateful
dankeschön	thanks very much
dunkel, dunkler, dunkelst-	dark, darker, darkest
die Erkältung, -en	cold (illness)
erlauben	to allow, permit
erstaunt sein	to be astonished
die Freiheit	freedom
die Freundlichkeit, -en	friendliness; favor
gern, lieber, liebst- (*adv.*)	gladly, rather, most of all
das Gespräch, -e	conversation
das Ferngespräch, -e	long distance telephone call
das Telefonegespräch, -e	telephone call, conversation
groß, größer, größt-	large, larger, largest
gut, besser, best-	good, better, best
der Handschuh, -e	glove
hängen (hängte, gehängt) (*with acc.*)	to hang (something)
er hängte das Bild an die Wand (hing, gehangen)	he hung the picture on the wall to hang, be suspended
das Bild hing an der Wand	the picture hung on the wall
hart	hard

die Härte	hardness
hoch, höher, höchst-	high, higher, highest
die Hoffnung, -en	hope
hoffnungsvoll	hopeful, full of hope
hoffnungslos	hopeless
die Höhe, -n	height; altitude
die Jugendherberge, -n	youth hostel
die Kälte	cold(ness)
die Krankheit, -en	illness, disease
leer	empty
die Möglichkeit, -en	possibility
der Nachbar, -n (n-noun)	neighbor
nah, näher, nächst-	near, close; closer; nearest, next
nee (*colloq.*) = **nein**	no
ohne . . . zu	without . . .
das Paket, -e	package
die Pension', -en	bed and breakfast inn
das Postamt, ¨er	post office
die Post (*no pl.*)	mail; post office; postal service
die Postleitzahl, -en	zip code
der Quatsch (*colloq.*)	nonsense
raten	to advise; to guess
der Rat (*no pl.*)	advice
reparieren	to repair
die Ruhe	rest, quietude
laß mich in Ruhe	leave me in peace (alone)

Dom in Halberstadt

die Sache, -n	matter, thing	**verbieten**	to forbid, prohibit
schreien	to scream	**Eingang verboten**	do not enter
schwach	weak	**Rauchen verboten**	no smoking
die Schwäche, -n	weakness	**verlangen**	to demand
selbst wählen	dial direct	**viel, mehr, meist-**	much, more, most
der Sinn, -e	sense	**der Volkswagen, - (der**	*lit.* people's car
(an)statt . . . zu	instead of . . .	**VW, die VWs)**	
stehen•bleiben (sein)	to stop; to remain standing	**die Vorstellung, -en**	introduction; (theater) performance; idea, representation
still	quiet, still		
der Sturm, ⁻e	storm		
das Telegramm, -e	telegram	**die Vorwahlnummer,**	area code
teuer, teurer, teuerst-	expensive	**-n**	
sich (*acc.*) **um•sehen**	to look around	**die Wärme**	warmth
der Unsinn	nonsense		

Strong Verbs

INFINITIVE	PRESENT	PAST TENSE	PERFECT	
befehlen	**befiehlt**	**befahl**	**befohlen**	to command, order
hängen		**hing**	**gehangen**	to hang, be suspended
raten	**rät**	**riet**	**geraten**	to advise; to guess
schreien		**schrie**	**geschrien**	to scream
stehen•bleiben		**blieb stehen**	**ist stehengeblieben**	to stop
sich um•sehen	**sieht um**	**sah um**	**umgesehen**	to look around
verbieten		**verbot**	**verboten**	to forbid, prohibit

Unit 17
Adjectives (Continued)

Berlin

Berlin, 750 years old in 1987, was the capital of Prussia and, from 1871 to 1945, of the German Reich. After the collapse of Nazi Germany in 1945, the city was occupied by the four Allied Powers. In the course of the Cold War, the Russian sector and the three western sectors gradually developed into two separate entities. The separation became complete when the East Germans built the wall in 1961.

When the German Democratic Republic was created in 1949, East Berlin became the capital and is now officially referred to as "Hauptstadt der Republik."

West Berlin, located within the GDR, 110 miles from the border of the Federal Republic, is legally and economically integrated into the Federal Republic, even though it is technically not one of the federal states. Legally, the Allied Powers are still the ultimate authority in Berlin. Despite its isolation, West Berlin remains a thriving cultural and industrial center in the German-speaking world.

750 JAHRE BERLIN

Übergänge von West- nach Ostberlin

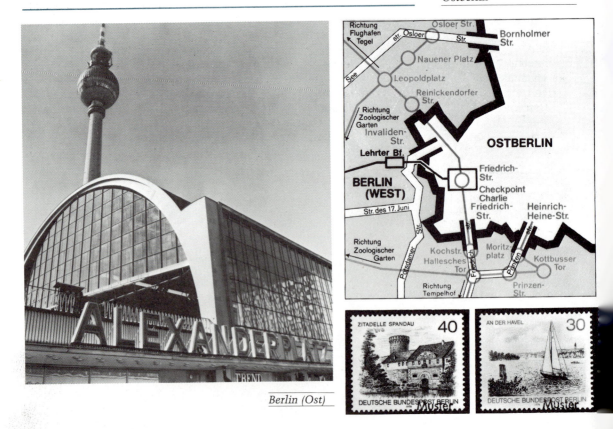

Berlin (Ost)

PATTERNS ONE

1/Adjectives Used as Nouns

In dem Zimmer lag ein Toter.

Die Polizei fand einen Toten im Zimmer.

Kein Mensch wußte, wer der Tote war.

Wer ist denn die Blonde da drüben?

Der junge Deutsche (die junge Deutsche) auf Zimmer Eins ist erst gestern angekommen.

Auf Zimmer Eins wohnt ein junger Deutscher (eine junge Deutsche).

Wir haben mit dem jungen Deutschen (mit der jungen Deutschen) zu Abend gegessen.

Den jungen Deutschen (Die junge Deutsche) habe ich noch nicht kennengelernt.

Auf Zimmer Zwei wohnen zwei junge Deutsche.

Die beiden jungen Deutschen habe ich noch nicht kennengelernt.

Er spricht ein gutes Deutsch.

Sie haben recht, er spricht wirklich gut Deutsch.

Auf Wiedersehen, und alles Gute.

Er hat viel Gutes getan.

Könnte ich noch etwas Warmes zu essen bekommen?

Ich habe etwas sehr Schönes erlebt.

Ich hoffe, ich habe nichts Wichtiges vergessen.

A dead man was lying in the room.

The police found a dead man in the room.

Nobody knew who the dead man was.

Who is the blond over there?

The young German (man/woman) in Room 1 arrived only yesterday.

A young German (man/woman) lives in Room 1.

We had dinner with the young German (man/woman).

I haven't met the young German (man/woman) yet.

Two young Germans are living in Room 2.

I haven't met the two young Germans yet.

He speaks good German.

You are right, he really does speak German well.

Good-bye, and all the best.

He has done much good.

Could I still get something hot to eat?

I've experienced something very beautiful.

I hope I haven't forgotten anything important.

2/Participles Used as Adjectives and Nouns

Wir standen vor der geschlossenen Tür.

Er kam mit einem gebrochenen Bein vom Schilaufen zurück.

Sie kam mit gebrochenem Herzen vom Schilaufen zurück.

We stood in front of the closed door.

He returned from skiing with a broken leg.

She returned from skiing with a broken heart.

In Verbindung bleiben...

...mit Freunden, Verwandten, Bekannten. Nur mal schnell hören, wie's geht, eine Verabredung treffen oder Glückwünsche durchgeben. Per Telefon!

Er war bei uns immer ein gern gesehener Gast.	He was always a welcome guest at our house (*lit.* he was a gladly seen guest).
Erich Merkle ist ein guter Bekannter von uns.	Erich Merkle is a close acquaintance of ours.
Frau Merkle ist eine gute Bekannte von meiner Frau.	Mrs. Merkle is a close acquaintance of my wife's.
Haben Sie Bekannte hier in der Stadt?	Do you have acquaintances here in town?
Haben Sie Verwandte in Westfalen?	Do you have relatives in Westphalia?
Otto Müller ist ein Verwandter von mir.	Otto Müller is a relative of mine.
Heidi ist eine entfernte Verwandte von mir.	Heidi is a distant relative of mine.
Das ist der amerikanische Gesandte.	That is the American ambassador.
Sein Vater war ein hoher Beamter bei der Bundesregierung.	His father was a high official in the federal government.
Alle deutschen Lehrer sind Beamte.	All German teachers are civil servants.
Hier auf der Post arbeiten über hundert Beamtinnen.	More than a hundred women civil servants work here at the post office.
Auch Frau Meyer ist eine Beamtin.	Mrs. Meyer is a civil servant too.

3/-d Adjectives

Wer war denn der gut aussehende junge Mann gestern abend?	Who was the good-looking young man last night?
Er hatte so ein gewinnendes Lächeln.	He had such a winning smile.
Alles um sich her vergessend, saßen sie mit klopfendem Herzen unter der blühenden Linde; und ihre vielsagenden Blicke aus leuchtenden Augen sagten mehr als ihre zurückhaltenden Worte.	Forgetting everything around them, they sat under the blooming linden tree, with their hearts pounding, and the meaningful glances of their shining eyes said more than their reserved words.

(from Schmidt-Ingelheim,
Die Frau mit dem Flamingo, p. 97)

ANALYSIS ONE

140/Adjectives Used as Nouns

In such English phrases as *the idle rich* and *he helped the poor*, the adjectives *rich* and *poor* are used as plural nouns. In German many adjectives can be used as nouns, frequently in the singular; they are then capitalized and take attributive adjective endings; thus, **der reiche Mann** becomes **der Reiche**.

SLOT 0	SLOT 1	SLOT 2	SLOT 3	
	der	Reiche		the rich man
	die	Alte		the old woman
	das	Gute		the good
mein	Alter			my old man
	die	Armen		the poor
	der	Tote		the dead man
	die	Tote		the dead woman
	die	Toten		the dead
ein	Toter			a dead man

When an adjective follows **nichts, etwas, viel,** and **wenig**, as in English *nothing new* or *something important*, the German adjective is capitalized and has a strong neuter singular ending.

Es gibt leider nichts Neues.
Ich habe etwas Wichtiges vergessen.
Das führt zu nichts Gutem.
Sie hat viel Gutes getan.
Er hat wenig Neues zu sagen.

NOTE: Of all nouns indicating nationality, **Deutsch** is the only one declined like an adjective.

der Deutsche   the German (man)
die Deutsche   the German (woman)
die Deutschen   the Germans

141/Participles Used as Adjectives and Nouns

In German, as in English, participles can be used as attributive adjectives.

SLOT 0	SLOT 1	SLOT 2	SLOT 3	
	die	geschlossene	Tür	the closed door
	eine	geschlossene	Tür	a closed door
	geschlossene		Türen	closed doors
ein	entwickelter		Film	a developed (processed roll of) film
	der	entwickelte	Film	the developed film

Both German and English can use participles as plural nouns. Unlike English, however, German can also use participles as singular nouns.

SLOT 0	SLOT 1	SLOT 2	SLOT 3	
	der/die	Angestellte		the employee
ein	Angestellter			an employee
	die	Angestellten		the employees

Similarly:

der Bekannte   acquaintance—from: **bekannt sein**   to be (well) known
die Bekannte
der Verwandte   relative—from: **verwandt sein**   to be related
die Verwandte
der Beamte   official, civil servant—from: **das Amt**   office
   (originally: **der Beamtete**   one who is given an office)

but

die Beamtin, plural: **die Beamtinnen**

142/-d Adjectives

Many German verbs can form attributive adjectives corresponding to English adjectives in *-ing* by adding **-d** to the infinitive. These forms are often referred to as "present participles."

SLOT 0	SLOT 1	SLOT 2	SLOT 3	
	das	schlafende	Kind	the sleeping child
ein	schlafendes		Kind	a sleeping child
	die	schlafenden	Kinder	the sleeping children
mit	wachsendem		Interesse	with growing interest

PRACTICE ONE

A. Complete the following sentences using the adjective in parentheses
as a noun.

1. Ein _____ und zwei Engländer wohnen hier. (deutsch)
2. Kennen Sie den _____? (deutsch)
3. Wie heißen die zwei _____ auf Zimmer Eins? (deutsch)
4. Ich gehe heute abend mit einer _____ ins Kino. (bekannt)
5. Ich habe meine _____ in Berlin besucht. (verwandt)
6. Ich muß dir etwas _____ sagen. (wichtig)
7. Unsere _____ haben im August Urlaub. (angestellt)
8. Sie hat uns nichts _____ gesagt. (neu)

Brandenburger Tor

B. Complete the following sentences by using the verb in parentheses either
as a participle or **d**-adjective.

1. Zum Frühstück hätte ich gerne ein weich _____ Ei. (kochen)
2. Er las den Roman mit _____ Interesse. (wachsen)
3. England und Japan sind _____ Länder. (entwickeln)
4. Karin stieg aus dem gerade _____ Zug. (ankommen)
5. Die in diesem Hotel _____ Gäste sind alle Ausländer. (wohnen)

PATTERNS TWO

4/derselbe

Ist das derselbe Wein, den wir gestern abend getrunken haben?

Is that the same wine that we drank last night?

Wir wohnen in demselben Hotel, in dem Fürstenbergs gewohnt haben.

We are staying in the same hotel in which the Fürstenbergs stayed.

Wir saßen gestern mit Fürstenbergs am selben Tisch.

Yesterday we sat at the same table with the Fürstenbergs.

Seit Jahren trägt er jeden Sonntag denselben Anzug.

For years he's been wearing the same suit every Sunday.

5/was für

Was für ein Wagen ist das denn?
Was ist denn das für ein Wagen?

What kind of car is that?

Was für einen Wagen hast du dir denn gekauft?
Was hast du dir denn für einen Wagen gekauft?

What kind of car did you buy?

Mit was für einem Wagen bist du denn gefahren?

What kind of car did you go in?

Was ist denn das für ein Wagen?

Hast du gesehen, was für einen unmöglichen Hut Tante Amalie schon wieder aufhat?	Did you see what an impossible hat Aunt Amalie has on again?
Weißt du noch, mit was für einem unmöglichen Hut sie damals im Theater war?	Do you remember what an impossible hat she came to the theater with?
Was für Wetter.	What weather.
Was für ein schöner Tag.	What a beautiful day.
Was für schöne Tage das waren.	What beautiful days those were.
Ich muß noch immer daran denken, was für wunderbare Tage wir an der Ostsee verbracht haben.	I still remember what wonderful days we spent at the Baltic Sea.

6/all, ganz

Alles Gute zum neuen Jahr wünscht Dir Deine Luise.	All good wishes for the New Year. Yours, Louise.
Was hilft ihm jetzt all sein schönes Geld?	What good does all his lovely money do him now?
Was hilft ihm denn jetzt das ganze Geld?	What good does all that money do him now?
Ich habe alle meine alten Freunde besucht.	I visited all my old friends.
All meine Freunde sind Ärzte.	All my friends are doctors.
Ich habe alle seine Romane gelesen.	I have read all his novels.
Ich habe seine Romane alle gelesen.	I have read all his novels.
Kannst du für uns alle *Kar*ten kaufen?	Can you buy tickets for all of us?
Kannst du Karten für uns *al*le kaufen?	Can you buy tickets for all of us?
Ich habe alle Karten gekauft, die noch zu haben waren.	I've bought all the tickets that were still to be had.

Alle guten Karten waren schon ausverkauft.	All the good tickets were sold out already.
Wir alle sind dir dankbar.	We are all grateful to you.
Wir sind dir alle dankbar.	We are all grateful to you.
Er hat den ganzen Tag auf mich gewartet.	He waited for me all day.
Fritzchen hat einen ganzen Apfel gegessen.	Fritzchen has eaten a whole apple.
Sie war ganz allein.	She was all alone.
Wie geht's dir denn? — Danke, ganz gut.	How are you? — Thanks, pretty well.
Wir sind durch ganz Österreich gefahren.	We drove through all of Austria.

7/viel, wenig

Meyer hat viel Geld.	Meyer has a lot of money.
Ja, aber das viele Geld macht ihn auch nicht glücklich.	Yes, but all that money doesn't make him happy either.
Sein vieles Geld macht ihn nicht glücklich.	All his money doesn't make him happy.
Heute ist Sonntag, und viele Leute fahren heute spazieren.	Today is Sunday, and many people go for a drive today.
Was haben Sie denn während der vielen langen Winternächte gemacht?	What did you do during the many long winter nights?
Ich habe viel zu wenig Geld, um jedes Jahr in die Schweiz fahren zu können.	I have far too little money to be able to go to Switzerland every year.
Mit dem wenigen Geld, das du mir schickst, kann ich nicht viel kaufen.	With the little money you send me I can't buy much.
Wir haben dieses Wochenende nur wenige Gäste im Hause. Bei dem Wetter bleiben die Leute zu Hause.	We have only a few guests here this weekend. In this weather, people stay at home.

8/ander-

So geht das nicht; das mußt du anders machen.	It won't work that way; you'll have to do it differently.
Aber Erich, du bist ja ganz anders als früher.	But Erich, you are so different from the way you used to be.
Erich soll ein ganz anderer Mensch geworden sein.	Erich supposedly has become a completely different person.
Er spricht von nichts anderem als von seiner Amerikareise.	He talks about nothing (else) but his trip to America.
Den einen Herrn kannte ich, aber wer war denn der andere?	One of the gentlemen I knew, but who was the other one?
Den anderen Herrn kenne ich auch nicht.	I don't know the other gentleman either.
Das muß jemand anders gewesen sein.	That must have been somebody else.
Das kann niemand anders gewesen sein als Meyer.	That can have been nobody (else) but Meyer.
Anderen hat er geholfen; sich selbst kann er nicht helfen.	Others he has helped; himself he cannot help.

9/ein paar, einige, mehrere

„In ein paar Tagen bin ich wieder hier", hatte er gesagt. Aber dann wurden aus den paar Tagen ein paar Jahre.	"I'll be back in a few days," he had said. But then the few days turned into a few years.
Es waren nur ein paar Leute da.	Only a few people were there.
Mit den paar Mark kannst du doch nicht nach Davos fahren.	You can't go to Davos with those few marks.

Ein paar schöne Tage haben wir ja gehabt, aber die meiste Zeit hat es geregnet.	We did have a few nice days, but most of the time it rained.
Ich hätte gerne ein paar kleine Würstchen zum Frühstück.	I'd like to have a few sausages for breakfast.
Bringen Sie mir doch bitte ein Paar Würstchen.	Could I have a couple of sausages (frankfurters), please?
Ich habe nur zwei Paar gute Schuhe mitgebracht.	I've only brought two pairs of good shoes.
Anton und Emma waren ein schönes Paar.	Anton and Emma were a lovely couple.
Einige von unseren Lesern möchten wissen, ob Ingelheim noch in Konstanz wohnt.	Some of our readers would like to know whether Ingelheim still lives in Constance.
Wir kamen durch mehrere alte Dörfer.	We came through several old villages.
Im Löwen kann man für ein paar Mark gut essen.	At the Lion Inn one can eat well for a few marks.
Ich habe auch schon einige Male da gegessen.	I've eaten there several times, too.
Letzte Woche habe ich mehrere Male im Löwen gegessen.	Last week I ate at the Lion several times.

ANALYSIS TWO

143/*derselbe*

There are two German adjectives to express English *the same*: **der gleiche** and **derselbe**. The forms of **derselbe** are written as one word unless the article is contracted with a preposition. Both **der-** and **selb-** must be declined.

> **Ist das derselbe Wein wie gestern?**
> **Ist das der gleiche Wein wie gestern?**
> **Wir trinken heute wieder denselben Wein wie gestern.**
> **Wir wohnen in derselben Stadt.**
> **Wir wohnen im selben Hotel.**
> **Wir wohnen im gleichen Hotel.**
> **Wir wohnen in demselben Hotel.**

Strictly speaking, **der gleiche** expresses similarity (the same kind), and **derselbe** expresses identity (the very same).

144/*was für*

There is no English structural equivalent for the frequently used construction with **was für**. The **für** in this fixed phrase does not influence the case of the following adjective or noun. **Was für** means *what kind of* or *what*.

In the nominative and accusative, **für** plus the noun or pronoun may either follow **was** immediately or stand in the inner field, usually right before the second prong.

> *Was für ein Wagen* **ist denn das da drüben?**
> *Was* **ist denn das** *für ein Wagen* **da drüben?**
> *Was* **ist denn das da drüben** *für ein Wagen?*

> *Was für einen Wagen* **hast du dir denn gekauft?**
> *Was* **hast du dir denn** *für einen Wagen* **gekauft?**

> *Was für Bücher* **hast du mir denn mitgebracht?**
> *Was* **hast du mir denn** *für Bücher* **mitgebracht?**

In the dative, the **was für** construction cannot be split, nor can it be split if it is preceded by a preposition.

> *Was für einem Mann* **gehört denn der Wagen?**
> *Mit was für einem Wagen* **bist du denn gefahren?**
> *Durch was für Dörfer* **seid ihr denn gefahren?**
> *Auf was für einen Mann* **wartest du denn?**

The **was für** construction also occurs in exclamations. If such exclamations are full clauses, the finite verb occurs in verb-last position.

> **Was für ein interessantes Buch!**
> **Was für ein interessantes Buch das ist!**

145/*all, ganz*

All is used with or without endings. When there is an ending, it is always strong; that is, it behaves like a **der**-word.

SINGULAR

(a) Forms with an ending are not used very frequently. They occur, immediately followed by a noun, in stereotyped phrases.

> **Ich wünsche dir alles Gute.**

and in proverbial expressions:

> **Aller Anfang ist schwer.**

(b) If used without an ending, **all** must be followed by a **der**-word or a possessive adjective.

> **all das schöne Geld**
> **all mein Geld**

Such phrases express bulk quantity, and **all** can be replaced by the attributive adjective **ganz.**

> **das ganze schöne Geld**
> **mein ganzes Geld**

PLURAL

(a) **All** with an ending is the plural of **jeder** and means "every single one of them"; it precedes nouns and follows pronouns.

> **Alle meine Brüder wohnen jetzt in der Stadt.**
> **Wir alle haben ihn gestern besucht.**

In the spoken language, it is usually separated from its noun or pronoun and placed in the inner field preceding the first item of news value.

> **Meine Brüder wohnen jetzt alle in der Schweiz.**
> **Wir haben ihn gestern alle besucht.**
> **Gestern haben wir ihn alle besucht.**

Note that **all-** is the only **der**-word that can be followed by another **der**-word or **ein**-word.

(b) **All** without an ending refers again to bulk quantity and means "the whole bunch of them." Again, it must be followed by a **der-** or an **ein**-word, but it cannot be separated from its noun.

> **Ich habe all meine Bücher verloren.**

Again, this "bulk" meaning of **all** can be replaced by the attributive adjective **ganz.**

> **Ich habe meine ganzen Bücher verloren.**

SLOT 0	SLOT 1	SLOT 2	SLOT 3
	alles	**Gute**	
all	**das**	**schöne**	**Geld**
	alle	**deutschen**	**Bücher**
	alle die	**deutschen**	**Bücher**
	alle meine	**deutschen**	**Bücher**
all	**meine**	**deutschen**	**Bücher**

Ganz, if not used as a replacement for **all**, is used in the following ways:

(a) As an attributive adjective meaning *whole* or *entire*.

Er hat den ganzen Tag auf mich gewartet.   He waited for me all day.

(b) As an adverb, meaning *completely*, modifying an adjective.

Sie war ganz allein.   She was all alone.

(c) As an *unstressed* adverb, meaning *quite* or *rather*, modifying such "praising" adjectives as **gut, glücklich, intelligent.**

Das Wetter war ja ganz gut, aber es hätte   The weather wasn't bad, but it could have
besser sein können.   been better.

Do not thank your hostess by saying **Das Essen war ganz gut.** This would mean that the food wasn't bad, but certainly nothing to rave about.

(d) Without an ending and preceding geographical names. It then means *all of.*

Wir sind durch ganz Österreich gefahren.

but

Wir sind durch die ganze Schweiz gefahren.

146/*viel, wenig*

Viel (*much;* plural: *many*) and **wenig** (*little;* plural: *few*) have the same characteristics.

(a) In the singular, **viel** and **wenig** express bulk and are usually used without endings.

Wir haben damals viel Fisch und wenig Fleisch gegessen.

Adjectives used after these endingless forms have strong endings.

Ich habe noch viel deutsches Geld.
Ich habe nur noch wenig deutsches Geld.

After definite articles, **viel** and **wenig**, still indicating bulk, take normal attributive adjective endings.

das viele Geld
mit dem wenigen Geld

Note, however, the expression **vielen Dank** (*thank you very much*).

(b) In the plural, **viele** means *many* and **wenige** *few*. They are treated as attributive adjectives.

	SLOT 1	SLOT 2	SLOT 3
	viele junge		**Leute**
	die	**vielen jungen**	**Leute**
mit	**wenigen**		**Worten**

(c) When used without an ending, **viel** and **wenig** are usually written as one word with **so, wie,** or **zu**. Inflected forms of **viel** and **wenig**, however, are written separately.

Es hat soviel geregnet wie schon lange nicht mehr.
Um wieviel Uhr ist sie gekommen?
Meyer hat schon wieder zuviel gegessen.
Wie viele Leute waren denn da?

NOTE: **soviel** is also used as a conjunction meaning *as far as*:

Soviel ich weiß, ist sie noch hier.	As far as I know, she's still here.

(d) **Viel** and **wenig** are used as adverbs preceding comparatives.

Er war viel älter als sie.
Er war nur wenig älter als sie.
Er hatte viel mehr Geld als ich.

Viel must not be confused with the adverb **sehr** (*very*), which sometimes corresponds to an English *very much.*

Ich habe sie sehr geliebt.	I loved her very much.
Ich ginge sehr gerne mit nach Köln.	I'd like very much to go along to Cologne.
Er war sehr krank.	He was very sick.
Die Amerikaner essen sehr viel Fleisch.	Americans eat a lot of (very much) meat.
Ich war sehr dagegen.	I was very much against it.
Es waren sehr viele Leute dort.	There were very many people there.

English *very* usually precedes *much, many,* or some other adjective or adverb. German **sehr**, on the other hand, is an independent adverb and does not have to be followed by anything.

Sie liebte ihn sehr.

147 /*ander-*

Ander- means *other, different,* or *else.* If used attributively or after **etwas** or **nichts**, it takes the same endings as any other attributive adjective and is often preceded by **ganz.**

Das eine Buch kenne ich, aber das andere habe ich noch nicht gelesen.
Erika kenne ich ja, aber wer war denn die andere Dame?
Dieser Herr war es nicht, es muß ein anderer gewesen sein.
Das ist natürlich etwas anderes. (*something else*)
Das ist etwas ganz anderes. (*something quite different*)

NOTE: For some unfathomable reason, no form of **ander-** is capitalized.

If **ander-** is used as an adverb or a predicate adjective, it always has the form **anders.**

Ich hätte das ganz anders gemacht.   I would have done that quite differently.
Er ist anders, als er früher war.   He is different than he used to be.

Note also the following frequently used phrases:

Das kann nicht mein Bruder gewesen sein, das muß *jemand anders* (*somebody else*) gewesen sein.
Das kann *niemand anders* (*nobody else*) gewesen sein als Anton Meyer.

148/mehrere, einige, ein paar

All three of these terms mean "more than two, but not many"; **mehrere** means *several*; **einige** and **ein paar** mean *a few* or *some*.

Because **mehrere** and **einige** are never used with an article, as is possible with English *the several states*, they always appear in slot one and behave like regular attributive adjectives. If there are additional attributive adjectives, they must also appear in slot 1.

The **ein** in **ein paar** is never inflected.

SLOT 0	SLOT 1	SLOT 2	SLOT 3
	mehrere junge		Leute
	einige deutsche		Bücher
ein paar	junge		Leute
ein paar	deutsche		Bücher

Do not confuse **wenige**, meaning *few* in the sense of *not many*, with **ein paar**, meaning *a few* in the sense of *some*.

Wenige Menschen wußten, wer er wirklich war.
Ein paar Menschen wußten, wer er wirklich war.
Ich komme in ein paar Minuten.
Er wollte in Berlin ein paar Freunde besuchen.
Er ist ein paar Tage in Berlin gewesen.
Wir haben ein paar schöne Tage an der Riviera verbracht.

After the definite article, **ein paar** becomes **paar.**

> **Die paar schönen Tage an der Riviera waren viel zu kurz.**

Note the difference between **ein paar** (*a few*) and **ein Paar** (*a couple, a pair*):

> **Wir aßen Suppe mit ein paar Würstchen.**
> **Wir aßen Suppe mit einem Paar Würstchen.**
> **Anton und Emma waren ein schönes Paar.**

149/Word Formation: Nouns Derived from Weak Verbs

The stem of some weak verbs appears as a noun of action—that is, a noun denoting the activity expressed by the verb. Feel free to use the nouns listed, but do not try to invent your own—they may not exist. Most of these nouns are masculine, but there are also a few feminines and neuters.

antworten	die Antwort,-en	das war eine gute Antwort
baden	das Bad,-̈er	ein heißes Bad
besuchen	der Besuch,-e	**Der Besuch der alten Dame** (Dürrenmatt)
blicken	der Blick,-e	ein vielsagender Blick
danken	der Dank (*no pl.*)	vielen Dank
fragen	die Frage,-n	das kommt nicht in Frage (*that's out of the question*)
glauben	der Glaube, *gen.* des Glaubens (*no pl.*)	Glaube, Hoffnung, Liebe
grüßen	der Gruß,-̈e	viele Grüße aus den Bergen
heiraten	die Heirat,-en	ich bin gegen diese Heirat
kaufen	der Kauf,-̈e	ein guter Kauf
küssen	der Kuß, die Küsse	mit Gruß und Kuß, Dein Julius
lieben	die Liebe (*no pl.*)	Liebe macht blind
reden	die Rede,-n	er hielt eine lange Rede
suchen	die Suche (*no pl.*)	die Suche nach dem Dieb
tanzen	der Tanz,-̈e	der Tanz um das goldene Kalb
versuchen	der Versuch,-e	ein chemischer Versuch
wünschen	der Wunsch,-̈e	alle guten Wünsche zum Neuen Jahr

The most common nouns of action are the feminine nouns in **-ung** (see Anal. 98, p. 305).

150/Word Formation: Nouns Derived from Strong Verbs

Theoretically, any one of the various forms of the stem of a strong verb can occur as a noun denoting the action of the verb, or the result of such action, or the thing used for such action.

> Action: **der Schlaf** sleep
> Result of action: **der Fund** the find
> Thing used for action: **der Sitz** the seat

Again, it is safe to use the nouns listed, but do not invent your own.
Note that of the nouns ending in **-t** and **-e**, most are feminine.

abfahren	die Abfahrt,-en	departure
anfangen	der Anfang,¨e	beginning
ankommen	die Ankunft,¨e	arrival
anrufen	der Anruf,-e	phone call
aufnehmen	die Aufnahme,-n	reception; photograph
ausgehen	der Ausgang,¨e	exit
beginnen	der Beginn (no pl.)	beginning
bitten	die Bitte,-n	request
fahren	die Fahrt,-en	drive, trip
fallen	der Fall,¨e	fall; case
gewinnen	der Gewinn,-e	profit, gain
helfen	die Hilfe,-n	help
liegen	die Lage,-n	situation
raten	der Rat,¨e	advice, counsel; counselor; council
schlafen	der Schlaf (no pl.)	sleep
schlagen	der Schlag,¨e	strike, stroke, hit
schneiden	der Schnitt,-e	cut
schreiben	die Schrift,-en	(hand)writing
	die Heilige Schrift	Bible, Holy Writ
sehen	das Gesicht,-er	face
sitzen	der Sitz,-e	seat
sprechen	die Sprache,-n	language; speech
springen	der Sprung,¨e	jump
stehen	der Stand,¨e	stand
trinken	das Getränk,-e	beverage
verbieten	das Verbot,-e	prohibition
verlieren	der Verlust,-e	loss
verstehen	der Verstand (no pl.)	reason, intelligence
ziehen	der Zug,¨e	train

PRACTICE TWO

C. Express in German.

1. What kind of car is that?
2. Oh, what a beautiful morning.
3. We're all very grateful to you, Mrs. Behrens.
4. Ingrid and I went to the same school.
5. Monika visited all her German relatives.

D. Insert the correct form of **viel**.

1. Ich habe nicht _____ Geld.
2. Was tut sie denn mit ihrem _____ Geld?

3. Wie _____ Kinder habt ihr denn?
4. Wie _____ Bier habt ihr denn getrunken?
5. Was machst du denn jetzt mit deinen _____ Büchern?
6. Er hat schon immer _____ gelesen.

E. Insert the correct form of **ander-**.

1. Es war ganz _____, als ich gedacht hatte.
2. Wer waren denn die _____ Herren?
3. Sie wohnen in einem _____ Hotel.
4. Ich war es nicht; es war jemand _____.
5. Dieses Buch war es nicht; es war ein _____.
6. Ich habe leider keinen _____ Mantel.
7. Alle _____ gingen nach Hause.
8. Ich hätte lieber etwas _____.

F. Express in German.

1. She bought several old books.
2. Some of those books were expensive.
3. She came back a few days later.
4. We spent a few nice days in Innsbruck.
5. I bought a pair of shoes.

CONVERSATIONS

I

How to Express What?

Below you will find colloquial, and mostly stereotypical, phrases that are used with high frequency in everyday conversation, to express such sentiments as astonishment, surprise, disbelief, doubt, anger, pleasure, urgency, etc. Almost all of these expressions have been used before; the list, therefore, can serve as a vocabulary review. They are arranged in vaguely alphabetical sequence; as you go through them, try to determine on what level of discourse—from fairly formal to highly colloquial—they may be used. In class, practice all of them in sentences or brief exchanges to make sure you use them right, and then, as you continue with the conversations of Units 17 and 18, use them as much as possible.

Aha!	I see; I get it.
Ach so.	Oh; now I get it.
Na also.	I told you so; why all the fuss?
Guten Appetit.	(said at beginning of a meal)
Mahlzeit.	

(Ganz) bestimmt.	Certainly; definitely.
So was Blödes.	How stupid; what a stupid (dumb) thing to have
Dummes.	happened, to do.
Wie kann man/ein Mensch nur so blöd sein?	How can anybody be so stupid?
Sei mir nicht böse, aber . . .	Don't be angry (mad at me, offended), but . . .
Danke ja/nein.	Thank you, yes/no.
Danke ebenfalls.	Thanks, and the same to you.
Dann ja!	If (X) is the case, then I agree.
Denk (dir) mal.	Just imagine, think.
Also doch!	So (X) is happening/going to happen after all.
Also gut!	OK, I give in; I'll go along.
Oh doch!	Oh yes! (contrary to expectation)
Ehrlich.	Honest, I mean it. (used mostly by young people)
Entschuldigung, entschuldigen Sie.	(I'm) sorry; beg your pardon; forgive me
Verzeihung.	
Ich bitte um Verzeihung/Entschuldigung.	
Ich bin total fertig.	I'm done in; I've had it.
Ich bin ganz mit den Nerven fertig/runter.	My nerves are shot.
Das ist ja alles falsch.	It's all wrong.
stimmt nicht.	
Das freut mich.	I'm glad/delighted (about that); I like that.
Ich fürchte, ja.	I'm afraid so.
nein.	not.
Ganz gut.	Not bad; so-so; OK.
Nicht schlecht.	
(Aber) (sehr) gerne.	Sure; I'll be glad to.
Genau.	Exactly.
(So) ein Glück!	Are we lucky!
Da haben Sie aber Glück (gehabt).	What luck; you sure were lucky.
Das glaubt (dir) doch kein Mensch.	Nobody is going to believe that, is going to buy that.
Gottseidank.	Thank God; thank goodness.
Mein Gott!	(Oh) My God; heavens! (unpleasant surprise)
Um Gottes willen!	For God's sake!
Um Himmels willen!	For heaven's sake!
Was hältst du denn davon?	What do you think of it/make of it?
Was soll denn das heißen?	What's that all about?
	What's going on (around here)?
Hören Sie, . . . hör mal, . . .	Listen, . . .
Gute Idee.	Good idea.
So ein Idiot.	What an idiot.
Na ja.	Well, I don't know, maybe; OK, it's all right with me, I don't care.
Na klar.	Sure; of course.
Das klingt gut.	That sounds good; that's all right (with me).
(Nun) komm schon.	Come on. (impatient)
Ich komm ja schon.	I'm coming.
Ich komme sofort/gleich.	I'll be with you in a minute.
Da kann ich nur lachen.	That (really) makes me laugh.
Leider nicht.	I'm sorry (but I can't . . .).
nein.	
(Das/Es) tut mir leid, aber . . .	

Lieber nicht.
Was ist (denn) los?
   Was ist denn los mit dir?
Jetzt/Gleich geht's los.
Nun mach schon.
   Eil dich.
Natürlich.
(Das ist doch) nicht möglich.
Nicht wahr?
(Da habe ich halt) Pech gehabt.
   So ein Pech.
Da haben Sie recht.
Das ist mir recht.
   Mir soll's recht sein.
Wenn's dir recht ist, dann . . .
Laß mich in Ruhe.
Sagen Sie, . . . sag mal, . . .
(Das ist) schade.
Sehen Sie, . . .
   (Austrian: schaun Sie)
Na, wir wollen mal sehen.
(Aber) sicher.
Ja/Na, so was.
(Das) stimmt.
   (Das ist) richtig.
Viel Spaß.
   Das macht Spaß/Freude.
Das ist (ja) interessant.
      großartig.
      prima.
      echt gut.
Na, wie wär's?
Na, wie war's?
Was ist denn?
(Bitte,) sei so nett/lieb, und . . .
Das war aber gar nicht nett von dir.
Tu (doch) nicht so.
Übrigens.
Du bist wohl verrückt?
        wahnsinnig?
Verdammt (noch mal).
Aber warum denn?
Weißt du, was?
Wirklich.
Auf Ihr Wohl!
  Prosit!
  Prost!
Kein Wunder.
Nun macht aber (mal) Schluß.
   Nun ist aber Schluß.
   Nun hört aber mal auf.

(You'd) better not; (I'd) rather not.
What's the matter?
   What's wrong with you?
Ready to go.
Come on, hurry up.

Sure; of course.
(That's) not possible/true; you don't mean it.
Right?
It didn't work out; too bad; I lost that one.
   Too bad; such bad luck.
You are *right* there.
That's all right with me.

If it's OK with you, then . . .
Leave me alone.
Say; tell me, . . .
Too bad.
You see, . . .

Well, let's see (how it'll turn out).
Sure.
Well, what do you know; I'll be darned.
(That's) right/correct.

Have fun.
   That's fun.
Isn't that interesting.
      great; marvelous.
      great; first-rate.
      real good.
Well, how about it?
Well, how was it?
What's the matter/wrong?
(Please) do me a favor, and . . .
That really wasn't nice of you.
Don't be funny; oh stop it; don't pretend.
By the way.
Are you out of your mind?
      crazy?
Dammit; damn.
But why?
(Do) you know what?
Really.
Here's to you. (said when raising glasses, but only
     with alcoholic beverages)

No wonder.
Stop it; come off it; cut it out;
   no more of this;
   I've had enough.

II

Have your class decide on some topics for conversation, discussion, and debate. With the aid of a dictionary and the help of your teacher, put together lists of appropriate vocabulary; then, as usual, have your teacher be the native speaker.

Some suggestions:

1. Kinder, Küche, Kirche—oder: die Ehe° früher und heute.   (institution of) marriage
2. Die Frauenbewegung: pro's und contra's.
3. Moderne Technologie: Hilfe oder Hindernis?
4. Atomkraft oder Sonnenenergie?
   Die Energiekrise und die Zukunft der Menschheit°.   mankind
5. Bevölkerungszuwachs°: null?   population increase
   oder: was soll mit all den Menschen werden?
6. Der industrialisierte Norden und die „Dritte Welt".
7. Linksradikalismus, Rechtsradikalismus und Terrorismus.

The Economy

In the wake of the near-total destruction caused by World War II, West Germany recovered astonishingly fast due in large part to the infusion of U.S. capital provided by the Marshall Plan.[1] Ironically, the recovery was helped by the influx of millions of people expelled from former eastern German territories who provided a pool of skilled labor. For the past few decades, the Federal Republic has been the strongest economic power in the European Community and the third largest in the western world after the U.S. and Japan.

The East German recovery had a much slower start, but as a member of COMECON (Council for Mutual Economic Assistance) the German Democratic Republic today ranks second in Gross National Product in the East Bloc after the Soviet Union and tenth worldwide.

Frankfurt am Main 1945 und 1985

[1]Established in 1947, the Marshall Plan provided funds for the reconstruction of Western Europe; it was named for Secretary of State George Marshall who first proposed it.

READING

PETER SCHNEIDER

Peter Schneider (born 1940 in Lübeck) has lived in West Berlin since 1961. The following selection is from his novel **Der Mauerspringer** (*The Wall Jumper*), published in 1982. It deals with the "German Question," that is, the situation of the two German states and their future, and the absurdity of the Berlin wall.

Der Mauerspringer

Herr Kabe, Mitte vierzig, arbeitslos, Sozialhilfeempfänger°, fiel° zum ersten Mal polizeilich auf°, als er, von Westen Anlauf neh-mend°, die Mauer mitten in Berlin in östlicher Richtung übersprang. Dicht° an der Mauer hatte er ein Gelände° entdeckt, auf dem Trüm-merreste° eine natürliche Treppe bildeten, die er soweit hinan- 5 steigen konnte, daß er sich nur noch mit den Armen hochzustem-men° brauchte, um sich auf die Mauer zu schwingen. Andere Berichte wissen von einem VW-Transporter°, dessen Dach Kabe als Sprungbrett° benutzt haben soll. Wahrscheinlicher ist, daß er auf diesen Einfall° erst später kam, als die Behörden° seinetwegen[2] 10 Aufräumungsarbeiten veranlaßten°.

Oben stand Kabe eine Weile im Scheinwerferlicht° der herbeige-eilten Weststreife°, ignorierte die Zurufe° der Beamten, die ihm in letzter Minute klar zu machen versuchten, wo Osten und Westen sei, und sprang dann in östlicher Richtung ab. Die Grenzer° des 15 anderen deutschen Staates nahmen° Kabe als Grenzverletzer° fest°. Aber auch in stundenlangen Verhören° ließ Kabe weder politische Absichten° noch einen ernsthaften° Willen zum Dableiben er-kennen. Gefragt, wer ihn geschickt habe, antwortete Kabe, er komme im eigenen Auftrag° und habe nur auf die andere Seite 20 gewollt. Im übrigen ermüdete° er seine Vernehmer°, die von ihm wissen wollten, warum er nicht einen Grenzübergang° benutzt habe, mit der wiederholten Erklärung, er wohne genau gegenüber, und der Weg über die Mauer sei der einzig gerade.

Seine Vernehmer wußten keine bessere Erklärung für diese merk- 25 würdige Verkehrung° der Sprungrichtung, als daß bei Kabe mehrere Schrauben locker säßen°. Sie brachten ihn in die psychiatrische Klinik Buch. Aber auch dort konnten die Ärzte an Kabe nichts außer einem krankhaften Bedürfnis° zur Überwindung° der Mauer ent-decken. In der Klinik genoß° Kabe die Sonderstellung° eines Sperr- 30 brechers°, der mit seinem Sprung die Himmelsrichtungen° neu benannt hatte.

Sozialhilfeempfänger°	welfare recipient
fiel° ... auf°	came to the attention of the police
Anlauf nehmend°	with a running start
Dicht°	close
Gelände°	area
Trümmerreste°	rubble
hochzustemmen°	lift
VW-Transporter°	van
Sprungbrett°	jumping board
Einfall°	idea
Behörden°	authorities
veranlaßten°	had the rubble cleaned up
Scheinwerferlicht°	spotlight
Weststreife°	**die Streife** patrol
Zurufe°	shouts
Grenzer°	border police
nahmen° ... fest°	**festnehmen** to arrest
Grenzverletzer°	violator
Verhören°	interrogations
Absichten°	intentions
ernsthaften°	serious
Auftrag°	behalf
ermüdete°	**ermüden = müde machen**
Vernehmer°	interrogators
Grenzübergang°	border crossing
Verkehrung°	odd reversal
Schrauben locker säßen°	had several screws loose
Bedürfnis°	pathological need
Überwindung°	surmounting
genoß°	enjoyed
Sonderstellung°	special position
Sperrbrechers°	barrier breaker
Himmelsrichtungen°	compass points

[2]**seinetwegen**, *on his account*; also **meinetwegen, deinetwegen**, etc.

Nach drei Monaten wurde° Kabe wohlgenährt° der Ständigen
Vertretung der Bundesrepublik Deutschland[3] übergeben°. Sie
brachte ihn im Dienstmercedes° nach Westberlin zurück. Dort las 35
er, ohne ein Gemütsbewegung° zu zeigen, die Zeitungsartikel, die
ein Nachbar gesammelt° hatte, und schloß sich in seiner Kreuz-
berger[4] Wohnung ein.

Die Einschätzung° in den östlichen Blättern° schwankte° zwischen
«Grenzprovokateur» und «verzweifelter° Arbeitsloser»; ein west- 40
liches Bildblatt spekulierte, daß Kabe von östlichen Geheimdien-
sten° für seinen Sprung bezahlt worden sei°, um endlich einmal
im Osten einen Flüchtling vorweisen° zu können, den man nicht
nur von hinten sehe. Diese Vermutung° erhielt neue Nahrung°
durch den Bericht eines Journalisten, der den in Kreuzberg unerreich- 45
baren Kabe in Paris ausfindig gemacht° haben wollte. Unmittelbar°
nach seiner Rückkehr° habe sich Kabe in die französische Metro-
pole abgesetzt° und in einem einschlägigen Stadtviertel Rech-
nungen quittiert, die mit einer Sozialrente kaum zu bestreiten
seien°.   50

Wahr an dieser Geschichte war soviel, daß Kabe, nachdem er drei
Monate in der psychiatrischen Klinik im Osten umsonst verpflegt
worden war°, auf seinem Konto° in Westberlin drei Monatszah-
lungen seiner Sozialrente vorfand. Diesen Betrag° hob° er ab°, um
sich einen alten Wunsch zu erfüllen°, und löste° eine Schlaf- 55
wagenkarte nach Paris. Sicher ist auch, daß Kabe, nachdem er sich
auf Kosten beider deutscher Staaten in Paris erholt hatte, nach Westberlin zurückkehrte und sofort wieder sprang.

Nach wiederum drei Monaten zurückgebracht, erwies sich° Kabe
als Rückfalltäter°. Die Versuche westberliner Behörden, Kabe 60
juristisch beizukommen°, schlugen fehl. Denn Kabe hatte ja eine
Staatsgrenze illegal überwunden, die nach Auffassung° der westdeutschen Regierung gar nicht existiert. Folgte man dem Sprach-
gebrauch der Verfassungsrechtler°, so hatte Kabe lediglich° von
seinem Recht auf Freizügigkeit° Gebrauch° gemacht.   65

Mit dieser Auskunft mochten sich die westberliner Behörden nicht
mehr begnügen°, als die ostberliner Klinik Rechnungen° über Kabes
Aufenthalte vorlegte°. Die Westberliner verfielen auf den Ausweg°,
Kabe wegen Selbstgefährdung° in das Krankenhaus Havelhöhe
zwangseinzuweisen°. Aber auch dieser Einfall° hielt näherer Be- 70
trachtung nicht stand°. Denn Kabe hatte durch seine Sprünge hin-
länglich° bewiesen, daß ein Überqueren° der Mauer in östlicher
Richtung möglich war, ohne Schaden an Leib und Seele° zu nehmen;
nebenbei drang° durch seine Sprünge ins Bewußtsein°, daß der

Marginal glosses:

well nourished
was turned over
government car
emotion
collected

assessment papers fluctuated desparate

secret service
had been paid show
speculation
nourishment
located immediately
return
removed himself, settled
signed bills in a part of
town which his
welfare payments
would hardly cover

had been fed account
sum took out
fulfill bought

turned out to be
repeat offender
to get at him legally
failed view

constitutional lawyers
merely freedom of
movement use

no longer satisfied with
bills presented
found the way out
self-endangerment
forcibly admit idea
did not withstand closer
  scrutiny
amply crossing
damage to body and soul

---

[3]Since West Germany and East Germany recognize each other as separate states, but
not as foreign countries, they do not maintain embassies in each other's capitals,
but rather **Ständige Vertretungen,** *Permanent Missions.*

[4]Kreuzberg, a West Berlin district.

Grenzstreifen° hinter der Mauer im Stadtgebiet nicht vermint° ist. 75
Der zuständige° Arzt fand an Kabe nichts weiter auszusetzen° als
den zügellosen Trieb°, die Mauer zu überwinden. Statt der Zwangs-
jacke° empfahl er, die Mauer als Grenze kenntlich° zu machen. Der
Einwand°, die Bundesrepublik Deutschland könne nicht einem Kabe
zuliebe° die Schandmauer° als Staatsgrenze anerkennen°, hielt° den 80
Arzt nicht davon ab°, Kabe für zurechnungsfähig° zu erklären.
Kabe wurde° aus der Klinik entlassen° und nahm den geraden Weg.
Insgesamt° sprang er fünfzehnmal. Er wurde zu einer ernsten
Belastung° für die deutsch-deutschen Beziehungen°. Nach einem
seiner letzten Sprünge kamen° die Behörden darauf°, Kabe fortzu- 85
bringen, möglichst weit weg von Berlin in stillere Gegenden°, wo
er seine Sprünge an alten Burgmauern fortsetzen° mochte. Im
Dienstmercedes wurde° er zu Verwandten nach Süddeutschland
gebracht°, benahm° sich dort zwei Tage lang ganz vernünftig, löste°
am dritten Tag eine Fahrkarte nach Berlin und sprang. 90

Über die Motive seiner Sprünge befragt, war aus Kabe nichts weiter
herauszubekommen als dies: «Wenn es so still in der Wohnung ist
und draußen so grau und so neblig und gar nichts ist los, da denke
ich: Ach springste° wieder mal über die Mauer.»

penetrated conscious-
  ness border strip
mined in charge
wrong unbridled desire
straitjacket
recognizable objection
for Kabe's sake wall of
  shame recognize
abhalten von to keep
  from
mentally competent
was discharged
all told
burden relations
had the idea
areas
continue

was taken behaved
bought

springste = springst du

REVIEW EXERCISES

G. Express in German.

1. We have two small children.
2. He lived with his old mother.
3. My grandmother was an intelligent woman.
4. She wrote him a long letter.
5. She never read his long letters.
6. Good coffee is very expensive.
7. He is an old friend of mine.
8. She is a good friend of mine.
9. Is that the new hotel?
10. Last week I was in Berlin.
11. She spent last Tuesday in Salzburg.
12. I am living with my German relatives.
13. I have a German aunt.
14. Do you know that we have a new director?
15. Dear Hans!

*Kaiser-Wilhelm-Gedächtniskirche
(Westberlin)*

H. Insert the words italicized in the first sentence as adjectives into the
second sentence.

1. Der Wind hatte die Brücke *zerstört*. Wir konnten nicht über die _____ Brücke fahren.
2. Wir alle hatten unsere Großmutter sehr *geliebt*. Unsere _____ Großmutter ist mit 89 Jahren gestorben.
3. Der Dieb hatte DM 50.000 *gestohlen*. Mit dem _____ Geld fuhr er nach Italien.
4. Die Maschine aus London ist gerade *gelandet*. Die gerade _____ Maschine hat 35 Minuten Verspätung.

I. Change the italicized inflected form of the verb into a **-d** adjective and
insert it into the second sentence.

1. Der *sieht* aber gut *aus*. Er ist ein gut _____ junger Mann.
2. Die Linden *blühten* noch; sie saßen unter einer _____ Linde.
3. Das Kind *schlief*, als er abfuhr. Er sah noch einmal auf das _____ Kind und fuhr dann ab.
4. Die Kinder *spielten* auf der Straße, aber der alte Mann sah die _____ Kinder nicht.

J. Change singular nouns in the following sentences to plurals.

1. Was für einen herrlichen Tag wir gehabt haben!
2. Was für ein Buch möchtest du denn gerne haben?
3. Was für eine schöne Tochter Sie haben!
4. Was ist denn das für ein Haus?

K. Change the plural nouns in the following sentences to singulars.

1. Was für schöne Kinder das sind! .
2. Was für schöne Tage das waren!
3. Was für interessante Kleider die Anita gekauft hat!
4. Was müssen das für Menschen sein!

L. Express in German.

1. Our dear old Aunt Dora died last week.
2. In which hotel did you live?
3. She really is a very interesting woman.
4. In this city we don't have one single good hotel.
5. We all went to the movies last night.
6. I have read all of his novels.
7. This is really a good wine.
8. My old friends are all dead.
9. All my old friends are dead.
10. She has married a young German.
11. He married a young German.
12. In the room above me lives a young German (man).
13. I have forgotten something very important.
14. Today I experienced something very beautiful.
15. When a man is thirty-nine, he is no longer a young man in the eyes of a young girl.

M. Composition.

After you have spent a few days in Germany, you decide to write to your cousin Hildegard again. Describe your stay in a small **Pension** and how surprised you were that they only serve breakfast, but how much you enjoyed the fresh **Brötchen** every morning. Tell her that you walked through the city and went to a couple of museums. Then tell her that you have tried to call your friend Barbara in Nürnberg, but haven't been able to reach her yet. You will try again and you hope that you'll be able to visit her. Ask Hildegard to write to you in Nürnberg and to let you know whether it is all right with her if you come to Munich in about two weeks.

VOCABULARY

ander-	different, other
jemand anders	somebody else
niemand anders	nobody else
etwas anderes	something else
der Anruf, -e	telephone call
an•stellen	to employ
der Angestellte, -n	employee (m.)
die Angestellte, -n	employee (f.)
der Anzug, ⸚e	(men's) suit
der Apfel, ⸚	apple
das Auge, -n	eye
der Ausgang, ⸚e	exit
ausverkauft	sold out
der Beginn (no pl.)	beginning
das Bein, -e	leg
der Bekannte, -n	acquaintance (m.)
die Bekannte, -n	acquaintance (f.)
die Bevölkerung, -en	population
sich (acc.) bewegen	to move
die Bewegung, -en	movement
die Bitte, -n	request
der Blick, -e	look, glance
blühen	to bloom, blossom, flower
böse	angry, mad; evil
ich bin ihm böse	I am mad at him
derselbe, dieselbe, dasselbe	the same
der Dieb, -e	thief
die Ehe, -n	(institution of) marriage
ehrlich	honest

eilen	to hurry
sich (acc.) eilen	to hurry
= sich (acc.) beeilen	
entdecken	to discover
entfernt	distant
entwickeln	to develop
die Erklärung, -en	explanation
fort	away
die Gegend, -en	area
der Glaube (n-noun, no pl.)	belief
grau	gray
großartig	wonderful, great, marvelous
halt	just
die Heirat, -en	marriage, wedding
herrlich	splendid, magnificent
das Herz, -en (n-noun) (gen. Herzens)	heart
der Himmel, -	sky; heaven
der Idiot', -en (n-noun)	idiot, fool
das Interes'se, -n	interest
das Kleid, -er	dress
die Kleider (pl.)	clothes
die Kraft, ⸚e	strength; force; power
das Krankenhaus, ⸚er	hospital
lächeln	to smile
das Lächeln	smile
die Mauer, -n	wall
mehrere	several
kein Mensch	nobody

das Pech	bad luck	das Verbot, -e	prohibition, ban
die Polizei' (*no pl.*)	police	der Verlust, -e	loss
die Rechnung, -en	bill	verrückt	crazy
die Rede, -n	speech	der Versuch, -e	experiment; attempt,
eine Rede halten	to give a speech		try
die Regierung, -en	government	verwandt	related
die Bundesregierung	Federal government	der Verwandte, -n	relative (*m.*)
die Richtung, -en	direction	die Verwandte, -n	relative (*f.*)
der Schlaf	sleep	verzeihen (*dat.*)	to forgive
schließen	to close; to end; to	Verzeihung!	excuse me, I'm sorry
	conclude	wachsen (sein)	to grow
der Schluß, die	conclusion, end	wahnsinnig	insane, crazy
Schlüsse		was für	what kind of
der Sitz, -e	seat	weich	soft
springen (sein)	to jump	der Wunsch, ⸚e	wish
stehlen	to steal	das Würstchen, -	(little) sausage
der Tanz, ⸚e	dance	zerstören	to destroy
tot	dead		
um . . . willen (*gen.*)	for the sake of . . .		

Strong Verbs

INFINITIVE	PRESENT	PAST TENSE	PERFECT	
schließen		schloß	geschlossen	to close; to end; to conclude
springen		sprang	ist gesprungen	to jump
stehlen	stiehlt	stahl	gestohlen	to steal
verzeihen		verzieh	verziehen	to forgive
wachsen	wächst	wuchs	ist gewachsen	to grow

Unit 18

The Passive—*es* in the Front Field— Pre-Noun Inserts

German Cars

The original VW "beetle" (**Käfer**) was designed by Professor Ferdinand Porsche in the 1930s as a "people's car," a **Volkswagen**. It was to be affordable and reliable like the Ford Model T ten years earlier. After World War II, the beetle became what was probably the most popular car in the world. Today Volkswagen also owns Audi and Porsche.

The oldest auto manufacturer is Daimler-Benz, which started building cars in 1890 and today produces not only the luxury Mercedes passenger cars but is also one of the largest manufacturers of trucks in the world. BMW (Bayrische Motorenwerke) produces expensive sporty sedans as well as precision-engineered motorcycles.

The German subsidiaries of General Motors (Opel) and of Ford produce over 40% of all the cars manufactured in the Federal Republic. Most of these are compacts and subcompacts.

DAIMLER-BENZ AG

Vorsprung durch Technik

Freude am Fahren

Volkswagen – da weiß man, was man hat.

ZUVERLÄSSIG IN DIE ZUKU...

HUNDERT JAHRE *AUTO*

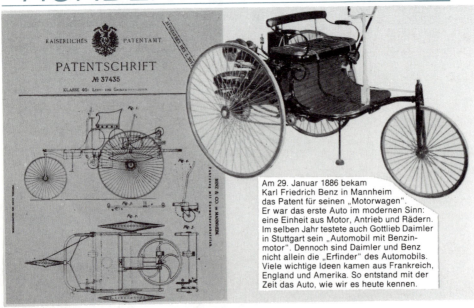

Am 29. Januar 1886 bekam Karl Friedrich Benz in Mannheim das Patent für seinen „Motorwagen". Er war das erste Auto im modernen Sinn: eine Einheit aus Motor, Antrieb und Rädern. Im selben Jahr testete auch Gottlieb Daimler in Stuttgart sein „Automobil mit Benzinmotor". Dennoch sind Daimler und Benz nicht allein die „Erfinder" des Automobils. Viele wichtige Ideen kamen aus Frankreich, England und Amerika. So entstand mit der Zeit das Auto, wie wir es heute kennen.

PATTERNS ONE

1/Active Voice and Passive Voice

ACT.   Ich hoffe, Dr. Brinker löst das Problem.
    I hope Dr. Brinker will solve the problem.

PASS.   Das Problem wird hoffentlich bald von Dr. Brinker gelöst.
    I hope the problem will soon be solved by Dr. Brinker.

ACT.   Dr. Brinker hat das Problem schon gelöst.
    Dr. Brinker has already solved the problem.

PASS.   Das Problem ist von Dr. Brinker gelöst worden.
    The problem has been solved by Dr. Brinker.

ACT.   Dr. Brinker kann das Problem bestimmt lösen.
    Dr. Brinker can certainly solve the problem.

PASS.   Ich bin sicher, das Problem kann von Dr. Brinker gelöst werden.
    I'm certain the problem can be solved by Dr. Brinker.

ACT.   Dr. Brinker soll das Problem gelöst haben.
    Dr. Brinker is said to have solved the problem.

PASS.   Das Problem soll von Dr. Brinker gelöst worden sein.
    The problem is said to have been solved by Dr. Brinker.

2/Passive Sentences with Agent

Wir kommen um fünf Uhr in Frankfurt an und (wir) werden von Tante Amalie am Bahnhof
    abgeholt.
    We arrive in Frankfurt at five o'clock and (we) are picked up at the train station by Aunt Amalie.

Der Roman erschien 1910 in London und (er) wurde von Helene Porter aus dem Englischen
    ins Deutsche übersetzt.
    The novel appeared in London in 1910 and (it) was translated from English into German by Helene
    Porter.

Das Heidelberger Schloß wird jedes Jahr von vielen Touristen besichtigt.
    The Heidelberg castle is viewed every year by many tourists.

Hier werden Sie vom Chef selbst bedient.
    Here you will be served by the chef himself.

Das neue Hochhaus wird von Schmidt und Co. gebaut werden.
    The new high rise will be built by Schmidt & Co.

In Bonn sind wir vom Bundeskanzler empfangen worden.
    In Bonn we were received by the Chancellor.

Die Rechnung muß bis zum ersten Januar bezahlt werden.
    The bill must be paid by the first of January.

Die Villa soll von einem reichen Ausländer gekauft worden sein.
    The villa is said to have been purchased by a rich foreigner.

3/Passive Sentences without Agent

Das Mittagessen wird um zwölf serviert.
> Dinner is served at 12.

Der Roman wurde 1909 in Afrika geschrieben und ist damals viel beachtet worden.
> The novel was written in Africa in 1909 and was given a lot of attention at that time.

Dieser Eingang war schon lange nicht mehr benutzt worden, als wir die Villa gekauft haben.
> This entrance had not been used for a long time when we bought the villa.

In diesem Buch wird die Stadt Hamburg beschrieben.
> In this book the city of Hamburg is described.

Die Universität Heidelberg wurde im Jahre 1386 gegründet.
> The University of Heidelberg was founded in 1386.

Auf unserem Parkplatz ist gestern ein Mercedes gestohlen worden.
> Yesterday a Mercedes was stolen from our parking lot.

Der gestohlene Wagen konnte bisher noch nicht gefunden werden.
> The stolen car could not be found up to now.

Um gewählt zu werden, braucht man mindestens fünfzig Prozent der Stimmen.
> In order to be elected, one needs at least fifty percent of the votes.

**Energie
muss gespart
werden**

Das ist Gesetz

4/Passive Sentences with Dative Objects

Dem Nobelpreisträger wurden von vielen Freunden Glückwunschtelegramme geschickt.
> The Nobel Prize winner was sent congratulatory telegrams by many friends.

Den Hotelgästen wird ein großes Frühstücksbuffet angeboten.
> The hotel guests are offered an extensive breakfast buffet.

Den Angestellten wurde vom Management eine Gehaltserhöhung versprochen.
> The employees were promised a salary increase by management.

Das ist mir von meinem Großvater erzählt worden.
> That was told to me by my grandfather.

Allen Achtzigjährigen wird vom Bürgermeister persönlich zum Geburtstag gratuliert.
> All eighty-year-olds are greeted personally on their birthday by the mayor.

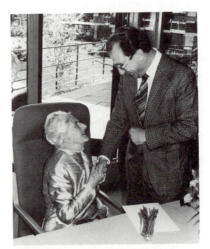

Was immer er sagt, ihm wird nicht geglaubt.
    Whatever he says, he is not believed.

Dem Verletzten konnte sofort geholfen werden.
Es konnte dem Verletzten sofort geholfen werden.
    The injured man could be helped immediately.

Es wurde mir erlaubt, die Dokumente zu lesen.
    I was permitted to read the documents.

Jemand hat mir gesagt, ich sollte um drei Uhr hier sein.
Mir wurde gesagt, ich sollte um drei Uhr hier sein.
Es wurde mir gesagt, ich sollte um drei Uhr hier sein.

5/Subjectless Passive

Hier wird gearbeitet.
Jeden Samstag abend wird dort getanzt.
In meinem Elternhaus ist viel musiziert worden.
In Kalifornien wird fast nur mit Gas geheizt.
Bei euch im Büro wird viel zu viel geredet.
Wann wird denn hier morgens gefrühstückt?
Es wird gebeten, nicht zu rauchen.

6/The Use of *von*, *durch*, and *mit* in Passive Sentences

Im Jahre 1906 wurde San Francisco durch ein Erdbeben zerstört.
    In 1906 San Francisco was destroyed by an earthquake.

Sie wurden durch den starken Verkehr gezwungen, sehr langsam zu fahren.
    They were forced by the heavy traffic to drive very slowly.

Das Obst wird mit der Bahn nach Norddeutschland geschickt.
    The fruit is sent to North Germany by train.

Karin ist von Herrn Enderle mit dem Wagen am Bahnhof abgeholt worden.
    Karin was picked up at the train station by Mr. Enderle with the car.

ANALYSIS ONE

151/The Passive Voice

FORMS OF THE PASSIVE

Both English and German verbs have an active and a passive voice.

English forms the passive with *to be* as an auxiliary, followed by a participle.

	ACTIVE VOICE	PASSIVE VOICE
PRESENT	**they elect him**	he is elected
PAST	**they elected him**	he was elected
PRES. PERF.	**they have elected him**	he has been elected
FUTURE	**they will elect him**	he will be elected

German forms the passive with **werden** as an auxiliary, followed by a participle in the second prong. In the passive, the participle of **werden** is **worden** rather than **geworden**. Remember that the auxiliary for **werden** is **sein**.

	ACTIVE VOICE	PASSIVE VOICE
PRESENT	**sie wählen ihn**	**er wird gewählt**
PAST	**sie wählten ihn**	**er wurde gewählt**
PERFECT	**sie haben ihn gewählt**	**er ist gewählt worden**
FUTURE	**sie werden ihn wählen**	**er wird gewählt werden**

Like the active voice, the passive has a present and past infinitive.

	ACTIVE	PASSIVE
PRESENT	**wählen** to elect	**gewählt werden** to be elected
PAST	**gewählt haben** to have elected	**gewählt worden sein** to have been elected

Der Präsident soll nächsten Monat gewählt werden.

The president is supposed to be elected next month.

Der Präsident soll schon gewählt worden sein.

The president is said to have been elected already.

NOTE:

1. Remember that in addition to its use as the passive auxiliary, **werden** is also used as the auxiliary for the future tense and as a verb in its own right (*to become*).

(a) **Dieser Film wird jetzt auch in Deutschland gezeigt.**

(b) **Ich fürchte, morgen wird es regnen.**

(c) **Unsere Tochter Monika wird Ärztin.**

2. Not all verbs that take objects can be used in the passive, for example, **haben**. A sentence like **Hans hat ein neues Buch** has no corresponding passive.

3. Intransitive verbs with **sein** as an auxiliary (for example, **bleiben, fahren, kommen**) normally cannot form a passive. Modals never form a passive.

USES OF THE PASSIVE

Consider the following two pairs of sentences:

ACTIVE The parliament elects the president.
   Das Parlament wählt den Präsidenten.

PASSIVE The president is elected by the parliament.
   Der Präsident wird vom Parlament gewählt.

A speaker's or writer's choice of active or passive is by no means arbitrary, but depends on the preceding context. Throughout this book, we have repeatedly referred to the principle of increasing news-value (see Anal. 10, p. 19 and Anal. 54, p. 142), and we have pointed out that most sentences begin with a topic that is followed by a comment (see Anal. 27, p. 70).

Thus the topic of the active sentence above is the parliament and what is said about the parliament is that it elects the president (the comment). The topic of the passive sentence is the president, and what is said about the president is that he is elected by parliament. The same topic (the president) can also be followed by a comment in the active voice, and in fact, both active and passive can appear in the same sentence.

The president is elected by parliament (passive)
   and serves a five-year term (active).

This sentence might be from the section of a constitution that deals with the presidency; what is "new" in the sentence is a) the election procedure and b) the length of term.

In most German sentences, the topic is either the subject or an adverb. If the topic is an object, contrast intonation tends to result.

The sentence

Den Präsidenten wählt das Parlament.

probably implies that there is another election, for example, one in which the representatives are elected by the general populace. However, no contrast is implied if the accusative object becomes the grammatical subject of a passive sentence.

Der Präsident wird vom Parlament gewählt.

The subject of the active sentence has now become the **von**-phrase (in English, the *by*-phrase) of the passive construction.

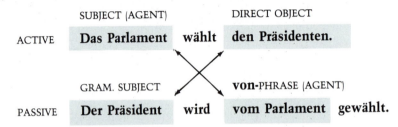

There is no **von**-phrase if the agent is unknown or unimportant. In fact, passive sentences are frequently used to avoid mentioning the agent.

Mein Wagen ist gestern gestohlen worden.	My car was stolen yesterday.
Das Mittagessen wird um 12 serviert.	Dinner is served at 12.

152/Dative Objects and the Passive

In English, verbs that take both indirect and direct objects can have two different passive equivalents:

ACTIVE
The president himself presented the prize to the winner.

PASSIVE
1. The prize was presented to the winner by the president himself.
2. The winner was presented the prize by the president himself.

Whether one uses passive sentence 1 or 2 depends on the preceding context which determines the topic of the sentence. Note that either the direct or indirect object of the active sentence can become the grammatical subject of the passive sentence.

In German, only the accusative object can become the grammatical subject of a passive sentence:

ACTIVE
Der Präsident selbst überreichte dem Sieger den Preis.

PASSIVE
Der Preis wurde dem Sieger vom Präsidenten selbst überreicht.

If the dative object becomes the topic of a passive sentence, it remains a dative object:

PASSIVE

DAT. OBJ.   GRAM. SUBJ.

Dem Sieger **wurde** **der Preis** vom Präsidenten selbst überreicht.

GRAM. SUBJ.   DIR. OBJ.

The winner was presented the prize by the president himself.

German verbs, such as **helfen**, that take only a dative object, follow the same pattern: the object must be in the dative in both the active and passive, but because there is no accusative object in the active, there cannot be a normal grammatical subject in the passive sentence.

Ihnen **konnte sofort geholfen werden.**

They could be helped immediately.

If, however, news value requires the dative object to be moved to the inner field, a meaningless **es** is placed in the front field as a "dummy" subject (see Anal. 155, p. 546). Whether there is a dummy **es** or not, the inflected verb must be in the third-person singular.

Es **konnte ihnen sofort geholfen werden.**

153/Subjectless (Impersonal) Passives

In English and in German, there are verbs, such as *to work*, **arbeiten**, that normally do not take any objects.

In English, such verbs cannot form passives, since there is no object in the active that can become the grammatical subject in the passive.

In German, however, these verbs can form passives to express that some activity is going on, but without a grammatical subject and normally without an agent, that is, without reference to particular participants.

Hier wird gearbeitet.

The form **wird gearbeitet**, structurally not possible in English, denotes the activity of **arbeiten** as such. **Hier wird gearbeitet** means "the activity of working is going on here"; *there's work going on here*.

The use of the passive to express "activity as such" is also possible with verbs that take an accusative object or a prepositional object.

> **Um zwölf Uhr wird gegessen.**
> **Es ist oft darüber geredet worden.**

With all subjectless passives, a dummy **es** can occupy the front field, and the verb can only be in the third-person singular.

154/The Use of *von, durch,* and *mit* in Passive Sentences

Many German passive sentences contain only the grammatical subject and no agent.

1. If a personal agent is mentioned, **von** is used.

> **Die Villa wurde von einem Arzt gekauft.**
> The villa was purchased by a doctor.

2. Abstract and impersonal causes are introduced by **durch.**

> **Sie wurden durch ein neues Gesetz gezwungen, das Land zu verlassen.**
> They were forced by a new law to leave the country.
> **Lissabon wurde durch ein Erdbeben zerstört.**
> Lisbon was destroyed by an earthquake.
> **Die Stadt wurde durch Bomben zerstört.**
> The city was destroyed by bombs.

3. **Mit** is used for things "handled" by a personal agent.

> **Abel wurde von Kain mit einem Stein erschlagen.**
> Abel was slain by Cain with a rock.
> **Das ganze Zimmer wurde mit Blumen geschmückt.**
> The whole room was decorated with flowers.

PRACTICE ONE

A. Restate the following active sentences in the passive. Keep the same tense and do not omit the agent.

Dr. Brinker löst das Problem.	**Das Problem wird von Dr. Brinker gelöst.**

1. Viele Arbeiter feiern den ersten Mai.
2. Willy Brauer fuhr den neuen Porsche.
3. Ein deutscher Archäologe hat diese antike Vase gefunden.
4. Auch Pan American fliegt jetzt den europäischen Airbus.
5. Cornelia Egelhold wird die Ophelia spielen.

B. Restate the following active sentences in the passive. Keep the same tense, but do not express the agent.

Er schrieb den Roman in Afrika.	**Der Roman wurde in Afrika geschrieben.**

1. Wir alle halten ihn für sehr intelligent.
2. Karl IV. gründete 1348 die Universität Prag.
3. Der Polizist fragte ihn nach seinem Namen.
4. Die Polizei hat den Dieb noch nicht gefunden.
5. Wir müssen das Frühstück morgen schon um sechs servieren.

»Liberal«
ist eine Zeitung,
wenn sie ständig
gefragt wird,
ob sie eigentlich
»rechts« oder »links«
steht.

Süddeutsche Zeitung

C. Express the following sentences in English.

1. Jedem Studenten wurden zwei Freikarten gegeben.
2. Allen Angestellten wurde die 35-Stunden-Woche versprochen.
3. Es wurde uns erlaubt, noch eine Woche zu bleiben.
4. Den Kindern wird jeden Abend eine Geschichte vorgelesen.

D. Change to actional passive, expressing "activity as such."

Wir spielen jeden Samstag Fußball.	**Es wird jeden Samstag Fußball gespielt.**

1. Wir arbeiten hier schwer.
2. Man hat hier noch nie getanzt.
3. Wir frühstücken hier um neun.
4. Und um eins essen wir zu Mittag.
5. In unserer Familie lachen wir viel.

PATTERNS TWO

7/The Impersonal *es*: The Filler *es*

Niemand war zu Hause.
Es war niemand zu Hause.

Jemand hat heute nachmittag nach Ihnen gefragt.
Es hat heute nachmittag jemand nach Ihnen gefragt.

Leider meldete sich niemand.
Es meldete sich leider niemand.

Jetzt werden wieder Häuser gebaut.
Es werden jetzt wieder Häuser gebaut.

Viele Leute waren da.
Es waren viele Leute da.

8/*es* with Impersonal Verbs

Es regnet schon seit Tagen.
Hier regnet es schon seit Tagen.

Es hat schon wieder gehagelt.
Hier hat es heute schon wieder gehagelt.

Es hat die ganze Nacht geschneit.
Heute morgen hat es ein bißchen geschneit.

Es hat stundenlang gedonnert und geblitzt, aber geregnet hat es nicht.

Wie geht es denn deinem Vater?—Danke, es geht ihm gut.
Dem Anton geht's immer gut.
Mir geht es heute gar nicht gut; mir geht's schlecht.
Guten Tag, Herr Müller. Ich habe Sie lange nicht gesehen; wie geht's Ihnen denn?

Was gibt's denn zum Mittagessen?
Es gibt jeden Tag Schweinebraten.
Das ist doch kein Schweinebraten, das ist Kalbsbraten.

Wieviele Hotels gibt es denn hier?
Heute gibt es nicht mehr viele Familien mit neun Kindern.

Vor hundert Jahren gab es noch keine Flugzeuge.
Da oben ist ein Flugzeug.

Ach Emma, du bist's!
Wer ist denn da?—Ich bin's, Emma.
Meyer kann es nicht gewesen sein.

Es sorgt für Sie

HERR MEYER

Rathaus in Markgröningen bei Ludwigsburg

9/The Anticipatory *es*

Es ist leider nicht erlaubt, vor dem Rathaus zu parken.
Leider ist es nicht erlaubt, vor dem Rathaus zu parken.

Es ist verboten, während der Fahrt die Türen zu öffnen.
Ist es verboten, während der Fahrt die Türen zu öffnen?

Es wurde vorgeschlagen, eine neue Brücke über den Rhein zu bauen.
Von allen Seiten wurde vorgeschlagen, eine neue Brücke über den Rhein zu bauen.

Es wurde beschlossen, endlich eine neue Klinik zu bauen.
Gestern abend wurde beschlossen, endlich eine neue Klinik zu bauen.

Es muß leider angenommen werden, daß er nicht mehr am Leben ist.
Leider muß angenommen werden, daß er nicht mehr am Leben ist.

Leider konnte nicht festgestellt werden, wer der Dieb ist.
Es konnte nicht festgestellt werden, wer der Dieb ist.
Wer der Dieb ist, konnte bis jetzt nicht festgestellt werden.

10/Action and State; The Statal Passive

Das alte Haus wurde gestern verkauft. Jetzt ist das Haus verkauft.
  The old house was sold yesterday. Now the house is sold.

Frau Ritter, Ihr Wagen wird heute nachmittag noch repariert.
  Mrs. Ritter, your car is going to be repaired this afternoon.

Bis morgen früh ist er bestimmt repariert. Sie können ihn um acht abholen.
  By tomorrow morning it'll definitely be repaired. You can pick it up at eight.

Die Stadt wurde während des Krieges zerstört.
  The city was destroyed during the war.

Mit dem Wiederaufbau der zerstörten Stadt wurde bald nach dem Krieg begonnen.
> The reconstruction of the destroyed city was begun soon after the war.

Heute ist die Stadt völlig wiederaufgebaut.
> Today the city is completely rebuilt.

Der Tisch ist gedeckt; jetzt kann gegessen werden.
> The table is set; now we can eat.

Ist dein Koffer schon gepackt, Tante Amalie?
> Is your suitcase packed already, Aunt Amalie?

So, der Tank ist gefüllt. Jetzt können wir losfahren.
> OK, the tank is filled. Now we can take off.

Ist mein Film schon entwickelt?
> Is my film developed already?

Wie viele Arbeiter sind hier beschäftigt?
> How many workers are employed here?

Die Briefe müssen bis morgen geschrieben sein.
> The letters must be written by tomorrow.

	ACTIVE INFINITIVE
PRESENT	Ingelheim will *Die Frau mit dem Flamingo* an den Exotica-Verlag verkaufen.
PAST	Ingelheim soll *Die Frau mit dem Flamingo* an den Exotica-Verlag verkauft haben.

	ACTIONAL PASSIVE INFINITIVE
PRESENT	In Kanada darf *Die Frau mit dem Flamingo* nicht verkauft werden.
PAST	Im letzten Jahr sollen über 100.000 Exemplare verkauft worden sein.

	STATAL PASSIVE INFINITIVE
PRESENT	Die ganze erste Auflage soll schon verkauft sein.
PAST	Haben Sie gehört, die ganze erste Auflage soll schon nach vier Wochen verkauft gewesen sein.

11/Other German Equivalents of the English Passive

Hier kann man uns nicht beobachten.
> We can't be observed here.

Den Dieb hat man nie gefunden.
> The thief was never found.

Man konnte sie leider nicht erreichen.
> She could unfortunately not be reached.

Man hat ihn in London gesehen.
> He was seen in London.

Man soll ihn in London gesehen haben.
> He is said to have been seen in London.

Man hatte sie gar nicht erwartet.
> She had not been expected at all.

Man muß sie schon gestern erwartet haben.
> She must have been expected yesterday already.

Warum hat man ihn denn nicht eingeladen?
> Why wasn't he invited?

Man wird ihn wahrscheinlich nicht eingeladen haben.
> He probably hasn't been invited.

Das ist einfach nicht zu glauben.
> That is simply not to be believed.

Da ist nichts mehr zu machen.
> Nothing can be done anymore.

Sie war nirgends zu sehen.	She was not to be seen anywhere.
Er war nicht zu finden.	He was not to be found.
Es war zu erwarten, daß er eines Tages zurückkommen würde.	It was to be expected that he would return one day.
Daß er eines Tages zurückkommen würde, war zu erwarten.	That he would return one day was to be expected.
Das läßt sich leicht entscheiden.	That is easily decided.
Das läßt sich leider nicht machen.	Unfortunately, that can't be done.
Diese Frage läßt sich leicht beantworten.	This question can be answered easily.
Ich bin sicher, daß sich ein Weg finden läßt, das zu machen.	I'm sure a way can be found to do that.
Die Zahl 12 läßt sich durch 3 oder 4 teilen.	The number 12 can be divided by 3 or 4.
Die Tür öffnete sich.	The door opened.
Gottseidank hat sich das Problem gelöst.	Thank goodness, the problem has been solved.
Das Heimatmuseum befindet sich im alten Rathaus.	The local history museum is located in the old city hall.

12/Pre-Noun Inserts

Parentheses are added here only to indicate the pre-noun inserts.

Dieser Roman, der den Kritikern nach[1] viel zu lang war, erhielt den Preis.
Dieser (den Kritikern nach viel zu lange) Roman erhielt den Preis.

Der Winter, der selbst für Norwegen ungewöhnlich kalt war, wollte gar kein Ende nehmen.
Der (selbst für Norwegen ungewöhnlich kalte) Winter wollte gar kein Ende nehmen.

Die Fluggäste, die soeben mit Lufthansa Flug Nummer 401 aus Frankfurt angekommen sind, werden gebeten, sich zum Ausgang A zu begeben.
Die (soeben mit Lufthansa Flug Nummer 401 aus Frankfurt angekommenen) Fluggäste werden gebeten, sich zum Ausgang A zu begeben.

Karthago, das von den Römern zerstört wurde, ist nicht wiederaufgebaut worden.
Das (von den Römern zerstörte) Karthago ist nicht wiederaufgebaut worden.

Aloys Hinterkofer, der seit Wochen von der Polizei gesucht wird, soll gestern in der Regina-Bar gesehen worden sein.
Der (seit Wochen von der Polizei gesuchte) Aloys Hinterkofer soll gestern in der Regina-Bar gesehen worden sein.

Die Züge, die im Sommer von München nach Italien fahren, sind meistens überfüllt.
Die (im Sommer von München nach Italien fahrenden) Züge sind meistens überfüllt.

Alle Studenten, die an dem Projekt interessiert waren, das Professor Behrens vorgeschlagen hatte, wurden gebeten, sich am nächsten Tag auf dem Sekretariat zu melden.
Alle (an dem von Professor Behrens vorgeschlagenen Projekt interessierten) Studenten wurden gebeten, sich am nächsten Tag auf dem Sekretariat zu melden.

---

[1]If the preposition **nach** follows a noun, it means *according to*.

ANALYSIS TWO

155/The Impersonal *es* in the Front Field

The pronoun **es** in the front field can, of course, refer to a neuter noun in the nominative.[2]

Das Haus gehörte früher meinem Onkel;

es **gehört jetzt meiner Mutter.**

Frequently, however, an **es** in the front field (or in the inner field) does not refer back to anything. This impersonal **es** has one of three functions: (1) It can be a meaningless filler to preserve verb-second position; (2) it can be the grammatical subject of an impersonal verb; and (3) it can be used to anticipate a following dependent clause or an infinitive phrase.

1.   THE USE OF **es** AS A FILLER

In a short sentence like

Niemand war zu Hause.

the inner field is empty. Both **war**, the first prong, and **zu Hause**, the second prong, are position-fixed. If the speaker, in order to put greater news value on **niemand**, decides to put **niemand** in the inner field, he must put something else in the front field; otherwise he would come up with the question

War niemand zu Hause?

Verb-second position, in these cases, can be preserved by filling the front field with a meaningless **es**. If the verb in sentences with a "dummy" **es** is a form of **sein**, the English equivalent uses a "dummy" *there*. With other verbs, however, English cannot use *there*.

Es war niemand zu Hause.   There was no one at home.
Es hat niemand angerufen.   No one has called.

This use of **es** as a filler is rather frequent with passives; it must be used when nothing else is available to fill the front field.

Es werden wieder Häuser gebaut.
Es wird wieder gearbeitet.

---

[2]If the accusative **es** is moved from the inner field to the front field, it becomes **das.**

  Ich weiß es nicht.
  Das weiß ich nicht.

In all these cases, the dummy **es** disappears when the front field is occupied by some other element.

> **Gestern war niemand zu Hause.**
> **Gestern hat niemand angerufen.**
> **Hier werden wieder Häuser gebaut.**
> **Hier wird wieder gearbeitet.**

NOTE: **Es** as a filler is also used in the standard introduction of German fairy tales and folk songs. **Es war einmal ein König** corresponds to *Once upon a time there was a king.* Since the entire news value is concentrated in **ein König**, the subject cannot stand in the front field.

> **Es war einmal eine alte Geiß.**
> **Es war ein König in Thule.**
> **Es waren zwei Königskinder.**
> **Es steht ein Baum im Odenwald.**

2. **es** AS THE GRAMMATICAL SUBJECT OF IMPERSONAL VERBS

Some frequently used impersonal constructions with **es** are:

> **Es regnet, es schneit, es donnert, es hagelt.**
> **Es geht mir (ihm, ihr, etc.) gut (schlecht).**
> **Es ist mir zu warm (zu kalt, zu heiß).**
> **Es ist zehn Uhr (schon spät, noch früh).**

In all these cases, **es** must appear in the inner field if the front field is occupied by some other element or if the sentence is a question.

> **Es hat gestern geregnet.**   **Gestern hat es geregnet.**
> **Es schneit schon wieder.**   **Schneit es schon wieder?**
> **Es ist zehn Uhr.**   **Jetzt ist es zehn Uhr.**

Also, the idiom **es gibt** belongs to this group of impersonal verbs. **Es gibt,** *there is* or *there are*, takes the accusative. In connection with a food term, it expresses what will be served. In other cases, it expresses that certain things exist as a part of the environment or of nature.

> **Heute mittag gibt es Kartoffelsuppe.**
> **In Afrika gibt es noch immer wilde Elefanten.**
> **In diesem Dorf gibt es keinen Arzt.**

Unlike English *there is*, **es gibt** can never be used to point at a specific thing or person.

> **[Da drüben gibt es ein Hotel.]**

But:

Da drüben ist ein Hotel.

The **es** used in identification sentences (see Anal. 50, p. 135) can appear either in the front field or immediately behind the first prong.

Es war nicht mein Bruder.
Mein Bruder war es nicht.

The **es** in such sentences means "the thing to be identified." **Ich bin's** corresponds to *it's me*, which cannot be expressed by **[Es bin ich]** or **[Es ist ich]**. Similarly, **Du bist's, er ist's**, and so on.

3. THE ANTICIPATORY **es**

The use of **es** to anticipate a following dependent clause is comparable to the use of English *it* in

I have *it* on good authority that Smith will be our next boss.
It simply is not true that he has gone to college.

where the *it*, which cannot be left out, anticipates the following *that*-clause.

The German anticipatory **es** refers forward to a dependent (subject) clause or to an infinitive phrase, and **es** is the grammatical subject of the main clause.

Es ist möglich, daß Frau Meyer nicht kommt.
Es tut mir leid, daß ich gestern nicht kommen konnte.
Es freut mich, daß Sie kommen konnten.
Es wird berichtet, daß der Präsident morgen nach Rom fliegt.
Es ist mir endlich gelungen, Julia zu erreichen.

As long as this anticipatory **es** precedes the clause it anticipates, it does not disappear when the front field is occupied by some other element.

Natürlich ist es auch möglich, daß Frau Meyer nicht kommt.
Natürlich tut es mir leid, daß ich gestern nicht kommen konnte.

If the dependent clause precedes the main clause, the anticipatory **es** disappears, because there is nothing left to anticipate.

Daß Frau Meyer heute kommt, ist unwahrscheinlich.

In impersonal passive phrases, however, **es** disappears when the front field is occupied by some other element.

Es wird berichtet, daß der Präsident morgen nach Rom fliegt.
Gestern wurde berichtet, daß der Präsident morgen nach Rom fliegt.

156/Action and State; The Statal Passive

All passive sentences introduced so far are in the "actional" passive, that is, they describe processes or events. There is another passive, the "statal" passive, that describes the state resulting from the actional passive. In English, both passives use a form of *to be* and are often ambiguous. For example, the sentence

> The car was sold.

can refer both to the action of selling the car and to the accomplished fact that the car has been sold. Only context will show whether *was sold* is an actional or a statal passive form.

ACTIONAL	The car was sold at auction yesterday afternoon.
STATAL	When I got there, the car was already sold.

In German the ambiguity between the actional and statal passive does not exist; a speaker must *always* distinguish between action and state. The actional passive introduced in Part 1 of this unit is expressed by a form of **werden** plus a past participle; the statal passive, on the other hand, is expressed by a form of **sein** plus a past participle. Context is not needed to make the distinction clear.

ACTIONAL	**Das Auto wurde verkauft.**
STATAL	**Das Auto war verkauft.**

The agent is rarely expressed in a statal passive sentence.

Because all English passives look like German statal passives, you may be tempted to use German statal passives where actional passives are required. Remember that the actional passive describes a process or an event and that the statal passive can only describe the result, that is, a state.

In statal passives, the participle functions like a predicate adjective and can also be used as an attributive adjective (see Anal. 141, p. 508).

Statal passives can be the result not only of actional passives, but also of some reflexives (see Anal. 124, p. 428) and of reflexive constructions with **lassen** (see Anal. 135, p. 479). However, only a few verbs can be used in all three of these patterns. One of these is the verb **überzeugen**, *to convince*.

	ACTIONAL	STATAL PASSIVE
PASSIVE	**er ist überzeugt worden** he has been convinced	**er ist überzeugt** he is convinced
REFLEXIVE	**er hat sich überzeugt** he has convinced himself	**er ist überzeugt** he is convinced
REFL. + **lassen**	**er hat sich überzeugen lassen** he has let himself be convinced	**er ist überzeugt** he is convinced

157/Other German Equivalents of the English Passive

German uses the passive less frequently than English, especially in everyday speech. In addition to the passive, German has several other constructions that deemphasize the agent and focus on the recipient of the action. Sentences with **man** are the most common of these constructions.

1. **man** + active voice

   Man kann dieses Problem leicht lösen.

2. **sein** + **zu** + infinitive

   Dieses Problem ist leicht zu lösen.

3. **sich lassen** + infinitive

   Das Problem läßt sich leicht lösen.

4. reflexive construction

   Das Problem löst sich leicht.

All four of these sentences correspond to the passive:

   Dieses Problem kann leicht gelöst werden.

158/Pre-Noun Inserts

Pre-noun inserts are elements that are inserted between an article and a noun. For clarity and illustration, these inserts are placed in parentheses in the following examples.

Frequently, such inserts are adjectives:

   ein (erfolgreicher) Film
   a (successful) film

These adjectives can be modified by adverbs:

   ein (unerwartet erfolgreicher) Film
   an (unexpectedly successful) film

Unlike English, however, German can continue to extend such pre-noun inserts. The following German phrase is perfectly normal, but its English equivalent is impossible.

   ein (trotz seiner ungewöhnlichen Länge unerwartet erfolgreicher) Film
   [a (despite its unusual length unexpectedly successful) film]

In German, pre-noun inserts of considerable length are characteristic of expository prose, but they are rarely used in spoken German. After

you have practiced pre-noun inserts in this unit, you should be able
to recognize them when you see them in print.

Both in English and in German, pre-noun inserts can be transformed
into relative clauses.

> **ein Film, der trotz seiner ungewöhnlichen Länge unerwartet erfolgreich ist, . . .**
> a film, which despite its unusual length is unexpectedly successful, . . .

When a relative clause is transformed into a pre-noun insert, it drops
its subject and the inflected verb belonging to it. Since this transformation changes a predicate adjective or a participle into an attributive adjective, the adjective requires an ending.

In German, pre-noun inserts, with the exception of 5 below, have
an inner field and a second prong with usual word order. Pre-noun
inserts can originate in the following ways:

1. The second prong is a predicate adjective.

> **Dieses (**   **) Mädchen, das (sehr intelligent) ist, . . .**
> **Dieses (sehr intelligente) Mädchen . . .**

2. The second prong is the participle of an intransitive verb like
ankommen, which forms its compound tenses with **sein.**

> **Der (**   **) Zug, der (vor einigen Minuten aus Salzburg angekommen)**
>   **ist, . . .**
> **Der (vor einigen Minuten aus Salzburg angekommene) Zug . . .**

3. The second prong is the participle used to form the actional or
statal passive.

> **Diese (**   **) Stadt, die (während des Krieges zerstört) wurde, . . .** (Actional
>   **Passive)**
> **Diese (während des Krieges zerstörte) Stadt . . .**

> **Diese (**   **) Stadt, die (heute völlig wiederaufgebaut) ist, . . .** (Statal
>   **Passive)**
> **Diese (heute völlig wiederaufgebaute) Stadt . . .**

The last two examples can be combined in one sentence.

> **Diese (während des letzten Krieges zerstörte) und (heute völlig wiederaufgebaute) Stadt**
>   **war einmal ein wichtiges Kulturzentrum.**

4. The second prong is the participle of a reflexive verb. The reflexive pronoun does not appear in the pre-noun insert.

> **Der (**   **) Student, der sich (gut vorbereitet) hat, . . .** (Action)
> **Der (**   **) Student, der (gut vorbereitet) ist, . . .**   (State)
> **Der (gut vorbereitete) Student . . .**

5. As long as it makes sense, any present and past form of the *active* voice may be changed into a **-d** adjective. This **-d** adjective, preceded by its inner field, can then be used as a pre-noun insert.

Alle (   ) Reisenden, die (nach Berlin fuhren), . . .
Alle (nach Berlin fahrenden) Reisenden . . .

159 / *jetzt* and *nun*

Though both **jetzt** and **nun** are frequently equivalent to English *now*, they are not always interchangeable. **Jetzt** is an adverb of time without any implications.

Es ist jetzt zwölf Uhr fünfzehn.
Meyer wohnt jetzt in München.

Nun, on the other hand, always implies a reference to something which precedes; it therefore contains the idea that one state of affairs is followed by another.

Und nun wohnt er in München.
(He used to live elsewhere.)

Bist du nun zufrieden?
(I know you were dissatisfied before.)

Und nun hören Sie zum Abschluß unserer Sendung „Eine kleine Nachtmusik" von Wolfgang Amadeus Mozart.
And now we conclude our broadcast with Mozart's "Eine kleine Nachtmusik."

Because of the connotation "this is something new," **nun mal (nun einmal)** has the flavor "you might as well get used to it."

Das *ist* nun einmal so.
That's the way it is.

Ich *bin* nun mal nicht so intelligent wie du.
You might as well accept the fact that I'm not as intelligent as you are.

Wolfgang Amadeus Mozart (1756–91)

Lippizaner, Lederhosen, and the Lorelei

If tourist brochures and posters are your only source of information, you will get a distorted view of modern-day Central Europe. Tourists are frequently attracted by the quaint, the romantic, and the relics of bygone eras. Medieval castles are more interesting than modern factories and folk costumes more than blue jeans. In order to promote tourism, Austria emphasizes its imperial past, for example, the Vienna Choir Boys and the Lippizaner (the famous white horses of the Spanish Riding School), but on the other hand, the Austrians also make strong efforts to promote an image of a thoroughly modern country. Similarly, the German tourist industry advertises oompah bands, Lederhosen, Mad King Ludwig's Neuschwanstein castle, and the Munich Oktoberfest, and tourists sing "Ich weiß nicht, was soll es bedeuten" as their Rhine steamer passes the Lorelei rock. While these tourist attractions may be fun to visit, you should, however, expect to find a very different reality surrounding them.

PRACTICE TWO

E. Restate these sentences, starting with **es.**

1. Jemand hat angerufen.
2. Nur wenige Leute haben davon gewußt.
3. Jemand hat mir gesagt, du wärst schon hier.

4. Ein paar Briefe sind hier für Sie, Frau Doktor.
5. Das Stuttgarter Kammerorchester spielt unter der Leitung von Karl Münchinger.

F. Express in German.

1. There's Wiener Schnitzel for dinner.
2. There's only one railroad station in this town.
3. There is the railroad station at last.

4. At that time there weren't any streetcars yet.
5. There is our streetcar.
6. Who's there? —It's me.

G. Restate the following sentences with an infinitive phrase. Begin each sentence with an anticipatory **es** and use the verb in parentheses.

> **Man darf hier nicht rauchen. (verboten)**
> **Es ist verboten, hier zu rauchen.**

1. Man wollte endlich eine neue Brücke bauen.   (beschließen)
2. Die Höchstgeschwindigkeit soll herabgesetzt werden.   (vorschlagen)
3. Man darf nicht mehr als 100 Stundenkilometer fahren.   (nicht erlauben)

H. Change the following actional passive sentences to the statal passive.

1. Ist die Stadt wiederaufgebaut worden?
2. Das Haus war schon verkauft worden.
3. Das müßte verboten werden.
4. Wird meine Schreibmaschine bald repariert?

I. Restate the following active sentences in the actional passive and then in the statal passive. Leave out the agent.

1. Mat hat die ganze Stadt zerstört.
2. Wir haben das Problem gelöst.
3. Sie hat das Haus verkauft.
4. Sie soll das Haus verkauft haben.

CONVERSATIONS

I

Zehn Aphorismen

Use as many of these aphorisms as time permits for discussions of their meaning and of their applicability in various situations.

1. Es ist einfacher, ein Atom zu spalten°, als ein Vorurteil° zu zerstören. (Einstein) — split prejudice
2. Gewalt° kann Paläste zerstören, aber noch keinen Schweinestall erbauen. — force, might
3. Das Leben ist so einfach, aber die Menschen sind so kompliziert.
4. Ein Spiegel ist besser als eine Ahnengalerie°. — **der Ahne** ancestor
5. Zuviel Vertrauen° ist oft eine Dummheit; zuviel Mißtrauen ist immer ein Unglück. — trust

6. Erzähle mir die Vergangenheit, und ich werde die Zukunft erkennen. (Konfuzius)
7. Alles was heute selbstverständlich ist, war einmal revolutionär.
8. Es ist besser, einen intelligenten Feind zu haben als einen dummen Freund. (Ben-Gurion)
9. Ewige Freizeit—das müßte die Hölle° auf Erden sein. (Shaw) hell
10. Die letzte Stimme, die gehört wird, bevor die Welt auseinanderfliegt°, wird von einem Sachverständigen° kommen, der sagt: „Das ist unmöglich!" (Peter Ustinov) blows up specialist

II

Vorschläge für weitere Gespräche und Diskussionen

As in Unit 17, decide on one or more topics to discuss with your fellow students and select appropriate vocabulary with the help of your teacher.

1. Wie wäre das Leben im Staat Oregon, der genau so groß ist wie die BRD, wenn er 60 Millionen Einwohner und 30 Millionen Autos hätte?
2. Verbrechen° im Fernsehen: Haben Crime-Shows einen Einfluß auf die zunehmende Kriminalität in den Industrieländern? crime
3. Was sind die Vorteile und Nachteile der modernen Reklame in Zeitungen und Zeitschriften und im Fernsehen?

Ach ja, der deutsche Wald

What many Germans in the U.S. miss about the "old country" is the forest, **der deutsche Wald**. This **Wald** plays a major role in Germanic mythology and in literature. Many of the famous Grimm fairy tales take place in the forest, and there are numerous poems romanticizing the forest. Thirty percent of the Federal Republic is covered by well cared for forests. Many miles of well maintained and carefully marked hiking paths (**Wanderwege**) provide one of the major recreational outlets for all age groups, a **Waldspaziergang**. Alas, in recent years the German forest has suffered severely from acid rain, which has devastated large sections of the famous **Schwarzwald** in the southwest of the Federal Republic.

READING

*Wilhelm Grimm
(1786–1859) und Jakob
Grimm (1785–1863)*

THE BROTHERS GRIMM

Der Wolf und die sieben Geißlein[3]

Es war einmal eine alte Geiß°, die hatte sieben junge Geißlein, und   goat
hatte sie lieb, wie eine Mutter ihre Kinder lieb hat. Eines Tages
wollte sie in den Wald gehen und etwas zu essen holen. Da rief sie
alle sieben ins Haus und sprach: „Liebe Kinder, ich will in den Wald.
Wenn der Wolf kommt, dürft ihr ihn nicht ins Haus lassen. Wenn er   5
hereinkommt, so frißt er euch alle. Der Bösewicht verstellt sich oft°,   the rascal often disguises
aber an seiner Stimme und an seinen schwarzen Füßen werdet ihr   himself
ihn gleich erkennen." Die Geißlein sagten: „Liebe Mutter, du brauchst
keine Angst zu haben." Da meckerte° die Alte und ging in den Wald.   bleated

Es dauerte nicht lange, so klopfe jemand an die Haustür und rief: 10
„Macht auf, ihr lieben Kinder, eure Mutter ist da und hat jedem von
euch etwas mitgebracht." Aber die Geißlein hörten an der Stimme,
daß es der Wolf war. „Wir machen nicht auf", riefen sie, „du bist
nicht unsere Mutter, die hat eine feine und liebliche° Stimme, aber   sweet
deine Stimme ist rauh°; du bist der Wolf." Da ging der Wolf fort und   15   rough
kaufte ein Stück Kreide°; die aß er und machte damit seine Stimme   chalk
fein. Dann kam er zurück, klopfte an die Haustür und rief: „Macht

---

[3]This story is taken, with very few changes, from the famous collection of fairy tales
by the brothers Grimm. The German of these fairy tales is highly sophisticated and
yet of classic simplicity. Every German child grows up with Grimm. The standard
introduction to German fairy tales, **Es war einmal** . . . , corresponds to the English
Once upon a time, there was . . . .

auf, ihr lieben Kinder, eure Mutter ist da und hat jedem von euch etwas mitgebracht." Aber der Wolf hatte seinen schwarzen Fuß in das Fenster gelegt; das sahen die Kinder und riefen: „Wir machen 20 nicht auf, unsere Mutter hat keinen schwarzen Fuß, wie du; du bist der Wolf." Da lief der Wolf zu einem Bäcker und sprach: „Ich habe etwas an meinem Fuß, kannst du etwas Teig° auf meinen Fuß   dough streichen°?" Und als der Bäcker den Teig auf seinen Fuß gestrichen   spread hatte, so lief er zum Müller und sprach: „Kannst du etwas Mehl° 25   flour auf meinen Fuß streuen°?" Der Müller dachte: „Der Wolf will einen   sprinkle betrügen°", und wollte es nicht tun; aber der Wolf sprach: „Wenn   deceive du es nicht tust, so fresse ich dich." Da bekam der Müller Angst und machte ihm den Fuß weiß. Ja, so sind die Menschen.[4]

Nun ging der Bösewicht wieder zu der Haustür, klopfte an und 30 sprach: „Macht auf, Kinder, euer liebes Mütterchen ist zurück und hat jedem von euch etwas aus dem Wald mitgebracht." Die Geißlein riefen: „Du mußt uns erst deinen Fuß zeigen, sonst wissen wir nicht, ob du unser liebes Mütterchen bist." Da legte er den Fuß ins Fenster, und als sie sahen, daß er weiß war, so glaubten sie, es wäre alles 35 wahr, was er sagte, und machten die Tür auf. Wer aber hereinkam, das war der Wolf.

Da bekamen sie alle Angst. Das eine sprang unter den Tisch, das zweite ins Bett, das dritte in den Ofen, das vierte in die Küche, das fünfte in den Schrank°, das sechste unter die Waschschüssel°, das 40   cupboard   washbowl siebte in den Kasten der Wanduhr. Aber der Wolf fand sie alle und fraß sie eins nach dem andern; nur das jüngste in dem Uhrkasten fand er nicht. Als der Wolf die sechs gefressen hatte, ging er fort, legte sich draußen vor dem Haus unter einen Baum und fing an zu schlafen.   45

Es dauerte nicht lange, da kam die alte Geiß aus dem Wald wieder nach Hause. Ach, was mußte sie da sehen! Die Haustür stand auf, Tisch, Stühle und Bänke waren umgeworfen. Sie suchte ihre Kinder, aber sie konnte sie nicht finden. Sie rief sie alle bei Namen, aber niemand antwortete. Endlich, als sie an das jüngste kam, da rief eine 50 feine Stimme: „Liebe Mutter, ich bin im Uhrkasten." Sie holte es heraus, und es erzählte ihr, daß der Wolf gekommen wäre und die anderen alle gefressen hätte. Da könnt ihr denken, wie sie über ihre armen Kinder geweint hat.[4]

Endlich ging sie hinaus, und das jüngste Geißlein lief mit. Als sie vor 55 das Haus kam, so lag da der Wolf unter dem Baum und schnarchte°,   snored daß die Äste° zitterten°. „Ach Gott", dachte sie, „vielleicht leben   branches   trembled meine Kinder doch noch." Da mußte das Geißlein ins Haus laufen und Schere°, Nadel° und Zwirn° holen. Dann schnitt sie dem Bösewicht   scissors, needle, and den Bauch° auf, und kaum hatte sie einen Schnitt getan, so steckte 60   thread schon ein Geißlein den Kopf heraus, und als sie weiter schnitt, so   belly

---

[4]Observe the change of tense: this sentence is not part of the story.

sprangen sie alle sechs heraus, und waren noch alle am Leben. Das
war eine Freude! Die Alte aber sagte: „Jetzt wollen wir Steine suchen,
mit denen füllen wir dem Bösewicht den Bauch, solange er noch
schläft." Da brachten die sieben Geißlein Steine herbei und steckten 65
sie ihm in den Bauch. Dann nähte° ihn die Alte wieder zu.   sewed

Als der Wolf endlich ausgeschlafen hatte, stand er auf, und weil ihn
die Steine in seinem Bauch durstig machten, so wollte er zu einem
Brunnen° gehen und trinken. Als er aber an den Brunnen kam und   well
trinken wollte, da zogen ihn die Steine in den Brunnen hinein, und 70
er mußte ertrinken°. Als die sieben Geißlein das sahen, da kamen   drown
sie herbeigelaufen°, riefen laut: „Der Wolf ist tot! der Wolf ist tot!"   they came running
und lachten und tanzten mit ihrer Mutter um den Brunnen.

FRANZ KAFKA

Die Prüfung

Ich bin ein Diener°, aber es ist keine Arbeit für mich da. Ich bin   servant
ängstlich° und dränge° mich nicht vor°, ja ich dränge mich nicht   timid   push forward
einmal in eine Reihe der andern, aber das ist nur die eine Ursache°   cause
meines Nichtbeschäftigtseins°, es ist auch möglich, daß es mit   **beschäftigt sein** be
meinem Nichtbeschäftigtsein überhaupt nichts zu tun hat, die 5   employed
Hauptsache ist jedenfalls°, daß ich nicht zum Dienst gerufen werde,   at any rate
andere sind gerufen worden und haben sich nicht mehr darum
beworben° als ich, ja haben vielleicht nicht einmal den Wunsch   applied
gehabt, gerufen zu werden, während ich ihn wenigstens manchmal
sehr stark habe.   10

So liege ich also auf der Pritsche° in der Gesindstube°, schaue zu   cot   servants' quarters
den Balken° auf der Decke° hinauf, schlafe ein, wache auf und   beams   ceiling
schlafe schon wieder ein. Manchmal gehe ich hinüber ins Wirtshaus,
wo ein saueres Bier ausgeschenkt° wird, manchmal habe ich schon   served
vor Widerwillen° ein Glas davon ausgeschüttet°, dann aber trinke 15   in disgust   poured out
ich es wieder. Ich sitze gern dort, weil ich hinter dem geschlossenen
kleinen Fenster, ohne von irgendjemandem entdeckt werden zu können, zu den Fenstern unseres Hauses hinübersehen kann. Man sieht
ja dort nicht viel, hier gegen die Straße zu° liegen, glaube ich, nur   on the streetside
die Fenster der Korridore und überdies° nicht jener° Korridore, die 20   furthermore   of those
zu den Wohnungen der Herrschaft° führen. Es ist möglich, daß ich   of the master and
mich aber auch irre, irgend jemand hat es einmal, ohne daß ich ihn   mistress
gefragt hätte, behauptet und der allgemeine Eindruck dieser Haus-
front bestätigt° das. Selten nur werden die Fenster geöffnet, und   confirms
wenn es geschieht, tut es ein Diener und lehnt° sich dann wohl auch 25   leans
an die Brüstung°, um ein Weilchen hinunterzusehn. Es sind also   sill
Korridore, wo er nicht überrascht werden kann. Übrigens kenne ich
diese Diener nicht, die ständig° oben beschäftigten Diener schlafen   permanently
anderswo°, nicht in meiner Stube°.   elsewhere   room

Einmal, als ich ins Wirtshaus kam, saß auf meinem Beobachtungs- 30
platz schon ein Gast. Ich wagte° nicht genau hinzusehn und wollte   dared
mich gleich in der Tür wieder umdrehn° und weggehn. Aber der   turn around
Gast rief mich zu sich, und es zeigte sich, daß er auch ein Diener
war, den ich schon einmal irgendwo gesehn hatte, ohne aber bisher
mit ihm gesprochen zu haben. „Warum willst du fortlaufen? Setz 35
dich her und trink! Ich zahl's." So setzte ich mich also. Er fragte mich
einiges, aber ich konnte es nicht beantworten, ja ich verstand nicht
einmal° die Fragen. Ich sagte deshalb: „Vielleicht reut es dich° jetzt,   not even   you regret
daß du mich eingeladen hast, dann gehe ich," und ich wollte schon
aufstehn. Aber er langte° mit seiner Hand über den Tisch herüber 40   reached
und drückte° mich nieder°; „Bleib," sagte er, „das war ja nur eine   pushed down
Prüfung. Wer die Fragen nicht beantwortet, hat die Prüfung be-
standen."

REVIEW EXERCISES

J. Change the following sentences from the active voice to the actional
passive. Do not change the tense. Omit the subject (**man**) of the active
sentence.

Man brachte ihn zurück.	**Er wurde zurückgebracht.**

1. Man führt uns durch den Garten.
2. Man schickte die Kinder zu den Großeltern.
3. Um acht Uhr schloß man die Tür.
4. Mich nimmt man nie mit.
5. Man suchte sie, aber man fand sie nicht.
6. Man hat ihn nach Hause geschickt.
7. Man hielt ihn für einen Spion.
8. Man brachte uns im Löwen unter.
9. Man hat uns wieder im Löwen untergebracht.
10. Man hat sie schon wieder gebeten, eine Rede zu halten.

K. In the following sentences, change the present actional passive forms
into (a) perfect actional passive forms and (b) present statal passive forms.

Die Stadt wird zerstört.	(a) **Die Stadt ist zerstört worden.**
	(b) **Die Stadt ist zerstört.**

1. Die Brücke wird schon gebaut.
2. Der Tisch wird gedeckt.
3. Der Brief wird schon geschrieben.

4. Es wird beschlossen.
5. Der Schlüssel wird gefunden.
6. Die Tür wird geschlossen.

L. Change the following active sentences into actional passive sentences.
Omit the subject of the active sentence.

> **Wir zeigen den Film jetzt auch in Deutschland.**
> **Der Film wird jetzt auch in Deutschland gezeigt.**

1. In den Vereinigten Staaten trinkt man mehr Bier als in Deutschland.
2. Mich lädt nie jemand ein.
3. In unserem Elternhaus haben wir viel musiziert.
4. Kolumbus hat Amerika 1492 entdeckt.
5. Wann hat Ihr Vater denn dieses Haus gebaut?
6. Sie konnten den Dieb nicht finden.

M. In the following sentences, supply **von, mit**, or **durch**.

1. Die Stadt wurde _____ ein Erdbeben völlig zerstört.
2. Das Hotel wurde _____ Feuer völlig zerstört.
3. Er ist _____ einem Stein erschlagen worden.
4. Er ist _____ seinem Bruder erschlagen worden.
5. Der Brief ist mir _____ meiner Mutter nachgeschickt worden.
6. Sie hat den Brief zwar unterschrieben, aber der Brief ist nicht _____ ihr sclbst geschrieben worden.
7. Sie hat alle ihre Briefe _____ der Schreibmaschine geschrieben.
8. Ich wurde _____ meinem Chef nach Afrika geschickt.
9. Amerika ist _____ Kolumbus _____ Zufall entdeckt worden.
10. Früher ist bei uns nur _____ Butter gekocht worden.

N. In the following sentences, supply either a form of **werden** or a form of **sein**.

1. Daß die Erde sich um die Sonne bewegt, _____ schon lange bewiesen.
2. Die Stadt _____ im Jahre 1944 zerstört.
3. Im Jahre 1950 _____ die Stadt noch nicht wieder aufgebaut.
4. Der weiße Mercedes _____ schon verkauft.
5. Das Haus neben der Kirche soll nächste Woche verkauft _____.
6. Der Film hat mir gar nicht gefallen. Ich _____ wirklich enttäuscht.

O. Express in German.

1. I wish they would invite us.
2. I wish we were invited.
3. I wish Ingrid had invited us.
4. I wish we had been invited by Ingrid.

Eine Litfaßsäule in Berlin

5. When is the film supposed to be shown here?
6. It (the film) can never be shown here.
7. Have you packed your suitcase? — Yes, it's packed.
8. Excuse me, when is breakfast served here?
9. I was told to be here at three o'clock. (Use **daß** and **sollte**.)
10. Somebody told me to be here at three o'clock. (Use **sollte** without **daß**.)
11. The bridge was built by an Austrian architect.
12. The letter must have been sent to Hamburg.
13. I'm sorry, this problem cannot be solved.
14. There's dancing here every weekend.

P. Change the following relative clauses into pre-noun inserts.

1. Der Zug, der soeben aus München angekommen ist, fährt in zehn Minuten weiter.
2. Für einen jungen Menschen, der in einem Dorf in den bayerischen Alpen großgeworden ist, ist es nicht leicht, sich an die Großstadt zu gewöhnen.
3. Hans ist jetzt Arzt, aber sein Bruder, der viel intelligenter ist, hat nie seinen Doktor gemacht.
4. Ingrids Vater war ein Architekt, der auch in Amerika bekannt war.
5. Die Städte, die während des Krieges zerstört wurden, sind heute fast alle wiederaufgebaut.
6. Den Airbus, der von einem europäischen Konsortium gebaut wird, sieht man heute auf vielen amerikanischen Flughäfen.
7. Der Juwelendieb, der seit Wochen von der Polizei gesucht wird, soll gestern in München gesehen worden sein.
8. Der Preis, der für diesen Rembrandt bezahlt worden ist, ist nach meiner Meinung viel zu hoch.
9. Seine Mutter, die noch immer in Berlin wohnte, hatte er seit Jahren nicht gesehen.
10. Er sah sie mit einem Blick an, der viel sagte.

VOCABULARY

ab•nehmen	to decrease, decline; to lose weight
an•bieten	to offer
auf•bauen	to construct
wiederauf•bauen	to reconstruct
auf•wachen (sein)	to wake up
beantworten (acc.)	to answer (a question, letter, etc.)
bedeuten	to mean; to signify
sich (acc.) befinden	to be located
beob'achten	to observe
beschäftigen	to employ
beschließen	to decide
beschreiben	to describe
besichtigen	to visit, look at, inspect
blitzen	to lighten
es blitzt	it is lightning
der Blitz, -e	lightning
der Bundeskanzler, -	Federal Chancellor
der Chef, -s	boss; chief; chef
donnern	to thunder
der Donner	thunder
der Eindruck, ¨e	impression
der Einfluß, die Einflüsse	influence
der Eingang, ¨e	entrance
der Einwohner, -	inhabitant
sich (acc.) entscheiden	to decide
enttäuschen	to disappoint
die Erde, -n	earth
das Erdbeben, -	earthquake
erfolgreich	successful
erscheinen (sein)	to appear
europä'isch	European
der Feind, -e	enemy
das Feuer, -	fire
die Freizeit, -en	leisure time
die Freude, -n	joy
füllen	to fill
die Geschwindigkeit, -en	speed
die Höchstge- schwindigkeit	maximum speed, speed limit
gewöhnlich	usual
ungewöhnlich	unusual

gratulieren (dat.)	to congratulate
hageln	to hail
der Hagel	hail
das Hochhaus, ¨er	high-rise building
der Koffer, -	suitcase
kompliziert	complicated
die Meinung, -en	opinion
meiner Meinung nach	in my opinion
nirgends	nowhere
nirgendwo	nowhere
nun	now
oben (adv.)	up, up above; upstairs
das Orchester, -	orchestra
das Kammer- orchester	chamber orchestra
packen	to pack
das Prozent, -e	percent
das Rathaus, ¨er	town hall, city hall
reich	rich
das Schloß, ¨er	castle
der Schlüssel, -	key
schneien	to snow
der Schnee	snow
selbstverständlich	self-evident, obvious, of course
senden	to send; to broadcast
der Sender, -	radio station, transmitter
die Sendung, -en	broadcast, trans- mission
sinken (sein)	to sink
den Tisch decken	to set the table
trennen	to separate
überraschen	to surprise
überzeugen	to convince
unten (adv.)	down, down below, downstairs
unterschreiben	to sign (a letter, document, etc.)
verletzen	to hurt (someone), injure
vor•lesen	to read aloud
die Zeitschrift, -en	magazine; journal
zu•nehmen	to increase; to gain weight

Strong Verbs

INFINITIVE	PRESENT	PAST TENSE	PERFECT	
ab•nehmen	nimmt ab	nahm ab	abgenommen	to decrease, decline; to lose weight
an•bieten		bot an	angeboten	to offer
sich befinden		befand	befunden	to be located
beschließen		beschloß	beschlossen	to decide
beschreiben		beschrieb	beschrieben	to describe
sich entscheiden		entschied	entschieden	to decide
erscheinen		erschien	ist erschienen	to appear
sinken		sank	ist gesunken	to sink
vor•lesen	liest vor	las vor	vorgelesen	to read aloud
zu•nehmen	nimmt zu	nahm zu	zugenommen	to increase; to gain weight

Appendix

PRINCIPAL PARTS: STRONG VERBS AND IRREGULAR WEAK VERBS

This table does not contain most compound verbs, since their principal parts are the same as those of the basic verbs. Thus, if you want to look up the forms of **ausgehen**, look under **gehen** and supply the additional information yourself:

gehen	ging	ist gegangen	to go
ausgehen	ging aus	ist ausgegangen	to go out

The table also does not show which verbs can or must be used with reflexive pronouns, nor does it show the use of prepositions with these verbs. For all such information, refer to the vocabulary beginning on p. A-5.

Present-tense forms are listed only for those verbs that change the stem vowel in the second- and third-person singular or, as with the modals and **wissen**, in all three singular forms. The word **ist** indicates that **sein** is used as the auxiliary in the perfect tense. All other verbs use **haben**. Words in parentheses are alternate forms.

INFINITIVE	PRESENT	PAST	AUX.	PERFECT	
anbieten		bot an		angeboten	to offer
anfangen	fängt an	fing an		angefangen	to start
anwenden		wandte an		angewandt	to use
backen	(bäckt)	backte (buk)		gebacken	to bake
befehlen	befiehlt	befahl		befohlen	to command
beginnen		begann		begonnen	to begin
begreifen		begriff		begriffen	to comprehend
bekommen		bekam		bekommen	to receive
beschließen		beschloß		beschlossen	to decide
beschreiben		beschrieb		beschrieben	to describe
bestehen		bestand		bestanden	to consist
beweisen		bewies		bewiesen	to prove
bitten		bat		gebeten	to ask
bleiben		blieb	ist	geblieben	to stay
braten	brät	briet		gebraten	to roast
brechen	bricht	brach	(ist)	gebrochen	to break
bringen		brachte		gebracht	to bring
denken		dachte		gedacht	to think
dürfen	darf	durfte		gedurft	to be permitted
einladen	lädt ein	lud ein		eingeladen	to invite
empfangen	empfängt	empfing		empfangen	to receive
empfehlen	empfiehlt	empfahl		empfohlen	to recommend

INFINITIVE	PRESENT	PAST	AUX.	PERFECT	
entscheiden		entschied		entschieden	to determine
entschließen		entschloß		entschlossen	to decide
entstehen		entstand	ist	entstanden	to originate
erfahren	erfährt	erfuhr		erfahren	to find out
erfinden		erfand		erfunden	to invent
erhalten	erhält	erhielt		erhalten	to receive
erkennen		erkannte		erkannt	to recognize
erscheinen		erschien	ist	erschienen	to appear
erschlagen	erschlägt	erschlug		erschlagen	to slay
essen	ißt	aß		gegessen	to eat
fahren	fährt	fuhr	ist	gefahren	to drive
fallen	fällt	fiel	ist	gefallen	to fall
finden		fand		gefunden	to find
fliegen		flog	ist	geflogen	to fly
fließen		floß	ist	geflossen	to flow
fressen	frißt	fraß		gefressen	to eat
geben	gibt	gab		gegeben	to give
gefallen	gefällt	gefiel		gefallen	to be pleasing
gehen		ging	ist	gegangen	to go
gelingen		gelang	ist	gelungen	to succeed
geschehen	geschieht	geschah	ist	geschehen	to happen
gewinnen		gewann		gewonnen	to win
haben	hat	hatte		gehabt	to have
halten	hält	hielt		gehalten	to hold
hängen		hing		gehangen	to hang
heben		hob		gehoben	to lift
heißen		hieß		geheißen	to be called
helfen	hilft	half		geholfen	to help
kennen		kannte		gekannt	to know
klingen		klang		geklungen	to sound
kommen		kam	ist	gekommen	to come
können	kann	konnte		gekonnt	to be able to
lassen	läßt	ließ		gelassen	to let
laufen	läuft	lief	ist	gelaufen	to run
leiden		litt		gelitten	to suffer
leihen		lieh		geliehen	to lend
lesen	liest	las		gelesen	to read
liegen		lag	(ist)[1]	gelegen	to lie
lügen		log		gelogen	to tell a lie
messen	mißt	maß		gemessen	to measure
mögen	mag	mochte		gemocht	to like
müssen	muß	mußte		gemußt	to have to
nehmen	nimmt	nahm		genommen	to take
nennen		nannte		genannt	to call
raten	rät	riet		geraten	to advise
rennen		rannte	ist	gerannt	to run
rufen		rief		gerufen	to call
schaffen		schuf		geschaffen	to create
scheiden		schied		geschieden	to separate

INFINITIVE	PRESENT	PAST	AUX.	PERFECT	
scheinen		schien		geschienen	to appear
schlafen	schläft	schlief		geschlafen	to sleep
schlagen	schlägt	schlug		geschlagen	to beat
schließen		schloß		geschlossen	to close
schneiden		schnitt		geschnitten	to cut
schreiben		schrieb		geschrieben	to write
schreien		schrie		geschrien	to scream
schweigen		schwieg		geschwiegen	to be silent
schwimmen		schwamm	ist	geschwommen	to swim
sehen	sieht	sah		gesehen	to see
sein	ist	war	ist	gewesen	to be
senden		sandte (sendete)		gesandt (gesendet)	to send
singen		sang		gesungen	to sing
sinken		sank	ist	gesunken	to sink
sitzen		saß	(ist)[1]	gesessen	to sit
sprechen	spricht	sprach		gesprochen	to speak
springen		sprang	ist	gesprungen	to jump
stehen		stand	(ist)[1]	gestanden	to stand
stehlen	stiehlt	stahl		gestohlen	to steal
steigen		stieg	ist	gestiegen	to climb
sterben	stirbt	starb	ist	gestorben	to die
stoßen	stößt	stieß		gestoßen	to push
streichen		strich		gestrichen	to spread
tragen	trägt	trug		getragen	to carry
treffen	trifft	traf		getroffen	to meet
trinken		trank		getrunken	to drink
tun		tat		getan	to do
unterbrechen	unterbricht	unterbrach		unterbrochen	to interrupt
verbieten		verbot		verboten	to forbid
verbringen		verbrachte		verbracht	to spend time
vergessen	vergißt	vergaß		vergessen	to forget
vergleichen		verglich		verglichen	to compare
verlassen	verläßt	verließ		verlassen	to leave
verlieren		verlor		verloren	to lose
versprechen	verspricht	versprach		versprochen	to promise
verstehen		verstand		verstanden	to understand
vertreiben		vertrieb		vertrieben	to displace
verwenden		verwandte (verwendete)		verwandt (verwendet)	to use
verzeihen		verzieh		verziehen	to forgive
vorschlagen	schlägt vor	schlug vor		vorgeschlagen	to suggest
wachsen	wächst	wuchs	ist	gewachsen	to grow
waschen	wäscht	wusch		gewaschen	to wash
werden	wird	wurde	ist	geworden	to become

[1]Austrians tend to use **liegen, sitzen,** and **stehen** with **sein** rather than with **haben.**

INFINITIVE	PRESENT	PAST	AUX.	PERFECT	
werfen	wirft	warf		geworfen	to throw
wissen	weiß	wußte		gewußt	to know
ziehen		zog		gezogen	to pull
ziehen		zog	ist	gezogen	to move
zwingen		zwang		gezwungen	to force

VOCABULARY: GERMAN-ENGLISH

This vocabulary is intended primarily for quick reference; it is not meant to be a substitute for a dictionary of the German language. The English equivalents given here do not include all the meanings of the corresponding German words that are found in a German dictionary. Most of the translations are limited to the meanings in which the German words are used in this book. Some low-frequency words which occur in the reading sections and are translated there have not been included here.

NOUNS

All nouns are listed with the definite article to indicate their gender:

der Mann, ̈er   die Frau, -en   das Kind, -er

Nouns for which no plural form is shown are not normally used in the plural. If the plural changes from ß to ss, the plural form is written out (e.g., **der Fluß, die Flüsse**). All n-nouns are identified with the notation (*n-noun*).

ACCENTUATION

Accent marks are used whenever the pronunciation of a word deviates from the standard German stress pattern (e.g., **das Thea'ter**). If the stress shifts to another syllable in the plural, the entire plural form is given (e.g., **der Dok'tor, die Dokto'ren**). Stress is not indicated for words in which the first syllable is an unaccented prefix such as **be-** or **er-**.

VERBS

All strong verbs and irregular weak verbs are indicated by an asterisk (e.g., ***kommen**). Their principal parts can be found in the list of strong verbs and irregular weak verbs (p. A-1), but note that not all verbs are listed there; compounds such as **mitfahren** can be looked up under **fahren**.

All verbs that take **sein** as an auxiliary are identified with (**sein**).

In compound verbs written as one word, a dot between complement and verb (e.g., **aus•gehen, nach•denken**) indicates that the two parts are separated in the present and past tenses (**er geht aus, er denkt nach**).

With reflexive verbs, the case of the pronoun is given, as with **sich** (*acc.*) **freuen**; with prepositional objects, the case is indicated only with two-way prepositions.

ABBREVIATIONS

abbrev.	abbreviation	*indef.*	indefinite
acc.	accusative	*m.*	masculine
adv.	adverb	*obj.*	object
colloq.	colloquial	*pers.*	person, personal
conj.	conjunction	*pl.*	plural
dat.	dative	*prep.*	preposition
demonstr.	demonstrative	*refl.*	reflexive
f.	feminine	*rel. pron.*	relative pronoun
gen.	genitive	*sent. adv.*	sentence adverb
impers.	impersonal	*sing.*	singular

ab off; from; as of
ab und zu now and then, occasionally
der Abend, -e evening
   abends in the evening, evenings
   (guten) Abend good evening
   das Abendessen, - supper
aber but, however
***ab•fahren (sein)** to leave, depart (on schedule)
   die Abfahrt, -en departure (by car, train, etc.)
der Abflug, ⸚e departure (by plane)
***ab•gehen von (sein)** to leave (school), to graduate
ab•hängen to detach a (railway) car, to uncouple
ab•holen to pick up (at station, airport, etc.)
das Abitur' final examination in secondary school
   der Abiturient', -en (*n-noun*) *Gymnasium* graduate
die Abkürzung, -en abbreviation
ab•legen to pass (an exam)
ab•reisen (sein) to leave, depart
   die Abreise, -n departure
***ab•schließen** to close, to lock up; to terminate; to conclude

der Abschluß, die Abschlüsse conclusion
ach oh
   ach ja oh yes, of course
   ach so oh, I see
acht eight
   acht Tage a week; eight days
   achtzehn eighteen
   achtzig eighty
(das) Afrika Africa
ähnlich similar
der Akade'miker, - university graduate
der Akt, -e act
die Aktentasche, -n briefcase
der Akzent', -e accent
akzeptieren to accept
alle all, all of us
die Allee', die Alle'en boulevard
allein alone
allerdings however
alles everything, all
allgemein general
   die Allgemeinbildung general education
die Alpen Alps
das Alphabet', -e alphabet
als as; when; than
   als ob, als wenn as if
also (*sent. adv.*) therefore; well; in other words
alt old
das Altenheim, -e old-age home
die Altstadt, ⸚e old city

(das) Amerika America
amerikanisch American
der Amerikaner, - American (*m.*)
die Amerikanerin, -nen American (*f.*)
die Amerikanis'tik American Studies
die Ampel, -n traffic light
an (*prep. with dat. or acc.*) at, on
die Ananas, - pineapple
***an•bieten** to offer
ander- different, other
   anders different
   anderswo elsewhere, somewhere else
***an•fangen** to begin, start
   der Anfang, ⸚e beginning
   der Anfänger, - beginner
angenehm pleasant
die Anglis'tik English Studies
die Angst, ⸚e fear, anxiety, angst
   Angst haben vor (*dat.*) to be afraid of
an•klopfen to knock (on a door)
***an•kommen (sein)** to arrive
   ***an•kommen auf** (*acc.*) to depend on
   das kommt darauf an that depends
die Ankunft, ⸚e arrival
an•machen to switch on, turn on (light, TV, etc.)

*an•nehmen to assume; to accept

*an•rufen to call (on the telephone)

der Anruf, -e (telephone) call

an•schauen to look at

sich (acc.) an•schnallen to fasten (seatbelt), to buckle up

*an•sehen to look at

*sich (dat.) etwas an•sehen to look at something

anstatt, statt (prep. with gen.) instead of

an•stellen to employ

der (die) Angestellte, -n employee

anstrengend strenuous

die Anthropologie' anthropology

der Anthropolo'ge, -n (n-noun) anthropologist

antworten (dat.) to answer

antworten auf (acc.) to reply to, to answer (a letter)

die Antwort, -en answer

*an•wenden to use, to apply

*sich (acc.) an•ziehen to dress; to get dressed

der Anzug, ⸚e (men's) suit

der Apfel, ⸚e apple

der Apfelsaft apple juice

die Apothe'ke, -n pharmacy

der Apparat', -e apparatus; instrument; telephone

am Apparat speaking (phone)

der Photoapparat, -e camera

der Appetit' (no pl.) appetite

die Apriko'se, -n apricot

der April' April

ara'bisch Arabian, Arabic

arbeiten to work

die Arbeit, -en work

der Arbeiter, - (blue-collar) worker; work-ingman (m.)

die Arbeiterin, -nen worker (f.)

der Arbeitgeber, - employer

der Arbeitnehmer, - employee, worker

arbeitslos unemployed

der Arbeitsplatz, ⸚e place of work

die Archäologie' archaeology

der Archäolo'ge, -n (n-noun) archaeologist

der Architekt', -en (n-noun) architect

die Architektur', -en architecture

sich (acc.) ärgern über (acc.) to be annoyed by, put out; to be mad at

arm poor

der Arm, -e arm

der Arzt, ⸚e physician, doctor (m.)

die Ärztin, -nen physician (f.)

(das) Asien Asia

der Assistent', -en (n-noun) assistant (m.)

die Assisten'tin, -nen assistant (f.)

die Assistentenstelle, -n assistantship

atmen to breathe

die Aubergi'ne, -n eggplant (pronounced as in French)

auch also, too

auf (prep. with dat. or acc.) on, upon

auf (adj.) open; up

auf•bauen to construct

wiederauf•bauen to reconstruct

*auf•bleiben (sein) to stay up

der Aufenthalt, -e stay, residence

auf•führen to perform, put on (a play)

die Aufführung, -en performance

auf•hören to stop, cease

die Auflage, -n printing (of a book)

auf•machen to open

*auf•nehmen to photograph

die Aufnahme, -n photograph, picture

sich (acc.) auf•regen über (acc.) to get upset, excited about

*auf•stehen (sein) to get up (out of bed), to rise

auf•wachen (sein) to wake up

*auf•weisen to show, to present

das Auge, -n eye

der Augenblick, -e moment, instant

(einen) Augenblick, bitte just a moment, please

der August' (month of) August

aus (prep. with dat.) out of

aus (adj.) over

die Ausbildung, -en training

die Ausfahrt, -en exit, off-ramp

*aus•fallen (sein) to be canceled

der Ausgang, ⸚e exit

*aus•geben to give out; to spend (money)

*aus•gehen (sein) to go out

mir war das Geld ausgegangen I had spent all my money

ausgezeichnet excellent

die Auskunft, ⸚e information

das Ausland (no pl.) foreign countries

im Ausland abroad; out of the country

der Ausländer, - foreigner (m.)

die Ausländerin, -nen foreigner (f.)

ausländisch foreign

aus•lachen to laugh at

aus•machen to switch off (light); to comprise

aus•probieren to try out

sich (acc.) aus•ruhen to rest

*sich (*acc.*) **aus•schlafen** to get enough sleep
*aus•sehen to appear, look
außer (*prep. with dat.*) besides, except for
  außer sich beside oneself
  ich bin außer mir I am beside myself
  außerdem moreover, in addition
  außerhalb (*prep. with gen.*) outside of
*aus•sprechen to pronounce
  die Aussprache, -n pronunciation
*aus•steigen (sein) to get off (a train, etc.)
aus•suchen to select, pick out
(das) Australien Australia
ausverkauft sold out
der Ausweis, -e identification paper, I.D. card
aus•wischen to wipe out
*aus•ziehen (sein) to move out
  *sich (*acc.*) **ausziehen** to undress
das Auto, -s car, automobile
  die Autobahn, -en superhighway, freeway
  der Autobus, -se bus
  der Automechaniker, auto mechanic (*m.*)
  die Automechanikerin, -nen auto mechanic (*f.*)
  das Automobil', -e car
  der Autounfall, ⁒e car accident
automatisch automatic

*backen to bake
  der Bäcker, - baker
  die Bäckerei, -en bakery
baden to bathe, to swim
  baden gehen to go swimming
  das Bad, ⁒er bath; bathroom
die Bahn, -en track; train; streetcar

der Bahnhof, die Bahnhöfe railway station
der Bahnsteig, -e platform (in station)
der Hauptbahnhof, ⁒e main railway station
die Straßenbahn, -en streetcar
bald soon
  baldig (*adj.*) soon
  auf baldiges Wiedersehen (hoping to) see you again soon
der Ball, ⁒e ball
der Fußball soccer
  das Fußballspiel, -e soccer game
die Bank, ⁒e bench
die Bank, -en bank
die Bar, -s bar, tavern
basieren auf (*dat.*) to be based on
  die Basis base, basis
bauen to build
  der Bau, die Bauten construction; building
  die Baufirma, die Baufirmen construction firm
  das Bauwerk, -e building
  der Weinbau winegrowing, viticulture
der Bauer, -n farmer (*m.*)
  die Bäuerin, -nen farmer (*f.*)
  bäuerlich rural
  das Bauernhaus, ⁒er farm house
  der Bauernhof, ⁒e farm
der Baum, ⁒e tree
(das) Bayern Bavaria
  bayerisch Bavarian
  der Bayer, -n Bavarian (*m.*)
  die Bayerin, -nen Bavarian (*f.*)
beachten to notice, take note of
der Beamte, -n civil servant (*m.*)
  die Beamtin, -nen civil servant (*f.*)

beantworten to reply to, answer
sich (*acc.*) **bedanken** to thank
bedeuten to mean; to signify
  die Bedeutung, -en meaning, importance
bedienen to wait on, to serve
sich (*acc.*) **beeilen** to hurry
beerdigen to bury
  die Beerdigung, -en funeral
*befehlen to command, to order
*sich (*acc.*) **befinden** to be located
befragen to ask
begabt (*adj.*) gifted, intelligent
*sich (*acc.*) **begeben** to proceed, go
begegnen (*dat.*) to meet (by chance)
*beginnen to start, begin
  der Beginn (*no pl.*) beginning
*begreifen to comprehend, understand
begrenzen to border; to limit
der Begriff, -e concept, idea, notion; term
behaupten to claim, maintain
bei (*prep. with dat.*) at; with, at the home of; near; while
  beim Essen while eating, during a meal
  Potsdam bei Berlin Potsdam near Berlin
beide both, both of; two
der Beifall applause
das Bein, -e leg
beinah(e) nearly, almost
das Beispiel, -e example
  zum Beispiel (z.B.) for example
bekannt (well) known
  unbekannt unknown
der (die) Bekannte, -n acquaintance
*bekommen to get, receive

beliebt well-liked
*benennen to name
benutzen to use
das Benzin' gasoline
beob'achten to observe
   die Beobachtung, -en observation
*bereit sein zu to be ready for
der Berg, -e mountain
   in die Berge to the mountains
berichten to report
   der Bericht, -e report
der Beruf, -e job, profession
sich (*acc.*) **beruhigen** to calm down
   beunruhigt sein to be worried
beschäftigen to employ
   beschäftigt sein to be busy; to be employed
*beschließen to decide
*beschreiben to describe
besetzen to occupy
   besetzt busy (telephone)
besichtigen to visit; look at; inspect
*besitzen to own
besonders especially
besser better
best- (*adj. or adv.*) best
   am besten (*adv.*) best
*bestehen to pass (an examination)
   *bestehen aus to consist of
bestellen to (place an) order
bestimmt certain; I'm sure
besuchen to visit; to attend (a school)
   der Besuch, -e visit
   der Besucher, - visitor (*m.*)
   die Besucherin, -nen visitor (*f.*)
betrachten to regard; to look at
   betrachten als to consider as
der Betrieb, -e place of work, plant, factory
das Bett, -en bed

die Bevölkerung, -en population
der Bevölkerungszuwachs population growth
bevor (*adv.*) before
sich (*acc.*) **bewegen** to move
   die Bewegung, -en movement
*beweisen to prove
bewundern to admire
bezahlen to pay (a bill)
die Bibel, -n Bible
die Bibliothek', -en library
das Bier, -e beer
das Bild, -er picture
bilden to form; to educate
   die Bildung education, training
   der (die) Gebildete, -n educated person
billig cheap
die Biologie' biology
   der Biolo'ge, -n (*n-noun*) biologist (*m.*)
   die Biolo'gin, -nen biologist (*f.*)
bis until; up to, as far as
   bis morgen until tomorrow; see you tomorrow
bißchen bit, little, little bit
bisher (*adv.*) up to now, so far
bitte, bitte sehr please; OK, go ahead
*bitten um to ask for, request
   die Bitte, -n request
blau blue
*bleiben (sein) to stay, remain
blicken to look, glance
   der Blick, -e look, glance
blind blind
blitzen to lighten
   es blitzt it is lightning
   der Blitz, -e lightning
blöd stupid, dumb
blond blond, blonde
blühen to bloom, blossom, flower
die Blume, -n flower

der Blumenkohl cauliflower
das Blut blood
   der Blutdruck blood pressure
der Bodensee Lake Constance
die Bohne, -n bean
   die Bohnensuppe, -n bean soup
die Bombe, -n bomb
das Boot, -e boat
   das Segelboot, -e sailboat
böse angry, mad; evil
   ich bin ihm böse I am mad at him
*braten to roast
brauchen to need; to use
   brauchbar usable
die Braut, ⁀e bride
der Bräutigam, -e groom
*brechen to break
   *sich (*dat.*) **den Arm brechen** to break one's arm
breit broad
   die Breite, -n breadth, latitude
der Brief, -e letter
   *einen Brief aufgeben to post (mail) a letter
   die Briefmarke, -n stamp
   der Briefträger, - mailman
   der Eilbrief, -e special-delivery letter
   der Einschreibebrief, -e registered letter
   der Luftpostbrief, -e airmail letter
*bringen to bring
das Brot, -e bread; loaf of bread; sandwich
   das Brötchen, - (hard) roll
die Brücke, -n bridge
der Bruder, ⁀ brother
das Buch, ⁀er book
   der Buchstabe, -n letter (of alphabet)
der Bund, ⁀e federation
   der Bundesbürger, - citizen (of FRG)

der Bundeskanzler, -
Federal chancellor
das Bundesland, ¨er
Federal state
die Bundespost Federal
post office
**der Bundespräsident,
-en** (*n-noun*) Federal
president
der Bundesrat Federal
Council (upper house
of parliament)
die Bundesregierung
Federal government
**die Bundesrepublik
Deutschland** Federal
Republic of Germany
die Bundesstraße, -n
Federal highway
der Bundestag Federal
Parliament (lower
house)
die Bundeswehr Federal
Armed Forces
die Burg, -en castle
der Bürgermeister, - mayor
(*m.*)
**die Bürgermeisterin,
-nen** mayor (*f.*)
der Bürgersteig, -e sidewalk
das Büro', -s office
der Bus, -se bus
die Butter (*no pl.*) butter

das Café, -s café, coffeehouse
der Campus campus
Celsius centigrade
der Chef, -s boss; chief; chef
die Chemie' chemistry
che'misch chemical
(das) China China
chinesisch Chinese
der Chinese, -n (*n-noun*)
Chinese (*m.*)
die Chinesin, -nen
Chinese (*f.*)
die Chirurgie' surgery

da (*adv.*) there; then; under
these circumstances;
(*conj.*) since, because

dabei' (*adv.*) moreover,
besides
*dabei•sein (sein) to be
present
das Dach, ¨er roof
dagegen in comparison with
that; on the other hand
daher from there; therefore,
for that reason, that's
why
dahin there, to that place
damals at that time, then
die Dame, -n lady
damit' (*conj.*) so that, in
order that
der Dampfer, - steamship
danken (*dat.*) to thank
   **danke (dankeschön,
   danke sehr)** thanks;
   thank you
   der Dank gratitude,
   thanks
   dankbar grateful
   die Dankbarkeit gratitude
   vielen Dank thank you
   very much
dann then
darum therefore; for that
reason
das the (*neuter*); that
(*demonstr.*); which,
that (*rel. pron.*)
daß (*conj.*) that
das Datum, die Daten date
(calendar)
   die Daten data
   der Datenverarbeiter, -
   data processor
   die Datenverarbeitung
   data processing
dauern to last; to take (time)
definieren to define
der Demokrat', -en (*n-noun*)
Democrat (*m.*)
   die Demokra'tin, -nen
   Democrat (*f.*)
   die Demokratie', -n
   democracy
   demokra'tisch democratic
*denken to think

*denken an (*acc.*) to
think of
*sich (*dat.*) **denken** to
imagine
   ich denke mir etwas I
   imagine
   die Denkweise, -n way
   of thinking
denn (*see* Anal. 12); (*conj.*)
because, for
dennoch yet; though, nevertheless
der the (*m.*); that (*demonstr.*);
which, that (*rel. pron.*)
derselbe, dieselbe, dasselbe,
pl. **dieselben** the same
deshalb (*adv.*) because of
that
(das) Deutschland Germany
deutsch German
(das) Deutsch(e) German
language
   der Deutsche, -n
   German (*m.*)
   die Deutsche, -n
   German (*f.*)
der Dezember December
der Dialekt', -e dialect
der Diamant', -en (*n-noun*)
diamond
dicht close; tight; dense
dick thick, fat
die the (*f.*); that (*demonstr.*);
which, that (*rel. pron.*)
der Dieb, -e thief
dienen (*dat.*) to serve; to be
used for
   der Diener, - servant
der Dienstag, -e Tuesday
der Diesel, - diesel car
dieser, diese, dieses, *pl.* **diese**
this; that
diesmal this time
das Ding, -e thing
direkt direct
der Direk'tor, die Direkto'ren
director (*m.*)
   die Direkto'rin, -nen
   director (*f.*)
die Diskothek', -en disco-
theque

doch (*sent. adv.*) (*see* Anal. 38)

der Dok'tor, die Dokto'ren doctor, physician (*m.*)

die Dokto'rin, -nen doctor, physician (*f.*)

der Doktorand', -en (*n-noun*) doctoral candidate (*m.*)

die Doktoran'din, -nen doctoral candidate (*f.*)

der Dollar, - dollar

der Dom, -e cathedral

die Domglocke, -n cathedral bells

die Donau the Danube

donnern to thunder

der Donner, - thunder

der Donnerstag, -e Thursday

das Dorf, ¨er village

dort there

draußen outside

drei three

dreizehn thirteen

dreißig thirty

dreiviertel sieben 6:45

dritt- third

das Drittel, - third (fraction)

drittens third(ly)

die Drogerie', -n drugstore

drüben on the other side

da (dort) drüben over there

dumm dumb, stupid

die Dummheit, -en stupidity

der Dummkopf, ¨e stupid person, dumbbell

dunkel dark

die Dunkelheit darkness

dünn thin

durch (*prep. with acc.*) through

*durch•fallen (sein) to flunk (an examination)

*dürfen to be permitted to

das darfst du nicht you mustn't do that

durstig thirsty

der Durst thirst

ich habe Durst I am thirsty

duschen to shower

die Dusche, -n shower

eben flat, even; just

die Ebene, -n plain, flatland

ebenfalls likewise, too

danke ebenfalls thanks, and the same to you

ebensogut just as well

echt genuine

die Ecke, -n corner

eckig cornered

dreieckig triangular

viereckig rectangular

egalitär' egalitarian

die Ehe, -n marriage

das Ehepaar, -e (married) couple

eher rather, sooner

ehrlich honest

das Ei, -er egg

eigen- own

eigentlich actually, really

eilen to hurry

sich (*acc.*) eilen to hurry

ein, eine, ein a; one (*indef. article*)

eins one (number)

einander each other

eineinhalb one and a half

sich (*dat.*) etwas einbilden to imagine something (falsely); to fancy

eingebildet sein to be conceited

der Eindruck, ¨e impression

einfach easy, simple

die Einfahrt entrance (way); driveway; on-ramp

der Einfluß, die Einflüsse influence

der Eingang, ¨e entry, entrance

die Einheit, -en entity; unit

einheitlich uniform, homogeneous

einig in agreement

einige some; a few

ein•kaufen to shop; to purchase

*einkaufen gehen to go shopping

*ein•laden to invite

die Einladung, -en invitation

einmal once; at some time

zweimal twice

dreimal three times

viermal four times

auf einmal at once

nicht einmal not once

noch einmal once more

nur einmal just once

*ein•schlafen (sein) to fall asleep

*ein•steigen (sein) to get on (a train, etc.), board

der Einwohner, - inhabitant

einzeln single, one at a time

einzig single; sole; solitary

das Eis ice; ice cream

die Eisenbahn, -en railroad, train

der Elefant', -en (*n-noun*) elephant

elf eleven

elitär' (*adj.*) elitist, selective

die Eltern (*pl. only*) parents

*empfangen to receive

*empfehlen (*dat.*) to recommend

die Empfehlung, -en recommendation

das Ende, -n end

endlich finally

die Energie', -n energy

eng narrow

(das) England England

englisch English

(das) Englisch(e) English (language)

der Engländer, - Englishman

die Engländerin, -nen Englishwoman

das Enkelkind, -er grandchild

der Enkel, - grandchild, grandson

die **Enkelin, -nen** grand-daughter
entdecken to discover
entfernt distant
die **Entfernung, -en** distance
entlang along
    am Rhein **entlang** along the Rhine
*sich (acc.) **entscheiden** to decide
die **Entscheidung, -en** decision
*sich (acc.) **entschließen** to decide, to make up one's mind
entschlossen sein to be determined
sich (acc.) **entschuldigen** to apologize; to excuse (oneself)
die **Entschuldigung, -en** excuse
    um Entschuldigung **bitten** to apologize
    (ich bitte um) Entschul-digung (I am) sorry; excuse me
    entschuldigen Sie excuse me
***entsprechen** to correspond to
***entstehen (sein)** to originate
enttäuschen to disappoint
entweder . . . oder either . . . or
entwickeln to develop
die **Entwicklung, -en** development
erblicken to see, catch sight of
die **Erde, -n** earth
    das **Erdbeben, -** earth-quake
sich **ereignen** to occur, happen
    das **Ereignis, -se** event, occurrence
***erfahren** to find out, learn; to experience
***erfinden** to invent
der **Erfolg, -e** success, result

erfolgreich successful
***erhalten** to receive; to preserve
sich (acc.) **erholen** to get a rest
    erholt sein to be well rested
die **Erholung** recreation; recuperation
erinnern an (acc.) to remind of
    sich (acc.) **erinnern an** (acc.) to remember
die **Erinnerung, -en** memory; remembrance
sich (acc.) **erkälten** to catch a cold
    erkältet sein to have a cold
die **Erkältung, -en** cold
***erkennen an** (dat.) to recog-nize by
erklären to explain; to declare
die **Erklärung, -en** explanation
erlauben to allow, permit
erleben to experience
erledigen to take care of
erreichen to reach (a desti-nation)
***erscheinen (sein)** to appear
***erschlagen** to slay, kill
erst only, not until
erst- (adj.) first
erst (= zuerst) (adv.) first
erstens first(ly)
erstaunt sein to be astonished
erwärmen to warm (up)
erwarten to expect
die **Erwartung, -en** expectation
erzählen to tell (a story)
    der **Erzähler, -** narrator
    die **Erzählung, -en** story; narration
***essen** to eat
    das **Essen, -** food; meal
etwa about; by any chance
etwas something, somewhat
    etwas anderes some-thing else

(das) **Euro'pa** Europe
    europä'isch European
ewig eternal, forever
das **Exa'men, -** examination
das **Exemplar, -e** copy (of a book)
das **Experiment', -e** experi-ment
exportieren to export

die **Fabrik', -en** factory
das **Fach, ⁻er** (academic) sub-ject, discipline; box
    der **Fachbereich, -e** group of academic departments
das **Fachwerkhaus, ⁻er** frame(work) house, half-timbered house
***fahren (sein)** to drive, to go (by car, train, boat, plane)
    der **Fahrplan, ⁻e** time-table
    die **Fahrt, -en** drive, trip
    die **Heimfahrt, -en** trip home
    der **Fahrer, -** driver
    der **Fahrgast, ⁻e** passen-ger
    die **Fahrkarte, -n** ticket (train, etc.)
    die **Rückfahrkarte, -n** round-trip ticket
***fallen (sein)** to fall
    der **Fall, ⁻e** fall; case
    auf jeden Fall at any case
    auf keinen Fall in no case
falsch wrong, false
die **Fami'lie, -n** family
die **Farbe, -n** color
fast almost
der **Februar** February
feiern to celebrate
    der **Feiertag, -e** holiday
fein fine, delicate
der **Feind, -e** enemy
das **Fenster, -** window
die **Ferien** (pl.) vacation

fern distant
  die Ferne distance
  das Ferngespräch, -e
    long-distance call
  *****fern•sehen** to watch TV
  das Fernsehen (*no pl.*)
    television
  der Fernseher, - televi-
    sion set
  der Fernsprecher, - tele-
    phone
fertig ready, finished
das Fest, -e celebration,
  party, festivity
fest•stellen to notice, find
  out; to determine
fett fat
das Feuer, - fire
das Fieber fever
der Film, -e film
*****finden** to find
die Firma, die Firmen firm,
  company
fischen to fish
  der Fisch, -e fish
flach flat
  die Fläche, -n area
die Flasche, -n bottle
das Fleisch (*no pl.*) meat
*****fliegen (sein)** to fly
  der Flieger, - flier, pilot
*****fließen (sein)** to flow
  fließend fluent; flowing
flüchten (sein) to flee; to
  escape
  der Flüchtling, -e refugee
der Flug, ˙e flight
  der Fluggast, ˙e (airline)
    passenger
  der Flughafen, ˙ airport
  der Flugkapitän, -e flight
    captain
  das Flugzeug, -e airplane
die Flunder, -n flounder
der Fluß, die Flüsse river
folgen (sein) (*dat.*) to follow
formen to form, mold
  die Form, -en form
  die Formel, -n formula
  das Formular', -e form,
    blank

fort away
  *****fort•gehen (sein)** to go
    away, leave
  fort•leben to live on; to
    survive
  die Fortsetzung, -en
    continuation
fragen to ask
  fragen nach to ask
    about, inquire after
  die Frage, -n question
der Franken, - (sFr) franc
  (Swiss)
(das) Frankreich France
  franzö'sisch French
  der Franzo'se, -n (*n-
    noun*) Frenchman
  die Franzö'sin, -nen
    Frenchwoman
die Frau, -en woman; wife;
  Mrs., Ms.
  Frau Meyer Mrs. Meyer,
    Ms. Meyer
  das Fräulein, - young
    (unmarried) woman,
    Miss, Ms.
  die Frauenbewegung, -en
    women's movement
frei free
  die Freiheit freedom
  die Freizeit leisure time
der Freitag, -e Friday
fremd strange, foreign
  der Fremdenverkehr
    tourism
  die Fremdsprache, -n
    foreign language
  der Fremdsprachenunter-
    richt foreign language
    instruction
  das Fremdwort, ˙er
    foreign word, non-
    German word
*****fressen** to eat (of animals),
  feed
die Freude, -n joy
sich (*acc.*) **freuen auf** (*acc.*)
  to look forward to
sich (*acc.*) **freuen über** (*acc.*)
  to be happy (glad)
  about

das (es) freut mich I'm
  glad, delighted
der Freund, -e friend (*m.*)
  die Freundin, -nen
    friend (*f.*)
  freundlich friendly
  unfreundlich unfriendly
  die Freundlichkeit, -en
    friendliness, kindness
  die Freundschaft, -en
    friendship
der Frieden peace
  der Friedhof, ˙e ceme-
    tery, graveyard
frisch fresh
froh glad, happy
  fröhlich cheerful
früh early
  früher earlier; formerly
  frühestens at the earliest
der Frühling spring
frühstücken to (eat, have)
  breakfast
  das Frühstück, -e break-
    fast
fühlen to feel
führen to lead, take
  der Führerschein, -e
    driver's license
füllen to fill
der Fund, -e find
fünf five
  fünfzehn fifteen
  fünfzig fifty
funktionieren to function;
  to work
für (*prep. with acc.*) for
furchtbar terrible
fürchten to fear
  sich (*acc.*) **fürchten vor**
    (*dat.*) to be afraid of
der Fürst, -en (*n-noun*) prince
  das Fürstentum, ˙er
    principality
der Fuß, ˙e foot
  zu Fuß (gehen) (to go)
    on foot
  der Fußgänger, - pedes-
    trian
  die Fußgängerzone, -n
    pedestrian zone

die **Gabel, -n** fork
die **Gans, ⸚e** goose
ganz all of; entire; quite
    ganz gut not bad
gar fully, even; quite, very
    gar nicht not at all
    gar nichts nothing at all
die **Gara′ge, -n** garage
garantiert guaranteed; I
    guarantee you
der **Garten, ⸚** garden
das **Gas, -e** gas
der **Gast, ⸚e** guest
    der **Gastarbeiter, -**
      foreign worker
    der **Gasthof, ⸚e** inn,
      restaurant
*****geben** to give
    es gibt there is, there are
das **Gebiet, -e** area
das **Gebilde, -** structure
geboren born
    die **Geburt, -en** birth
    der **Geburtstag, -e** birth-
      day
gebrauchen to use
    der **Gebrauch, ⸚e** use;
      custom, habit
der **Gedanke, -n** (*gen.* **des**
    Gedankens) (*n-noun*)
    thought
das **Gedicht, -e** poem
*****gefallen** (*dat.*) to be pleasing
    to
    es gefällt mir I like it
gegen (*prep. with acc.*)
    against; around
    gegen neun around nine
      o'clock
    gegenüber (*prep. with
      dat.*) opposite
    gegenüber dem Bahnhof
      or **dem Bahnhof ge-**
      genüber opposite
      (across from) the
      station
die **Gegend, -en** area
der **Gegensatz, ⸚e** contrast
gegenseitig reciprocal,
    mutual
das **Gegenteil, -e** opposite

im Gegenteil on the
    contrary
die **Gegenwart** present (time)
das **Gehalt, ⸚er** salary
    die **Gehaltserhöhung,**
      -en salary increase
*****gehen** (sein) to go; to walk
    wie geht's? wie geht es
      dir/euch/Ihnen? how
      are you? how are
      things going?
gehören (*dat.*) to belong to
    (possession)
    gehören zu to belong
      to, be a member of
das **Geld, -er** money
geliebt beloved
*****gelingen** (sein) (*impers.*)
    (*dat.*) to succeed
    es gelingt mir I succeed
gemein common
    gemeinsam common,
      mutual
    die **Gemeinschaft, -en**
      community
    die **Europäische Gemein-**
      schaft (E.G.) European
      Community (E.C.)
    die **Gemeinde, -n** (reli-
      gious or civic) com-
      munity
das **Gemüse, -** vegetable
gemütlich cozy
genau exact(ly)
die **Generation′, -en** genera-
    tion
genug enough
gerade straight; just
    geradeaus straight,
      straight ahead
gerecht just
    ungerecht unjust
das **Gericht, -e** dish, course
    (food)
germanisch Germanic
    der **Germanist′, -en**
      (*n-noun*) Germanist,
      German scholar (*m.*)
    die **Germanis′tin, -nen**
      Germanist, German
      scholar (*f.*)

die **Germanis′tik** study
    of German (academic
    discipline)
gern(e) (*adv.*) gladly
    ich esse gern I like to
      eat
der **Gesandte, -n** ambassador
das **Geschäft, -e** business,
    store
    die **Geschäftsfrau, -en**
      businesswoman
    der **Geschäftsmann,** *pl.*
      die **Geschäftsleute**
      businessman
*****geschehen** (sein) (*impers.*)
    (*dat.*) to happen
das **Geschenk, -e** present
die **Geschichte, -n** story;
    history
der **Geschmack** taste
geschweige not to mention
die **Geschwindigkeit, -en**
    speed
    die **Höchstgeschwindig-**
      keit maximum speed,
      speed limit
die **Geschwister** (*pl. only*)
    brothers and sisters,
    siblings
das **Gesetz, -e** law
das **Gesicht, -er** face
das **Gespräch, -e** conversation
gestern yesterday
    gestern abend last night
    gestern morgen yester-
      day morning
gesund healthy
    die **Gesundheit** health
    Gesundheit! (said when
      someone sneezes)
das **Getränk, -e** beverage
das **Getreide, -** grain
    das **Getreidefeld, -er**
      grainfield
das **Gewicht, -e** weight
*****gewinnen** to win
gewiß certainly
sich (*acc.*) **gewöhnen an**
    (*acc.*) to get used to
    gewöhnt sein an (*acc.*)
      to be used to

gewöhnlich usual
der Gigant', -en (n-noun) giant
die Gitar're, -n guitar
das Glas, -̈er glass
glauben an (acc.) to believe in
  der Glaube (gen. **des Glaubens**) (n-noun) belief
gleich equal, same, like; right away
gliedern to arrange, to divide
die Glocke, -n bell
das Glück luck, fortune
  Glück haben to be lucky
  glücklich happy
  glücklicherweise fortunately
  der Glückwunsch, -̈e congratulation
gnädig gracious
  gnädige Frau madam (formal address)
das Gold (no pl.) gold
  die Goldmedaille gold medal
der Gott, -̈er god
  die Göttin, -nen goddess
  gottseidank thank goodness
der Grad, -e degree
das Gramm (no pl.) (metric) gram
  das Deka(gramm) ten grams (Austrian)
  das Kilo(gramm) 1000 grams
gratulieren (dat.) to congratulate
grau gray
die Grenze, -n border, limit
(das) Griechenland Greece
  griechisch Greek
  der Grieche, -n Greek (m.)
  die Griechin, -nen Greek (f.)
grillen to grill, barbecue
die Grippe flu
der Groschen, - (smallest unit of Austrian currency)

groß large, big, tall, great
großartig wonderful, great, marvelous
die Größe, -n size; greatness
die Großeltern grandparents
  die Großmutter, -̈ grandmother
  der Großvater, -̈ grandfather
die Großfamilie, -n extended family
die Großstadt, -̈e large city, metropolis
***groß•werden (sein)** to grow up
grün green
gründen to found; to start
grüßen to greet, say hello
  der Gruß, -̈e greeting
gut good; OK
das Gymnasium, die Gymnasien German secondary school, grades 5–13

das Haar, -e hair
  ***sich** (dat.) **die Haare schneiden lassen** to have one's hair cut, to get a haircut
***haben** to have
hageln to hail
halb half
  halb zehn half past nine, 9:30
  die Hälfte, -n half
die Halle, -n hall; lobby
***halten** to hold; to stop, halt; keep (of animals)
  halt just; stop
  ***halten für** to consider
  ich halte ihn für dumm I think he's stupid
  ***halten von** to have an opinion about
  was halten Sie von Meyer? what do you think of Meyer?
die Hand, -̈e hand
  ***sich** (dat.) **die Hände**

waschen to wash one's hands
der Handschuh, -e glove
der Hang, -̈e slope
hängen (hängte, gehängt) (with acc. obj.) to hang (something)
  er hängte das Bild an die Wand he hung the picture on the wall
  auf•hängen to hang up
***hängen (hing, gehangen)** to hang, be suspended
  das Bild hing an der Wand the picture hung on the wall
hart hard
  die Härte hardness
häßlich ugly
Haupt- (prefix) main
  das Hauptfach, -̈er (academic) major (subject)
  die Hauptsache, -n main thing
  hauptsächlich mainly, primarily
  die Hauptstadt, -̈e capital (city)
das Haus, -̈er house
  ich bin zu Hause I am at home
  ich gehe nach Hause I am going home
  die Hausfrau, -en housewife
  die Haustür, -en front door
  das Hochhaus, -̈er high rise
***heben** to lift; to raise
die Heimat home, native land
  der Heimatstaat, -en home state
  die Heimatstadt, -̈e home town
die Heimfahrt trip home
heimlich secret, hidden
heiraten to marry; to get married
  die Heirat, -en marriage

heiß hot
*heißen to be called
    wie heißen Sie? what's
      your name?
    das heißt (d.h.) that is,
      i.e.
heizen to heat
*helfen (dat.) to help, give
    help to
hell light, bright
her from (toward the
    speaker)
    wo kommst du her?
      where do you come
      from?
herab down
    herab•setzen to lower
*heraus•finden to find out
der Herbst autumn, fall
herein in; come in!
der Hering, -e herring
der Herr, -en (n-noun) man,
    gentleman, Mr.
    die Herrschaften (pl.)
      ladies and gentlemen
herrlich splendid, magnifi-
    cent
das Herz, -en (gen. des
    Herzens) (n-noun)
    heart
    das Herzklopfen palpita-
      tion of the heart
    herzlich cordial
    herzlos heartless
der Herzog, ⸚e duke
heterogen' heterogeneous
heute today
    heute abend tonight;
      this evening
    heute morgen this
      morning
hier here
    hierher (adv.) here
      (hither); to this place
die Hilfe help, aid
der Himmel, - sky; heaven
hin there (away from the
    speaker)
    ich gehe hin I am going
      there
    hin und her back and
      forth

das Hindernis, -se hindrance,
    obstacle
*hin•kommen (sein) to get
    there
hin•stellen to put, to place
hinten (adv.) in the back
hinter (prep. with dat. or
    acc.) behind
historisch historical
die Hitze heat
das Hobby, -s hobby
hoch high
    (das) Hochdeutsch High
      (Standard) German
    die Hochschule, -n uni-
      versity; institution of
      higher learning
    höher higher
    die höhere Schule
      secondary school,
      Gymnasium
    höchst- highest
    höchstens at the most
    die Höhe, -n height;
      altitude
die Hochzeit, -en wedding
    die Hochzeitsgesell-
      schaft, -en wedding
      party
der Hof, ⸚e yard; court; farm
    der Bauernhof, ⸚e farm
hoffen auf (acc.) to hope for
    hoffentlich (sent. adv.) I
      hope, hopefully
    die Hoffnung, -en hope
höflich polite
    unhöflich impolite
    die Höflichkeit polite-
      ness
holen to get, fetch
homogen' homogeneous
    die Homogenität' homo-
      geneity
hören to hear
    der Hörer, - telephone
      receiver; listener
das Hotel', -s hotel
    der Hotelführer, - hotel
      guide; guidebook
hübsch pretty
der Hügel, - hill
das Huhn, ⸚er chicken

der Hund, -e dog
hundert hundred
der Hunger hunger
    ich habe Hunger I am
      hungry
    hungrig hungry
    ich bin hungrig I am
      hungry
der Hut, ⸚e hat

die Idee', die Ide'en idea
iden'tisch identical
    die Identität', -en iden-
      tity
der Idiot', -en (n-noun) idiot,
    fool
immer always
    immer noch, noch
      immer still
in (prep. with dat. or acc.)
    in
die Industrie', -n industry
    das Industriegebiet, -e
      industrial area
der Ingenieur', -e engineer
    (m.)
    die Ingenieu'rin, -nen
      engineer (f.)
innerhalb (prep. with gen.)
    inside of
instinktiv' instinctive
das Institut', -e institute
intellektuell' intellectual
intelligent' intelligent
interessant' interesting
    uninteressant uninter-
      esting
    interessanterweise in-
      terestingly
    das Interes'se, -n interest
    sich (acc.) interessieren
      für to be interested in
irgendetwas something; any-
    thing
irgendjemand somebody;
    anybody
irgendwo somewhere; any-
    where
iro'nisch ironic
sich (acc.) irren to err, be in
    error
    irr(e) insane

der (die) Irre, -n insane person
(das) Ita′lien Italy
 italie′nisch Italian
 der Italiener, - Italian (m.)
 die Italienierin, -nen Italian (f.)

ja yes
die Jacke, -n jacket
das Jahr, -e year
 jahrelang for years
 die Jahreszeit, -en season
 das Jahrhun′dert, -e century
der Januar January
(das) Ja′pan Japan
 japa′nisch Japanese
 der Japaner, - Japanese (m.)
 die Japanerin, -nen Japanese (f.)
je (jemals) ever
jeder, jede, jedes, pl. **alle** each, every, pl. all
 jedesmal every time
 jedesmal, wenn whenever
jemand somebody, someone
 jemand anders somebody else
jetzt now
der Job, -s job
der Joghurt yogurt
die Jugend (time of) youth
 die Jugendherberge, -n youth hostel
 das Jugendzentrum, die Jugendzentren youth center
(das) Jugoslawien Yugoslavia
 jugoslawisch Yugoslavian
 der Jugoslawe, -n Yugoslavian (m.)
 die Jugoslawin, -nen Yugoslavian (f.)
der Ju′li July
jung young
der Junge, -n (n-noun) boy
der Ju′ni June
juris′tisch legal

der Kaffee coffee
das Kalb, ̈er calf
 das Kalbfleisch veal
 der Kalbsbraten, - veal roast
kalt cold
 die Kälte cold(ness)
die Kamera, -s camera
der Kanton, -e canton (Swiss)
kaputt′ (colloq.) busted, broken
der Karneval carnival, season before Lent
die Karot′te, -n carrot
die Karte, -n card; map; ticket
die Kartof′fel, -n potato
der Käse, - cheese
die Kasse, -n cash register
der Kasten, ̈ box, case
katho′lisch Catholic
 der Katholik′, -en (n-noun) Catholic (m.)
 die Katholi′kin, -nen Catholic (f.)
die Katze, -n cat
kaufen to buy, purchase
 der Kauf, ̈e buy, purchase
 der Käufer, - buyer, purchaser
 das Kaufhaus, ̈er department store
kaum hardly
kein, keine, kein, pl. **keine** no, not any
der Kellner, - waiter
 die Kellnerin, -nen waitress
*****kennen** to know, be acquainted with
 kennen•lernen to meet, to get acquainted with, to get to know
 das Kennzeichen identification symbol; license plate
kichern to giggle
der Kilometer, - kilometer
 der Quadratkilometer, square kilometer
das Kind, -er child

kindlich childlike
das Kino, -s movie theater
 wir gehen ins Kino we are going to the movies
die Kirche, -n church
klar clear
die Klasse, -n class
das Klavier, -e piano
kleiden to dress
 das Kleid, -er dress
 die Kleider (pl.) clothes
klein small
das Klima climate
klingeln to ring (the bell)
*****klingen** to sound
klopfen to knock
knapp scarce, tight
 knapp bei Kasse low on cash
die Kneipe, -n pub
der Knödel, - dumpling
 der Leberknödel, - liver dumpling
 die Leberknödelsuppe liver dumpling soup
kochen to boil; to cook
 der Koch, ̈e cook (m.)
 die Köchin, -nen cook (f.)
der Koffer, - suitcase
das Kolleg′, -s (university) class, lecture
komisch funny; odd; comical
das Komma, -s comma
*****kommen (sein)** to come
komplex′ complex
das Kompliment′, -e compliment
kompliziert complicated
die Konditorei′, -en pastry shop
der König, -e king
*****können** to be able to; to know (a language)
konservativ′ conservative
das Konzert′, -e concert
der Kopf, ̈e head
 die Kopfschmerzen (pl.) headache
 das Kopftuch, ̈er scarf, kerchief
der Korkzieher, - corkscrew
kosten to cost

die Kraft, ⁻e strength; force; power
das Kraftfahrzeug, -e motor vehicle
das Kraftfahrzeugkennzeichen, - license plate
krank sick
das Krankenhaus, ⁻er hospital
die Krankheit, -en illness
die Krankenkasse, -n health insurance, medical plan
die Kreide chalk
der Kreis, -e circle; county
der Landkreis, -e rural county
der Krieg, -e war
kriegen (*colloq.*) to get, receive
der Krimi, -s detective novel; TV cop show
der Kriminal'roman, -e detective novel
die Krise, -n crisis
der Kritiker, - critic
die Krone, -n crown
die Küche, -n kitchen; cuisine
der Kuchen, - cake
der Kugelschreiber, - ballpoint pen
die Kuh, ⁻e cow
die Kultur', -en culture
kulturell' cultural
die Sub'kultur, -en subculture
der Kunde, -n (*n-noun*) customer
die Kunst, ⁻e art
der Künstler, - artist
kurz short
die Kürze shortness; brevity
kürzlich recently
die Kusi'ne, -n cousin (*f.*)
küssen to kiss
der Kuß, die Küsse kiss
die Küste, -n coast
die Kutsche, -n coach; jalopy

das Labor', -s lab
das Laborato'rium, die Laborato'rien laboratory
der Laborant', -en (*n-noun*) lab technician (*m.*)
die Laboran'tin, -nen lab technician (*f.*)
lächeln to smile
lachen to laugh
die Lage, -n situation; site (particular location of a vineyard)
das Land, ⁻er country; land; state
er wohnt auf dem Land he lives in the country
landen (sein) to land
die Landung, -en landing
lang long
lange for a long time
die Länge, -n length
langsam slow
langweilen to bore
langweilig boring
sich (*acc.*) **langweilen** to be bored
*****lassen** leave; let, allow; cause
lateinisch Latin
*****laufen (sein)** to run; to walk
der Läufer, - runner
laut loud
läuten to ring
leben to be alive, live
das Leben life
am Leben sein to be alive
*****ums Leben kommen (sein)** to lose one's life
der Lebensinhalt content of life
die Lebensmittel (*pl.*) groceries, food
das Lebensmittelgeschäft, -e grocery store
die Leber liver
der Leberkäse (kind of) meatloaf
die Leberwurst, ⁻e liverwurst

die Lederwaren (*pl. only*) leather goods
leer empty
legen to lay (flat), place
sich (*acc.*) **legen** to lie down
lehren to teach, instruct
der Lehrer, - teacher (*m.*)
die Lehrerin, -nen teacher (*f.*)
der Lehrling, -e apprentice
leicht easy; light
*****leid tun** to be sorry
es tut mir leid I'm sorry
er tut mir leid I feel sorry for him
*****leiden an** (*dat.*) to suffer from
*****leiden** to tolerate
ich kann sie nicht leiden I can't stand her
leider (*sent. adv.*) unfortunately
*****leihen** to lend; to borrow
ich leihe ihm ein Buch I lend him a book
er leiht das Buch von mir he borrows the book from me
leise quiet(ly)
leiten to lead, direct; to pipe
der Leiter, - head; leader
die Leitung direction, leadership
lernen to learn
*****lesen** to read
der Leser, - reader (*m.*)
die Leserin, -nen reader (*f.*)
letzt- last
leuchten to shine
die Leute (*no sing.*) people
das Licht, -er light
lieben to love
lieb dear
die Liebe love
lieber (*adv.*) rather, preferably
am liebsten (*adv.*) (would like) most of all

der Liebling, -e favorite; darling
Lieblings- favorite
*****liegen** to lie (flat); to be situated
die Linde, -n linden tree
die Li'nie, -n line
link- left
links to the left
der Liter, - liter
die Literatur', -en literature
der Löffel, - spoon
das Lokal', -e restaurant
los loose; going on
was ist hier los? what's going on here?
was ist los mit dir? what's the matter with you
lösen to solve; to dissolve
der Löwe, -n (*n-noun*) lion
die Luft, -e air
*****lügen** to lie
der Lügner, - liar
die Lust desire
ich habe keine Lust I don't feel like it

machen to do; to make
mach's gut so long; take care; see you
das Mädchen, - girl
die Mahlzeit, -en meal
der Mai May
mal once; times; for a change
mal (= einmal) once
diesmal, dieses Mal this time
man (*dat.* **einem,** *acc.* **einen**) (*indef. third-person pron.*) you, we, people, they, one
mancher (**der**-word) many a
manchmal sometimes
der Mann, -er man; husband
der Mantel, - coat
das Märchen, - fairy tale
die Margari'ne margarine
die Mark (*no pl.*) mark (money)
DM = die Deutsche

Mark (basic unit of West German currency)
der Markt, -e market
der Marktplatz, -e market square
der Supermarkt, -e supermarket
die Marmela'de, -n (any kind of) jam
der März (month of) March
die Maschi'ne, -n machine; airplane
das Maß, -e measure, measurement
die Mathematik' mathematics
die Mauer, -n (outside) wall
die Maus, -e mouse
der Mechaniker, - mechanic
die Medizin' medicine; science of medicine
das Meer, -e ocean
das Mehl flour
die Mehlspeise, -n dish made with flour; dessert (Austrian)
mehr more
mehr als more than
nicht mehr no longer
mehrere several
die Meile, -n mile
die Quadrat'meile, -n square mile
meinen to think, express an opinion; to say
die Meinung, -en opinion
meist- most
am meisten most
meistens in most cases
melden to report
sich (*acc.*) **melden** to answer (the phone); to report
die Menge, -n lot; crowd
die Mensa, die Mensen student cafeteria
der Mensch, -en (*n-noun*) human being, person
kein Mensch nobody
menschlich human
die Menschlichkeit humaneness, humanity

das Menü, -s complete dinner (i.e., not à la carte)
*****messen** to measure
das Messer, - knife
der (*or* **das**) **Meter, -** meter
der Metzger, - butcher
die Metzgerei, -en butcher shop
die Metzgersfrau, -en butcher's wife
die Milch (*no pl.*) milk
die Militär'regierung, -en military government
die Milliar'de, -n billion
die Million', -en million
der Millionär', -e millionaire
mindestens at least
die Minu'te, -n minute
mischen to mix
mit (*prep. with dat.*) with
*****mit•bringen** to bring (along)
*****mit•fahren** (sein) to ride with, come along
*****mit•gehen** (sein) to go with, come along
*****mit•nehmen** to take along
das Mitglied, -er member
das Fami'lienmitglied, -er family member
der Mittag, -e noon
das Mittagessen, - noonday meal, dinner
die Mitte middle, center
(das) Mitteleuropa Central Europe
der Mitteleuropäer, - Central European
mitteleuropäisch Central European
mitteleuropäische Zeit (MEZ) Central European time
mitten in in the middle of
die Mitternacht midnight
der Mittwoch, -e Wednesday
möblieren to furnish (a room)

die **Möbel** (pl.) furniture
modern' modern
*__mögen__ to like to
möglich possible
    unmöglich impossible
    möglicherweise possibly
    die **Möglichkeit, -en**
      possibility
der **Moment', -e** moment
der **Monat, -e** month
der **Montag, -e** Monday
der **Morgen, -** morning
    morgens in the morn-
      ing, mornings
    (**guten**) **Morgen** good
      morning
    morgen tomorrow
    morgen abend tomor-
      row night
    morgen früh tomorrow
      morning
die **Mosel** Moselle River
    der **Moselwein, -e**
      Moselle wine
der **Motor', -en** motor
müde tired
    die **Müdigkeit** tiredness
der **Müller, -** miller
mündlich oral(ly)
das **Muse'um, die Muse'en**
    museum
die **Musik'** music
    musizieren to make
      music
*__müssen__ to have to
die **Mutter, ⁻** mother
    mütterlich motherly

na well
nach (prep. with dat.) to,
    toward; after
    nach wie vor as always
der **Nachbar, -n** (n-noun)
    neighbor
nachdem (conj.) after
*__nach•denken__ to reflect
    *__nach•denken über__ (acc.)
      to think about, medi-
      tate on
*__nach•gehen__ (sein) to be
    (run) slow (of a clock)

*__vor•gehen__ (sein) to be
    (run) fast
nachher afterwards, later
der **Nachmittag, -e** afternoon
    nachmittags in the
      afternoon
die **Nachricht, -en** report,
    message
    die **Nachrichten** (pl.)
      news (radio, TV, etc.)
nach•schicken to forward
*__nach•sehen__ to check, inves-
    tigate
nächst- next
    nächstens in the near
      future
die **Nacht, ⁻e** night
    nachts at night
    eines Nachts one night
der **Nachteil, -e** disadvantage
der **Nachtisch, -e** dessert
nackt naked, nude
nah near, close by
    die **Nähe** vicinity, prox-
      imity, closeness
    in der Nähe nearby
der **Name, -n** (gen. **des**
    Namens) (n-noun)
    name
nämlich to be specific; you
    see; namely
die **Natur'** nature
    natür'lich natural; natu-
      rally, of course
der **Nebel, -** fog
    neblig foggy
neben (prep. with dat. or
    acc.) beside, next to
    nebenan next door
    nebeneinander next to
      each other, side by side
*__nehmen__ to take
nein no
    nee (colloq.) no
*__nennen__ to call; to name
der **Nerv, -en** nerve
    nervös nervous
    die **Nervosität'** nervous-
      ness
nett nice
neu new

neun nine
    neunzehn nineteen
    neunzig ninety
neutral' neutral
nicht not
nichts nothing
nie (niemals) never, not ever
    nie mehr never again
die **Niederlande** (pl.) The
    Netherlands
niedrig low
niemand nobody
    niemand anders nobody
      else
nirgends nowhere
das **Niveau, -s** level
noch still
    noch ein one more, an
      additional
    noch nicht not yet
    noch nie never yet
der **Norden** north
    nördlich northern
    die **Nordsee** North Sea
normal' normal
    normalerweise normally
(**das**) **Norwegen** Norway
    norwegisch Norwegian
    der **Norweger, -** Nor-
      wegian (m.)
    die **Norwegerin, -nen**
      Norwegian (f.)
nötig necessary
der **November** November
die **Nudel, -n** noodle
die **Null, -en** zero
die **Nummer, -n** number
    das **Nummernschild, -er**
      license plate
nun now; (sent. adv.) well
nur only

ob whether; if
oben (adv.) up, above, up-
    stairs
der **Ober, -** waiter
das **Obst** (no pl.) fruit (col-
    lective noun)
obwohl even though, al-
    though
der **Ochse, -n** (n-noun) ox

das Ochsenfleisch beef
oder or
der Ofen, ⁻ oven, stove
offen open
öffentlich public
offiziell′ official
öffnen to open
oft often
ohne (*prep. with acc.*) without
der Oktober October
das Öl, -e oil
die Oma, -s grandma
der Opa, -s grandpa
der Onkel, - uncle
die Oper, -n opera
die Oran′ge, -n orange
der Orangensaft orange juice
das Orches′ter, - orchestra
das Kammerorchester, chamber orchestra
die Ordnung, -en order
in Ordnung all right, OK
orientieren to orient
der Ort, -e town; place
der Ortsrand, ⁻er edge of town
die Ortszeit local time
der Osten east
östlich eastern
der Ostblock East Bloc
die Ostsee Baltic Sea
(das) Ostern Easter
die Osterferien Easter vacation
(das) Österreich Austria
österreichisch Austrian
der Österreicher, - Austrian (*m.*)
die Österreicherin, -nen Austrian (*f.*)

das Paar, -e pair, couple
ein Paar Schuhe a pair of shoes
ein paar a few, some
packen to pack
das Paket, -e package
der Park, -s park
parken to park

das Parkhaus, ⁻er parking garage
der Parkplatz, ⁻e parking lot
die Partei′, -en (political) party
die Party, -s party
der Paß, die Pässe passport
die Paßkontrolle, -n passport control
passieren (sein) (*impers.*) (*dat.*) to happen
die Pause, -n pause, stop, break, intermission
das Pech bad luck
die Pension′, -en bed and breakfast inn
die Perle, -n pearl
die Person′, -en person
der Personenzug, ⁻e local train
persön′lich personal(ly)
pessimistisch pessimistic
der Pfeffer pepper
der Pfarrer, - minister, pastor
der Pfennig, -e penny
das Pfingsten Pentecost
die Pflanze, -n plant
die Pflicht, -en duty
das Pfund, -e pound
das Phänomen′, -e phenomenon
die Philosophie′, -n philosophy
der Philosoph′, -en (*n-noun*) philosopher (*m.*)
die Philoso′phin, -nen philosopher (*f.*)
photographie′ren (*also:* **fotografieren**) to photograph
die Physik′ physics
der Phy′siker, - physicist (*m.*)
die Phy′sikerin, -nen physicist (*f.*)
der Platz, ⁻e place; seat
Platz nehmen to sit down, have a seat
plaudern to chat
plötzlich suddenly

(das) Polen Poland
polnisch Polish
der Pole, -n (*n-noun*) Pole (*m.*)
die Polin, -nen Pole (*f.*)
die Politik′ politics
poli′tisch political
die Politik′wissenschaft political science
die Polizei′ (*no pl.*) police
der Polizist′, -en (*n-noun*) policeman
die Polizis′tin, -nen policewoman
die Post mail; post office
das Postamt, ⁻er post office
die Postkarte, -n postcard
die Postleitzahl, -en zip code
praktisch practical
der Präsident, -en (*n-noun*) president (*m.*)
die Präsidentin, -nen president (*f.*)
der Preis, -e price; prize
prima excellent, tops, first-rate
primitiv′ primitive
das Prinzip′, die Prinzi′pien principle
privat′ private
das Problem′, -e problem
die Produktion, -en production
der Profes′sor, die Professo′ren professor (*m.*)
die Professo′rin, -nen professor (*f.*)
das Programm′, -e program
der Programmierer programmer
programmieren to program
das Projekt′, -e project
promovieren to get a doctorate
Prosit (Prost) cheers! here's to you!
protestan′tisch protestant

der **Protestant'**, **-en** (*n-noun*) Protestant (*m.*)
die **Protestan'tin**, **-nen** Protestant (*f.*)
provinziell' provincial
das **Prozent**, **-e** percent
die **Prüfung**, **-en** examination
die **Psychologie'** psychology
der **Punkt**, **-e** point, dot
pünktlich on time; punctually
die **Pünktlichkeit** punctuality
putzen to clean

der **Quark** soft curd cheese
der **Quatsch** (*colloq.*) nonsense
die **Quittung**, **-en** receipt

das **Rad**, **˙er** wheel; bicycle
das **Fahrrad**, **˙er** bicycle
das **Motor'rad**, **˙er** motorcycle
das **Radio**, **-s** radio
rapid' rapid
der **Rappen**, **-** (smallest unit of Swiss currency)
rasen (**sein**) to race, to speed
sich (*acc.*) **rasieren** to shave
*****raten** to advice, counsel; to guess
der **Rat** (*no pl.*) advice, counsel; council
der **Rat**, **˙e** counselor
das **Rathaus**, **˙er** town hall, city hall
der **Ratskeller**, **-** restaurant in city hall
rauchen to smoke
der **Raucher**, **-** smoker
der **Nichtraucher**, **-** nonsmoker
räuchern to smoke (meat)
der **Raum**, **˙e** room; space
*****raus•fahren** (= **hinaus•fahren**) (**sein**) to go out, drive out
reagieren auf (*acc.*) to react to
rechnen to figure, to calculate

der **Rechner**, **-** calculator, computer
die **Rechnung**, **-en** bill, account
recht- right
rechts to the right
das ist mir recht that's OK with me
rechteckig rectangular
*****recht•haben** to be right
rechtzeitig on time
reden to talk, speak
der **Redner**, **-** speaker
die **Rede**, **-n** speech
*****eine Rede halten** to give a speech
regelmäßig regular
regieren to govern
die **Regierung**, **-en** government
regnen to rain
der **Regen** (*no pl.*) rain
der **Regenmantel**, **˙** raincoat
der **Rehrücken**, **-** saddle of venison
reich rich
der **Reifen**, **-** tire
der **Hinterreifen**, **-** rear tire
der **Vorderreifen**, **-** front tire
die **Reihe**, **-n** row; series
*****rein•lassen** (= **herein•lassen**) to let in
der **Reis** rice
reisen (**sein**) to travel
die **Reise**, **-n** trip
die **Durchreise** transit
auf der Durchreise in transit
die **Geschäftsreise**, **-n** business trip
eine Reise machen to take a trip
der **Reisende**, **-n** traveler
der **Reisescheck**, **-s** traveler's check
die **Rekla'me** advertising
relativ relative(ly)
die **Religion'**, **-en** religion

*****rennen** (**sein**) to run
reparieren to repair
die **Republik'**, **-en** republic
die **Bundesrepublik Deutschland** Federal Republic of Germany
die **Deutsche Demokratische Republik** German Democratic Republic
der **Republikaner**, **-** Republican (*m.*)
die **Republikanerin**, **-nen** Republican (*f.*)
das **Restaurant'**, **-s** restaurant
das **Rezept**, **-e** recipe
der **Rhein** Rhine River
der **Rheinwein**, **-e** Rhine wine
richtig correct, right
die **Richtung**, **-en** direction
das **Rippchen**, **-** cured and smoked pork chop
der **Rock**, **˙e** skirt; jacket
die **Rolle**, **-n** role
der **Roman'**, **-e** novel
der **Romanist'**, **-en** (*n-noun*) student of Romance languages
romantisch romantic
der **Römer**, **-** Roman
die **Rose**, **-n** rose
rosig rosy
rot red
der **Rotkohl** red cabbage
der **Rucksack**, **˙e** backpack
*****rufen** to shout, call out
die **Ruhe** rest, quietude
laß mich in Ruhe leave me alone
ruhig quiet, restful; (*sent. adv.*) it won't bother me, I'll stay calm about it
(**das**) **Rumänien** Romania
rund round
der **Rundfunk** radio, broadcasting
runter (*adv.*) (= **hinunter, herunter**) down
(**das**) **Rußland** Russia

russisch Russian
der Russe, -n (n-noun)
Russian (m.)
die Russin, -nen Russian (f.)

die Sache, -n matter; thing
der Saft, ⸚e juice
sagen to say; to tell
sag mal tell me, say
der Salat, -e salad
salzen to salt
das Salz (no pl.) salt
der Samstag, -e Saturday
sarkastisch sarcastic
sauer sour
das Sauerkraut sauerkraut
schade too bad, what a shame
das Schaf, -e sheep
der Schafskäse sheep's cheese
*schaffen to create, to make; to accomplish, to manage
die Schallplatte, -n record (music)
schauen to look
auf Wiederschauen good-bye (Bavarian, Austrian)
die Scheibe, -n (glass) pane, windshield; slice
*scheiden to separate; to divide
*sich (acc.) scheiden lassen to get a divorce
die Scheidung, -en divorce
*scheinen to seem; to shine
schenken to give (as a present)
schicken to send
das Schiff, -e ship
*schi•laufen (sein) to ski
das Schild, -er sign
der Schilling, -e (öS) schilling (Austrian currency)
der Schinken, - ham
*schlafen to sleep

*schlafen gehen (sein) to go to bed
der Schlaf sleep
*schlagen to hit, strike, beat
der Schlag, ⸚e hit, strike; stroke; bang
schlecht bad
*schließen to close; to end; to conclude
schließlich finally, after all
schlimm bad
das Schloß, die Schlösser castle
der Schluß, die Schlüsse conclusion, end
der Schlüssel, - key
der Hausschlüssel, - house key
schmecken to taste
schmücken to decorate
der Schnaps, ⸚e (hard) liquor, schnapps
*schneiden to cut
schneien to snow
schnell fast
der Schnitt, -e cut
das Schnitzel, - cutlet
die Schokola'de, -n chocolate
schön pretty, beautiful
die Schönheit, -en beauty
schon already, earlier than expected
der Schrank, ⸚e cupboard; closet
*schreiben to write
die Schreibmaschine, -n typewriter
der Schreibtisch, -e desk
*schreien to scream
die Schrift, -en writing
schriftlich in writing
der Schriftsteller, - writer, author
der Schuh, -e shoe
die Schule, -n school
der Schüler, - pupil, (Gymnasium) student (m.)
die Schülerin, -nen pupil, student (f.)

die Schulter, -n shoulder
schütteln to shake
den Kopf shütteln to shake one's head
(das) Schwaben Swabia
schwäbisch Swabian
der Schwabe, -n (n-noun) Swabian (m.)
die Schwäbin, -nen Swabian (f.)
schwach weak
die Schwäche, -n weakness
schwarz black
der Schwarzwald Black Forest
(das) Schweden Sweden
schwedisch Swedish
der Schwede, -n (n-noun) Swede (m.)
die Schwedin, -nen Swede (f.)
*schweigen to be silent
das Schwein, -e pig, swine
der Schweinebraten, - pork roast
das Schweinefleisch pork
die Schweiz Switzerland
schweizerisch Swiss
der Schweizer - Swiss (m.)
die Schweizerin, -nen Swiss (f.)
schwer heavy; difficult, hard
die Schwester, -n sister
schwierig difficult, hard
die Schwierigkeit, -en difficulty, trouble
*schwimmen (sein) to swim
*schwimmen gehen (sein) to go swimming
sechs six
sechzehn sixteen
sechzig sixty
der See, Se'en lake
die See (no pl.) sea, ocean
segeln (sein) to sail
*sehen to see
sehr very
*sein (sein) to be

seit (*prep. with dat.*) since
  seit einer Woche for a week
  seitdem (*adv.*) since then, since that time
  seitdem, seit (*conj.*) since
die Seite, -n page; side
  einseitig one-sided
  die Seitenstraße, -n side street
das Sekretariat', -e department office
die Sekun'de, -n second
selbst, selber -self; even
selbstverständlich self-evident, obvious, of course
der Sellerie celery (root)
selten rare, rarely
das Semester, - semester
das Seminar', -e seminar
*****senden (sandte, gesandt)** to send
  senden (sendete, gesendet) to broadcast
  der Sender, - radio station, transmitter
  die Sendung, -en broadcast, transmission
der September September
servieren to serve
setzen to set; to seat
  sich (*acc.*) **setzen** to sit down
sich (*refl. pron.*) himself; herself; itself; oneself; themselves
sichern to secure, make safe
  sicher certain, certainly; sure
  die Sicherheit safety, security; certainty
sieben seven
  siebzehn seventeen
  siebzig seventy
die Siedlung, -en housing development
der Sieger, - winner
*****singen** to sing
*****sinken (sein)** to sink
  der Sinn, -e sense

die Sitte, -n custom
*****sitzen** to sit
  *****sitzen•bleiben (sein)** to stay seated; to stay behind (in school), to have to repeat a grade
  der Sitz, -e seat
  der Sitzplatz, ⸚e seat
so so
soe'ben just (now); this moment
das Sofa, -s sofa
sofort right away, immediately
sogar even
der Sohn, ⸚e son
solch- such
der Soldat', -en (*n-noun*) soldier
sollen to be supposed to
der Sommer, - summer
  die Sommerzeit daylight saving time
sondern but
der Sonnabend, -e (= **Samstag**) Saturday
die Sonne, -n sun
der Sonntag, -e Sunday
  sonntags on Sundays
sonst otherwise
  sonst nichts nothing else
sowieso anyhow, in any case
sozial' social
soziali'stisch socialist
sozusagen so to speak, as it were
(das) Spanien Spain
  spanisch Spanish
  der Spanier, - Spaniard (*m.*)
  die Spanierin, -nen Spanish woman (*f.*)
sparen to save
der Spaß, ⸚e fun; joke
  Spaß haben to have fun
  Spaß machen to joke
  das macht Spaß that's fun
spät late
  spätestens at the latest
die Spätzle (*pl.*) kind of noodle (Swabian specialty)

*****spazieren•gehen (sein)** to go for a walk
die Speisekarte, -n menu
der Spezialist', -en (*n-noun*) specialist
die Spezialität', -en specialty
der Spiegel, - mirror
  das Spiegelei, -er fried egg
spielen to play
der Spinat spinach
der Spion, -e spy
der Sport (*no pl.*) sport(s)
  Sport treiben to exercise
  das Sportgeschäft, -e sporting goods store
  der Sportler, - athlete (*m.*)
  die Sportlerin, -nen athlete (*f.*)
  sportlich athletic
die Sprache, -n language
  deutschsprachig German-speaking
*****sprechen** to speak
  *****sprechen über** (*acc.*) to talk about
  *****sprechen von** to talk about
*****springen (sein)** to jump
  der Sprung, ⸚e jump
der Staat, -en state
die Stadt, ⸚e town, city
  städtisch municipal, urban
  die Stadtverwaltung, -en city administration
  die Innenstadt inner city, downtown
stammen aus to come from, be a native of
der Stammkunde, -n (*n-noun*) regular customer
der Stammtisch, -e table reserved for regular guests
stark strong
  die Stärke, -n strength
starten (sein) to start
*****statt•finden** to take place; occur

die Stauung, -en traffic jam, back-up, congestion
stecken to stick; to put
***stehen** to stand
  ***stehen•bleiben (sein)** to stop; to remain standing
***stehlen** to steal
***steigen (sein)** to climb
der Stein, -e stone
  steinig stony
stellen to put, place (upright)
  sich (*acc.*) **stellen** to place oneself; to stand (up)
  die Stelle, -n place, spot, position
  an deiner Stelle in your place
  die Stellung, -en position
***sterben (sein)** to die
  sterblich mortal
die Stereoanlage, -n stereo system
still quiet, still
  die Stille quietness
  der Stillstand standstill
  zum Stillstand kommen to (come to a) stop
die Stimme, -n voice; vote
stimmen (*impers.*) to be correct
  das stimmt that is correct
das Stipen'dium, die Stipen'dien stipend, scholarship, fellowship
der Stock, *pl.* die Stockwerke floor (of a building)
  im ersten Stock on the second floor
  achtstöckig with eight stories
stolz proud
  stolz sein auf (*acc.*) to be proud of
stören to disturb
***stoßen** to push; to shove; to strike
der Strafzettel, - traffic ticket
die Straße, -n street

die Straßenkarte, -n road map
***streichen** to spread
die Struktur', -en structure
die Stube, -n room
das Stück, -e piece; (theatrical) play
studie'ren to study, to attend a university, to be a student (at a university)
  der Student', -en (*n-noun*) university student (*m.*)
  die Studen'tin, -nen university student (*f.*)
  das Studentenheim, -e student residence, dormitory
  das Studium, die Studien (period of) study
  der Studienrat, ¨e *Gymnasium* teacher (*m.*)
  die Studienrätin, -nen *Gymnasium* teacher (*f.*)
der Stuhl, ¨e chair
die Stunde, -n hour
  stundenlang for hours
der Sturm, ¨e storm
suchen to look for, search
(das) Südamerika South America
der Süden south
  südlich southern
die Suppe, -n soup
süß sweet
sympa'thisch likeable
das System', -e system
die Szene, -n scene

die Tafel, -n blackboard
der Tag, -e day
  (guten) Tag hello
  den ganzen Tag all day
  tagelang for days
tanken to get gas, fill up
  der Tank, -s tank
  die Tankstelle, -n gas station
  der Tankwart, -e gas station attendant

die Tante, -n aunt
tanzen to dance
  der Tanz, ¨e dance
die Tasse, -n cup
tatsächlich in fact, indeed
taufen to baptize
  die Taufe, -n baptism
tausend thousand
das Taxi, -s taxi
technisch technical
  der Techniker, - engineer, technician
die Technische Hochschule institute of technology
der Tee (*no pl.*) tea
teilen to divide
  geteilt durch divided by
  der Teil, -e part, piece
telefonie'ren to talk on the telephone, to make a telephone call
  das Telefon, -e telephone
  das Telefongespräch, -e telephone conversation
das Telegramm', -e telegram
der Teller, - plate
die Temperatur', -en temperature
das Tennis tennis
  der Tennisschuh, -e tennis shoe
die Terras'se, -n terrace
das Testament', -e testament; (last) will
teuer expensive
das Thea'ter, - theater
das Thema, die Themen topic; theme
die Theorie', -n theory
das Tier, -e animal
der Tisch, -e table
  den Tisch decken to set the table
der Titel, - title
die Tochter, ¨ daughter
der Tod death
  tot dead
toll crazy; great
der Tourist', -en (*n-noun*) tourist

der Touris'mus tourism
die Tradition', -en tradition
traditionell' traditional
*tragen to carry; to wear
(clothes)
träumen to dream
traurig sad
die Trauung, -en marriage
ceremony, wedding
*treffen to hit; to meet
der Treffpunkt, -e meet-
ing place
trennen to separate
die Treppe, -n stairs; stair-
case
*trinken to drink
das Trinkgeld, -er tip
trotz (prep. with gen.) in
spite of
trotzdem nevertheless
die Tschechoslowakei'
Czechoslovakia
tschüß (colloq.) bye
*tun to do
die Tür, -en door
die Türkei' Turkey
türkisch Turkish
der Türke, -n (n-noun)
Turk (m.)
die Türkin, -nen Turk (f.)
der Typ, -en type; model

die U-Bahn, -en (= die Untergrundbahn) subway
üben to practice
über (prep. with dat. or
acc.) over
überall everywhere
überfüllt overcrowded, over-
flowing
überhaupt in general; altogether
überhaupt nicht not at
all
überlegen to wonder, con-
sider
sich (dat.) überlegen to
think (meditate); to
wonder
übermorgen day after to-
morrow

überraschen to surprise
überraschend surprising(ly)
überreichen to present
übersetzen to translate
die Übersetzung, -en
translation
überzeugen to convince
übrigens by the way, inci-
dentally
die Übung, -en exercise;
practice
die Uhr, -en clock, watch
um ein Uhr, um eins at
one o'clock
der Uhrmacher, - watch-
maker
um (prep. with acc.) at;
around
um . . . herum around
um . . . willen (prep.
with gen.) for the
sake of
die Umgebung surroundings
umgekehrt vice versa, conversely
um•rechnen to convert
(currency)
*sich (acc.) um•sehen to
look around
umsonst in vain; for
nothing
*um•steigen (sein) to change
(trains, etc.)
*sich (acc.) um•ziehen to
change (clothes)
*um•ziehen (sein) to
move (from one place
to another)
unbedingt absolutely
und and
der Unfall, ¨e accident
(das) Ungarn Hungary
ungarisch Hungarian
der Ungar, -n (n-noun)
Hungarian (m.)
die Ungarin, -nen Hun-
garian (f.)
ungeduldig impatient
ungefähr approximately
unglaublich unbelievable,
incredible

das Unglück, -e bad luck,
misfortune; accident
unglücklich unhappy
die Universität', -en university
der Unsinn nonsense
unten (adv.) down, down
below; downstairs
unter (prep. with dat. or
acc.) under
*unterbrechen to interrupt
*unter•bringen to house
untereinander among each
other, among them-
selves
unterrichten to instruct,
teach
der Unterricht instruction
der Unterschied, -e difference
*unterschreiben to sign (a
letter, document, etc.)
unzugänglich impenetrable
die Urbanisierung urbanization
der Urlaub leave; vacation
usw. (und so weiter) and so
on, etc.

der Vater, ¨ father
sich (acc.) verändern to
change
die Veränderung, -en
change
verarbeiten to process
die Verarbeitung pro-
cessing
verbessern to improve,
make better; to
correct
*verbieten to prohibit
das Verbot, -e prohibi-
tion
verboten forbidden, not
allowed, prohibited
*verbringen to spend (time)
verdammt damned
verdammt noch mal
dammit
verdienen to earn; to deserve
Geld verdienen to make
money

vereinigen to unify, unite
   die Vereinigten Staaten United States
*****sich** (*acc.*) **verfahren** to get lost (driving)
die Vergangenheit past
*****vergessen** to forget
   vergeßlich forgetful
   unvergeßlich unforgettable
*****vergleichen mit** to compare with
das Vergnügen, - pleasure
verheiratet sein (mit) to be married (to)
verkaufen to sell
   der Verkauf, ̈e sale
   der Verkäufer, - salesman
   die Verkäuferin, -nen saleswoman
der Verkehr traffic
   der Berufsverkehr commuter traffic, rush hour
der Verlag, -e publishing house
verlangen to ask for, demand
*****verlassen** (*with acc. obj.*) to leave
   *****sich** (*acc.*) **verlassen auf** (*acc.*) to rely on
*****sich** (*acc.*) **verlaufen** to get lost (walking), to lose one's way
verletzen to hurt (someone)
sich (*acc.*) **verlieben in** (*acc.*) to fall in love with
   verliebt sein in (*acc.*) to be in love with, to be infatuated
*****verlieren** to lose
sich (*acc.*) **verloben mit** to get engaged to
   verlobt sein mit to be engaged to
   der (die) Verlobte, -n fiancé(e)
   die Verlobung, -en engagement
der Verlust, -e loss

das Vermögen, - fortune, estate
die Vernunft (*no pl.*) (power of) reason
   vernünftig reasonable
verpassen to miss, to fail to make a connection
verreisen (sein) to go on a trip
verrückt crazy
verschieden different
die Verschmutzung pollution
die Verspätung, -en delay
   Verspätung haben to be late (train, plane, etc.)
*****versprechen** to promise
*****verstehen** to understand
   der Verstand (*no pl.*) reason, intelligence
versuchen to try
   der Versuch, -e experiment; attempt, try
verteilen to distribute
*****vertreiben** to displace, chase away
   der (die) Vertriebene, -n expellee
der Verwaltungsbezirk, -e administrative district
verwandt related
   der (die) Verwandte, -n relative
*****verwenden** to use, make use of, put to use
verwöhnen to spoil, pamper (someone); to take good care (of someone)
*****verzeihen** to forgive
   Verzeihung! excuse me, I'm sorry
verzollen to declare; to pay duty on
verzweifeln to despair
   verzweifelt in despair
der Vetter, -n cousin (*m.*)
viel much
vielleicht perhaps
vier four
   vierzehn fourteen
   vierzehn Tage two weeks; fourteen days

vierzig forty
das Viertel, - quarter
das Volk, ̈er people
der Volkswagen, - (der VW, -s) Volkswagen
voll full; crowded
   voll machen to fill up
völlig completely
von (*prep. with dat.*) from
   von . . . aus from (and out of)
vor (*prep. with dat. or acc.*) in front of; ago (*only dat.*)
   vor allem above all, particularly
voraus ahead
   *****voraus•fahren (sein)** to drive ahead
vorbei past
   *****vorbei•gehen (sein)** to pass by
sich (*acc.*) **vor•bereiten auf** (*acc.*) to prepare for
   die Vorbereitung (auf) preparation (for)
vorgestern the day before yesterday
vorher before; earlier
   ein Jahr vorher a year earlier
vorhin a while ago
*****vor•kommen (sein)** to appear
*****vor•lesen** to read aloud
   die Vorlesung, -en lecture (university)
der Vormittag, -e forenoon
vorne (*adv.*) in front
der Vorort, -e suburb
*****vor•schlagen** to suggest, propose
   der Vorschlag, ̈e proposal
die Vorsicht precaution
   vorsichtig careful
sich (*acc. or dat.*) **vor•stellen** to introduce; to imagine
   ich stelle mich vor I introduce myself
   ich stelle mir vor I imagine

die Vorstellung, -en introduction; (theater) performance; idea, representation
der Vorteil, -e advantage
der Vortrag, ⸚e (formal) lecture
die Vorwahl(nummer, -n) area code
vorwärts forward

*****wachsen (sein)** to grow, increase
der Wagen, - car; cart
wählen to choose, decide; elect; dial (telephone)
selbst wählen dial direct
wahnsinnig insane, crazy
wahr true
nicht wahr? isn't that so?, aren't you?, don't you?, etc.
die Wahrheit truth
während (*prep. with gen.*) during
während (*conj.*) while
wahrscheinlich probably
der Wald, ⸚er forest
die Wand, ⸚e wall (of a room)
wandern (sein) to hike
die Wanderung, -en hike
wann at what time, when
warm warm
die Wärme warmth
warten auf (*acc.*) to wait for
warum why
was (= **etwas**) something
was what
was für what kind of
*****waschen** to wash
die Waschmaschine, -n washing machine
das Wasser water
das WC, -s (water closet), toilet
wechseln to change (money)
wecken to awaken (someone)
weder . . . noch neither . . . nor
weg away

*****weg•fahren (sein)** to leave, depart (by car, etc.), drive away
*****weg•gehen (sein)** to go away, leave
der Weg, -e way; path
wegen (*prep. with gen.*) because of
weich soft
(die) Weihnachten Christmas
die Weihnachtsferien Christmas vacation
weil because
die Weile while, short time
der Wein, -e wine
der Weinbau wine-making, viticulture
der Weinberg, -e vineyard
der Weinkenner, - judge of wines, wine connoisseur
weinen to cry, shed tears
weiß white
weit far
weiter further
welcher, welche, welches, *pl.* **welche** which
die Welt, -en world
weltbekannt world-famous
der Weltkrieg, -e world war
weltlich worldly, secular
wenig little
wenige (*pl.*) few
weniger less; minus
wenigstens at least
wenn when; if; whenever
wer who
*****werden (sein)** to become
*****werfen** to throw
werktags weekdays
der Westen west
westlich western
das Wetter (*no pl.*) weather
der Wetterbericht, -e weather report
wichtig important
wie how
wieso why, how come

wieder again
*****wieder•sehen** to see again
auf Wiedersehen see you again; good-bye
auf Wiederschaun (Austrian for **auf Wiedersehen**)
auf Wiederhören good-bye (telephone)
wiederholen to repeat
*****wieder•kommen (sein)** to return
die Wiese, -n meadow
wieviel how much
wieviel Uhr what time
wild wild
der Wind, -e wind
der Winter, - winter
winzig tiny
wirklich real; really
die Wirklichkeit, -en reality
der Wirt, -e landlord; innkeeper
die Wirtin, -nen landlady; innkeeper
das Wirtshaus, ⸚er inn, restaurant
die Wirtschaft (*no pl.*) economy
das Wirtschaftswunder economic miracle
*****wissen** to know (facts)
das Wissen (*no pl.*) knowledge
das Unwissen ignorance
wo where
die Woche, -n week
wochenlang for weeks
das Wochenende, -n weekend
woher (wo . . . her) where from
wohin (wo . . . hin) where (to)
wohl (*sent. adv.*) probably
sich (*acc.*) **wohl fühlen** to feel well
das Wohl well-being, good health

auf Ihr Wohl to your health

der Wohlstand wealth, affluence, prosperity

wohnen to live, reside

die Wohnung, -en apartment

der Wolf, ⸚e wolf

wollen to intend to

das Wort, ⸚er {or **-e**} word

das Wörterbuch, ⸚er dictionary

das Wunder, - miracle

wunderbar marvelous, wonderful

wunderschön wonderful, very beautiful

sich {acc.} **wundern** to be amazed

wünschen to wish

der Wunsch, ⸚e wish

die Wurst, ⸚e sausage

das Würstchen, - frankfurter

die Zahl, -en number, figure

die gerade Zahl even number

die ungerade Zahl odd number

zahlen, bezahlen to pay

zählen to count

der Zahn, ⸚e tooth

der Zahnarzt, ⸚e dentist

der Zaun, ⸚e fence

zehn ten

zeigen to show

die Zeit, -en time

zur Zeit at the moment, right now; for the time being

das Zeitalter, - age, epoch

eine Zeitlang a short time

die Zeitschrift, -en magazine; journal

die Zeitung, en newspaper

das Zelt, -e tent

der Zement cement

das Zentrum, die Zentren center

zerstören to destroy

das Zeugnis, -se report card, school report

***ziehen** to pull **(haben)**; to move {from one place to another} **(sein)**

ziemlich rather

die Zigaret'te, -n cigarette

das Zimmer, - room

das Eßzimmer, - dining room

das Schlafzimmer, - bedroom

das Wohnzimmer, - living room

der Zirkus, -se circus

der Zoll, ⸚e customs; duty

die Zollnummer, -n customs plate {for car}

der Zoo, -s zoo

zu {prep. with dat.} to; at; {adv.} too; {adj.} closed

der Zucker sugar

zuerst' at first

der Zufall, ⸚e chance, accident

***zufrieden sein mit** to be satisfied with

der Zug, ⸚e train

der (die) Zugewanderte, -n immigrant

zugleich at the same time, simultaneously

***zu•kommen auf** {acc.} **(sein)** to approach

die Zukunft {no pl.} future

zuletzt last, lastly, finally

zu•machen to close, shut

***zu•nehmen** to increase; to gain weight

zurück back

zurückhaltend reserved

zusammen together

der Zustrom, ⸚e influx

zuviel too much

zwanzig twenty

zwar indeed, to be sure

zwei two

zweit- second

zweitens second{ly}

***zwingen** to force

zwischen {prep. with dat. or acc.} between

zwölf twelve

VOCABULARY: ENGLISH-GERMAN

This list includes only words that appear in the Express-in-German exercises. Only basic forms are listed.

able: to be able to können
above über
across über
to act (as if) tun (als ob)
again wieder
against gegen
ago vor
airport der Flughafen
all alle
allowed: to be allowed erlaubt sein
alone allein
along mit
already schon
also auch
although obwohl
always immer
annoyed: to be annoyed with sich ärgern über
another noch ein
to answer antworten
(not) anything nichts
apartment die Wohnung
arm der Arm
around um; gegen
to arrive ankommen
to ask fragen; bitten
astonished: to be astonished erstaunt sein
at an
aunt die Tante
Austria Österreich
auto mechanic der Automechaniker
autumn der Herbst

back zurück
bad schlecht
bank die Bank, -en
to be sein
beautiful schön
because weil
to become werden
bed das Bett

beer das Bier
to begin anfangen, beginnen
behind hinter
to believe glauben; denken
to belong to gehören
best best-
better besser
between zwischen
birthday der Geburtstag
book das Buch
bored: to be bored sich langweilen
both beide
bottle die Flasche
boy der Junge
bread das Brot
to break brechen
breakfast das Frühstück
bridge die Brücke
brother der Bruder
to build bauen
bus der Bus
but aber; sondern
butter die Butter
to buy kaufen
by the way übrigens

cake der Kuchen
to call (up) anrufen
called: to be called heißen
to calm down (sich) beruhigen
camera die Kamera, der Photoapparat
car der Wagen
to catch a cold sich erkälten
chair der Stuhl
to change (sich) verändern
to change (clothes) sich umziehen
for a change mal, einmal
cheese der Käse
child das Kind
Christmas Weihnachten
church die Kirche

city die Stadt
coat der Mantel
coffee der Kaffee
cold kalt
to come kommen
corner die Ecke
to cost kosten
country das Land
    in the country auf dem Land
    to the country aufs Land
of course natürlich
cup die Tasse
customer der Kunde

to dance tanzen
daughter die Tochter
day der Tag
dead tot
dear lieb
to decide sich entschließen
to die sterben
different(ly) ander-; anders
dinner das Essen; das Mittagessen; das Abendessen
divorce: to get a divorce sich scheiden lassen
to do machen, tun
doctor der Arzt; der Doktor
dog der Hund
door die Tür
dorm das Studentenheim
downtown in die Stadt; in der Stadt
to dress, get dressed (sich) anziehen
to drink trinken
to drive fahren
driver der Fahrer
dumbbell der Dummkopf
during während

each jeder, jede, jedes
each other sich, einander
early früh
to eat essen
either auch; entweder
end das Ende
engaged: to get engaged sich
    verloben
evening der Abend
ever je
every jeder, jede, jedes
everything alles
every time jedesmal
exam die Prüfung
excuse me Entschuldigung
to expect erwarten
expensive teuer
to experience erleben
eye das Auge

fast schnell
father der Vater
few wenige
    a few ein paar; einige
finally endlich; schließlich
first erst-
flu die Grippe
to fly fliegen
to follow folgen
for (conj.) denn
foreigner der Ausländer
to forget vergessen
French (lang.) Französisch
Friday der Freitag
friend der Freund, die
    Freundin
friendly freundlich
in front of vor

garden der Garten
German (lang.) Deutsch
to get up aufstehen
girl das Mädchen
to give geben
to give (as a present)
    schenken
to go gehen; fahren
to go out ausgehen
glass das Glas
glove der Handschuh
good gut

grandfather der Großvater
grandmother die Großmutter
grateful dankbar

haircut: to get a haircut sich
    die Haare schneiden
    lassen
to hang hängen
to happen geschehen,
    passieren
happy glücklich
hat der Hut
to have haben
    to have to müssen
healthy gesund
to hear hören
to help helfen
here hier
home (adv.) nach Hause
    at home zu Hause
to hope hoffen
    hopefully (I hope)
    hoffentlich
hour die Stunde
house das Haus
how wie
human being der Mensch
(to be) hungry Hunger
    haben
to hurry up sich eilen, sich
    beeilen
husband der Mann

if wenn
to imagine sich
    vorstellen
immediately sofort
important wichtig
instead of statt (. . . zu)
intelligent intelligent
interested: to be interested in
    sich interessieren für
interesting interessant
to introduce (oneself) (sich)
    vorstellen
to invite einladen
Italy Italien

January der Januar
Japanese (lang.) Japanisch
June der Juni

kind: what kind of was für
kitchen die Küche
to know (a person) kennen
    to know (facts) wissen
    to know (a language)
    können

large groß
last letzt-; zuletzt
at last endlich
late spät
to learn lernen
least: at least mindestens,
    wenigstens
to leave abfahren; lassen
to let lassen
letter der Brief
to lie liegen
to lie down sich legen
to like mögen
    I would like to ich
    möchte
    I like it es gefällt mir
little klein; wenig
to live wohnen; leben
liver sausage die Leberwurst
living room das Wohnzimmer
long lang; (adv.) lange
to look (appear) aussehen
to look at ansehen
to look forward to sich
    freuen auf
to lose one's way sich ver-
    laufen; sich verfahren
love: to fall in love with sich
    verlieben in

mad: to be mad at sich
    ärgern über
man der Mann
many viele
married: to be married
    verheiratet sein
to marry, to get married
    heiraten
medicine die Medizin
to meet kennenlernen; treffen
milk die Milch
to be mistaken sich irren
moment der Augenblick
money das Geld

month der Monat
more (than) mehr (als)
morning der Morgen
most meist-
mother die Mutter
motorcycle das Motorrad
mountain der Berg
movie (house) das Kino
　　to the movies ins Kino
much viel
museum das Museum

name der Name
　　my name is ich heiße
to need brauchen
never nie
new neu
newspaper die Zeitung
next nächst-
　　next to neben
nice nett
night die Nacht
　　last night gestern abend
not nicht
　　not until erst
　　not yet noch nicht
nothing nichts
novel der Roman
now jetzt
number die Nummer

o'clock: at (three) o'clock
　　um (drei) Uhr
October der Oktober
often oft
old alt
once einmal; früher
　　once more noch einmal
only nur; erst
in order to um . . . zu
other ander-
overcoat der Mantel

to pack packen
pair das Paar
parents die Eltern
to park parken
　　parking lot der Parkplatz
park der Park
to pay bezahlen

peace: to leave in peace in
　　Ruhe lassen
people die Leute
perhaps vielleicht
permitted: to be permitted to
　　dürfen
to pick up, meet abholen
picture das Bild
piece das Stück
please bitte
policeman der Polizist
potato die Kartoffel
pound das Pfund
to prefer (to do) lieber (tun)
to prepare (oneself) for (sich)
　　vorbereiten auf
to promise versprechen
psychology die Psychologie
to put setzen; stellen; legen

quite ganz

railroad station der Bahnhof
rain der Regen
to rain regnen
to reach erreichen
to read lesen
really wirklich; eigentlich
to recommend empfehlen
to recover sich erholen
relative der Verwandte
to remember sich erinnern an
to rest sich ausruhen
to ring (a telephone) klingeln
(hard) roll das Brötchen
room das Zimmer
run rennen, laufen

salesman der Verkäufer
same derselbe, dieselbe,
　　dasselbe
sausage die Wurst
secretary die Sekretärin
school die Schule
to see sehen
to seem scheinen
semester das Semester
to send schicken
to serve servieren
several mehrere

to shave sich rasieren
to shine scheinen
shoe der Schuh
short kurz
to show zeigen
sick krank
simple einfach
since seit
single einzig
sister die Schwester
to sit sitzen
to sit down sich setzen
to sleep schlafen
　　to get enough sleep (sich)
　　　ausschlafen
slow langsam
small klein
to smoke rauchen
to solve lösen
some einige; ein paar;
　　　manche; etwas
somebody jemand
something etwas
son der Sohn
soon bald
sorry: I'm sorry es tut mir leid
sour sauer
to speak sprechen
to spend verbringen
in spite of trotz
to stand stehen
station der Bahnhof
to stay bleiben
still noch
stop halten; stehenbleiben
story die Geschichte
straight ahead geradeaus
street die Straße
streetcar die Straßenbahn
student der Student, die
　　　Studentin
to study studieren
such solch
to suggest vorschlagen
suitcase der Koffer
summer der Sommer
　　next summer nächsten
　　　Sommer
sun die Sonne
Sunday der Sonntag

supper das Abendessen
supposed: to be supposed to sollen
to swim schwimmen
Swiss cheese der Schweizerkäse
Switzerland die Schweiz

table der Tisch
to take nehmen
to talk reden; sprechen
tea der Tee
teacher der Lehrer
telephone das Telefon
to tell sagen; erzählen
to thank danken
  thank you danke
then dann
there dort, da
to think (of) denken (an); halten von
third dritt-
thousand tausend
through durch
time die Zeit
  at that time damals
tired müde
today heute
tomorrow morgen

tomorrow evening morgen abend
tonight heute abend
too auch; zu
town die Stadt
train der Zug
trip die Reise
to try versuchen
Tuesday der Dienstag

under unter
to understand verstehen
to undress (sich) ausziehen
unfortunately leider
United States die Vereinigten Staaten
until bis
  not until erst
to upset, get upset (about) (sich) aufregen (über)
to get used to sich gewöhnen an

very sehr
Vienna Wien
to visit besuchen
  visit der Besuch

to wait (for) warten (auf)
to walk (zu Fuß) gehen

to want to wollen
to want (wish) (sich) wünschen
war der Krieg
watch die Uhr
weather das Wetter
Wednesday der Mittwoch
week die Woche
weekend das Wochenende
well gesund; gut
when wann
where wo; wohin
whether ob
white weiß
who wer
why warum
wife die Frau
wine der Wein
winter der Winter
with mit; bei
without ohne
woman die Frau
to work arbeiten
to write schreiben
writer der Schriftsteller

year das Jahr
yesterday gestern
yet noch; schon
young jung

Index

This index provides quick references to the grammar topics treated in the analysis sections. Numbers refer to pages.

Mitteleuropa

0	50	100	200	300

Meilen

0	50	100	200	300	400	500

Kilometer

V E R E I N I G T E

MITTELEUROPA

S T A A T E N

Mitteleuropa und die Vereinigten Staaten
(drawn at the same scale)